TO

HAROLD S. PRINCE

who has the enviable distinction of having produced and/or directed since 1954 over 50 musicals, plays and operas, and having been rewarded with 20 "Tony" Awards and a Pulitzer Prize...a record unequaled by any other Broadway producer or director. May his talent and genius continue to be recognized and honored with many more tokens of appreciation from a grateful audience.

For the record: producer and/or director of "The Pajama Game" (1954 Tony), "Damn Yankees" (1955 Tony), "New Girl in Town", "West Side Story", "Fiorello!" (1959 Tony/Pulitzer Prize), "Tenderloin", "A Call on Kuprin", "Take Her, She's Mine", "A Funny Thing Happened on the Way to the Forum" (1962 Tony), "She Loves Me", "Fiddler on the Roof" (1964 Tony), "Baker Street", "Poor Bitos", "Flora the Red Menace", "It's a Bird, It's a Plane, It's Superman!", "Zorba", "Cabaret" (1966 Tony), "Company", (1970 producer and director Tonys), "Follies" (1972 Tony), "The Visit", "The Great God Brown", "A Little Night Music" (1973 Tony), "Love for Love", "Candide" (1974 Tony), "Pacific Overtures", "Side by Side by Sondheim", "Some of My Best Friends", "On the 20th Century", "A Family Affair", "Sweeney Todd" (1978 Tony), "Evita" (1988 Tony), "Merrily We Roll Along", "A Doll's Life", "Play Memory", "End of the World", "Diamonds" (off Broadway), "Grind", "Phantom of the Opera" (1988 Tony), "Roza, Grandchild of Kings" (off Broadway), "Show Boat" (1995 Tony)."

Ellen McLaughlin and Stephen Spinella in "Angels in America: Millennium
Approaches," winner of 1993 "Tonys" for Best Play, Leading Actor in a Play
(Ron Leibman), Featured Actor in a Play (Stephen Spinells), Direction of a Play
(Joan Marcus Photo)

John Willis

Theatre World

1992-1993 SEASON

VOLUME 49

APPLAUSE

NEW YORK • LONDON

THEATRE BOOK PUBLISHERS

211 WEST 71 STREET • NEW YORK •10023

LIBRARY OF CONGRESS CATALOG CARD NO. 73-82953
ISBN 1-55783-203-X (cloth)
ISBN 1-55783-204-8 (paper)

CONTENTS

EDITOR: JOHN WILLIS
ASSISTANT EDITOR: TOM LYNCH

Assistants: Herbert Hayward, Jr., Barry Monush, Stanley Reeves, John Sala
Staff Photographers: Gerry Goodstein, Michael Riordan, Michael Viade, Van Williams
Computer Imaging and Layout: Christopher Weir

BROADWAY PRODUCTIONS

(June 1, 1992-May 31, 1993)

THE REAL INSPECTOR HOUND

and

THE FIFTEEN MINUTE HAMLET

By Tom Stoppard; Director, Gloria Muzio; Sets, John Lee Beatty; Costumes, Jess Goldstein; Lighting, Pat Collins; Sound, Douglas J. Cuomo; Fights, Steve Rankin; General Manager, Ellen Richard; Stage Managers, Kathy J. Faul, Matthew T. Mundinger; Presented by Roundabout Theatre Company (Todd Haimes, Producing Director; Gene Feist, Founding Director); Press, Chris Boneau/Adrian Bryan-Brown, Susanne Tighe, Bob Fennell, Jackie Green, Cabrini Lepis, Craig Karpel; Previewing from Wednesday July 29; Opened in the Criterion Center Stage Right on Thursday, August 18, 1992*

CASTS

FIFTEEN MINUTE HAMLET
Shakespeare/Claudius/Polonius ....Jeff Weiss
Francisco/Horatio/Laertes ....Rod McLachlan
Marcellus/Bernardo/Ghost/Gravedigger/Osric/Fortinbras...........................David Healy
Ophelia ....J.Smith-Cameron
Gertrude ....Patricia Conolly+1
Hamlet ....Simon Jones

REAL INSPECTOR HOUND
Moon ....Simon Jones
Birdboot ....David Healy
Mrs. Drudge ....Patricia Conolly
Simon ....Anthony Fusco +2
Felicity...J.Smith-Cameron
Cynthia ....Jane Summerhays
Magnus/Radio Announcer's Voice ....Jeff Weiss
Inspector Hound ....Rod McLachlan
The Body ....Gene Silvers

UNDERSTUDIES: Brennan Brown (Shakespeare/Claudius/Polonius/Moon/Magnus/Inspector), Charles Gorder (Francisco/Horatio/Laertes/ Marcellus/Bernardo/Ghost/Gravedigger/Orsic/Fortinbras/Hamlet/Simon), Rod McLachlan (Birdboot), Shan Willis (Ophelia/Gertrude/Drudge/Felicity/ Cynthia)

A double-bill of comedies. ...Hamlet takes place at Elsinore Castle.

Variety recorded 8 favorable, 2 mixed and 4 negative notices. *Times* (Mel Gussow): "...devious theatrical comedy, nimbly revived...", *News* (Howard Kissel): "The idea is more amusing than its execution" (Doug Watt) "...exhibits both Stoppard's strongest and most treacherous qualities." *Post* (Jerry Tallmer): "...done again, beautifully, hilariously...", *Newsday* (Jan Stuart): "...more pleasing in the contemplation than the experiencing."

*Closed October 4, 1992 after 61 performances and 16 previews.

+Succeeded by: 1. Shan Willis 2. Joseph Adams

Martha Swope Photos

Top: Anthony Fusco, Jane Summerhays, David Healy, Simon Jones
Center: Jeff Weiss, David Healy, Jane Summerhays, J.Smith-Cameron
Bottom: J. Smith-Cameron, David Healy, Patricia Conolly,
Rod McLachlan, Jeff Weiss, Simon Jones

ANNA KARENINA

Music, Daniel Levine; Lyrics/Book, Peter Kellogg; Adapted from the novel by Leo Tolstoy; Director, Theodore Mann; Musical Staging, Patricia Birch; Orchestrations, Peter Matz; Musical Director/Dance Arrangements, Nicholas Archer; Music Coordinator, Seymour Red Press; Sets, James Morgan; Costumes, Carrie Robbins; Lighting, Mary Jo Dondlinger; Sound, Fox and Perla; Associate Choreographer, Jonathan Cerullo; Dramaturg, Nancy Bosco; Stage Managers, Wm. Hare, Jack Gianino; Company Manager, Susan Elrod; Casting, Judy Henderson, Alycia Aumuller; Presented by Circle in the Square Theatre (Mr. Mann, Artistic Director; Robert A. Buckley, Managing Director; Paul Libin, Consulting Producer); Press, Maria Somma, Patty Onagan; Previewed from Tuesday, August 11; Opened in the Circle in the Square Uptown on Wednesday, August 26, 1992*

CAST

Count Alexis Vronsky	Scott Wentworth
Anna Karenina	Ann Crumb
Constantine Levin	Gregg Edelman
Train Conductor/Fyodor/Basso/Foreman	David Pursley
Prince Stephen Oblonsky (Stiva)	Jerry Lanning
Princess Kitty Scherbatsky	Melissa Errico
Dunyasha/Party Woman	Naz Edwards
Korsunsky/Party Man/Peasant	Gabriel Barre
Vasily/Station Guard/Man at Ball	Larry Hansen
Masha/Gina	Amelia Prentice
Seryozha Karenin, Anna's son	Erik Houston Saari
Annushka, Karenin's maid	Darcy Pulliam
Nicolai Karenin, Anna's husband	John Cunningham
Princess Elizabeth Tversky (Betsey)	Jo Ann Cunningham
Prince Yashvin/Finance Minister/Man at Ball	Ray Wills

UNDERSTUDIES: Melissa Errico (Anna), Ray Wills (Vronsky), Amelia Prentice (Kitty), Larry Hansen (Karenin), Gabriel Barre (Levin), David Pursley (Stiva) SWINGS: Jonathan Cerullo, Audrey Lavine EXTRAS: Jeremy Black, Billy Hipkins

MUSICAL NUMBERS: On a Train, There's More to Life than Love, How Awful, Would You?, In a Room, Waltz and Mazurka, Nothing Has Changed, Lowlands, Rumors, How Many Men?, We Were Dancing, I'm Lost, Karenin's List, Waiting for You, This Can't Go On, This Will Serve Her Right, Everything's Fine, Only At Night, Finale DURING PREVIEWS: Peasant's Idyll

A musical in two acts with 19 scenes. The action takes place in Russia and Italy, 1870s.

Variety recorded 2 favorable, 2 mixed and 6 negative reviews. *Times* (Gussow): "...a series of misperceptions and errors in judge-ment...",*News* (Kissel) "...the score has an occasional melodic surge and there is some skillful ensemble writing..." *Post* (Tallmer): "Gregg Edelman..has a splendid voice-well, they all do...Melissa Errico..truly enchanting..." *Newsday* (Stuart): "Restraint is an ample but dubious asset..." *Variety* (Jeremy Gerard): "What goes wrong, goes wrong immediately."

*Closed October 4, 1992 after 46 performances and 18 previews.

Martha Swope Photos

Gregg Edelman, Melissa Errico
Top: Ann Crumb
Left: Scott Wentworth, Ann Crumb

OBA OBA '93

Oba Oba '93

Musical Director, Wilson Mauro; Choreography, Robert Abrahao; Stage Manager, Monica Goncalves; Presented by Franco Fontana; Press, Peter Cromarty/David Lotz, David Katz; Previewed from Thursday, September 10; Opened in the Marquis Theatre on Thursday, October 1, 1992*

CAST

Ailto Souza ....FormiguinhaMonica Acioli
Ana Careca ....GamoNelaci Costa
Ana Paula Dos Reis ....Giovani RamosNilton Maravilha
Angela Mara..Ilson HelvecioPatricia Dantras
Arlindo Pipiu...Iris Da RochaPatricia Moreira
Carlos Leca ....Jaime SantosPaulo W. Takase
Carlos Oliveira..Jones SantanaR. Malaguti
Carlos Silva ....Jorge Boa MorteRay Do Pandeiro
Casemiro Raposo...Jorge RumRatinho
Chico Filho ....Julio PeluchiRita Nobre
Claudia Lisboa ....Lu VianaRoberto Silva
Claudio Nascimento ....Luciano RibeiroRodman Clayson
Claudio Sampaio..MacRose Perola
Claudio Santos..Marcia Labios De MelSergio Rocha
Cobrinha Mansa...Marcio Do RepeniqueSete Mola
Cristiane Moreira ....Marquinho Da GeraldaSonia Regina
Edgar Aguiar ....Mauricio De SouzaToco Preto
Edval Boa Morte ....Mercia AlexandreValeria Matos
Eliane Garcia...Messias Bastos
....Wellington Gusmao
Emerson Bernardes ....Wilson Mauro
and Eliana Estevao

PROGRAM: Origins of Brazil, Homage to Chorinho, Samba De Roda, Lambada, Samba Reggae, Homage to the Northeast, Brazil Cappella, Homage to the Bossa Nova and the Seventies, Tribute to Carmen Miranda-the Brazilian Bombshell, Macumba, Afro-Brazilian Folk Songs and Dances, Partido Alto, Rhythm Beaters, Show of Samba Dancers, Grand Carnival

A musical revue in two parts.

Variety recorded 4 favorable and 2 mixed notices.

*Closed October 18, 1992 after 22 performances and 24 previews.

Sophie Hayden, Pat Carroll, Laura Esterman in "the Show-Off"

THE SHOW-OFF

By George Kelly; Director, Brian Murray; Sets, Ben Edwards; Costumes, David Charles; Lighting, Peter Kaczorowski; Sound, Douglas J. Cuomo; General Manager, Ellen Richard; Casting, Pat McCorkle, Richard Cole; Stage Managers, Kathy J. Faul, Matthew T. Mundinger; Presented by the Roundabout Theatre Company (Todd Haimes, Producing Director; Gene Feist, Founding Director); Press, Chris Boneau/Adrian Bryan-Brown, Susanne Tighe; Previewed from Wednesday, October 14; Opened in the Criterion Center Stage Right on Thursday, November 5, 1992*

CAST

Clara Fisher Hyland	Laura Esterman
Mrs. Fisher	Pat Carroll
Amy Fisher	Sophie Hayden
Frank Hyland	Edmund C. Davys
Mr. Fisher	Richard Woods
Joe Fisher	Tim DeKay
Aubrey Piper	Boyd Gaines
Mr. Gill	Kevin McClarnon
Mr. Rogers	J.R. Horne

UNDERSTUDIES/STANDBYS: Patricia Kennell Carroll (Mrs. Fisher), Trent Bright (Joe/Gill/Rogers), Edmund C. Davys (Aubrey), J.R. Horne (Mr. Fisher)

A new production of a 1924 comedy in three acts. The action takes place in the Fisher's home, North Philadelphia, 1922. For the 1967 Broadway production, see Theatre World Vol. 24.

Variety recorded 8 favorable, 2 mixed and 2 negative reviews. *Times* (Gussow): "...a popular comedy that is close to foolproof..." (Richards): "...some bumpy sledding.", *News* (Kissel): "...a triumphant performance by Pat Carroll..." (Watt): "...an exemplary piece of comedy construction...", *Post* (Barnes): "It is a period place of timeless charm." *Newsday* (Linda Winer): "...a big step backward with this three-act theatrical antique.", *Variety* (Gerard): "...can't breathe any life into it."

*Closed December 13, 1992 after 45 performances and 25 previews.

Carol Rosegg/Martha Swope Photos

Sophie Hayden, Boyd Gaines
Top: Sophie Hayden, Boyd Gaines, Laura Esterman, Pat Carroll

Stacy Keach

SOLITARY CONFINEMENT

By Rupert Holmes; Director, Marshall W. Mason; Based on original Direction by Kenneth Frankel; Sets/Art Direction, William Barclay; Lighting, Donald Holder; Costumes, Kathleen Detoro; Sound, Jack Allaway; Fights, David Leong; Music Production, Deborah Grunfeld; Production Manager, Roy Sears, Jr.; General Managers, Niko Associates; Stage Managers, Artie Gaffin, Joe Cappelli; Presented by Gladys Nederlander, James M. & Charlene Nederlander, Roger L. Stevens in association with Normand Kurtz; Press, Jeffrey Richards/Tom D'Ambrosio; Previewed from Thursday October 27; Opened in the Nederlander Theatre on Sunday, November 8, 1992*

CAST

Richard Jannings ....Stacy Keach
Fillip...Samuel Tate
Conroy..Art Calvin
Girard ....Yves Konstantine
Eldridge ....Edward Allesandro
Fleischer..Carl Huffman
Miss Davis ....Jane Rollins

A thriller in two acts. The action takes place in the residence of Richard Jannings, atop the Jannings Industries building in Albuquerque, New Mexico.

Variety recorded 4 favorable, 5 mixed and 5 negative reviews. *Times* (Gussow): "...a tepid attempt at a mystery, offering neither chills nor thrills..."(Richards): "Mr. Keach ends up carrying the lion's share of the evening..." *News* (Kissel) "..the stage manager, though never seen, is a role that requires virtuoso talents." (Watt): "All it really has to recommend it is...Stacy Keach...", *Post* (Barnes): "...not so much a whodunit as a whatwasit.", *Newsday* (Winer): "...less a thriller than an extended riddle...", *Variety* (Gerard): "...happy to provide an audience with a couple of hours of suspense, sprinkled with a couple of jolting surprises."

*Closed November 29, 1992 after 25 performances and 15 previews.

Joan Marcus Photos

3 FROM BROOKLYN

Conception/Direction, Sal Richards; Original Music/Lyrics, Sandi Merle and Steve Michaels; Musical Director, Mr. Michaels; Sets, Charles E. McCarry; Lighting, Phil Monat; Sound, Raymond D. Schilke; General Manager, Michael Frazier; Company Manager, Peter Bogyo; Stage Managers, Laura Kravets, Bern Gautier; Presented by Mr. Frazier, Larry Spellman and Don Ravella; Press, Judy Jacksina/Robin Constantine; Previewed from Thursday, November 12; Opened in the Helen Hayes Theatre on Thursday, November 19, 1992*

CAST

The BQE Dancers (Guy Richards, John Michaels, Damon Rusignola)
Raymond Serra as "Cosmo the Cabbie"
Adrianne Tolsch
Roslyn Kind
Bobby Alto & Buddy Mantia
Sal Richards

A musical revue performed without intermission. The action takes place on a street in Brooklyn.

Variety noted 2 mixed and 10 negative reviews.*Times* (Gussow): "...shopworn revue...", *News* (Kissel): "...a series of lounge acts masquerading as a Broadway show."(Watt): "..less than top-notch...", *Post* (Barnes): "...it's a lot better than you might think...", *Newsday* (Winer): "...extremely variable, mostly minor..." Variety (Gerard): "Producers stuck with a sure prospect for Broadway floptitude used to open in the weeks between Thanksgiving and Christmas in order to dun the tourist trade; hence the term turkey. Should 3 From Brooklyn still be running when this notice is published, the wisdom of that ploy will have been proved..."

*Closed December 27, 1992 after 45 performances and 8 previews.

**Left: Adrianne Tolsch, Sal Richards, Roslyn Kind
Bottom Left: Bobby Alto, Buddy Mantia
Bottom Right: John Michaels, Damon Rusignola, Guy Richards**

SOMEONE WHO'LL WATCH OVER ME

By Frank McGuiness; Director, Robin Lefevre; Design, Robin Don; Lighting, Natasha Katz; Sound, T. Richard Fitzgerald; Production Supervisor, Jeremiah J. Harris; Company Manager, Thomas P. Santopietro; Stage Managers, Sally Jacobs, Dan Hild; Produced originally at the Hampstead Theatre; Presented by Noel Pearson and The Shubert Organization in association with Joseph Harris; Press, Shirley Herz/Sam Rudy; Previewed from Thursday, November 19; Opened in the Booth Theatre on Monday, November 23, 1992*

CAST

Edward ....Stephen Rea +1
Adam ....James McDaniel +2
Michael ....Alec McCowen +3

UNDERSTUDIES: Tom Tammi (Edward), Chuck Cooper (Adam), Denis Holmes (Michael)

A drama in two acts. The action takes place in a basement somewhere in the Middle East.

Variety recorded 4 favorable, 4 mixed and 4 negative reviews. *Times* (Frank Rich): "...sporadically amusing without being riveting...The actors are first rate."(Richards): "...any drama that features Alec McCowen...has already taken a major step toward minimizing it's potential trouble spots." *News* (Kissel): "McGuinness' flights of fancy are beguiling. So is his dialogue..."(Watt): "Most of the buoyancy is generated by Stephen Rea...", *Post* (Barnes): "...absorbing, life-assertive and unexpectedly funny...", *Newsday* (Winer): "...tenderly written and exquisitely performed..awfully tidy for such an agonizing mess of a situation..."*Variety* (Gerard): "...won't have an easy time finding the audience it deserves."

*Closed June 13, 1993 after 232 performances and 5 previews. Winner of 1993 New York Drama Critics Circle for Best Foreign Play.

+Succeeded by: 1.David Dukes 2.Chuck Cooper 3.Michael York

Tom Lawlor Photos

Left: Stephen Rea, Alec McCowen

James McDaniel

Stephen Rea

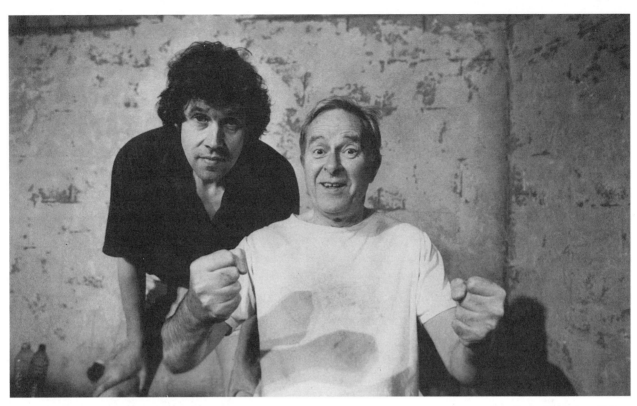

Stephen Rea, Alec McCowen in "Someone Who'll Watch Over Me"

GYPSY PASSION

Music/Lyrics, Traditional; Writer and Director, Tomas Rodriguez-Pantoja; Artistic/Musical Director, Manuel Morao; Choreography, Gitanos de Jerez; Sets, David Sumner; Lighting, Tom Sturge; Costumes, Mercedes Muniz; Sound, Otts Munderloh; Production Supervisor, Carlos Gorbea; Company Manager, Lisa M. Poyer; Producer, Roy A. Somlyo; Presented by Andalucia Productions; Press, Max Eisen/Madelon Rosen; Opened in the Plymouth Theatre on Tuesday, November 17, 1992*

CAST

First Generation ....Manuel Morao, Lorenzo Galvez, Manuel Moneo, Juana La Del Pipa
Second Generation ....Antonio El Pipa, Sara Baras, Concha Vargas, Juan Antonio Ogalla, Pepe De La Joaquina, Luis Moneo, Antonio Moreno, Carmen De La Jeroma
Third Generation...Manuela Nunez, Mercedes Ruiz, Patricia Valdes, Estefania Aranda

MUSICAL NUMBERS: Tona, Villancico, Solea, Cantina, Tangos, Tanguillos, Seguirillas. Zapateado, Taranto, Bulerias, Alegrias, Alborea, El Polo de Tobalo, Martinetes, Finale

A Flamenco musical from Spain in two acts. The story of the gypsies of Andalucia, Spain.

Variety noted 6 favorable and 1 mixed review.

*Closed January 2, 1993 after 55 performances.

Martha Swope/William Gibson Photos

Left: Estefania Aranda, Patricia Valdes, Manuela Nuniz, Mercedes Ruiz

Jon Voight, Tony Roberts

Ethan Hawke, Laura Linney

THE SEA GULL

By Anton Chekhov; Translation, David French; Director, Marshall W. Mason; Sets, Marjorie Bradley Kellogg; Costumes, Laura Crow; Lighting, Richard Nelson; Sound, Stewart Werner, Chuck London; Music, Peter Kater; Production Supervisor, Bonnie Panson; Casting, Georgianne Walken & Sheila Jaffe; Technical Adviser, Christopher C. Smith; General Manager, Niko Associates; Stage Managers, James Harker,John M. Atherlay, Glen Gardali; Executive Producer, Manny Kladitis; Presented by National Actors Theatre (Tony Randall, Founder/Artistic Director; Michael Langham, Artistic Adviser); Press, John Springer/Gary Springer; Previewed from Tuesday, November 17; Opened in the Lyceum Theatre on Sunday, November 29, 1992*

CAST

Konstantin	Ethan Hawke
Medvedenko	Zane Lasky
Masha	Maryann Plunkett
Sorin	John Franklyn-Robbins
Yakov	Danny Burstein
Nina	Laura Linney
Polina	Joan MacIntosh
Dr. Dorn	Tony Roberts
Shamrayev	Russel Lunday
Madame Arkadina	Tyne Daly
Trigorin	Jon Voight
The Cook	John Beal
Servants	Kam Metcalf, Kevin Shinick, David Watson

UNDERSTUDIES: William Leone (Medvedenko/Yakov/Cook), Elizabeth Marvel (Masha), Daisy White (Nina), Rand Mitchell (Sorin/Shamrayev), Bill Camp (Konstantin), Delphi Harrington (Polina/Arkadina), Tom Stechschulte (Trigorin).

Chekhov's 1896 play in four acts (performed with two intermissions).

Variety reported 2 mixed and 13 negative reviews. *Times* (Rich): "...waste of resources and talent...", *News* (Kissel): "Even the title character-a dead bird- has a faintly absurd glimmer in its eye.", *Post* (Barnes): "...does indeed find a happy medium of enduring humanity between the excessive polarities of broad comedy and soft-toned tragic sentiment." *Newsday* (Winer): "The two best elements are the young actors, Hawke and Laura Linney..."*Variety* (Gerard): "...another travesty of a sacred theatrical text..."

*Closed January 10, 1993 after 48 performances and 16 previews.

Joan Marcus Photos

Right:Ethan Hawke, Tyne Daly
Bottom Left: Jon Voight, Maryann Plunkett
Bottom Right: Jon Voight, Laura Linney

MY FAVORITE YEAR

Music, Stephen Flaherty; Lyrics, Lynn Ahrens; Book, Joseph Dougherty; Based on the film *My Favorite Year* with Screenplay by Norman Steinberg and Dennis Palumbo; Story, Mr. Palumbo; Director, Ron Lagomarsino; Musical Staging, Thommie Walsh; Orchestrations, Michael Starobin, Danny Troob, Michael Gibson; Musical Director, Ted Sperling; Sets, Thomas Lynch; Costumes, Patricia Zipprodt; Lighting, Jules Fisher; Sound, Scott Lehrer; Cast Recording, RCA; Dance Arrangements, Wally Harper; Fights, B.H. Barry; Hairstylist, Angela Gari; General Manager, Steven C. Callahan; Production Manager, Jeff Hamlin; Stage Managers, Robin Rumpf, Dale Kaufman; Presented by Lincoln Center Theater in association with AT&T OnStage; Press, Merle Debuskey/Susan Chicoine; Previewed from Saturday, October 31; Opened in the Vivian Beaumont Theater on Thursday, December 10, 1992*

CAST

Benjy Stone	Evan Pappas
King Kaiser	Tom Mardirosian
Sy Benson	Josh Mostel
K.C. Downing	Lannyl Stephens
Alice Miller	Andrea Martin
Herb Lee	Ethan Phillips
Belle Steinberg Carroca	Lainie Kazan
Leo Silver	Paul Stolarsky
Alan Swan	Tim Curry
Rookie Carroca	Thomas Ikeda
Tess	Katie Finneran
Uncle Morty	David Lipman
Aunt Sadie	Mary Stout

Ensemble......Maria Calabrese, Kevin Chamberlin, Colleen Dunn, Ms. Finneran, James Gerth, Michael Gruber, Mr. Lipman, Roxie Lucas, Nora Mae Lyng, Michael McGrath, Alan Muraoka, Jay Poindexter, Russell Ricard, Ms. Stout, Thomas Titone, Bruce Winant, Christina Youngman

UNDERSTUDIES/STANBYS: Michael McGrath (Benjy/Kaiser), Thomas Titone (Benjy/Herb), Bruce Winnant (Kaiser/Sy/Leo), Kevin Chamberlin (Sy/ Herb), Katie Finneran (K.C.), Roxie Lucas(Alice), Mary Stout (Alice/Belle), Nora Mae Lyng (Belle), James Gerth (Leo/Alan), Alan Muraoka (Rookie), Michael O'Gorman (Alan) SWINGS: Robert Ashford, Amiee Turner

MUSICAL NUMBERS: Twenty Million People, Larger Than Life, Musketeer Sketch, Waldorf Suite, Rookie in the Ring, Manhattan, Naked in Bethesda Fountain, Gospel According to King, Rehearsal, Funny/The Duck Joke, Welcome to Brooklyn, If the World Were Like the Movies, Entracte, Exits, Shut Up and Dance, Professional Showbizness Comedy, The Lights Come Up, Maxford House, Sketch Finale, My Favorite Year

A musical in two acts with 15 scenes. The setting is New York City, 1954.

Variety recorded 4 favorable, 3 mixed and 13 negative reviews.

Times (Rich): "...a missed opportunity, a bustling but too frequently flat musical...a superior supporting cast led by Andrea Martin and Lainie Kazan..."(Richards): "Maybe we can no longer subscribe to the notion that a man can be blissfully intoxicated.", *News* (Kissel): "Particulary winning is Evan Pappas..Tim Curry gives Swann all the flourishes...There are two great comediennes...", *Post* (Barnes): "...it's a good story. Some people might have made a good musical out of it. But these people haven't.", *Newsday* (Winer): "..so devoid of originality it seems to disappear as you're watching it."*Variety* (Gerard): "there are 18 musical numbers, and several of them are right on target. But none of them is memorable..."

*Closed January 10, 1993 after 37 performances and 44 previews. Winner of 1993 "Tony" for Featured Actress in a Musical (Andrea Martin).

Left: Tim Curry   Top: Evan Pappas

Thomas Ikeda, Mary Stout, Tim Curry, David Lipman, Lanie Kazan, Evan Pappas and Ensemble

Josh Mostel, Evan Pappas, Andrea Martin, Ethan Phillips

Lannyl Stephens, Evan Pappas

A CHRISTMAS CAROL

By Charles Dickens; Adapted and Staged by Patrick Stewart; Lighting, Fred Allen; General Managers, R. Tyler Gatchell, Jr., Peter Neufeld; Stage Manager/Executive Producer, Kate Elliott; Presented by Timothy Childs; Press, Chris Boneau/Adrian Bryan-Brown, Bob Fennell; Previewed from Tuesday, December 15; Opened in the Broadhurst Theatre on Thursday, December 17, 1992*

CAST

PATRICK STEWART

A solo performance of the 1843 Christmas classic, in two acts.

News (Kissel): "..with a star like Stewart, you don't really need a stage full of actors...I have never seen a full-fledged production of this work that captures as much of it's richness..." *Newsday* (Aileen Jacobson): "...an engrossing tale about loneliness, heartlessness and redemption that strides well beyond a dramatic reading."

*Closed January 3, 1993 after 22 limited performances and 2 previews. This production played last season at the Eugene O'Neill Theatre.

Jim Farber Photo

TOMMY TUNE TONITE!

A Song & Dance Act

Director, Jeff Calhoun; Musical Director, Michael Biagi; Set, Tony Walton; Costumes, Willa Kim; Lighting, Jules Fisher, Peggy Eisenhauer; Sound, David Dansky; General Manager, Stuart Thompson; Company Manager, Alan R. Markinson; Stage Manager, Jay Rabins; Associate Producers, Phillip Oesterman, David Wolfe; Presented by Pierre Cossette, James M. Nederlander, William E. Simon; Press, Chris Boneau/Adrian Bryan-Brown/ Craig Karpel; Previewed from Friday, December 25; Opened in the Gershwin Theatre on Sunday, December 27, 1992*

CAST

TOMMY TUNE
Robert Fowler   Frantz Hall

A musical revue performed without intermission.

Variety reported 4 favorable and 6 mixed notices. *Times* (Stephen Holden): "If Tommy Tune could wave a magic scepter, Broadway would be transformed..into an immaculate thoroughfare of diamond-studded glamour and endless high spirits.", *News* (David Hinckley): "...a fine Christmas present to Broadway.", *Post* (Barnes): "...a rare and extraordinarily uncluttered glimpse of a man who has become a Broadway legend...", *Newsday* (Stuart): "...a Tommy-gun blast of Broadway pizzazz..."

*Closed January 3, 1993 after limited run of 10 performances and 4 previews.

Carmen Schiavone Photos

Natasha Richardson, Liam Neeson

ANNA CHRISTIE

By Eugene O'Neill; Director, David Leveaux; Sets, John Lee Beatty; Costumes, Martin Pakledinaz; Lighting, Marc B. Weiss; Composer/Sound, Douglas J. Cuomo; Fights, Steve Rankin; Casting, Pat McCorkle, Richard Cole; General Manager, Ellen Richard; Stage Managers, Kathy J. Faul, Bill McComb; Presented by Roundabout Theatre Company (Todd Haimes, Artistic Director; Gene Feist, Founding Director); Press, Chris Boneau/ Adrian Bryan-Brown, Susanne Tighe; Previewed from Wednesday, December 3, 1992; Opened in the Criterion Center Stage Right on Thursday, January 14, 1993*

CAST

Johnny-the-Priest ....Christopher Wynkoop
Larry ....Barton Tinapp
Chris Christopherson..Rip Torn
Marthy Owen..Anne Meara
Anna Christopherson..Natasha Richardson
Mat Burke ....Liam Neeson

UNDERSTUDIES: Barton Tinapp (Mat), Christopher Wynkoop (Chris), Jeffrey Shore (Johnny/Larry), Angelica Torn (Anna/Marthy)

Performed in four acts with one intermission. The action takes place on the New York City waterfront, Provincetown, Mass. and Boston.

Variety reported 9 favorable, 3 mixed and 2 negative reviews. *Times* (Rich): "...a thrilling staging..astonishing Natasha Richardson..gives what may prove to be the performance of the season..." (Richards) "...O'Neill's 1921 drama has aged badly...", *News* (Kissel): "..Liam Neeson, an actor of tremendous prescence bounds about the stage with a rough, virile energy balanced by enormous physical grace." (Watt): "brilliantly incisive...a giant step beyond any of the company's previous offerings..." *Post* (Barnes): "...a strange ramshackle classic. However with these two knockout star turns..Leveaux's clever and minutely delicate staging..makes this a classic infinitely well worth seeing.", *Newsday* (Winer): "...blazingly self-assured production..with flinty, shuddering chemistry..." *Variety* (Gerard): "It has a lot of life in it..."

*Closed February 28, 1993 after 54 performances and 24 previews. Winner of 1993 "Tony" for Best Revival.

Origional Production with Pauline Lord, George Marion and Frank Shannon opened Nov. 2, 1921 in the Vanderbilt Theatre and played 177 performances. It received the 1922 Pulitzer Prize. Last revival Apr. 14, 1977 in the Imperial Theatre with Liv Ullmann, John Lithgow and Mary McCarthy, and played a limited engagement of 124 performances.

Carol Rosegg/Martha Swope Photos

Right: Natasha Richardson, Rip Torn
Bottom Left: Rip Torn, Anne Meara
Bottom Right: Natasha Richardson, Liam Neeson

SAINT JOAN

Top: Maryann Plunkett

By Bernard Shaw; Director, Michael Langham; Sets, Marjorie Bradley Kellogg; Costumes, Ann Hould-Ward; Lighting, Richard Nelson; Sound, T. Richard Fitzgerald; Music, Stanley Silverman; Hairstylist, Robert Fama; Casting, Georgianne Walken, Sheila Jaffe; Production Supervisor, Bonnie Panson; Fights, J. Allen Suddeth; General Managers, Niko Associates; Stage Managers, Perry Cline, Marjorie Horne; Executive Producer, Manny Kladitis; Presented by National Actors Theatre (Tony Randall, Founder/Artistic Director; Michael Langham, Artistic Advisor) by special arrangement with Duncan C. Weldon; Press, John and Gary Springer; Previewed from Monday, January 8; Opened in the Lyceum Theatre on Sunday, January 31, 1993*

CAST

Robert de Baudricourt/Soldier	Edmund C. Davys
Steward/Roman Delegate	Ivar Brogger
Joan	Maryann Plunkett
Bertrand De Poulengey	Rod McLachlan
Archbishop of Rheims/Executioner	John Franklyn-Robbins
La Tremouille/D'Estivet	Tom Lacy
Court Page/De Courcelles	Peter McRobbie
Gilles de Rais (Bluebeard)	Bill Camp
Capt. La Hire	Helmar Augustus Cooper
The Dauphin (Charles VII)	Michael Stuhlbarg
Duchesse de la Tremouille	Elizabeth Marvel
Dunois, Bastard of Orleans	Jay O. Sanders
Dunois' Page	Danny Burstein
Richard de Beauchamp, Earl of Warwick	John Neville
Chaplain de Stogumber	Remak Ramsay
Peter Cauchon, Bishop of Beauvais	Louis Turenne
Warwick's Page	David Adkins
The Inquisitor	Nicholas Kepros
Brother Marin Ladvenu	Lorne Kennedy
Knights, Soldiers, Scribes	Charles Geyer, Richard Holmes, Emily Baer, Ted Brunson, Roslyn Cohn, Kam Metcalf, Kevin Shinick, David Watson

UNDERSTUDIES: Elizabeth Marvel (Joan), Danny Burstein (Bluebeard), Lorne Kennedy (Page), Rod McLachlan (De Courcelles), Bill Camp (Dauphin), Alan Mixon (Cauchon/Archbishop/Executioner), Leo Leyden (Inquisitor/de Stogumber), David Rainey (Steward/Page/La Hire), Richard Holmes (Poulengey/Dunois), Charles Geyer (Baudricourt/Soldier/ Tremouille/D'Estivet), David Adkins (Page/Ladvenu/Roman Delegate)

Performed in two parts, with six scenes and epilogue. The action takes place 1429-1456.

Variety noted 13 favorable and 3 mixed reviews. *Times* (Gussow): "Ms. Plunkett strides into her role with an impudence to match her confidence" (Richards): "...a safe, unadventurous production of a classic.", *News* (Kissel): "...actors who can convey both the drama of Shaw's ideas and the intense musicality of his writing." (Watt): "Always welcome, Bernard Shaw is back on Broadway..." *Post* (Barnes): "...the playing of the title role..seems oddly wrong...a very interesting time." *Newsday* (Jacobson): "Leave it to Bernard Shaw to create an entertaining and often comic play about a heroine who gets burned at the stake.", *Variety* (Gerard): "...a play whose rewards remain compelling..."

Original New York production with Winifred Lenihan opened Dec. 28, 1923 in the Garrick Theatre.

*Closed March 14, 1993 after 49 performances and 15 previews.

Joan Marcus Photos

Louis Turenne, Remak Ramsay, John Neville

Maryann Plunkett, Michael Stuhlbarg

John Franklyn-Robbins, Richard Holmes, Maryann Plunkett, Helmar Augustus Cooper
Top: Jay O. Sanders, Maryann Plunkett

David Shiner, Bill Irwin

David Shiner, Bill Irwin(also below)

FOOL MOON

Created by Bill Irwin and David Shiner; Set, Douglas Stein; Costumes, Bill Kellard; Lighting, Nancy Schertler; Sound, Tom Morse; Flying by Foy; Production Associate, Nancy Harrington; Company Manager, Daniel Kearns; Stage Manager, James Harker; General Managers, Fremont Associates; Presented by James B. Freydberg, Kenneth Feld, Jeffrey Ash, Dori Berinstein; Press, Chris Boneau/Adrian Bryan-Brown, Jackie Green; Previewed from Friday, February 12; Opened in the Richard Rodgers Theatre on Thursday, February 25, 1993*

CAST

DAVID SHINER   BILL IRWIN
Red Clay Ramblers

An entertainment in two acts.

Variety recorded 5 favorable, 7 mixed and 2 negative notices. Times (Rich): "To that short list of unbeatable combinations that includes bacon and eggs, bourbon and soda, and Laurel and Hardy, you can now add Shriner and Irwin."(Richards): "...it racks up more laughs per minute than any endeavor on Broadway right now...", News (Kissel): "Irwin and Shriner obviously have zany courage in spades..." (Watt): "they rattle around on stage like lost souls on Broadway." Post (Barnes): "...two shades of clowning, darker and lighter...", Newsday (Winer): "...an inspired, helium-weight treasure..."Variety (Gerard): "...art that is sweetly comforting and at the same time challenging."

*Closed September 5, 1993 after 207 performances and 15 previews.

Joan Marcus Photos

THE GOODBYE GIRL

Music, Marvin Hamlisch; Lyrics, David Zippel; Book, Neil Simon based on his 1977 screenplay; Director, Michael Kidd; Musical Staging, Graciela Daniele; Orchestrations, Billy Byers, Torrie Zito; Musical Director, Jack Everly(During Chicago tryout, Gene Saks was the director.); Dance Arrangements, Mark Hummel; Sets/Costumes, Santo Loquasto; Lighting, Tharon Musser; Sound, Tom Clark; Asst. Choreographer, Willie Rosario; Production Supervisor, Peter Lawrence; Casting, Jay Binder; General Manager, Leonard Soloway; Cast Recording, Columbia; Stage Managers, Thomas A. Bartlett, Greta Minsky; Assoc. Producer, Kaede Seville; Presented by Office Two-One, Gladys Nederlander, Stewart F. Lane, James M. Nederlander, Richard Kagan and Emanuel Azenberg; Press, Bill Evans/ Jim Randolph, Erin Dunn, Sandy Manley; Previewed from Saturday, February 13; Opened in the Marquis Theatre on Thursday, March 4, 1993*

CAST

Lucy	Tammy Minoff
Paula	Bernadette Peters +1
Billy	Scott Wise
Donna	Susann Fletcher
Jenna	Cynthia Onrubia
Cynthia	Erin Torpey
Melanie	Lisa Molina
Mrs. Crosby	Carol Woods
Elliot	Martin Short
Mark/Ricky Simpson	John Christopher Jones
Stage Manager	Darlesia Cearcy
First Man at Theatre	Larry Sousa
Woman at Theatre	Mary Ann Lamb
2nd Man/TV Manager/Announcer	Rick Crom
Mark's Mother	Ruth Gottschall
Richard III Cast	Barry Bernal, Ms. Cearcy, Jamie Beth Chandler, Dennis Daniels, Denise Faye, Nancy Hess, Joe Locarro, Rick Manning, Ms. Onrubia, Linda Talcott, Mr. Wise
Richard III Audience	Mr. Crom, Ruth Gottschall, Sean Grant, Ms. Lamb, Mr. Sousa

UNDERSTUDIES/STANDBYS: Betsy Joslyn, Nancy Hess (Paula), Michael McGrath (Elliot), Rick Crom (Elliot/Mark/Ricky), Erin Torpey, Lisa Molina (Lucy), Darlesia Caercy (Mrs. Crosby), Ruth Gottschal (Donna), Ibijoke Akinola (Melanie/Cynthia) SWINGS: Ned Hannah, Michele Pigliavento

MUSICAL NUMBERS: This Is as Good as It Gets, No More, A Beat Behind, My Rules, Elliot Garfield Grant, Good New Bad News, Footsteps, How Can I Win?, Richard Interred, Too Good to Be Bad/2 Good 2 B Bad, Who Would've Thought?, Paula (An Improvised Love Song), I Can Play This Part, Jump for Joy, What a Guy, Finale DURING TRYOUT: I'm Outta Here

A musical comedy in two acts with 21 scenes. The action takes place in New York City.

Variety recorded 1 favorable, 5 mixed and 12 negative notices. *Times* (Rich): "In their heroic and tireless effort to put over the dull musical at the Marquis, these stars would serve the audience dinner and fill out its 1040 forms if given the chance." (Richards): "Mr. Hamlish's score is easy enough to listen to, and Mr. Zippel's lyrics..can be smart and funny...Mr. Short is eager to please...",*News* (Kissel): "...everybody is trying too hard..Graciela Daniele's choreography has an angular jocularity, and she has given Scott Wise some great steps." (Watt): "...particularly disappointing." *Post* (Barnes): "...Martin Short..deserves to be the toast of the town, and his already beloved co-star Bernadette Peters ain't chopped liver either." *Newsday* (Winer): "...more than a little confused about whether to be a glitzy musical-comedy with dancing girls or a chamber musical about modern relationships." *Variety* (Chicago tryout-Lewis Lazare): "There's some good news on the way to Broadway..in pretty good shape." (NY-Gerard): "...wonder how things could have gone so wrong..the musical never sings."

*Closed August 15, 1993 after 188 performances and 23 previews.

+Succeeded by: 1. Betsy Joslyn (during illness)

Left: Bernadette Peters Top: Bernadette Peters, Martin Short

Mark Linn-Baker, Jane Krakowski in "Face Value"

FACE VALUE

By David Henry Hwang; Director, Jerry Zaks; Sets, Loy Arcenas; Costumes, William Ivey Long; Lighting, Paul Gallo; Sound, Tony Meola; Music, Michael Starobin; Hairstylist, Angela Gari; Casting, Joanna Merlin; Production Supervisor, Jeremiah J. Harris; Production Manager, Steven Beckler; Company Manager, Beth Riedmann; Stage Manager, Joe Cappelli; Presented by Stuart Ostrow, Scott Rudin and Jujamcyn Theatres; Press, John and Gary Springer; Previewed from Tuesday, March 9, 1993*

CAST

Linda Anne Wing	Mia Korf
Randall Lee	B.D. Wong +1
Pastor	Gus Rogerson
Glenn Ebens	Jeff Weiss
Bernard Sugarmann	Mark Linn-Baker
Andrew Simpson	Michael Countryman
Jessica Ryan	Jane Krakowski
Marci Williams	Gina Torres

UNDERSTUDIES: Jennifer Lam (Linda), Marcus Olson (Bernard/Pastor), Alene Dawson (Marci), Mark Zimmerman (Glenn/Andrew), Susan Wood (Jessica)

A comedy in two acts with 9 scenes. The action takes place on opening night of a new musical (The Real Manchu) that is being protested by Asian activists and Asian-bashing extremists.

*Closed March 14, 1993 after 8 previews.

+1. Played by Dennis Dun during Boston tryout.

Joan Marcus Photos

Bernadette Peters (center) and Ensemble
Center: Carol Woods
Top Left: Martin Short, Bernadette Peters

THE SISTERS ROSENSWEIG

By Wendy Wasserstein; Director, Dan Sullivan; Sets, John Lee Beatty; Costumes, Jane Greenwood; Lighting, Pat Collins; Sound, Guy Sherman/ Aural Fixation; Casting, Daniel Swee; General Manager, Steven C. Callahan; Production Manager, Jeff Hamlin; Stage Managers, Roy Harris, Elise-Ann Konstantin; Produced by Lincoln Center Theater (Andre Bishop, Bernard Gersten, Directors); Press, Merle Debuskey/Susan Chicoine; Previewed from Tuesday, March 2; Opened in the Ethel Barrymore Theatre on Thursday, March 18, 1993*

CAST

Tess Goode ....Julie Dretzin+1
Pfeni Rosensweig ....Christine Estabrook+2
Sara Goode ....Jane Alexander+3
Geoffrey Duncan...John Vickery+4
Mervyn Kant ....Robert Klein+5
Gorgeous Teitelbaum..Madeline Kahn+6
Tom Valiunus ....Patrick Fitzgerald+7
Nicholas Pym ....John Cunningham+8

STANDBYS: Chiara Peacock (Tess), Robin Moseley (Sara/Pfeni), Lucy Martin (Gorgeous/Sara), Stephen Stout (Geoffrey/Nicholas), Stan Lachow (Mervyn/Nicholas), Jonathan Friedman (Tom)

A comedy in two acts. The action takes place in a sitting room in Queen Anne's Gate, London during August, 1991.

Variety recorded 8 favorable reviews. *Times* (Gussow): "A captivating look at three uncommon women and their quest for love, self-determination and fulfillment." *News* (Kissel): "...moved to Broadway with all its hilarity intact..as thoughtful as it is comic." (Watt): "Daniel Sullivan's direction remains letter-perfect.", *Post* (Barnes) "...Christine Estabrook..is as accomplished and delicious as Jane Alexander and Madeline Kahn...", *Newsday* (Winer): "...enormously good natured and confident..."

*Closed July 16, 1994 after 556 performances and 18 previews at the Barrymore preceeded by 142 performances and 29 previews Off- Broadway. Winner of 1993 "Tony" for Leading Actress in a Play (Madeline Kahn).

Suceeded by : 1. Amy Ryan, 2.7Joanne Camp, 3.Michael Learned, 4.Tom Hewitt 5.Hal Linden, 6.Linda Lavin, Deborah Rush, 7.Brian F. O'Byrne, 8.Rex Robbins, John Cunningham

Martha Swope Photos

Left: Patrick Fitzgerald, Jane Alexander, John Vickery, Julie Dretzin (front)
Top Left: Robert Klein, Jane Alexander

Robert Klein, Madeline Kahn, Christine Estabrook, John Cunningham
Top: Madeline Kahn, Jane Alexander, Christine Estabrook

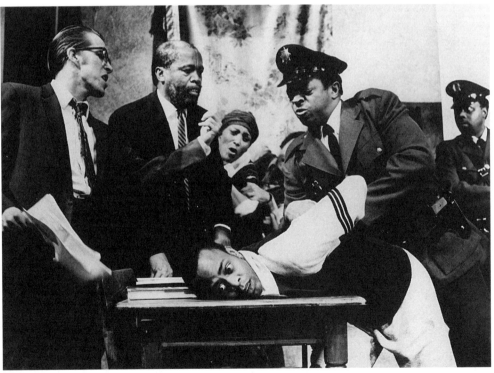

Nicholas Wodtke, Zakes Mokae, Pat Bowie, Cedric Young, Seth Sibanda, K. Todd Freeman (on table)
Top: Ladysmith Black Mambazo

THE SONG OF JACOB ZULU

Tania Richard, Erika L. Heard, K. Todd Freeman, (behind) Leelai Demoz,
Gary DeWitt Marshall, Seth Sibanda
Bottom: (front) K. Todd Freeman

By Tug Yourgrau; Music/Lyrics, Ladysmith Black Mambazo; Lyrics, Mr. Yourgrau; Director, Eric Simonson; Sets, Kevin Rigdon; Costumes, Erin Quigley; Lighting, Robert Christen; Sound, Rob Milburn; Stage Managers, Malcolm Ewen, Femi Sarah Heggie; Presented by Steppenwolf Theatre Company, Randall Arney, Stephen Eich, Albert Poland, Susan Liederman, Bette Cerf Hill, in association with Maurice Rosenfield; Press, David Rothenberg/ Hugh Hayes, Manuel Igrejas, Terence Womble; Previewed from Wednesday, March 17; Opened in the Plymouth Theatre on Wednesday, March 24, 1993*

CAST

Marty Frankel	Garry Becker
Mrs.Zulu/Mrs.Ngobese/Ma Bythelezi/Guerilla	Pat Bowie
Judge Neville	Robert Breuler
John Dawkins/Dr. Shaw	David Connelly
Jacob Zulu	K. Todd Freeman
Mrs. Sabelo/Beauty Dlamini/Guerilla	Erika L. Heard
Mr. Vilakazi/Fumani/Guerilla	Danny Johnson
Student/Policeman/Mbongeni/Michael Dube/Guerilla	Gary DeWitt Marshall
Rev. Zulu/Mr. X/ Itshe	Zakes Mokae
Magistrate/Mr. Van Heerden/Mr. Jeppe	Daniel Oreskes
Student/Aunt Miriam/Ruth Dube/Guerilla	Tania Richard
Interpreter/Policeman/Jacob's Superior	Seth Sibana
Anthony Dent/Lt. Malan	Alan Wilder
Michael Jeppe/Lt. Kramer	Nicholas Cross Wodtke
Uncle Mdishwa/Teacher/Police/Percy/Commissar	Cedric Young

and

LADYSMITH BLACK MAMBAZO
Joseph Shabalala
Jubulani Dubazana, Abednego Mazibuko, Albert Mazibuko,
Geophrey Mdletshe, Russel Mthembu, Inos Phungula
Jockey Shabalala, Ben Shabalala

UNDERSTUDIES/STANDBYS: David Connelly, Leelai Demoz, Erika L. Heard, Gary DeWitt Marshall, Daniel Oreskes, Seth Sibanda, Tania Richard, Nicholas Cross Wodtke, Cedric Young

A drama with music performed in two acts. This fictional play is inspired by actual events.

Variety recorded 3 favorable and 3 negative reviews. *Times* (Rich): "..a worthy drama about apartheid that lacks the poetic texture, eloquence, surprises and deep feeling-in short, the voice-of its music." (Richards): "...the a capella singing group Ladysmith Black Mambazo produce a lovely sound..They are the song.", *News* (Kissel): "...a work rationalizing an act of terrorism."(Watt): "Jacob Zulu, attractively set forth by K. Todd Freeman..Most impressive of all was the accomplished and winning Zakes Mokae.", *Post* (Barnes): "...the music is what leaves its lasting, fleeting impression...", *Newsday* (Winer): "...the show has the most important-not to mention lovable-score of any musical so far this season.", *Variety* (Gerard): "...plays slack and full of lulls despite the story and the vibrant music..."

*Closed May 9, 1993 after 53 performances and 11 previews.

Jack Mitchell Photos

CANDIDA

By George Bernard Shaw; Director, Gloria Muzio; Set, David Jenkins; Costumes, Jess Goldstein; Lighting, Peter Kaczorowski; Sound, Douglas J. Cuomo; Casting, Pat McCorkle, Richard Cole; General Manager, Ellen Richard; Stage Managers, Jay Adler, Kathy J. Faul; Presented by Roundabout Theatre Company (Todd Haimes, Artistic Director; Gene Feist, Founding Director); Press, Chris Boneau/Adrian Bryan-Brown, Susanne Tighe; Previewed from Friday, March 5; Opened in the Criterion Center Stage Right on Thursday, March 25, 1993*

CAST

Miss Prosperine Garnett .... Ann Dowd
The Reverend James Mavor Morell .... Robert Foxworth
The Reverend Alexander Mill .... Simon Brooking
Mr. Burgess .... William Duff-Griffin
Candida .... Mary Steenburgen
Eugene Marchbanks .... Robert Sean Leonard

UNDERSTUDIES: Vivian Nesbitt (Candida/Prosperine), Simon Brooking (Marchbanks)

Shaw's 1894 play in three acts. The action takes place in St. Dominic's parsonage, London.

Variety noted 1 favorable, 4 mixed and 4 negative reviews. *Times* (Gussow): "Mary Steenburgen..is genial and winsome. What she misses is the character's self-centeredness..her cunning..Robert Sean Leonard earns most of the evening's laughs..." (Richards): "Gloria Muzio is responsible for the direction ..indicating that Candida, for all her wit and wisdom, may have made the wrong choice. Now there's an interesting notion for you." *News* (Kissel): "...the low comedy... undermines the dignity of the characters...", *Post* (Barnes): "It is difficult to stage what is esentially a sex comedy that possesses no sense of sexuality." *Newsday* (Winer): "...Leonard..has the comic timing of a romantic clown..We go to see Steenburgen; we leave remembering Leonard." *Variety* (Gerard): "There have doubtless been many memorable Candidas..but I've never encountered one..."

*Closed May 2, 1993 after a limited engagement of 45 performances and 23 previews.

Carol Rosegg/Martha Swope Photos

Left: Robert Sean Leonard, Robert Foxworth

Robert Foxworth, Mary Steenburgen, Robert Sean Leonard

Mary Steenburgen, Robert Sean Leonard

REDWOOD CURTAIN

By Lanford Wilson; Director, Marshall W. Mason; Set, John Lee Beatty; Costumes, Laura Crow; Lighting, Dennis Parichy; Sound, Chuck London/ Stewart Werner; Music, Peter Kater; Fights, Nels Hennum; Casting, Meg Simon; Stage Managers, Fred Reinglas, Denise Yaney; Associate Producers, Susan Sampliner, Nick Scandalios; Presented by Robert Cole, Benjamin Mordecai, Deborah D. Matthews, James M. Nederlander, James D. Stern, William P. Sutter, Circle Repertory Company (Tanya Berezin, Artistic Director); Press, Bill Evans/Jim Randolph, Erin Dunn, Sandy Manley; Previewed from Friday, March 13; Opened in the Brooks Atkinson Theatre on Tuesday, March 30, 1993*

CAST

Lyman..Jeff Daniels
Geri...Sung Yun Cho
Geneva ....Debra Monk

UNDERSTUDIES: Pamela Dunlap (Geneva)

A drama performed without intermission. The action takes place in a redwood forest, near Arcata, California, not long ago.

Variety recorded 5 favorable, 3 mixed and 8 negative notices. *Times* (Rich): "That Mr. Wilson writes with enormous wit and compassion..will come as no surprise..a real yarn with a satisfying old-fashioned mousetrap of a plot..."(Richards): "Mr. Wilson is really writing about the torn fabric of our society, about people uprooted and what the uprooting does to them..." *News* (Kissel): "...always seems to be straining the author's resources..."(Watt): "...often haunting but weakly resolved...", *Post* (Barnes): "...a lengthy, obvious and rather boring metaphor."*Newsday* (Winer): "...stunningly thin..an odd little play... haunting set...", *Variety* (Gerard): "Filling the emptiness..is John Lee Beatty's set...The saving grace in all of this is Monk's performance..."

*Closed May 2, 1993 after 40 performances and 11 previews. Winner of 1993 "Tony" for Featured Actress in a Play (Debra Monk).

Ken Howard Photos

**Right: Jeff Daniels
Bottom Left: Debra Monk
Bottom Right: Sung Yun Cho**

Madeline Kahn

BROADWAY CANTEEN SEVENTH ANNUAL EASTER BONNET COMPETITION

Book/Lyrics, Bill Russell; Original Music, Henry Krieger; Director/ Choreographer, Robert Longbottom; Costumes, Bobby Pearce; Orchestrations/Dance Music, David Chase; Music Supervision/Vocal Arrangements, Phil Hall; Assisitant Choreographer, Barry Finkel; Production Supervisor, Tom Capps; Bonnet Coordinator, Andrea Cohen; Stage Manager, Deborah Porazzi; Associate Producer, Lyle Jones; Presented by Suzanne Ishee and Miss Saigon , Press, Chris Boneau/ Adrian Bryan-Brown, Hillary Harrow, Performed at the Broadway Theatre on Tuesday, April 6 and Wednesday, April 7, 1993*

HOSTS:

Bill Irwin

Nathan Lane & Faith Prince

Christopher Durang & Michael Rupert

Madeline Kahn

Marla Maples & Jason Opsahl

Bernadette Peters & Martin Short

Laurie Beechman

The Hunnies

(Mamie Duncan-Gibbs, Stephanie Pope, Allison Williams)

BROADWAY GI'S: Alan Ariano, Randy Davis, David Elder, Robert Fowler, Ramon Galindo, John Ganun, Joel Goodness, Aldrin Gonzalez, Michael Gruber, Frantz Hall, Devanand Janki, John MacInnis, Ken Nagy, Mason Rogers, George Smyros, Steven Sofia, Sergio Trujillo, Randy Wojcik, Kelly Woodruff

CANTEEN CUTIES: Paula Leggett Chase, Pascale Faye, Laurie Gamache, Eileen Grace, Ida Henry, Greta Martin, Lori MacPherson, Maryellen Scilla, Darlene Wilson, Christina Youngman

THEATRES OF WAR (PROGRAM): Sisters Rosensweig (Christine Estabrook, Jane Alexander), Jeffrey (John Michael Higgins, Tom Hewitt & cast), Goodbye Girl (Carol Woods, Tammy Minoff, Bernadette Peters, Martin Short), Hello Muddah Hello Fadduh , Fool Moon (David Shiner, Bill Irwin), Guys and Dolls, Three Men on a Horse (Julie Hagerty, Nora Mae Lyng), Falsettos (Heather MacRae sings "I Need a Little Sugar in My Bowl" with cast), Jelly's Last Jam, Crazy For You (Jodi Benson & cast), Madeline Kahn "Bunny" song, Five Guys Named Moe, Blue Man Group, Will Rogers Follies ("In the Navy"), Forever Plaid ("Bunny Hop"), Miss Saigon, Bernadette Peters & Martin Short ("I Can Play This Part"), Les Miserables ("We Want to Be Happy"), Nunsense (("Praise the Lord and Pass the Ammunition"), Phantom of the Opera ("Operatic Officer of Co. B"), Roundabout/Candida (Robert Sean Leonard, Mary Steenburgen), She Loves Me (Boyd Gaines), Show-Off (Sophie Hayden), Cats, Laurie Beechman ("Your Show is Going On")

*2 limited performances to benfit Broadway Cares/Equity Fights AIDS.

William Gibson/Martha Swope Photos

Opening Number
Center: Blue Man Group
Top: Christopher Durang, Michael Rupert

Elaine Stritch
Bottom: Reunion Cast: *Brian Hamill,*

Phillip Davies Photos

COMPANY
THE ORIGINAL CAST IN CONCERT

Music/Lyrics, Stephen Sondheim; Book, George Furth; Originally Directed /Produced by Harold Prince; Director, Barry Brown; Musical Staging, George Martin; Musical Director, John McDaniel; Orchestrations, Jonathan Tunick; Set (from My Favorite Year), Thomas Lynch; Lighting, Natasha Katz; Sound, John Weston; Stage Manager, John M. Gallo; Associate Producers, John V. Fahey, Rodger McFarlane and Tom Viola; Presented by Barry Brown, Broadway Cares/Equity Fights AIDS, New York Magazine, in association with Lincoln Center Theater; Press, Chris Boneau/Adrian Bryan-Brown; Performed in the Vivian Beaumont Theater on Sunday, April 11, 1993 and Monday, April 12, 1993*

CAST

Sarah ....Barbara Barrie
April ....Susan Browning
David ....George Coe
Peter ....John Cunningham
Paul ....Steve Elmore
Larry...Stanley Grover
Amy...Beth Howland
Robert...Dean Jones
Harry...Charles Kimbrough
Susan ....Merle Louise
Kathy...Donna McKechnie
Marta ....Pamela Myers
Jenny ....Teri Ralston
Joanne ....Elaine Stritch
Host...Patti LuPone

Vocal Minority, Eileen Barnett, Cathy Corkill, Marilyn Saunders, Dona D. Vaughn

MUSICAL NUMBERS: Company, The Little Things You Do Together, Sorry-Grateful, You Could Drive a Person Crazy, Have I Got a Girl for You, Someone is Waiting, Another Hundred People, Getting Married Today, Side by Side, What Would We Do Without You, Poor Baby, Tick-Tock, Barcelona, The Ladies Who Lunch, Being Alive, Finale

A staged concert of the 1970 musical featuring the original cast (and Stanley Grover replacing the late Charles Braswell as he did during the original run). The concert was also performed January 23, 1993 at the Terrace Theater in Long Beacg California, with Alice Cannon instead of Merle Louise and with Angela Lansbury and George Hearn hosting. For original Broadway production see *Theatre World* Vol. 26.

Tony Randall, Jack Klugman

THREE MEN ON A HORSE

By John Cecil Holm and George Abbott; Director, John Tillinger; Sets, Marjorie Bradley Kellogg; Costumes, Ann Hould-Ward; Lighting, Richard Nelson; Sound, T. Richard Fitzgerald; Music Direction, John Kander; Hair-stylist, Robert Fama; Fights, Jerry Mitchell; Casting, Georgianne Walken and Sheila Jaffe; Production Supervisor, Bonnie Panson; General Managers, Niko Associates; Stage Managers, Bob Borod, Glen Gardali, David John O'Brien; Executive Producer, Manny Kladitis; Presented by National Actors Theatre (Tony Randall, Founder/Artistic Director; Michael Langham, Artistic Advisor); Press, John and Gary Springer; Previewed from Tuesday, March 23; Opened in the Lyceum Theatre on Tuesday, April 13, 1993*

CAST

Audrey Trowbridge	Julie Hagerty
The Tailor	John Beal
Erwin Trowbridge	Tony Randall
Clarence Dobbins	Ralph Williams
Delivery Boy	Danny Burstein
Harry	Joey Faye
Charlie	Jerry Stiller
Frankie	Zane Lasky
Patsy	Jack Klugman
Mabel	Helmar Augustus Cooper
Gloria	Leslie Anderson
Mr. Carver	John Franklyn-Robbins
Al/Radio Announcer	Michael Stuhlbarg
Hotel Maid	Heather Harlan
Sylvia, the Chanteuse	Nora Mae Lyng
Gus, the Piano Player	David Geist
Racetrack Announcer	Dave Johnson

UNDERSTUDIES: Andrew Bloch (Patsy/Charlie/Harry), Danny Burstein (Tailor/Al), Edmund C. Davys (Erwin/Clarence/Carver), Margery Murray (Audrey/Mabel), Michael Stuhlbarg (Frankie/Delivery Boy)

A new production of the 1935 comedy. Performed in two acts with seven scenes. The action takes place in and around New York City.

Variety noted 2 favorable, 3 mixed and 7 negative reviews. *Times* (Gussow): "...the show is as dim and contrived a play as could be imagined.", *News* (Kissel): "...you have to be touched by the fact that Tony Randall has invited his old friend and colleague to appear with him..." (Watt): "...shoddy production, ill cast..." *Post* (Barnes): "...it happily reunites the American stage's oddest but most adored odd couple...", *Newsday* (Winer): "...this strangely cautious revival has too much logic and not enough ballons. Things don't threaten to blow up..." *Variety* (Greg Evans): "Steady improvement, but unspectacular."

*Closed May 16, 1993 after 40 performances and 24 previews.

Joan Marcus Photos

Tony Randall, Julie Hagerty

Tony Randall, Ellen Greene

THE NORMAL HEART

By Larry Kramer; Director, Jerry Zaks; Assistant Director, Lori Steinberg; Stage Manager, George Darveris; General Manager, Ellen Richard; Associate Producer, James Calleri; Made possible in part by a grant from Broadway Cares/Equity Fights AIDS; Presented by David Binder and David G. O'Connell; Press, Chris Boneau/Adrian Bryan-Brown, Craig Karpel; Performed for 1 night only in the Criterion Center/Roundabout Theatre on Sunday May 18, 1993

CAST

Craig Donner/Hiram Keebler/Examining Doctor ....Kevin Bacon
Mickey Marcus..John Turturro
Ned Weeks ....Eric Bogosian
David/Grady..Kevin Geer
Dr. Emma Brookner..Stockard Channing
Bruce Niles ....Harry Hamlin
Felix Turner..D.W. Moffett
Ben Weeks ....Tony Roberts
Tommy Boatwright ....David Drake
Stage Directions ....Jonathan Hadary

with introduction by Barbra Streisand

   A staged reading of the 1985 drama to benefit the Treatment and Data Network of ACT UP. D.W. Moffett originated his role at the Public Theatre with Brad Davis (see Theatre World Vol.41).

Eric Bogosian

Barbra Streisand

Stockard Channing

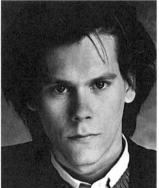

Kevin Bacon

Mike Burstyn, Maureen McNamara Above: Debbie Shapiro Gravitte in "Ain't Broadway Grand"

Jerry Bauer, Martha Swope Photos

38

AIN'T BROADWAY GRAND

Music, Mitch Leigh; Lyrics, Lee Adams; Book, Thomas Meehan, Mr. Adams; Director, Scott Harris; Choreography, Randy Skinner; Orchestrations, Chris Bankey; Musical Director, Nicholas Archer; Musical Supervision/Vocal Arrangements, Neil Warner; Dance Arrangements, Scot Wooley; Sets, David Mitchell; Costumes, Suzy Benzinger; Lighting, Ken Billington; Sound, Otts Munderloh; Hair/Make-Up, Masarone; Cast Recording, Music Makers; Casting, Gayle Kenerson; Production Supervisor, Jeremiah J. Harris; General Manager, Peter H. Russell; Stage Managers, Frank Marino, John Actman; A Tra La La Production; Presented by Arthur Rubin; Press, Fred Nathan/William Schelble; Previewed from Friday, March 26; Opened in the Lunt-Fontanne Theatre on Sunday, April 18, 1993*

CAST

Bobby Clark	Gerry Vichi
Gypsy Rose Lee	Debbie Shapiro Gravitte
Mike Todd	Mike Burstyn
Harriet Popkin	Alix Korey
Lou, the Stage Manager	Bill Nabel
Murray Pearl	Mitchell Greenberg
Reuben Pelish	David Lipman
Joan Blondell	Maureen McNamara
Marvin Fischbein	Gabriel Barre
Waldo Klein	Bill Kux
Wally Farfle	Scott Elliott
Dexter Leslie	Richard B. Shull
Jaeger	Merwin Goldsmith
Lindy's Waiters	Bill Corcoran, Jerold Goldstein, Bill Nabel
Thelma	Caitlin Carter
Floyd	Patrick Wetzel
Rocco	Luis Perez +1
Frankie, the Bartender	Scott Fowler
Herbie, the Office Boy	Jerold Goldstein

Of The People Cast I

President & His Cabinet ....Timothy Albrecht, Mr. Corcoran, Mr. Elliott, Mr. Fowler, Mr. Goldstein, Joe Istre, Rod McCune, Mr. Nabel, Mr. Perez, Mimi Cichanowicz Quillin, Mr. Wetzel
Riverside Drive Streetwalker ....Beverly Britton
Lili ....Ginger Prince
Sheryl ....Jennifer Frankel
Linda ....Ms. Quillin

Of The People Cast II

President & His Cabinet.................Leslie Bell, Ms. Britton, Ms. Carter, Colleen Dunn, Ms. Frankel, Lauren Golar-Kosarin, Elizabeth Mills, Ms. Prince, Ms. Quillin, Carol Denise Smith
Ensemble...Mr. Albrecht, Ms. Bell, Ms. Britton, Ms. Carter, Mr. Corcoran, Ms. Dunn, Mr. Elliott, Mr. Fowler, Ms. Frankel, Mr. Goldstein, Ms. Goler-Kosarin, Mr. Istre, Mr. McCune, Ms. Mills, Mr. Nabel, Mr. Perez, Ms. Prince, Ms. Quillin, Ms. Smith, Mr. Wetzel

UNDERSTUDIES/STANDBYS: P.J. Benjamin (Mike), Mimi C. Quillin (Gypsy), Beverly Britton (Joan), Jerold Goldstein (Bobby/Reuben), Scott Elliott (Marvin/Waldo), Bill Nabel (Murray/Jaeger), Ginger Prince (Harriet), Merwin Goldsmith (Dexter) SWINGS: Kelli Barclay, James Horvath, Lynn Sullivan

MUSICAL NUMBERS: Girls Ahoy!, Ain't Broadway Grand, Class, The Theatre The Theatre, Lindy's, It's Time to Go, Waiting in the Wings, You're My Star, A Big Job, They'll Never Take Us Alive, On the Street, The Man I Married, Maybe Maybe Not, Tall Dames and Low Comedy, He's My Guy, Finale

A musical in two acts with 18 scenes. The action takes place in New York and Boston, 1948. An earlier version of this show was titled "Mike."

Variety recorded 2 favorable and 13 negative notices. *Times* (Gussow): "Originality..is a key ingredient missing..Mr. Leigh's score..is listenable and recognizable." (Richards): "...isn't good enough–or bad enough–to be much fun.", *News* (Kissel): "My heart went out to the talented chorus, who work so hard injecting cheer and zest...", *Post* (Barnes): "...the evening brightens whenever Alix Korey and Mitchell Greenberg show up..inability of the show to grab and maintain the interest." *Newsday* (Winer): "...songs that sound remarkably like '40s standards...", *Variety* (Gerard): "No, it ain't."

*Closed May 9, 1993 after 25 performances and 27 previews.

+Succeeded by: 1. Peter Gregus

Grossman/Goldsmith/Schnier Photos

Maureen McNamara, Mike Burstyn, Debbie Shapiro Gravitte, Gerry Vichi
Center: Ensemble
Top: Mike Burstyn, Mimi Cichanowicz Quillin, Coleen Dunn, Jennifer Frankel

WILDER, WILDER, WILDER

THREE BY THORNTON WILDER

Director, Edward Berkeley; Set, Miguel Lopez-Castillo; Costumes, Dede Pochos, Fiona Davis; Lighting, Steven Rust; Company Manager, Susan Elrod; Stage Managers, Wm. Hare, James Marr; Presented by Circle in the Square (Theodore Mann, Artistic Director; George Elmer, Managing Director; Paul Libin, Consulting Producer) and Willow Cabin Theatre Company (Mr. Berkeley, Artistic Director; Adam Oliensis, Maria Radman, Producing Directors); Press, Bruce Cohen/Patty Onagan; Previewed from Friday, April 9; Opened in the Circle in the Square Uptown on Wednesday, April 21, 1993*

CASTS

THE LONG CHRISTMAS DINNER

Lucia 1	Linda Powell
Roderick 1	Ken Forman
Mother Bayard/Lucia 2	Sabrina Boudot
Cousine Brandon	Jonathan Sea
Nurse	Rebecca Killy
Charles	Adam Oliensis
Genevieve	Angela Nevard
Leonora	Fiona Davis
Cousine Ermengarde	Cynthia Besteman
Sam	David Goldman

THE HAPPY JOURNEY TO TRENTON AND CAMDEN

Stage Manager	Michael Rispoli
Ma Kirby	Maria Radman
Arthur	Craig Zakarian
Caroline	Dede Pochos
Elmer	Laurence Gleason
Beulah	Tasha Lawrence

PULLMAN CAR HIAWATHA

Stage Manager	Michael Rispoli
Lower #1	Dede Pochos
Lower #3	Peter Killy
Lower #7	Adam Oliensis
Lower #9	Jonathan Sea
Porter	Patrick Huey
Harriet	Angela Nevard
Phillip	Craig Zakarian
Insane Woman	Tasha Lawrence
Nurse	Linda Powell
Attendant	Stephen Mora
Grover's Comer, Ohio/Mercury	David Goldman
The Field/Mars	Laurence Gleason
Parkersburgh, Ohio/Venus	Cynthia Besteman
The Tramp	Ken Forman
The German Workman	Bjarne Hecht
The Watchman	John Billeci
The Weather	Charmaine Lord
10 O'Clock	Sabrina Boudot
11 O'Clock	Rebecca Killy
12 O'Clock	Fiona Davis
Archangel Gabriel	Timothy McNamara

Three one-act plays written in 1931.

Variety recorded 2 favorable, 4 mixed and 1 negative review. *Times* (Wilborn Hampton): "...Thornton Wilder was perhaps the American theatre's greatest innovative genius.", *Post* (Barnes): "...a strong visual fascination.", *Newsday* (Jacobson): "...Grand Hotel, ..the musical..was cheery compared to Wilder, Wilder, Wilder ...", *Variety* (Gerard): "...charming production..youthful company..refreshing to behold.."

*Closed May 16, 1993 after 30 performances and 14 previews on Broadway. The production played 46 performances at the Second Stage and 21 performances at the Harold Clurman Theatre earlier in the season.

Carol Rosegg/Martha Swope, Edward Berkeley Photos

Top: Maria Radman, Dede Pochos, Craig Zakarian, Laurence Gleason

Maria Radman, Dede Pochos, Craig Zakarian, Laurence Gleason

Michael Cerveris in "Tommy"

THE WHO'S TOMMY

Music/Lyrics, Pete Townshend; Book, Mr. Townshend, Des McAnuff; Director, Mr. McAnuff; Additional Music/Lyrics, John Entwistle, Keith Moon; Choreography, Wayne Cilento; Orchestrations, Steve Margoshes; Musical Supervision/Direction, Joseph Church; Musical Coordinator, John Miller; Sets, John Arnone; Costumes, David C. Woolard; Lighting, Chris Parry; Projections, Wendall K. Harrington; Sound, Steve Canyon Kennedy; Video, Batwin + Robin Productions; Hairstylist, David H. Lawrence; Special Effects, Gregory Meeh; Flying by Foy; Fights, Steve Rankin; Cast Recording, RCA; Company Manager, Sandy Carlson; Stage Managers, Frank Hartenstein, Karen Armstrong; Executive Producers, David, Strong, Warner, Inc., Scott Zieger/Gary Gunas; Associate Producer, John F. Kennedy Center for the Performing Arts; Presented by PACE Theatrical Group and DODGER Productions with Kardana Productions; Press, Chris Boneau/Adrian Bryan-Brown/Susanne Tighe; Previewed from Monday, March 29; Opened in the St. James Theatre on Thursday, April 22, 1993*

CAST

Mrs. Walker ....Marcia Mitzman
Captain Walker ....Jonathan Dokuchitz
Uncle Ernie ....Paul Kandel
Minister/Mr. Simpson ....Bill Buell
Minister's Wife ....Jody Gelb
Nurse ....Lisa Leguillou
Officer #1/Hawker ....Michael McElroy
Officer #2 ....Timothy Warmen
Allied Soldier #1/1st Pinball Lad ....Donnie Kehr
Allied Soldier #2 ....Michael Arnold
Lover/Harmonica Player...Lee Morgan
Tommy, Age 4 ....Carly Jane Steinborn,Crysta Macalush
(alternating performances)
Tommy...Michael Cerveris
Judge/Kevin's Father/*News* Vendor/DJ ....Tom Flynn
Tommy, Age 10 ....Buddy Smith
Cousin Kevin ....Anthony Barrile
Kevin's Mother ....Maria Calabrese
Local Lads/Security Guards ....Mr. Arnold, Paul Dobie,
Christian Hoff, Mr. Kehr, Mr. McElroy, Mr. Warmen
Local Lasses ....Ms. Calabrese, Tracy Nicole Chapman,
Pam Klinger, Lisa Leguillou, Alice Ripley, Sherie Scott
The Gypsy ....Cheryl Freeman
2nd Pinball Lad ....Christian Hoff
Specialist ....Norm Lewis
Specialist's Assistant ....Alice Ripley
Sally Simpson ....Sherie Scott
Mrs. Simpson ....Pam Klinger
Ensemble.....................................Mr. Arnold, Mr. Buell, Ms. Calabrese, Ms. Chapman,
Mr. Dobie, Mr. Flynn, Ms. Gelb, Mr. Hoff, Mr. Kehr, Ms. Klinger, Ms. Leguillou,
Mr. Lewis, Mr. McElroy, Mr. Morgan, Ms. Ripley, Ms. Scott, Mr. Warmen

UNDERSTUDIES: Donnie Kehr, Roman Fruge (Tommy/Cousin Kevin), Ari Vernon (Tommy,10), Alice Ripley, Jody Gelb (Mrs. Walker), Paul Dobie, Timothy Warmen, Todd Hunter (Walker), Bill Buell, Tom Flynn (Ernie), Tracy Langran, Nicole Chapman (Gypsy) SWINGS: Victoria Lecta Cave, Roman Fruge, Todd Hunter, Tracey Langran

MUSICAL NUMBERS: Overture, Captain Walker, It's a Boy, We've Won, Twenty-One, Amazing Journey, Sparks, Christmas, See Me Feel Me, Do You Think It's Alright, Fiddle About, Cousin Kevin, Sensation, Eyesight to the Blind, Acid Queen, Pinball Wizard, Underture (Entr'act), There's a Doctor, Go to the Mirror, Listening to You, Tommy Can You Hear Me, I Believe My Own Eyes(new song), Smash the Mirror, I'm Free, Miracle Cure, Tommy's Holiday Camp, Sally Simpson, Welcome, We're Not Going to Take It, Finale

A musical in two acts with 22 scenes. The action takes place mostly in London between 1941-63. Tommy originated as a 1969 rock opera album.

Variety recorded 13 favorable, 6 mixed and 4 negative reviews. *Times* (Rich): "...at long last the authentic rock musical that has eluded Broadway for two generations..for two hours it makes the world seem young." (Richards): "On a bare platform, a musical like My Fair Lady would still make sense. Tommy wouldn't..", *News* (Kissel): "...the actors are incidental to the constantly changing visuals..." (Jim Farber): "...it thrills...", *Post* (Barnes): "...came around to the St. James theatre last night in blazing triumph, and Broadway..will never be the same again..", *Newsday* (Winer): "The audience was on it's feet, whooping and cheering..I've seldom felt so alone in a theatre.." *Variety* (Gerard): "Seeing..is believing..the best rock 'n' roll show..ever produced on Broadway."

*Still playing May 31, 1993. Winner of 1993 "Tonys" for Direction of a Musical, Scenic Design, Lighting Design, Choreography, and Best Score (tie).

The Ensemble
Center: Jonathan Dokuchitz, Buddy Smith, Marcia Mitzman
Top: Donnie Kehr, Anthony Barrile, Christian Hoff

Marcus/Bryan-Brown Photos

BLOOD BROTHERS

**Con O'Neill, Mark Michael Hutchinson
Bottom: The Company**

Music/Lyrics/Book, Willy Russell; Directors, Bill Kenwright and Bob Tomson; Arrangements, Del Newman; Production Musical Director, Rod Edwards; Musical Director, Rick Fox; Musical Coordinator, Mort Silver; Sets/Costumes, Andy Walmsley; Lighting, Joe Atkins; Sound, Paul Astbury; Casting, Pat McCorkle; General Manager, Stuart Thompson; Company Manager, Bruce Klinger; Stage Managers, Mary Porter Hall, John Lucas; Associate Producer, Jon Miller; Presented by Mr. Kenwright; Press, Philip Rinaldi/Kathy Haberthur; Previewed from Wednesday, April 14; Opened in the Music Box Theatre on Sunday, April 25, 1993*

CAST

Mrs. Johnstone	Stephanie Lawrence
Narrator	Warwick Evans
Mrs. Lyons	Barbara Walsh
Mr. Lyons	Ivar Brogger
Mickey	Con O'Neill
Eddie	Mark Michael Hutchinson
Sammy	James Clow
Linda	Jan Graveson
Perkins	Sam Samuelson
Donna Marie/Miss Jones	Regina O'Malley
Policeman/Teacher	Robin Haynes
Brenda	Anne Torsiglieri
Ensemble	Mr. Brogger, Kerry Butler, Mr. Clow, Mr. Haynes, Philip Lehl, Ms. O'Malley, Mr. Samuelson, John Schiappa, Ms. Torsiglieri, Douglas Weston

UNDERSTUDIES: Regina O'Malley (Mrs. Johnstone/Mrs. Lyons), Philip Lehl (Mickey), John Schiappa (Sammy/Narrator), Sam Samuelson (Eddie), Anne Torsiglieri (Linda), Robin Haynes (Mr. Lyons), Kerry Butler (Donna)

MUSICAL NUMBERS: Marilyn Monroe, My Child, Easy Terms, Shoes Upon the Table, Kids Game, Prelude, Long Sunday Afternoon/My Friend, Bright New Day, That Guy, I'm Not Saying a Word, Take a Letter Miss Jones, Light Romance, Madman, Tell Me It's Not True

A musical in two acts. The action takes place in and around Liverpool. The show originally premiered in London's West End in January, 1983 and was revived there in 1988.

Variety noted 2 favorable, 1 mixed and 10 negative reviews. *Times* (Rich): "..rousing theatre ionly in spurts..score is tuneful..but spread thin..." (Richards): "Strained as the premise is, it allows Mr. Russel to illustrate his conviction...", *News* (Kissel): "...pathetically melodramatic plot..."(Watt): "...overall, it's as dull as dishwater.", *Post* (Barnes): "...heavy handed, heavy footed...", *Newsday* (Winer): "There is much one wants to embrace..heart, social conscience, simplicity...", *Variety* (Gerard): "...a weird effect..while it's bad theatre, I didn't regret having spent time with these people..."

*Still playing May 31, 1993.

Joan Marcus, Phil Cutts Photos

Stephanie Lawrence, Con O'Neill

SHAKESPEARE FOR MY FATHER

Conceived and Written by Lynn Redgrave; Director/Producer, John Clark; Lighting, Thomas R. Skelton; Sound, Duncan Edwards; Associate Lighting Designer, Beverly Emmonds; Production Supervisor, David Bosboom; Company Manager, Roy Gabay; Stage Manager, C. A. Clark; Press, John and Gary Springer/Jeffrey Richards; Previewed from Tuesday, April 20; Opened in the Helen Hayes Theatre on Monday, April 26, 1993*

CAST

LYNN REDGRAVE

A reminiscence of life with Sir Michael Redgrave interspersed with scenes from Shakespeare.

Variety recorded 10 favorable and 3 mixed reviews. *Times* (Gussow): "...a revealing and often rueful account of life without father in a stagestruck family."(Richards): "...the actress possesses a bracing honesty, welcome wit and an unforced intelligence...", *News* (Kissel): "...elegantly written and acted memoir."(Watt) "...touched with shadows...", *Post* (Barnes): "...her anecdotes are hilarious.", *Newsday* (Winer): "...surprisingly engaging, touching, easygoing...", *Variety* (Evans): "...argues convincingly for Lynn's status as a Redgrave."

*Closed January 2, 1994 after 266 performances and 8 previews.

**Right: Lynn Redgrave, Sir Michael Redgrave
Top: Lynn Redgrave**

TANGO PASION

Conception, Mel Howard; Choreography, Hector Zaraspe; Orhestrations/Arrangements/Musical Direction, Jose Libertella and Luis Stazo; Sets based on paintings by Ricardo Carpani; Costumes/Scenic Design, John Falabella; Lighting, Richard Pilbrow, Dawn Chiang; Sound, Jan Nebozen-ko; Stage Manager, Joe Lorden; Executive Producer, Norman Rothstein; Presented by Mel Howard, Donald K. Donald, Irving Schwartz; Press, Chris Boneau/Adrian Bryan Brown/Ellen Levene; Previewed from Friday, April 23; Opened in the Longacre Theatre on Wednesday, April 28, 1993*

CAST

Ricardo (The Artist) ....Alberto del Solar
Pedro Montero ....Jorge Torres
Lila Quintana ....Pilar Alvarez
Lucas (The Maitre d') ....Osvaldo Ciliento
Juan Larossa ....Gustavo Russo
Senorita Virginia ....Veronica Gardella
Carmela (The Waitress) ....Alejandra Mantinan
Julio Camargo ....Marcelo Bernadaz
Dr. Bertolini ....Luis Castro
Senora Rosalinda Bertolini ....Claudia Mendoza
Carlos Bronco ....Armando Orzuza
Senora Dora Bronco ....Daniela Arcuri
Grisel (Carlos' Mistress) ....Graciela Garcia
Romero Brandan (The Spoiler) ....Jorge Romano
Rosendo Frias (Pool Player) ....Fernando Jimenez
Angela (Rosendo's Girlfriend) ....Judit Aberastain
Rodolfo (The Club Singer) ....Daniel Bouchet
Flora Rosa (The Club Singer) ....Yeni Patino
Zully (The Lieutenant's Date) ....Viviana Laguzzi
The Lieutenant...Juan Corvalan
Ludmilla Orlinskaya (European Movie Star) Gunilla Wingquist and THE SEXTETO MAYOR TANGO ORCHESTRA

A dance musical in two acts. The action takes place in the late 1940s (Act I) and the present (Act II).

Variety noted 3 mixed and 7 negative reviews. *News* (Joan Acocella) "..dull material being half-saved by the people performing it.", *Post* (Barnes): "...faintly bizarre.", *Variety* (Evans): "Rescuing tango from the discard heap of kitsch is an order far too tall for Tango Pasion."

*Closed May 2, 1993 after 5 performances and 6 previews.

Jo Winstead Photos

Viviana Laguzzi, Juan O. Corvalan

KISS OF THE SPIDER WOMAN

Music, John Kander; Lyrics, Fred Ebb; Book, Terrence McNally; Based on the novel by Manuel Puig; Director, Harold Prince; Orchestrations, Michael Gibson; Musical Director, Jeffrey Huard; Dance Music, David Krane; Choreography, Vincent Paterson; Additional Choreography, Rob Marshall; Sets/Projections, Jerome Sirlin; Costumes, Florence Klotz; Lighting, Howell Bikley; Sound, Martin Levan; Mr. Prince's Assistant, Ruth Mitchell; Cast Recording (London), RCA; Casting, Johnson-Liff & Zerman; Company Manager, Jim Brandeberry; Stage Managers, Beverly Randolph, Clayton Phillips; Presented by Livent (U.S.); Press, Mary Bryant; Previewed from Monday, April 19; Opened in the Broadhurst Theatre on Monday, May 3, 1993*

CAST

Molina	Brent Carver
Warden	Herndon Lackey
Valentin	Anthony Crivello
Esteban	Philip Hernandez
Marcos	Michael McCormick
Spider Woman/Aurora	Chita Rivera
Aurora's Men/Prisoners	Keith McDaniel, Robert Montano, Dan O'Grady, Raymond Rodriguez
Molina's Mother	Merle Louise
Marta	Kirsti Carnahan
Escaping Prisoner	Colton Green
Religious Fanatic/Prisoner	John Norman Thomas
Amnesty Int'l Observer/Prisoner Emilio	Joshua Finkel
Prisoner Fuentes	Gary Schwartz
Gabriel/Prisoner	Jerry Christakos
Window Dresser at Montoya's/Prisoner	Aurelio Padron

STANDBYS/UNDERSTUDIES: Dorothy Stanley (Spider Woman/Aurora/Marta), Lorraine Foreman (Mother), Joshua Finkel (Molina), Philip Hernandez (Valentin), Gary Schwartz (Valentin/Esteban/Observer), John Norman Thomas (Marcos), Michael McCormick (Warden), Dan O'Grady (Gabriel) SWINGS: Gregory Mitchell, Colton Green (partial)

MUSICAL NUMBERS: Prologue, Her Name Is Aurora, Over the Wall, Blubloods, Dressing Them Up/I Draw the Line, Dear One, Where You Are, Marta, Come, I Do Miracles, Gabriel's Letter/My First Woman, Morphine Tango, You Could Never Shame Me, A Visit, She's a Woman, Gimme Love, Russian Movie/Good *Times*, The Day After That, Mama It's Me, Anything for Him, Kiss of the Spider Woman, Only in the Movies

A musical in two acts with 19 scenes and prologue. The action takes place in a prison in Latin America, sometime in the recent past.

Variety recorded 10 favorable, 3 mixed and 3 negative notices. *Times* (Rich): "...a shiver of pure theatre..consumates the showmanship of a director who wrote the book on how to spread a web of white heat through a Broadway house." (Richards): "..the last musical of the season, is far and away the most thrilling..Brent Carver..electrifying Broadway debut..Chita Rivera..significantly closer to legendary status.", *News* (Kissel): "Kander and Ebb have written one of their most pungent and original scores." (Watt): "...brilliantly orchestrated by Michael Gibson...",*Newsday* (Winer): "For all the spectacle..Puig's connections between sexual repression, totalitarianism and rebellion are sorely missed.", *Variety* (Gerard): "..will undoubtedly divide critics and audiences alike..."

*Still playing May 31, 1993. Winner of 1993 "Tony" Awards for Best Musical, Leading Actor in a Musical (Brent Carver), Leading Actress in a Musical (Chita Rivera), Featured Actor in a Musical (Anthony Crivello), Book of a Musical, Costume Design, and Best Score (tie). Winner of New York Drama Critics Circle for Best

**Left: Chita Rivera, Brent Carver, Kristi Carnahan, (lying) Anthony Crivello
Center: Chita Rivera and Cast Members
Top: Chita Rivera, Brent Carver**

Chita Rivera

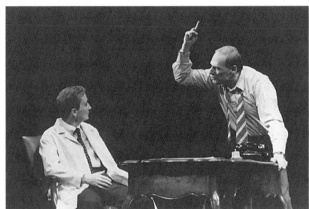

Marcia Gay Harden, Stephen Spinella
Center Left: Stephen Spinella, David Marshall Grant, Marcia Gay Harden,
Joe Mantello
Top Left: Joe Mantello, Stephen Spinella

Ron Leibman
Center Right: Kathleen Chalfant, Ron Leibman
Top Right: David Marshall Grant, Ron Leibman

ANGELS IN AMERICA
MILLENNIUM APPROACHES
A Gay Fantasia On National Themes

By Tony Kushner; Director, George C. Wolfe; Sets, Robin Wagner; Costumes, Toni-Leslie James; Lighting, Jules Fisher; Original Music, Anthony Davis; Additional Music, Michael Ward; Sound, Scott Lehrer; Hair/Make-Up, Jeffrey Frank; Production Supervision, Gene O'Donovan/Neil A. Mazzella; Casting, Meg Simon, Stanley Soble; Company Manager, Lisa M. Poyer; Stage Managers, Perry Cline, Mary K. Klinger, Michael Passaro; Produced in association with The New York Shakespeare Festival; Executive Producers, Benjamin Mordecai and Robert Cole; Presented by Jujamcyn Theatres, Mark Taper Forum/Gordon Davidson, Margo Lion, Susan Quint Gallin, Jo B. Platt, The Baruch-Frankel-Viertel Group, Frederick Zollo, Herb Alpert; Press, Chris Boneau/Adrian Bryan-Brown/ Bob Fennell; Previewed from Tuesday April 13; Opened in the Walter Kerr Theatre on Tuesday, May 4, 1993*

CAST

Rabbi Chemelwitz/Henry/Hannah Pitt/Ethel Rosenberg............	...Kathleen Chalfant
Roy Cohn/Prior 2	Ron Leibman
Joe Pitt/Prior 1/Eskimo	David Marshall Grant
Harper Pitt/Martin Heller	Marcia Gay Harden
Mr. Lies/Belize	Jeffrey Wright
Louis Ironson	Joe Mantello
Prior Walter/Man in Park	Stephen Spinella
Emily/Ella Chapter/So.Bronx Woman/The Angel	Ellen McLaughlin

UNDERSTUDIES: Jay Goede (Prior/Joe/Louis), Matthew Sussman (Roy Cohn /Louis), Susan Bruce (Harper/Angel), Beth McDonald (Hannah/Angel), Darnell Williams (Belize)

A drama in three acts. The action takes place in New York City, Salt Lake City and Elsewhere. Millennium Approches is the first of two parts of Angels In America.

Variety recorded 15 favorable and 4 mixed reviews. Times (Rich): "...the most thrilling American play in years..speaks so powerfully..." (Richards) "...everywhere Mr. Kushner looks he sees people fleeing responsibilities, blocking out the truth. America, as a whole, would seem to have gone deaf, dumb and blind.", News (Kissel): "It is a wild, savagely comic journey..That Kushner is a major voice seems beyond doubt." (Watt) "A striking combination of ferocity, vision, daring and compassion..", Post (Barnes): "...the quick laugh can detract from the playwright's more serious purpose...", Newsday (Winer): "...a fierce and wonderful play..as intimate and entertaining as it is monumental and spiritual.", Variety (Gerard): "...restoring..Broadway's fading lustre as the preeminent venue for important work..smartly ambitious, unabashedly sprawling, glintingly provocative, frequently hilarious and urgently poignant play is as revelatory as the title suggests..."

*Still playing May 31, 1993. Winner of the 1993 Pulitzer Award for drama. Winner of 1993 "Tony" Awards for Best Play, Leading Actor in a Play (Ron Leibman), Featured Actor in a Play (Stephen Spinella), Direction of a Play. Winner of 1993 New York Drama Critics Circle for Best Play.

Joan Marcus Photos

**Top Right: Ellen McLaughlin
Below: Jeffrey Wright
Bottom: Stephen Spinella
Above: Kathleen Chalfant**

CATS

Music, Andrew Lloyd Webber; Based on Old Possum's Book Of Practical Cats by T.S. Eliot; Orchestrations, David Cullen, Lloyd Webber; Prod. Musical Director, David Caddick; Musical Director, Edward G. Robinson; Sound, Martin Levan; Lighting, David Hersey; Design, John Napier; Choreography/Associate Director, Gillian Lynne; Director, Trevor Nunn; Original Cast Recording, Geffen; Casting, Johnson-Liff & Zerman; General Managers, Gatchell & Neufeld; Company Manager, James G. Mennen; Stage Managers, Peggy Peterson, Tom Taylor, Suzanne Viverito; Presented by Cameron Mackintosh, The Really Useful Co., David Geffen, and The Shubert Organization; Press, Fred Nathan/Michael Borowski; Opened in the Winter Garden Theatre on Thursday, October 7, 1982*

Liz Callaway

CAST

Alonzo ....Stephen M. Reed +1
Bustopher/Asparagus/Growltiger ....Jeffrey Clonts
Bombalurina ....Marlene Danielle
Cassandra ....Leigh Webster +2
Coricopat ....Johnny Anzalone +3
Demeter..Mercedes Perez
Grizabella..Laurie Beechman +4
Jellylorum/Griddlebone..Nina Hennessey
Jennanydots..Rose McGuire
Mistoffelees ....Kevin Poe +5
Mungojerrie..Roger Kachel
Munkustrap..Bryan Batt +6
Old Deuteronomy ....Larry Small +7
Plato/Macivity/Rumpus Cat ....Randy Wojcik +8
Pouncival ....Devanand N. Janki +9
Rum Tum Tiger ....Bradford Minkoff +10
Rumpleteazer ....Kristi Lynes +11
Sillabub..Lisa Mayer +12
Skimbleshanks..George Smyros
Tantomile ....Michelle Artigas
Tumblebrutus ....John Vincent Leggio +14
Victoria ....Claudia Shell
Cat Chorus......................................John Briel, Jay Aubrey Jones, Susan
....Powers, Heidi Stallings

STANDBYS/UNDERSTUDIES: Michael Arnold, Brian Andrews, Kevin Berdini, Dawn Marie Church, Angelo H. Fraboni, Wade Laboissonniere, John Vincent Leggio, David E. Liddell, Joe Locarro, Jack Magredey, Rusty Mowery, Jim Raposa, Sarah Solie Shannon, Michelle Schumacher, Lynn Shuck, Lynn Sterling, Sally Ann Swarm, Suzanne Vivertito, Leigh Webster, Lily-Lee Wong

MUSICAL NUMBERS: Jellicle Songs for Jellicle Cats, Naming of Cats, Invitation to the Jellicle Ball, Old Gumbie Cat, Rum Tum Tugger,Grizabella the Glamour Cat, Bustopher Jones, Mungojerrie and Rumpleteazer, Old Deuteronomy, Aweful Battle of the Pekes and Pollicles, Memory, Moments of Happiness, Gus the Theatre Cat, Growltiger's Last Stand, Skimbleshanks, Macavity, Mr. Mistoffolees, Journey to the Heavyside Layer, Ad-dressing of Cats

A musical in two acts with 20 scenes.

*Still playing May 31, 1993. The musical celebrated it's tenth Broadway anniversary on October 7, 1992 with more than 4000 performances. Winner of 1983 "Tonys" for Best Musical, Score, Book, Direction, Costumes, Lighting, and Featured Actress in a Musical (Betty Buckley as Grizabella). For original 1982 production see Theatre World Vol.39.

+Succeeded by: 1. Randy Wojcik 2. Darlene Wilson, Leigh Webster 3. Cholsu Kim 4. Diane Fratantoni, Laurie Beechman, Liz Callaway, Laurie Beechman, Heidi Stallings, Liz Callaway 5. Gen Horiuchi, Lindsay Chambers 6. Robert Amirante, Bryan Batt, Dan McCoy, Bryan Batt, Dan McCoy 7. Ken Prymus 8. Robb Edward Morris 9. Joey Pizzi, Devanand N. Janki 10.B K Kennelly 11. Christine DeVito 12. Joyce Chittick, Lisa Mayer 13. Lynn Sterling, Michelle Artigas 14. Michael Giacobbe, Marc Ellis Holland

Martha Swope Photos

Jeffrey Clonts, Dan McCoy

CONVERSATIONS WITH MY FATHER

By Herb Gardner; Director, Daniel Sullivan; Sets, Tony Walton; Costumes, Robert Wojewodski; Lighting, Pat Collins; Sound, Michael Holten; Casting, Meg Simon; General Manger, James Walsh; Company Manager, Florie Seery; Stage Managers, Warren Crane, Anna Jo Gender; Presented by James Walsh; Press, Jeffrey Richards/David LeShay, Ben Gutkin; Previewing from Thursday, March 3; Opened in the Royale Theatre on Sunday, March 29, 1992*

CAST

Charlie	Tony Shalhoub +1
Josh/Joey	Tony Gillan +2
Eddie	Judd Hirsch +3
Gusta	Gordana Rashovich
Zaretsky	David Margulies+4
Young Joey	Jason Biggs +5
Hannah Di Blindeh	Marilyn Sokol
Nick	William Biff McGuire +6
Finney the Book	Peter Gerety
Jimmy Scalso	John Procaccino +7
Blue	Richard E. Council
Young Charlie	David Krumholtz +8

UNDERSTUDIES/STANDBYS: Sidney Armus (Zaretsky), Robert Canaan (Josh/Joey), Richard E. Council (Scalso), Cheryl Giannini (Gusta/Hannah), John Procaccino (Charlie), Michael M. Ryan (Nick/Blue/Finney), Tristan Smith (Young Charlie/Young Joey)

A drama in two acts. The action takes place on Canal St. in New York City between 1936-76.

*Closed March 14, 1993 after 402 performances and 30 previews. Winner of 1992 "Tony" Award for Best Actor in a Play (Judd Hirsch).

Succeeded by: 1. James Sutorius 2. Robert Canaan 3.James Belushi 4. Richard Libertini during previews 5. Rick Faugno 6. Alan North 7. Joseph Siravo 8. Jason Woliner

Marc Bryan-Brown Photos

Tony Gillan, Judd Hirsch   Top: James Belushi, Gordana Rashovich

CRAZY FOR YOU

Music, George Gershwin; Lyrics, Ira Gershwin, Gus Kahn, Desmond Carter; Book, Ken Ludwig; Conception, Mr. Ludwig and Mike Ockrent, inspired by material by Guy Bolton and John McGowan; Director, Mr. Ockrent; Choreography, Susan Stroman; Orchestrations, William D. Brohn, Sid Ramin; Musical Director, Paul Gemignani; Musical Consultant, Tommy Krasker; Dance/Incidental Arrangements, Peter Howard; Sets, Robin Wagner; Costumes, William Ivey Long; Lighting, Paul Gallo; Sound, Otts Munderloh; Casting, Julie Hughes, Barry Moss; Cast Recording, Broadway Angel; Fights, B.H. Barry; Hairstylist, Angela Gari; General Manager, Gatchell & Neufeld; Prod. Manager, Peter Fulbright; Company Manager, Abbie M. Strassler; Stage Managers, Steven Zweigbaum, John Bonanni; Associate Producers, Richard Godwin, Valerie Gordon; Presented by Roger Horchow and Elizabeth Williams; Press, Bill Evans/Jim Randolph, Susan L. Schulman, Erin Dunn; Previewing from Friday, January 31; Opened in the Shubert Theatre on Wednesday, February 19, 1992*

CAST

Tess	Beth Leavel
Patsy	Stacey Logan
Bobby Child	Harry Groener
Bela Zanger	Bruce Adler
Sheila	Judine Hawkins Richard
Mitzi	Paula Legget
Susie	Ida Henry
Louise	Jean Marie
Betsy	Peggy Ayn Maas
Margie	Salome Mazard
Vera	Louise Ruck
Elaine	Pamela Everett
Irene Roth	Michele Pawk
Mother	Jane Connell
Perkins/Custus	Gerry Burkhardt
Moose	Brian M. Nalepk	The Manhattan
Mingo	Tripp Hanson	Rhythm
Sam	Hal Shane	Kings
Junior	Casey Nicholaw
Pete	Fred Anderson
Jimmy	Michael Kubala
Billy	Ray Roderick
Wyatt	Jeffrey Lee Broadhurst
Harry	Joel Goodness
Polly Baker	Jodi Benson
Everett Baker	Ronn Carroll
Lank Hawkins	John Hillner
Eugene	Stepehn Temperley
Patricia	Amelia White

UNDERSTUDIES: Michael Kubala (Bobby/Lank/Bela), Beth Leavel (Polly), Paula Leggett (Irene), Gerry Burkhardt (Everett), Amelia White (Mother), Casey Nicholaw (Eugene), Peggy Ayn Maas (Pastsy), John Jellison (Everett/Eugene/Zangler), Ida Henry (Tess), Angelique Ilo (Patricia)

MUSICAL NUMBERS: Original sources follow in parentheses: K-ra-azy for You (Treasure Girl, 1928), I Can't Be Bothered Now (Film: A Damsel in Distress, 1937), Bidin' My Time (Girl Crazy, 1930), Things Are Looking Up (A Damsel in Distress,), Could You Use Me (Girl Crazy), Shall We Dance (Film: Shall We Dance, 1937), Someone to Watch Over Me (Oh Kay, 1926), Slap That Bass (Shall We Dance), Embraceable You (Girl Crazy), Tonight's the Night (previously unused), I Got Rhythm (Girl Crazy), The Real American Folk Song Is a Rag (Ladies First, 1918), What Causes That? (Treasure Girl), Naughty Baby (previously unused), Stiff Upper Lip (A Damsel in Distress), They Can't Take That Away From Me (Shall We Dance), But Not for Me (Girl Crazy), Nice Work If You Can Get It (A Damsel in Distress), Finale

A musical comedy, inspired by Girl Grazy (1930), in two acts with 17 scenes. The action takes place in New York City and Deadrock, Nevada in the 1930's.

*Still playing May 31, 1993. Winner of 1992 "Tonys" for Best Musical, Best Choreography and Best Costumes. The show has now passed it's 500th Broadway performance.

Joan Marcus Photos

Left: Harry Groener, Jane Connell
Center: The Finale
Top: Harry Groener with Showgirls

FALSETTOS

Music/Lyrics, William Finn; Book, Mr. Finn, James Lapine; Director, Mr. Lapine; Arrangements, Michael Starobin; Musical Director, Scott Frankel; Sets, Douglas Stein; Costumes, Ann Hould-Ward; Lighting, Frances Aronson; Sound, Peter Fitzgerald; Hairstylist, Phyllis Della; Musical Contractor, John Monaco; Cast Recording, DRG (one-acts); Casting, Wendy Ettinger, Susan Howard, Amy Schecter; Prod. Supervisor, Craig Jacobs; General Manager, Barbara Darwall; Company Manager, Kim Sellon; Stage Manager, Karen Armstrong; Produced in association with James and Maureen O'Sullivan Cushing and Masakazu Shibaoka Broadway Pacific; Associate Producer, Alecia Parker; Presented by Barry and Fran Weissler; Previewing from Wednesday, April 8; Opened in the John Golden Theatre on Wednesday, April 29, 1992*

CAST

Marvin ....Michael Rupert +1
Whizzer ....Stephen Bogardus +2
Mendel ....Chip Zien +3
Jason....................................Jonathan Kaplan +4, Andrew Harrison Leeds +5
Trina...Barbara Walsh +6
Charlotte...Heather Mac Rae
Cordelia...Carolee Carmello +7

STANBYS:UNDERSTUDIES: Philip Hoffman, John Ruess, Maureen Moore, Susan Goodman, Sal Viviano, Jordan Leeds, Jay Montgomery

MUSICAL NUMBERS: Four Jews in a Room Bitching, A Tight Knit Family, Love is Blind, Thrill of First Love, Marvin at the Psychiatrist, Everyone Tells Jason to See a Psychiatrist, This Had Better Come to a Stop, I'm Braking Down, Jason's Therapy, A Marriage Proposal, Trini's Song, March of the Falsettos, Chess Game, Making a Home, Games I Play, Marvin Goes Crazy, I Never Wanted to Love You, Father to Son, Welcome to Falsettoland, Year of the Child, Miracle of Judaism, Sitting Watching Jason Play Baseball, A Day in Falsettoland, Everyone Hates His Parents, What More Can I Say, Something Bad Is Happening, Holding to the Ground, Days Like This I Almost Believe in God, Cancelling the Bar Mitzvah, Unlikely Lovers, Another Miracle of Judaism, You Gotta Die Sometime, Jason's Bar Mitzvah, What Would I Do ?

A musical in two acts. The action takes place in 1979 and 1981.

*Closed June 27, 1993 after 487 performances and 23 previews. Winner of 1992 "Tonys" for Best Score and Best Book for a Musical.

+Succeeded by:1.Mandy Patinkin, Gregg Edelman 2.Sean McDermot 3. Jason Graae 4.Sivan Cotel 5.Jeffrey Landman 6. Randy Graff 7.Maureen Moore

Carol Rosegg/Martha Swope Photos

Left: Mandy Patinkin, Sean McDermott
Top Left: (top) Michael Rupert, Jonathan Kaplan
Top Right: Mandy Patinkin, Sivan Cotel, Barbara Walsh

FIVE GUYS NAMED MOE

Music/Lyrics by Louis Jordan with Leo Hickman, Dallas Bartley, Larry Wynn, Jerry Breslen, Morry Lasco, Dick Adams, Claude Demetriou, Jon Hendricks, Lora Lee, Johnny Burke, Jimmy Van Heusen, Sid Robin, Bill Davis, Don Wolf, Johnny Lange, Hy Heath, Joe Willoughby, Dr. Walt Merrick, Ellis Walsh, Busby Meyers, R. McCoy, C. Singleton, Browley Bri, Sam Theard, Spencer Lee, Joan Whitney, Alex Kramer, Jo Greene, Vaughn Horton, Denver Darling, Milton Gabler, Joseph Meyer, Buddy Bernier, Robert Emmerich, S. Austin; Book, Clarke Peters; Director/Choreographer, Charles Augins; Orchestrations, Neil McArthur; Vocal Arrangements/Musical Supervision, Chapman Roberts; Musical Director/Supervisor, Reginald Royal; Design, Tim Goodchild; Lighting, Andrew Bridge; Costumes, Noel Howard; Sound, Tony Meola/Autograph; Cast Recording, Columbia; Casting, Johnson-Liff & Zerman; General Manager, Alan Wasser; Company Manager, Michael Sanfilippo; Stage Managers, Marybeth Abel, Gwendolyn M. Gilliam, Roumel Reaux; Executive Producer, Richard Jay -Alexander; Presented by Cameron Mackintosh; Press, Merle Frimark/Marc Thibodeau; Previewing from Friday, March 20; Opened in the Eugene O'Neill Theatre on Wednesday, April 8, 1992*

CAST

Nomax	Jerry Dixon +1
Big Moe	Doug Eskew
Four-Eyed Moe	Milton Craig Nealy
No Moe	Kevin Ramsey
Eat Moe	Jeffrey D. Sams
Little Moe	Glenn Turner

UNDERSTUDIES: Phillip Gilmore (Nomax/Four Eyed/Eat Moe), Michael Leon Wooley (Big Moe/Eat Moe), W. Ellis Porter (Four-Eyed/No Moe/ Little Moe)

MUSICAL NUMBERS: Early in the Morning, Five Guys Named Moe, Beware Brother Beware, I Like 'em Fat Like That, Messy Bessy, Pettin' and Pokin', Life is so Peculiar, I Know What I've Got, Azure Te, Safe Sane and Single, Push Ka Pi Shi Pie, Saturday Night Fish Fry, What's the Use of Getting Sober, If I Had Any Sense, Dad Gum Your Hide Boy, Let the Good *Times* Roll, Reet Petite and Gone, Caldonia, Ain't Nobody Here But Us Chickens, Don't Let the Sun Catch You Crying, Choo Choo Ch'boogie, Look Out Sister, Hurray Home/Is You Is or Is You Ain't My Baby?, Finale

A musical in two acts.

*Closed May 2, 1993 after 445 performances and 19 previews.

+Succeeded by: 1. Weyman Thompson

Joan Marcus Photos

Milton Craig Nealy, Jeffrey Sams, Kevin Ramsey, Glenn Turner
Top: Jeffrey Sams, Kevin Ramsey, Doug Eskew, Milton Craig Nealy, Glen Turner, (Front) Jerry Dixon

GUYS AND DOLLS

A Musical Fable Of Broadway

Music/Lyrics, Frank Loesser; Book, Jo Swerling and Abe Burrows; Director, Jerry Zaks; Choreography, Christopher Chadman; Orchestrations, (original) George Bassman, Ted Royal, (new) Michael Starobin, Michael Gibson; Musical Supervision, Edward Strauss; Sets, Tony Walton; Costumes, William Ivey Long; Lighting, Paul Gallo; Dance Music, Mark Hummel; Sound, Tony Meola; Asst. Choreographer, Linda Haberman; Musical Coordinator, Seymour Red Press; Hairstylist, David H. Lawrence; Casting, Johnson-Liff & Zerman; Prod. Manager, Peter Fulbright; Company Manager, Marcia Goldberg; Stage Managers, Steven Beckler, Clifford Schwartz, Joe Deer; Cast Recording, RCA Victor; Executive Producer, David Strong Warner; Associate Producers, Playhouse Sq. Center, David B.Bode; Presented by Dodger Productions, Roger Berlind, Jujamcyn Theatres/TV ASAHI, Kardana Prod., and Kennedy Ceneter for the Performing Arts; Press, Chris Boneau/Adrian Bryan-Brown, John Barlow, Jackie Green; Previewed from Monday, March 16; Opened in the Martin Beck Theatre on Tuesday, April 14, 1992*

CAST

Nicely-Nicely Johnson	Walter Bobbie
Benny Southstreet	J.K. Simmons +1
Rusty Charlie/Guy	Timothy Shew
Sarah Brown	Josie de Guzman
Arvide Abernathy	John Carpeneter +2
Agatha	Eleanor Glockner
Calvin/Gu	Leslie Feagan
Martha	Victoria Clark +3
Harry the Horse	Ernie Sabella
Lt. Brannigan	Steve Ryan
Nathan Detroit	Nathan Lane +4
Angie the Ox/Joey Biltmore/Guy	Michael Goz
Miss Adelaide	Faith Prince
Sky Masterson	Peter Gallagher +5
Hot Box MC/Guy	Stan Page
Mimi/Doll	Denise Faye +6
Gen. Matilda B. Cartwright	Ruth Williamson
Big Jule	Herschel Sparber
Drunk/Guy	Robert Michael Baker +7
Waiter/Guy	Kenneth Kantor
Havana Dance Specialty	Sergio Trujillo, Nancy Lemenager
Crapshooter Dance Lead/Guy	Scott Wise

Other Guys........Randy Bettis, Larry Cahn, Lloyd Culbreath, R.F. Daley, Randy Andre Davis, Mark Esposito, Leslie Feagan, Aldrin Gonzalez, Dale Hensley, Carlos Lopez, John MacInnis
Other Dolls..............Tina Marie DeLeone, Pascale Faye, Jennifer Lamberts, Nancy Lemenager, Greta Martin, Holly Raye

UNDERSTUDIES: Jeff Brooks, Larry Cahn (Nathan/Benny/Harry), Robert Michael Baker (Sky), Leslie Feagan (Harry), Michael Goz (Jule), Kenneth Kantor (Brannigan), Stan Page (Arvide), Timothy Shew (Nicely/Brannigan), Steven Sofia (Calvin), Scott Wise (Charlie), Victoria Clark (Adelaide/Agatha), Eleanor Glockner (Cartwright), Tina Marie DeLeone (Mimi), Denise Faye (Agatha), Nancy Lemenager (Martha) SWINGS: Mr. Cahn, Susan Misner, Mr. Sofia

MUSICAL NUMBERS: Fugue for Tinhorns, Follow the Fold, The Oldest Established, I'll Know, A Bushel and a Peck, Adelaide's Lament, Guys and Dolls, Havana, If I Were a Bell, My Time of Day, I've Never Been in Love Before, Take Back Your Mink, More I Cannot Wish You, Crapshooter's Dance, Luck Be a Lady, Sue Me, Sit Down You're Rockin' the Boat, Marry the Man Today, Finale

A new production of the 1950 musical in two acts with seventeen scenes. The action takes place in "Runyonland" around Broadway and in Havana, Cuba. The original production (Theatre World Vol.7) opened at the Forty-Sixth St. Theatre on Nov.24, 1950 featuring Vivian Blaine, Robert Alda, Sam Levene, Isabel Bigley and Stubby Kaye , running 1200 performances.

*Still playing May 31, 1993. Winner of 1992 "Tonys" for Best Revival, Best Actress - Musical (Faith Prince), Best Director-Musical, Best Scenic Design

+Succeeded by 1. Jeff Brooks 2. Conrad McLauren 3. Jennifer Allen 4.Adam Arkin, Nathan Lane, Jonathan Hadary 5. Tom Wopat, Burke Moses 6.Tina Marie DeLeone 7.Jere Shea 8. Michael Berresse

Martha Swope Photos

Right: Tom Wopat, Josie de Guzman
Top: Jennifer Allen, Jonathan Hadary

JELLY'S LAST JAM

Music, Jelly Roll Morton, Luther Henderson; Lyrics, Susan Birkenhead; Book/Direction, George C. Wolfe; Choreography, Hope Clarke; Tap Choreography, Gregory Hines, Ted L. Levy; Musical Adaptation/Orchestrations/Musical Supervision, Mr. Henderson; Musical Director, Linda Twine; Sets, Robin Wagner; Costumes, Toni-Leslie James; Lighting, Jules Fisher; Musical Coordinator, John Miller; Sound, Otts Munderloh; Cast Recording, Mercury; Masks/ Puppets, Barbara Pollitt; Hairstylist, Jeffrey Frank; Casting, Hughes/Moss & Stanley Soble; General Manager, David Strong Warner; Company Manager, Susan Gustafson; Stage Managers, Arturo E. Porazzi, Bernita Robinson, Bonnie L. Becker; Associate Producers, Peggy Hill Rosenkranz, Marilyn Hall, Dentsu Inc; Presented by Margo Lion and Pamela Koslow in association with Polygram Diversified Entertainment, 126 Second Ave. Corp., Hal Luftig, Rodger Hess, Jujamcyn Theatres, TV Asahi and Herb Alpert; Press, Richard Kornberg/Carol R. Fineman; Previewing from Tuesday, March 31; Opened in the Virginia Theatre on Sunday, April 26, 1992*

CAST

Chimney Man	Keith David +1
The Hunnies	Mamie Duncan-Gibbs, Stephanie Pope, Allison M. Williams
The Crowd	Ken Ard +2, Adrian Bailey, Sherry D. Boone, Brenda B. Braxton, Mary Bond Davis, Ralph Deaton, Melissa Haizlip, Cee-Cee Harshaw, Ted L. Levy, Stanley Wayne Mathis, Victoria Gabrielle Platt, Gil Pritchett III, Michele M. Robinson
Jelly Roll Morton	Gregory Hines +3
Young Jelly	Savion Glover
Sisters	Cee-Cee Harshaw, Victoria Gabrielle Platt, Sherry D. Boone
Ancestors	Adrian Bailey+2, Mary Bond Davis, Ralph Deaton, Ann Duquesnay, Melissa Haizlip
Miss Mamie	Mary Bond Davis
Buddy Bolden	Ruben Santiago-Hudson
Too-Tight Nora	Brenda Braxton
Three Finger Jake	Gil Pritchett III
Gran Mimi	Ann Duquesnay
Jack the Bear	Stanley Wayne Mathis
Foot-in-Yo-Ass Sam	Ken Ard +4
Anita	Tonya Pinkins +5
Melrose Brothers	Don Johanson, Gordon Joseph Weiss

UNDERSTUDIES/STANDBYS: Lawrence Hamilton (Jelly), Ken Ard (Chimney Man), Jimmy W. Tate (Young Jelly), Stephanie Pope (Anita), Ralph Deaton (Jack-the-Bear), Adrian Bailey (Buddy/Chimney Man), Clare Bathe (Mimi/Maimie), Melissa Haizlip (Hunnies), Bill Brassea (Melrose Bros.) SWINGS: Ken Roberson, Keith L. Thomas, Janice Lorraine-Holt, La-Rose Saxon, Rosa Curry

MUSICAL NUMBERS: Jelly's Jam, In My Day, The Creole Way, The Whole World's Waitin' to Sing Your Song/Street Scene, Michigan Water, Get Away Boy/Lonely Boy Blues, Somethin' More, That's How You Jazz, The Chicago Stomp, Play the Music for Me, Lovin' Is a Lowdown Blues, Dr. Jazz, Good Ole New York, Too Late Daddy, That's the Way We Do Things in New Yawk, Jelly's Isolation Dance, Last Chance Blues, The Last Rites

A musical in two acts with twelve scenes. The action takes place in The Jungle Inn, a lowdown club somewhere's 'tween Heaven 'n' Hell on the eve of Jelly Roll Morton's death.

*Closed September 5, 1993 after 207 performances and 15 previews. Winner of 1992 "Tony" awards for Best Actor in a Musical (Gregory Hines), Best Featured Actress/Musical (Tonya Pinkins) and Best Lighting

+Succeeded by: 1. Ken Ard, Ben Vereen 2. Adrian Bailey 3. Brian Mitchell

4. Ken Roberson 5. Phylicia Rashad

Martha Swope Photos

Left: Gregory Hines, Stanley Wayne Mathis
Top: Ben Vereen

LES MISERABLES

By Alain Boublil and Claude-Michel Schonberg; Based on the novel by Victor Hugo; Music, Mr. Schonberg; Lyrics, Herbert Kretzmer; Original French Text, Mr. Boublil and Jean-Marc Natel; Additional Material, James Fenton; Direction/Adaptation, Trevor Nunn and John Caird; Orchestral Score, John Cameron; Musical Supervisor, Robert Billig; Musical Director, Jay Alger; Design, John Napier; Lighting, David Hersey; Costumes, Andreane Neofitou; Casting, Johnson-Liff & Zerman; Original Cast Recording, Geffen; General Manager, Alan Wasser; Company Manager, Robert Nolan; Stage Managers, Thom Schilling, Mary Fran Loftus, Gregg Kirsopp; Executive Producer, Martin McCallum; Presented by Cameron Mackintosh; Press, Marc Thibodeau/Merle Frimark; Previewed from Saturday, February 28; Opened in the Broadway Theatre on Thursday, March 12, 1987* and moved to the Imperial Theatre on October 16, 1990.

CAST

PROLOGUE: Mark McKerracher +1(Jean Valjean), Richard Kinsey +2 (Javert), J.C. Sheets, Joel Robertson, Alan Osburn, Ken Krugman, Matt McClanahan, Drew Eshelman, Lawrence Anderson, Michael Berry, Michael Sutherland Lynch (Chain Gang), Douglas Webster (Farmer), Mr. Krugman (Labourer), Lucille DeCristofaro (Innkeeper's Wife), Gary Lynch (Innkeeper), Kenny Morris (Bishop), Tom Donoghue, Paul Avedisian (Constables)

MONTREUIL-SUR-MER 1823: Rachel York +3 (Fantine), Mr. Robertson (Foreman), Mr. Webster, Mr. McClanahan (Workers), Jean Fitzgibbons, Jessica Sheridan, Cissy Lee Cates, Madeleine Doherty (Women Workers), Jessie Janet Richards (Factory Girl), Mr. Berry, Mr. Sheets, Mr. McClanahan (Sailors), Ms. DeCristofaro, Ms. Doherty, Ms. Cates, Lisa Ann Grant, Ms. Richards, Tia Riebling, Jennifer Lee Andrews, Sarah E. Litzsinger (Whores), Ms. Fitzgibbons (Old Woman), Ms. Sheridan (Crone), Mr. Morris (Pimp/Fauchelevent), Alan Osburn (Bamatabois)

MONTFERMEIL 1823: Lacey Chabert, Jessica Scholl, Savannah Wise (Young Cosette/Young Eponine), Evalyn Baron (Mme. Thenardier), Drew Eshelman (Thenardier), Mr. Webster (Drinker), Mr. Krugman, Ms. Litzsinger (Young Couple), Mr. Lynch (Drunk), Paul Avedisian, Ms. Doherty (Diners), Mr. Morris, Mr. Osburn, Mr. Sheets, Ms. Fitzgibbons, Ms. Richards, Ms. DeCristofaro (Drinkers), Mr. Berry (Young Man), Ms. Cates, Ms. Grant (Young Girls), Ms. Sheridan, Mr. McClanahan (Old Couple), Mr. Robertson, Mr. Donohue (Travelers)

PARIS 1832: Brian Press, Michael Shulman (Gavroche), Ms. DeCristofaro (Beggar Woman), Ms. Richards (Young Prostitute), Mr. Lynch (Pimp), Michele Maika +4 (Eponine), Mr. Krugman (Montparnasse), Mr. Donoghue (Babet), Mr. Sheets (Brujon), Mr. Morris (Claquesous), Lawrence Anderson (Enjolras), Eric Kunze +5 (Marius), Melissa Anne Davis +6 (Cosette), Mr. Robertson (Combeferre), Mr. Berry (Feuilly), Mr. Webster (Courfeyrac), Mr. McClanahan (Joly), Mr. Osburn (Grantaire), Mr. Avedisian (Lesgles), Mr. Lynch (Jean Prouvaire)

UNDERSTUDIES: J.C. Sheets, Joel Robertson, Douglas Webster (Valjean), Gary Lynch, Alan Osburn (Javert), Paul Avedisian, Bruce Thompson (Bishop), Jessie Janet Richards, Jean Fitzgibbons (Fantine), Kenny Morris, Ken Krugman (Thenardier), Ms. Fitzgibbons, Jessica Sheridan (Mme. Thenardier), Lisa Ann Grant, Sara Litzsinger (Eponine), Tom Donoghue, Matt McClanahan (Marius), Ms. Litzsinger, Cissy Lee Cates (Cosette), Mr. Avedisian, Michael Berry (Enjolras), Gregory Grant, Lacey Chabert (Gavroche) SWINGS: Lorraine Goodman, Christa Justus, Wayne Scherzer, Mr. Thompson

MUSICAL NUMBERS: Prologue, Soliloquy, At the End of the Day, I Dreamed a Dream, Lovely Ladies, Who Am I?, Come to Me, Castle on a Cloud, Master of the House, Thenardier Waltz, Look Down, Stars, Red and Black, Do You Hear the People Sing?, In My Life, A Heart Full of Love, One Day More, On My Own, A Little Fall of Rain, Drink with Me to Days Gone By, Bring Him Home, Dog Eats Dog, Soliloquy, Turning, Empty Chairs at Empty Tables, Wedding Chorale, Beggars at the Feast, Finale

A dramatic musical in two acts with four scenes and prologue.

*Still playing May 31, 1993. Winner of 1987 "Tonys" for Best Musical, Best Score, Best Book, Best Featured Actor and Actress in a Musical (Michael Maguire, Frances Ruffelle), Direction of a Musical, Scenic Design and Lighting.

+ Succeeded by: 1. Donn Cook 2. Chuck Wagner 3. Donna Kane 4. Brandy Brown, Lea Salonga, Tia Riebling 5. Michael Sutherland Lynch 6. Jennifer Lee Andrews

Joan Marcus Photos

Left: Lacey Chabert
Top: Mark McKerracher

MISS SAIGON

Music, Claude-Michel Schonberg; Lyrics, Richard Maltby ,Jr., Alain Boublil; Adapted from Boublil's French lyrics; Book, Mr. Boublil, Mr. Schonberg; Additional Material, Mr. Maltby, Jr.; Director, Nicholas Hytner; Musical Staging, Bob Avian; Orchestrations, William D. Brohn; Musical Supervisors, David Caddick, Robert Billig; Associate Director, Mitchell Lemsky; Design, John Napier; Lighting, David Hersey; Costumes, Andreane Neofitou; Sound, Andrew Bruce; Conductor, Dale Rieling; Stage Managers, Fred Hanson, Sherry Cohen, Tom Capps; Cast Recording (London), Geffen; Presented by Cameron Mackintosh; Press, Fred Nathan/Marc Thibodeau, Merle Frimark; Previewed from Saturday, March 23; Opened in the Broadway Theatre on Thursday, April 11, 1991*

CAST

SAIGON - 1975
The Engineer..Herman Sebek
Kim...Leila Florentino, Annette Calud
Gigi...Marina Chapa
Mimi...Sala Iwamatsu +1
Yvette..Imelda De Los Reyes
Yvonne..Lyd-Lyd Gaston
Bar Girls............................Emy Baysic, Mirla Criste, Cheri Nakamura,
Jade Stice, Melanie Mariko Tojio, Sharon Leal
Chris..Sean McDermot +2
John..Alton F. White +3
Marines...Reed Armstrong, Robert Bartley,
Craig Bennett, Alvin Crawford, Matthew Dickens, Paul Dobie,
Jim Harrison, Jamie, Leonard Joseph, Paul Matsumoto,
Kevin Neil McCready, Michael McElroy,
Thomas James O'Leary, Grant Norman, Matthew Pederson,
Jeff Reid, Bruce Winant
Barmen ....Zar Acayan, Alan Ariano, Yancey Arias
Vietnamese Customers ....Tito Abeleda, Denis Akiyama, Francis J.
Cruz, Darrell Autor, Rob Narita, Ray Santos,
Corey Smith, Nephi Jay Wimmer
Army Nurse...Anne Torsiglieri +4
Thuy...Jason Ma
Embassy Workers, Vendors, etc...Company
HO CHI MINH CITY (Formerly Saigon)-April 1978
Ellen...Jane Bodle
Tam... Jeffrey Chang, Michael Ordinario
Guards.....................................Tony C. Avanti, Mr. Cruz, Mr. Narita
Dragon Acrobats ....Mr. Autor, Mr. Harrison, Mr. Smith
Asst. Commissar ....Mr. Arias
Soldiers ....Mr. Abeleda, Mr. Acayan, Mr. Ariano, Mr.
Matsumoto, Mr. Santos, Mr. Smith, Mr. Wimmer
Citizens, Refugees ....Company
USA - September 1978
Conference Delegates ....Company
BANGKOK - October 1978
Hustlers ....Mr. Acayan, Mr. Arias, Mr. Matsumoto,
Mr. Santos, Mr.Smith, Mr. Wimmer
Moulin Rouge Owner ....Mr. Cruz
Inhabitants, Bar Girls, Vendors, Tourists ....Company
SAIGON - April 1975
Shultz ....Thomas James O'Leary +5
Doc ....Mr. McElroy +6
Reeves ....Mr. Bennett +7
Gibbons...Mr. Dobie+8
Troy ....Mr. Joseph
Nolen...Jamie
Huston ....Matthew Pederson
Frye ....Reed Armstrong +9
Marines, Vietnamese..Company
BANGKOK - October 1978
Inhabitants, Moulin Rouge Customers ....Company

UNDERSTUDIES: Denis Akiyama, Paul Matsumoto, Ray Santos, (Engineer), Emy Baysic, Imelda de los Reyes, Melanie Mariko Tojio (Kim), Reed Armstrong, Grant Norman (Chris), Michael McElroy, Leonard Joseph (John), Jade Stice, Anne Torsiglieri (Ellen), Zar Acayan, Yancey Arias, Marc Oka (Thuy) SWINGS: Eric Chan, Sylvia Dohi, Zoie Lam, Kevin Neal McReady, Henry Menendez, Marc Oka, Todd Zamarripa

MUSICAL NUMBERS: The Heat Is on in Saigon, Movie in My Mind, The Transaction, Why God Why?, Sun and Moon, The Telephone, The Ceremony, Last Night of the World, Morning of the Dragon, I Still Believe, Back in Town, You Will Not Touch Him, If You Want to Die in Bed, I'd Give My Life for You, Bui-Doi, What a Waste, Please, Guilt Inside Your Head, Room 317, Now That I've Seen Her, Confrontation, The American Dream, Little God of My Heart

A musical in two acts. The action takes place in Saigon, Bangkok, and the USA between 1975-79.

*Still playing May 31, 1993. Winner of 1991 "Tonys" for Leading Actor in a Musical (Jonathan Pryce), Leading Actress in a Musical (Lea Salonga) and Featured Actor in a Musical (Hinton Battle).

+ Succeeded by: 1. Zoie Lam 2. Jarrod Emick, Christopher Peccaro 3. Timothy Robert Blevins 4. Alisa Gyse Dickens 5. Craig Bennett 6. Michael Gruber 7. Alvin Crawford 8. Kevin Joseph McCready 9. Mat-thew Dickens

Joan Marcus/Michael LePoer Trench Photos

Timothy Robert Blevins
Center: Sean McDermott, Leila Florentino
Top: Jarrod Emick

THE PHANTOM OF THE OPERA

Music, Andrew Lloyd Webber; Lyrics, Charles Hart; Additional Lyrics, Richard Stilgoe; Book, Mr. Stilgoe, Mr. Lloyd Webber; Director, Harold Prince; Musical Staging/Choreography, Gillian Lynne; Orchestrations, David Cullen, Mr. Lloyd Webber; Based on the novel by Gaston Leroux; Design, Maria Bjornson; Lighting, Andrew Bridge; Sound, Martin Levan; Musical Direction/Supervision, David Caddick; Casting, Johnson-Liff & Zerman; General Manager, Alan Wasser; Company Manager, Michael Gill; Stage Managers, Steve McCorkle, Bethe Ward, Frank Marino; Presented by Cameron Mackintosh and The Really Useful Theatre Co.; Press, Merle Frimark, Marc Thibodeau; Previewed from Saturday, January 9; Opened in the Majestic Theatre on Tuesday, January 26, 1988*

CAST

The Phantom of the Opera	Mark Jacoby +1
Christine Daae	Karen Culliver +2
	Luann Aronson (Mon/Wed eves.)
Raoul, Vicomte de Chagny	Hugh Panaro
Carlotta Giudicelli	Marilyn Caskey +3
Monsieur Andre	Jeff Keller
Monsieur Firmin	George Lee Andrews
Madame Giry	Leila Martin
Ubaldo Piangi	Gary Rideout
Meg Giry	Catherine Ulissey +4
M. Rever	Gary Barker +5
Auctioneer	Richard Warren Pugh
Porter/Marksman	Gary Lindemann
M. Lefevre	Kenneth Waller
Joseph Buquet	Philip Steele
Don Attilio/Passarino	Thomas Sandri +6
Slave Master	David Loring
Flunky/Stagehand	Wesley Robinson
Solo Dancer	Thomas Terry
Policeman	Charles Rule +7
Page	Patrice Pickering
Porter/Fireman	Maurizio Corbino
Spanish Lady	Diane Ketchie
Wardrobe Mistress/Confidante	Mary Leigh Stahl
Princess	Raissa Katona
Madame Firmin	Dawn Leigh Stone
Innkeeper's Wife	Rebecca Eichenberger +8
Ballet Chorus of the Opera Populaire	Tener Brown, Harriet M. Clark, Alina Hernandez, Cherllyn Jones, Lori MacPherson, Tania Philip, Kate Solmssen, Christine Spizzo

UNDERSTUDIES: Gary Barker (Phantom/Andre), Jeff Keller, Hugh Panaro (Phantom), Raissa Katona (Christine), Gary Lindemann, James Romick (Raoul), Peter Atherton, Paul Laureano (Firmin), Richard Warren Pugh (Firmin/Piangi), George Lee Andrews, James Thomas O' Leary, Mr. Romick (Andre), Elena Jeanne Batman, Rebecca Eichenberger, Dawn Leigh Stone, Diane Ketchie (Carlotta), Suzanne Ishee (Carlotta/Giry), Patrice Pickering, Mary Leigh Stahl (Giry), Maurizio Corbino, Mr. Pugh (Piangi), Tener Brown, Cherllyn Jones, Kate Solmssen, Lori MacPherson (Meg), Wesley Robinson (Master/Dancer) SWINGS: David P. Cleveland, Ms. Ishee, Mr. Laureano, Mr. Romick, Laurie Gayle Stephenson

MUSICAL NUMBERS: Think of Me, Angel of Music, Little Lotte/The Mirror, Phantom of the Opera, Music of the Night, I Remember/Stranger Than You Dreamt It, Magical Lasso, Notes/Prima Donna, Poor Fool He Makes Me Laugh, Why Have You Brought Me Here?/ Raoul I've Been There, All I Ask of You, Masquerade/Why So Silent?, Twisted Every Way, Wishing You Were Somehow Here Again, Wandering Child/Bravo Bravo, Point of No Return, Down Once More/Track Down This Murderer, Finale

A musical in two acts with nineteen scenes and a prologue. The action takes place in and around the Paris Opera house, 1881-1911.

*Still playing May 31, 1993. Winner of 1988 "Tonys" for Best Musical, Leading Actor in a Musical (Michael Crawford), Featured Actress in a Musical (Judy Kaye), Direction of a Musical, Scenic Design and Lighting.

Phantom has given more than 2,000 Broadway performances to date and the title role has been played by Michael Crawford, Timothy Nolen, Cris Groenendaal, Steve Barton, Jeff Keller, Kevin Gray, Mark Jacoby and Marcus Lovett.

+Succeeded by: 1. Marcus Lovett 2. Mary D'Arcy 3. Elena Jeanne Batman 4. Tener Brown 5. Thomas James O'Leary 6. Peter Atherton 7. Stacey Robinson 8. Teresa Eldh

Joan Marcus Photos

Hugh Panaro, Karen Culliver
Center: The Ensemble
Top: Mark Jacoby

THE WILL ROGERS FOLLIES

Music/Arrangements, Cy Coleman; Lyrics, Betty Comden and Adolph Green; Book, Peter Stone; Director/Choreographer, Tommy Tune; Orchestrations, Billy Byers; Musical Director, Eric Stern; Musical Contractor, John Miller; Sets, Tony Walton; Costumes, Willa Kim; Lighting, Jules Fisher; Original Cast Recording, Columbia; Sound, Peter Fitzgerald; Projections, Wendall K. Harrington; Wigs, Howard Leonard; General Manager, Marvin A. Krauss; Casting, Julie Hughes, Barry Moss; Stage Managers, Peter von Mayrhauser, Patrick Ballard; Presented by Pierre Cossette, Martin Richards, Sam Crothers, James M. Nederlander, Stewart F. Lane, Max Weitzenhoffer in association with Japan Satellite Broadcasting; Press, Richard Kornberg; Previewed from Monday, April 1; Opened in the Palace Theatre on Wednesday, May 1, 1991*

CAST

Indian Sun Goddess	Jillana Urbina
Ziegfeld's Favorite	Marla Maples +1
Indian of the Dawn	Jerry Mitchell
Indian Solist	Jeanne Jones
Will Rogers	Mac Davis +2
Unicyclist/Roper	Vince Bruce
Wiley *Post*	David M. Lutken
The Will Rogers Wranglers	John Ganun, Troy Britton Johnson, Jerry Mitchell, Jason Opsahl
Clem Rogers	Dick Latessa +4
Will's Sisters/Betty's Sisters	Maria Calabrese, Rebecca Downing, Kimberly Hester, Luann Leonard, Lynne Michele, Kathy Trageser
Stage Manager	Tom Flagg
Betty Blake	Nancy Ringham
Wild West Show/Trainers/Madcap Mutts	Tom & Bonnie Brackney with B.A., Cocoa, Gigi, Rusty, Trixie, Zee
Will Rogers, Jr.	James Zimmerman
Mary Rogers	Candace N. Walters
James Rogers	Buddy Smith
Freddy Rogers	Jeffrey Stern
Vaudeville Announcer	Jason Opsahl
Radio Engineer	John Ganun
New Ziegfeld Girls	Ms. Calabrese, Heather Douglas, Ms. Downing, Sally Mae Dunn, Ganine Giorgione, Eileen Grace, Amy Heggins, Ms. Hester, Ms. Jones, Ms. Leonard, Ms. Michele, Carol Denise Smith, Ms. Trageser, Susan Trainor, Ms. Urbina, Christina Youngman
Voice of Mr. Ziegfeld	Gregory Peck

UNDERSTUDIES/STANDBYS: David M. Lutken (Will), Belle Calaway (Betty), Buddy Smith (Will Jr.), Jack Doyle (Wiley/Stage Mgr.) Tom Flagg (Clem/ Wiley), Eden Riegel (Mary/James/Freddy) SWINGS: Mary Lee DeWitt, Mr. Doyle, Angie L. Schworer

MUSICAL NUMBERS: Let's Go Flying, Will-a-Mania, Give a Man Enough Rope, It's a Boy, So Long Pa, My Unknown Someone, We're Heading for a Wedding, Big Time, My Big Mistake, Powder Puff Ballet, Marry Me Now/I Got You, Wedding Finale, Look Around, Favorite Son, No Man Left for Me, Presents for Mrs. Rogers, Without You, Never Met a Man I Didn't Like

A musical inspired by the words of Will and Betty Rogers, in two acts with twelve scenes and prelude. The action takes place in Broadway's Palace Theatre at present.

*Closed September 5, 1993 after 983 performances and 34 previews. Winner of 1991 "Tonys" for Best Musical, Best Score, Best Direction of a Musical, Best Costumes, Best Lighting, Best Choreography. Selected by the NY Drama Critics Circle as Best Musical of 1990-91.

+Succeeded by:1. Lisa Niemi 2. Larry Gatlin 3. David N. Dinkens, Rush Limbaugh, Frank Gifford, John McLaughlin, Johnny Cash, Mort Zuckerman, Riddick Bowe, Robert Preston Tisch, Arthur Schlesinger, Jr. and others guested in this role 4.Robert Fitch, Mickey Rooney

Martha Swope, Edward Patino Photos

**Right: Marla Maples and the Company
Top: Nancy Ringham, Mac Davis**

BEAU JEST

By James Sherman; Director, Dennis Zacek; Design, Bruce Goodrich; Costumes, Dorothy Jones; Lighting, Edward R.F. Matthews; Company Manager, Laura Heller; Stage Manager, Jana Llynn; Presented by Athur Cantor, Carol Ostrow, Libby Adler Mages; Press, Mr. Cantor; Opened at the Lambs Theatre on Wednesday, October 2, 1991*

CAST

Sara Goldman ....Laura Patinkin +1
Chris...John Michael Higgins +2
Bob..Tom Hewitt +3
Joel ....Larry Fleischman
Miriam ....Rosalyn Alexander +4
Abe...Bernie Landis

UNDERSTUDIES: Paul Amodeo (Chris/Bob/Joel), Herbert Rubens (Abe), Molly Stark (Miriam)

A comedy in three acts. The action takes place in Sarah's apartment in the Lincoln Park area of Chicago, Illinois.

*Closed May 1, 1994 after 1077 performances.

+Succeeded by: 1. Cindy Katz 2. Bill Doyle 3.Joe Warren Davis, Jeffrey Edward Peters, Sal Viviano 4. Catherine Wolf

Carol Rosegg/Martha Swope Photos

Laura Patinkin, Tom Hewitt
Top: Cindy Katz, Joe Warren Davis

THE FANTASTICKS

Music, Harvey Schmidt; Lyrics/Book, Tom Jones; Director, Word Baker; Original Musical Director/Arrangements, Julian Stein; Design, Ed Wittstein; Musical Director, Dorothy Martin; Stage Managers, Kim Moore, James Cook, Steven Michael Daly, Christopher Scott; Presented by Lore Noto; Associate Producers, Sheldon Baron, Dorothy Olim, Jules Field, Cast Recording, MGM/Polydor; Opened in the Sullivan Street Playhouse on Tuesday, May 3, 1960*

CAST

The Boy ....Matthew Eaton Bennett
The Girl ....Marilyn Whitehead
The Girl's Father ....William Tost
The Boy's Father ....George Riddle
Narrator/El Gallo ....Scott Willis
Mute ....Christopher Scott
Old Actor ....Bryan Hull
Man Who Dies ....Earl Aaron Levine

MUSICAL NUMBERS: Overture, Try to Remember, Much More, Metaphor, Never Say No, It Depends on What You pay, Soon It's Gonna Rain, Abduction Ballet, Happy Ending, This Plumb is Too Ripe, I Can See It, Plant a Radish, Round and Round, They Were You, Finale

A musical in two acts.

*Still playing May 31, 1993. The world's longest running musical. For origional production, see Theatre World Volume 16.

Steve Young Photos

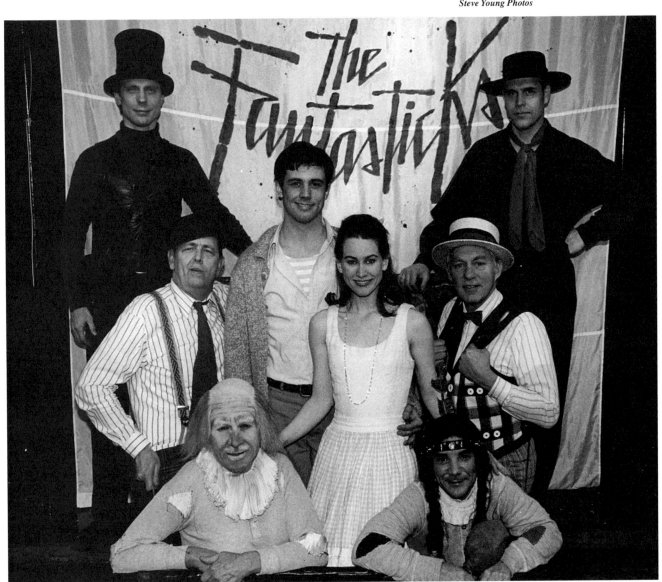

"Fantasticks" company

FORBIDDEN BROADWAY

1992-93 Season Edition

Susanne Blakeslee	Brad Ellis	Gina Kreiezmar
Dorothy Kiara	Brad Oscar	Craig Wells

Created/Written/Directed by Gerard Alessandrini; Musical Director, Brad Ellis; Asst. Director, Phillip George; Costumes, Erika Dyson; Wigs, Teresa Vuoso; Consultant, Pete Blue; Stage Manager, Jim Griffith; Cast Recordings, DRG; Press, Shirley Herz/Glenna Freedman; Presented by Jonathan Scharer; Originally opened at Palssons (now Steve McGraw's) on January 15, 1982 and moved to Theatre East on September 15, 1988*

PROGRAMS: Forbidden Christmas (Dec.1-27, 1992) Forbidden Broadway 1993 (Jan.7, 1993-)

SELECTIONS INCLUDED: Imitation Is the Sincerest Form of Flattery, Forbidden Bdwy 1993, Fuge for Scalpers, Guys and Dolls (I Know I've Seen This Show Before), Crazy for You (Replaceable You), Marla Maples, Michael Crawford, Five Guys Named Moe (Push da Drinky-Drink), Les Miserables (God It's High), Rosyln Kind, Close a Little Faster, Anna Karenina (On the Ashabad, Tiblesi and Kiev Express), Julie Andrews, Disney (Be Depressed), Falsettos, Mandy Patinkin, Miss Saigon (Tonight Who will Play Miss Saigon), Tommy Tune, Shirley MacLaine & Frank Sinatra, Barbra Streisand, Spring Preview, Heart, Ta-ta

*Closed January 2, 1994.

Carol Rosegg/Martha Swope Photos

Brad Oscar, Dorothy Kiara, Craig Wells, Susanne Blakeslee, Gerard Alessandrini

FOREVER PLAID

Written/Directed/Choreographed by Stuart Ross; Music/Lyrics, Various; Musical Arrangements/Continuity/Supervision, James Raitt; Sets, Neil Peter Jampolis; Lighting, Jane Reisman; Costumes, Debra Stein; Musical Director, David Chase; Sound, Marc Salzberg; Original Cast Recording, RCA; Stage Manager, Connie Drew; Presented by Gene Wolsk in association with Allen M. Shore and Steven Suskin; Press, Shirley Herz/Miller Wright, Glenna Freedman, Sam Rudy; Opened in Steve McGraw's on Friday, May 4, 1990*

CAST

Jinx	Paul Binotto +1
Smudge	Gregory Jbara +2
Sparky	Michael Winther +3
Francis	Neil Nash +4

ALTERNATES: Paul Castree, Drew Geraci, Steve Gunderson, Nick Locilento

MUSICAL NUMBERS: Anniversary Song, Catch a Falling Star, Chain Gang, Crazy 'bout Ya Baby, Cry, Day-O, Dream Along with Me, Gotta Be This or That, Heart and Soul, Jamaica Farewell, Kingston Market, Lady of Spain (Ed Sullivan Show spoof), Love Is a Many Splendored Thing, Magic Moments, Matilda, Moments to Remember, No Not Much, Papa Loves Mambo, Perfidia, Rags to Riches, Round and Round, Shangri-La, She Loves You, Sing to Me Mr. C, Sixteen Tons, Temptation, Theme from The Good the Bad the Ugly, Three Coins in the Fountain, Undecided

A musical for the "good guys" performed without intermission. The action takes place in 1964 and now.

*Closed June 12, 1994.

+Succeeded by: 1. Ryan Perry 2. Tom Cianfichi 3. David Benoit, Daniel Eli Friedman 4. Robert Lambert, Drew Geraci

Carol Rosegg/Martha Swope Photos

The Original Cast: David Engel, Guy Stroman, Stan Chandler, Larry Raben
Top: Gregory Jbara, Neil Nash, Paul Binotto, Michael Winther

NUNSENSE

Music/Lyrics/Book/Direction by Dan Goggin; Choreography, Felton Smith; Sets, Barry Axtell; Lighting, Susan A. White; Musical Director, Michael Rice; General Manager, Roger Alan Gindi; Casting, Joseph Abaldo; Stage Managers, Paul Botchis, Nancy Wernick; Original Cast Recording, DRG; Presented by The Nunsense Theatrical Co. in association with Joseph Hoesl, Bill Crowder & Jay Cardwell; Press, Shirley Herz/Pete Sanders, Glenna Freedman, Sam Rudy, Miller Wright, Robert Larkin; Opened in the Cherry Lane Theatre on Tuesday, December 3, 1985* then transferred to Circle Repertory Theatre and then to the Douglas Fairbanks Theatre

CAST

Sister Mary Regina ....Julie J. Hafner/Terri Mazzarella
Sister Mary Hubert ....Alvaleta Guess/Jennifer Perry
Sister Robert Anne ....Lin Tucci
Sister Mary Amnesia...Sarah Knapp/Jennifer Jay Myers
Sister Mary Leo ....Alicia Miller/Valerie DePena

UNDERSTUDIES: Susan J. Jacks, Teri Gibson

MUSICAL NUMBERS: Nunsense Is Habit-Forming, A Difficult Transition, Benedicte, Biggest Ain't the Best, Playing Second Fiddle,, So You Want to Be a Nun, Turn Up the Spotlight, Lilacs Bring Back Memories, Tackle That Temptation with a Time Step, Growing Up Catholic, We've Got to Clean Out the Freezer, Just a Coupl'a Sisters, Soup's On, Dying Nun Ballet, I Just Want to Be a Star, The Drive In, I Could've Gone to Nashville, Gloria in Excelsis Deo, Holier Than Thou, Finale

A musical in two acts. The action takes place in Mt. Saint Helen's School Auditorium in Hoboken, New Jersey at the present time.

*Still playing May 31, 1993.

Carol Rosegg Photos

PERFECT CRIME

By Warren Manzi; Director, Jeffrey Hyatt; Set, Chris Pickart; Costumes, Barbara Blackwood; Lighting, Patrick Eagleton; Sound, David Lawson; Stage Manager, George E.M. Kelly; Press, Michelle Vinvents, Paul Lewis, Jeffrey Clarke; Opened in the Courtyard Playhouse on April 18, 1987* and later transferred to the Second Stage, 47th St. Playhouse, Intar, Harold Clurman Theatre, and since January 3, 1991, Theatre Four

CAST

Margaret Thorne Brent...Catherine Russell
James Ascher ....Warren Manzi
Lionel McAuley...Trip Hamilton/J.A. Nelson
W. Harrison Brent ....Graeme Malcolm/Mark Johannes
David Breuer...Dean Gardner

   A mystery.

*Still playing May 31, 1993.

Catherine Russell in "Perfect Crime"

Sharon Angela, Lee Mazzilli in "Tony 'N' Tina..."

TONY 'N' TINA'S WEDDING

By Artificial Intelligence; Conception, Nancy Cassaro (Artistic Director); Director, Larry Pellegrini; Supervisory Director, Julie Casari; Musical Director, Debra Barsha; Choreography, Hal Simons; Design/Decor, Randall Thropp; Costumes/Hairstyles/Makeup, Juan DeArmas; General Manager, Leonard A. Mulhern; Company Manager, James Hannah; Stage Managers, K.A. Smith, Bernadette McGay; Presented by Joseph Corcoran & Daniel Cocoran; Press, David Rothenberg/Terence Womble; Opened in the Washington Square Church & Carmelita's on Saturday, February 6, 1988*

CAST

Valentia Lynne Nunzio, the bride ....Sharon Angela
Anthony Angelo Nunzio, the groom ....Rick Pasqualone +1
Connie Mocognì, maid of honor..Susan Laurenzi
Barry Wheeler, best man ....Timothy Monagan
Donna Marsala, bridesmaid..Susan Campanero
Dominick Fabrizzi, usher ....Lou Martini, Jr.
Marina Gulino, bridesmaid...Celeste Russi
Johnny Nunzio, usher/brother of groom...Ken Garito
Josephine Vitale, mother of the bride ....Nancy Timpanaro
Joseph Vitale, brother of the bride...Paul Spencer
Luigi Domenico, great uncle of the bride ....Allen Lewis Rickman
Rose Domenico, aunt of the bride...Wendy Caplan
Sister Albert Maria, cousin of bride...Fran Gennuso
Anthony Angelo Nunzio, Sr., father of groom ....Dan Grimaldi
Madeline Monroe, Mr. Nunzio's girlfriend......................................Georgienne Millen
Grandma Nunzio, grandmother to groom.....................................Bonnie Rose Marcus
Michael Just, Tina's ex-boyfriend...Anthony T. Lauria
Father Mark, parish priest ....Gary Schneider
Vinnie Black, caterer...Tom Karlya
Loretta Black, wife of the caterer...Victoria Constan
Mick Black, brother of the caterer...Tony Palellis
Nikki Black, daughter of the caterer ....Maria Gentile
Mikie Black, son of the caterer..Anthony Luongo
Pat Black, sister of the caterer...Jody Oliver
Rick Demarco, the video man ....Marc Romeo
Sal Antonucci, the photographer ....Glenn Taranto

   An environmental theatre production. The action takes place at a wedding and reception.

*Still playing May 31, 1993 after moving to St. John's Church and Vinnie Black's Coliseum.

+Succeeded by: 1. Lee Mazzilli

Linda Alaniz Photos

TUBES

Created and Written by Matt Goldman, Phil Stanton, Chris Wink; Director, Marlene Swartz; Artistic Coordinator; Caryl Glaab; Sets, Kevin Joseph Roach; Lighting, Brian Aldous; Costumes, Lydia Tanji, Patricia Murphy; Sound, Raymond Schilke; Computer Graphics, Kurisu-Chan; Stage Manager, Kevin Cunningham; Press, David Rothenberg; Opened at the Astor Place Theatre on Thursday, November 7, 1991*

CAST

Blue Man Group (Matt Goldman, Phil Stanton, Chris Wink)

An evening with the performance group, without intermission.

*Still playing May 31, 1993.

Martha Swope Photos

PRODUCTIONS FROM PAST SEASONS THAT CLOSED DURING THIS SEASON

Production	Opened	Closed	Performances
Catskills on Broadway	12/5/91	1/3/93	452 & 23 previews
Chinese Coffee	6/29/92	8/1/92	9 & 14 previews
Conversations With My Father	3/29/92	3/14/93	462 & 30 previews
Dancing at Lughnasa	10/24/91	10/25/92	421& 15 previews
Death and the Maiden	3/17/92	8/2/92	159 & 33 previews
Five Guys Named Moe	4/8/92	5/2/93	445 & 19 previews
Jake's Women	3/24/92	10/25/92	245 & 14 previews
Julie Halston's Lifetime	1/15/92	6/7/92	125 & 20 previews
Lips Together Teeth Apart	5/28/91	6/27/92	250 (MTC)169 Lortel
Lost In Yonkers	2/21/91	1/3/93	780 & 11 previews
Man of La Mancha	4/24/92	7/26/92	108 & 28 previews
Marvin's Room	2/28/92	9/6/92	214 & 7 previews
The Most Happy Fella	2/13/92	8/30/92	229 & 23 previews
Pageant	5/2/91	6/27/92	462 & 10 previews
The Price	6/10/92	7/19/92	47 & 25 previews
Ruthless	3/13/92	1/24/93	302 & 40 previews
Salome	6/28/92	7/29/92	18 & 16 previews
The Secret Garden	4/25/91	1/3/93	706 & 22 previews
A Small Family Business	4/27/92	6/7/92	48 & 31 previews
Song of Singapore	5/7/91	6/30/92	459 & 18 previews
Spike Heels	5/12/92	7/4/92	56 performances
A Streetcar Named Desire	4/12/92	8/9/92	137 & 31 previews
The Substance of Fire(Newhouse)	1/31/92	7/26/92	205 performances
Two Trains Running	4/13/92	8/30/92	160 & 7 previews
Weird Romance	5/12/92	7/2/92	50 performances

Lucie Arnaz in "Lost in Yonkers" (*Martha Swope*)

Gene Hackman, Richard Dreyfuss, Glenn Close in "Death and the Maiden"
(*Joan Marcus*)

(counter-closckwise from lower right) Roxanne Hart, Jonathan Hadary, Hillary
Bailey Smith, Anthony Heald in "Lips Together, Teeth Apart" (*Gerry Goodstein*)

Alec Baldwin, Jessica Lange in "Streetcar Named Desire" (*Brigitte Lacombe*)

OFF BROADWAY PRODUCTIONS

JUNE 1, 1992-MAY 31, 1993

(Jerusalem Group Theatre) Monday, June 1-28, 1992 (16 performances) Alan Jacobson presents:
REMEMBER MY NAME by Joanna Halpert Kraus; Director, Shela Xoregos; Set, Murphy Gigliotti; Lighting, David J. Lander; Costumes, Kenneth J. Wyrtch; Sound, Kenn Dovel; Stage Manager, Lori A. Brown; Press, Isadora O'Gorman CAST: Ruth Bender (Pauline Simon), Alan Barr (Leon Simon), Orli Cotel (Rachel Simon), Kerry Wolf (Pere Antoine), Jane K. Hamilton (Yvette Reynaud), Glen Lincoln (Marie-Therese Barbiere), Paul David Ross (Gerard LaSalle), Elizabeth Striker (Suzanne Fleury), Pierre Lang (Hans Schmidt), Pierre Lang (Julien Delacour), Jonathan Freiman (Julien Delacour), Ruth Bender (Vendor), Bruce Wall (British Radio Voice)
   A drama in two acts. The action takes place in France, 1942-44.

(Westside Theatre) Tuesday, June 2-Aug.2, 1992 (56 performances and 16 previews/re-opened for Sun. night shows only) The N.N.N. Co. presents:
BALANCING ACT with Music/Lyrics/Book by Dan Goggin; Directors, Tony Parise, Mr. Goggin; Musical Director, Michael Rice; Orchestrations, Mr. Rice, David Nyberg; Sets, Barry Axtell; Costumes, Mary Peterson; Lighting, Paul Miller; Sound, Craig Zaionz; Stage Manager, Paul Botchis; Press, Pete Sanders CAST: Craig Wells succeeded by Robert Stella (Ambitious Side), Diane Fratantoni succeeded by Cindy Benson (Sensitive Side), Christine Toy (Optimistic Side), J.B. Adams (Skeptical Side), Suzanne Hevner (Humorous Side), Nancy E. Carroll (Everybody Else)
MUSICAL NUMBERS: Life Is a Balancing Act, Next Stop New York City, Home Sweet Home, Play Away the Blues, My Bio Is a Blank, A Tough Town, I Left You There, A Twist of Fate, Casting Call, The Fifth from the Right, You Heard It Here First, A Long Long Way, Woman of the Century, Welcome Bienvenue, Where is the Rainbow, I am Yours, That Kid's Gonna Make It, Chew Chewy Chow, Hollywood 'n' Vinyl, California Suite, I Knew the Music
   A musical in two acts. The action takes place in Hometown, USA, New York and Hollywood.

Christine Toy, Craig Wells, Suzanne Hevner, Diane Frantantoni, J.B. Adams in
"Balancing Act" (*Carol Rosegg/Martha Swope*)

(Irish Arts Center) Wednesday, June 3, 1992 Marianne Delaney and Donald Kelly present:
BOBBY SANDS, M.P. by Judy GeBauer; Director, Nye Heron; Set/Lighting, Rick Butler; Costumes, Carla Gant; Music, Brian O'Neill Mor, Nicholas Kean; Stage Manager, Kurt Wagemann CAST: Brenda Daly, Robin Howard, Brian Mallon, Fionna McCormac, Seamus McDonagh, Barry McEvoy, D.J. O'Neill, Donal J. Sheehan, Jimmy Smallhorne
   A drama in two acts. The action takes place in a Belfast prison.

Skip Kennon, Jane Smulyan, Joseph Kolinski, Maureen Silliman in "Picking Up the Pieces" (*Michael Ian*)

(Via Theatre) Wednesday, June 3-28, 1992

THE BITTER TEARS OF PETRA von KANT by Rainer Werner Fassbinder; Director, Brian Jucha; Set, Sarah Edkins; Lighting, Roma Flowers CAST: Tina Shepard (Petra von Kant), Sheryl Dold, Tamar Kotoske, Karla Silverman, Lisa Welti, David Kellet, Anne McKenna, Megan Spooner

(Eighty Eights) June-July 26, 1992 Eighty Eight's presents:
PICKING UP THE PIECES; with Music by Skip Kennon; Words, Richard Enquist, Ellen Fitzhugh, Terrence McNally, David Spencer, Mr. Kennon; Director, Sara Louise Lazarus; Lighting/Sound, Matt Berman; Press, Jim Baldassare CAST: Joseph Kolinski, Maureen Silliman, Jane Smulyan, Skip Kennon
MUSICAL NUMBERS: Plaisir D'Amour : Love at First Sight, Vows/The First Year, Loads of Time, It was Like Fire Did You Ever Have One of those Years? : Did You Ever Have One of Those Years, That's the Good News, What's a Body, Picking Up the Pieces, We'll Do It Again Fairy Tales and Legends : Small Words, Spring Day, As I'd Like to Be, I Had to Come from Somewhere The Music of Love : Music of Love, Time and Time Again, I Almost Cry, A Mother (Louise), It's All Too Beautiful, Its's Onlt the Best Yet, So When the Time Comes
   Four mini-musicals.

(Samuel Beckett Theatre) Thursday, June 4-21, 1992 MMM Inc. presents:
BUNDY; Written and Performed by Dan Metelitz; Director, Seth Gordon; Set, Allen Moyer; Lighting, Paul Palazzo; Costumes, Yoko Metelitz
   A one-act monodrama about the serial killer.
(Theatre for the New City) Thursday, June 4-July 5, 1992 (20 performances)
ANNA, THE GYPSY SWEDE; Written and Performed by Viveca Lindfors; Director, Cate Caplin; Music, Patricia Lee; Costumes, Franne Lee; Lighting, Vivien Leone; Press, Ellen Zeisler/Kevin P. McAnarney
   A monodrama in two acts. The action takes place in Sweden and Minnesota, mid-1800s.

(Third Step Theatre) Thursday, June 4-21, 1992 (11 performances)
CORNERPIECES; Directors, Al D'Andrea, Erica Gould, Ellen Lewis, Elfin Frederick Vogel; Sets, Alex Biagioli; Costumes, Jennifer Anderson; Lighting, Mr. Vogel; Sound, Gayle Jeffery CAST: Don Cummings, Charls Hall, Andrea Fletcher, Barbara A. Goodison, Denise M. Kennedy, Raan Lewis, Alexandria Sage, Alba Sanchez, Carol Spencer, Judy Unger, Karen Elaine Wells, Joe Wesley, Lee Winston, Billy Joe Young
PROGRAM: NOTES and STREETSIDE SERENADE by Noel Katz; TIME'S HERE by Darryl Curry; GREAT X-ING by Margit Ahlin; ECLIPSE by Fred Rohan Vargas; CITY CRIERS by Vincent Sessa; HELLFIRE AND SPERM GLO by Pat Kaufman
  Seven short plays.

(Westbeth Theatre) Thursday, June 4-14, 1992 (12 performances) Six Figures presents:
WAITING FOR THE PARADE by John Murrell; Director, Maggie da Silva; Set, Kim Kachougian; Lighting, Laura Glover; Sound, Jim Van Bergen; Press, David Rothenberg CAST: Tricia Bastian, Andria Laurie, Tara Leigh, Sheila Schmidt, Susan Vaughn
  A drama set in Canada during World War II.

(Dwyer Warehouses) Friday, June 5-27, 1992 (11 performances) En Garde Arts presents:
VANQUISHED BY VOODO; Written and Directed by Laurie Carlos; Music, Don Meissner; Choreography, Marlies Yearby; Set, Kyle Chepulis; Costumes, Natalie Walker; Lighting, Brian Aldous; Sound, Tim Palmer; Stage Manager, Keith Jones; Press, Ted Killmer CAST: Avis Brown (Tara), Dor Green (Zabane), DeWarren Moses (Aaron), Cynthia Oliver (Lisa), Carl Hancock Rux (Culpepper), Viola Sheely (Momo)
  A sitr-specific dance/music/theatre piece.

(29th St. Playhouse) Friday, June 5-21, 1992 (15 performances) Annette Moskowitz and Alexander E. Racolin present:
BILLINGS FOR THE DEFENSE by Calvert Parlato; Director, Richmond Shepard; Set/Lighting, Timothy Glasby; Costumes, Elizabeth Elkins; Press, Peter Cromarty/Lynne McCreary CAST: Suzanne Farkas, Avi Ber Hoffman, Miguel Sierre, Whit Vernon
  A detective mystery.

(Ballroom) Sunday, June 7-23, 1992 (18 performances)
CASINO PARADISE with Music by William Bolcom; Lyrics, Arnold Weinstein; Musical Director, Roger Trefousse; Press, Tony Origlio CAST: Joan Morris, Andre De Shields, Steven Goldstein
  A cabaret opera.

(John Houseman Theatre) Monday, June 8, 1992 Eric Krebs presents:
ETHEL MERMAN'S BROADWAY; Director, Christopher Powich; Musical Director, Robert Bendorff Press, David Rothenberg CAST: Rita McKenzie

(St. Mark's Theatre) Tuesday, June 9, 1992 Pancham Vedic presents:
OTTAYAN, THE LONE ELEPHANT by Kavalam Narayana Panikkar; Director, Erin B. Mee; Music, Skip LaPlante CAST: Teviot Fairservis, Robert Maniscalco, Karren Williams

(Perry St. Theatre) Tuesday, June 9, 1992-June 27, 1993 Sean Strub in association with Tom Viola presents:
THE NIGHT LARRY KRAMER KISSED ME by David Drake; Director, Chuck Brown; Set, James Morgan; Lighting, Tim Hunter; Sound, Raymond Schilke; Music, Steven Sandberg; Stage Manager, Ali Sherwin; Press, Chris Boneau/Adrian Bryan-Brown/Susanne Tighe, Craig Karpel; Philip Rinaldi CAST: David Drake succeeded by Eric Paeper
VIGNETTES: The Night Larry Kramer Kissed Me, Owed to the Village People, Why I Go to the Gym, 12" Single, A Thousand Points of Light, The Way We Were
  A monodrama performed without intermission.

(Carnegie Hall) Wednesday, June 10, 1992 (1 performance only)

SONDHEIM: A CELEBRATION AT CARNEGIE HALL; Musical Director, Paul Gemignani; Writer, David Thompson; Director, Scott Ellis; Choreography, Susan Stroman; Cast Recording/Video, RCA CAST: Bill Irwin, Madeline Kahn, George Lee Andrews, Richard Muenz, Michael Jeter, James Naughton, Robert LaFosse, Leslie Brown, Patti LuPone, The Tonics, Dorothy Loudon, Betty Buckley, Boy's Choir of Harlem, Billy Stritch, Liza Minnelli, Karen Ziemba, Jerry Hadley, Carolann Page, Eugene Perry, Herbert Perry, Harolyn Blackwell, Patrick Cassidy, Victor Garber, Daisy Eagan, BETTY, Bernadette Peters, Kevin Anderson, Ron Baker,Peter Blanchet, Glenn Close, Mark Jacoby, Beverly Lambert, Jeanne Lehman, Carol Meyer, Maureen Moore, Susan Terry, Bronwyn Thomas, Blythe Walker, Stephen Sondheim
PROGRAM: Sweeney Todd Suite, Getting Married Today, Waiting For the Girls Upstairs, Love I Hear, Live Alone and Like It, Someone Is Waiting, Barcelona, Being Alive, Good Thing Going, Losing My Mind/You Could Drive a Person Crazy, Our Time, Children Will Listen, Anyone Can Whistle, Water Under the Bridge (Premiere), Back in Business, Comedy Tonight, Sooner or Later, Pretty Lady, Green Finch and Linnet Bird, Ballad of Booth, Broadway Baby, I Never Do Anything Twice, With So Little to Be Sure Of, Not a Day Goes By, Weekend in the Country, Send in the Clowns, Old Friends, Sunday
  A gala benefit.

David Drake in "The Night Larry Kramer Kissed Me" (*Christopher Makos*)

Liza Minnelli in "Sondheim: A Celebration..."(*Steve J. Sherman*)

(John Houseman Studio) Wednesday, June 10-21, 1992 (12 performances)
CIRCUMSTANTIAL EVIDENCE by Michael McCarthy; Director, John Margulis; Lighting, Ellen Bone; Costumes, Beverly Bullock CAST: Brian Backer, William Hallmark, Craig Noble, Marc Phillips, Bersaida Vega, JoAnn Wahl

(Actors' Playhouse) Friday, June 12, 1992 Michael Davis presents:
RED DIAPER BABY; Wriiten and Performed by Josh Kornbluth; Director, Joshua Mostel; Set, Randy Benjamin; Lighting, Pat Dignan; Costumes, Susan Lyall; Stage Manager, Tracy Dedrickson; Press, David Rothenberg
   A recollection of growing up with Communist parents. Presented last season at Second Stage.

(Vineyard Theatre) Tuesday, June 16-28, 1992 (16 performances) re-opened at American Place Theatre Thursday, Oct.29-Nov.22, 1992 (20 performances) Ananse Productions presents:
SISTER! SISTER!; Arranged/Adapted/Performed by Vinie Burrows; Costumes, Dada's Works; Stage Manager, Ken Starrett; Press, Peter Cromarty/David Bar Katz; David Rothenberg
   A collage of women's voices from around the world.

Vinie Burrows in "Sister Sister"

(American Place Theatre) Sunday, June 21, 1992 (1 performance only)
A POSTER OF THE COSMOS and THE MOONSHOT TAPE by Lanford Wilson
CASTS: Alec Baldwin (Cosmos), Judith Ivey (Moonshot)
   Two one-act monlogues.

(Courtyard Playhouse) Wednesday, June 24-Nov.29, 1992 The Glines presents:
MURDER IN DISGUISE by John Glines; Director, Pip Carpenter; Set, Bill Wood; Lighting, Tracy Dedrickson; Costumes, Charles Cantanese, Gene L. Lauze; Music, Tom Haffelwander; Press, Chris Boneau/Adrian Bryan-Brown CAST: John Carhart III, Sean Flanigan, John Jason, Wayne Markover, Steve Silver, Philip Stoehr
   A comedy murder mystery.

(Wings Theatre) Saturday, June 27-Aug.9, 1992 (28 performances)
TEN NIGHTS IN A BAR-ROOM by William W. Pratt; Based on novel by T.S. Arthur; Director, Michael Hillyer; Musical Director, Paul Novosel; Olios, Bill Wheeler; Sets, Edmond Ramage; Costumes, Jeffrey Wallach; Lighting, John-Paul Szczepanski; Press, Jeffery Corrick CAST: Tom Grasso (Mr. Romaine), Stephen Wyler (Simon Slade), Terrance Sullivan (Willie Hammond), Burton Fitzpatrick (Sample Swichel), Robert Zaleski (Harvey Green), Don Buff (Frank Slade), Dan Leventritt (Joe Morgan), Nomi Tichman (Mrs. Slade), Elsie James (Mrs. Morgan), Princess Sandlin (Mary Morgan), Connie Carnes (Mehitable Cartright), Peter Diskin, Sally Dymek, Vera E. Chazen, Arthur Walker, Bill Wheeler
   An 1852 temperance drama.

(Theatre Arielle) Tuesday, July 7-Aug.1, 1992 (28 performances) Michael Ross and Eric Krebs present:
THE WORLD OF KURT WEILL; Conceived and Performed by Juliette Koka; Musical Director, David Wolfson; Arrangements, Elliot Finkel; Dialogue, Mr. Finkel, Mille Janz; Staging, Sharon Miller; Lighting, David Meade; Stage Manager, Steven Jay Cohen; Press, Pete Sanders/ Matt Lenz

MUSICAL NUMBERS: Sing Me Not a Ballad, American Love Medley, Pirate Jenny, Barbara Song, Bilbao, Je Ne T'aime Pas, That's Him, Greening Time, Surabaya Johnny, Nana's Lied, Rise & Fall of the City of Mahagonny, War Medley: Buddy's on the Night Shift/Soldier's Wife/Schickelgrubber, How Can You Tell an American, Lost in the Stars, Lady in the Dark, September Song

Juliette Koka in "World of Kurt Weill"

(Del's Down Under) Tuesday, July 7-Oct.25, 1992 ADF Productions presents:
THE NEWS IN REVUE by Nancy Holson; Director, Terry Long; Musical Director, Stephen A. Sasloe; Executive Producer/Press, Becky Flora CAST: Monique Lareau, Jack Plotnick, Richard Rowan, Linda Strasser, Stan Taffel

   The musical comedy scoop on the news performed without intermission.
(Lincoln Center) Tuesday, July 7-30, 1992 (18 performances)
SERIOUS FUN! AT LINCOLN CENTER; Press, Ellen Zeisler/Judith Keenan
PROGRAMS: DR. FAUSTUS LIGHTS THE LIGHTS by Robert Wilson; MO' MOVES with Jamale Graves and Dancers, Rhythm Technicians, Rock Steady Crew; THE FLASH AND CRASH DAYS by Gerald Thomas; DOG SHOW with Eric Bogosian; 49 BLUES SONGS FOR A JEALOUS VAMPIRE by The Hittite Empire, A CERTAIN LEVEL OF DENIAL with Karen Finley; MUSIC WHILE WAGING VICTORY with John Kelly; DAVID SHINER with guests Bill Irwin, Red Clay Ramblers; MY MATHEMATICS with Rose English and Rex the Horse; MEGADANCE, works by Lucinda Childs, Douglas Dunn, Simone Forti, Meredith Monk, Rudy Perez, Yvonne Rainer, Gus Solomons jr., Paul Taylor, James Waring/Elizabeth Walton
   The sixth festival of contemporary work.

Angel Salazar, Daphne Rubin-Vega in "El Barrio '92"

(Rainbow & Stars) Tuesday, July 7-Sept.26, 1992 (120 performances) Steve Paul and Greg Dawson present:
SAY IT WITH MUSIC...THE IRVING BERLIN REVUE; Press, Jessica Miller/David Lotz CAST: Kaye Ballard, Liz Callaway, Joe Cocuzzo, Jason Graae, Jay Leonhart, Ron Raines, Fred Wells

(Village Gate) Wednesday, July 8, 1992 (continuing Wed. Nights) Check It Out Productions and Art D'Lugoff present:
EL BARRIO '92 (EL BARRIO USA); Book, Angel Salazar, Andrew Smith; Director, Mr. Salazar; Set, Joanne Barry; Lighting, Fermen Suarez; Costumes, Yolanda Dobles; Press, Max Eisen/Madelon Rosen CAST: Angel Salazar, Daphne Rubin-Vega, J.J. Ramirez, Kenya Bennett, Andres Fernandez, Santi Suaviro, Mel Gorham, Alexandra Reichler, Iraida Polanco, Al Romero
    Musical comedy revue on life in New York through Hispanic eyes.

(Intar Theatre) Wednesday, July 8-Aug.2, 1992 (28 performances) Gerald A. Goehring in association with Daniel E. Heffernan present:
DAY DREAMS: THE MUSIC AND MAGIC OF DORIS DAY with Book by Jim Murphy; Original Music/Lyrics, David Levy and Darren Cohen; Director/Choreography, Helen Butleroff; Set, John Scheffler; Lighting, Brian Nason; Costumes, Julie Doyle; Sound, Duncan Edwards; Musical Director/Orchestrations, Mr. Cohen; Press, Peter Cromarty/Lynne McCreary CAST: Marijane Sullivan (Doris-1975), Jeannine Moore (Alma Kappelhoff), Michelle Opperman (Young Doris), Christopher Scott (Terry Melcher/Les Brown/Others), Patty Carver (Doris Day), Danny Rutigliano (Barney Rapp/Mary Melcher/Others), Steve Fickinger (Frankie Laine /Others), Billy Miller, Michelle Blakely, Catherine Dupuis (Varied roles)
MUSICAL NUMBERS: (originals) You've Got Something, The Girl Back Home, In My Hands, The Girl You Always Wanted Me to Be, (standards) Whatever Will Be Will Be, Life Is Just a Bowl of Cherries, Jeepers Creepers, Day after Day, Booglie Wooglie Piggy, Chocolate Sundae, My Dreams Are Getting Better, Sentimental Journey, I Wish I Didn't Love You So, Love Somebody, It Had to Be You, It's Magic, Secret Love, I'm in Love, Bewitched Bothered and Bewildered, Shanghai, Everybody Loves a Lover, Purple Cow, Love Me or Leave Me, Ten Cents a Dance, Others
A musical biography in two acts.

Patty Carver, Steve Fickinger, Michelle Blakely, Billy Miller, Catherine DuPuis in "Day Dreams" (*Carol Rosegg/Martha Swope*)

(The Spot at Cafe Arielle) Sunday, July 12, 1992 (1 performance only)
ARMOR; Written and Directed by William Neish; Lighting, Graeme F. McDonnell; Sound, Peter Millrose CAST: Kenneth Laurents (Paul), Dan Tyler (Sammy)
    Two young men drift together and apart in Boston, 1985.

(Nat Horne Theatre) Thursday, July 16-Aug.1, 1992 (14 performances and 1 preview) Love Creek Productions present:
PIE SUPPER; Written and Directed by Le Wilhelm; Set/Lighting, Bill Schwartz; Costumes, Caren Alpert; Press, Francine L. Trevens CAST: Caren Alpert, Cynthia L. Brown; Jackie Jenkins, Nancy McDoniel, Tracy Newith, Katherine Parks, Kirsten Walsh, Dustye Winniford

(Sheridan Sq. Playhouse) Saturday, July 18-27, 1992 (8 performances) New Stages Musical Arts (Joe Miloscia, Artistic/Producing Director) presents:
NEW AMERICAN MUSICAL WRITERS FESTIVAL; Festival Director, Robert J. Weston; Festival Manager, Rikki Josephson

Karen Ziemba in "110 in the Shade" (*Carol Rosegg/Martha Swope*)

SOME SUMMER NIGHT with Music by Joel Adlen; Lyrics, Steve Josephson, Mr. Adlen; Book, Mr. Josephson; Director, Joe Miloscia; Musical Director, Maria Delgado CAST: Carolan Berman (Snug), Beth Blatt (Hippolyta Heartstop), Bill Brooks (Theseus Killington), Wells Cornelius (Demetrius Killington), Nanette DeWester (Helena Troy), Daniel Ely (Robin Good-fellow), Dennis Holly (Oberon Fairly), Debra Joy (Peaseblossom Hummingtree), Lora Jean Martens (Titania Fairly), Adam Michenner (Egeus Upham-Downs), Joseph Ricci (Lysander Lovelorn), Lisa Rochelle (Hermia Upham-Downs), Kevin Scullin (Nick Bottom)
JUNGLE QUEEN DEBUTANTE with Music/Lyrics by Thomas Tierney; Book, Sean S. O'Donnell; Director, Gene Fotte; Music Director, Wendy Bobbitt CAST: Nora Brennan (Norris Westwood), Linda Gabler (Jungle Queen), Peter Kapetan (Sinclair Alcott), B.K. Kennelly (Rocco/Skip/Loppy/Minion) Nancy Leach (Bangles Jolie), Aliza Loewy (Lacey), Lori Putnam (Sara Westwood), Tom Souhrada (Sal/Trip/Porter/Minion), Andy Taylor (Richard Duvalle), Annette Verdolino (Tiffy), Jay Brian Winnick (Dominick Zeppoli)
FINALE! with Music/Lyrics/Book/Direction by Robert Ost; Music Director, C. Colby Sachs CAST: Virl Andrick (Cosmo Delaney), Carolan Berman (Lotti/Glory Jean Johnson), Edwin Bordo (Wilbur Shulman), Bill Brooks (Warren), Martha Cotton (Salesgirl), Jo Ann Cunningham (Allison Edwards), Rebecca Fasanello (Rosa Perez), David Gurland (Gordon/Guard) Jonathan Hadley (Craig Lawrence), Helen Hanft (Gladys), Francine Lobis (Donna Plotnick), Amanda Lord (Mrs. Shulman), Harold Mason (Jeremiah Trumbull), Ethelmae Mason (Charlotte Trumbull), Vickie Phillips (Bobbi/ Kikki McDonald), Rob Rushton (Randy/Feminicci), Allan Stevens (Paul Edawrds), James Weatherstone (Dorian)

(Lincoln Center/New York State) Saturday, July 18-November 15, 1992 (performances in repertory) New York City Opera presents:
110 IN THE SHADE with Music by Harvey Schmidt; Lyrics, Tom Jones; Book, N. Richard Nash based on his play *The Rainmaker* ; Director, Scott Ellis; Conductor, Paul Gemignani; Choreography, Susan Stroman; Orchestrations, Hershy Kay, William D. Brohn; Sets, Michael Anania; Costumes, Lindsay W. Davis; Lighting, Jeff Davis CAST: Robert Mann Kayser (Tommy), Jennifer Paulson Lee, Craig Innes (Dance Couple), Richard Muenz (File), David Aaron Baker (Jimmy Curry), Walter Charles (Noah Curry), Henderson Forsythe (H.C. Curry), Karen Ziemba (Lizzie Curry), Crista Moore (Snookie Updegraff), Brian Sutherland (Bill Starbuck)
MUSICAL NUMBERS: Gonna Be Another Hot Day, Lizzie's Comin' Home, Love Don't Turn Away, Overheard, Poker Polka, Why Can't They Leave Me Alone(new song-cut from original), Come on Along(unused in original), Rain Song, You're Not Foolin' Me (new ending), Cinderella, Raunchy, A Man and a Woman, Old Maid, Come on Along, Everything Beautiful Happens at Night, Shooting Star(new song), Melisande, Simple Little Things, Little Red Hat, Is It Really Me?, Wonderful Music, Finale
    A new production of the 1963 musical. The action takes place in a Western state during a drought.

(Village Theatre Company) Wednesday, July 22, 1992 Village Theatre Co. and Randy Kelly present:
ROLEPLAY with Music by Adryan Russ; Lyrics, Ms. Russ, Doug Haverty; Book, Mr. Haverty; Director/Set, Henry Fonte; Musical Director, Mark York; Choreography, Karen Luschar; Lighting, David Edwardson, Costumes, Brenda D. Renfroe; Stage Manager, Lisa Jean Lewis
CAST: Kimberly Schultheiss, Alyson Reim, Kate Bushmann, Marj Feenan, Elizabeth Silon, Anita Lento
MUSICAL NUMBERS: Why Join a Group?, First, Thin, Let It Go, If You Really Loved Me, Things Look Different, Behind Dena's Back, Grace's Nightmare, Reaching Up, Never Enough, I Don't Say Anything, Passing of a Friend, Do It at Work, Do It at Home, Love Again, Finale
    A two-act musical about five women in group therapy.

Jordan Lage, David Wolos-Fonteno, Ray Anthony Thomas, Giamcarlo Esposito, Todd Weeks, Jack Wallace in "Distant Fires" (*William Gibson/Martha Swope*)

Geoffrey C. Ewing in "Ali" (*William Gibson/Martha Swope*)

Ray Kaspar, Michael Gump, Terry Flynn in "Cata strophe"
(*Carol Rosegg/Martha Swope*)

(Quaigh Theatre) Wednesday, July 29-Aug.15, 1992 (20 performances)
THE BEST OF QUAIGH'S ANNUAL DRAMATHON; Lighting, Winifred Powers; Sound, George Jacobs; Set, Tobi Furukawa; Stage Manager, Jonathan Polk; Press, Francine L. Trevens
PROGRAM: AT LIBERTY by Tennessee Williams; Director Bill Lipscomb; with Kim Dickens (Gloria LaGreen), Patricia Dodd (Mother); THE LOCAL STIGMATIC by Heathcote Williams; Director, Will Lieberson; with Ned Salisbury (Graham), Robert P. King (Ray), Edward Charles Lynch (Man in street), Tom Fountain (David); THE DICKS by Jules Fieler; Director, Mary Tierney; with Ron Roth (Ed), Jean-Robert Cledet (Young Man); THE TIES THAT BIND by Matthew Witten; Director, Bill Lipscomb; with Tom Fountain (David), Kim Dickens (Sandy), Claudine Kielson (Eileen); NOW DEPARTING by Robert Mearns; Director, Will Lieberson; with Derek Le Dain (Tommy), Edward Charles Lynch (Frank); BREAKING IN by James T. McCartin; Director, Edward Charles Lynch; with Mardina Parker (Mary), Karen Dumas (Beatrice)

(Circle in the Square Downtown) Tuesday, Aug.18-Oct.4, 1992 (56 performances) The Herrick Theatre Foundation presents:
DISTANT FIRES by Kevin Heelan; Director, Clark Gregg; Sets, Kevin Rigdon; Costumes, Sarah Edwards; Lighting, Howard Werner; Stage Manager, James FitzSimmons; Press, Peter Cromarty/David Bar Katz CAST: David Wolos-Fonteno (Raymond), Todd Weeks (Angel), Giancarlo Esposito (Foos), Ray Anthony Thomas (Thomas), Jordan Lage (Beauty), Jack Wallace (General)
A construction crew drama in two acts. The action takes place in Ocean City, MD.

(John Houseman Studio) Wednesday, Aug.5-Sept.6 (30 performances) moved to Sheridan Square Playhouse on Tuesday, Sept.15, 1992 Eric Krebs Theatrical Management presents:
ALI; Conceived and Performed by Geoffrey C. Ewing; Written by Mr. Ewing and Graydon Royce; Director, Stephen Henderson; Boxing Choreography, Ron Lipton; Sets, Sirocco D. Wilson; Costumes, Ann Rubin; Lighting, Robert Bessoir; Sound, Tom Gould; Stage Manager, Patricia Flynn
A biography of Muhammad Ali in two acts.

(Ubu Repertory Theatre) Thursday, Aug.13-31, 1992 (14 performances) King Spike Theatre presents:
THERE YOU ARE; Director, Randy Sharp; Lighting/Sound, Michael Birnbaum, Mr. Sharp; Press, Peter Cromarty/Lynne McCreary
PROGRAM: CATASTROPHE by Samuel Beckett; with Ray Kaspar (Director), Terrance Flynn (Asst.), Michael Gump (Protagonist); THE MAN WITH THE FLOWER IN HIS MOUTH by Luigi Pirandello; with Mr. Gump (Man), Mr. Flynn (Peaceful Customer); CATASTOPHE 2 by Samuel Beckett; with Mr. Kaspar, Mr. Flynn, Mr. Gump
Three plays about the realm of the universe.

(Alice's Fourth Floor) Aug.13-Sept.4, 1992 Alice's Fourth Floor (Susann Brinkley, Artistic Director) and Angels w/o Wings Productions (Lyle J. Jones and Daniel J. Adkins, Executive Producers) present:
THE MELVILLE BOYS by Norm Foster; Director, Susann Brinkley; Sets/Lighting, The Big Deal Productions; Costumes, Elizabeth Elkins; Stage Manager, David Smith; Press Chris Boneau/Adrian Bryan-Brown, Craig Karpel CAST: Richard Joseph Paul (Owen Melville), Mark Tymchyshyn (Lee Melville), Katherine Leask (Mary), Kellie Overbey (Loretta)
A comedy in two acts. The action takes place during a Michigan fall.

(Ballroom) Monday, Aug.17-Sept.27, 1992
LYPSINKA! NOW IT CAN BE LIP-SYNCHED; Created and Performed by John Epperson; Director, Kevin Malony; Gowns, Anthony Wong; Sets, Russ Clower; Lighting, Randolph F. Wilson; Sound, Mark Bennett
Lip-synching performance art.

(Theatre for the New City) Thursday, Aug.27-Sept.13, 1992 Theatre for the New City presents:
WHO COLLECTS THE PAIN by Sean O'Connor; Director, Manucher Harsini; Press, Jonathan Slaff CAST: Tai Bennett, Mykeko Bryant, Samanthia E. Carroll, Vladimir France, Derek Lively, Manny Perez, Jake Torem, Donald Viscardi
An interracial romance drama.

Richard Joseph Paul, Kellie Overbey, Mark Tymchyshyn in "Melville Boys"
(*William Gibson/Martha Swope*)

(Charles Ludlam Theater) Wednesday, Sept.2, 1992-Jan.3, 1993 The Ridiculous Theatrical Co. (Everett Quinton, Artistic Director; Steve Asher, Managing Director) presents:
BROTHER TRUCKERS by Georg Osterman; Director, Everett Quinton; Sets, Mark Beard; Costumes, Elizabeth Fried; Lighting, Terry Alan Smith; Sound, Mark Bennett; Stage Manager, Karen Ott; Press, Peter Cromarty/ David Bar Katz CAST: James Lamb (Lech Fabrinski), Georg Osterman (Billie Wilson), Eureka (Harry Balskin), Everett Quinton (Lyla Balskin), Maureen Angelos (Flem Fabrinski), Lisa Herbold (Bina Fabrinski), Stephen Pell (Frenchy DuVey), Noelle Kalom (Trixie Fabu), Adam Weitz (Prosecutor)
   A new "film noir" set in New York City.

(Studio Theatre 4A) Thursday, Sept.3-20, 1992 (15 performances) Helicon Players present:
FREE FALL by Laura Harrington; Director, Alma Becker; Set, J.C. Svec; Costumes, Ryan Dunn; Lighting, Chad McArver; Sound, Debra Whitford-Gallo; Stage Manager, Kimberly N. Fajen; Press, Howard and Barbara Atlee CAST: Paul Frediani (Lou), Emily Caigan (Sam), Don Owen (Norman), Eve Laurel (Patti)
   A drama in two acts. The action takes place in Maine.

(Bouwerie Lane Theatre) Friday, Sept.4-Nov.13, 1992 (15 performances) Jean Cocteau Repertory presents:
AN OLD ACTRESS IN THE ROLE OF DOSTOYEVSKY'S WIFE by Edvard Radzinsky; Translation, Alma H. Law; Director, Eve Adamson; Set/Lighting, Giles Hogya; Costumes, Susan Soetaert; Stage Manager, Harold A. Mulanix; Press, Jonathan Slaff CAST: Jere Jacob (Old Actress), Craig Smith (Fedya)
   A 1986 Russian drama performed without intermission. The setting is an old-age home.

Paul Frediani, Emily Caigan in "Freefall" (*Christie Mullen*)

(Public Theatre) Monday, Sept.7-20, 1992 The Jim Henson Foundation presents:
PUPPETRY AT THE PUBLIC; featuring Bread and Puppet Theatre (Vermont), Roman Paska (NY), Stuffed Puppet Theatre (Netherlands), Theatre Drak (Czechoslovakia), Diablomundo (Argentina), Paul Zaloom (NY), Green Apple Puppet Theatre (Finland), Theodora Skipitares (NY), Hystopolis Puppet Theatre (Chicago), Eric Bass/Sandglass Theatre (Vermont), Theatre Im Wind (Germany), Jusaburo Tsujimura (Japan), Compagne Philippe Genty (France), Janie Geiser and Co. (NY), George Latshaw Puppets (Ohio), Paul Vincent Davis (Mass.), Yang Feng (China)
   The first New York international festival of puppet theatre.

(Westside Theatre Downstairs) Tuesday, Sept.8-Oct.11, 1992 (40 performances) George Elmer/Phase Three Prods. present
CUTTING THE RIBBONS with Music by Cheryl Harwick and Mildred Hayden (additional) Nancy Ford; Lyrics, Mae Richard; Director, Sue Lawless; Choreography, Sam Viverito; Musical Director, Sande Campbell; Orchestrations, Ms. Campbell, Patti Wyss, Ron Zito; Sets/Lighting, Michael Hotopp; Costumes, Terence O'Neill; Sound, Tom Sorce; Stage Manager, Allison Sommers; Press, Peter Cromarty/ David Lotz CAST: Georgia Engel, Barbara Feldon, Donna McKechnie
MUSICAL NUMBERS: Overture, She Loves You, Kick Me Again, Mommy Number Four, Let Her Go, The Door Is Closed, Period Piece, Lookin' Good, It's a Party, Four-Two-Two, Two-Two-Four, Because of Her, Try Not to Need Her, Balancing, Mom Will Be There, Am I Ready for This, Instinct, T'ai Chi, Bed, Isabel, That Woman in the Mirror, Where's My Picture, I Dare You Not to Dance, Her Career, I Just Can't Move in Her Shadow, Cut the Ribbons
   A mother-daughter musical in two acts.

James Lamb, Georg Osterman, Maureen Angelos in "Brother Truckers"
(*Anita & Steve Shevett*)

Georgia Engel, Barbara Feldon, Donna McKechnie in "Cut the Ribbons"
(*Martha Swope*)

(Actors' Playhouse) Tuesday, Sept.8-Oct.4, 1992 (27 performances and 1 preview each) The Irish Repertory Theatre Co.(Charlotte Moore, Ciaran O'Reilly, Artistic Directors) and One World Arts Foundation present:
JOYICITY by Ulick O'Connor; Director, Caroline FitzGerald; Music, Noel Eccles; Set, David Raphel; Lighting, Gregory Cohen; Stage Manager, Chris Kelly; Press, Chris Boneau/Adrian Bryan-Brown CAST:Vincent O'Neil
and
FRANKLY BRENDAN; Adapted by Chris O'Neill from the works of Frank O'Connor and Brendan Behan; CAST: Chris O'Neill
Two one-man shows in repertory.

(Theatre for the New City) Thursday, Sept.10-Oct.11, 1992 (20 performances) Theatre for the New City presents:
BLUE HEAVEN; Written and Directed by Karen Malpede; Design, Leonardo Shapiro; Music, Gretchen Langheld; Choreography, Lee Nagrin; Costumes, Karen Young; Lighting, Brian Aldus; Video, Maria Venuto; Stage Manager, Sue Jane Stoker; Press, Jonathan Slaff CAST: George Bartenieff, Lailah Hanit Bragin, Christen Clifford, Shelia Dabney, Joseph Kellough, Lee Nagrin, Nicki Paraiso, Rosalie Triana, Beverly Wideman
A multi-media play.

(St. Mark's Theatre) Thursday, Sept.10-27, 1992 (14 performances) Target Margin Theatre Presents:
LITTLE EYOLF by Henrik Ibsen; Translation, Rolf Fjelde; Director, David Herskovits; Sets, Erika Belsey; Lighting, Lenore Doxsee; Costumes, Tom Broeker CAST: Thomas Jay Ryan (Alfred), Mary Neufeld (Rita), Mairhinda Groff (Asta), Neil Bradley (Borghejm), Linda Donald (Rat Wife), Clifton Munz-Phelps (Little Eyolf)

(Theatre Row Theatre) Thursday, Sept.10, 1992 Merry Enterprises Theatre presents:
A RAG ON A STICK AND A STAR with Music by Elliot Weiss; Lyrics/Book, Eric Blau; Director, Richard Ziman; Musical Director, Woody Regan; Dances, Shaelyn Ament; Set, Don Jensen; Lighting, Graeme McDonnell; Costumes, Traci Di Gesu; Press, M.J. Boyer CAST: William Youmans (Rev.Hechler), Daniel Neiden (Dori/Herzl), Courtenay Collins (Julie), David Pevsner (Newlinski), Jeff Gardner (Bokov), Steve Irish (Lueger, others), Catherine Dupuis (Lulu, others), Adriana Maxwell (Party Guest, others), Shaelyn Ament (Queen Victoria, others), Hart MacCardell-Fossel (Child)
MUSICAL NUMBERS: Oh Lead Us Now, Oh Vienna, Wishing for a Victory, Farewell Soft Life, Appearances, A Rag on a Stick and a Star, On the Way Home to the Old Land, Let's Play the Game, Actress on the Stage, Abdullah, In the Wildest Dream, I'm a Very Patient Man, When It Grows Dark My Lord, All My Anguish and My Sorrow, We Have Come So Far, A World without Us, Let Them Bleed, What Happened Here?, This Is My Promise, Do You Know What the Children Were Doing Today?, There Is a Bird, We Are Dancing in the Temple
A two act musical about Israel's founder.

(John Houseman Studio) Friday, Sept.11-Oct.4, 1992 (17 performances) Playmarket and Annette Moskowitz & Alexander E. Racolin present:
THE MYSTERY OF ANNA O by Jerome Coopersmith and Lucy Freeman; Director, Yanna Kroyt Brandt; Set, John Farrell; Costumes, Tay Cheek; Lighting, Heather Rogan; Choreography, Amy Coopersmith; Stage Manager, Uriel Menson; Music, Anthony Brandt; Press. Peter Cromarty/ David Bar Katz CAST: Peter Tate (Breuer/Jones), Ariane Brandt (Anna O), C.C. Loveheart (Stephanie/Bertha), Bernard Barrow (Gestapo, others), Marilee Warner (Jenny, others), Bobbi Randall (Maria, others), Barbara Hilson (Mathilde, others), David Mazzeo (Bloch/ Sigmund Freud)
A drama taking place between the 19th century and 1956.

C.C. Loveheart, Peter Tate, Ariane Brandt in "Mystery of Anna O" (*Martha Swope*)

Jean Stapleton, Rochelle Oliver in "Roads to Home" (*Michael Bailey*)

(Lamb's Little Theatre) Friday, Sept.11-Oct.31, 1992 Lamb's Theatre Co. presents:
THE ROADS TO HOME; Written and Directed by Horton Foote; Sets, Peter Harrison; Lighting, Kenneth Posner; Costumes, Gweneth West; Stage Manager, Lori M. Doyle; Press, Chris Boneau/Adrian Bryan-Brown, Cabrini Lepis CAST: Jean Stapleton (Mabel Votaugh), Rochelle Oliver (Vonnie Hayhurst), Hallie Foote (Annie Gayle Long), Michael Hadge (Mr. Long), Emmett O'Sullivan-Moore (Jack Votaugh), William Alderson (Eddie Hayhurst), Devon Abner (Dave Dushon), Frank Girardeau (Cecil Henry), Dan Mason (Greene Hamilton)
A drama in three acts. The action takes place in Texas, 1924-28.

(McGinn/Cazale Theatre) Sunday, Sept.13-27, 1992 (16 performances) Paassha Productions presents:
WUTHERING HEIGHTS: A Romantic Musical; Music/Lyrics/Book by Paul Dick; Based on Emily Bronte's novel; Director, Jack Horner; Musical Director, Christopher McGovern; Choreography, Jean Shepard; Lighting, David Forni; Stage Manager, Lee O'Connor; Press, Wesley Stevens CAST: Ellen Beattie (Isabella), Paul Bellantoni (Earnshaw), Sharon Claveau (Mrs. Linton), Karen DiConcetto (Young Cathy), Rob Evan (Lockwood/ Robert), Colin Fisher (Young Heathcliff), Steve Gray (Edgar Linton), Ron Keith (Linton), John LaLonde (Heathcliff), Jeffrey Landman (Young Hindley), Genette Lane (Nellie Dean), Robert Manzari (Hindley Earnshaw), Jerry Rodgers (Joseph), Beth Thompson (Cathy)
MUSICAL NUMBERS: Hymn to the House, Catherine's Come Home, Gift from Liverpool, How Could You, How Could I?, Dance on the Moor, Heathcliff's Love, Flesh and Blood, From Now On, More Like a Lady, Never Seen Anthing Like It Before, Outside/Inside, Cath'rine, I Can Hardly Believe It's You, If I Were Edgar, Dusting Now?, Go if You Want, Caught, Hymn to Her, Choose Love, I Love Him, Will I Wake Tomorrow, I Thought Only of You, Fair Fight, Deal Choose Throw Lose, From the Very First Day, Come with Me, A Life without Love, Twenty Years from Now, Never to Go, Be There, Wuthering Heights
A musical in two acts. The action takes place in and around Wuthering Heights, early nineteenth century.

John LaLonde, Beth Thompson in "Wuthering Heights"
(*Blanche Mackey/Martha Swope*)

(Atlantic Theatre) Saturday, Sept.12-30, 1992 (16 performances) Common Ground Stage and Film Co. present:
THE KING OF INFINITE SPACE by Andrew C. Ordover; Director, David Crommett; Sets, James Wolk; Costumes, Rosi Zingalis; Lighting, Laura Menteuffel; Press, Jeffrey Richards/Tom D'Ambrosio CAST: Craig Addams, Christopher Burns, Dwight Donaldson, C. Francis Blackchild, Tiffany Fraser, Nancy Gartlan, Ken Glickfeld, Joan Green, Mark McCoy, M.J. Sawyer, Erik Sherr, David Valcin
A drama set in a mythic, post-apocalyptic future.

(John Houseman Theatre) Tuesday, Sept.15, 1992-Jan.30, 1992 David G. Richenthal and Georganne Aldrich Heller present:
REMEMBRANCE by Graham Reid; Director, Terence Lamude; Sets, Bill Stabile; Costumes, Barbara Forbes; John McLain; Sound, Tom Gould; Stage Manager, Susan Whelan; Press, Jeffrey Richards/David LeShay CAST: Milo O'Shea (Bert Andrews), John Finn (Victor Andrews), Frances Sternhagen (Theresa Donaghy), Caroleen Feeney (Joan Donaghy), Terry Donnelly (Deirdre Donaghy), Mia Dillon (Jenny Andrews)
A drama in two acts. The action takes place in Ireland.

(Judith Anderson Theatre) Wednesday, Sept.16-27, 1992 (12 performances) Thomas L. Collins and Performing Arts Perservation Assoc. present:
THE YES WORD by John Tobias; Director, Andre Ernotte; Set, James Noone; Costumes, Muriel Stockdale; Lighting, Phil Monat; Sound, Phil Lee, David Lawson; Music, Stan Davis; Lryics, Mr. Tobias; Stage Manager, Althea Watson CAST: Paul Ukena, Jr. (Nick), Matthew Arkin (Ernie), Cornelia Mills (Feathers), Stephen Lee (Wing), Geoff Pierson (Lenny)
A two-act comedy set in a Manhattan warehouse.

(Kampo Cultral Center) Wednesday, Sept.16-Oct.4, 1992 (15 performances) The Seven Artists Co. presents:
ACADEMY STREET by Richard Andrew Gaeta; Director, John Eisner; Set, Charles Golden; Lighting, Marcus Abbott; Music, Joe Gaeta; Costumes, Annie Saposnick; Stage Manager, Lisa Gavaletz; Press, Lisa McNellis CAST: Jaime Sanchez (Don), Philip Levy (Ted), Jane Jakimetz (Sandy), John DiGennaro (Henry), Karen Lynn Gorney (Barbara), Erza Barnes (Brent), Lenore Loveman (Mom)
A drama in two acts. The action takes place in a home for developmentally disabled adults.

(Theatre for the New City) Thursday, Sept.17-Oct.18, 1992 Bartenieff/Fields presents the Nu Matt production:
MONK 'n' BUD by Laurence Holder; Director, Jasper McGruder; Lighting, Stewart Wagner; Costumes, Rome Neal; Stage Manager, Cheryl Jones CAST: Alvin Alexis (Thelonius Monk), Tony Jackson (Bud Powell), Marie McKinney (Nellie Monk)
The action takes place on a hot summer evening, 1951.

(Promenade Theatre) Thursday, Sept.17-Oct.18, 1992 (38 performances) John A. McQuiggan and Donald L. Taffner in association with Diana Bliss and W. Scott & Nancy McLucas present:
THE HOLY TERROR; Written and Directed by Simon Gray; Sets, David Jenkins; Costumes, David Murin; Lighting, Beverly Emmons; Stage Manager, George Darveris; Press, Chris Boneau/Adrian Bryan-Brown, Cabrini Lepis CAST: Daniel Gerroll (Mark Melon), Michael McGuire (Edward Ewart Gladstone), Lily Knight (Samantha Eggerley), Anthony Fusco (Michael/Jacob/Rupert/Graeme), Noel Derecki (Josh Melon), Kristine Nielsen (Gladys Powers), Kristin Griffith (Kate Melon)
A drama in two acts. The action takes place in the Cheltenham Women's Institute over a 15 yr period.

Milo O'Shea, Mia Dillon in "Remembrance" (*Marc Bryan-Brown*)

Marie McKinney, Alvin Alexis, Tony Jackson in "Monk 'n' Bud" (*KAJ*)

(Theatre for the New City) Thursday, Sept.17-Oct.3, 1992 (15 performances) Chester Fox and Kaflama Prod. present:
FORTY-DEUCE by Alan Bowne; Director, Tom O'Horgan; Set, Perry Arthur Kroeger; Costumes, Todd Tomarrow; Lighting, Adrienne De Guevara; Sound, Alexander Brofsky; Stage Manager, Johanna Staray CAST: Vince Castellanos (Blow), Russell Coyne (Augie), Peter Craig (Roper), Christopher Zane Gordon (Crank), Sam Koppelman (John Anthony), Bobbie Miller (Mitchell), Thom Vallette (Ricky)
The 1981 drama about Times Square male hustlers.

(One Dream) Friday, Sept.18-Oct.10, 1992 (16 performances) Young Dog Ensemble present:
THE DEPRESSION SHOW! by Thomas Keith & Jane Young; Music, Marc Steinberg; Director, George Hewit; Design, Ronald Gottschalk; Musical Director, Michael Shenker; Stage Manager, David Alan Comstock; Press, Peter Cromarty/David Bar Katz CAST: James Adlesic, William Flatley, Brian Keane, Thomas Keith, Randy Lilly, Christine Malik, Pamela Newkirk, Marc Reeves, Michael Shenker, Gwen Torry-Owens, Jane Young

(55 Grove St.) Friday, Sept.18-Nov.27, 1993
DANGEROUS DUETS; Musical Director, Christopher Howatt; Artistic Manager, Peter De La Cruz; Production Design, Brian Rardin CAST: Jeff Loeffelholz, Michael Tidd

(West Bank Cafe) Wednesday, Sept.23-Oct.4, 1992 (8 performances)
THINGS THAT SHOULD BE SAID; Written and Produced by Philip Carlo; Sets, Kevin Joseph Roach; Music, Tim Carosi; Lighting, Tammy Richardson; Stage Manager, Michael Kelleher; Press, Les Schecter CAST: Rebecca Boyd, Mario D'Elia, Currie Graham, Andrew Heckler, Mary Lynn Hetsko, Paul Herman, Ray Karl, Mike Mahon, Ron Maccone, Marie Marshall, Annie Meisels, Gemma Nanni, Bill Prael, Tim Quill, Michael Santoro, Tony Sirico, Anastasia Traina, Chuck Zito
PROGRAM: *For Whom The Bell Really Tolls* and *Blind Eye* Director, Frank Rainone; *Multiple* and *I've Got The Applicatia'* and *Everythin'* Director, Sheila Jaffe; *Unspeakable Ways* and *Punk City* Director, John A. Gallagher; Walk Alone Director, Philip Carlo
Seven one-acts on sexual abuse.

Daniel Gerroll and cast in "The Holy Terror" (*Joan Marcus*)

(Harold Clurman Theatre) Wednesday, Sept.23, 1992 Red Light District presents:
THE TEMPEST by William Shakespeare; Director, Marc Geller; Music, Daniel T. Denver; Lighting, Raymond Reehill; Set, Mary Jane McNamara; Stage Manager, Emily Schriebl CAST: Meliisa Osborn (Ariel),Bart Tangredi (Boatswain), Oleg Passer (Ship Master), Bill Roulet (Gonzalo), Morrow Wilson (Alonso), Alan Denny (Sebastian), Brian McCormack (Antonio), Russell Stevens (Prospero), Karen Wexler (Miranda), Marc Geller (Caliban), Tom Delling (Ferdinand), John Little (Trinculo), Gregg Dubner (Stephano), Gemma DeBiase (Juno/Spirit), Amy Boyer, Jackob G. Hoffman, Kevin Kennedy, Christina Lisi, Colleen Ward

Ian Betts, Suzanne Gregoire in "Le Cabaret Risque" (*Michael Sean Edwards*)

(Time Cafe) Thursday, Oct.1-15, 1992 (3 performances) Cirque Gregoire presents:
LE CABARET RISQUE by Robin Noble; Choreography/Director, Suzanne Gregoire; Songs, Timothy J. Anderson & Debra Kaye; Musical Director, Debra Kaye; Guest Choreographer, Peter diFalco; Press Jim Baldassare CAST: Robert Cardazone (Zizi), Delice Neals (Roxanne), Debra Kaye (Jou Jou), Cody Smolik (Myra), Jeremy Peterson (Pierre), Fabienne Bongard (Pierette), Suzanne Gregoire (Sebastienne), Ian Betts (Lord Richard), J.S. Anderson (Armand), Charles Haack, Daniel Holodyk (Freddie), Stephanie Godino, Claire Posada (Gretchen), Laurence Rawlins (L'Incroyable), Kyle Larsen (Lolaboa)
MUSICAL NUMBERS: Le Cabaret Risque, Room of Madagascar, Pierre Et Pierrette Tango, Sebastienne Et Lord Richard's Tango, La Ultima Curda, Freddie und Gretchen Polka, L'Incroyable's Numero, Je Ne T'aime Pas, Taunting Song, Lolaboa's Boa, Wonderful Nightmare
   The action takes place in a Paris nightclub, 1930s.

(St Mark's Theatre) Thursday, Oct.1-4, 1992 (4 performances) Creation presents:
THE WINDOW MAN with Music by Bruce Barthol and Greg Pliska; Book/Lyrics, Matthew Maguire; Set/Lighting, Kyle Chepulis CAST: Tom Cayler, Joe Daly, Verna Hampton, Eisaku Takami

(Dont Tell Mama) Thursday Oct.1-Nov.26, 1992 (9 performances)
BEYOND THE WINDOW; Written and Directed by Michael Schubert; Photography, Hazen B. Reed; Press, Peter Cromarty/Julie Taylor CAST: Maggi-Meg Reed
   A music theatre piece.

(Jerusalem Group Theatre) Thursday, Oct.1-25, 1992 (16 performances) Alan and Mellissa Boher Jacobson present:
TWO BY CHAIM POTOK; Director, Shela Xoregos; Set/Lighting, David J. Lander; Sound, Kenn Dovel; Costumes, Elly Van Horne; Stage Manager, Kelli Stich
PROGRAM: THE CARNIVAL CAST: Kenny Kamlet (Alex), Ben Frimmer (Michael), Pierre Lang (Pitchman), Lenny Singer (Old Man) THE GALLERY CAST: Alan Jacobson (Asher Lev), Glen Lincoln (Rivkeh Lev), Albert Makhtsier (Aryeh Lev), Emile Titone (Asher at 7), Vivien Landau (Anna Schaeffer), Ben Frimmer (Jonathan), Kenny Kamlet (Asher at 16/Asst.), Lenny Singer (Jacob Kahn)

Richmond Hoxie, Larry Pine in "Dolphin Position" (*Marvin Einhorn*)

(Primary Stages) Oct.1-Nov.1, 1992 (24 performances)
THE DOLPHIN POSITION by Percy Granger; Director, Casey Childs; Set, Ray Recht; Costumes, Bruce Goodrich; Lighting, Deborah Constantine; Sound, One Dream; Stage Manager, Tony Luna; Press, Anne Einhorn, Bob Ganshaw CAST: Larry Pine (Jerry Tremendous), Charlotte d'Amboise (Cheryl), Richmond Hoxie (Paul), Anna Holbrook (Woman), Randell Haynes (Tilly/Bohan/Cal), Andrew Weems (Mike/Bernie/Simon), Ilene Kristen (J.J.), Justin Zaremby (Ronnie/B.J.)
   A play in two acts. The time is the eternal present.

(Holy Trinity) Thursday, Oct.1-26, 1992 (20 performances) Triangle Theatre Co. presents:
DEMOCRACY AND ESTHER by Romulus Linney; Director, Elisabeth Lewis Corley; Set, Bob Phillips; Costumes, Amanda J. Klein; Lighting, Nancy Collings; Stage Manager, Cathy Diane Tomlin; Press, Susan Chicoine CAST: Frank Anderson (Ulysses S. Grant), Maureen Silliman (Julia Grant), Paul Urcioli (Rev. Hazard), Kathleen Dennehy (Ester Dudley), Kathryn Eames (Lydia Dudley), John Woodson (Sen. Raitcliffe), Priscilla Shanks (Mrs. Lee), Fred Burrell (Baron Jacobi), Mary Beth Peil (Mrs. Samuel "Essy" Baker)
   A drama in two acts set in Washington, DC, 1875.

(Village Gate) Thursday, Oct.1, 1992-Feb.7, 1993 Blue Curl Prod., Phylis Raskind, Harold L. Strauss, and Stuart Zimberg present:
JAQUES BREL IS ALIVE AND WELL AND LIVING IN PARIS; Based on Brel's lyrics and commentary; Music by Jaques Brel, Francois Rauber, Gerard Jouannest, Jean Corti; Director, Elly Stone; Conception/English Lyrics/Additional Material, Eric Blau and Mort Shuman; Musical Director, Annie Lebeauz; Set, Don Jensen; Lighting, Graeme F. McDonnell; Costumes, Mary Brecht; Additional Movement, Gabriel Barre; Press, M.J. Boyer CAST: Gabriel Barre, Andrea Green, Joseph Neal, Karen Saunders
MUSICAL NUMBERS: My Childhood, Overture, Marathon, Alone, Madelaine, I Loved, Mathilde, Bachelor's Dance, Timid Friede, My Death, Girls and Dogs, Jackie, Statue, Desperate Ones, Sons Of, Port of Amsterdam, The Bulls, Old Folks, Marieke, Brussels, Fanette, Funeral Tango, Middle Class, No Love You're Not Alone, Next, Carousel, If We Only Have Love
   Twenty-fifth anniversary revival of the musical revue. The original production debuted Jan.22, 1968 at the same theatre.

John Woodson, Priscilla Shanks in "Democracy and Esther"

(Westside Theatre) Friday, Oct.9, 1992-Jan.24, 1993 (86 performances and 17 previews) Westside Theatre, Marshall B. Purdy and Michael S. Bregman present:
SPIC-O-RAMA; Written and Performed by John Leguizamo; Developed/ Directed by Peter Askin; Sets, Loy Arcenas; Lighting, Natasha Katz; Sound, Dan Moses Schreier; Video, Dennis Diamond; Musical Supervisor, Jellybean Benitez; Stage Manager, Michael Robin
    The saga of the damaged Gigante family performed without intermission.

(Actors' Playhouse) Friday, Oct.9-Nov.1, 1992 (29 performances) The Irish Repertory Theatre and One World Arts Foundation present:
THE MADAME MacADAM TRAVELLING THEATRE by Thomas Kilroy; Director, Charlotte Moore; Set, David Raphel; Lighting, Kenneth Posner; Costumes, David Toser; Sound, James M. Bay; Stage Manager, Pamela Edington; Press Chris Boneau/Adrian Bryan-Brown, Susanne Tighe CAST: Denise duMaurier (Mde. MacAdam), Michael Judd (Bun Bourke), Denis O'Neill(LDF man/Chamberlain), Brian F. O'Byrne (Ldf man/Slipper/Simon/Maher), Fiona McCormac (Marie Therese), Rosemary Fine (Jo), Atilla (Dog), Michael O'Sullivan (Sergeant), W.B. Brydon (Lyle Jones), Ellen Adamson (Sally), Ciaran O'Reilly (Rabe)
    A comic drama in two acts. The setting is a small Irish village, 1941.

(Kampo Cultral Ceneter) Thursday, Oct.9-Nov.1, 1992 (16 performances) Signature Theatre Company presents:
FORTINBRAS by Lee Blessing; Director, Jeanne Blake; Set, David Birn, Judy Gailen; Costumes, Teresa Snider-Stein; Lighting, Jeffrey S. Koger; Stage Manager, Dean Gray; Press, James Morrison, Thomas Proehl CAST: Keith Reddin (Fortinbras), Samantha Mathis (Ophelia), Don Reilly (Hamlet), Albert Macklin (Orsic), Timothy Wheeler (Horatio), William Cain (Polonius/Ambassador), Steven Guevera (Capt.), Anthony Michael Ruivivar (Marcellus), Kevin Elden (Barbardo), Archer Martin, Kim Walsh (Maidens), William Metzo (Claudius), Celia Howard (Gertrude), Josh Sebers (Laertes)
    A play picking up where *Hamlet* left off. The action takes place in the Elsinore Castle.

(Synchronicity Space) Friday, Oct.9, 1992- The Stillwaters Theatre Co. presents:
THE OEDIPUS CHRONICLES by Peter Manos; Director, Charles R. Johnson; Set, Andrea Grahm; Lighting, David Alan Comstock CAST: James Brill (Creon), Kate Schlesinger (Jocasta), Andrea Kooharian (Daphne), Maura Clifford (Hebejebe), Henry Tenney, Kevin McClatchy, Christopher Murphy, Scott Zak, Evelyn Hatahway, Susan Kurowski, Anne Lilly
    A comedy applying the Oedipus story to American politics.

(Sanford Meisner Theatre) Friday, Oct.9-31, 1992 Malaparte presents:
A JOKE by Luigi Pirandello; Adaptation/Direction, Keith Bunin; from a literal translation by Susan Tenaglia; Producers, Ami Armstrong, Briar Faure; Sets, Gadi Harel; Lighting, Michael Butts; Music Composed/ Performed by Lisa Loeb; Stage Manager, Gwenn Morreale CAST: Ethan Hawke (Memmo Speranza), Josh Hamilton (Magnasco), Jonathan Marc Sherman (Grizzoffi), Austin Pendleton (Il Signor Barranco), Cynthia Nixon (Gasparina Torretta), Nadia Dajani (Loletta Festa), Jose Zuniga (Il Pro-fessor Virgadamo), Jenny Robertson (La Maestrina Terrasi), Linda Larkin (Rosa), Kevin Breznahan (Vico Lamanna)
    American premiere of a 1918 play in three acts. The action takes place in a small Italian town during the early 1900s. The first production of a new theatre company.

(Sceond Stage Theatre) Tuesday, Oct.13, 1992-Jan 3., 1993 (84 performances) Second Stage Theatre (Carole Rothman, Artistic Director; Suzanne Schwartz Davidson, Producing Director) presents:
A...MY NAME IS STILL ALICE; Conception/Direction by Joan Micklin Silver and Julianne Boyd; Material by Marion Adler, Dan Berkowitz, Douglas Bernstein, Francesca Blumenthal, Craig Carnelia, Randall Courts, John Gorka, Carol Hall, Georgia Bogardus Holof, Doug Katsaros, Michael John LaChiusa, Christine Lavin, Lisa Loomer, Denis Markell, Amanda McBroom, David Mettee, Lynn Nottage, Mary Bracken Phillips, Jimmy Roberts, Mark Saltzman, Stephen Schwartz, Kate Shein, June Siegel, Carolyn Sloan, Mark St. Germain, Steve Tesich; Musical Director/ Arranger, Ian Herman; Orchestrations, Brian Besterman; Choreography, Hope Clark; Set, Andrew Jackness; Lighting, David F. Seagal; Costumes, David C. Woolard; Stage Manager, Renee Lutz; Press, Richard Kornberg CAST: Roo Brown, Laura Dean, Cleo King, KT Sullivan, Nancy Ticotin

PROGRAM: Two Steps Forward, It Ain't Over, Non-Bridaled Passion, Once and Only Thing, Cover Up #1, Why Doesn't She Call on Me?, Juanita Craiga, So Much Rain, The Group, Ida Mae Cole Takes a Stance, Wheels, Sorghum Sisters, Painted Ladies, Sensitive New Age Guys, Lovely Little Life, Play Nice, Gross Anatomy Lecture, Hard Hat Woman, Cover Up #2, Baby, Women Behind Desks, What Did I Do Right, Life Lines, Finale
    A musical revue in two acts. A sequel to 1984's *A...My Name is Alice* .

John Leguizamo in "Spic-o-rama" (*William Gibson*/*Martha Swope*)

Keith Reddin, Samantha Mathis in "Fortinbras" (*Susan Johann*)

Rebecca Pidgeon, William H. Macy

(Orpheum Theatre) Tuesday, Oct.13, 1992-Jan.16, 1994 (513 performances) Frederick Zollo, Mitchell Maxwell, Alan J. Schuster, Peggy Hill Rosenkranz, Ron Kastner, Thomas Viertel, Steven Baruch, Frank & Woji Gero, Patricia Wolff, and the Back Bay Theatre present:

OLEANNA; Written and Directed by David Mamet; Set, Michael Merritt; Costumes, Harriet Voyt; Lighting, Kevin Rigdon; Stage Manager, Carol Avery; Press, Bill Evans CAST: William H. Macy succeeded by Treat Williams, Jim Frangione (John), Rebecca Ridgeon succeeded by Mary McCann (Carol)

A drama in two acts. The action concerns a blunt and sometimes violent interchange between a middle-aged professor and his young woman student.

William H. Macy

Rebecca Pidgeon

Treat Williams, Mary McCann

Brigitte Lacombe, Gerry Goodstein Photos

(29th St. Rep. Theatre) Tuesday, Oct.13-Nov.7, 1992 (20 performances) 29th St. Repertory, Annette Moskowitz/Alexander E. Racolin, Play Producers and Scarborough Prod. present:
UNDER CONTROL by Paul Walker; Director, Jonathan Silver; Set, Anna Louizos; Costumes, Jeffrey Wallach; Lighting, David Smart; Sound, Stuart J. Allyn; Design, Victor Stabin; Stage Manager, Eileen M. Rooney; Press, Jim Baldassare CAST:Danna Lyons (Holly Wheeler), Anita Pratt Morris (Diane McIntyre), Amy Pierce (Loretta Wheeler), Milton Carney (Earl Wheeler), Diane Martella (Rose Wheeler), Linda June Larson (Ann Reilly), Chris Burmester (Jack Casey), David Mogentale (Richard Hornby), Alison Lani Broda (Dr. Anderson), Tim J. Corcoran (Judge voice)
   A drama in two acts. The action, inspired by real life events, concerns a young gay woman who survives a serious accident and the struggle between her lover and family.

(Michael's Pub) Tuesday, Oct.13, 1992-Mar.13, 1993 (203 performances)

VERNEL BAGNERIS PRESENTS JELLY ROLL MORTON: A ME-MORIAL; Musical Director, Morten Gunnar Larsen; Press, Terry M. Lilly/David J. Gersten CAST: Vernel Bagneris
MUSICAL NUMBERS: Perfect Rag, Mamie's Blue's, La Miserere, Mister Jelly Lord, Aaron Harris, Pep, Wolverine Blues, Whinin' Boy, Don't Leave Me Here/Alabama Bound, Fingerbuster, Animule Dance, Dr. Jazz, Sweet Substitute, Jelly Roll Blues
   One-man tribute based on Morton's 1938 Library of Congress interviews.

Ellen Gould in "Bubbe Meises" (*Carol Rosegg/Martha Swope*)

(Cherry Lane Theatre) Tuesday, Oct.13, 1992-Mar.21, 1993 (166 performances and 15 previews) Richard Frankel, Paragon Park Prod., and Renee Blau present:
BUBBE MEISES, BUBBE STORIES; Written and Performed by Ellen Gould; Songs, Holly Gewandter and Ms. Gould; Director, Gloria Muzio; Musical Director/Arrangements, Bob Goldstone; Sets, David Jenkins; Lighting, Peter Kaczorowski; Costumes, Elsa Ward; Sound, Raymond D. Schilke; Stage Manager, Stacey Fleischer; Press, Chris Boneau/Adrian Bryan-Brown, Jackie Green
MUSICAL NUMBERS: Bubbe Meises Bubble Stories, Fifty-Fifty, Oy How I Hate That Fella Nathan, Oy I Like Him, You're Dancing Inside Me, It's a Bubbe Meise, The Road I'm Taking, Bridge Song, Goldstein Swank & Gordon, Take More Out of Life, Chocolate Covered Cherries
   A one-woman musical performed without intermission. A granddaughter recalls her immigrant grandmothers.

(Intar Theatre) Wednesday, Oct.14-18, 1992 (6 performances) Intar presents:
DAEDALUS IN THE BELLY OF THE BEAST (DEDALO EN EL VIENTRE DE LA BESTIA) by Marco Antonio de la Parra; Translation, Joanne Pottlitzer; Director, Alfredo Castro; Music, Miguel Miranda; Press, Peter Cromarty/ Judy Rabitcheff CAST: Pablo Schwartz, Rodrigo Perez, Paulina Urrutia, Eric Beatty
   A bilingual production based on ancient Greek myth.

Paulina Urrutia, Eric Beatty in "Daedalus in the Belly of the Beast" (*B. Stanley*)

(Vineyard Theatre) Wednesday, Oct.14-Nov.15, 1992 (34 performances) The Vineyard Theatre (Douglas Aibel, Artistic Director; Barbara Zinn Krieger, Executive Director; Jon Nakagawa, Managing Director) presents:
JUNO with Music/Lyrics by Marc Blitzstein; Additional Lyrics, Ellen Fitzhugh; Book, Joseph Stein; Based on the play *Juno and the Paycock* by Sean O'Casey; Director, Lonny Price; Musical Supervision/ Direction/ Adaptation, Grant Sturiale; Choreography Joey McKneely; Sound, Bruce Ellman; Set, William Barclay; Lighting, Phil Monot; Costumes, Gail Brassard; Stage Manager, Kenneth J. Davis; Press, Shirley Herz/Sam Rudy CAST: Anita Gillette (Juno Boyle), Dick Latessa (Capt. Jack Boyle), Ivar Brogger (Joxer Daly), Anne O'Sullivan (Mrs. Madigan), Verna Jeanne Pierce (Mrs. Brady), Jeanette Landis (Mrs. Coyne), James Clow (Charlie Bentham), Bill Nabel (Reilly/IRA), Andy Taylor (Jerry Devine), Erin O'Brien (Mary Doyle), Malcolm Gets (Johnny Boyle), Stephen Lee Anderson (IRA), Tanny McDonald (Mrs. Tancred), Frank O'Brien (Nugent), Justin Malone, Tony Valentine
MUSICAL NUMBERS: We're Alive, We Can Be Proud, Liffey Waltz, Daarlin' Man, Song of the Ma, I Wish It So, One Kind Word, Old Sayin's, His Own Peculiar Charm, On a Day Like This, You Poor Thing, My True Heart, Bird Upon the Tree, Music in the House, It;s Not Irish, Hymn, Ireland's Eye, Farewell Me Butty, For Love, Where?, Finale
   A revised version of the 1959 musical featuring songs not used in the original production. The action takes place in Dublin, 1921.

(Atlantic Theatre) Wednesday, Oct.14-Nov.21, 1992 (33 performances) Atlantic Theatre Company presents:
NOTHING SACRED by George F. Walker; Based on *Fathers and Sons* by Ivan Turgenev; Director, Max Mayer; Set, David Gallo; Lighting, Donald Holder; Costumes, Harry Nadal; Stage Manager, Matt Silver; Press, Jim Baldassare CAST: Robert Bella (Gregor), Damian Young (Bailiff), Matt McGrath (Arkady), Clark Gregg (Bazarov), Daniel De Raey (Nikolai), David Pittu (Piotr), Mary McCann succeeded by Robin Spielberg (Fenichka), Larry Bryggman (Pavel), Steven Goldstein (Sitnikov), Heidi Kling (Anna), Nick Phelps (Sergei)
   A play in two acts. The action takes place in Russia, 1859.

Matt McGrath, Clark Gregg in "Nothing Sacred" (*Carol Rosegg/Martha Swope*)

(Judith Anderson Theatre) Thursday, Oct.15-25, 1992 (10 performances) Cintone Productions presents:
IMPASSIONED EMBRACES by John Pielmeier; Director, David Briggs; Sets, Nancy Deren; Lighting, David Weiner; Costumes, Carol Ann Pelletier; Sound, Jessica Murrow; Stage Manager, Elizabeth Brady Davis; Press, Chris Boneau/Adrian Bryan-Brown, Bob Fennell CAST: Tom Aulino, Cynthia Carrafa, Beth Howland, Daniel Pardo, Jeff Robins, Sarah Zinsser
PROGRAM: Sado-Monologue, Chapeter Twelve:The Frog, Emotional Recall, Cheek to Cheek, An Intellectual Discussion (or the Poor Man's Samuel Beckett), My Life in Art, Splatter Flick, On Forgetting, Pick-up Artist, Backer's Audition, Goober's Descent, Mondo Vee-Day-O, Vas Difference, Acting Olympics
    Fourteen short plays.

(Ohio Theatre) Thursday, Oct.15-Nov.1, 1992 (14 performances) Project III in association. with Waterfront Ensemble present:
THE MEN ARE AFRAID OF THE WOMEN by John Kaplan; Director, Dennis Delaney; Set, Bennet Averyt; Lighting, Adrienne Shulman; Costums, Deborah Edelman; Sound, Greg Rajczewski; Stage Manager, Colleen Davis; Press, Jonathan Slaff CAST: Kevin Agnew (Student), Tim Barrett (Max), Dina Dillon (Gloria), Funda Duyal (Joan), Joseph McKenna (Satan), Mary McLain (Mary), Jeff Morris (Peter)
    A dark comedy in two acts.

(One Dream Theatre) Thursday, Oct.15-Nov.7, 1992 (12 performances) Under One Roof Theatre Company presents:
POT MELTING; Written and Performed by Danny Hoch; Director, Greg Freelon; Press, David Rothenberg/Terence E. Womble
    One man explores prejudice.

(National Shakespeare Conservatory) Thursday, Oct.15-Dec.19, 1992 (39 performances) Mosaic Productions present:
FLOWERS OF WAR; Written and Directed by Bob Jude Ferrante; Music, Jamie Lokoff, Paul Casanova CAST: Rachele Bailey, Jacqueline Donohue, Don Fletcher, Tangela Hall, Liz Martinez, Michael Myers, Neill Schill
    The action takes place in an Iraqi fallout shelter during "Operation Desert Storm".

(Atlantic Theatre) Friday, Oct.16-31, 1992 (6 performances) Atlantic Theatre Company presents:
VOX POP; Producers, Hilary Hinckle, Bill Wrubel, Todd Weeks; Video, Michael Louden; Lighting, Howard Werner; Sets, Dan Shefelman; Stage Manager, Katherine Lumb; Press, Jim Baldassare
PROGRAM:*The Happy Camper* by Charlie Schulman; Director, Bill Wrubel; with Todd Weeks (Dan Quale); *The Gettysburg Soundbite* by Ted Tally; Director, Mr. Weeks; with Damian Young (Lincoln), Kristen Johnston (Sue), Robert Bella (Dick), Jordan Lage (Roger); *The Ballad of H. Ross Perot* with Music by Craig Addams; Lyrics, Mr. Wrubel; with Mr. Addams, Neil Pepe; *Ceaucesceau's Dog* by Warren Leight; Director, Mr. Pepe; with David Pittu (Man), Mr. Lage (Dog); *Imagining America* ;Written and Directed by Howard Korder; with Clark Gregg (Bob Clinton), Chris Jones (Steve Davis); *The Debate* by Robert Bella; Director, Daisy Mayer; with Mr. Addams (Candidate), David Valcin (Handler); *The Ark* with Music by Jeanine Levenson; Lyrics, Wendy Riss; with Mr. Pittu; *A Bird in the Hand* by Madleine Olneck; Director, Hilary Hinckle; with Ms. Johnston (Joan), Karen Kohlhaas (Jill), Robin Spielberg (June), Kathleen Dennehy (Joleen), Mr. Pittu (Barbara); *A Moment with Chuck* ; Written and Performed by Michael Louden (Charlton Heston); Eating Goober Peas ; with Mr. Addams, Mr. Pepe; *A Speech for Michael Dukakis* by David Mamet; with W.H. Macy; *A Song* performed by Rebecca Pidgeon and Anthony Chote; *Glengarry Glen Ross Perot* by Jay Martel; Director, Mr. Bella; with Mr. Louden (George Bush), Mr. Pepe (Bill Clinton), Mr. Weeks (Perot)

Tom Aulino, Daniel Pardo, Beth Howland, Cynthia Carrafa, Jeff Robins in "Impassioned Embraces" (*Carol Rosegg/Martha Swope*)

Tim Barrett, Funda Duyal, (top) Joe McKenna in "Men Are Afraid of the Women" (*Jonathan Slaff*)

(Weill Recital Hall) Sunday, Oct.18-19 (2 performances)
THE WORLD OF RUTH DRAPER; Performed by Patricia Norcia; Director, David Kaplan; Press, Chris Boneau/Adrian Bryan-Brown, Bob Fennell
    Monolgue theatre by Draper.

(Naked Angels) Monday, Oct.19-Nov.7, 1992
A SUFFERING COLONEL by Kenneth Longeran; Director, Matthew Broderick CAST: Timothy Britten Parker, Frank Whaley, Bruno Kirby, Nicole Burdette
    A comedy involving a police colonel getting bitten by the show biz bug.

(Samuel Beckett Theatre) Tuesday, Oct.20-Nov.1, 1992 (12 performances) The Basic Theatre presents:
LOVE'S LABOUR'S LOST by William Shakespeare; Director, David Ganon; Music/Sound, Lewis Flinn; Set, Walt Spangler; Lighting, Marc D. Malamud; Costumes, Jared Hammond, Patty Burke, Clint Ramos; Stage Manager, Susan Gutmann CAST: John Edmond Morgan (King Ferdinand), Ed Altman, Tony Cormier, David Zabel (Lords), Gary Cowling (Dull), David Goldman (Costard), Darryl Croxton (Don Adriano), Samuel D. Cohen (Moth), Sandy Porter (Jaquenetta), Jared Hammond (Boyet), Margaret Burnham (Princess of France), Joanne Comerford, Carol Dunne, Loretta Toscano (Ladies), Kevin Dwyer (Holofernes), Thom Haneline (Sir Nathaniel), Kevin Durkin (Marcade)

(American Place Theatre) Friday, Oct.23-Nov. 1992   American Place Theatre (Wynn Handman, Director; Dara Hershman, General Manager) presents
DOG LOGIC by Thomas Strelich; Director, Darrell Larson; Set/Costumes, Kert Lundell; Lighting, Jan Kroeze; Music, Paul Lacques, Richard Lawrence; Sound, Tristan Wilson; Stage Manager, Anne Marie Paolucci; Press, David Rothenberg/Meg Gordean, Manuel Igrejas, Terence Womble CAST: Darrell Larson (Hertel), Joe Clancy (Dale), Karen Young (Kaye), Lois Smith (Anita)
    A dark comedy in two acts set in a run-down pet cemetery

Darrell Larson, Karen Young, Lois Smith in "Dog Logic" (*Gerry Goodstein*)

(Threshold Theatre) Sunday, Oct.25-Nov.8, 1992 (16 performances) Threshold Theatre Company presents:
NO CONDUCTOR and **IN SHADOW** by Geza Paskandi; Director, Pamela Billig; Costumes, Anita Ellis; Lighting, Stephen P. Edelstein; Press, Jeffrey Richards CAST: Robert Katims, Colin Garrey, Cornelia Mills, Eleanor Ruth, Evan Thompson
    American premieres of plays by Hunarian political figure.

(Theatre Row Theatre) Sunday, Oct.25, 1992- M & J Entertainment presents:
THEM...WITHIN US by Todd David Ross; Director, Allan Carlsen; Set, Ray Recht; Lighting, F. Mitchell Dana; Costumes, Chelsea Harriman; Sound, Bob Lazaroff, Mr. Ross; Stage Manager, Lisa Ledwich; Press, Peter Cromarty/Julie Taylor CAST: Bonnie Black (Susan), Marcus Olson (Roger), Steven Sennett (Tommy), Marceline Hugot (Sarah)
    A science-fiction comedy of manners. The action takes place in a Vermont cabin. Known as *Dimensia* in earlier stagings.

(224 Waverly Place) Wednesday, Oct.28-Nov.22, 1992 (27 performances) Interborough Rep. Theatre presents:
THE BOY WHO SAW TRUE; Written and Performed by Glen Williamson; Director, Penelope Smith; Lighting, Karlee Dawn; Press, David Rothenberg
    Adapted from the 19th century diary of a Victorian schoolboy.

(St. Clement's Playhouse) Wednesday, Oct.28-Nov.29, 1992 (29 performances) Pan Asian Repertory presents:
CAMBODIA AGONISTES; Text/Lyrics by Ernest Abuba; Music, Louis Stewart; Director, Tisa Chang; Sound, Jim van Bergen; Lighting, Deborah Constantine; Set, Robert Klingelhoefer; Costumes, Juliet Ouyoung; Choreography, Sam-Oeun Tes, H.T. Chen; Orchestrations, Jack Jarrett, Kevin Kashka, Mr. Stewart; Stage Manager, Robert Mark Kalfin CAST: June Angela, Ron Nakahara, John Baray, Richard Ebihara, Lou Ann Lucas, Virginia Wing, Sam-Oeun Tes, Hai Wah Yung
    A music-theatre epic.

(Town Hall) Wednesday, Oct.28-Dec.27, 1992 (54 performances) Mazel Musicals, Lawrence Toppall, Alan & Kathi Glist present:
THE SHEIK OF AVENUE B; Written and Conceived by Isaiah Sheffer; Director/Musical Staging, Dan Siretta; Musical Direction/Arrangements, Larry Meyers; Sets, Bruce Goodrich; Lighting, Robert Bessoir; Costumes, Deirdre Burke; Stage Manager, Don Christy; Press, Max Eisen/Madelon Rosen CAST:Paul Harman (Don Gonfalon), Judy Premus (Becky Barrett), Jack Plotnick (Kevin Bailey), Amanda Green (Gretta Genug/Diana Darling), Michele Ragusa (Sally Small), Mark Nadler (Pinky Pickles), Virginia Sandifur (Fanny Farina), Larry Raiken (Willie Wills)
MUSICAL NUMBERS: Doin' the Neighborhood Rag, Ish-ga Bibble, Matinee Girl, Cookin' Breakfast for the One I Love, Nathan Nathan What are You Waitin' for?, Serenade Me Sadie with a Ragtime Tune, Rosie Rosenblatt Stop the Turkey Trot, Yiddisha Jazz, My Yiddisha Colleen, Beckie Stay in Your Own Backyard, Jake the Ball Player, Nize Baby, Sam You Made the Pants Too Long, Yiddisha Charleston, Rosenthal ain't Rosenthal No More, Yiddisha Nightingale, Abie and Me and the Baby, Cohen Owes Me 97 Dollars. If You Want the Rainbow You Must Have the Rain, Yiddisha Luck and Irisha Love, A Rabbi's Daughter, Whose Izzy Is He, When a Women Loves a Man, Since Henry Ford Apologized to Me, The Sheik of Avenue B
    A ragtime and jazz era musical comedy revue with songs of the period.

Susanna Page, Ennis Smith in "Romeo + Juliet" (*Roberto Langella*)

Bonnie Black, Marcus Olson, Steven Sennett, Marceline Hugot in "Them..Within Us"

Michele Ragusa, Paul Harman, Jack Plotnick in "Sheik of Avenue B" (*Carol Rosegg/Martha Swope*)

(St. Peter's Theatre) Thursday, Oct.29-Nov.15, 1992 (15 performances) St. Bart's Players present:
FIORELLO! with Music by Jerry Bock; Lyrics, Sheldon Harnick; Book, Jerome Weidman and George Abbott; Director, Christopher Catt; Musical Director, Raphael; Choreography, Michelle Jacobi; Sets, Michael Daughtry; Costumes, Estella Marie; Lighting, Karen Spahn; Press, Peter Cromarty/Julie Taylor CAST: Keith Garsson, Kenneth Ashford, Melissa Broder, Randall E. Lake, Jane Larkworthy, James T. Mullins, Stacey Nye, Paul Seymour, Merrill Vaughan
    A new production of the 1959 musical.

(Sanford Meisner Theatre) Thursday, Oct.29-Nov.14, 1992 (13 performances) Daedalus & Son presents:
SPINDRIFT by Lannie Hill; Director, Michele Pearce; Set/Lighting, Tom Simitzes; Music, Salvator Pisano; Press, Francine L. Trevens CAST: Paul Barry, Mel Williams
    A drama about two men who discover a common past.

(Cornelia St. Cafe/Studio K) Thursday, Oct.29, 1992 (12 performances) Quaigh Theatre presents:
A MAP AND A CAP; Written and Performed by Stuart Warmflash
    Comic monologue performed without intermission.

(Synchronicity Space) Friday, Oct.30-Nov.15, 1992 (13 performances) Art & Work Ensemble presents:
ROMEO + JULIET by William Shakespeare; Director, Lisa Juliano; Set, Gene Gardella; Scenic Artist, David Cunningham; Lighting, J. Michael Gottlieb; Costumes, Jimmy Hurley; Fights, Ian Marshall CAST: Reggei Monique Holland (Lady Montague), Steven Rahav (Sampson/Watchman), Peter Soares (Gregory/Servant/Watchman), Reuben M. Rasheed (Balthasar), T.S. Grant (Abram), Christopher Grossett (Benvolio), Brian Sullivan (Tybalt), Laura Gillis (Citizen), James R. Bianchi (Capulet), Ann Guilford-Grey (Lady Capulet), Larney Rutledge (Montague), Mary F. Unser (Escalus), Ennis Smith (Romeo), Lawrence Kopp (Paris), Nancy Castle (Nurse), Susanna Page (Juliet), David Frank (Mercutio/Apothecary/Citizen), Curtis Anderson (Friar Laurence)
    Adaptation set in summer of 1992.

(Lone Star Theatre) Saturday, Oct.31, 1992-
MADISON AVENUE with Music/Lyrics by Gary Cherpakov and Robert Moehl; Book/Lyrics, Paul Streitz; Director/Choreography, David C. Wright; Musical Director, Joel Maisano; Sets/Lighting, Chris O'Leary; Costumes, Brenda Burton; Sound, Frank Papitio; Music/Vocal Arrangements, Robert Marks; Stage Manager, Lisa Anne Kofod; Press, Bobby Reed, Jeffrey Richards/David LeShay CAST: Randi Cooper, Michelle McDermott, Sarah Laine Terrell (Women on the Move), Jordan Church (Alice O'Connor), Bill Goodman (J. Quinby IV), Donald Fish (Bruce Singer), Nicole Sislian (Honeydew Plushbottom), Tony Rossi (Media Rep)
MUSICAL NUMBERS: Women on the Move, A Woman at Home, Something for Me, All a Matter of Strategy, Thirty Seconds, Client Service, L.A. Freeway, Office Romance, Typical American Consumer, Residuals, Leonardo's Lemonada/Lennie's Lemonade, Leonard's Lemonade, It's Not a Commercial It's Art, Squeeze Squeeze Squeeze, The Look, Upper East Side Blues, Madison Avenue
   A musical in two acts that takes a madcap look at the advertising biz.

(Fez/Time Cafe) Monday, Nov.2, 1992 (1 performance only) Cultral Elite Against Nine Committee presents:
NO TO NINE; with John Cameron Mitchell, Daisy Eagan, Julie Halston, Frank Maya, Five Lesbian Brothers, Maggie Moore, BETTY
   Benefit to fight Oregon's anti-gay measure.

(Theatre 1010) Tuesday, Nov.3-22, 1992 (16 performances) Prufrock Productions presents:
TOM & VIV by Michael Hastings; Director, Catherine Gaffigan; Costumes, Martha Bromelmeier; Lighting, David Castaneda; Set, Sarah Edkins; Effects/Stage Manager, Paul Norton; Press, Jim Baldassare CAST: Karen Eterovich (Vivienne Haigh-Wood), David Perrine (Viv's Dance Partner/ Charles Marion Todd), David A. Green (Tom "T.S." Eliot), David James O'Brien (Maurice Haigh-Wood), Therese McLaughlin (Louise Purdon), Sheila Mart (Rose Haigh-Wood), David Dawson (Charles Haigh-Wood), Louisa Geswaldo, Peter Walton (Guests), Joseph Scott (William Leonard James), Thomas P. Keough (Barrister)
   A drama in two acts. The action takes place in England, 1915-47 and involves the first marriage of T.S. Eliot.

(47th St. Theatre) Wednesday, Nov.4-22, 1992 Opening Doors Productions present:
ANYONE CAN WHISTLE with Music/Lyrics by Stephen Sondheim; Book, Arthur Laurents; Director, Tom Klebba; Choreography, Barry McNabb; Musical Director, Darren R. Cohen; Sets/Lighting, Ray-On; Costumes, Wade Laboissonniere; Stage Managers, Mike Bucco, Gail Eve Malatesta; Press, David Roggensack CAST: Tim Connell (Narrator), Rusty Mowery (Sandwich Man), Merete Muenter (Drunk Nurse), Jim Fitzpatrick (Treasurer Cooley), Mark Enis (Chief Magruder), Joseph Gram (Controller Schub), Magery Beddow (Cora Hoover Hooper), Paul Brown, Doug Carabe, Paul Cole, Tim Foster (The Boys), Jennifer Cody (Baby Joan), Elizabeth Green (Mrs. Schroeder), Wendy Oliver (Fay Apple), Chris Innvar (J. Bowden Hapgood), Eileen Connolly (Dr. Detmold), David Eye (George), Meera Popkin (June), Paul Cole (John), Tim Foster (Telegraph Boy), Elizabeth Green (Soprano), Melissa Jane Martin (Velma), Eileen Kaden (Osgood)
MUSICAL NUMBERS: I'm Like the Bluebird, Me and My Town, Miracle Song, There Won't Be Trumpets, Simple, A-1 March, Come Play wiz Me, Anyone Can Whistle, A Parade in Town, Everybody Says Don't Ballet, I've Got You to Lean On, See What It Gets You, Waltzes, With So Little to Be Sure Of
   A new production of the 1964 musical in three acts.

(Ballroom) Wednesday, Nov.4-15, 1992 (15 performances) The Loman Company in association with Susan Dietz & Joan Stein present:
LOVE AND SHRIMP; Words, Judith Viorst; Music, Shelly Markham; Director/Producer, Marilyn Shapiro; Choreography, Gene Castle; Musical Director, Ms. Markham; Lighting/Sound, Steve Visscher; Stage Manager, Pamela Singer; Press, David Rothenberg CAST: Eileen Barnett, Bonnie Franklin, Mariette Hartley
   A musical involving the lives of three women.

(Variety Arts Theatre) Wednesday, Nov.4-Dec.6, 1992 (17 performances and 22 previews) Dick Feldman and Ralph Roseman in assoc. with Frederick M. and Patricia Supper present:
PROGRAM FOR MURDER by George W. George and Jeff Travers; Director, Allen Schoer (succeeding Larry Arrick); Sets, Edward Gianfrancesco; Costumes, Deborah Shaw; Lighting, Natasha Katz; Special Effects, Gregory Meeh; Sound, Guy Sherman/Aural Fixation; Stage Manager, Brian Meister; Press, Jeffrey Richards/David LeShay CAST: Anthony Cummings (Jeremy), Colleen Quinn (Brenda), Mary Kay Adams (Elizabeth), Stephen Van Benschoten (Frank), Jon Krupp (Alan), Jill Susan Margolis (Denny)
   A mystery in two acts. The setting is a Victorian house in Cambridge, MA.

"Madison Avenue" (*Carol Rosegg*)

(clockwise from left) David Dawson, David James O'Brien, Karen Eterovich, Sheila Mart in "Tom and Viv" (*Carol Rosegg/Martha Swope*)

Chris Innvar, Wendy Oliver in "Anyone Can Whistle"
(*Blanche Mackey/Martha Swope*)

(Harold Clurman Theatre) Wednesday, Nov.4-8, 1992 (5 performances) Downtown Express Productions presents:
SMOKE RINGS by Blanche Blakeny, Drew Pacholyk, William Perry Morgan CAST: Jane Brockman, Candy Joseph, Ray Luetters, Dewey Moss
   A musical revue about two couples' romantic delights and dilemmas.

(Samuel Beckett Theatre) Friday, Nov.6-22, 1992 (16 performances) Africa Arts Theatre Co. presents:
THE BLACK HERMIT by Ngugi Wa Thiong'o; Director/Choreographer, Shela Xoregos; Sets, Andre C. Durette; Lighting, David J. Lander; Costumes, Elly Van Horne; Sound, Kenn Dovel; Stage Manager, Debra D. Holt; Press, Jonathan Slaff CAST: Jonathan Dewberry (Remi), Jessie Saunders (Nyobi), Alicia Monique Allen (Thoni), William Francis-Smith (Omage), Jacqueline Pennington (Jane), Ahmat Jallo (Pastor), Jimmy Antoine (Leader), Hudson Pillow (Elder/Dancer), Lawrence D. Rushing (Elder), Wasi Mekuria (Thoni's Friend/Dancer), Gordon H. Brooks (Elder/Flutist), Adam Otokiti (Elder/Drummer)
   A 1962 African Greek tragedy.

(INTAR Theatre) Wednesday, Nov.11-Dec.13, 1992 (30 performances) INTAR presents:
WORDS DIVINE; Translation/Adaptation, Lorenzo Mans; Based on *Divinas Palabras* by Ramon del Valle Inclan; Director, Max Ferra; Design, Rimer Cardillo; Music, William Harper; Lighting, Mark McCullough; Sound, Fox and Perla; Press, Peter Cromarty/Steve Grenyo CAST: Philip Arroyo, Susan Batson, Luz Castafios, Josie Chavez, Monique Cintron, Christopher Coucill, Shelton Dane, Ron Faber, Peter McCabe, Ofelia Medina, Alec Murphy, Irma St. Paule
   A miracle play written in 1913.

(Harriman Playhouse) Thursday, Nov.12-15, 1992 (4 performances) The Boys' Club of New York presents:
COMPANY with Music/Lyrics by Stephen Sondheim; Book, George Furth; Director, Bruce Campbell; Musical Director, Rick Page; Lighting, Luis Rosado CAST: Marcus Kettles (Robert), Anna Bernstein (Sarah), John McDermott (Harry), Philippa Kaplan (Susan), Jay Smith (Peter), Stacey Ursta (Jenny), Michael Kuhn (David), Beth Walters (Amy), Joseph Danisi (Paul), Maggie Ryan Egan (Joanne), Al Turner II (Larry), Mary Purdy (Marta), Susanne Skrobarczyk (Kathy), Justine Lambert (April)
   The 1970 musical set in New York City.

(Soho Rep Theatre) Thursday, Nov.12-29, 1992 (16 performances) Soho Rep presents:
CROSS-DRESSING IN THE DEPRESSION by Erin Cressida Wilson; Director, Marcus Stern; Set, James Schuette; Lighting, Scott Zielinski; Costumes, Allison Koturbash; Sound, John Huntington; Stage Manager, Kristen Harris CAST: Mark Margolis (old Wilder), Erin Cressida Wilson (The Women), Jan Leslie Harding (Young Wilder)
   Performed without intermission. The sexual awakening of a 12 year old boy in Denver during the depression.

(One Dream Theatre) Thursday, Nov.12-15, 1992 (5 performances) Sheethouse Music Productions present:
CHOICES with Music by Michael Filak; Lyrics/Book, Howard Danzinger; Director, Andrew Barrett; Musical Director, Neil Ginsberg; Press, Penny Landau CAST: Jean Marie Barnwell, Jane Ann Bartell, Andrea Bianchi, Natalie Hershlag, Anthony Inneo, Kris Koop, Spencer Leunberger, Michael L. Marra, Lora Jeanne Martens, Gerald McCullouch, Alisa Reyes, Randy Slovacek, Jamison Stern
   A musical about a young man's journey to the mythical land of Edentine.

(Irish Arts Center) Monday, Nov.16, 1992-
THE LAMENT OF ARTHUR CLEARY by Dermot Bolger; Director, Nye Heron CAST: David Herlihy (Arthur Cleary), Jenny Conroy, Chris O'Neill
   Loosely based on a Gaelic epic poem of the 1700s.

(Joyce Theatre) Tuesday, Nov.17-29, 1992 (14 performances)
AMERICAN BALLROOM THEATRE; Artistic Directors, Pierre Dulaine and Yvonne Marceau; Design/Costumes, Martin Pakledinaz; Lighting, Michael Chybowski; Press, Peter Cromarty/Steve Grenyo COMPANY: Danny Carter and Lori Brizzi, Alex Chassov and Natasha Uzhvak, Victor Kanevsky and Dee Quinones, Stanley McCalla and Jennifer Ford, Gary Pierce and Gaye Bowidas, Jeff and Donna Shelly
PROGRAM: The Silver Screen, Ballroom, Latin For You, Swing

(Minetta Lane Theatre) Wednesday, Nov.18-Dec.6, 1994 (24 performances) Polygram Diversified Theatrical Entertainment and Controlled Entopy Entertainment present:
CBS LIVE; New Material by Bob Bejan, Ben Garant, Michael Schwartz, S. Sydney Weiss; Director, Mr. Bejan; Sets/Mixed Media, Cubic B's; Costumes/Hair/Makeup, Thomas Augustine; Lighting, Peggy Eisenhauer; Video, Ira H. Gallen; Stage Manager, Allison Sommers; Press, Peter Cromarty/David Bar Katz, Diane L. Blackman CAST: Bob Ari (Ralph Kramden), Jonathan Bustle (Ed Norton/Ross), Kim Cea (Female Cover), Suzanne Dawson (Lucy/Mrs. Stevens), Patricia Masters (Trixie), Marcus Neville (Carlos Sanchez/Ricky/Cop), Hardy Rawls (Mr. Manicotti /Fred /Stage Manager/ Musician/Butcher), Sue Rihr (Mrs. Manicotti/Ethel), Dana Vance (Alice)
   Episodes of tv shows *I Love Lucy* and *The Honeymooners* are followed by a mix-up of characters from the shows.

Alicia Monique Allen, Jessie Saunders in "The Black Hermit" (*Jonathan Slaff*)

Ofelia Medina, Ron Faber, Monique Cintron in "Words Divine" (*Carol Rosegg*)

Sue Rihr, Suzanne Dawson, Marcus Neville in "CBS Live" (*Carol Rosegg/Martha Swope*)

Towns, Michele Shay, Minelva Nanton, Vincent Campbell in "Christchild"
(*Bert Andrews*)

Robert Tate, Tony Fair in "Lightin' Out" (*Carol Rosegg/Martha Swope*)

(Henry St. Settlement) Friday, Nov.20-Dec.20, 1992 (26 performances) New Federal Theatre presents:
CHRISTCHILD by J.E. Franklin; Director, Irving Vincent; Sets, Felix Cochren; Costumes, Judy Dearing; Lighting, Jeff Guzlik; Sound, Bill Toles; Stage Manager, Fred Seagraves; Press, Max Eisen/Madelon Rosen CAST: Patti Brown (Gertie), Vincent La Mar Campbell (Benny Jr), Lee Roy Giles (Benjamin), Minerva Nanton (Addie), Michele Shay (Katherine), Terri Towns (Joyce), Charles Malik Whitfield (Tom)
   An allegorical play set in Houston during the Roosevelt years.

(Judith Anderson Theatre) Friday, Nov.20-Dec.20, 1992 (18 performances and 13 previews) The Dauphin Co. presents:
LIGHTIN' OUT with Music by Walt Stepp and John Tucker; Lyrics/Book, Mr. Stepp; Director, Kevin Cochran; Musical Director/Arrangements, Robert Meffe; Set, Campbell Baird; Costumes, Thom J. Peterson; Lighting, Paul Bartlett; Sound, Jim van Bergen; Stage Manager, Marjorie Goodsell Clark; Press, Jim Baldassare CAST: Gordon Stanley (Mark Twain), Robert Tate (Huckleberry Finn), Tony Fair (Jim), Karen Looze (Jane Clemens / Judith Loftus/Livy Clemens), Beth Blatt (Miss Lyons/Clara Clemens /Emmeline Grangerford), Robert Roznowski (Duke/Tom Sawyer)
MUSICAL NUMBERS: Overture, Nothing Left But You, I Got De Raff, Mother I Am Not a Christian, So Says I, Ain't No Trouble, Fog Song, Dat Truck Da Is Trash, Blue Jeans and Misery, One Sweet Chile, Don't Take Off Your Mask in Bricksville, Follow the Drinkin' Gourd, I'll Be Gone to Freedom, Entrace, Home Is a State of Mind, Stephen Dowling Botts, Every Day's An Invention Youth, Belle of New York, Rip Around, Call This a Guverment?, It Was Kind of Lazy and Jolly, Awful Word and Awful Thoughts, Negro Prison Songs, Murderer's Home, Satan's Song, Poor Pitful Rascals, Finale
   A musical in two acts about Mark Twain and his characters.

(Holy Trinity) Thursday, Nov.19-Dec.13, 1992 (19 performances) Triangle Theatre Co. presents:
MARRY ME A LITTLE with Music/Lyrics by Stephen Sondheim; Conception/Development, Craig Lucas, Norman Rene; Director, Alex Dmitriev; Musical Director, Steven D. Bowen; Set, Bob Phillips; Costumes, Amanda J. Klein; Lighting, Peter Portnoy; Stage Manager, Cathy Diane Tomlin; Press, Susan Chicoine
   The 1980 musical utilizing previously unused Sondheim songs is set in Brooklyn. Performed without intermission.

(Rainbow & Stars) Tuesday, Nov.24, 1992-Jan.3, 1993 Steve Paul and Greg Dawson present:
MAKE SOMEONE HAPPY! THE JULE STYNE REVUE; Director, Fred Greene; Musical Director/Arrangements, William Roy; Lighting, Tim Flannery; Sound, Alexander Carney; Costumes, Gail Cooper-Hecht; Logistics, Alexander Carney; Creative Consultant, Jule Styne; Press, David Lotz CAST: Ann Hampton Callaway, Gregg Edelman, David Garrison, Jay Leonhart, Kay McClelland, William Roy
MUSICAL NUMBERS: As Long as There's Music, Let Me Entertain You, All I Need Is the Girl, If Momma Was Married, Small World, You'll Never Get Away from Me, Together, Just in Time, Music That Makes Me Dance, Absent Minded Me, You Mustn't Feel Discouraged, Long Before I Knew You, Catch Our Act at the Met, I Fall in Love Too Easily, Guess I'll Hang My Tears Out to Dry, Conchita Marquita Rosita Lolita Pepita Juanita Lopez, Who Are You Now?, Sunday, It's Magic, I'm Atingle I'm Aglow, Time After Time, Ev'ry Streets a Boulevard, Bye Bye Baby, People, Never Never Land, Capt. Hook's Waltz, Don't Rain on My Parade, It's Been a Long Long Time, I've Heard That Song Before, There Goes That Song Again, I'll Walk alone, I Don't Want to Walk Without You, Saturday Night Is the Loneliest Night, Make Someone Happy, Everything's Coming Up Roses

(Circle in the Square Downtown) Thursday, Nov.24, 1992-June27, 1993 (235 performances and 9 previews) Diane F. Krausz, Jennifer R. Manocherian and David A. Blumberg present:
HELLO MUDDAH, HELLO FADDUH!; Conceived and Written by Douglas Bernstein and Bob Krausz; Director/Choreographer, Michael Leeds; Musical Director/Vocal Arrangements, David Evans; Orchestrations, David Lawrence; Sets, Michael E. Downs; Lighting, Howard Werner; Costumes, Susan Branch; Sound, Tom Morse; Stage Manager, R. Wade Jackson; Press, Peter Cromarty/David Bar Katz CAST: Stephen Berger, Tovah Feldshuh, Jason Graae, Paul Kreppel, Mary Testa
MUSICAL NUMBERS: Opening Goulash, Sarah Jackman, Disraeli, Sir Greenbaum's Madrigal, Good Advice, I Can't Dance, Kiss of Myer, Hello Muddah Hello Fadduh, No One's Perfect, One Hippopotami, Phil's Medley, Harvey and Sheila, Shake Hands with Your Uncle Max, Here's to the Crabgrass, Harvey Bloom, Mexican Hat Dance, Grow Mrs. Goldfarb, Jump Down Spin Around, Crazy Downtown, Did I Ever Really Live?, Like Yours, Down the Drain, Ballad of Harry Lewis
   Vignettes inspired by musical comedy parodies of the late Alan Sherman. Also including 3 songs from Sherman's one Broadway musical *The Fig Leaves Are Falling* .

Julia Kiley, Robert Vincent Smith in "Marry Me a Little" (*Carol Rosegg*)

Jason Graae, Tovah Feldshuh, Stephen Berger, Mary Testa, Paul Kreppel in "Hello Muddah, Hello Fadduh" (*Carol Rosegg*)

David Garrison, Ann Hampton Callaway in "Make Someone Happy" (*Carol Rosegg/Martha Swope*)

Keith A. Brush, Joe Sharkey in "Lake Street Extension" (*Susan Johann*)

(Kampo Cultural Center) Thursday, Nov.27-Dec.20, 1992 (16 performances) Signature Theatre Co. presents:
LAKE STREET EXTENSION by Lee Blessing; Director, Jeanne Blake; Set, E. David Cosier; Costumes, Teresa Snider-Stein; Lighting, Jeffrey S. Koger; Stage Manager, Dean Gray; Press, James Morrison, Thomas Proehl CAST: Keith A. Brush (Trace), Joe Sharkey (Fuller), Rick Telles (Gregorio)
A drama performed without intermission. The action takes place in a basement room of a northern city, 1982 and 1992.

(American Theatre of Actors) Wednesday, Dec.2-12. 1992 (9 performances) Knucklehead Productions presents:
THE CELLAR by Deborah Stamos; Director, Peter J. Tomasi CAST: Nick Stavrides, Kevin Otto, Daniel Nalbach, Kyle Holt, Jan Ross, H.J. Tomasi

(Theatre for the New City) Thursday, Dec.3-20, 1992 (12 performances) Theatre for the New City presents:
MY ANCESTORS' HOUSE by Bina Sharif; Director, Francisco G. Rivela; Set, J. Antonio Rouco; Lighting, Adam Silverman; Press, Peter Cromarty CAST: Madhur Jaffrey, Sunita Mukhi, Glenn Athaide, Karim Panjwani
A New Yorker travels back to Pakistan and is trapped between the two worlds.

(Theatre for the New City) Thursday, Dec.3-20, 1992
TIMES SQUARE ANGEL by Charles Busch CAST INCLUDES: Charles Busch, Jim Borstelmann, Andy Halliday, Arnie Kolodner
Holiday revival of comedy.

(Soho Rep Theatre) Thursday, Dec.3-13, 1992 (10 performances) New York Ensemble Workshop and Under One Roof present:
STEALING FIRE by Diana Son; Director, Deborah Oster Pannell; Music, Joy Askew; Set, Christine Jones; Lighting, Ellen Waggett; Costumes, Cynthia DuMont; Press, Kate Whoriskey CAST: Holley Stewart (Procne), Claire Dorsey (Philomela), Barney Fitzpatrick (Tereus), Crystal Bock, Susan Gerardi, Kim Ima, T.W. King, Carol Lonnie, John McKie, Frank Nastasi, Rob Rowe, Richard Saint-Joy, Michelle Zangara
A modern, ironic reworking of myth.

(Westbeth Theatre Center) Friday, Dec.4-20, 1992 (14 performances) Playwrights' Preview Productions presents:
A CHRISTMAS CAROL with Music by Douglas Yetter; Lyrics/Book, Michael Hulet; Director, Margaret Mancinelli-Cahill; Musical Director, Jean Norton; Sets, Peter R. Feuche; Costumes, Kevin Brainard; Lighting, Sandy Ross; Press, Susan Goodell CAST: Ruth Adams (Christmas Past/Sally), Constance Boardman (M. Cratchit/M.Diber), Pamela Brown (Belinda/Charity Girl), Matt Goldstein (Peter/YoungScrooge/Boy/Beggar) , Wayne Gordy (Bob Cratchit), Will Hao (Old Joe/Fessiwig), Christine Little (Mary/Fan), Chuck Muckle (Marley/Topper), Nick Plakias (Scrooge), T.L. Reilly (Fred/Young Scrooge), Stephanie Sweeney (Christmas Present / Beggar/Mrs. Fessiwig), Claudio St. John (Tiny Tim), Sandy Yen (Belle / Martha)
MUSICAL NUMBERS: Spirit of Christmas, Ours for the Keeping, Link by Link, Christmas at Home, Hand in Hand & Arm in Arm, Take My Heart, Nightmare, Touch My Robe, Anything at All, Family Christmas Recipe, Yes or No, It All Goes Around, Finale
A new two-act musical adaptation of Dickens' novel.

(Lamb's Little Theatre) Friday, Dec.4, 1992-Jan.3, 1993 (32 performances) Lamb's Theatre Company presents:
THE GIFTS OF THE MAGI with Music/Lyrics by Randy Courts; Book/ Lyrics, Mark St. Germain; Director, Scott Harris; Musical Staging, Janet Watson; Sets, Peter Harrison; Costumes, Kathryn Wagner; Lighting, Michael Gilliam; Musical Director, Lynn Crigler; Stage Manager, Donna A. Drake; Press, Chris Boneau/Adrian Bryan-Brown, Cabrini Lepis CAST: Michael J. Farina (The City-Him), Lou Williford (The City-Her), Eddie Korbich (Willy Porter), John Hickok (Jim Dillingham), Kathleen Bloom (Della Dillingham), Herb Foster (Soapy Smith)
MUSICAL NUMBERS: Star of the Night, Gifts of the Magi, Jim and Della, Christmas to Blame, How Much to Buy My Dream, The Restaurant, Once More, Bum Luck, Greed, Pockets, The Same Girl, Gift of Christmas, Finale
A musical holiday tradition (since 1984) performed without intermission. The action takes place in New York City, December 1905.

Madhur Jaffrey, Tamir in "My Ancestors' House" (*Claudia Thompson*)

Eddie Korbich in "Gifts of the Magi" (*Carol Rosegg/Martha Swope*)

Adam Oliensis, Fiona Davis in "Wilder, Wilder, Wilder" (*Edward Berkeley*)

Mercedes Ruehl   Victor Garber
"A Christmas Memory"

Michael Kessler, Melinda Jackson in "Manhattan Moves"

(Harold Clurman Theatre) Friday, Dec.4-28, 1992 (21 performances) transferred to Second Stage on Friday, Feb.19-Apr.4, 1993(46 performances and to Broadway's Circle in the Square on Friday, April 9, 1993 Willow Cabin Theatre Company presents:
WILDER, WILDER, WILDER - THREE BY THORNTON; Director, Edward Berkeley; Sets, Miguel Lopez-Castillo; Costumes, Fiona Davis, Dede Pochos; Press, Jim Baldassare CAST: Cynthia Besteman, Sarah Braun, Sabrina Boudot, Fiona Davis, David Folwell, Ken Forman, Laurence Gleason, Joel Goldes, David Goldman, Deborah Greene, Bjarne Hecht, Patrick Huey, Jon Kellam, Peter Killy, Rebecca Killy, Tasha Lawrence, Charmaine Lord, Tim McNamara, Jerry Mettner, Stephen Mora, Angela Nevard, Adam Oliensis, Dede Pochos, Linda Powell, Maria Radman, Michael Rispoli, Jayson Veduccio, Craig Zakarian
 Three short plays by Thornton Wilder: The Long Christmas Dinner, The Happy Journey to Trenton and Camden and Pullman Car Hiawatha.

(William Redfield Theatre) Tuesday, Dec.8-19, 1992 (10 performances) Curious Theatre Company presents:
IN THIS ROOM; Director, Allen Coulter; Sets, Rick Sobel; Lighting, Joe Saint; Press, David Rothenberg
PROGRAM: THE STAIN by Frank Pugliese CAST: Elizabeth Ann Daniels, Adam Trese BLACKOUT by Tom McClelland CAST: Alexandra Styron, Gareth Williams
 Two one-acts in which life-changing experiences take place in a single room.

(Playhouse 91) Wednesday, Dec.9, 1992-Jan.3, 1993 (28 performances) Light Opera of Manhattan presents:
HOME FIRES by Linda Thorsen Bond and William Repicci; Director, Robert Stewart; Musical Director, Jeffrey Buchsbaum; Orchestrations, Bob McDowell; Costumes, Robert Mackintosh; Choreography, Barry McNabb
 A musical set during WWII and featuring period songs.

(Book-Friends Cafe) Friday, Dec.11-20, 1992 (6 performances) David Binder and Karen Fricker present:
A CHRISTMAS MEMORY by Truman Capote; Press, Chris Boneau/Adrian Bryan-Brown, Craig Karpel CASTS: Olympia Dukakis & Christopher Durang (Dec.11), Christine Baranski & Matthew Broderick (Dec.12), Linda Lavin & David Marshall Grant (Dec.13), Mercedes Ruehl & Terrence McNally (Dec. 19), Tyne Daly & Adam Arkin (Dec.20)
 A holiday benefit for Broadway Cares/Equity Fights AIDS.

(Open Eye Theatre) Saturday, Dec.12, 1992- Open Eye Theatre presents:
THE WISE MEN OF CHELM by Sandra Fenichel Asher; Direction/Design, Amie Brockway; Choreography, Adina Popkin; Musical Director, Richard Henson; Press, Shirley Herz/Sam Rudy CAST: Judy Dodd, Stacie Chaikin, George Colangelo, Larry Hirschhorn, Scott Facher, Andy Rogow
 A comedy from Jewish folklore.

(Joyce Theatre) Tuesday, Dec.15, 1992-Jan.3, 1993 (21 performances) Pick Up Performance Company presents:
THE MYSTERIES AND WHAT'S SO FUNNY? with Music by Philip Glass; Written and Directed by David Gordon; Visual Design, Red Grooms; Music Director, Alan Johnson; Lighting, Dan Kotlowitz; Sound, David Meschter; Press, Ellen Zeisler/Suzanne Ford CAST: Scott Cohen (Young Sam), Scott Cunningham (Anger I), Norma Fire (Detective/Only Oldest Child), Karen Graham (Young Rose), Jane Hoffman (Fanny), Alan Johnson (Pianist), Bill Klux (Mr. Him), Jerry Matz (Old Sam), Dean Moss (Young Artist), Lola Pashalinski (Old Rose), Alice Playten (Actor/Grandfather/Father etc..), Adina Porter (Anger II), Tisha Roth (Mrs. Him), Valda Setterfield (Marcel Duchamp)
 The mysteries of who we are, what we aspire to, and what motivates us. Performed without intermission.

(American Place Theatre) Wednesday, Dec.16, 1992-Jan.17, 1993 (40 performances) M & M American Dance Theatre, David H. Peipers, Virginia L. Dean present:
MANHATTAN MOVES; Directed and Choreographed by Michael Kessler; Lighting, Randy Becker; Costumes, Geff Rhian; Sound, Ted Rothstein; Arrangements, Jon Gordon; Press, Susan L. Schulman CAST: Melinda Jackson, Michael Kessler, Adrienne Armstrong, Kevin Gaudin, Andre George, El Tahra Ibrahim, Barry Wizoreck
 All-dancing theatrical entertainment in two acts.

(One Dream Theatre) Wednesday, Jan.6-31, 1993 (20 performances) Under One Roof Theatre Company presents:
WHITE COTTON SHEETS with Music/Lyrics/Book by Tom Judson; Director, Michael Sexton; Set, Jed Johnson, Alan Wanzenberg; Costumes, John A. Robelen; Lighting, Brian MacDevitt; Stage Manager, Beth Bornstein; Press, David Rothenberg CAST: Bobby Reed (Bobby Singleton), Dori Kiplock (Ruby Pearl), Tom Judson (Elmer), Stephen Pell (Mr. LaBarge), David Pittu (Clarence), Francine Lobis (Edwina), Chris Odo (Delancey), Keith Davis (Billy Racine), Ellen Mittenthal (Doris Racine)
 A musical set in Southern hotel on a hot August night, 1931.

Mark Shannon, Lee Brock in "Tales from Hollywood" (*Joan Marcus*)

Mark Rylance in "Henry V" (*Gerry Goodstein*)

Joel Aroeste, Harlin C. Kearsley, Erika Johnson Newell in "Slow Dance on the Killing Ground" (*Tim Raab/Northern*)

(La MaMa) Thursday, Jan.7-24, 1993 (12 performances) La Mama and the Barrow Group present:
TALES FROM HOLLYWOOD by Christopher Hampton; Director, Seth Barrish; Set, Markas Henry; Costumes, Nina Canter; Lighting, Eileen H. Doughtery; Sound, One Dream; Stage Manager, Eric Eligator CAST: Lee Brock (Nelly Man), Marcia DeBonis (Toni Spuhler), Keely Eastley (Helen Schwartz), Tom Riis Farrell (Charles Money), Aaron Goodwin (Art Nicely), Shannon Lee Jones (Helene Weigal/Greta Garbo), Phil Kaufman (Hal/ Tarzan), Judith Kinsey (Heinrich Mann), Denis O'Hare (Lomakhin), Michael Warren Powell (Thomas Mann), Wendee Pratt (Angel), Paul Rice (Young Man), Jeff Robins (Harpo Marx), Natalie Ross (Marta Feuchwanger), Mark Shannon (Horvath), Stephen Singer (Bertolt Brecht), John Ventimiglia (Chico Marx)
A drama in two acts. The action involves German intellectuals who flee to Hollywood to escape Nazism, 1938-50.

(St. Mark's Theatre) Thursday, Jan.7, 1993-
SAMUEL'S MAJOR PROBLEMS; Written/Directed/Designed by Richard Foreman; Sound, John Collins; Stage Manager, Christine Lemme CAST: Thomas Jay Ryan (Samuel), Jill Dreskin (Maria Helena), Steven Rattazzi (Dr. Martino)
A fable of identity.

(Kraine Theatre) Thursday, Jan.7, 1993- Antrobus Group presents:
WILD DESIRES: THE STORY OF MADAME BOVARY by Gustave Flaubert; Adaptation, Sandra Laub; Director, Dan Oliverio; Design, Deborah L. Jensen, Buddy Saunders; Press, Judy Jacksina/Robin Constantine CAST: Sandra Laub (Emma Bovary), Suzanna Byrne, Buddy Saunders, Caren Browning, L.J. Ganser, Marty Pistone
A sensual adaptation of Flaubert's novel.

(Intar Theatre) Friday, Jan.8-30, 1993 (26 performances) Zena Theatre Group presents:
STRANGERS ON EARTH by Mark O'Donnell; Director, Matthew Ames; Sets, Sean McCarthy; Lighting, Amy Appleyard; Sound, Matthew Ames; Costumes, Kathleen Hardgrove; Press, Chris Boneau/Adrian Bryan-Brown , Bob Fennell, Jamie Morris CAST: Elizabeth Daly (Priscillsa Fairburn), Jeremy Gold (Hank Knox), Johanna Pfaelzer (Margaret Gaminski), Shaun Powell (Pony Crocker), Jesse Wolfe (Mutt Vespucci)
A two-act romantic comedy set in New York City.

(St. Clement's) Tuesday, Jan.12-Feb.20, 1993 (23 performances and 4 previews) Theatre for a New Audience presents:
HENRY V by William Shakespeare; Director, Barry Kyle; Sets, Marina Draghici, Jay Durrwachter; Costumes, Ms. Draghici, Hwa Kyoung C. Park; Music, Deniz Ulben; Lighting, Steve Woods; Fights, J. Allen Suddeth; Stage Manager, Carol Dawes; Press, Shirley Herz/ Miller Wright CAST: Mark Rylance (Henry), Scott Howard Allen (Bardolph/Erpingham), Graham Brown (Charles), John Henry Cox (Duke of Exeter), Curzon Doball (Montjoy), David Dossey (Nym/Jamy/Bates), Miriam Healy-Louie (Katherine/Boy/Chorus), Francis E. Hodgins (Westmoreland/MacMorris/ Court), John McConnell (Pistol), Joyce Lynn O'Connor), Mark Niebuhr (Gower/Scroop/Burgandy), Alec Phoenix (Bedford/Orleans), John Prince (Ely/Cambridge/Constable/Harfleur), Mary Lou Rosato (Quickley/York/Chorus), Michael Rudko (Canterbury/Grey/Fluellen), Trellis Stepter, Jr. (Gloucester/Williams), Timothy D. Stickney (Dauphin)
Performed with one intermission.

(NYU University Theatre) Tuesday, Jan.12-19, 1993 (9 performances) New York State Theatre Institute presents:
SLOW DANCE ON THE KILLING GROUND by William Hanley; Director, Ed. Lange; Set, Victor A. Becker; Costumes, Brent Griffin; Lighting, Victor En Yu Tan; Sound, Dan Toma; Stage Manager, Michael A. Bartuccio; Press, Susan L. Schulman CAST: Joel Aroeste (Glas), Harlin C. Kearsley (Randall), Erika Johnson Newell (Rosie)
The 1964 drama in two acts. The action takes place in Brooklyn.

(224 Waverly Place Theatre) Thursday, Jan.14-Mar.7, 1993 (39 performances) Poor Folk Theatre Company presents:
ST. VITUS DANCE; Written and Directed by John Regis; Lighting, David Brody; Costumes, Elizabeth Reiss; Press, David Rothenberg CAST: Chris Cappiello, Eleonora Kihlberg-Graham, Neale Harper, Art Suskin, Suzanne Rose
Adaptation of Dostoevsky's *The Idiot* .

(Open Eye Theatre) Saturday, Jan.16, 1993- Open Eye Theatre presents:
FREEDOM IS MY MIDDLE NAME by Lee Hunkins; Director, Ernest Johns; Music, Kyle Williams; Press, Shirley Herz/Sam Rudy CAST: Mary Cushman, John Di Leo, Byron Easley, Keith Johnston, Sheryl Greene Leverett, Stephanie Marshall
A play with a rap score about a group of students going back in time to meet African-Americans who changed history.

(St. Peter's Theatre) Thursday, Jan.21-Feb.7, 1993 (15 performances) St. Bart's Players presents:
THE MUSICAL COMEDY MURDERS OF 1940 by John Bishop; Director, Christopher Catt; Set, Vicki Neal, Richard Kendrick; Costumes, Estella Marie; Lighting, Karen Spahn; Press, Peter Cromarty/Julie Taylor CAST: Ken Altman, Barbara Blomberg, Tracey Cassidy, Paul Seymour, Steve Ross, Steven Sabowitz, Maren Swenson, Richard Van Slyke, Catherine Winters, Nancy Young
The case of the stage door slasher.

(Puerto Rican Traveling Theatre) Wednesday, Jan.13-Feb.21, 1993 (30 performances)
Puerto Rican Traveling Theatre presents:
THE BOILER ROOM by Reuben Gonzalez; Spanish Translation, Manuel Martin; Director, Alex Colon; Set, Edward Gianfrancesco; Lighting, Rachel Budin; Sound, Sergio Garcia Marruz; Stage Manager, James Marr; Press, Max Eisen/Madelon Rosen CAST: Miriam Colon (Olga), Joe Quintero (Anthony), Rosalinde Milan (Olivia), Ed Trucco (Doug)
A drama in two acts. The action takes place in a New York City boiler room, 1968.

(Theatre Row Theatre) Friday, Jan.22, 1993 (1 performance) The Cheshire Company presents:
ADORING THE MADONNA by Allan Havis; Director, Christopher Hanna; Set, Judy Gailen; Lighting, Mary Louise Geiger; Costumes, Virginia M. Johnson; Stage Manager, Kristen Harris; Press, Jim Baldassare CAST: Patricia Mauceri (Lydia), John Gould Rubin (Rudy), Jon Manfrellotti (Sal), Ed Setrakian (Fiducci), Erin Cressida Wilson (Minnie)
A "callous comedy with heart" about the movie business.

(Fairbanks Theatre Studio) Friday, Jan.22-31, 1993 (9 performances) First Theatre Company presents:
JULIUS CAESAR by William Shakespeare; Director, Marc Raphael; Sets, Mary T. Creede; Costumes, Elly Van Horne; Music, Deborah Hurwitz; Stage Manager, Cheryl McNear CAST: Bob O'Melia (Caesar), Mary Rose Synek (Brutus), Robin Cornett (Cassius), Nicholas Martin-Smith (Anthony), Kendall Caornell, Linda Green, Angela Hailey, Meredith Hlafter, Jim Heisel, Tom Kulesa, Lina Patel, Khea Williams
A feminist-inspired interpretation of the text.

(Actors Playhouse) Monday, Jan.25, 1993 (1 performance only) Postage Stamp Xtravaganzas and the Glines present:
MISS GULCH RETURNS; Written and Performed by Fred Barton; Lighting, Tracy Dedrickson; Stage Manager, Michael Henderson
MUSICAL NUMBERS: Take Me Please, You're the Woman I'd Wanna Be, I'm the Bitch, Born on a Bike, Pour Me a Man, Everyone Worth Taking, It's Not My Idea of a Gig, Don't Touch Me, I'm Your Bitch, I Poured Me a Man, Give My Best to the Blonde, Finale
Encore performance for popular club act bring to life *Wizard of Oz* character.

(Union Sq. Theatre) Tuesday, Jan.26-Mar.7, 1993 (19 performances and 23 previews) Rowan Joseph & Kevin Eberly, EMI Music Publishing, Robert B. Shaffer and Daryl Roth in assoc. with Shane T. Partlow and Neal Roberts present:
TAPESTRY: THE MUSIC OF CAROLE KING with Music by Carole King; Lyrics, Ms. King, Gerry Goffin, T. Stern, D. Palmer; Director, Jeffrey Martin; Musical Staging, Ron Navarre; Musical Supervision/Arrangements, John Kroner; Musical Director, Kathy Sommer; Orchestrations, David Lawrence; Set, David Jenkins; Costumes, Debra Stein; Lighting, Peter A. Kaczorowski; Sound, Terry Van Richardson; Stage Manager, Adele House; Press, Shirley Herz/Sam Rudy CAST: Lawrence Clayton, Mary Gutzi, Pattie Darcy Jones, Vanessa A. Jones, Frank Mastrone, Jim Morlino, (understudies) Lon Hoyt, Rozz Morehead
MUSICAL NUMBERS: Music, Where You Lead, Sweet Seasons, Been to Canaan, Up on the Roof, Growing Away from Me, I Feel the Earth Move, So Far Away/Home Again, Jazzman, Early Years, Speeding Time, No Easy Way Down, Where Does Love Go, Beautiful, Smackwater Jack, Tapestry, Will You Love Me Tomorrow, Some Kind of Wonderful, Natural Woman, Hi De Ho, Way Over Yonder, You've Got a Friend
Musical revue performed without intermission.

Rosalinda Milan, Miriam Colon, Ed Trucco in "The Boiler Room" (*Peter Krupenye*)\

Matt McGrath, Peter Maloney in "The Dadshuttle" (*Jayne Wexler*)

Craig Dudley in "Ursula's Permanent"

(Atlantic Theatre) Tuesday, Jan.26-Feb.20, 1993 (26 performances) Atlantic Theatre Company presents:
DOWN THE SHORE/THE DADSHUTTLE by Tom Donaghy; Director, William H. Macy; Sets, James Wolk; Lighting, Howard Werner; Costumes, Sarah Edwards; Music, Ari Frankel; Fights, Rick Sordelet; Stage Manager, Matt Silver; Press, Jim Baldassare

THE DADSHUTTLE with Matt McGrath (Junior), Peter Maloney (Senior)
The action takes place en route to 30th St. Station, Philadelphia
DOWN THE SHORE with Neil Pepe (MJ), Kathryn ERbe (Luke), Todd Weeks (Phippsey), Peter Maloney (Stan Man)
The action takes place outside a Philly church on a summer night.

(Kraine Theatre) Wednesday, Jan.27-Feb.27, 1993 (12 performances) Mr. and Mrs. Smith Productions in assoc. with The Theatre Barn present:
URSULA'S PERMANENT; Written and Directed by Adam Rapp and Anthony Rapp; Sets, Sherri Adler; Costumes, Guyah Clark; Lighting, Tim Walsh; Ursula's Ditty Arranged by Adam Wolfensohn; Stage Manager, Samantha Reynolds CAST: Tom Burka (Reed), Greg Pierotti (Brian/Ben/ Stewart), Tish Williamson (Dorothy), Craig Dudley (Tony G), Kimberly Wood (Nan), Scott Lucy (Matthew), Maude Mitchell (Ursula)
The action takes place in a magical cafe, one late evening.

(Circle Rep Theatre) Thursday, Jan.28, 1993- Jesse L. Devore Jr. in assoc. with Circle Repertory presents:
FAITH JOURNEY by Jo Jackson; Director/Choreographer, Bernard Marsh; Musical Director, Ladd Johnson; Sets, Billy Graham; Lighting, Marshall Williams; Costumes, Estella Marie; Press, David Rothenberg CAST: Mark Hall (Martin Luther King Jr.), Dee B. Cook, Yvette Doughty, Lance Gross, Deb Harris, Michael Lewis, Forrest McClendon, Hilda Willis

A musical look at the Civil Rights Movement usuing traditional and contemporary songs.

(Pulse Ensemble Theatre) Thursday, Jan.28-Feb.15, 1993 (15 performances) Pulse Ensemble presents:
A WORM IN THE HEART by Paul Minx; Director, William Roudebush; Lighting, Ellen J. Kramer; Costumes, Fran Cole; Stage Manager, Tim Farley; Press, Max Eisen, Madelon Rosen CAST: Karla Silverman (Darlene Fischer), Keith R. Smith (Serge Toussaint), Kelly Champion (Donna Jean Fischer), Denise Burse-Mickelbury (Isabel Banks), Thomas Roy (Karl Fischer)

A drama in two acts. The action takes place in Indianapolis, IN, 1964.

(Holy Trinity) Thursday, Jan.28-Feb.21, 1993 (16 performances and 2 previews) Triangle Theatre Company presents:
PLAYING WITH FIRE (AFTER FRANKENSTEIN) by Barbara Field; Director, Charles R. Johnson; Costumes, Amanda J. Klein; Lighting, Nancy Collings; Set, Evelyn Sakash; Stage Manager, Cathy Diane Tomlin; Press, Susan Chicoine CAST: Jeff Sugarman (Frankenstein), Aloysius Gigl (The Creature), Jennifer Petsche (Elizabeth), Paul Anthony Stewart (Victor), Garrison Phillips (Prof. Krempe), Doug Von Nessen (Adam/Creature)

A drama in two acts.The final meeting between Dr. Frankenstein and his creation is set in the barren wastes of the North Pole.

(Hudson Guild Theatre) Saturday, Jan.30-Feb.28, 1993 (23 performances) Roundabout Theatre Conservatory Ensemble Company presents:
A MIDSUMMER NIGHT'S DREAM by William Shakespeare; Director, Gene Feist; Set/Lighting, Charles Ard; Costumes, Hattie Fischer; Sound, Leon Walker CAST: David Bander (Quince), DeBanne Browne (Peaseblossom), Veronica Caldwell (Puck), Joe Hackett (Snout), Alica Harding (Mustardseed), Carol Hexner (Hippolyta), David Heymann (Lysander), Tom Hitchcock (Theseus), Matthew Karas (Bottom), Christopher King (Snug), Dana Kramer (Oberon), M. William Lettich (Egeus), Stephen C. Marshall (Philostrate), Sharon Nordlinger (Helena), Mary Elizabeth O'Connor (Titania), Awilda Rivera (Moth), Peter C. Ruvolo (Flute), Joanna Sabath (Cobweb), Dennis Southers (Starvveling), Christopher Springer (Demetrius), Allyson Surprenant (Hermia)

Performed in two acts.

(Manhattan Class Company) Wednesday, Feb3-Mar.21, 1993 Manhattan Class Co. presents:
FIVE WOMEN WEARING THE SAME DRESS by Alan Ball; Director, Melia Bensussen; Sets, Rob Odorisio; Lighting, Howard Werner; Costumes, Karen Perry; Sound, Bruce Ellman; Stage Manager, Hazel Youngs; Press, Peter Cromarty/David Bar Katz CAST: Dina Spybey (Frances), Amelia Campbell (Meredith), Ally Walker (Trisha), Betsy Aidem (Georgeanne), Allison Janney (Mindy), Thomas Gibson (Tripp)

A comedy in two acts. The action takes place in Knoxville, TN during June.

(Downtown Art Co.) Thursday, Feb.6-21, 1993 (14 performances)
BREATHING IT IN; Written and Directed by Eduardo Machado; Set/ Lighting, Paul Clay; Costumes, Kasia Walkicka-Mainmone CAST: Leslie Nipkow, Leland F. Grant, Alba Oms, Barry Sherman, Leslie Lyles, Lazaro Perez

Jeff Sugarman, Aloysius Gigl, (top) Doug Van Nessen, Paul Anthony Stewart in "Playing with Fire (After Frankenstein)" (*Carol Rosegg/Martha Swope*)

Dina Spybey, Ally Walker, Amelia Campbell, Allison Janney, Betsy Aidem in "Five Women Wearing the Same Dress" (*David Taffit*)

The action takes place in a small cult community where female energy is worshiped.

(Primary Stages) Thursday, Feb.4-Mar.7, 1993 (19 performances and 4 previews) Primary Stages presents:
BARGAINS by Jack Heifner; Director, Casey Childs; Set/Costumes, Bruce Goodrich; Lighting, Deborah Constantine; Stage Manager, Sally Plass; Press, Anne Einhorn CAST: T. Scott Cunningham (Michael Mead), Raynor Scheine (Dennis Pugh), Sally Sockwell (Sally Banks), Jacqueline Lucid (Tish Elmore), Celia Weston (Mildred Latner), Gregory Grove (Lothar Latner)

A comedy in two acts. The action is set in a Central Texas town.

(Tribeca Lab) Thursday, Feb.4-27, 1993 (12 performances) Tribeca Lab and Hexen Prod. present:
HEXEN; Written/Directed/Adapted by Danny Ashkenasi; Original German Script, Peter Lund; Press, Audrey Ross CAST: Kimberly Gambino (Margaret Hutchinson), Priscilla Quinby (Leona Gail)

A chamber musical about two witches living out the eighth of their nine lives.

Gregory Grove, Celia Weston in "Bargains" (*Andrew Leynse*)

(Theatre for the New City)Thursday, Feb.4-21, 1993 (12 performances) Theatre for the New City presents:
RISING SUN FALLING STAR by Yolanda Rodriguez; Director, Robert Landau; Set, Charles McClennahan; Lighting, Richard Shaefer; Stage Manager, Jean Mitchell; Sound, Michael Roark CAST: Rafael Alvarez (Georgie), Gloria Galo (Mimi), Joe Gonzalez (Pedro), Raul Martinez (Herman/The Man), David Medina (Carlos), Benny Nieves (Tito), Marilyn Sanabria (Sonia/Voice), Jaime Sanchez (Papi)
    A drama in two acts. The action takes place in Manhattan's lower east side.

(Promenade Theatre) Tuesday, Feb.9-June 27, 1993 James B. Freydberg, Jeffrey Ash and William P. Miller present:
WRONG TURN AT LUNGFISH by Garry Marshall and Lowell Ganz; Director, Mr. Marshall; Set, David Jenkins; Costumes, Erin Quigley; Lighting, Peter Kaczorowski; Sound, Tom Morse; Stage Manager, Wm. Hare; Press, Chris Boneau/Adrian Bryan-Brown, Cabrini Lepis CAST: George C. Scott succeeded by Stephen Pearlman (during illness), Garry Marshall, Fritz Weaver (Peter Ravenswaal), Kelli Williams succeeded by Kathleen Marshall (Nurse), Jami Gertz succeeded by Calista Flockhart (Anita Merendino), Tony Danza succeeded by Michael E. Knight (Dominic De Caesar)
    A comedy in two acts set in a New York City hospital room.

(Playhouse 91) Wednesday, Feb.10-Mar.28, 1993 (49 performances) INTAR Hispanic American Arts Center and Light Opera of Manhattan present:
NOSTALGIA TROPICAL; Conceived/Directed by Max Ferra; Musical Direction/Arrangements, Meme Solis; Choreography, Victor Cuellar; Set, Riccardo Hernandez; Costumes, Randy Barcelo; Lighting, Jennifer Tipton; Sound, Fox & Perla; Stage Manager, Sergio Cruz; Press, Peter Cromarty/ David Bar Katz CAST: Hector Miguel "Ringo" Barrera, Merly Bordes, Aimee Cabrera, Claudina Montenegro, Gilberto C. Peralta, Marden Ramos, Orlando "Puntilla" Rios, Meme Solis, Victor Sterling, Ramoncito Veloz Jr.
    An Afro-Cuban Musical revue.

(29th St. Playhouse) Wednesday, Feb.10, 1993- Annette Moskowitz and Alexander E. Racolin present:
WALLENBURG STILL LIVES by Carl Levine; Director, David LeBarron; Set, David Guthan; Costumes, Tanya Serdiuk; Lighting, Stewart Wagner; Press, Bruce Cohen/Maria Somma CAST: Gary Brennan (Wallenberg), Tiffany Yates (Anna), Paula Boyajian, John Corrigan, Rose Anne Fahey, James Gordon, Brad Gore, David Greenwood, Jason Jacobs, Greg Kanczes, Eric Perlmutter, Jeff Sass
    A drama about the last days of Raoul Wallenberg.

(La MaMa) Thursday, Feb.11-28, 1993 (16 performances) La MaMa presents:
GHOSTS: LIVE FROM GALILEE (The Scottsboro Boys Blues Opera) with Music by Genji Ito; Libretto, Edgar Nkosi White; Director, George Ferencz; Lighting, Howard Thies; Costumes, Sally Lesser; Press, Jonathan Slaff CAST: Lynnard Edwin Williams (Clarence Norris), Phyllis Nannyoung (Donna Lee), Jonathan Goldstein (Samuel Leibowitz), Judy Bady, Donna Coulter, Earl McKay, Valmont Miller, Peter McCabe, Stephen C. Croce, Charles Britt, Nancy K. Anderson, Jennifer FlemingAn opera about a civil rights trial in Georgia, 1930s.
    An opera about a civil rights trial in Georgia, 1930s.

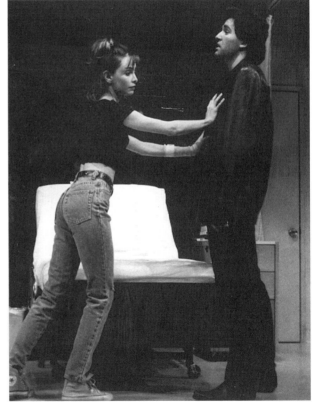

Calista Flockhart, Michael E. Knight
Top: George C. Scott, Jami Gertz, Tony Danza in "Wrong Turn at Lungfish"
(Joan Marcus)

(Kampo Cultral Center) Friday, Feb.12-Mar.7, 1993 (18 performances) Signature Theatre Company presents:

TWO ROOMS by Lee Blessing; Director, James Houghton; Set, E. David Cosier; Costumes, Teresa Snider-Stein; Lighting, Jeffrey S. Koger; Music, Hum This Music; Stage Manager, Bethany Ford; Press; James Morrison CAST: Jeffrey Hayenga (Michael), Laura Esterman (Lainie), A. Bernard Cummings (Walker), Madhur Jaffrey (Ellen)

A drama about an American couple in Beirut.

(Harold Clurman Theatre) Wednesday, Feb.17-Mar.7, 1993 (20 performances) Opening Doors presents:

ANYTHING COLE with Music/Lyrics by Cole Porter; Director, Tom Klebba; Choreography, Lynnette Barkley; Musical Director, Robert A. Berman; Sets/Lighting, Trad A Burns; Costumes, Susan Branch; Stage Manager, Mike Bucco CAST: Elizabeth Green, Stacey Todd Holt, David Lowenstein, Michael Malone, Wendy Oliver, Jane Wasser, Jim Weaver

MUSICAL NUMBERS: You're the Tops, Let's Fly Away, No Cure Like Travel/Bon Voyage, Lost Liberty Blues, Come Along with Me, Come to the Supermarket in Old Peking, Greek to You, Wunderbar, Kate the Great, Do You Want to See Paris?, Quadrille/Allez-vous en, Who Said Gay Paree?, Why Don't We Try Staying Home?, Take Me Back to Manhattan, I Happen to Like New York, Thank You So Much Mrs Losborough-Goodby, Ozarks Are Callin'Me Home/Don't Fence Me In, Please Don't Monkey with Broadway, Big Town, Shootin' the Works for Uncle Sam, Military Maids, You'd be So Nice to Come Home to, I'm in Love with a Soldier Boy, Ev'ry Time We Say Goodbye, Leader of a Big-Time Band, Wake Up and Dream, Lets Do It, All of You, It's Bad for Me, A Lady Needs a Rest, I'm a Gigolo, Love for Sale, Why Can't You Behave, Most Gentlemen Don't Like Love, Dream-Dancing, My Heart Belongs to Daddy, Let's Not Talk About Love, All I've Got to Get Now Is My Man, Down in the Depths, Make It Another Old-fashioned Please, Always True to You in My Fashion, Is It the Girl?, I Like Pretty Things, Anything Goes

A musical revue in two acts.

(Lambs Little Theatre) Thursday, Feb.18-Mar.28, 1993 (41 performances) Lamb's Theatre presents:

THE VIEW FROM HERE by Margaret Dulaney; Director, Matt Williams; Sets, Michael Anania; Lighting, Michael Gilliam; Costumes, Elsa Ward; Sound, Tristan Wilson; Press, Chris Boneau/Adrian Bryan-Brown, Cabrini Lepis CAST: Angelina Fiordellisi, Lily Knight, Adam LeFevre, Tudi Roche

A comedy about a happy agoraphobic.

(Henry St. Settlement) Thursday, Feb.18-Mar.20, 1993 (28 performances) New Federal Theatre presents:

ROBERT JOHNSON: TRICK THE DEVIL by Bill Harris; Director, Woodie King, Jr.; Music, Guy Davis; Set, Richard Harmon; Costumes, Judy Dearing; Lighting, Antoinette Tynes; Arrangements, Grenoldo Frazier; Stage Manager, Malik; Press, Max Eisen/Madelon Rosen CAST:James Curt Bergwall (Kimbrough), Denise Burse-Mickelbury (Georgia), Guy Davis (Robert Johnson), Grenoldo Frazier (Stokes), Herman Levern Jones (Lem)

A drama about a professor's search for the blues musician. The setting is Georgia's Colored Jook Joint, late 1920s.

(Primary Stages) Saturday, Feb.20-23, 1993 (4 performances)
HOW SHE PLAYED THE GAME by Cynthia L. Cooper; CAST: Susan Stevens

Six great female athletes are brought to life.

(John Houseman Studio) Tuesday, Feb.23, 1993- Eric Krebs presents:
TALKING THINGS OVER WITH CHEKHOV by John Ford Noonan; Director, Maureen Heffernan; Costumes, Mimi Maxmen; Lighting, Robert Bessoir; Sound, Tom Gould; Stage Manager, Patricia Flynn Press, David Rothenberg CAST: Lou Sumrall(Jeremy), Roma Maffia(Marlene)

A revision of the 1990 play.

(P.S.122) Wednesday, Feb.24-27, 1993 (6 performances) Performance Space 122 (Managing Director, Dominick Balletta) presents:
POUNDING NAILS INTO THE FLOOR WITH MY FOREHEAD; Written and Performed by Eric Bogosian; Director, Jo Bonney; Production Manager, David Herrigel

New performance pieces.

(Village Theatre) Wednesday, Feb.24-Mar.20, 1993 (18 performances) The Village Theatre Company presents:
THE BEST OF SEX AND VIOLENCE by Thomas Hinton; Director/Set, Henry Fonte; Lighting, Douglas O'Flaherty; Costumes, Marj Feenan; Sound, Richard L. Sirois CAST: Christopher Bailey (Jarret), Julia McLaughlin (Marion), Michael Curran (Robert), Bill Christ (Randell), Barbara Berque (Karen), Michelle Berke (Cindy)

A two-act comedy of manners set in Connecticut.

Laura Esterman, Jeffrey Hayenga in "Two Rooms" (*Susan Johann*)

Elizabeth Green, Stacey Todd Holt, Robert Berman, David Lowenstein, Jane Wasser, Wendy Oliver, Michael Malone, Jim Weaver in "Anything Cole" (*Blanche Mackey/Martha Swope*)

Guy Davis, Denise Burse-Mickelbury in "Robert Johnson: Trick the Devil" (*Martha Holmes*)

Adrian Pasdar, Ron Eldard, Michael Imperioli in "Aven'U Boys" (*Carol Rosegg/Martha Swope*)

(John Houseman Theatre) Tuesday, Feb.23-Apr.18, 1993 (49 performances and 16 previews) Ron Kastner, William B. O'Boyle, Sonny Everett, and Evangeline Morphos present:
AVEN' U BOYS by Frank Pugliese; Director, Frederick Zollo; Sets, Kert Lundell; Costumes, Carol Oditz; Lighting, Jan Kroeze; Sound, John Kilgore; Fights, B.H. Barry; Stage Manager, Eric S. Osbun; Press, Bill Evans /Jim Randolph CAST: Lili Taylor (Wendy), Lucinda Jenney (Ann), Cynthia Martells (Linda), Ron Eldard (Ed), Michael Imperioli (Charlie), Adrian Pasdar (Rocky)
    A drama in two acts set in Brooklyn.

(Westside Theatre/Upstairs) Wednesday, Feb.24-Apr.11, 1993 (42 performances and 14 previews) Stonebridge Presentations, Producers Circle & Pyramid Enterprises by arrangement with Michael Redington present:
THE BEST OF FRIENDS by Hugh Whitemore; Director, William Partlan; Sets, Robert Klingelhoefer; Costumes, Edi Giguere; Lighting, Tina Charney; Sound, Michael Croswell; Stage Manager, Ed Fitzgerald; Press, Shirley Herz/Glenna Freedman CAST: Michael Allinson (Sir Sydney Cockrell), Roy Dotrice (George Bernard Shaw), Diana Douglas (Dame Laurentia McLachlan)
    The action takes place in England, 1924-62.

(Judith Anderson Theatre) Thursday, Feb.25-Mar.14, 1993 (16 performances) Miranda Theatre Company presents:
SOMEWHERE I HAVE NEVER TRAVELED by Daniel Macivor; Director, Daniel Selznick; Set, Ted LeFevre; Lighting, Scott Griffin; Costumes, Rodney Munoz; Sound, Jim van Bergen; Stage Manager, Sally Frontman; Press, Peter Cromarty/Michael Hartman CAST: Raymond Haigler (Joseph), Brad Sullivan (Buck), Aideen O'Kelly (Rose), Ibi Janko (Dolly), Julie Follansbee (Agnes), Jerry Mettner (Gene)
    A drama in two acts. The action takes place in Eastern Canada.

(Samuel Beckett Theatre) Friday, Feb.26-Mar.14, 1993 (14 performances) The Basic Theatre presents:
OFF THE BEAT N PATH 2: NO KITCHEN SINKS; Sets/Lighting, Marc D. Malamud; Costumes, Jared Hammond, Patty Burke; Stage Manager, Susan "Q" Gutmann CAST:Eric Brandenburg, Betty Burdick, Gary Cowling, Sheri Delaine, Sarah Ford, David Goldman, Jared Hammond, Spruce Henry, Tom Spivey, Elizabeth Ann Townsend

PROGRAM:*Victoria Station* by Harold Pinter; Director, Tom Spivey; *Let Us Go Out Into The Starry Night* by John Patrick Shanley; Director, Lester Shane; *The Messenger's Assistant* by Michael Frayn; Director, Robert Lee Martini; Downtown by Jeffrey Hatcher; Director, John Edmond Morgan; *Gertrude! The Prequel* by M. Van Buren; Director, Susan Jacobson

(Primary Stages) Sunday, Feb.28-Mar.2, 1993 (3 performances)
OLIVIA'S OPUS; Written and Performed by Nora Cole
    A collection of remembrances from the mid-sixties, somewhere near the Mason-Dixon line.

Roy Dotrice, Michael Allinson, Diana Douglas in "Best of Friends" (*Martha Swope*)

Brad Sullivan, Raymond Haigler in "Somewhere I Have Never Traveled" (*William Gibson/Martha Swope*)

(Algonquin Hotel Oak Room) Tuesday, Mar.2-27, 1993 (28 performances)
OVER THE RAINBOW; with Bill Daugherty and Robin Field

Daugherty and Field sing the songs of Harold Arlen.I Happen to Like New York, their previous show was performed late night weekend shows.

(Rainbow & Stars) Tuesday, Mar.2-Apr.10, 1993 (60 performances) Greg Dawson and Steve Paul present:
A GRAND NIGHT FOR SINGING! THE RODGERS & HAMMERSTEIN REVUE; Director, Walter Bobbie; Musical Director, Fred Wells; Press, David Lotz CAST: Victoria Clark, Jason Graae, Martin Vidnovic, Lynne Wintersteller, Karen Ziemba

(St Clement's) Wednesday, Mar.3-Apr.3, 1993 (17 performances and 3 previews) Theatre for a New Audience presents:
LOVE'S LABOR'S LOST by William Shakespeare; Director, Michael Langham; Set, Douglas Stein; Costumes, Ann Hould-Ward; Lighting, Matthew Frey; Music, Alexandra Harwood; Choreography, Jill Beck; Sound, Jim van Bergen; Fights, J. Allen Suddeth; Stage Manager, Mark Cole; Press, Shirley Herz/Miller Wright CAST: Samuel Baird, Melissa Bowen, Kathleen Christal, Courtenay Collins, Jim Donovan, Zachary Ehrenfreund, Enid Graham, Christina Haag, Francis E. Hodgins, Peter Jacobson, Mark Niebuhr, Alec Phoenix, Gregory Poretta, Linda Powell, Bruce Racond, Frani Ruch, Michael Rudko, Trellis Stepter Jr., Eric Swanson

(Puerto Rican Traveling Theatre) Wednesday, Mar.3-Apr.25, 1993 Puerto Rican Traveling Theatre presents:
THE TOOTHBRUSH by Jorge Diaz; Translation/Direction, Alba Oms; Set, Miguel Lopez-Castillo; Lighting, Bill Simmons; Sound, Sergio Garcia-Marruz; Stage Manager, Fernando Quinn CAST: Maria Cellario, Chris de Oni
A day in the life of a married couple is turned upside down.

(One Dream Theatre) Thursday, Mar.4-14, 1993 (8 performances) Under One Roof Theatre Company presents:
INSIDE THE CREOLE MAFIA; Created and Performed by Roger Guenveur and Mark Broyard; Press, David Rothenberg/Terence E. Womble
Performance incorporating rap, movement and Creole food.

(Atlantic Theatre) Friday, Mar.5-Apr.3, 1993 (22 performances and 6 previews) Daryl Roth presents:
THE ROOT by Gary Richards; Director, Matthew Penn; Set, Deborah Jansien; Lighting, Donald Holder; Costumes, David Loveless; Sound, Doug Cuomo; Stage Manager, Chris DeCamillis; Press, Jim Baldassare CAST: Giancarlo Esposito (Willie), Joseph Siravo (Vinny), Jude Ciccolella (Jerry), Tony Hoty (Chick)
A drama in two acts. The action takes place in a gas station at the foot of the Williamsburg Bridge.

(St. Peter's Theatre) Thursday, Mar.4-21, 1993 (15 performances) St. Bart's Players presents:
BABES IN ARMS with Music by Richard Rodgers; Lyrics, Lorenz Hart; Book, George Oppenheimer; Director, Christopher Catt; Musical Director, Raphael Crystal; Choreography, Jeff Peters; Set, Richard Kendrick; Costumes, Estella Marie; Lighting, Karen Spahn; Sound, Andrew Skomorowsky; Press, Peter Cromarty/David Bar Katz CAST INCLUDES: Joann Baney, Melissa Broder, Andrea Capalaces, Deidre Curry, Bruce Lloyd, Mark Modano, Brian Myers, Lucas Torres, Lizzie Yawitz
A new production of the 1937 musical.

(INTAR Theatre) Friday, Mar.5-Apr.4, 1993 (32 performances) Serendipity Productions in association with Andrew C. McGibbon and Steven M. Levy presents:
WINTER LIES by Robert Clyman; Director, Larry Arrick; Set/Costumes, G.W. Mercier; Lighting, Rachel Budin; Stage Manager, Andrea Testani; Press, Shirley Herz/Wayne Wolfe CAST: Jerry Grayson (Ross), Robert LuPone (Karl), Amanda Peet (Dawn), Darby Townsend (Kate)
A thriller involving the murder of a young prostitute.

(Trocadero Cabaret and Don't Tell Mama) Friday, Mar.5-Oct.3, 1993 (41 performances) SDD Productions presents:
ONE FOOT OUT THE DOOR with Music/Lyrics/Book/Musical Direction by Stephen Dolginoff; Director, Cheryl Katz; Press, Seth Goldman CAST: Laurie Alyssa Myers succeeded by Beth Baur (Shelly),Kyle Dadd succeeded by Denis Jones, Garth Kravits (Bryan), Elizabeth Richmond succeeded by Melinda Berk, Lauren Cohn (Marissa), Patrick Peterson succeeded by Joel Carlton, Brian T. Cahill (Therapist)
MUSICAL NUMBERS: Prelude, Therapy, Night That I Met Phil, Here I Am, Barbie and Ken, What He'd Say, Eddie Always Here, One Foot Out the Door, Penalty, Not Anymore, House on Coney Island, Like the Skyline, My Deepest Thoughts, When I'll Miss Him, Conclusions.
A musical about three people who meet in group therapy.

Victoria Clark, Martin Vidnovic, Lynne Wintersteller, (front) Karen Ziemba, Jason Graae in "Grand Night for Singing" (*Carol Rosegg/Martha Swope*)

Joseph Siravo, Tony Hoty, Giancarlo Esposito in "The Root" (*Carol Rosegg/Martha Swope*)

Laurie Alyssa Myers, Joel Carlton, Denis Jones, Melinda Berk in "One Foot Out the Door"

(Minetta Lane Theatre) Saturday, Mar.6, 1993-Jan.16, 1994 Thomas Viertel, Richard Frankel, Steven Baruch, Jack Viertel, Mitchell Maxwell, Alan Schuster, and the WPA Theatre present:

JEFFREY by Paul Rudnick; Director Christopher Ashley; Sets/Projections, James Youmans; Lighting, Donald Holder; Costumes, David C. Woolard; Sound, Donna Riley; Musical Staging, Jerry Mitchell; Wigs/Hairstylist, David H. Lawrence; Stage Manager, John F. Sullivan; Press, Chris Boneau/ Adrian Bryan-Brown, Craig Karpel CAST: John Michael Higgins succeeded by Jeffrey Hayenga (Jeffrey), Patrick Kerr succeeded by Albert Macklin (Man in Bed/Gym Rat/Skip Winkly/Casting Director/ Headdress Waiter/Man #2 with Debra/Man in Chaps/Thug #2/ Dave/ Angelique), Scott Whitehurst succeeded by Demitri Corbin (Man in Bed/Gym Rat/ Salesman/ Boss/ Man #1 with Debra/Jockstrap Man/ Thug #1/ Young Priest/ Sean), Richard Poe succeeded by Keith Langsdale (Man in Bed/Gym Rat/Don/Tim/Dad/Father Dan/Chuck Farling), Bryan Batt succeeded by Greg Louganis (Darius/Man in Bed), Edward Hibbert succeeded by Peter Bartlett (Sterling/Man in Bed), Tom Hewitt succeeded by Anthony M. Brown (Steve/Man in Bed), Harriet Harris succeeded by Theresa McElwee, Anne Lange (Woman in Bed/ Showgirl/Ann Marwood Bartle/Debra Moorhouse/Sharon/Mom/Mrs. Marcangelo)

A romantic comedy in two acts. The action takes place in New York City.

Top: John Michael Higgins, Tom Hewitt
Center: John Michael Higgins, Edward Hibbert, Bryan Batt
Bottom: Greg Louganis
William Gibson/Martha Swope Photos

(UBU Repertory) Tuesday, Mar.9-Apr.4, 1993 (28 performances) UBU Repertory Theatre presents:
THE FREE ZONE by Jean-Claude Grumberg; Translation, Catherine Temerson; Director, Francoise Kourlisky; Set, Watoku Ueno; Lighting, Greg MacPherson; Costumes, Carol Ann Pelletier; Music/Sound, Genji Ito; Stage Manager, Jenny Peek; Press, Peter Cromarty/David Bar Katz CAST: Bernie Passeltiner (Maury), Polly Adams (Lea), Mildred Clinton (Mrs. Schwartz), Patti Perkins (Mauricette), Oren J. Sofer (Henri), Ronald Guttman (Simon), J.D. Hyman (Grandchild), Michael Ingram (Apfelbaum), Jodi Lynne McClintock (Daughter-in-Law), Dan Daily, Ian Cohen (Police), Ivan Borodin (Young German)
  A drama set in France during WWII.

(American Place Theatre) Wednesday, Mar.10, 1993- American Place Theatre (Wynn Handman, Artistic Director; Dara Hershman, General Manager) presents:
THE CONFESSIONS OF STEPIN FETCHIT by Matt Robinson; Director, Bill Lathan; Set, Kert Lundell; Lighting, Shirley Prendergast; Sound, Robert LaPierre; Movement, Hank Smith; Stage Manager, Jacqui Casto; Press, David Rothenberg CAST: Roscoe Orman (Lincoln Perry)
  A monodrama on the black actor of the 1920s-30s.

(Ohio Theatre) Thursday, Mar.11-28, 1993 (15 performances and 4 previews) Watermark Theater presents:
THE ARRANGEMENT by Susan Kim; Director, Nela Wagman; Lighting, Betsy Finston; Set, Jon Waldo; Stage Manager, Colleen Davis; Press, Fred Nathan/Michael Borowski CAST: Jordan Lage (Jack), Claudia Silver (Kara), Richard Long (Gary), Seth Herzog (Jerry/Waiter)
  A dark comedy in two acts about love and obsession.

(Club 53) Thursday, Mar.11-Sept.11, 1993 Daryl Roth, Hal Luftig, Alan D. Perry, Jim David and Kathy Najimy present:
BACK TO BACHARACH AND DAVID; Music, Burt Bacharach; Lyrics, Hal David; Director, Kathy Najimy; Conceived/Arranged by Steve Gunderson; Set, Peter Rogness; Costumes, David Loveless; Lighting, Maura Sheridan; Musical Staging, Javier Velasco; Stage Manager, Todd Gajdusek; Press, Shirley Herz/Miller Wright CAST: Melinda Gilb, Steve Gunderson, Sue Mosher, Lillias White
MUSICAL NUMBERS: A House Is Not a Home, Alfie, Always Something There to Remind Me, Another Night, Any Old Time of the Day, Anyone Who Had a Heart, Are You There with Another Girl, Close to You, Do You Know the Way to San Jose, Don't Make Me Over, I Just Have to Breathe, I Say a Little Prayer for You, I'll Never Fall in Love Again, Just Don't Know What to Do with Myself, Knowing When to Leave, Let Me Be Lonely, Let Me Go to Him, Message to Michael, My Little Red Book, Nikki, One Less Bell to Answer, Promises Promises, Reach Out for Me, April Fools, The Look of Love, This Empty Place, This Guy's in Love with You, Trains and Boats and Planes, 24 Hours from Tulsa, Walk on By, What the World Needs Now, Whoever You Are I Love You, You'll Never Get to Heaven
  A musical revue.

(Theatre for the New City) Thursday, Mar.11-28, 1993 (12 performances) Theatre for the New City presents:
SMALL TOWN GIRLS WITH BIG PROBLEMS by Larry Myers; Director, Roger Mrazek; Costumes, Myrna Duarte; Set, Michelle Sibilia; Lighting, David Alan Comstock; Stage Manager, Diana Trimble CAST: Maria Bello, Angel Dean, Marilyn Duryea, Diane Jean-George
  A comedy set in a small town trailer park.

(Actors' Playhouse) Sunday, Mar.14, 1993- Thomas Weekley and Tomarq Productions presents:
THE SECOND ANNUAL HEART O'TEXAS ECZEMA TELETHON by Mark Dunn; Director, Amy Brentano; Set, Robert Alan Harper; Lighting, Stewart Wagner; Costumes, Don Newcomb; Stage Manager, Thom Fudal; Press, Shirley Herz/Miller Wright CAST: Todd Chayet (Mickey Cutler), Anthony Marchionda, Jr. (Drummer), Raymond Bally (Guitarist), Beverly Jean-Favre (Gladiola Pilbeam), Stephen Bauer (Russ Roulez), Jennifer Rose (Pristine Gibbons), Julie Hays (Eve Adams), Nancy Flom (Sue Kwan Ling), Jennifer Tulchin (Arletta Kirby), Deny Staggs (Buddy Towers), Elizabeth Ragsdale (Tanya Towers), Christopher Casoria (Mime), Wallace Wilhoit (Jordan Isles), Adam J. Weinberg (Ricky Duval), Alison Korman (Beauty Bandit), Chris Northup, Stephanie K. Bennett (Camera People)
  A comedy involving a small town telethon.

(U.S. Customs House) Tuesday, Mar.16-Apr.11, 1993 (24 performances) En Garde Arts presents:
STRANGE FEET by Mac Wellman; Director, Jim Simpson; Music, David Van Tieghem; Set, Kyle Chepulis; Lighting, Brian Aldous; Sound, Eric Liljestrand; Press, David Rothenberg CAST: Yusef Bulos, Elzbieta Czyzewska, Jan Leslie Harding, Steve Mellor, Vagabond Children's Choir
  A site-specific play with music where dinosaurs give primordial perspective on the mysteries of the planet.

(Beacon Theatre) Tuesday, Mar.16-Apr.11, 1993 (28 performances) Atlanta's Theatre

Oren Sofer, Polly Adams, Patti Perkins, Mildred Clinton(seated), Ronald Guttman, Bernie Passeltiner in "Free Zone" (*Carol Rosegg/Martha Swope*)

Jordan Lage, Claudia Silver, Richard Long in "The Arrangement" (*Peter C. Cook*)

Lillias White, Melinda Gilb, Steve Gunderson, Sue Mosher in "Back to Bacharach and David" (*William Gibson/Martha Swope*)

97

of the Stars and Robert L. Young & Assoc. present:

THE WIZ with Music/Lyrics by Charlie Smalls; Book, William F. Brown; Director/Choreographer, George Faison; Musical Director/Dance Arrangements, Timothy Graphenreed; Sets, Randel Wright; Lighting, John McLain; Costumes, Jonathan Bixby; Sound, Abe Jacob; Stage Manager, Matthew G. Marholin; Press, Jeffrey Richards/Irene Gandy CAST: Stephanie Mills (Dorothy), Andre De Shields (Wiz), Eugene Fleming (Tinman), H. Clent Bowers (Lion), Garry Q. Lewis (Scarecrow), Ella Mitchell (Evillene), Ebony Jo-Ann (Addaperle), Toni Seawright (Glinda/Aunt Em), Maurice Lautner (Uncle Henry/Lord High Underling), Evelyn Thomas (Tornado), Inaya Jafan Davis, Bobby Daye, Kellie Turner, Virginia Ann Woodruff, Christopher Davis, James A. Ervin, Cornell Ivey, Neil Whitehead, Evelyn Ebo, Gina Renee Ellis, Roland Hayes, Frederick Moore, April Nixon, John Eric Parker, Katherine J. Smith, Rachel Tecora Tucker
MUSICAL NUMBERS: Feeling We Once Had, Tornado Ballet, He's the Wiz, Soon as I Get Home, I Was Born on the Day Before Yesterday, Ease on Down the Road, Mean Ole Lion, Kalidah Battle, Be a Lion, Lion's Dream. Emerald City Ballet. So You Wanted to Meet the Wizard, If I Could Feel, No Bad News, Funky Monkeys, Everybody Rejoice, Who Do You Think You Are, Believe in Yourself, Y'all Got It, Rested Body is a Rested Mind, Home

A new production of the 1975 musical with the original leading lady.

(Public/Anspacher Theatre) Tuesday, Mar.16-May 2, 1993 (55 performances) Second Stage Theatre (Carole Rothman, Artistic Director; Suzanne Schwartz Davidson, Producing Director) presents:
ONE SHOE OFF by Tina Howe; Director, Carole Rothman; Set, Heidi Landesman; Lighting, Richard Nelson; Costumes, Susan Hilferty; Sound, Mark Bennett; Stage Manager, Gregg Fletcher; Press, Richard Kornberg CAST: Jeffrey DeMunn (Leonard), Mary Beth Hurt (Dinah), Jennifer Tilly (Clio), Daniel Gerroll (Tate), Brian Kerwin (Parker)
A comedy in two acts. The setting is a Greek revival farm house in upstate New York.

(Alices's Fourth Floor) Thursday, Mar.18-Apr.10, 1993 (15 performances and 3 previews) Alice's Fourth Floor presents:
LEMONADE; Written and Directed by Eve Ensler; Press, Chris Boneau/ Adrian Bryan-Brown; Jaime Morris CAST: Anette Hunt, Bill Moor, Julia Martin, Alex Fitzsimmons
A dark comedy about a reclusive gardener and a killer.

(Judith Anderson Theatre) Thursday, Mar.18-Apr.4, 1993 (16 performances) Leahy Productions presents:
PETS by Marion Adler, Adele Ahronheim, Raphael Crystal, Rick Cummins, Richard Enquist, Faye Greenberg, Alison Hubbard, Dan Kael, Kim Oler, Jimmy Roberts, Ben Schaechter, June Siegel, Carolyn Sloan, Thomas Tierney, Thomas Edward West, Greer Woodard; Director/Choreographer, Helen Butleroff; Asst. Choreographer, Thom Warren; Musical Direction/ Orchestrations, Albert Ahronheim; Set/Lighting, Fred Kolo; Costumes, Debra Stein; Stage Manager, D.C. Rosenberg; Press, Peter Cromarty/ Michael Hartman CAST: David Beach, Barbara Broughton, Tim Connell, Janine LaManna, Cheryl Stern
MUSICAL NUMBERS: Pets, Take Me Home with You, Don't Worry 'bout Me, I Walk Ze Dogs, Perpetual Care, There's a Bagel on the Piano, Cool Cats, Dear Max, First Cat, What About Us?, Peculiar, Franklin, Mice of Means, Night of the Iguana, If You Can Stay, All in a Day's Work, Finale
Musical revue in two acts.

(29th St. Rep. Theatre) Friday, Mar.19-31, 1993 (12 performances) Third Step Theatre Company presents:
THE KNIGHTS OF THE ROUND TABLE by Christoph Hein; Translation, Beate Hein Bennett; Director, Moshe Yassur CAST: Catherine Argo, Erica McFarquhar, Bobbi Randall, Larry Swansen, Lee Winston, Richard Dahlia
A loose re-telling of the tales with reference to the fall of Eastern Europe's communist regimes.

Mark Tenore in "The Interview"

Brian Kerwin, Jennifer Tilly in "One Shoe Off" (*Susan Cook*)

David Beach in "Pets!" (*Carol Rosegg/Martha Swope*)

(Nat Horne Studio) Saturday, Mar.20-Apr.10, 1993 (13 performances) Aboutface Theatre Company presents:
THE HISTORY OF PRESIDENT JOHN FITZGERALD KENNEDY, PART ONE by Sean Burke; Director, Ron O'Connor; Design, Marty Fluger; Stage Manager Jonathon Fishman; Press, Francine L. Trevens CAST: Mark La Mura (JFK), G Rogers (Henry Cabot Lodge), Mel Boudrot (Joe Kennedy), Tracy Brenner, Jason Duchin, John Elsen, Allison Jones, David MacDonald, Dean Marisco, Chuck Poole Yvette Thor, Whit Vernon
A drama which parallels Shakespeare's *King Henry IV*. The action takes place during the 1952 Kennedy-Lodge senatorial race.

(224 Waverly Place) Wednesday, Mar.24-Apr.10, 1993 (11 performances)
THE INTERVIEW by Thom Thomas; Director, Leo Leyden CAST: Edmund Lyndeck, Mark Tenore

(Eighty Eights) Wednesday, Mar.24-June 23, 1993 Music-Theatre Group presents:
HEY, LOVE; with Music by Mary Rodgers; Lyrics, Marshall Barer, Martin Charnin John Forster, Richard Maltby, Jr., Shakespeare, Stephen Sondheim Conception/Direction, Richard Maltby, Jr.; Musical Direction/ Arrangements, Patric S. Brady; Press, Jim Baldassare CAST: Karen Mason, Marcus Lovett, Mark Waldrop
Cabaret revue on the songs of Mary Rodgers.

(Downtown Art Co.) Wednesday, Mar.24-Apr.4, 1993 (10 performances) Downtow Art Co. presents:
HEARTBREAK HOUSE by George Bernard Shaw; Director, Ryan Gilliam; Set, Da Hurlin; Lighting, Paul Clay; Costumes, Anna Thomford CAST: David Abaire (Randa Utterword), Will Badgett (Hector Hushabye), Jim Calder (Burglar), Lenor Champagne (Nurse Guiness), Anne Darragh (Hesione Hushabye), Kyle DeCam (Capt. Shotover), Dan Hurlin (Boss Mangan), Kirk Jackson (Mazzini Dunn), Chri Lindsay (Ellie Dunn), Oliver Wadsworth (Lady Utterword)

(Harold Clurman Theatre) Thursday, Mar.25-Apr.4, 1993 (11performances) Carava Theatre Co. and Prima Artists New York present:
DANDO BOHICA; Written/Directed by Peter B. Hodges; Stage Manager, Kevin C Ewing CAST: Marie Andrews, David DeBesse, Randall Rapstine, Wendy Scharfma Robert Sonderskov, Ken Threet, Jennifer Dorr White

Courtyard Playhouse) Friday, Mar.26-May 9, 1993 (40 performances) The Up to Mischief Players and the Glines presents:
MEET MARVIN by Robert Patrick; Director, Lawrence Lane; Costumes, Wade Laboissonniere; Sets, John Willis, David M. Jensen, LouAnne Gilleland; Lighting, Tracy Dedrickson; Press, Betsy Hunt/Maria Pucci CAST: David Blackman, Neil Butterfield, Erich Schmidt, Casey Wayne
Three short plays: *Meet Marvin, Evan on Earth, T-Shirts* .

Battery Park City) Tuesday, Mar.30-June 6, 1993 (90 performances) Cirque du Soleil presents:
SALTIMBANCO; Artistic Director, Franco Dragone; Creative Director, Gilles Ste-Croix; Choreography, Debra Brown; Music, Rene Dupere; Costumes, Dominique Lemieux; Set, Michael Crete; Press, Ellen Zeisler/ Kevin P. McAnarney
Latest edition of the Cirque du Soleil. The title is a sixteenth century Italian word meaning "skilled street performers".

Theatre for the New City) Thursday, Apr.1-11, 1993 (8 performances)Theatre for the New City presents:
NEW JERSEY/NEW YORK; Written/Directed/Sets by Richard Hoehler; Lighting, Mark London; Stage Manager, Deborah Natoli; Press, Jonathan Slaff CAST: Richard Hoehler (Richard), Bill Corsair (Tony/Vinnie/Father), David Joe Wirth (Phil/Zero/Ugly Fucker), Mary Foster Conklin (Sheryl Heffernan)
Five thematically-linked pieces.

Theatre for the New City) Thursday, Apr.1-25, 1993 (16 performances) Theatre for the New City presents:
SPAIN; Written/Directed by Romulus Linney; Set, Mark Marcante; Lighting, Jeffrey S. Koger; Costumes, Teresa Snider-Stein; Stage Manager, Lauren McConnell; Press, Jonathan Slaff CAST: Frank Anderson (Brother Miguel de Puyal), Peter Ashton Wise (Bishop Atanasio), Fred Burrell (Tomas de Torquemada), T. Cat Ford (Francisca Mendez), Russel Lunday (Fosco Mendez), Mary Beth Peil, Gretchen Walther (Anna Rey), Michael Burrell (Bradley Smith)
Performed without intermission. The action takes place at the Monastery of St Thomas, Spain and at an American psychoanalyst's office, 1490 and 1993.

(Synchronicity Space) Friday, Apr.2-18, 1993 (13 performances) Red Earth Ensemble presents:
THOSE PEOPLE by Richard Gaeta; Sets/Lighting, Richard Lichte CAST: Joe Anania, Richard Mark Arnold, John DiGennaro, Janet Giradeau, Salty Loeb, Dorothy Nixon, Robert Poletick PROGRAM: **Don the Working Man** , Director, Christopher Nunnally; I'm Thirty-six Years Old and I Can Smoke If I Want, Director, Harvey Huddleston
Two one-act plays.

(Wings Theatre) Saturday, Apr. 3-May 16, 1993 Wings Theatre Company (Artistic Director, Jeffery Corrick; Associate Director, Michael Hillyer) presents:
THERE'S A WAR GOING ON by Ken Krauss CAST INCLUDES: Gordon Gauntlett, Jr., Stephen Bienskie

(Antrobus Group Theatre) Thursday, Apr.8-17, 1993 (7 performances)
CRUSHED:TALES FROM THE TWENTYNOTHING GENERATION; Written and Performed by Lee Rosenthal; Director, Forrest Brakeman; Press, Chris Boneau/Adrian Bryan-Brown, Jamie Morris
A humorous monologue on the "baby bust" generation.

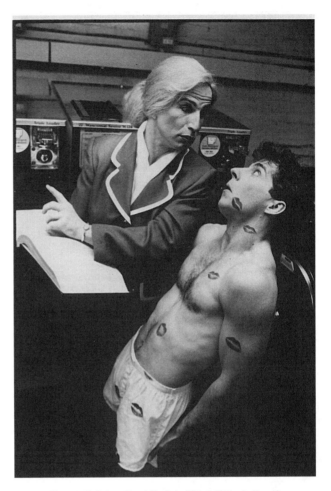

Everett Quinton, Grant Neale in "Linda" (*Paula Court*)

(William Redfield Theatre) Tuesday, Apr.13-25, 1993 (14 performances) Seventh Seal Ensemble presents:
"..'til death do us part." Press, Judy Jacksina/Tracy Strann CAST:Chris Bruno, Alicia Coppola, Felicia Dyer, Lonnie Quinn, Laura Botsacos, Kevin Cutts, Marjorie Hirsch, Greg Houston, David Jeffryes, Frank J. Kali, Tom Miscia, Jill Pixley, Bill Potts, Beth Shachat, Jennifer A. Skinner, Natalya Sokiel, Cheri M. Spriggs
PROGRAM: Anchors, Talk Shows, Love and Poetry Without Motion by Peter Mercurio; Director, Tony Marando, Electric Roses by David Howard; Director, Scott Segall, Sane Reaction by Lisa Morton; Director, James Lish, The House With Nobody In It by Jennifer A. Skinner; Director, Alexander Harrington
Four one-acts.

(Charles Ludlam Theater) Wednesday, Apr.14-May 30, 1993 (42 performances) The Ridiculous Theatrical Company presents:
LINDA with Music by Mark Bennett; Lyrics, Everett Quinton, Mr. Bennett; Book, Mr. Quinton; Director, David Ganon; Sets, Greenfield; Costumes, Toni Nanette Thompson; Lighting, Richard Currie; Wigs/ Makeup, Zsamiro Ronquillo; Stage Manager, Karen Ott; Press, Peter Cromarty/David Bar Katz CAST:Chris Tanner (Tetchen), Grant Neale (Gabriel), Lisa Herbold (Linda), Bobby Reed, Mr. Ganon (Mrs. Jones/ Zeke/Devil/Nurse), Everett Quinton (Rev. Mrs. Charlotte Drum), Brenda Cummings (Lizzie), Eureka (Armitage Shanks), Eureka, Ms. Cummings, Mr. Quinton, Mr. Neale (Devilettes)
MUSICAL NUMBERS:Wash-a-Day World, Lizzie the Lezzie, A Whole Lotta Them, If God Had Call Waiting (He'd Put You on Hold), I'm Gonna Cry Cry Cry, No Flies on You, Aryan Nation March, There's Gotta Be a Place, Heatin' Up This Hell Hole Tonight, End of the Line Lady, Ain't No Sin, The Girl I Love, Peace of Mind
A country musical in two acts. The action takes place in Dead Man's Gulch, Colorado.

Michael Burrell, Mary Beth Piel in "Spain" (*Jonathan Slaff*)

Prince Edward with "Ragged Child" cast

Rae C. Wright, Deb Margolin in "The Breaks"

John Epperson as Lypsinka (*Martha Swope*)

(Judith Anderson Theatre) Wednesday, Apr.14-May 2, 1993 (15 performances) Blue Heron Theatre and National Black Touring Circuit present:
THEM THAT'S GOT by Robyn Hatcher; Director, Charles Dumas; Music, David Lulow; Set, John Douglas; Lighting, James Fulton; Costumes, Lesley Neilson-Bowman; Stage Manager, Kit Holiday CAST: Robyn Hatcher (Diane Cooper), Phyllis Bash (Helen Cooper), Kim Sykes (Sharon Cooper), Kurt Rhoads (Michael Jacobs), Burnadair Lipscomb (Hallie Richards), Mone Walton (Crystal Harrison), William Christian (Adrian Harrison), Sharon Hope (Mae Harrison)
A two-act drama set in Philadelphia.

(Acting Co. Studio) Wednesday, Apr.14, 1993-
EINSTEIN; Written/Directed by Joel Selmeier; Press, David Rothenberg/ Terence Womble CAST: Richard Davis Springle (Einstein)
A monodrama about the inventor of the theory of relativity.

(New Group Theatre) Wednesday, Apr.14-May 2, 1993 New Group Theatre presents:
MAKE UP YOUR MIND by Kurt Vonnegut; Director, Sam Schacht; Design, Zaniz CAST: Richard Brandon, Tom Brannum (Otis Fletcher), Rod McLachlan (Roland Stackhouse), Miranda Sinclair (Karen)
A comedy performed without intermission.

(Cucaracha Theatre) Thursday, Apr.15-May 9, 1993 (16 performances) Cucaracha Theatre presents:
A VAST WRECK; Written/Directed by Richard Caliban; Music Composed/Performed by John Hoge; Sets, Kyle Chepulis; Lighting, Brian Aldous; Costumes, Mary Myers CAST: Lauren Hamilton, Carolyn McDermott; Chuck Montgomery, Mollie O'Mara, Dale Orlandersmith, Hugh Palmer, Thomas Pasley, David Simonds

A journey through Our Town for our times.

(Triplex) Thursday, Apr.15-17, 1993 (5 performances) The Triplex/BMCC and National Youth Music Theatre of Great Britain present:
THE RAGGED CHILD by Jeremy James Taylor and Frank Whately; Music, David Nield; Musical Directors, John Pearson, Mr. Nield; Choreography, Wendy Cook; Set, Christopher Richardson; Costumes, Sheila Darlington; Lighting, Peter Walters; Press, Ted Killmer CAST: Tim Vincent-Smith, James Sturgess, Layla Harrison, Polly Tracey, Greg Morton, Steven Dunlop, Stephen Graham, Laurence Taylor, Naomi Taylor, Dorian Clark, Timothy Goodwin, Zoe Mason, Tom Hollis, Charley Pugsley, Nick Saich, Laura Tristram, Rebecca Ryan, Michael Dovey, Barnaby Davies, Jonathan Gow, Madeleine Reeves, Emma Trow, Emma Roskilly, Stephanie Eckhardt, Sarah Brown, Rebecca Weeks, Danny Nutt, Michelle Thomas, Tim Steeden, Tiffany Gore, Rebecca Lock, Edward Pascall, Oliver Thornton, Andrew Walkinshaw, Josephine Morgan, Adam Keeper, James Clare, Ashley Cox, Andrew Robinson, Alastair Bird, Ben Lumsden, Alex Robinson, Daniel Dalton
MUSICAL NUMBERS: Opening Sentence, Botany Bay, Ballad of Joe Cooper, Now Ain't That a Bloomin' Shame, There'll Come a Day, Banquet Scene, Sores of London, Deep Below the City Streets, Cholery, Let Them Starve, Up and Be Doing, Work Boys Work, London Town, There's a Friend for Little Children, Here's to the Bootblacks, Home Sweet Home, Paddy Lay Back, Come Rude Boreas, Come Away, Closing Sentence
A musical in two acts. The setting is London, 1850-51.

(Interart Theatre) Thursday, Apr.15-May 23, 1993 (25 performances) Interart Theatre presents:
THE BREAKS by Deb Margolin and Rae C. Wright; Director, Cheryl Katz; Sets, Christina Weppner; Lighting, Jeff Zeidman; Costumes, Linda Gui; Stage Manager, Dan Geist; Press, Peter Cromarty/Michael Hartman CAST: Rae C. Wright (Betty), Deb Margolin (Marian)
Two women bond in a Pennsylvania nursing home.

(Cherry Lane Theatre) Thursday, Apr.15, 1993- Sam Rudy, Michael O'Rand, Howard Danziger in assoc. with Barbara Carrellas and Denise Cooper and New York Theatre Workshop present:
LYPSINKA! A DAY IN THE LIFE; Created by John Epperson; Director/Choreographer, Michael Leeds; Set, James Schuette; Costumes, Anthony Wong; Lighting Mark McCullough; Sound, James M. Bay; Puppet Maker, Randy Carfagno; Stage Manager, Kate Broderick; Press, Shirley Herz/Sam Rudy CAST: John Epperson(Lypsinka), Enrico Kuklafraninalli Puppets, Standyby: Eve Harrington
An all-too-typical day in the life of Lypsinka.

(Danny's Skylight Room) Friday, Apr.16-May 1, 1993 (6 performances)
STRANDED IN THE PLAYGROUND by Cynthia Adler, Evan Matthews and Wally Strauss; Director, Mr. Strauss; Musical Director, Daryl Kojak; Press, Jim Baldassare CAST: Cynthia Adler, Evan Matthews
Songs (original and standard) and sketches.

(American Place Theatre) Monday, Apr.19-May 23, 1993 (31 performances) American Place Theatre (Wynn Handman, Director; Dara Hershman, General Manager) presents:
ON THE WAY HOME; Written/Collected/Performed by Stephen Wade; Directoin/Set/Lighting, Milton Kramer; Stage Manager, Michael Robin; Press, David Rothenberg
Musical journeys through America.

Evan Handler in "Time on Fire" (*Susan Cook*)

Leslie Castay, Brian Sutherland, Nick Wyman in "Hunchback of Notre Dame" (*Carol Rosegg/Martha Swope*)

David Lewman, Peter Burns, Rob Riley, Joe Liss, George Wendt in "Wild Men!" (*William Gibson/Martha Swope*)

Jon DeVries, Robin Morse, Richard Bekins in "Patient A" (*Susan Johann*)

(Second Stage Theatre) Tuesday, Apr.20-June 3, 1993 (45 performances) Second Stage (Carole Rothman, Artistic Director; Suzanne Schwartz Davidson, Producing Director) presents:
TIME ON FIRE; Written and Performed by Evan Handler; Director, Marcia Jean Kurtz; Lighting, Kenneth Posner; Set, Rob Odorisio; Sound, Aural Fixation; Stage Manager, Jenny Peek; Press, Richard Kornberg
    The actor's account of beating "incurable" leukemia.

(Westbeth Theatre Center) Thursday, Apr.22-May 15, 1993 (19 performances) Westbeth presents:
THE HUNCHBACK OF NOTRE-DAME with Music by Byron Janis; Lyrics, Hal Hackady; Book, Anthony Scully; Director, Brian Murray; Choreography, Karen Azenberg; Musical Director, Tom Fay; Set, Bob Phillips; Costumes, Franne Lee; Lighting, Nancy Collings; Sound, Peter Fitzgerald; Stage Manager, Jane E. Neufeld; Press, David Lotz CAST: Steve Barton (Quasimodo), Leslie Castay (Esmeralda), Ed Dixon (Clopin), Laura Kenyon (Meral), Brian Sutherland (Phoebus), Nick Wyman (Frollo), Angel Caban (Marie), Tony Capone (Hungadi), Colleen Durham (Francoise), Anne Rickenbacher (Magda), Lorna Shane (Fatma), Fiddle Viracola (Faifou), Mark Ankeny, Douglas Carabe, Joyce Chittick, Andrei Clark, Lenny Daniel, Kathleen Lamb, Pavel Lempert, Dore Manasevit, Mary Jo McConnell, Michael John McGann, Vince Pesce, Alex Sharp, Thomas Titone
MUSICAL NUMBERS: Notre-Dame Prelude, Welcome to Paris, A Little Love, Because of Me, A Kiss Like That, Auction, Let Me Make Love to You, Like Any Man, I'll Die Happy, Keep an Eye on Me, You Are More, I Can't Lose You, Steal Another Day, Sanctuary, Look at Me It's Better with a Man, Madonna Mia, Esmeralda, On to Notre Dame, All That's Left of Love
    A musical in two acts. The setting is medieval Paris.

(Studio 4-A) Thursday, Apr.22, 1993- Antrobus Group presents:
MAD LOVE by Jennifer Maisel; Director, Dan Oliverio; Costumes, Adele Mattern; Sets, Mathew Maraffi; Lighting, Jennifer Houston; Sound, Daniel Kramer; Press, Judy Jacksina/Tracy Strann, Joanne Tanguay CAST: Rosemary Keough (Diane), Paul Beauvais (Colt), Elisa Donovan (Jace), Michael Stacy (Ted), Tamar Schoenberg (Becca), Kevin Cristaldi (Ken), Stewart Walker (Ben)
    A drama performed without intermission.

(Westside Theatre/Downstairs) Friday, Apr.23-June 27, 1993 (59 performances and 15 previews) James D. Stern in assoc. with Doug Meyer presents:
WILD MEN! by Peter Burns, Mark Nutter, Rob Riley and Tom Wolfe; Music/Lyrics by Mr. Nutter; Director, Mr. Riley; Set, Mary Griswold; Costumes, John Paoletti; Lighting, Geoffrey Bushor; Musical Director, Lisa Yeargun; Choreography, Jim Corti; Sound, Domenic Bucci; Stage Manager, Mary McAuliffe; Press, Chris Boneau/Adrian Bryan-Brown, Jackie Green CAST: George Wendt (Ken Finnerty), Rob Riley (Stuart Penn), David Lewman (Donnie Lodge), Peter Burns (Greg Neely), Joe Liss (Artie Bishop)
MUSICAL NUMBERS: Come Away, What Stuart Has Planned, True Value, Wimmins, Ooh That's Hot, We're Wild Men, Lookit Those Stars, The 'Un' Song, It's You, My Friend My Father, Get Pissed, Now I Am a Man, Finale
    A "musical...sort of" in two acts. The setting is the north woods.

(Kampo Cultral Center) Friday, Apr.23-May 23, 1993 (21 performances) Signature Theatre Company presents:
PATIENT A by Lee Blessing; Director, Jeanne Blake; Costumes, Teresa Snider-Stein; Lighting, Jeffrey S. Koger; Stage Manager, Kurt Engstrom; Press, James Morrison CAST: Robin Morse (Kimberly), John DeVries (Lee), Richard Bekins (Matthew)
    A drama performed without intermission. Based on the experience of Kimberly Bergalis, who may have contracted AIDS from her dentist.

(Mazur Theatre) Friday, Apr.23-25, 1993 (4 performances) Musicals in Concert presents:
THE HIGH LIFE with Music by Arthur Schwartz; Lyrics, Howard Dietz; Book, Fay and Michael Kanin based on Arthur Schnitzler's *The Affairs of Anatol* ; Director, BT McNicholl; Musical Director, James Stenborg; Choreography, Courtney Conner; Lighting, Jennifer Houston; Wardrobe, Linda Grant; Stage Manager, Bryan Gill; Press, Rob Hargraves CAST: Joseph DiSalle (Baron/Gaston), Heidi Heller (Baroness/Anna/Salka), Bonnie Rapp (Young Woman), Russell Goldberg (Max), Gregory Schultz (Usher/Photographer/Proprietor), Neal Mayer (Priest/Performing Anatol/Accountant), Michael Licata (Anatol), John-Charles Kelly (Franz), Patricia Masters (Helene), John Easterlin (Attendant/Helmut), Joyce Lynn (Frau Brandel), Clark Gesner (Herr Brandel), Leslie Beauvais (Liesl), Christine Siracusa (Girl/Nurse/Cissy), Kobi Shaw (Girl/Franzl), Catherine Anne Gale (Girl/Celestina/Steffi), Catherine Minn, Michael Dalton (Liebchen Dancers), Gregory Bossler (Proprietor/Doorman), Joanne Lessner (Mimi), Brian Runbeck (Otto/Oscar), Jeanne Grant (Grandmother), Dave Hugo (Lawyer), Melinda Thompson (Magda), Carl Nicholas (Tenor)
MUSICAL NUMBERS: What a Charming Couple, Why Go Anywhere at All?, Bring Your Darling Daughter, Now I'm Ready for a Frau, Magic Moment, Who Can? You Can, Oh Mein Liebchen, This Kind of Girl, Bloom Is off the Rose, I'm Glad I'm Single, Something You Never Had Before, You Will Never Be Lonely, You're Not the Type, Come a-Wandering with Me, I Never Had a Chance, I Wouldn't Marry You, For the First Time, Finale
    A concert version of the 1961 musical *The Gay Life* under a new title.

(Theatre Arielle) Tuesday, Apr.27-30, 1993 (4 performances) Thomas Sinclair presents:
JACK AND JILL with Music by Hal Schaefer; Lyrics/Book, Bob Larimer; Director, Miriam Fond; Musical Director, Wes McAfee CAST: Michael Scott (Jack Miller), Julia Lema (Jill Donovan), John Steber (Brad Donovan), Marilyn J. Johnson (Ruby Donovan), Ennis Smith (Ernie Harris), Raymond Thorne (Ben Miller), Sheila Smith (Ruth Miller)
MUSICAL NUMBERS: J-a-z-z, First Time I Heard Ella, Black and White People, Woulda Coulda Shoulda, First Time I Heard Ellington, A Little Bit, Old Mom and Pop Lament, He's Waltzing You Around, After All, On Your Own, In Between Gigs, Finale
   A jazz musical.

(Village Theatre) Wednesday, Apr.28-May 22, 1993 (17 performances) Village Theatre Company presents:
AUNT MARY by Pam Gems; Director, Gigi Rivkin; Set, Michael Blau; Costumes, Marj Feenan; Lighting, Susan M. Kelleher; Sound, Jim Harrington; Stage Manager, Lisa Jean Lewis CAST: Julia McLaughlin (Muriel), Allyn Burrows (Martin), Bill Christ (Mary), Michael Curran (Cyst), David McConnell (Jack), Kimberly Schultheiss (Alison), Scott Facher (Frogman/Man Out of Petrol)
   A British play in two acts. The action takes place in Birmingham, England in summer 1980.

(Playhouse 46) Wednesday, Apr.28-May 22, 1993 (19 performances and 4 previews) Pan Asian Repertory Theatre (Tisa Chang, Artistic Director) presents:
A DOLL HOUSE by Henrik Ibsen; Adaption/Direction, John R. Briggs; Set, Robert Klingelhoefer; Lighting, William Simmons; Costumes, Juliet Ouyoung CAST: Karen Tsen Lee, Daniel Dae Kim, Mel Duane Gionson, Lou Ann Lucas, Ron Nakahara
   This version sets the story on Long Island in the 1970s.

(John Houseman Theatre) Wednesday, Apr.28-July 1993 Eric Krebs presents:
BUYA AFRICA (COME BACK AFRICA); Musical Director, Emma; Lighting, Robert Bessoir; Sound, Charles McIntyre; Set, E.F. Morrill; Stage Manager, Margo Barkdull; Press, David Rothenberg CAST: Thuli Dumakude
   An African journey in music, performed in two acts.

(Primary Stages) Thursday, Apr.29-May 23, 1993 (23 performances) Primary Stages presents:
WASHINGTON SQUARE MOVES by Matthew Witten; Director, Seth Gordon; Set, Bruce Goodrich; Lighting, Deborah Constantine; Costumes, Amanda J. Klein; Stage Manager, Christine Catti; Press, Anne Einhorn CAST: Dion Graham (Al), Jack Stehlin (Bobby), Joe Quintero (Sammy D), Ascanio Sharpe (Randall), Angela Bullock (Margie), Dawn McClendon (Homeless Woman/Cop/Waitress), Bert Goldstein (John/Passerby)
   A drama in two acts. The action takes place at Washington Sq. Park, New York City.

(La Guardia Performing Arts Center) Friday, Apr.30-May 23, 1993 (22 performances) Negro Ensemble Company presents:
LAST NITE AT ACE HIGH by Kenneth Hoke-Witherspoon; Director, Douglas Turner Ward; Set, Michael Green; Costumes, Judy Dearing; Sound, Richard Turner; Lighting, Shirley Prendergast; Stage Manager, Sandra Ross; Press, Howard and Barbara Atlee CAST: Douglas Turner Ward (Daddy John), William Jay Marshall (Lucius), Michael Wright (Tommie), Jeannie M. Collins, Maggie Cooke, O.L. Duke, Brian Shnipper, Iris Little , Leonard Thomas, Ed Wheeler, Curt Williams, Darryl Williams
   A drama set in a Baltimore bar.
(Harold Clurman Theatre) Wednesday, May 5-29, 1993 (26 performances) Opening

Angela Bullock, Jack Stehlin, Dion Graham in "Washington Square Moves"
(*Andrew Leynse*)

Jennifer Prescott, Joseph Culliton in "On a Clear Day..."
(*Blance Mackey/Martha Swope*)

Doors presents:
ON A CLEAR DAY YOU CAN SEE FOREVER with Music by Burton Lane; Lyrics/Book, Alan Jay Lerner; Director, Tom Klebba; Musical Director, Robert Berman; Sets/Lighting, Trad A Burns; Costumes, Susan Branch; Choreography, David Lowenstein; Artistic Consultant; Burton Lane; Stage Manager, Mike Bucco CAST: Jennifer Prescott (Daisy/Melinda), Jim Madden (Mark), Jim Gricar (Edward/Preston), Tom Dusenbury (Warren/ Hubert), Joseph Culliton (Conrad/Sir Richard), Melissa Aggeles (Muriel/Flora), Evan Edwards (Hamilton/Airline Official), David Eye (Welles/Millard), Paul Gallagher (Solicitor/Airline Official), Susan Hackett (Joanne/Airline Official), Nicole Halmos (Miss Hatch/Mrs. Welles)
MUSICAL NUMBERS: Hurry It's Lovely Up Here, Solicitor's Song, I'll Not Marry, On a Clear Day, On the S.S. Bernard Cohn, Don't Tamper with My Sister, She Wasn't You, Melinda, When I Come Around Again, What Did I Have, Wait till We're Sixty-Five, Come Back to Me, Finale
   A revised version of the 1965 musical featuring songs not heard in the original.

(Ensemble Studio Theatre) Wednesday, May 5-June 13, 1993 (42 performances) Ensemble Studio Theatre presents:
MARATHON '93; Producer, Kevin Confoy; Artistic Director, Curt Dempster; Sets, H. Peet Foster; Costumes, Martha Bromelmeier, Julie Doyle; Lighting, Greg MacPherson; Sound, Jeff Taylor; Stage Manager, Erika Feldman
SERIES A: LONG AGO AND FAR AWAY by David Ives; Director, Christopher A. Smith; with Crista Moore, John Ottavino, Baxter Harris; BED AND BREAKFAST by Richard Dresser; with Jenny O'Hara, Daniel Ziskie; IRON TOMMY by James Ryan; JACKIE by David Rasche; with Cecilia de Wolf, Ted Neustadt
SERIES B: A FAREWELL TO MUM by Julie McKee; Director, Margaret Mancinelli-Cahill; with Ms. McKee, Matthew Mutrie; TUNNEL OF LOVE by Jacquelin Reingold; Director, Ethan Silverman; with Amelia Campbell, Bill Cwikowski, David Eigenberg, Christine Farrell, Karen Kandel, Angela Pietropinto; FORE! by Frank D. Gilroy; Director, David Margulies; with Barbara Andres, Sam Coppola, Ted Neustadt, M. Emmet Walsh; RING OF MEN by Adam Oliensis; Director, Jamie Richards; with Jesse L. Martin, Corey Parker, Michael Louis Wells
SERIES C: COSMO'S IN LOVE by Bill Bozzone; Director, Shirley Kaplan; with Shirl Bernheim, Zach Grenier, Ilene Kristen, Robert Pastorelli; SEVENTH WORD, FOUR SYLLABLES by Susan Kim; Director, Melia Bensussen; with Richmond Hoxie, Gordana Rashovich, Sara Rue, Rocco Sisto, Janet Zarish; WHERE'S MAMIE? by Michael John LaChiusa; Director, Kirsten Sanderson; Choreography, Janet Bogardus; with Jennifer Chase, Alice Playten, Debra Stricklin, David Wasson; THE REHEARSAL by Joyce Carol Oates; Director, Kevin Confoy; with Chris Ceraso, Kristin Griffith, Richmond Hoxie
   Sixteenth annual festival of one-act plays.
(St. Mark's Studio) Thursday, May 6, 1993- Michael Hyman presents:

HOMO ALONE:LOST IN COLORADO by The Planet Q Players; Director/Set, Chrisanne Eastwood; Choreography, Eric Rockwell; Lighting, Deborah Malkin; Press, Peter Cromarty/David Bar Katz CAST: Walter Barnett, Kelly J. Brower, Nora Burns, Stephen Earley, Chrisanne Eastwood, Terrence Michael, Eric Rockwell

   Comedy revue on today's headlines by the queer troupe.

(West End Theatre) Thursday, May 6-23, 1993 (12 performances) Centerfold Productions presents:
A MIND IS A TERRIBLE THING TO LOSE; Conception/Direction, Robert Armin CAST: Dawn Akiyama, Bob Celli, Mary Grace, Jay Hammer, Andrea Kolb, Lucy McMichael, Kristine Nevins, Gary Trahan, David Vogel, M.C. Waldrep
PROGRAM: *Harlan Ellison's Shatterday*; Adaptation, Mr. Armin; *Restaurant* by Dan Greenburg; *You're On the Air* by Andrea Kolb; *Genghis Khan* by Mr. Armin; *Toxic Schlock*; Written/Directed by Barb Rhodes; *Now Here This* with Music/Lyrics by Josh Rosenblum

(Kaufman Theatre) Thursday, May 6-22, 1993 Martin R. Kaufman presents:
SPIKE HEELS by Theresa Rebeck; Director, Nancy Hancock; Lighting, Eric Haugen; Sets, John Farrell; Costumes, Catherine Small; Press, Judy Jacksina/Tracy Strann, Joanne Tanguay CAST: Nellie Sciutto, Jonathan Sweet, Vincent Angell, Kay O'Connell

   A comedy set in Boston.

(Playhouse 91) Saturday, May 8-30, 1993 (15 performances and 9 previews) Eclectic Theatre Company presents:
SHARON with Music by Franklin Micare; Lyrics/Book/Direction, Geraldine Fitzgerald; Based on *Sharon's Grave* by John B. Keane; Production Supervisor, Johnny King; Choreography, Pamela Sousa; Orchestrations, Ned Ginsburg; Musical Director, Bruce W. Coyle; Set, Mich R. Smith; Costumes, Mary O'Donnell; Lighting, Mark F. Connor; Fights, B.H. Barry; Sound, Scott Stauffer; Stage Manager, Bruce Greenwood; Press, Shirley Herz/Wayne Wolfe CAST:Arthur Anderson (Lawyer/Tom Shawn), Sinead Colreavy (Miss Dee), Mark Doerr (Neelus), Patrick Farrelly (Fr. Riordan), Christina Gillespie (Mague), Ken Jennings (Dinzie Conlee), Kurt T. Johns (Patrick Minogue), Michael Judd (Jack Conlee), Ruth Kulerman (Moll), John McDonough (Pats Bo Bwee), David K. Thome (Guarda Mooney/Donal Conlee), Deanna Wells (Trassie Conlee), Leslie Blumenthal, Tim Connell, Karen Faistl, Steven Garrett, Mary Beth Griffith (Ensemble)
MUSICAL NUMBERS: For the Money, Song of Sharon, It's a Sin, Rim of a Rainbow, Hear the Birds, I'm Blest, Hurry Uncle Donal, Two Eyes, God Bless Everyone, Grand Man, That's How It Goes, Dreaming, Hail Mary, Let's Pretend, Boots on the Floor, Someone, Forgiveness, Never, The Man Below, Journey's in the Mind, Sharon's Waltz, Finale

   A musical drama in two acts. The action takes place in New York and Ireland, 1927.

(Primary Stages) Sunday, May 9-11, 1993 (3 performances)
A NORMAL GUY; Written and Performed by Jim Fyfe
   Interconnected comic monologues.

(Classic Stage Company) Tuesday, May 11-30, 1993 Working Theatre presents:
I AM A MAN by OyamO; Director, Bill Mitchelson; Music, Olu Dara; Sets, Charles McClennahan; Costumes, B. Christine McDowell; Sound, Serge Ossorguine; Fights, J. Allen Suddeth; Projections, Jan Hartley; Stage Manager, Crystal Huntington CAST: Paul Butler (T.O. Jones), Larry Keith (Solomon), Myra Taylor (Alice Mae Jones), Mark Kenneth Smaltz (Rev. Moore), Monte Russell (Swahili), Harold Perrineau, Jr. (Cinnamon), Guy Davis(Song performance), Robert Arcaro, A. Bernard Cummings, James Murtaugh, Howard Samuelsohn

   A drama set in Memphis, 1968.

Terrence Michael in "Homo Alone" (*Carol Rosegg/Martha Swope*)

Kurt Johns, Deanna Wells in "Sharon" (*Carol Rosegg/Martha Swope*)

(Courtyard Playhouse) Wednesday, May 12, 1993- The Glines presents:
EARL, OLLIE, AUSTIN & RALPH by Glenn Rawls; Director, Michael Henderson; Set, Louanne Gilleland; Lighting, Tracy Dedrickson; Costumes, Pat Robler; Stage Manager, Ricky Hill; Press, Susan L. Schulman CAST: Mitch Florer (Austin), Scott Kelly (Ralph), Barry Crewdson (Rogers), David John Dean (Earl), Bill Wood (Ollie)

   A two-act comedy about the gay generation gap. The action takes place at a South Carolina hotel.

(Samuel Beckett Theatre) Wednesday, May 12-June 6, 1993 (21 performances) The Basic Theatre in association with Pamela Mobilia presents:
SHAVIANA by Marty Martin; Director, Lester Shane; Set, Walt Spangler; Lighting, Marc D. Malamud; Costumes, Patty Burke, Jared Hammond; Stage Manager, Robert Lemieux; Press, Chris Boneau/Adrian Bryan-Brown, Bob Fennell CAST: Timothy Altmeyer (George Bernard Shaw), Steve Boles (George Carr Shaw), Sheri Delaine (Mrs. Lucinda Elizabeth Shaw), Kevin Dwyer (Vanderleur Lee), Mary Jasperson (Nurse Hill), Marilyn Salinger (Lucy Shaw)

Timothy Altmeyer, Marilyn Salinger in "Shaviana" (*Vibeke Toft*)

The story of the young Shaw and family is set in Ireland, 1872.

(One Dream Theatre) Thursday, May 13-June 6, 1993 (19 performances) Barrow Group and One Dream present:
LOW LEVEL PANIC by Clare McIntyre; Director, Leonard Foglia; Set, Michael McGarty; Costumes, Nina Canter; Lighting, Russell Champa; Sound, One Dream; Stage Manager, Jude Domski; Press, Shirley Herz/ Wayne Wolfe CAST: Marcia Debonis (Jo), Wendee Pratt (Mary), Christina Denzinger (Celia)

A drama performed without intermission. The setting is London's East End.

(Theatre for the New City) Thursday, May 13-June 20, 1993 Theatre for the New City and Play Producers present:
MASTER & MARGARITA by Mikhail Bulgakov; Interpretation, Jean-Claude van Itallie; Director, David Willinger; Set, Mark Symczak; Lighting, Tommy Barker; Costumes, Tanya Serdiuk; Music, Arthur Abrams; Stage Manager, Colin Rudd; Press, Jonathan Slaff CAST: Arthur Abrams (Bengalsky), Eran Bohem (Master), Lisa Nicholas (Margarita), Jonathan Teague Cook (Woland), Gary Kimble (Koroviev/Arthanius), Kolawole Ogundiran (Cat/Legionnaire), Eric Rasmussen (Ivan/Mathew), Cesar Rodriguez (Nazarene), Alison Lani Broda (Natasha/others), Milton Carney (Berlioz/others), Matthew Dudley (Rimsky/others), Tom Dale Keever (Pilate/others), Rafael Mateo (Varenukha/others)

The devil comes to Moscow in this two-act fantasy comedy.

(Nat Horne Theatre) Friday, May 14-June 6, 1993 (20 performances) Love Creek Productions and Le Wilhelm present:
FESTA ITALIANA DE THEATRO; Translations, Lynne Romeo Erspamer, Kay McCarthy, John Christopher Jones, Patrizia La Fonte, Renato Giordano, Dina Morrone; Press, Chris Boneau/Adrian Bryan-Brown, Jamie Morris, Hillary Harrow CAST: Caren Alpert, Olga Bagnasco, Antonia Banewicz, John Beaird, CaSandra Brooks, Michael Cannis, Barbara Costigan, Laura D'Arista, Henry Marsden Davis, Loris Diran, Sharon Fallon, Tristan Fitch, Cecelia Frontero, Michael Gilpin, Richard Kent Green, Robyn Hartman, Duffy Hudson, Jackie Jenkins, Paul Kawecki, Bob Manus, John Marino, Jenny Martel, Nancy McDoniel, Katherine Parks, Gloria Ptak, Taryn Quinn, Kevin Reifel, Debbie Rochon, Jonie Schumacher, Scott Sparks, Thomas Sullivan, John Unruh, Kirsten Walsh, Vicki Weidman, Dustye Winniford, Kate Zahorsky
PROGRAM 1: Director, Philip Galbraith; A DAY OFF by Maria Letizia Campatangelo; COMPUTHERAPY by Leonardo Franchini; TALKING ABOUT GRIEG by Eva Franchi; LOOK AT ME, LISTEN TO ME, KISS ME by Stefania Porrino
PROGRAM 2: Director, Diane Hoblit; HALF AND HALF and OUR CHILDREN by Antonio Gavino Sanna
PROGRAM 3: Director, Sharon Fallon; BYE BYE CELLULITE, IF THIS IS THE FUTURE COUNT ME OUT, and SUMMER AT CASA MAGNI by Patrizia Monaco
PROGRAM 4: Director, Jeffrey J. Albright; A SMALL CONCERT FOR A LADY by Alida Maria Sessa, ROCK AND ROLL HELL by Renata Giordano; ARTHUR by Rosario Galli

One-act plays newly translated from the Italian.

(Horace Mann Theatre) Friday, May 14-27, 1993 (9 performances) Nicky Genovese presents:
BEDROOM FARCE by Alan Ayckbourn; Director, Harland Meltzer; Costumes, Carol Brys; Lighting, Jeffrey Segal; Stage Manager, Barry Ravitch CAST: Marie Andrews (Delia), Peter Williamson (Ernest), John Eisner (Nick), Jennifer Dorr White (Jan), Marion Markham (Kate), Patrick White (Malcolm), John Heath Stewart (Trevor), Pamela Wiggins (Susannah)

Estelle Parsons in "Extended Forecast" (*Carole Rosegg/Martha Swope*)

Christina Denzinger, Wendee Pratt, Marcia DeBonis in "Low Level Panic" (*Joan Marcus*)

A comedy in two acts. The action is set in three bedrooms.
(Town Hall) Saturday, May 15-16, 1993 (2 performances)
LA GRAN SCENA OPERA CO.; Artistic Director, Ira Siff; Press, Tony Origlio/William McLaughlin CAST INCLUDES: Ira Siff (Mme. Vera Galupe-Borszkh, traumatic soprano), Joe Simmons (Sylvia Bills, America's Most Beloved Retired Diva), Keith Jurosko(Gabriella Tonnoziti, World's Oldest Living Diva), Johnny Maldonado (Carmelita della Vaca Browne), David St. Jude Sabella (Mirella Frenzi), Philip Koch (Philene Wannelle), Ross Barentyne (Francesco Folinari-Soave-Coglioni)

Spoof of the Met's 1993 season.

(Primary Stages) Sunday, May 16-18, 1993 (3 performances)
TWO THEATRE PIECES by Frank Gagliano; *Hanna: A Run-On Odyssey* and *My Chekhov Light* with Sara Romersberger

(Union Sq. Theatre) Tuesday, May 18-July 11, 1993 (48 performances) Frank & Woji Gero and Mark Gero present:
THE INVISIBLE CIRCUS; Press, Bill Evans; with Victoria Chaplin, Jean Baptiste Thierree, James Spencer Thierree

An intimate family circus.

(Theatre for the New City) Thursday, May 20-June 5, 1993 Theatre for the New City presents:
THE HOUSEGUESTS by Harry Kondoleon; Director, Tom Gladwell; Sets, Chris Fields; Costumes, David Zinn; Stage Manager, Jason Knapp CAST: Birgit Darby (Vera), Melissa Hurst (Gale), Tom Ledcke (John), Albert Macklin (Manny)

A dark comedy.

(Soho Rep) Thursday, May 20-June 13, 1993 (16 performances) Soho Rep presents:
DAVID'S REDHAIRED DEATH by Sherry Kramer; Director, Julian Webber; Set, Robert Odorisio; Lighting, Don Holder; Costumes, Maggie Morgan; Sound, John Collins; Choreography, Ain Gordon; Stage Manager, Kristen Harris CAST: Jan Leslie Harding(Jean), Deidre O'Connell(Marilyn)

(Soho Rep) Friday, May 21-June 15, 1993 Soho Rep presents:
THREE AMERICANISMS and **TERMINAL HIP** by Mac Wellman; Directors, Jim Simpson, Mr. Wellman; Sets/Lighting, Kyle Chepulis; Stage Manager, Kristen Harris; Music, Mike Nolan CASTS: (Americanisms) Jan Leslie Harding, Ron Faber, Mark Margolis (Hip) Steve Mellor

Performed in repertory.

(Primary Stages) Sunday, May 23-25, 1993 (3 performances)
THE BEST THINGS IN LIFE; Written and Performed by Lenora Champagne; Director, Robert Lyons

A look at modern values through remade fairy tales.

(La MaMa) Friday, May 28-June 12, 1993 (14 performances) La MaMa E.T.C. presents:
EXTENDED FORECAST by Franz Xaver Kroetz; Translation, Erica Bilder, Estelle Parsons; Director, Ms. Bilder; Set/Lighting, Watoku Ueno; Costumes, Theodora Skipitares; Stage Manager, Shigeko Suga; Press, Jonathan Slaff, Richard Kornberg CAST: Estelle Parsons

American premiere of German drama.

OFF BROADWAY COMPANY SERIES

AMERICAN JEWISH THEATRE

Nineteenth Season

Artitic Director, Stanley Brechner; Associate Artistic Director, Lonny Price; Resident Director, Richard Sabellico; General Manager, George Elmer; Production Stage Manager, Joseph Millet; Press, Jeffrey Richards/Tom D'Ambrosio
Saturday, Nov.21-Dec.20, 1992 (31 performances)
A BACKER'S AUDITION with Music/Lyrics/Book by Douglas Bernstein & Denis Markell; Based on idea by Martin Charnin, Bernstein & Markell; Director, Leonard Foglia; Musical Director, Michael Sansonia; Set, James Noone; Costumes, Deborah Shaw; Lighting, Russell Champa CAST: Sheila Smith (Esther Kanner), Alice Spivak (Nellie), Tom Ligon (Roger Freed), Arthur J. Kalodner (Charles Goff), Stan Free (Andrew Marks), Ray Wills (Don Costello), Gretchen Kingsley (Kim Terry), Tom Riis Farrell (Leonard), Lon Hoyt (Eli Friedman)
    A musical comedy in two acts.
Saturday, Jan.9-Feb.21, 1993 (45 performances)
BORN GUILTY by Ari Roth; Based on the book by Peter Sichrovsky; Director, Jack Gelber; Set, James Wolk; Costumes, Pamela Scofield; Lighting, Susan A. White CAST: Zach Grenier (Peter), Jennie Moreau (Anna), Amy Wright (Susanne/Edda), Greg Germann (Dieter/Johannes/Egon), Victor Slezak (Rudolph/Horst), Lee Wilkof (Rainer/Herbert/ Gerhard), Maggie Burke (Brigitte)
    A drama set in Austria, Germany and London, 1990-present.
Saturday, Mar.13-May 9, 1993 (59 performances)
ANOTHER TIME by Ronald Harwood; Director, Stanley Brechner; Set/Lighting, Paul Wonsek; Costumes, Lee Austin; Sound, Bruce Ellman CAST: Malcolm McDowell (Ike Lands/Leonard Lands), James Waterston (Leonard Lands/Jeremy Lands), Joan Copeland (Belle Lands), Marian Seldes (Rose Salt), Michael Lombard (Prof. Zadook Salt), J. Max Sullivan (Technician)
A drama in two acts. The action takes place in South Africa and London, and spans the 1950s to the present.
Saturday, May 15-June 1993
TOTIE with Music/Lyrics by Robert Bendorff; Book, Bobby Pearce and Nancy Timpanaro; Director, Richard Sabellico; Set, Brian Nason CAST: Nancy Timpanaro (Totie Fields)
    Solo musical about the late comedienne.

Gerry Goodstein, Carol Rosegg Photos

Sheila Smith, Charles Goff, Stan Free in "A Backer's Audition"

James Waterston, Malcolm McDowell in "Another Time"

Lena Endre in "Peer Gynt"

BROOKLYN ACADEMY OF MUSIC

(Opera House) Tuesday, June 9-21, 1992 (14 performances)
RICHARD III by William Shakespeare; Director, Richard Eyre; Design, Bob Crowley; Lighting, Jean Kalman; Music, Dominic Muldowney CAST: Ian McKellen (Richard III), Keith Bartlett (Brackenbury/Scrivener), Paul Bazely (Marquess of Dorset), David Neames (Catesby), Sam Beazley (Lord Mayor/Ghost Henry VI), Simon Blake, Oliver Grig, Tom Penta, Richard Puddifoot (Edward, Prince of Wales/Page), Richard Bremmer (Stanley), Sebastian Brennan, James Graves,Richard Lawrence, Marco Williamson (Richard, Duke of York), Charlotte Cornwell (Queen Elizabeth), Peter Darling (Henry/Lord Grey), David Foxxe (Bishop of Ely/Blunt), Anastasia Hille (Anne), Dominic Hingorani (Murderer/Lovel), Rosalind Knight (Duchess of York), Phil McKee (Murderer), Tim McMullan (Tyrrel), Antonia Pemberton (Queen Margaret), Alan Perrin (Rivers), Bruce Purchase (King Edward/Earl of Oxford), Terence Rigby (Duke of Buckingham), Richard Simpson (Hastings/Herbert), Malcolm Sinclair (George), Chris Walker (Keeper/Citizen), Olivia Williams (Maid/Mistress), Tristram Wymark (Ratcliffe)
  This production takes place in England during the 1930s.

(Park Slope Armory) Thursday, Oct.1-11, 1992 (12 performances)
LES ATRIDES; Director, Ariane Mnouchkine; Translation, William M. Hoffman; Music, Jean-Jacques Lemetre; Set, Guy-Claude Francois; Masks, Erhard Stiefel; Costumes, Nathalie Thomas CAST: Theatre du Soleil
PROGRAM: *Iphigenia in Aulis* by Euripides; *Agememnon, The Libation Bearers*, T*he Eumenides* by Aeschylus
  A Parisian theatre company presents a ten hour, epic four play cycle. Performed in French with translation head sets available.

(Opera House) Tuesday, May 11-15, 1993 (5 performances)
PEER GYNT by Henrik Ibsen; Director, Ingmar Bergman; Sets/Costumes, Lennart Mork; Choreography, Donya Feuer; Music, Bohuslav Martinu; Lighting, Hans Akesson CAST: Borje Ahlstedt, Bibi Andersson, Lena Endre and Royal Dramatic Theatre of Sweden
  Dramatic poem performed in Swedish with translation avaliable.

(Carey Playhouse) Thursday, May 20-22, 1993 (3 performances)
MADAME DE SADE by Yuko Mishima; Director, Ingmar Bergman; Sets/ Costumes, Charles Koroly; Choreography, Donya Feuer; Music, Ingrid Yoda; Lighting, Sven-Erik Jacobson CAST: Stina Ekblad (Renee), Anita Bjork (Madame de Montreuil), Marie Richardson (Anne), Margaretha Bystrom (Baroness de Simiane), Agneta Ekmanner (Countess de Sain-Fond), Helena Brodin (Charlotte)
  Performed in Swedish in three acts. The action takes place from 1777-90.

John Haynes Photos

Ian McKellen in "Richard III"

Michael McCormick, Stanley Tucci in "Scapin"

CLASSIC STAGE COMPANY
Twenty-sixth Season

Artistic Director, David Esbjornson; Managing Director, Patricia Taylor; Development Director, Catherine Pages; Company Manager, Kelly Voorhees; Production Manager, Jeffrey Berzon; Production Stage Manager, Crystal Huntington; Press, Jeffrey Richards, Denise Robert

Tuesday, Oct.13-Nov.22, 1992 (33 performances and 8 previews)
GOODNIGHT DESDEMONA (GOOD MORNING JULIET) by Ann-Marie MacDonald; Director, David Esbjornson; Set, Donald Eastman; Costumes, C.L. Hundley; Lighting, Brian MacDevitt; Sound, John Kilgore; Fights, Byron Jennings CAST: Liev Schreiber (Chorus/Iago/Romeo/Ghost), Cherry Jones (Constance Ledbelly), Hope Davis (Student/Soldier of Cyprus/ Juliet), Robert Joy (Othello/ Prof. Claude Night/Tybalt/Juliet's Nurse), Saundra McClain (Ramona/Mercutio /Desdimona/Servant)
    A two-act comedy about a dreamy drama professor journeying into Shakespeare's unruly world.

Friday, Oct.23-24, 1992 (2 performances late night)
STUFF AS DREAMS ARE MADE ON; Written and Performed by Fred Curchack
    A whimsical adaptation of The Tempest .
Tuesday, Jan.12-Mar.7, 1993 (48 performances and 9 previews)
SCAPIN by Moliere; New Version, Shelly Berc & Andrei Belgrader; Music/Lyrics, Rusty Magee; Director, Andrei Belgrader; Set, Anita Stewart; Costumes, Candice Donnelly, Elizabeth Hope Clancy; Lighting, Stephen Strawbridge CAST: Stanley Tucci (Scapin), Alexander Draper (Octave), Ken Cheeseman (Silvestre), Sarah McCord Williams (Hyacinte), Michael McCormick (Argante), Walker Jones (Geronte), Joshua Fardon (Leandre), Mary Testa (Zerbinette), Roberta Kastelic (Nerine), John August, Denis Sweeney (Porters), Jules Cohen (Musician)
MUSICAL NUMBERS: Scapin, Another Girl, Heir to My Fortune, The Way I Got, What? What? What?, Monsieur, Vile Thing, Act I Finale, Gypsy Song, Money and Family
A two-act musical version of the 1671 comedy.

Monday, Mar.29-Apr.17, 1993 (19 performances and 2 previews)
KRAPP'S LAST TAPE by Samuel Beckett; Direction/Design, David Esbjornson; Costumes, Jessica Grace; Lighting, Brian MacDevitt; Sound, Dan Moses Schreier CAST: John Seitz
    Beckett's 1958 monodrama performed without intermission. A bitter man becomes obsessed with his taped diaries.

T. Charles Erickson Photos

Robert Joy, Cherry Jones in "Goodnight Desdemona"

CIRCLE REPERTORY COMPANY

Artistic Director, Tanya Berezin; Managing Director, Abigail Evans; Associate Artistic Director, Mark Ramont; Production Manager, Jody Boese; Development Director, Virginia Finn Lenhardt; General Manager, Meredith Freeman; Marketing Director, Phillip Matthews; Press, Bill Evans/Jim Randolph, Erin Dunn

(Lucille Lortel Theatre) Wednesday, Sept.30, 1992-Mar.21, 1993 (175 performances and 22 previews)

THE DESTINY OF ME by Larry Kramer; Director, Marshall W. Mason; Sets, John Lee Beatty; Costumes, Melinda Root; Lighting, Dennis Parichy; Music, Peter Kater; Sound, Chuck London, Stewart Werner; Stage Manager, Fred Reinglas CAST: John Cameron Mitchell succeeded by Anthony Rapp (Alexander Weeks), Jonathan Hadary (Ned Weeks), Oni Faida Lampley (Nurse Hanniman), Bruce McCarty succeeded by Mark Robert Myers during vacation (Dr. Anthony Della Vida), David Spielberg succeeded by Ralph Waite, Robert Stattel (Richard Weeks), Piper Laurie succeeded by Carole Shelley (Rena Weeks), Peter Frechette succeeeded by Tom McBride (Benjamin Weeks)

   A drama in three acts. The action takes place just outside Washington, D.C., in the past and present. After the Circle Rep subscription run ended Nov.15, Lucille Lortel, Rodger McFarlane and Tom Viola continued the run as a commercial production.

(Circle Rep Theatre) Friday, Nov.27, 1992-Jan.3, 1993 (23 performances and 18 previews)

ORPHEUS IN LOVE with Music by Gerald Busby; Words, Craig Lucas; Director, Kirsten Sanderson; Musical Director, Charles Prince; Sets, Derek McLane; Costumes, Walker Hicklin; Lighting, Debra J. Kletter; Hairstylist/ Wigs, Bobby H. Grayson; Stage Manager, M.A. Howard CAST: Bradley Garvin, Steven Goldstein, Diane Ketchie, Belinda Pigeon

   A new opera in two acts.

Friday, Mar.19-Oct.10, 1993 (231 performances and 21 previews)

THREE HOTELS by Jon Robin Baitz; Director, Joe Mantello; Sets, Loy Arcenas; Costumes, Jess Goldstein; Lighting, Brian MacDevitt; Sound, Scott Lehrer; Music, Rick Baitz; Stage Manager, M.A. Howard CAST: Ron Rifkin (Kenneth Hoyle), Christine Lahti succeeded by Debra Monk (Barbara Hoyle)

   A drama in three parts. The action takes place in hotels in Morocco, the Virgin Islands, and Mexico.

(Lucille Lortel Theatre) Wednesday, Apr.14-May 23, 1993 (32 performances and 15 previews)

AND BABY MAKES SEVEN by Paula Vogel; Director, Calvin Skaggs; Sets, Derek McLane; Lighting, Peter Kaczorowski; Costumes, Walker Hicklin; Sound, Donna Riley; Music, Evan Morris; Stage Manager, Leslie Loeb CAST: Peter Frechette (Peter), Mary Mara (Ruth), Cherry Jones (Anna)

   A comedy in two acts set in a New York City loft.

Gerry Goodstein, Martha Swope/William Gibson Photos

Cherry Jones, Peter Frenchette, Mary Mana in " And Baby Makes Seven"

Christine Lahti, Ron Rifkin, Debra Monk in "Three Hotels"

Jonathan Hadary, John Cameron Mitchell, Piper Laurie in "The Destiny of Me"   Top: John Cameron Mitchell

JEWISH REPERTORY THEATRE

Nineteenth Season

Artistic Director, Ran Avni; Associate Director, Edward M. Cohen; General Manager, Steven M. Levy; Press, Shirley Herz/Glenna Freedman, Sam Rudy, Miller Wright

(New home at Playhouse 91) Saturday, Oct.24-Nov.15, 1992 (24 performances)
GOD OF VENGEANCE by Sholem Asch; Adaptation, Stephen Fife; Director, Ran Avi; Set, Rob Odorisio; Costumes, Gail Cooper-Hecht; Lighting, Betsy Finston; Music/Sound, Raphael Crystal; Stage Manager, D.C. Rosenberg CAST: Christine Burke (Rivkele), Marilyn Chris (Sore), Lee Wallace (Yankel), Stephen Singer (Shloyme), Robin Leslie Brown (Hindl), Bernie Passeltiner (Reb Elye), Maury Cooper (Scribe), Bernadette Quigley (Manke), Jodi Baker (Basha), Deborah Laufer (Reyzl), Roy Cockrum (Groom's Father)
   A three-act drama set in Poland, 1905.

Sunday, Jan.9-31, 1993 (15 performances and 9 previews)
THEDA BARA AND THE FRONTIER RABBI with Music by Bob Johnston; Lyrics, Mr. Johnston, Jeff Hochhauser; Book, Mr. Hochhauser; Director/ Choreographer, Lynne Taylor Corbett; Musical Director, Michael Rafter; Orchestrations, Steve Margoshes; Set, Michael R. Smith; Costumes, Tom Reiter; Lighting, Tom Sturge; Sound, Scott Stauffer; Stage Manager, Kevin Brannick CAST: Jonathan Brody (Marv/Adolph Zukor/Cowboy), Christopher Coucill (Gordon Edwards), Frank DiPasquale (Morris Flushing/Sam Goldfish/Cowboy), Mark Frawley (D.W. Griffith/Groom/Cowboy), Jonathan Hadley (Isaac Birnbaum), Robin Irwin (Head Foremother), Jeanine LaManna (Theda Bara), Iris Lieberman (Fanny Flushing/ Fore-mother), Ellen Margulies (Rachel Birnbaum), Rita Rehn (Irene/ Foremother), Allen Lewis Rickman (Selwyn Farp)
MUSICAL NUMBERS: Father I Have Sinned, There Are So Many Things That a Vampire Can't Do, Frontier Rabbi, It's Like a Movie, Velcome to Shul, Bolt of Love, Sermon, Scene with the Grapes, Another Rabbit Outta the Hat, There Are So Many Things That a Vampire Can Do, If She Came Back Again, Waiting for the Kiss to Come, Oh Succubus, Finale
   A musical comedy in two acts. The setting is Hollywood, 1917.

Saturday, Apr.3-25, 1993 (24 performances)
THE KING OF CARPETS by Joel Hammer; Director, Edward M. Cohen; Set, Ray Recht; Costumes, Brenda Rousseau; Lighting, Brian Nason; Sound, Michael Grumer; Stage Manager, Geraldine Teagarden CAST: Sam Graty (Dad), Matthew Arkin (Jamey), David Thornton (Barry), Wendy Kaplan (Sheila), Elaine Rinehart (Nancy)
   A two-act comedy set in Akron, OH.

Jonathan Hadley, Jeanine LaManna in "Theda Bara and the Frontier Rabbi"

Lee Wallace, Christine Burke, Marilyn Chris in "God of Vengeance"

Matthew Arkin, Wendy Kaplan, Sam Gray in "King of Carpets"

Martha Swope/Carol Rosegg Photos

LINCOLN CENTER THEATER
Eighth Season

Artistic Director, Andre Bishop; Executive Producer, Bernard Gersten; Resident Director, Gregory Mosher; General Manager, Steven C. Callahan; Development Director, Hattie K. Jutagir; Production Manager, Jeff Hamlin; Dramaturg, Anne Cattaneo; Musical Theatre Program, Ira Weitzman; Press, Merle Debuskey/Susan Chicoine

Friday, Sept.25, 1992-Feb.28, 1993 (142 performances and 31 previews) transferred to Ethel Barrymore Theatre Mar.3 1993 (see Broadway Calendar)
THE SISTERS ROSENSWEIG by Wendy Wasserstein; Director, Daniel Sullivan; Sets, John Lee Beatty; Costumes, Jane Greenwood; Lighting, Pat Collins; Sound, Guy Sherman, Aural Fixation; Stage Manager, Roy Harris CAST: Julie Dretzin (Tess Goode), Frances McDormand succeeded by Christine Estabrook (Pfeni Rosensweig), Jane Alexander (Sara Goode), John Vickery (Geoffrey Duncan), Robert Klein (Mervyn Kant), Madeline Kahn (Gorgeous Teitelbaum), Patrick Fitzgerald (Tom Valiunus), Rex Robbins (Nicholas Pym)

A comedy in two acts. The action takes place in London, 1991.
Thursday, Apr.8-July 25, 1993 (89 performances and 37 previews)
PLAYBOY OF THE WEST INDIES by Mustapha Matura; Director, Gerald Gutierrez; Sets, John Lee Beatty; Costumes, Paul Tazewell; Lighting, James F. Ingalls; Sound, Serge Ossorguine; Music, Andre Tanker; Fights, David Leong; Stage Manager, Michael Brunner CAST: Lorraine Toussaint (Peggy), Darryl Theirse succeeded by Michael Potts (Stanley), Arthur French (Phil), Akin Babatunde (Jimmy), Antonio Fargas (Mikey), Victor Love (Ken), Michele Shay (Mama Benin), Kelly Taffe (Alice), Melissa Murray (Ivy), Terry Alexander (Mac), Lou Ferguson, Elain Graham, Simi Junior, Adrian Roberts (Citizens)

Performed in three acts. Matura's version of J. M. Synge's 1921 *Playboy of the Western World* is set in Trinidad, 1950.

For other Lincoln Center Theater production, *My Favorite Year* , see Broadway Calendar.

Martha Swope Photos

**Top: Madeline Kahn, Jane Alexander, Frances McDormand
Center: Robert Klein, Alexander in "Sisters Rosensweig"
Left: Victor Love, Lorraine Toussaint in "Playboy of the West Indies"**

Welker White, Stephen Mailer in "The Innocent's Crusade"

Frank Whaley, Julie Hagerty in "The Years"

MANHATTAN THEATRE CLUB

Twenty-first Season

Artistic Director, Lynne Meadow; Managing Director, Barry Grove; General Manager, Victoria Bailey; Associate Artistic Director, Michael Bush; Play Development Director, Kate Loewald; Business Director, Michael P. Naumann; Company Manager, Patricia Decker; Production Manager, Michael R. Moody; Press, Helene Davis/Deborah Warren

(Stage II) Tuesday, June 2-July 5, 1992 (40 performances)
THE INNOCENT'S CRUSADE by Keith Reddin; Director, Mark Brokaw; Sets, Bill Clarke; Costumes, Ellen McCartney; Lighting, Michael R. Moody; Sound, Janet Kalas; Stage Manager, James Fitzsimmons CAST: Stephen Mailer (Bill), Harriet Harris (Ms. Connell/Waitress/Ms. Cabot/Wendy/Helen), James Rebhorn (Karl), Debra Monk (Mame), Tim Blake Nelson (Tommy/ Mr.Clancy/Mr. Cooper/Evan/Teller/Stephen), Welker White (Laura)
A dark comedy in two acts.

(Stage I) Tuesday, Sept.22-Nov.29, 1992 (80 performances)
MAD FOREST by Caryl Churchill; Director, Mark Wing-Davey; Sets/ Costumes, Marina Draghici; Lighting, Christopher Akerlind; Sound, Mark Bennett; Fights, David Leong; Dialects, Deborah Hecht; Stage Manager, Thom Widmann CAST: Rob Campbell (Securitate/Angel/Patient/Toma/Ghost/Waiter/Boy), Randy Danson (Irina/Grandmother/Flower Seller), Garret Dillahunt (Ianos/Painter), Lanny Flaherty (Bogdan/Soldier/ Translator), Calista Flockhart (Lucia/Student/Doctor), Mary Mara (Florina/Girl), Christopher McCann (Mihai/Dog/Bulldozer Driver/Wayne), Tim Blake Nelson (Gabriel/Boy), Mary Shultz (Flavia/Painter/Grand-mother/Rodica), Rocco Sisto (Vampire/Grandfather/Soldier/Priest/Securitate/SoreThroat Man/Old Aunt), Jake Weber (Radu/Soldier)
A three-act drama set against the 1989 Romanian uprising. The New York Theatre Workshop production from last season is revived.

(Stage II) Tuesday, Oct.27-Dec.20, 1992 (72 performances)
JOINED AT THE HEAD by Catherine Butterfield; Director, Pamela Berlin; Set, James Noone; Costumes, Alvin B. Perry; Lighting, Natasha Katz; Sound, John Kilgore; Stage Manager, Karen Moore CAST: Ellen Parker (Maggie Mulroney), Neal Huff (College Boy/Bill/others), Michael Wells (College Boy/Salesman/others), Sharon Washington (Political Woman/Doctor/others), Elizabeth Perry (Political Woman/Nora/others), John C. Vennema (Engaged Man/Raymond Terwilliger/others), Becca Lish (Engaged Woman/Coat Check/others), Kevin O'Rourke (Jim Burroughs), Catherine Butterfield (Maggy Burroughs)
A play in two acts set in and around Boston.

(Stage I) Monday, Dec.21, 1992-Feb.14, 1993 (64 performances)
THE YEARS by Cindy Lou Johnson; Director, Jack Hofsiss; Sets, Loren Sherman; Costumes, Lindsay W. Davis; Lighting, Peter Kaczorowski; Sound, John Kilgore; Fights, Jerry Mitchell; Stage Manager, Thomas A. Kelly CAST: Ron Eldard succeeded

Kevin Spacey, Frankie Faison in "Playland"

Garret Dillahunt, Tim Blake Nelson, Jake Weber in
"Mad Forest"

Steven Collins, Christopher Durang, Julie Andrews, Rachael York,
Michel Ruppert in "Putting It Together"

by Paul McCrane (Bartholomew), Rebecca Miller succeeded by Ashley Crow, Nancy Hower (Andrea), Marcia Gay Harden (Isabella), Frank Whaley (Andrew), Julie Hagerty (Eloise), William Fichtner (Jeffrey)

A two-act drama spanning sixteen years.
(Stage II) Tuesday, Jan.5-Feb.28, 1993 (64 performances)
THE LAST YANKEE by Arthur Miller; Director, John Tillinger; Set, John Lee Beatty; Costumes, Jane Greenwood; Lighting, Dennis Parichy; Sound, Scott Lehrer; Stage Manager, Diane DiVita CAST: John Heard (Leroy Hamilton), Tom Aldredge (John Frick), Charlotte Maier (Patient), Frances Conroy (Patricia Hamilton), Rose Gregorio (Karen Frick)

A drama performed without intermission. The action takes place in a state mental hospital. An earlier version was seen at Ensemble Studio Theatre last season.

(Stage I) Tuesday, Mar.2-May 23, 1993 (96 performances)
PUTTING IT TOGETHER with Music/Lyrics by Stephen Sondheim; Devised by Mr. Sondheim and Julia McKenzie; Direction, Ms. McKenzie; Musical Staging, Bob Avian; Arrangements, Chris Walker; Musical Director, Scott Frankel; Set, Robin Wagner; Costumes, Theoni V. Aldredge; Lighting, Tharon Musser; Sound, Scott Lehrer; Stage Manager, Franklin Keysar; Presented by arrangement with Cameron Mackintosh; Cast Recording, RCA CAST: Julie Andrews, Stephen Collins, Christopher Durang, Michael Rupert succeeded by Patrick Quinn, Rachel York
MUSICAL NUMBERS: Invocations and Instructions, Putting It Together, Rich and Happy, Merrily We Roll Along, Lovely, Everybody Ought to Have a Maid, Sooner or Later, I'm Calm, Impossible, Ah But Underneath, Hello Little Girl, My Husband the Pig/Every Day a Little Death, Have I Got a Girl for You, Pretty Woman, Now, Bang!, Country House, Could I Leave You?, Entr'acte/Back in Business, Night Waltzes, Gun Song, Miller's Son, Live Alone and Like It, Sorry-Grateful, Sweet Polly Plunkett, I Could Drive a Person Crazy, Marry Me a Little, Getting Married Today, Being Alive, Like It Was, Old Friends

A party is the setting for this two act revue of Sondheim songs

(Stage II) Two plays in repertory (60 performances together)
Monday, Mar.23-May2, 1993
JENNY KEEPS TALKING by Richard Greenberg; Director, Risa Bramon Garcia; Set, Shelly Barclay; Costumes, Rita Ryack; Lighting, Brian Nason; Sound, Bruce Ellman; Stage Manager, Buzz Cohen CAST: Leslie Ayvazian (Jenny/Claudia/Grandmother)

Two estranged sisters turn to their eccentric grandmother.
Friday, Mar.26-Apr.29, 1993
PRETTY FIRE; Written and Performed by Charlayne Woodard; Director, Pamela Berlin; Other Credits same as above except for Stage Manager, Allison Sommers
Five autobiographical stories (Birth, Nigger, Pretty Fire, Bonesy, Joy) in two acts.

(Stage II) Tuesday, May 18-June 27, 1993 (48 performances)
PLAYLAND; Written/Directed by Athol Fugard; Sets/Costumes, Susan Hilferty; Lighting, Dennis Parichy; Sound, David Budries; Stage Manager, Sandra Lea Williams
CAST: Frankie R. Faison (Martinus Zoeloe), Kevin Spacey (Gideon Le Roux), Bill Flynn (Barking Barney Voice)
A drama performed without intermission. The action takes place in a South African amusement park on New Year's Eve, 1989.

Gerry Goodstein, Joan Marcus Photos

Left: Charlayne Woodard in "Pretty Fire"
Right: Leslie Ayvazian in "Jenny Keeps Talking"

NEW YORK SHAKESPEARE FESTIVAL

Artistic Director, JoAnne Akalaitis; Producing Director, Jason Steven Cohen; Associate Artistic Director, Rosemary Tichler; General Manager, Sally Campbell Morse; Development Director, Christine S. Peck; Literary Consultant, Gail Merrifield; Literary Manager, Jason Fogelson; Production Manager, Andrew Mihok; Press, Bruce Campbell/Barbara Carroll, James Morrison

(Delacorte/Central Park) Thursday, July 2-26, 1992 (16 performances and 6 previews) **AS YOU LIKE IT** by William Shakespeare; Director, Adrian Hall; Sets, Eugene Lee; Costumes, Melinda Root; Lighting, Natasha Katz; Music, Richard Cumming CAST: Larry Bryggman (Duke Frederick), Stan Cahill (Jacques de Boys), Rob Campbell (Silvius), Viola Davis (Denise), Siobhan Fallon (Phebe), Peter Jay Fernandez (Oliver), Richard Libertini (Jaques), Boris McGiver (Mar-Text), Elizabeth McGovern (Rosalind), Kathryn Meisle (Celia), Donald Moffat (Touchstone), George Morfogen (Duke Senior), Kristine Nielson (Audrey), John Scanlan (Adam), Jim Shanklin (Lord to Senior), Jere Shea (Amiens), Mark Kenneth Smaltz (Charles), Trellis Stepter Jr (Lord to Frederick), Michael Stuhlbarg (William/Lord to Senior), Brad Sullivan (Corin), Gregory Wallace (Le Beau), Jake Weber (Orlando), Nancy Hower
    The action takes place in Oliver's House, at Court, and in the Forest of Arden. Production #20 in the NYSF Shakespeare marathon.

(Delacorte/Central Park) Thursday, Aug.6-30, 1992 (13 performances and 9 previews) **THE COMEDY OF ERRORS** by William Shakespeare; Director, Caca Rosset; Sets/Costumes, Jose de Anchieta Costa; Lighting, Peter Kaczorowski; Music, Mark Bennett; Movement, David Leong; Special Participation, Antigravity; Stage Manager, Pat Sosnow CAST: Simon Billig (Officer), Larry Block (Angelo), Karla Burns (Nell), Helmar Augustus Cooper (Duke Solinus), Elizabeth Franz (Abbess), Boyd Gaines (Antipholus of Syracuse), Stephen Hanan (Pinch), John Michael Higgins (Antipholus of Ephesus), Peter Jacobson (Dromio of Syracuse), Kati Kuroda (Courtesan), Kathleen McNenny (Luciana), Joseph Palmas (Merchant), Frank Raiter (Aegeon), Howard Samuelsohn (Dromio of Ephesus), Marisa Tomei (Adriana), Michael Ambrozy, Andrea Arden, Robert David Carroll, Christopher Harrison, Lauren Monte, Andrew Pacho, Paul Christopher Simon, Andrea Weber
    Shakespeare's 1594 comedy performed in two acts. Production #21 in the NYSF Shakespeare marathon.

(Public/Martinson Hall) Tuesday, Sept.29-Nov.1, 1992 (25 performances and 15 previews)
YOU COULD BE HOME NOW; Written and Performed by Ann Magnuson; Director, David Schweizer; Music, Tom Judson; Choreography, Jerry Mitchell; Set, Bill Clarke; Lighting, Heather Carson; Costumes, Pilar Limosner; Sound, Eric Liljestrand; Supervisor, Bill Barnes
    Performance art on the importance of "home". A co-production with Women's Project & Productions.

(Public)Thursday, Oct.8, 1992 and continuing through season
PUBLIC FRINGE/NO SHAME; Late night performance series featuring Frank Maya, Emmet Foster, Stephen Patterson, Late Bloomers, Chris Glenn, Scott Blakeman, Twin Fish, David Cale,Mental Furniture, Dead Clown Circus, Zel Rebels, Poster Boys, Stanley Allen Sherman, Washboard Jungle, Tom Cayler, Patricia Scanlon, and others.

(Public/Shiva Theater) Tuesday, Oct.20-Nov.22, 1992 (25 performances and 15 previews)
TEXTS FOR NOTHING by Samuel Beckett; Adaptation, Joseph Chaikin and Steven Kent; Director, Mr. Chaikin; Set, Christine Jones; Costumes, Mary Brecht; Lighting, Beverly Emmons; Sound, Gene Ricciardi; Stage Manager, Ruth Kreshka CAST: Bill Irwin
Adaptation of Beckett's 1955 *Texts for Nothing* and 1961's *How It Is* . Produced in 1981 by NYSF under the title Texts .

Top Right: Jake Weber, Kathryn Meisle, Elizabeth McGovern in "As You Like It"
Below: Boyd Gaines, Peter Jacobson, Kathleen McNenny, Marisa Tomei in "Comedy of Errors"
Bottom: Bill Irwin in "Texts for Nothing"
Above: Ann Magnuson in "You Could Be Home Now"

(Public/Newman Theater) Monday, Nov.23, 1992-Jan.3, 1993 (32 performances and 15 previews)
WOYZECK by Georg Buchner; Translation, Henry J. Schmidt; Director, JoAnne Akalaitis; Set, Marina Draghici; Costumes, Gabriel Berry; Lighting, Mimi Jordan Sherin; Sound, John Gromada; Music, Philip Glass; Lyrics, Paul Schmidt; Fights, David Leong; Stage Manager, Mireya Hepner CAST: Jesse Borrego (Woyzeck), Bruce Beatty (Andres), David E. Cantler (Christian), Robert Cicchini (Apprentice/Carnival Worker), Michael Early (Sergeant), Zach Grenier (Captain), Anita Hollander (Margaret), Ashley MacIsaac (Musician), Ruth Maleczech (Grandmother), Camryn Manheim (Carnival Worker), Pauline E. Meyer (Friend), Lou Milione (Drum Major), Denis O'Hare (Doctor/Soldier), Imani Parks (Girl), Richard Spore (Karl/ Carnival Showman), Michael Stuhlbarg (Barker/Soldier/Apprentice), Sheila Tousey (Marie), Louis Tucci (Musician/Soldier), LaTonya Borsay, Lynn Hawley (Townspeople)
  A drama, written in 1836-37, performed without intermission.

(Public/Martinson Hall) Tuesday, Feb.3-Mar.14, 1993 (31 performances and 15 previews)
ON THE OPEN ROAD by Steve Tesich; Director, Robert Falls; Set, Donald Eastman; Costumes, Gabriel Berry; Lighting, Kenneth Posner; Sound, John Gromada; Stage Manager, Peggy Imbrie CAST: Anthony LaPaglia (Angel), Byron Jennings (Al), Ilana Seagull (Little Girl), Henry Stram (Monk), Andy Taylor (Jesus)
  A two-act drama set during a Civil War.

(Public/Newman Theater) Tuesday, Feb.23-Apr.18, 1993 (47 performances and 16 previews)
WINGS with Music by Jeffrey Lunden; Lyrics/Book, Arthur Perlman; Based on Arthur Kopit's play; Director, Michael Maggio; Musical Director, Bradley Vieth Set/Projections, Linda Buchanan; Costumes, Birgit Rattenborg Wise; Lighting, Robert Christen; Sound, Richard Woodbury; Stage Manager, Deya S. Friedman CAST: Linda Stephens, Rita Gardner (Emily), William Brown (Doctor/Mr. Brambilla), Ora Jones (Nurse/Mrs. Timmins), Hollis Resnik (Amy), Ross Lehman (Billy)
  A musical drama performed without intermission.

(Public/Shiva Theater) Thursday Apr.1-25, 1993 (18 performances and 3 previews)
DEEP IN A DREAM OF YOU; Written and Performed by David Cale; Music, Roy Nathanson; Director, David Petrarca; Design, Linda Buchanan; Sound, Rob Milburn; Stage Manager, Liz Dreyer
  Twelve monologues on erotic obsession.

(Public/LuEsther Hall) Tuesday, Apr.6-May 2, 1993 (28 performances)
SECONDS OUT by Aidan Barry, Noel O'Keeffe, Josie Buckley, Noel O'Driscoll, Kieran Wiseman, Trevor O'Herlihy, Denis Butler, and William Martin; Director, Jack Hofsiss; Set, David Jenkins; Lighting, Beverly Emmons; Costumes, Julie Weiss; Choreography, Jerry Mitchell; Stage Manager, Thomas A. Kelly CAST: Brian F. O'Byrne (James Hennessy), Des Keogh (Governor/O'Riordan), Colin Lane (O'Mahoney/Christy), Sean Michael McCarthy (Flynn/Kevin), Chris O'Neill (Warden/Doctor/Father), Paul Ronan (Warden/Costello), Terry Donnelly (Debbie/Mother)
  A prison drama by eight Irish teenagers.
and **MY OEDIPUS COMPLEX** by Frank O'Connor; Performed by Chris O'Neill
  A curtain raiser.

(Public/Martinson Hall) Tuesday, May 4-June 6, 1993 (22 performances and 18 previews)
MARISOL by Jose Rivera; Director, Michael Greif; Set, Debra Booth; Costumes, Angela Wendt; Lighting, Kenneth Posner; Violence Director, David Leong; Sound, David Budries; Music, Jill Jaffe; Stage Manager, Lori M. Doyle CAST: Danitra Vance (Angel), Cordelia Gonzalez (Marisol), Doris Difarnecio (Young Woman), Skipp Sudduth (Golf Club Man/Ice Cream Man/Lenny/Scar Tiisue Man), Anne O'Sullivan (June), Phyllis Somerville (Woman with Furs/Announcer), Decater James, Robert Jiminez, Ms. Difarnecio, Ms. O' Sullivan, Ms. Somerville (Homeless), Chris Cunningham (Guitarist)
  An apocalyptic urban fantasy in two acts. The setting is a New York City winter.

Martha Swope, Paula Court, Liz Lauren, Eric Y. Exit Photos

Top:Byron Jennings, Anthony LaPaglia in "On the Open Road"
Below: William Brown, Ross Lehman, Hollis Resnik, Ora Jones, Linda Stephens in "Wings"

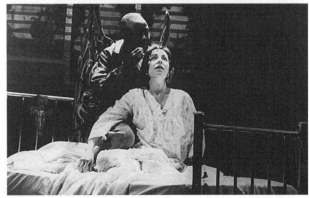

Bottom: Danitra Vance, Cordelia Gonzalez in "Marisol"
Above: Brian F. O'Byrne in "Seconds Out"

NEW YORK THEATRE WORKSHOP

Artistic Director, James C. Nicola; Managing Director, Nancy Kassak Diekmann Associate Artistic Director, Christopher Grabowski; General Manager, Esther Cohen Development Director, Glen Knapp; Press, Richard Kornberg

(New home at former Truck and Warehouse Theatre) Friday, Oct.9-Nov.8, 1992 (33 performances)
C. COLOMBO INC., EXPORT/IMPORT, GENOA by Leo Bassi; Director Christopher Grabowski; Set/Costumes/Lighting, Anita Stewart; Sound, Mark Bennett; Stage Manager, Liz Small CAST: Leo Bassi, Steve Elm, Edwin Newman
Performed without intermission. A businessman becomes obsessed with building a monument to Columbus.

Friday, Mar.5-May 23, 1993 (Owners) (38 performances) and (Traps) Friday, Mar.12-May 23, 1993 (37 performances)
OWNERS and TRAPS by Caryl Churchill; Sets, Derek McLane; Costumes, Gabriel Berry; Lighting, Christopher Akerlind; Sound, John Gromada; Fights, David Leong; Dialects, Elizabeth Smith; Stage Manager, Thom Widman
OWNERS; Director, Mark Wing-Davey CAST: John Curless (Clegg), Robert Stanton (Worsely), J. Smith-Cameron (Marion), Lynn Hawley (Lisa), Tim Hopper (Alec), Irma St. Paule (Alec's Mother/Customer), Melinda Mullins (Mrs. Arlington/Customer)
    A 1972 drama set in a developing bit of North London.

TRAPS; Director, Lisa Peterson CAST: Melinda Mullins (Syl), David Alford (Jack), John Curless (Albert), Robert Stanton (Reg), Tim Hopper (Del), J. Smith-Cameron (Christie)
    A 1977 drama set in a squat in England, 1976.

Martha Swope Photos

Left: Leo Bassi in "C. Colombo Inc."
Bottom Left: J. Smith-Cameron, John Curless in "Owners"
Bottom Right: J. Smith-Cameron, Robert Stanton in "Traps"

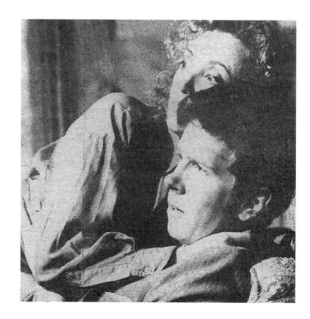

PEARL THEATRE COMPANY

Ninth Season

Artistic Director, Shepard Sobel; General Manager, Parris Relkin; Development Director, Larry Auld; Artistic Associate, Joanne Camp; Resident Set Designer, Robert Joel Schwartz; Resident Sound Designer, Donna Riley; Resident Company: Robin Leslie Brown, Arnie Burton, Joanne Camp, Frank Geraci, Anna Minot; Interns: Belynda Fay Hardin, Christopher Raymond; Press, Chris Boneau/Adrian Bryan-Brown/Bob Fennell

Wednesday, Sept.9-Oct.24, 1992 (47 performances)
A MOON FOR THE MISBEGOTTEN by Eugene O'Neill; Director, Allan Carlsen; Lighting, A.C. Hickox; Costumes, Lyn Carroll; Fights, Rick Sordelet CAST: Joanne Camp (Josie Hogan), Hank Wagner (Mike Hogan), Frank Lowe (Phil Hogan), Paul O'Brien (James Tyrone, Jr.), Arnie Burton (T. Stedman Harder).
   O'Neill's last play, written in 1943, in three acts.

Friday, Oct.30-Dec.19, 1992 (58 performances)
OTHELLO by William Shakespeare; Director, Clinton Turner Davis; Costumes, Chelsea Harriman; Lighting, David Castaneda CAST: Raphael Nash (Othello), Arnie Burton (Iago), Celeste Ciulla (Desdemona), Rose Stockton (Emilia), Belynda Fay Hardin (Bianca), Kurt Rhoads (Cassio), K. Bruce Harpster (Roderigo), Frank Lowe (Brabantio/Lodovico), Richard Bourg (Duke/Gratiano), Chris Raymond (Messenger/Gentleman), David S. Mills (Officer/Sailor/Montano), Doug Ladendorf (Senator/Gentleman), Barry Cassidy (Herald/Senator/Gentleman)
Performed in two acts. The action takes place in Venice and Cyprus.

Saturday, Dec.26, 1992-Feb.6, 1993 (47 performances)
THE GOOD NATUR'D MAN by Oliver Goldsmith; Director, Anthony Cornish; Costumes, Deborah Rooney; Lighting, Laura Perlman; Stage Manager, Joe Kops CAST: Frank Loew (Sir William Honeywood), Frank Geraci (Jarvis/Timothy Twitch),Kurt Rhoads (Mr. Honeywood), Anthony Lawton (Philip/ M. Dubardieu/Flanigan/Solomon), Robert Hock (Nicholas Croaker), Robin Leslie Brown (Miss Richland), Bella Jarrett (Mrs. Croaker), Sean Pratt (Leontine Croaker), Celeste Ciulla (Olivia), Belynda Fay Hardin (Mrs. Garnet), Jeff Woodman (Jack Lofty), Anna Minot (Landlady)
   A 1768 comedy set in suburban London.

Friday, Feb.12-Mar.20, 1993 (28 performances and 11 previews)
PHAEDRA by Jean Racine; Translation, Margaret Rawlings; Director, Shepard Sobel; Lighting, Thomas C. Hase; Costumes, Julie Abels Chevan; Stage Manager, Liz Dreyer CAST: Sean Pratt (Hippolytus), Robert Hock (Theramenes), Bella Jarrett (Oenone), Joanne Camp (Phaedra), Belynda Hardin (Panope), Celeste Ciulla (Aricia), Sheri Galan (Ismene), Seth Jones (Theseus)
   A 1667 drama, in a new translation, performed without intermission.

Friday, Mar.26-May 9, 1993 (51 performances)
WIDOWERS' HOUSES by Bernard Shaw; Director, Grey Johnson; Lighting, A.C. Hickox; Costumes, Chelsea Harriman; Sound, Jim van Bergen; Stage Manager, Mary-Susan Gregson CAST: Seth Jones (William de Burgh Cokane),Sean Pratt (Dr. Harry Trench), Ben Roberts (Waiter), Paul O'Brien (Sartorius), Edmund Wilkinson (Porter), Julie DePaul (Blanche Sartorius), Edward Seamon (Lickcheese), Belynda Hardin (Parlormaid)
   This 1892 comedy was Shaw's first produced play.

Carol Rosegg/Martha Swope Photos

Bella Jarrett, Joanne Camp, Sean Pratt in "Phaedra"
Center: Sean Pratt, Julie DePaul in "Widowers' Houses"
Top Left: Frank Geraci, Robin Leslie Brown, Belynda Fay Hardin in
"Good Natur'd Man"
Top Right: Arnie Burton, Raphael Nash, Celeste Ciulla in "Othello"

PLAYWRIGHTS HORIZONS

Twenty-second Season

Artistic Director, Don Scardino; Executive Director, Paul S. Daniels; Associate Artistic Director, Nicholas Martin; Production Manager, David A Milligan; Development Director, Lesley J. Kranz; Literary Manager, Tim Sanford; Press, Philip Rinaldi

Tuesday, June 9-July 19, 1992 (52 performances)
FLAUBERT'S LATEST by Peter Parnell; Director, David Saint; Set, James Noone; Costumes, Jane Greenwood; Lighting, Kenneth Posner; Music/Sound, John Gromada; Choreography, Paul Lester; Fights, Rick Sordelet; Stage Manager, William Joseph Barnes CAST: Mark Nelson (Felix), Mitchell Anderson (Colin), Sam Stoneburner (Howard), Mary Louise Wilson (Ursula), Leila Fazel (Kuchuk Hanem), John Bedford Lloyd (Gustave), Jean DeBaer (Louise), Gil Belows (Jace)
     A two-act comedy about a writer torn between his current love and his current project. The action takes place in a Connecticut country house.

Tuesday, Sept.15-Oct.11, 1992 (30 performances)
THE 1992 YOUNG PLAYWRIGHTS FESTIVAL; Artistic Director, Nancy Quinn; Managing Director, Sheri M. Goldhirsch; Sets, Loy Arcenas; Costumes, Elsa Ward; Lighting, Pat Dignan; Sound, Janet Kalas; Stage Managers, Jana Llynn, Paul J. Smith; Selection Committee, Christopher Durang, Ruth Goetz, Carol Hall, Murray Horwitz, David Henry Hwang, Marsha Norman, Nancy Quinn, Mary Rodgers, Don Scardino, Stephen Sondheim, Alfred Uhry, Wendy Wasserstein, John Weidman, George C. Wolfe

THE P.C. LAUNDROMAT by Aurorae Khoo; Director, Richard Caliban CAST: Peter Jay Fernandez (#1), Christina Moore (#2), Erika Honda (#3), Olga Merediz (#4)
     A political poem set to the rhythm of washers and dryers.
TAKING CONTROL by Terrance Jenkins; Director, Clinton Turner Davis CAST: Peter Jay Fernandez (Joe), Elain Graham (Mom), Novella Nelson (Nana), Afi McClendon (Nikki), Felicia Wilson (Kelly), Bahni Turpin (Tarae), Seth Gilliam (Tom)
     A sixteen year old attemps to survive her dysfunctional family.
MOTHERS HAVE NINE LIVES by Joanna Norland; Director, Gloria Muzio CAST: Erika Honda (Kelly), Danielle Ferland (Christie), Jennie Moreau (Louise/Wendy/Mia), Kim Yancy (Gina/Katherine/Marge), Olga Merediz (Margaret/Kim/Anna)
     An unusual look at mother-daughter relationships.
MRS. NEUBERGER'S DEAD by Robert Levy; Director, Michael Mayer CAST: Neal Huff (Jim), Margaret Welsh (Marah), Felicia Wilson (Jackie), Seth Gilliam (Aaron)
A young couple fights addiction, poverty, and each other.
The eleventh annual Young Playwrights Festival.

Campbell Scott, Cynthia Nixon in "On the Bum"
Top: Gil Bellows, Mitchell Anderson, Mark Nelson in "Flaubert's Latest"

118

Friday, Oct.30-Dec.13, 1992 (52 performances)
ON THE BUM or *The Next Train Through* by Neal Bell; Director, Don Scardino; Set, Allen Moyer; Costumes, Sharon Lynch; Lighting, Kenneth Posner; Sound, John Gromada; Stage Manager, Dianne Trulock CAST: Bill Buell (Stagehand/Elmo/Out-of-Work Man/Fisherman/Bumfork Tramp/ Spectacle Inspector), William Duell (Western Union/Winston),Jim Fyfe(Archie/Gresham/Cop/Out-of-Work Man/Fisherman/Bumfork Tramp), Kevin Geer (Tramp/Harry), John Benjamin Hickey (Oskar), Robert Hogan (Burly/Victor), Cynthia Nixon (Eleanor Ames), James Rebhorn (Tramp/Gil), Joyce Reehling (Lila/Jessie), Ross Salinger (Tramp/Out-of-Work Man/Fisherman/Bumfork Tramp/Headless Ghost/Hansford), Campbell Scott (Farker/Frank), Maureen Shay (Maud/Lula), J.Smith-Cameron (Norma).

A comedy in two acts. The action takes place in New York and Bumfork in the Midwest, 1938.

Wednesday, Dec.9-20, 1992 (14 performances)
MAN IN HIS UNDERWEAR by Jay Tarses; Director, Kevin Dowling; Set, Rob Odorisio; Costumes, Therese A. Bruck; Lighting, Michael Lincoln; Sound, Jeremy Grody; Stage Manager, Liz Small CAST: Debra Monk (Jan Kirkland), Dann Florek (Al Kirkland), Cordelia Richards (Lana Kirkland), Robert Joy (Larry Plays-with-Antelopes), Jennifer Van Dyck (Gracie Shannon), Cynthia Vance (Myra Kirkland), Dick Latessa (Daniel Shannon)

A comedy in two acts. The action takes place in Baltimore over a year's period.

Friday, Feb.5-Mar.21, 1993 (52 performances)
THE HELIOTROPE BOUQUET BY SCOTT JOPLIN & LOUIS CHAUVIN by Eric Overmyer; Based on Overmyer libretto from idea of Roger Trefousse; Director, Joe Morton; Choreography, Louis Johnson; Set, Richard Hoover; Costumes, Judy Dearing; Lighting, Phil Monat; Sound, Bruce Odland; Arrangements, Terry Waldo; Stage Manager, Lloyd Davis, Jr. CAST: Delroy Lindo (Joplin), Donna Biscoe (Lotte/Belle), Tonye Patano (Hannah), Amber Kain (Spice), Lisa Arrindell (Joy), Kim Yancey (Felicity), Ramon Moses (Disappearing Sam), Mike Hodge (Turpin), Steve Harris (Keeler), Duane Boutte (Chauvin), Herb Foster (Stark)

A play with ragtime music performed without intermission. The action takes place in Harlem, St. Louis, and Chicago, 1905-17.

Wednesday, Mar.17-28, 1993 (14 performances)
SOPHISTRY by Jonathan Marc Sherman; Director, Nicholas Martin; Set, Allen Moyer; Costumes, Michael Krass; Lighting, Kenneth Posner; Sound, Jeremy Grody; Stage Manager, Christopher Wigle CAST: Dick Latessa (Whitey McCoy), Steve Zahn (Willy), Jonathan Marc Sherman (Igor Konigsberg), Linda Atkinson (Quintana Matheson), Ethan Hawke (Xavier Ex Reynolds), Katherine Hiler (Robin Smith), Anthony Rapp (Jack Kahn), Nadia Dajani (Debbie), Scarlett Johannson (Child)

A new two-act play about the search for truth. The action takes place on the campus of a small New England college, 1990-91.

Friday, Apr.30-July 11, 1993 (84 performances) transferred to Westside Theatre on Aug.9, 1993
LATER LIFE by A.R. Gurney; Director, Don Scardino; Set, Ben Edwards; Costumes, Jennifer Von Mayrhauser; Lighting, Brian MacDevitt; Sound, Guy Sherman/Aural Fixation; Hairstylist/Wigs, Daniel Platten; Stage Manager, Dianne Trulock CAST: Maureen Anderman (Ruth), Charles Kimbrough succeeded by Edmond Genest (Austin), Carole Shelley (Other Women), Anthony Heald (Other Men)

Performed without intermission. The setting is a high-rise terrace overlooking Boston.

Joan Marcus, Gerry Goodstein, Martha Swope

T. Charles Erickson Photos

Top Right:Jonathan Marc Sherman, Ethan Hawke, Stephen Zahn in "Sophistry"
Center: Donna Biscoe, Delroy Lindo in "The Heliotrope Bouquet..."
Bottom: Charles Kimbrough, Carole Shelley, Maureen Anderman in "Later Life"

WPA THEATRE

Artistic Director, Kyle Renick; Managing Director, Donna Lieberman, Lori Sherman; Press, Jeffrey Richards/Tom D'Ambrosio, David LeShay

Thursday, Oct.20-Nov.22, 1992 (40 performances)
CAMP PARADOX by Barbara Graham; Director, Melia Bensussen; Set, Edward T. Gianfrancesco; Lighting, Craig Evans; Costumes, Mimi Maxmen; Sound, Guy Sherman/Aural Fixation; Hairstylist, Bobby H. Grayson; Stage Manager, John Frederick Sullivan CAST: Meredith Scott Lynn (Cory), Alix Korey (Edith), Emily Schulman (C.J.), Danielle Ferland (Renee), Russell Koplin (Iris), Christina Haag (Donna), Liann Pattison (Carla)

A play in two acts set at an Upstate New York summer camp, 1963.

Thursday, Dec.31, 1992-Feb.14, 1993 (47 performances) transferred to Minetta Lane Theatre Mar.6, 1993
JEFFREY by Paul Rudnick; Director, Christopher Ashley; Sets, James Youmans; Lighting, Donald Holder; Costumes, David C. Woolard; Sound, Donna Riley; Musical Staging, Jerry Mitchell; Stage Manager, John Frederick Sullivan CAST: John Michael Higgins (Jeffrey), Tom Hewitt (Steve/Man #6 in Bed), Patrick Kerr (Man #1 in Bed/Gym Rat/ Skip Winkly/ Casting Director/Headdress Waiter/Man #2 with Debra/Jock-strap Man/Thug #2/Dave/Angelique), Darryl Theirse (Man #2 in Bed/Gym Rat/Salesman/Boss/Man #1 with Debra/Chaps man/Thug#1/ Young Priest/Sean), Richard Poe (Man #3 in Bed/Gym Rat/Don/Tim/Dad/ Fr. Dan/ Chuck Farling), Bryan Batt (Darius/Man#4 in Bed), Edward Hibbert succeeded by Peter Bartlett (Sterling/Man#6 in Bed), Harriet Harris (Woman in Bed/Showgirl/Ann Marwood Bartle/Debra Moorhouse/Sharon /Mom/Mrs. Marcangelo)

A two-act comic odyssey through New York City gay life today.

Thursday, Mar.18-Apr.18, 1993 (33 performances)
LAUREEN'S WHEREABOUTS by Larry Ketron; Director, Dann Florek; Set, Edward T. Gianfrancesco; Lighting, Phil Monat; Costumes, Jonathan Green; Sound, Guy Sherman/Aural Fixation; Stage Manager, Liz Small CAST: Kevin O'Rourke (Joe), Mark Blum (Tom), Carolyn McCormick (Sharon), Mia Dillon (Laureen), Scott Sowers (Whitlock)

A drama in two acts. The setting is a South Carolina haunted house.

Tuesday, May 25-June 27, 1993 (35 performances)
TEN BELOW by Shem Bitterman; Director, Stephen Zuckerman; Set, Edward T. Gianfrancesco; Lighting, Richard Winkler; Costumes, Mimi Maxmen; Sound, Guy Sherman/Aural Fixation; Stage Manager, Karen Moore CAST: Anthony Edwards (Homer Beacon), Kevin Conway (The Kid)

A two-act drama set in a Harlem apartment on a January night.

Martha Swope/Carol Rosegg, William Gibson Photos

Mark Blum, Kevin O Rourke, Mia Dillon, Carolyn McCormick in "Lauren's Whereabouts"
Top: Emily Schulman, Russel Koplin, Christina Haag, Danielle Ferland, Meredith Scott Lynn in "Camp Paradox"

John Michael Higgins, Tom Hewitt, Harriet Harris, PatrickKerr, Darryl Theirse in "Jeffrey"

YORK THEATRE COMPANY

Twenty-fourth Season

Producing Director, Janet Hayes Walker; Managing Director, Molly Pickering Grose; Artistic Advisors, John Newton, James Morgan; Assistant Director, Terry Gibson; Scenic Designs, James Morgan; Lighting Designs, Mary Jo Dondlinger; Fights, Dale Girard; Press, Keith Sherman/Chris Day/Jim Byk

(York Theatre) Friday, Oct.2-25, 1992
SIX WIVES with Music by Edward Thomas; Lyrics/Book, Joe Masteroff; Direction/Choreography, Maggie L. Harrer; Musical Director, Norman Weiss; Costumes, Barbara Beccio; Lighting, Fred Hancock; Stage Manager, John Kennelly CAST: Steve Barton (Henry), Kim Crosby (Anne Boleyn/Kathryn Howard/Jane Seymour), Buddy Crutchfield (Messenger/others), Tovah Feldshuh (Katherine of Aragon/Anne of Cleves/Catherine Parr), Rex D. Hays (Minister)

A chamber musical performed without intermission.

(St. Peter's) Tuesday, Nov.24-Dec.20, 1993 (28 performances)
NOEL AND GERTIE; Devised by Sheridan Morley; Director, Brian Murray; Musical Director, Michael Kosarin; Costumes, Barbara Beccio; Choreography, Janet Watson; Stage Manager, John Kennelly CAST: Michael Zaslow (Noel Coward), Jane Summerhays (Gertrude Lawrence)
An entertainment celebrating the work of Coward and Lawrence.

(York Theatre) Friday, Jan.15-Feb.7, 1993
A DISTANCE FROM CALCUTTA; Written/Directed by P.J. Barry; Costumes, Barbara Beccio; Stage Manager, Cathleen Wolfe CAST: Beth Dixon (Maggie Conroy), Sally Parrish (Mama), Julie Boyd (Ann Donovan), Connor Smith (John Conroy), Daniel Hagen (Buddy McCormack).
A drama in two acts set in a Rhode Island village, 1923-24.

(St. Peter's) Tuesday, Mar.9, 1993 (1 performance only)
A MUSICAL ROLLER COASTER RIDE with Russel Nype
One-man retrospective of Nype's life and career.

(St. Peter's) Wednesday, Mar.31-May 2, 1993 (34 performances)
CARNIVAL with Music/Lyrics by Bob Merrill; Book, Michael Stewart; Based on material by Helen Deutsch; Direction/Choreography, Pamela Hunt; Musical Director, Darren R. Cohen; Costumes/Puppets, Michael Bottari, Ronald Case; Stage Manager, Joseph V. De Michele CAST: David Arthur (Grobert/Dr. William Glass), Robert Michael Baker (Paul Berthalet), Glory Crampton (Lili), Susan Guinn (Irin), William Linton (B.F. Schlegel), Robert Lydiard (Jacquot), Karen Mason (The Incomparable Rosalie), Paul Schoeffler (Marco the Magnificent), Bruce Anthony Davis, Teri Furr, Sandra Purpuro, Rusty Reynolds (Roustabouts)
MUSICAL NUMBERS: Direct from Vienna, A Very Nice Man, Fairyland, I've Got to Find a Reason, Mira, Sword and a Rose and a Cape, Humming, Yes My Heart, Everybody Likes You, Magic Magic, Carnival Ballet, Love Makes the World Go Round, Yum Tickey, We're Rich, Her Face, Grand Imperial Cirque de Paris, I Hate Him, Always Always You, She's My Love
The 1961 musical in two acts.

Martha Swope/Carol Rosegg, Blanche Mackey Photos

Top: Steve Barton, Tovah Feldshuh in "Six Wives"
Below: Michael Zaslow, Jane Summerhays in "Noel and Gertie"
Bottom: Glory Crampton in "Carnival"
Above: Connor Smith, Julie Boyd
in "Carnival"

ACTORS THEATRE OF LOUISVILLE

Louisville, Kentucky

Twenty-ninth Season

Producing Director, Jon Jory; Executive Director, Alexander Speer; Associate Director, Marilee Hebert-Slater; Production Manager, Frazier W. Marsh; Development Director, J. Christopher Wineman; Public Relations Director, James Seacat
RESIDENT COMPANY: Bob Burrus, Mark Sawyer-Dailey, Ray Fry, V. Craig Heidenreich, Michael Kebin, Fred Major, William McNulty, Adale O'Brien

PRODUCTIONS & CASTS

THE BEAUX STRATAGEM by George Farquhar; Director, Jon Jory; Sets, Virginia Dancy, Elmon Webb; Lighting, Karl E. Haas; Costumes, Laura A. Patterson CAST: Michael Kevin (Boniface/Bellair), Barbara Gulan (Cherry/Country Woman), Keith Hamilton Cobb (Thomas Aimwell), V. Craig Heidenreich (Franci Archer), Peggity Price (Mrs. Sullen), Holley Stewart (Dorinda), Fred Major (Mr. Sullen), Alan Pottinger (Scrub), Bob Burrus (Gibbet), Adele O'Brien (Lady Bountiful), Josh Hopkins (Hounslow), Joshua W. Coleman (Bagshot), Mark Sawyer-Dailey (Sir Charles), Sarah Agnew (Maid)
BRIEF LIVES by John Aubrey; Adaptation, Patrick Garland; Director, Ray Fry; Set, Paul Owen; Lighting, Karl E. Haas; Costumes, Hollis Jenkins-Evans CAST: William McNulty (Aubrey)
THE PASSION OF DRACULA by Bob Hall and David Richmond; Based on Bram Stoker's novel; Director, Frazier W. Marsh; Sets, Paul Owens; Costumes, Laura A. Patterson; Lighting, Karl E. Haas CAST: Ray Fry (Dr. Seward), Mark Sawyer-Dailey (Jameson), Fred Major (Van Helsing), Adale O'Brien (Dr. Van Zandt), Michael Kevin (Godalming), William McNulty (Renfield), Barbara Gulan (Wilhelmina), Keith Hamilton Cobb (Harker), V. Craig Heidenreich (Dracula)
GIVE 'EM HELL, HARRY by Samuel Gallu; Director, Scott Zigler; Set, Paul Owen; Costumes, Hollis Jenkins-Evans; Lighting, Rob Dillard CAST: Bob Burrus (Harry S. Truman)
A CHRISTMAS CAROL by Charles Dickens; Adaptation, Jon Jory, Marcia Dixcy; Director, Larry Deckel; Sets, Virginia Dancy, Elmon Webb; Lighting, Karl E. Haas; Costumes, Lewis D. Rampino, Hollis Jenkins-Evans; Music, Peter Ekstrom CAST: Michael Kevin (Scrooge), Vaughn McBride, William McNulty, Ann Hodapp, Fred Major, Mara Swanson, Adale O'Brien, Mark Sawyer-Dailey, V. Craig Heidenreich, Bob Burrus, Carlos Ramos, Jeffrey Roth, Liz Burmester, Keith Hamilton Cobb, Brian Worrall, Barbara Gulan, Jennifer Hubbard, Jennifer Carta, Pepper Stebbins, Joshua W. Coleman, Benji Taylor, Larry Barnett, Daniel Zakem, Sean Thomas McGill, Victor Gonzalez, Christopher Murphy
THE GIFT OF THE MAGI by O. Henry; Adaptation/Music/Lyrics by Peter Ekstrom; Director, Frazier W. Marsh; Sets, Paul Owen; Lighting, Matthew J. Reinert; Costumes, Hollis Jenkins-Evans CAST: Emily Loesser (Della), Don Stephenson (Jim)
PICNIC by William Inge; Director, Anne Bogart; Sets, John Conklin; Costumes, Laura Patterson; Lighting, Mimi Jordan Sherin CAST: Adale O'Brien (Helen Potts), J. Ed Araiza (Hal Carter), Karenjune Sanchez (Millie Owens), Christopher Murphy (Bomber), Ellen Lauren (Madge), Peggy Cosgrave (Flo), Diane D'Aquila (Rosemary), W. Josh Hopkins (Alan), Nailah Jumoke (Irma), Glory Kissel (Christine), William McNulty (Howard), Brooke Channon, Katie Furth, Victor Gonzalez, Jason Butler Harner, Tracey Maloney (Students)
LA BETE by David Hirson; Director, Jon Jory; Sets, Paul Owen; Costumes, Laura Patterson; Lighting, Karl E. Haas CAST: Michael Kevin (Elomire), Ray Fry (Bejart), Peter Zapp (Valere), Jessica Givelber (Dorine), V. Craig Heidenreich (Prince Conti), Susan Barnes (Madeleine), Fred Major (De Brie), Sandra Sydney (Catherine), Bob Burrus (Du Parc), Rachel Fowler (Marquise), Mark Sawyer-Dailey (White Clown), Nicole Scherzinger (Acolyte)
SHIRLEY VALENTINE by Willy Russell; Direction, Jon Jory based on Patrick Swanson's staging; Set, Paul Owen; Lighting, Matthew J. Reinert; Costumes, Hollis Jenkins-Evans CAST: Tina Packer (Shirley)

Top: Karenjune Sanchez, Ellen Lauren in "Picnic"
Center: William McNulty in "Brief Lives"
Bottom: Michael Kevin, Kevin Kling, William McNulty in "Ice Fishing Play"

STANTON'S GARAGE(PREMIERE) by Joan Ackermann; Director, Steven Albrezzi; Set, Paul Owen; Costumes, Laura Patterson; Lighting, Karl E. Haas CAST: Peter Zapp (Ron), Rob Kramer (Harlon), Bob Burrus (Silvio), V. Craig Heidenreich (Denny), Priscilla Shanks (Lee), Jessica Jory (FRannie), Adale O'Brien (Mary), Susan Barnes (Audrey)

SHOOTING SIMONE(PREMIERE) by Lynne Kaufman; Director, Laszlo Marton; Set, Paul Owen; Costumes, Laura Patterson; Lighting, Karl E. Haas CAST: Fred Major (Jean-Paul Sartre), Janni Brenn (Simone de Beauvoir), Kathleen Dennehy (Olga/Kate), Brett Rickaby (Alphonse/Rick), Christopher Murphy, Brian Worrall (Garons)

VARIOUS SMALL FIRES (PREMIERE) by Regina Taylor; Director, Novella Nelson; Sets, Paul Owen; Costumes, Toni-Leslie James; Lighting, Marcus Dilliard JENNINE'S DIARY Cast: Elain Graham (Jennine), Judy Tate (Driver /Esther/Rose), Nailah Jumoke (Karen), Kalimi A. Baxter (Terrinika), Yvette Hawkins (Madear) WATERMELLON RINDS Cast: Roger Robinson (Jes), Kalimi A. Baxter (Lottie), Donald Griffin (Willy), Regina Byrd Smith (Liza), Elain Graham (Pinkie), Ray Johnson (Papa), Yvette Hawkins (Mama), Judy Tate (Marva)

THE ICE FISHING PLAY (PREMIERE) by Kevin Kling; Director, Michael Sommers; Set, Paul Owen; Costumes, Toni-Leslie James; Lighting, Karl E. Haas CAST: Fred Major (Tim voice), Ray Fry (Paul voice), Kevin Kling (Ron), Pepper Stebbins (Shumway), Victor Gonzalez (Francis), Susan Barnes (Irene), Michael Kevin (Duff), William McNulty (Junior), Collin Sherman (Young Ron)

DEADLY VIRTUES (PREMIERE); Adapted/Directed by Brian Jucha; Sets, Paul Owen; Costumes, Laura Patterson; Lighting, Marcus Dilliard; Created and Performed by Tamar Kotoske, Barney O'Hanlon, Steven Skybell, Regina Byrd Smith, Andrew Weems

KEELY AND DU (PREMIERE) by Jane Martin; Director, Jon Jorry; Sets, Paul Owen; Costumes, Laura Patterson; Lighting, Marcus Dilliard CAST: Anne Pitoniak (Du), Bob Burrus (Walter), Julie Boyd (Keely), J. Ed Araiza (Cole), Janice O'Rourke (Guard), Jeremy Brisiel, Jeff Sexton (Orderlies)

TEN MINUTE PLAYS (PREMIERES); *What We Do With It* by Bruce MacDonald; Director, Frazier W. Marsh; with Ray Fry, Priscilla Shanks; *Tape* by Jose Rivera; Director, Scott Zigler; with Fred Major, Kalimi A. Baxter; *Poof* by Lynn Nottage; Director, Seret Scott; with Elain Graham, Yvette Hawkins

BORN YESTERDAY by Garson Kanin; Director, Ray Fry; Sets, Paul Owen; Costumes, Hollis Jenkins-Evans; Lighting, Karl E. Haas CAST: Ann Hodapp (Helen), V. Craig Heidenreich (Paul), Mark Sawyer-Dailey (Eddie), Fred Major (Harry), Vaughn McBride (Asst. Manager/Barber), Peggity Price (Billie Dawn), William McNulty (Ed), Michael Kevin (Sen. Hedges), Adale O'Brien (Mrs. Hedges), Jason Butler Harner, Sean Thomas McGill (Bellhops)

SUDS; Created/Written by Melinda Gilb, Steve Gunderson, Will Roberson, Bryan Scott; Musical/Vocal Arrangements, Mr. Gunderson; Director, Will Roberson; Choreography, Javier Velasco; Music Director, Tom Wojtas; Sets, Paul Owen; Costumes, Laura Patterson; Lighting, Karl E. Haas CAST: Jennifer Naimo (Cindy), Julie Prosser (Dee Dee), Adinah Alexander (Marge), Daniel Baum (Everyone Else)

Richard C. Trigg Photos

Top: "La Bete" cast
Center: Anne Pitoniak, Julie Boyd in "Keely and Du"
Bottom: Janni Brenn, Fred Major in "Shooting Simone"

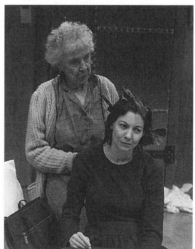

ALLENBERRY PLAYHOUSE

Boiling Springs, Pennsylvania

Producer, John J. Heinze; Artistic Director, Michael Haney; Production Stage Manager/Lighting Design, Richard J. Frost; Production Coordinator, Cate Van Wickler; Sets, Robert Klingelhoefer; Costumes, Jennifer Eve Flitton; Musical Director, Robert Felstein

PRODUCTIONS & CASTS

NUNSENSE with Music/Lyrics/Book by Dan Goggin; Director, Michael Haney; Choreography, Katherine Harber CAST: Karen Looze (Mary Regina), Debbie Lee Jones (Mary Hubert), Katherine Harber (Robert Anne), Helen Hedman (Mary Amnesia), Deborah Caitlyn (Mary Leo)
THE SOUND OF MUSIC by Rodgers and Hammerstein, Howard Lindsay, Russel Crouse; Director, Michael Haney; Choreography, Rebecca Timms CAST: Cynthia Marty (Maria), Deborah Caitlyn, Debbie Lee Jones, Emily Smith (Sisters), Karen Looze (Mother Abbess), Greg Zerkle (Capt. Von Trapp), Bob Tron (Franz), Deighna De Riu (Frau Schmidt), Rebecca Timms (Liesl), Ed Hammond (Friedrich), Nina Genzel (Louisa), Todd Berkich (Kurt), Julie Eyer (Brigitta), Kelly Fisher (Marta), Lindsay K. Mauck (Gretl), Bob Bucci (Rolf), Katherine Harber (Elsa), Bob Del Pazzo (Max), Neal Arluck (Zeller), Cort Huckabone (Baron), John Heinze (Admiral), Fern-Marie Aames, Dawn Fuller, Kevin Gillespie, Tina Guice, Adam Lang, Lee Neibert, Heather Robinson, Sarah Timms
KISS ME KATE by Cole Porter, Sam and Bella Spewack; Director, John Raymond; Choreography, David Wanstreet CAST: Greg Zerkle (Fred/Petruchio), Cynthia Marty (Lilli/Katherine), Rebecca Timms (Lois/Bianca), O.V. Vargas (Bill/Lucentio), Bob Tron (Harry/Baptista), Neal Arluck, Bob Del Pazzo (Gangsters), Dennis Stowe (Paul), Debbie Lee Jones (Hattie), Bob Bucci (Hortensio), Michael Levesque (Gremio), John Heinze (Harrison), Walt Kiser (Ralph), Adam Lang (Dave), Ed Hammond (Nathaniel), Lee Neibert (Gregory), Cort Huckabone (Haberdasher), Kevin Gillespie (Driver/Phillip), Robert Felstein (Conductor), Fern-Marie Aames, Deighna De Riu, Tina Guice, Heather Robinson, Emily Smith, Sarah Timms
UPROAR IN THE HOUSE by Anthony Marriott and Alistair Foot; Director, David Brubaker CAST: Ed Hammond (Cyril), Debbie Lee Jones (Monica), Fern-Marie Aames (Yvonne), Rebecca Timms (Melanie), Bob Tron (Bernard), Paul DeBoy (Nigel), Richert Easley (Sir Lindsay), Catherine Blaine (Lady Cooper), Neal Arluck (David), Bob Del Pazzo (Andrew), Deighna De Riu (Audrey), Kevin Gillespie (Photographer), Emily Ann Smith (Isabel)
TOWARDS ZERO by Agatha Christie; Director, Richard J. Frost CAST: Neal Arluck (Thomas), Julia Kelly (Kay), Emily Ann Smith (Mary), David Brubaker (Matthew), Paul DeBoy (Neville), Jeanne Tron (Lady Tressilian), Kathleen Conroy (Audrey), Cort Huckabone (Ted), Richert Easley (Battle), Ed Hammond (Leach), Kevin Gillespie (Benson)
MY FAT FRIEND by Charles Laurence; Director, Kathleen Conry CAST: Neal Arluck (James), Richert Easley (Henry), Gail Gustafson (Vicky), Paul DeBoy (Tom)
BAREFOOT IN THE PARK by Neil Simon; Director, Michael Haney CAST: Pamela Cecil (Corie), James Hayney (Repair Man), Ed Hammond (Delivery), Paul Carlin (Paul), Mary Rausch (Mother), George Holmes (Victor)
OUT OF ORDER by Ray Cooney; Director, Richard J. Frost CAST: George Holmes (Richard), David Brubaker (Manager), James Hayney (Waiter), Fern-Marie Aames (Maid), Pamela Cecil (Jane), Jason Graham (Body), Paul Carlin (George), Rich Hatch (Ronnie), Amy Warner (Pamela), Catherine Blaine (Gladys)
LETTICE AND LOVAGE by Peter Shaffer; Director, Michael Rothhaar CAST: Nancy Linehan Charles (Lettice Douffet), Amy Warner (Charlotte Schoen), Helen Hedman (Miss Framer), George Holmes (Bardolph), Fern-Marie Aames, Greg Edsell, Jason Graham, Rich Hatch, Jennifer Haroutounian, Gene Sexton, Brad Watson, Susan Webb

Top: Paul Carlin, George Holmes, Mary Rausch, Pamela Cecil in
"Barefoot in the Park"
Center: Karen Looze, Cynthia Marty in "Sound of Music"

George Holmes, David Brubaker, Paul Carlin, Jason Graham in
"Out of Order"

ALLEY THEATRE

Houston, Texas

Forty-fifth Season

Artistic Director, Gregory Boyd; Executive Director, Stephen J. Albert; Associate Director, Michael Wilson; Associate Artists, Edward Albee, Jose Quintero, Frank Wildhorn, Robert Wilson; Literary Director, Christopher Baker; Development Director, Heather Simpson; Production Stage Manager, M. Pat Hodge

PRODUCTIONS & CASTS

THE FRONT PAGE by Ben Hecht and Charles MacArthur; Director, Gregory Boyd; Sets, Hugh Landwehr; Costumes, David C. Woolard; Lighting, Howell Binkley CAST: Alex Allen Morris (Wilson), Jim McQueen (Endicott), Peter Webster (Murphy), Jeffrey Bean (McCue), Jamie Callahan (Kruger), Charles Sanders (Bensinger), Annalee Jefferies (Mrs. Schlosser), John Feltch (Diamond Louis), Thomas Derrah (Hildy), Dorothy Wilkes (Jennie), Shelley Williams (Molly), Charles Krohn (Hartman), Lee Merrill (Peggy), Bettye Fitzpatrick (Mrs. Grant), William Hardy (Mayor), Patrick Mitchell (Pincus), Mark Feltch (Earl Williams), James Black (Walter Burns), Glenn Dickerson, Matthew Rippy (Police)

DANTON'S DEATH by Georg Buchner; Translation, Robert Auletta; Conception/Direction/Sets/Lighting, Robert Wilson; Costumes, John Conklin; Lighting, Stephen Strawbridge; Music, Chuck Winkler CAST: Richard Thomas (Danton), Marissa Chibas (Julie), John Feltch (Sechelles), Jennifer Arisco (Adelaide), Emily York (Rosalie), Gage Tarrant, Katherine Pew (Women), Scott Rabinowitz (Camille), Jamie Callahan (Phillipeau), James Black (Street Man/Warder/Carter), Lou Liberatore (Robespierre), Willis Sparks (Legendre), Jeffrey Bean (Lacroix), Annalee Jefferies (Marion), Jon David Weigand (St. Just), Thomas Derrah(Fouquier/Gentle-man), Wade Mylius (Gentleman), Melissa Bowen (Lucille), Peter Webster (Herman), Gregory Boyd (Paine), Bettye Fitzpatrick (Jailer/Executioner), Jason Meisse (Boy), Peter Baquet, Glenn Dickerson, Matthew Rippy

A CHRISTMAS CAROL by Charles Dickens; Adaptation/Direction, Michael Wilson; Sets, Jay Michael Jagim; Costumes, Ainslie Brunmeau; Lighting, Howell Binkley; Music, John Dickson CAST: James Black (Scrooge), Jeffrey Bean, John Feltch, Peter Webster, Alex Allen Morris, Charles Sanders, Seth Collins, Blake Stokes, Matthew Rippy, Jennifer Arisco, Mia Havel, Gabby Turner, Bettye Fitzpatrick, Charles Krohn, Thomas Derrah, Emily York, Matthew Stokes, Robert Perkins, Jamie Callahan, Naomi Castillo, Jamaiya Havel, Dee Dee Byrd, German Leon, Aaron Krohn, Shelly Williams, Lanna Mathis, Jeanann Seidman, Joshua Pop, Ronald Sandrock, Katie Lynn Agular, Natalie Ann Agular, Major Johnson Finley, Amy Price, Camille Warren, Cynthia Camacho, William Balch, Stewart Guenther

LIPS TOGETHER, TEETH APART by Terrence McNally; Director, Michael Wilson; Set, Hugh Landwehr; Costumes, Steffani Compton; Lighting, Howell Binkley CAST: Annalee Jefferies (Chloe), James Black (Sam), Peter Webster (John), Shelly Williams (Sally)

OUR TOWN by Thornton Wilder; Director, Jose Quintero; Sets/Lighting, Kevin Rigdon; Costumes, Noel Taylor CAST: Bettye Fitzpatrick (Stage Manager), Thomas Derrah (Dr. Gibbs), Alexander White (Joe Crowell), Jeffrey Bean (Howie), Karen MacDonald (Mrs. Gibbs), Annalee Jefferies (Mrs. Webb), Mark Guin (George Gibbs), Kelley Ann Foy (Rebecca), Steven Powell (Wally), Calista Flockhart (Emily), Joe McHale (Willard/Dead Man), James Black (Mr. Webb), Shelly Williams (Balcony Woman/Dead Woman), John Feltch (Auditorium Man/Dead Man), Claire Hart-Palumbo (Box Lady/Dead Woman), Charles Sanders (Stimson), Marjorie Carroll (Mrs. Soames), Charles Krohn (Constable), Gary Minyard (Crowell/Baseball Player), Dennis Turney (Baseball Player), Whitney Rassbach (Player/Townsperson), Jamie Callahan (Sam), Patrick Mitchell (Stoddard), Bill French, Rebecca Harris, Stan Kansas, Aaron Krohn, Barbra Lasater,, Ted Pfister, Ellen Preston, Robin Proett, Joseph Royce, Kenneth L. Tireman, Sr., Paige Witte

DRACULA, A MUSICAL NIGHTMARE with Music/Musical Direction by John Aschenbrenner; Lyrics/Book/Direction, Douglas Johnson; Sets, Richard H. Young; Costumes, Susan Tsu; Lighting, Mary Louise Geiger; Choreography, Chesley Krohn CAST: Lisa Albright (Faith), Diane Pennington (Hope), Nita Moore (Chastity), John Feltch (DeVille), Charles Krohn (Harker), Shelley Williams (Mina), Kimberly King (Lucy), Ken Grantham (Seward), Thomas Derrah (Renfield), Richard Kinsey (Morris), James Black (Van Helsing), Dracula (Dracula)

Top: Peter Webster, Richard Thomas, Matthew Rippy in "Danton's Death"
Below: Jamie Callahan, Shelly Williams, Peter Webster, Alex Allen Morris, Jim McQueen, Thomas Derrah, Jeffrey Bean in "Front Page"

MACBETH by Shakespeare; Director, Gregory Boyd; Sets, Vincent Mountain; Costumes, Judith Anne Dolan; Lighting, Howell Binkley CAST: Bettye Fitzpatrick, Lona McManus, Paige Witte (Witches), James Black (Macbeth), John Feltch (Banquo), Jeffrey Bean (Ross/Porter), Shelley Williams (Lady Macbeth), Jamie Callahan (Seyton), Scott Rabinowitz (Duncan/Macduff), Aaron Krohn (Donalbain), Eric Morse, Adam Mesinger (Fleance), Charles Sanders (Lennox), Alex Allen Morris, Michael Ballard (Murderers), Suzanne Savoy (Lady Macduff/Gentlewoman), Danielle Odom, Katy Lu Siciliano(Macduff Daughter), Stephen Smith, George Allen Druck (Macduff Son), Greg Lehman, Alexander White, Gary Minyard, Jeff Miller (Soldiers), Vicki Weathersby (Gentlewoman)

ONE FLEW OVER THE CUCKOO'S NEST by Dale Wasserman; Based on the novel by Ken Kesey; Director, Gregory Boyd; Sets, Richard H. Young; Costumes, Steffani Compton; Lighting, Howell Binkley CAST: Davi Jay (Warren), Donis Leonard (Williams), Annalee Jefferies (Ratched), Lisa McEwen (Flinn), Charles Krohn (Spivey), Michael Marich (Aide), James Hamsen Prince (Technician), Alex Allen Morris (Turkle), Raul Flores (Bromden), John Feltch (Harding), Jeffrey Bean (Billy), Akin Babatunde (Scanlon), Charles Sanders (Cheswick), Peter Webster (Martini), Jamie Callahan (Ruckly), James Black (McMurphy), Stan Kansas (Sefelt), Pat Michell (Fredericks), Shelly Williams (Candy), Vicki Weathersby (Sandra)

FROM THE MISSISSIPPI DELTA by Dr. Ida Mae Hllland; Director, Seret Scott; Sets, Jane La Motte; Costumes, Lisa Vollrath; Lighting, York Kennedy CAST: Kena Tangi Dorsey (Woman One), Kim Brockington (Woman Two), Sheila Ramsey (Woman Three)

BILLY BISHOP GOES TO WAR; Written/Composed by John Gray in collaboration with Eric Peterson; Director, Gregory Boyd; Set, Robert N. Schmidt; Costumes, Steffani Compton; Lighting, Christina Giannelli CAST: Jeffery Bean (Billy Bishop/Everybody), Bill Bartlett (Piano)

DEATH AND THE MAIDEN by Ariel Dorfman; Director, Kent Grantham; Set, Robert N. Schmidt; Costumes, Steffani Compton; Lighting, Noele Stollmack CAST: Annalee Jefferies (Paulina), Thomas Derrah (Gerardo), Peter Webster (Roberto)

Jim Caldwell Photos

125

AMERICAN CONSERVATORY THEATRE

San Francisco, California

Twenty-seventh Season

Artstic Director, Carey Perloff; Managing Director, John Sullivan; Associate Artistic Directors, Richard Seyd, Benny Sato Ambush; General Manager, Dianne Pritchard; Production Manager, Jim Haire; Public Relations Director, Hollis Ashby

PRODUCTIONS & CASTS

CREDITORS by August Strindberg; Translation, Paul Walsh; Director, Carey Perloff; Sets, Donald Eastman; Costumes, Callie Floor; Lighting, Frances Aronson CAST: William Converse-Roberts (Adolf), Charles Lanyer (Gustav), Joan McMurtrey (Tekla), Debra Blondheim, Julia Falvey (Women), Christopher Schedler (Porter)

THE POPE AND THE WITCH (U.S. PREMIERE) by Dario Fo; Translation, Joan Holden; Director, Richard Seyd; Sets/Lighting, Kent Dorsey; Costumes, Christine Dougherty CAST: Joe Bellan (Friar/Caresi/Drunk), Gloria Weinstock (Nun/Addict), Ray Reinhardt (Cardinal Pialli/Goon), Maureen McVerry (Sister Gabriella/Carla), Howard Swain (Fr. Faggio/Goon), Dan Hiatt (Dr. Ridolfi), Sharon Lockwood (Elisa, the Healer), John Reynolds (Capt./Addict/Cardinal), Geoff Hoyle (Pope), Andrew DeAngelo (Guard/ Addict), John Martone, Craig Mason (Black Friars/Cardinals)

MISS EVERS' BOYS by David Feldshuh; Director, Benny Sato Ambush; Sets, Jefferson Sage; Costumes, Alvin Perry; Lighting, Clifton Taylor CAST: Judith Moreland (Eunice Evers), Steven Anthony Jones (Brodus/ Administration), Dennis Barnett (Dr. Douglass), Kent Gash (Willie Johnson), Wendell Pierce (Caleb Humphries), Fracaswell Hyman (Hodman Bryan), Charles Branklyn (Ben Washington)

THE DUCHESS OF MALFI by John Webster; Director, Robert Woodruff; Sets, George Tsypin; Costumes, Sandra Woodall; Lighting, James F. Ingalls CAST: Sam Tsoutsouvas (Ferdinand), Lawrence Hecht (Cardinal), Victor Mack (Antonio), Luis Oropeza (Delio), Mario Arrambide (Daniel de Bosola), Lane Nishikawa (Malateste), Victor Talmadge (Castruchio), Michael McFall (Marquis), John Reynolds (Grisolan), David Maier (Silvio/ Doctor), Randy Danson (Duchess of Malfi), Sharon Omi (Cariola), Gloria Weinstock (Julia), Roberta Callahan (Old Woman), J. Todd Adams, Charla Cabot, Andrea Carvajal, Tracey Huffman, Zachary Barton, Karen Garvey, Dan Johnson, Tom Lenoci, Brian Russell, Chanelle Schaffer, Sharr White, Jenny Woo

ANTIGONE by Sophocles; Translation/Adaptation, Timberlake Wertenbaker; Director, Carey Perloff; Music, David Lang; Sets, Kate Edmunds; Lighting, Peter Maradudin; Costumes, Donna Zakowska CAST: Elizabeth Pena (Antigone), Vilma Silva (Ismene), Joy Carlin, Ken Grantham, Gerald Hiken (Chorus), Ken Ruta (Kreon), Mo-Fracaswell Hyman (Guard), Wendell Pierce (Haimon), Steven Anthony Jones (Teiresias), Kay Kostopoulos (Eurydike)

DINNER AT EIGHT by George S. Kaufman and Edna Ferber; Director, Albert Takazauckas; Costumes, Deborah Nadoolman; Lighting, Kurt Landisman CAST: Frances Lee McCain (Millicent Jordan), Cynthia Lynch (Dora), Kent Gash (Gustave), Nicholas Hormann (Oliver Jordan), Nancy Carlin (Paula Jordan), Luis Oropeza (Ricci/Fitch), Joan Mankin (Hattie Loomis), Roberta Callahan (Miss Copeland), Jan Miner (Carlotta Vance), Lawrence Hecht (Dan Packard), Maureen McVerry (Kitty Packard), Charla Cabot (Tina), Richard Butterfield (Dr. Talbot), Peter Donat (Larry Renault), Andrew DeAngelo (Bellboy), J. Todd Adams (Waiter), Ed Hodson (Max Kane), Nino DeGennaro (Mr. Hatfield), Julie Eccles (Miss Alden), Judith Moreland (Lucy Talbot), Roberta Callahan (Mrs. Wendel), Bruce Williams (Jo Stengel), Frank Ottiwell (Ed Loomis), Jeff Brookner, Henry Gevurtz, Nicholas Greene

THE LEARNED LADIES by Moliere; Translation/Adaptation, Freyda Thomas; Director, Richard Seyd; Sets, Ralph Funicello; Costumes, Beaver Bauer; Lighting, Peter Maradudin; Music, Gina Leishman CAST: Joy Carlin (Belise), Julia Gibson (Henriette), Lorri Holt (Armande), L. Peter Callender (Clitandre), Gerald Hiken (Ariste), Sydney Walker (Chrysale), Delia MacDougall, Tracey Huffman (Martine), Jean Stapleton (Philamente), Brad DePlanche (lepine), Tony Amendola (Trissotin), Howard Swain (Valdius/Judge), Tradd David Keaton (Tutors/Servant)

Ken Friedman,Tom Chargin, Larry Merkle Photos

Top: Sharon Omi, Victor Mack, Randy Danson in "Duchess of Malfi"
Center:Elizabeth Pena, Vilma Silva in "Antigone"
Bottom: Maureen McVerry, Dan Hiatt, Geoff Hoyle, Sharon Lockwood,
Ray Reinhardt in "Pope and the Witch"

AMERICAN REPERTORY THEATRE

Cambridge, Massachusetts

Fourteenth Season

Artistic Director, Robert Brustein; Managing Director, Robert J. Orchard; Associate Artistic Director, Ron Daniels; Development Director, Charles Marz; General Manager, Jonathan Seth Miller; Marketing Director, Henry Lussier; Production Stage Manager, Abbie H. Katz

RESIDENT COMPANY: Patti Allison, Christian Baskous, Candy Buckley, Thomas Derrah, Alvin Epstein, Christine Estabrook, Jeremy Geidt, Margaret Gibson, Gustave Johnson, Cherry Jones, Christopher Lloyd, Royal E. Miller, Stephanie Roth, Tracy Sallows, Derek Smith, Jack Willis, William Young

PRODUCTIONS & CASTS

BLACK SNOW by Keith Dewhurst; Based on Mikhail Bulgakov's novel; Director, Richard Jones; Sets/Costumes, Antony McDonald; Lighting, Scott Zielinski CAST: Patti Allison (Augusta/Natasya), Christian Baskous (Likospastov/Patrikeyev), Candy Buckley (Annushka/Polixena/Margarita), Alvin Epstein (Vasilyevich), Raymond Fox (Singing Actor/Yermolai/Dream Figure), Jeremy Geidt (Rudolfi/Gornostayev/Romanus), Margaret Gibson (Lyudmilla), Gustave Johnson (Kuzmich/ General), Royal E. Miller (Bombardov), Kerry O'Malley (Nurse/Dream), John Payne (Guard/Yelagin /Chauffer), Matthew Rauch (Guard/Doctor/Felt Boots/Adalbert), Tracy Sallows (Yevlampia/Veshnyakova), Derek Smith (Maksudov), Jack Willis (Panin), William Young (Gavril/Audrey)

HEARTBREAK HOUSE by George Bernard Shaw; Director, David Wheeler; Sets, Derek McLane; Costumes, Catherine Zuber; Lighting, Howell Binkley CAST: Jeremy Geidt (Shotover), Patti Allison (Nurse Guinness), Tracy Sallows (Ellie), Candy Buckley (Lady Utterword), Margaret Gibson (Hesione Hushabye), Gustave Johnson (Mazzini), Royal Miller (Hector Hushabye), Jack Willis (Mangan), Christian Baskous (Randall Utterword), William Young (Burgler)

DREAM OF THE RED SPIDER by Ronald Ribman; Director, Ron Daniels; Sets, Riccardo Hernandez; Costumes, Catherine Zuber; Lighting, Frances Aronson CAST: Remo Airaldi (Rosas), Patti Allison (Antonia), Candy Buckley (Mistress of Ceremonies), Alvin Epstein (Valverde), Jonathan Fried (Gutierrez), Gustave Johnson (Cesteros), Timothy Karcher (Dwoff/Lorenzo), Kristen Lee Kelly (Josande), Lisa Louise Langford (Lena), Jennifer London (Cleo), Royal Miller (Cripple), Gino Montesinos (Bellevisage), Daniel Passer (Jockimo/Calista), Maggie Rush (Violet), Jack Willis (Uyttersprot)

ORPHEÉ by Philip Glass; Based on the film by Jean Cocteau; Adaptation, Mr. Glass; Editing, Robert Brustein; Director, Francesca Zambello; Music Director/Conductor, Martin Goldray; Sets, Robert Isreal; Costumes, Catherine Zuber; Lighting, Pat Collins CAST: James Ramlet (Older Poet), Wendy Hill (Princess), Richard Fracker (Heurtebise), Paul Kirby (Cegeste), Eugene Perry, Leroy Villanueva (Orphee), John Kuether (Police/Commisioner/Judge), Elizabeth Futral, Lynn Torgove (Eurydice), Janice Felty (Aglaonice), Brian Mirabile (Reporter/Glazier)

CAKEWALK by Peter Feibleman; Director, Ron Daniels; Sets, Tony Straiges; Costumes, Catherine Zuber; Lighting, Howell Binkley; Music, Carly Simon; Arrangements, Matthias Gohl CAST: John Slattery (Cuff), Elaine Stritch (Lilly), Stephanie Roth (Other Women), Matthew Rauch (Other Men)

THE CARETAKER by Harold Pinter; Director, David Wheeler; Set, Derek McLane; Costumes, Catherine Zuber, Kenneth Mooney; Lighting, John Ambrosone CAST: Mark Zeisler (Mick), Jack Willis (Aston), Jeremy Geidt (Davies)

SILENCE, CUNNING, EXILE(PREMIERE) by Stuart Greenman; Director, Ron Daniels; Set, Christine Jones; Costumes, Karen Eister; Lighting, John Ambrosone CAST: Stephanie Roth (Suzie), Royal Miller (Donald), Jonathan Fried (Frank), Candy Buckley (Beryl), Tresha Rodriguez (Nicole/Emaciated Model), Leslie Beatty (Kiki), Alvin Epstein (Party Man/Isaac), John Payne (Transvestite/Acquaintance), Richard Similio (Boyfriend/Transient/ Inert Man), Remo Airaldi (Prostitute)

THE L.A. PLAYS (PREMIERE) by Han Ong; Director, Steven Maler; Set, Christine Jones; Costumes, Gail A. Buckley; Lighting, John Ambrosone *In a Lonely Country* CAST: Han Ong (Greg), Jonathan Fried (Voice/Andrew), Gino Montesinos (Black Man), Starla Benford (Woman/Marilyn Monroe), Matthew Rauch (Bill/Nicholas), Raymond Fox (Ken), Faran Tahir (Nick), John Payne (John) *A Short List of Alternate Places* CAST: Mr. Ong (Greg), Mr. Fried, Mr. Payne, Mr. Fox, Mr. Montesinos, Ms. Benford, Mr. Tahir

THOSE THE RIVER KEEPS: Written/Directed by David Rabe; Sets, Loren Sherman; Costumes, Gail A. Buckley; Lighting, John Ambrose; Music, Jason Rabe CAST: Paul Guilfoyle (Phil), Rebecca Tilney (Susie), Jack Willis (Sal), Candy Buckley (Janice)

Richard Feldman Photos

Top: John Slattery, Elaine Stritch in "Cakewalk"
Center: Jonathan Fried, Candy Buckley in "Dream of the Red Spider"
Bottom: Paul Guilfoyle, Rebecca Tilney in "Those the River Keeps"

ARENA STAGE

Washingston, D.C.

Forty-second Season

Artistic Director, Douglas C. Wager; Executive Director, Stephen Richard; Founding Director, Zelda Fichandler; Production Manager, Dennis A. Blackledge; Publicity Director, Ann Greer

RESIDENT COMPANY: Richard Bauer, Casey Biggs, Teagle F. Bougere, Ralph Cosham, Terrence Currier, Gail Grate, M.E. Hart, Tana Hicken, Michael W. Howell, Jurian Hughes, David Marks, Pamela Nyberg, Henry Strozier, Jeffery V. Thompson, Halo Wines, Wendell Wright

PRODUCTIONS & CASTS

OF THEE I SING with Music by George Gershwin; Lyrics, Ira Gershwin; Book, Mr. Kaufman and Morrie Ryskind; Director, Douglas C. Wager; Choreography, Marcia Milgrom Dodge; Musical Director, William Huckaby; Sets, Zack Brown; Lighting, Allen Lee Hughes; Costumes, Marjorie Slaiman CAST: Gary Beach (Wintergreen), Lauren Mitchell (Mary), Terry Burrell (Diana), Richard Bauer (Fulton), David Marks (Throttlebottom), Terrence Currier (Ambassador/Justice), Jeffery V. Thompson (Gilhooley), Michael L. Forrest (Sen. Lyons), Richard Dix (Sen. Jones), Keith Savage (Jenkins), Lawrence Redmond (Lippman), Kyme (Miss Benson).
THE WAY OF THE WORLD by William Congreve; Director, Kyle Donnelly; Movement, Michael Sokoloff; Sets, Loy Arcenas; Lighting, Allen Lee Hughes; Costumes, Paul Tazewell CAST: Ralph Cosham (Congreve/Sir Wilfull Witwoud), Henry Strozier (Fainall), Casey Biggs (Mirabell), Gary Sloan (Witwoud), Brian Reddy (Petulant), Wendell Wright (Waitwell), Teagle F, Bougere (Messenger/Servant), Halo Wines (Lady Wishfort), Gail Grate (Millamant), Pamela Nyberg (Marwood), Jurian Hughes (Mrs. Fainall), Tana Hicken (Foible), Carol Monda (Mincing), Rosemary Knower (Peg/Attendant)
AVNER THE ECCENTRIC with Avner Eisenberg
BLOOD KNOT by Athol Fugard; Director, Tazewell Thompson; Sets, Douglas Stein; Costumes, Paul Tazewell; Lighting, Allen Lee Hughes CAST: Jed Diamond (Morris), Jonathan Earl Peck (Zachariah)
THE AFRICAN COMPANY by Carlyle Brown; Director, Tazewell Thompson; Sets, Douglas Stein; Costumes, Paul Tazewell; Lighting, Allen Lee Hughes CAST: Jed Diamond (Price), LaDonna Mabry (Sarah), Gail Grate (Ann), Leon Addison Brown (Hewlett), Wendell Wright (Papa Shakespeare), Jonathan Earl Peck (Brown), David Marks (Constable-Man), Ed Eaton, Paul Niebanck (Constabulary)
IT'S THE TRUTH (IF YOU THINK IT IS) by Luigi Pirandello; Director/Sets, Liviu Ciulei; Costumes, Marina Draghici; Lighting, Nancy Schertler CAST: Richard Bauer (Lamberto), Halo Wines (Amalia), Pamela Nyberg (Dina), Teagle F. Bougere (Butler), Jeffery V. Thompson (Sirelli), Trazana Beverley (Signora Sirelli), Vivienne Shub (Signora Cini), Ralph Cosham (Agazzi), Tana Hicken (Frola), Henry Strozier (Ponza), Jean Schertler (Nenni), Michael W. Howell (Police) Commissioner), Terrence Currier (Governor), Jurian Hughes (Signora Ponza)
ANTIGONE IN NEW YORK (PREMIERE) by Janusz Glowacki; Director, Laurence Maslon; Sets, Katherine Jennings; Costumes, Marjorie Slaiman; Lighting, Christopher Lewton CAST: Richard Bauer (Sasha), Ralph Cosham (Flea), Jeffery V. Thompson (Police), Tom Simpson (Paulie), Sheila M. Tousey (Anita)
SUMMER AND SMOKE by Tennessee Williams; Director, Kyle Donnelly; Sets, Marina Draghici; Costumes, Marjorie Slaiman; Lighting, Nancy Schertler CAST: Henry Strozier (Rev. Winemiller), Tana Hicken (Mrs. Winemiller), Casey Biggs (John), Pamela Nyberg (Alma), Alina Arenal (Rosa), Jackie Mari Roberts (Nellie), Rob Leo Roy (Roger), Terrence Currier (Roger), Halo Wines (Mrs. Bassett), David Hilder (Vernon), Carol Monda (Rosemary), Richard Salamanca (Dusty), Carlos Juan Gonzales (Gonzales), Michael Chaban (Archie)
THE FLYING KARAMAZOV BROTHERS IN THE BROTHERS KARAMAZOV by Paul Magid; Director, Daniel Sullivan; Music, Doug Wieselman, Gina Leishman; Lyrics, Howard Patterson; Sets, Andrew Wood Boughton; Costumes, Caryn Neman; Lighting, Allen Lee Hughes; Choreography, Doug Elkins CAST: Paul Magid (Dmitri), Howard Patterson (Ivan), Michael Preston (Alyosha), Sam Williams (Smerdyakov), Larry Block (Director/ Fyodor), Joanna Glushak (Grushenka), Cathy Sutherland (Katerina), Bob Amaral (Maurice/Mr. Bear), David Laduca (Guest/Dick/Fishbowl Lady), Gina Leishman (Brunhilda Barkwursthanbyte)
THE SKIN OF OUR TEETH by Thornton Wilder; Director, Douglas C. Wager; Sets, Thomas Lynch; Costumes, Paul Tazewell; Lighting, Nancy Schertler CAST: Saundra Quarterman (Sabina), Jeffery V. Thompson (Fitzpatrick), Halo Wines (Mrs. Antrobus), Carol Monda (Dinosaur/Majorette), M.E. Hart (Mammoth), David Marks (Telegraph Boy), Jurian Hughes (Gladys), Teagle F. Bougere (Henry), Richard Bauer (Antrobus), Ralph Cosham (Doctor/ Official/ Tremayne), Rob Leo Roy (Professor/Announcer/Official), Wendell Wright (Judge/Announcer), Terrence Currier (Homer/Fred), Pamela Nyberg (Miss E. Muse/Hester), Cynyhia Hood (Miss T. Muse), Gail Grate (Miss M. Muse/Ivy), Crystal Simone Wright (Majorette), Tana Hicken (Fortune Teller), Michael W. Howell (Chair Pusher)

Joan Marcus, Stan Barouh Photos

LaDonna Mabry, Gail Grate in "African Company"
Center: Gail Grate, Casey Biggs in "Way of the World"
Top: Lauren Mitchell, Gary Beach in "Of Thee I Sing"

ARIZONA THEATRE COMPANY

Tucson & Phoenix, Arizona

Managing Director, Robert Aplaugh; Artistic Director, David Ira Golsdtein; Assoiciate Artistic Director, Matthew Wiener; Marketing Director, Rob Sweibel; Public Relations Directors, Prindle Gorman-Oomens, Michele Robins

PRODUCTIONS & CASTS

ONE CRAZY DAY OR THE MARRIAGE OF FIGARO; (premiere) Translation /Adaptation, Roger Downey; Based on the play by Beaumarchais; Director, David Ira Goldstein; Musical Director, Nicolas Reveles; Sets, Greg Lucas; Costumes, David Kay Mickelesen; Lighting, Don Darnutzer; Choreography, Gema Sandoval CAST: David Asher (Marquez de Almaviva), Suzanne Bouchard (Rosina), Al Rodrigo (Figaro), Leticia Vasquez (Susanna), Kurt Knudson (Bankhead), Alma Martinez (Marcelina), Samantha Follows (Querubin), Roberto Guajardo (Antonio), Kristine Goto (Frasquita), Roberta Garcia (Pedrillo), Bill Anderson (Padre), Norma Medina (Campesina), Gaye Lynn Scott (Cook), John Aldecoa, Ruben M.Moreno, Larry J. Suarez

THE ALL NIGHT STRUT; Conception, Fran Charnas; Staging/Choreography, Steve Tomkins; Musical Director, Jerry Wayne Harkey; Sets, Greg Lucas; Costumes, David Kay Mickelsen; Lighting, Tracy Odishaw CAST: Robert Clater, Lesia Kaye, Paula Newsome, Michael Vodde

NORA; Adapted by Ingmar Bergman from Ibsen's A Doll's House ; Director, Matthew Wiener; Sets, R. Michael Miller; Costumes, Laura Crow; Lighting, Scott Zielinski; Music/Sound, Dan Moses Schreier CAST: Susan Gibney (Nora), Robertson Dean (Torvald), Faye M. Price (Mrs. Linde), Kirk Jackson (Nils), Apollo Dukakis (Dr. Rank)

FERTILITY RIGHTS (PREMIERE) by Michael Michaelian; Director, David Ira Goldstein; Sets, Jeff Thomson; Costumes, Rose Pederson; Lighting, Tracy Odishaw CAST: Lauren Tewes (Beth), Mark Bramhall (Ernie), Brian Brophy (Leo), Robert Nadir (Phil)

M. BUTTERFLY by David Henry Hwang; Director, Dennis Bigelow; Sets, William Bloodgood; Costumes, Deborah Dryden; Lighting, Robert Peterson CAST: Laurence Ballard (Gallimard), Francis Jue (Song Liling), Jonathan Emerson (Marc/Sharpless), Liisa Ivary (Renee/Party Woman), Jeanne Sakata (Comrad/Suzuki/Shu-Fang), Judy Jean Berns (Helga), David de Berry (Toulon/Judge), Jonathan Bush, Paul Keoni Chun (Kurogo/Dancers), Mei Kui Ding (Dancer)

WILLI, AN EVENING OF WILDERNESS AND SPIRIT by John Pielmeier; Director, David Ira Goldstein; Sets, Greg Lucas; Costumes, Carolyn Keim; Lighting, Rick Paulsen CAST: James Harper (Willi Unsoeld)

Tim Fuller Photos

James Harper in "Willi"

Bottom Left: (clockwise from L) Lesia Kaye, Michael Vodde, Paula Newsome, Robert Clater in "All Night Strut!"
Bottom Right: Kirk Jackson, Susan Gibney in "Nora"

BARN THEATRE

Augusta, Michigan

Forty-seventh Season

Producer, Jack Ragotzy; Producer's Assistant Brendan Ragotzy; Associate Producers, Betty Ebert Ragotzy, Dusty Reeds; Directors, Messrs. Ragotzy, Dusty Reeds; General Manager, Howard McBride; Stage Manager, Gregg Rehrig; Sets, Dusty Reeds, Michael Baggessi; Music Director, David Young; Lighting, Ann Marie Loomis; Choreography, Ann Marie Loomis

RESIDENT COMPANY: Joe Aiello, Penelope Alex, Scott Burkell, Betty Ebert, Louis Girard, Howard McBride, Charlie Misovye, Brendan Ragotzy, Joellyn Cox Young GUEST ARTIST: Tom Wopat

PRODUCTIONS: Perfectly Frank, Rumors, Kiss Me Kate, M. Butterfly, Phantom (Yeston & Kopit), Social Security, Man of La Mancha, Rocky Horror Show

CALWELL THEATRE COMPANY

Boca Raton, Florida

Seventeenth Season

Artistic/Managing Director, Michael Hall; Resident Set Designer, Frank Bennett; Company Manager, Patricia Burdett; Press, Paul Perone; Education/Publications Director, Christopher Cooper; Development Director, Joe Ancker; Marketing Director, Kathy Walton; Stage Manager, Bob Carter; Resident Costume Designer, Bridget Bartlett

PRODUCTIONS & CASTS

SMOKE AND MIRRORS by Will Osborne and Anthony Herrera; Director/Costumes, Michael Hall; Sets, Frank Bennett; Lighting, Mary Jo Dondlinger CAST:Peter Bradbury (Clark Robinson), Tim Hodgin (Leroy P. Lumpkin), Michael Minor (Hamilton Orr), Pat Nesbit (Barbara Orr), Don Robinson (Derek Coburn)
THE CURIOUS SAVAGE by John Patrick; Director, Michael Hall; Sets, Frank Bennett; Lighting, Kenneth Posner CAST: Viki Boyle (Mrs. Paddy), Kim Cozort (Miss Willie), John Felix (Hannibal), John Gardiner (Dr. Emmett), Joy Johnson (Ethel), Pat Nesbit (Lily), Andrea O'Connell (Florence), Tim Powell (Samuel), John G. Preston (Jeffrey), Maura Soden (Fairy May), Joe Warik (Titus)
A FEW GOOD MEN by Aaron Sorkin; Director, Kenneth Kay; Sets, James Morgan; Lighting, Mary Jo Dondlinger CAST: John Archie (Cmdr. Stone), Peter Bradbury (Lt. Daniel Kaffee), Jeffrey Blair Cornell (Lt. Sam Weinberg), Tom Disney (Lt. Kendrick), Peter Haig (Capt. Markinson), Kenneth Kay (Capt. Whitaker), Billy Langley (Lance Cpl. Dawson), Prudencio Montesino (Pfc. Santiago), Robert E. Riley (Lt. Col. Jessep), Jim Ryan (Pfc. Downey), Loretta Shanahan (Lt. Cmdr. Galloway), Tyson Stephenson (Lt. Ross), Clarence Thomas (Capt. Randolph), Tom Wahl (Col. Howard), Brandon Adams, Colin Jones, Vincent Larusso, Albert Leon, John Sama, Michael Strano (Marines, Lawyers, etc.)
THE LITTLE FOXES by Lillian Hellman; Director, Michael Hall; Sets, Frank Bennett; Lighting, Kenneth Posner CAST: John Archie (Cal), Viki Boyle (Birdie), John Felix (Benjamin), John Gardiner (William), Peter Haig (Horace), Kenneth Kay (Oscar), Jilanne Marie Klaus (Alexandra), Pat Nesbit (Regina), Jim Ryan (Leo), Avery Sommers (Addie)
SIGHT UNSEEN by Donald Margulies; Director, Michael Hall; Sets, James Morgan; Lighting, Mary Jo Dondlinger CAST: Peter Bradbury (Waxman), Barbara Bradshaw (Grete), John Fitzgibbon (Nick), Pat Nesbit (Patricia)
THE BOY FRIEND; Music/Lyrics/Book, Sandy Wilson; Director, Michael Hall; Music Director, Kevin Wallace; Choreography, Tina Paul; Sets, Frank Bennett; Lighting, Mary Jo Dondlinger CAST: Joan Susswein Barber (Dubonnet), Eric Bohus (Tony), Karl Christian (Bobby), Gregory Garrison (Michael), Julia Gregory (Maisie), Jerry Gulledge (Percival), Joy Johnson (Lady Brockhurst), Jilanne Marie Klaus (Fay), Jayme McDaniel (Pierre), John Messenger (Brockhurst), Rita Rehn (Hortense), Merry Simkins (Nancy), Meghan Strange (Dulcie), Tracy Venner (Polly), Robert Weber (Alphonse), Albert Leon (Gendarme)
BOOGIE WOOGIE BUGLE BOYS; Arrangements, Kevin Wallace; Choreography, Gregory Garrison; Lighting, Chip Latimer, Ken Melvin CAST: Mark Aldrich, William Selby, Deanna Surber

Paul Perone Photos

Barn Theatre: Top Left: Scott Burkell, Jill Walmsley in "Phantom"
Bottom: Joellyn Cox Young, Penelope Alex, Betty Ebert in "Rumors"
Caldwell Theatre: Right Top: Loretta Shanahan, Peter Bradbury, Jeffrey Blair Cornell in "A Few Good Men"
Center:Pat Nesbit, Peter Bradbury in "Sight Unseen"
Bottom: Joan Susswein Barber, Jerry Gulledge in "The Boy Friend"

CENTER STAGE

Baltimore, Maryland

Artistic Director, Irene Lewis; Managing Director, Peter W. Culman; Production Manager, Katharyn Davies; Stage Managers, Keri Muir, Julie Thompson; Technical Director, Tom Rupp; Resident Dramaturg, James Magruder; Public Relations Director, Linda Geeson

PRODUCTIONS

SERVANT OF TWO MASTERS by Carlo Goldoni; Director, Irene Lewis with Robert Dorfman, Nina Humphrey, David J. Steinberg
T BONE N WEASEL by Jon Klien with Damien Leake, Brian Tarantina, James Noah
A MOON FOR THE MISBEGOTTEN by Eugene O'Neill; Director, Lisa Peterson with Cherry Jones, James Parks, James J. Lawless, Stephen Markle, Keith Langsdale
ESCAPE FROM HAPPINESS by George F. Walker; Director, Irene Lewis with Marin Hinkle, Lois Smith, William Youmans, Annette Helde, Jack Wallace, James Noah, Alexandra Gersten, Pippa Pearthree, Liev Schreiber, Dan Moran
LADY DAY AT EMERSON'S BAR AND GRILL by Lanie Robertson; Director, George Faison with Pamela Isaacs, David Alan Bunn
ARMS AND THE MAN by Shaw; with Helen Carey, Mari Nelson, Lisa C. Arrindell, Robert Westenberg, Bruce R. Nelson, Thomas Ikeda, James J. Lawless, Morgan Strickland

Richard Anderson Photos

Pamela Isaacs, (foreground) David Alan Bunn in "Lady Day..."
Above: Alexandra Gersten, Lois Smith in "Escape From Happiness"

CENTER THEATRE GROUP/AHMANSON THEATRE

UCLA JAMES A. DOOLITTLE THEATRE

Los Angeles, California

Twenty-sixth Season

Producing Director, Gordon Davidson; Managing Director, Charles Dillingham; General Manager, Douglas C. Baker; Press/Advertising, Tony Sherwood; Press Assistant, Nicole Gorak; Audience Development Director, Robert Schlosser; Development Director, Christine Fiedler; Casting Director, Stanley Soble; Technical Director, Robert Routolo

PRODUCTIONS & CASTS

SIX DEGREES OF SEPARATION by John Guare; Director, Jerry Zaks; Sets, Tony Walton; Costumes, William Ivey Long; Lighting, Paul Gallo; CAST: Marlo Thomas (Ouisa), John Cunningham (Flan), Ntare Mwine (Paul), Holly Barron (Kitty), Ian Blackman (Police/Doorman), David Burke (Doug), James DuMont (Hustler), Brian Evers (Detective), Patrick Fabian (Rick), Philip LeStrange (Larkin), Deirdre Lovejoy (Elizabeth), Colin Mitchell (Woody), Adam Philipson (Woody), Adam Philipson (Ben), Victor Raider-Wexler (Dr. Fine), Isabel Rose (Tess), Sam Stoneburner (Geoffrey), Richard Wofford (Trent), Rachel Babcock, Mark Daniel Cade, Kathleen McKiernan, Rainn Wilson

MONEY AND FRIENDS by David Williamson; Director, Michael Blakemore; Sets/Costumes, Hayden Griffin; Lighting, Martin Aronstein CAST: Lisa Banes (Vicki), John Getz (Alex), Michael Gross (Peter), Lizbeth Mackay (Penny), John McMartin (Conrad), Sean O'Bryan (Justin), David Selby (Stephen), Linda Thorson (Margaret), Julie White (Jaquie), George McDaniel, Elizabeth Norment, Jeff Phillips, Marcus Smythe, Deborah Taylor

JAKE'S WOMEN by Neil Simon; Director, Gene Saks; Sets/Costumes, Santo Loquasto; Lighting, Tharon Musser CAST: Alan Alda (Jake), Helen Shaver (Maggie), Brenda Vaccaro (Karen), Talia Balsam (Sheila), Kate Burton (Julie), Genia Michaela (Molly at 12), Maura Russo (Molly at 21), Joyce Van Patten (Edith), Nike Doukas, Lynsey Fischer, Ileen Getz, Munson Hicks, Alexana Lambros

FIVE GUYS NAMED MOE by Clarke Peters; Music, Louis Jordan and various; Director/Choreography, Charles Augins; Musical Director, Reginald Royal; Design, Tim Goodchild; Lighting, Andrew Bridge; Costumes, Noel Howard CAST: Kevyn Brackett (Eat Moe), Doug Eskew (Big Moe), Milton Craig Nealy (Four-Eyed Moe), Jeffrey Polk (Little Moe), Kirk Taylor (No Max), Keith Tyrone (No Moe)

Jay Thompson Photos

Top Left: Alan Alda, Helen Shaver in "Jake's Women"
Top Right: Ntare Mwine, Marlo Thomas in "Six Degrees of Separation"
Center: Sean O'Bryan, Linda Thorson in "Money and Friends"
Bottom: Linda Thorson, Julie White, Lizbeth Mackay, Lisa Banes in "Money and Friends"

CENTER THEATRE GROUP/MARK TAPER FORUM

Los Angeles, California

Twenty-sixth Season

Artistic Director/Producer, Gordon Davidson; Managing Director, Charles Dillingham; Producing Director, Robert Egan; Resident Director, Oskar Eustis; Mangers, Karen S. Wood, Michael Solomon; Staff Producer, Corey Beth Madden; Production Supervisor, Frank Bayer; Press, Nancy Hereford, Phyllis Moberly, Evelyn Kiyomi Emi, Ken Werther

PRODUCTIONS & CASTS

ANGELS IN AMERICA: Part One **MILLENNIUM APPROACHES** and Part Two **PERESTROIKA** : A Gay Fantasia on National Themes (PREMIERE of *Perestroika*) by Tony Kushner; Directors, Oskar Eustis with Tony Taccone; Sets, John Conklin; Costumes, Gabriel Berry; Lighting, Pat Collins CAST: Kathleen Chalfant (Hannah Pitt), K. Todd Freeman (Belize), Jeffrey King (Joe Pitt), Ron Leibman (Roy Cohn), Cynthia Mace (Harper Pitt), Joe Mantello (Louis Ironson), Ellen McLaughlin (Angel), Stephen Spinella (Prior Walter), Pauline Lepor, Eve Signall (Heavenly Attendants)

THE SUBSTANCE OF FIRE by Jon Robin Baitz; Director, Dan Sullivan; Sets, John Lee Beatty; Costumes, Jess Goldstein; Lighting, Arden Fingerhut CAST: Patrick Breen (Martin), Ron Rifkin (Isaac Geldhart), Gena Rowlands (Marge), Jon Tenney (Aaron), Kelley Wolf (Sarah)

SCENES FROM AN EXECUTION (U.S. PREMIERE) by Howard Barker; Director, Robert Allan Ackerman; Scenic Concept, Richard Macdonald; Sets, Yael Pardess; Costumes, Dona Granata; Lighting, Arden Fingerhut CAST: Tony Abatemarco (Lasagna/Mustafa/Workman/Official), Don Amendolia (Prodo), Michael Cumpsty (Carpeta), Olivia d'Abo (Supporta), Alexander Enberg, Greg Naughton, Carlos Papierski (Sailors/Workmen), Michael Forest (Man),Richard Frank (Ostensibile), Francois Giroday (Sordo/Man in Cell), Ben Hammer (Suffici), Frank Langella (Urgentiono), Robert Machray (Pastaccio/Jailer), Jodie Markell (Dementia), Natalija Nogulich (Rivera), Juliet Stevenson (Galactia), Francis DiMase, Marcia Firesten, Roger Kern

TWILIGHT: LOS ANGELES, 1992 (PREMIERE) Conceived/Written/Performed by Anna Deavere Smith; Director, Emily Mann; Sets, Robert Brill; Costumes, Candice Donnelly; Lighting, Allen Lee Hughes; Music, Lucia Hwong

LIPS TOGETHER, TEETH APART by Terrence McNally; Director, John Tillinger; Sets, John Lee Beatty; Costumes, Jane Greenwood; Lighting, Ken Billington CAST: Andrea Martin (Chloe), Nathan Lane succeeded by Ethan Phillips (Sam), John Glover (John), Roxanne Hart (Sally)

Jay Thompson Photos

Top: Anna Devere Smith in "Twilight: Los Angeles 1992"
Second Photo: Joe Mantello, K. Todd Freeman in "Angels in America"
Bottom Left: Frank Langella, Juliet Stevenson in
"Scenes from an Execution"
Bottom Right: Nathan Lane, Andrea Martin, John Glover, Roxanne Hart in
"Lips Together, Teeth Apart"
Above: Ron Rifkin, Gena Rowlands in "Substance of Fire"

Brent Sudduth, Leon Addison Brown, Lou Ferguson in "Master Harold..."

Reed Birney, Lisa Fugard in "Scotland Road"

Bottom: Lisa Gay Hamilton, David Harum in "Our Country's Good"

CINCINNATI PLAYHOUSE IN THE PARK

Cincinnati, Ohio

Thirty-third Season

Producing/Artistic Director, Edward Stern; Executive Director, Buzz Ward; Production Manager, Phil Rundle; Technical Director, Shawn Nolan; Business Manager, Gail Lawrence; Development Director, Cynthia Colebrook; Marketing Director, Kimberly Cooper; Public Relations Director, Peter Robinson; Production Stage Manager, Tom Lawson

PRODUCTIONS & CASTS

HOT 'N' COLE with Music/Lyrics by Cole Porter; Devised by David Holdgrive, Mark Waldrop, George Kramer; Director/Choreographer, Mr. Holdgrive; Set, James Leonard Joy; Costumes, Mariann Verheyen; Lighting, Kirk Bookman CAST: Deb G. Girdler, Mark Martino, Pamela Myers, Amelia Prentice, Jonathan Smedley, Mark Waldrop

LADY DAY AT EMERSON'S BAR AND GRILL by Lanie Robertson; Director, Jonathan Wilson; Set, Joseph P. Tilford; Lighting, Kirk Bookman CAST: Ernestine Jackson (Billie Holiday), Dennis L. Moorman (Jimmy), Jim Anderson (Art)

"MASTER HAROLD"...AND THE BOYS by Athol Fugard; Director, Stephen Hollis; Set/Costumes, David Crank; Lighting, Kirk Bookman CAST: Lou Ferguson (Sam), Leon Addison Brown (Willy), Brent Sudduth (Hally)

THE HOUSE OF BLUE LEAVES by John Guare; Director, Edward Stern; Set, David Potts; Costumes, Michael Krass; Lighting, Kirk Bookman CAST: D'Jamin Bartlett (Bunny), Glynis Bell (Bananas), Michael Conn (Man in White), Charles E. Gerber (Billy), Adrienne Hill (2nd Nun), Russ Jolly (Ronnie), Leslie Scarlett Mason (Corrinna), Mack Miles (M.P.), Robert Walden (Artie), Olivia Williams (Head Nun), Mona Wyatt (Little Nun)

SHIRLEY VALENTINE by Willy Russell; Director, Linda Atkinson; Set, Robert Barnett; Costumes, Lisa Molymeux; Lighting, Jeffrey M. Gress CAST: Brooks Almy (Shirley)

A CHRISTMAS CAROL by Charles Dickens; Adaptation/Director, Howard Dallin; Sets, James Leonard Joy; Lighting, Kirk Bookman CAST: Tom Dunlop (Scrooge), Claire E. Cundiff, Sarah G. Fischer, Michael Haney, James Harris, Katie Harris, Matthew Harris, Rosie Harris, Sarah Harris, Rita Hirsch, Michael Ingram, Timothy Kuhlmann, Tif Luckenbill, Allison Mayer, Alan Mixon, Gregory Procaccino, Mary Proctor, Regina Pugh, Clive Rosengren, Ben Sands, Kathryn Rose Schwarz, Ronald James Strong III, Jim Stump, Tia Marie Talbert, Jonathan Tanzman, Carolan Turner, Isaac B. Turner, Amy Warner, Kathryn Gay Wilson, Joel Winston, Don Sterling Wong

OUR COUNTRY'S GOOD by Timberlake Wertenbaker; Director, Edward Stern; Sets, Andrew Jackness, David Crank; Lighting, Christopher Akerlind; Costumes, Candice Donnelly, Elizabeth Hope Clancy CAST: Kathleen Mahony-Bennett (Meg/Mary/Lt.Dawes), Lisa Gay Hamilton (Lt. Johnson/Duckling), David Harum (2nd Lt. Clark), Dale Hodges (Dabby/2nd Lt. Faddy), Bruce Longworth (Sideway/Capt. Collins), Christopher McHale (Midshipman Brewer/Capt.Campbell/Arscott), Eric Steven Mills (Aboriginal/Black Caesar/Capt. Tench), Carol Schultz (Liz/Rev. Johnson), Richard Thompson (Wisehammer/Capt, Phillip), Patrick Page (Major Ross/Freeman)

SCOTLAND ROAD (PREMIERE) by Jeffrey Hatcher; Director, Edward Stern; Set, Karen TenEyck; Costumes, Delmare L. Rinehart Jr.; Lighting, Kirk Bookman; Composer, Ronald Melrose CAST: Reed Birney (John), Margo Skinner (Halbrech), Lisa Fugard (The Woman), Betty Low (Frances Kittle)

THE IMMIGRANT by Mark Harelik; Director, Charles Towers; Set, Bill Clarke; Costumes, Candice Cain; Lighting, Nancy Schertler CAST: Nesbitt Blaisdell (Milton), Scott Freeman (Haskell), Beverly May (Ima), Rose Stockton (Leah)

SEPARATION by Tom Kempinski; Director, Susan Kerner; Set, Ursula Belden; Costumes, D. Bartlett Blair; Lighting, Jeffrey M. Gress CAST: Walter Charles (Joe), Liann Pattison (Sarah)

A MOON FOR THE MISBEGOTTEN by Eugene O'Neill; Director, Amy Saltz; Set, John Ezell; Costumes, D. Bartlett Blair; Lighting, Jackie Manassee; Music, Douglas J. Cuomo CAST: J. Kenneth Campbell (James Tyrone), Michael Crider (Harder), Giulia Pagano (Josie), Joe Wein (Mike), John Woodson (Phil)

SMOKE ON THE MOUNTAIN by Connie Ray; Conception/Direction, Alan Bailey; Set, Peter Harrison; Costumes, Don Bolinger; Lighting, Victor En Yu Tan CAST: David Hemsley Caldwell (Oglethorpe), Lucinda Blackwood (June), Richard Glover (Burl), Barbara Larsen (Vera), Don Bryant Bailey (Stanley), Jennifer Piech (Denise), Jeffrey Currier (Dennis)

AIN'T MISBEHAVIN'; Music, Fats Waller; Conception, Murry Horowitz and Richard Maltby, Jr.; Director, Carl Jablonski; Musical Director, Kevin Toney; Set/Costumes, Eduardo Sicangco; Lighting, Kirk Bookman CAST: Karen Anice Long, Jewel Tompkins, Dale E. Turner, Jerald Vincent, Kathy Wade

Sandy Underwood Photos

THE CLEVELAND PLAYHOUSE

Cleveland, Ohio

Seventy-seventh Season

Artistic Director, Josephine R. Abady; Managing Director, Dean R. Gladden; Artistic General Manager, Don Roe; Artistic Administrator, Susan Henry; Company Manager, Brint Learned; Production Stage Manager, Robert S. Garber

PRODUCTIONS & CASTS

OF THEE I SING with Music by George Gershwin; Lyrics, Ira Gershwin; Book, George S. Kaufman, Morrie Ryskind; Director, Peter Mark Schifter; Choreography, Ted Pappas; Musical Director, Evans Haile; Sets, Lawrence Miller; Costumes, David C. Paulin; Lighting, Richard Winkler CAST: Julie Marie Boyd (Bellhop), Daniel Marcus (Lippman), Michael Cone (Gilhooley), Scott Robertson (Fulton/Ambassador), Larry Collis (Sen. Jones), David O. Frazier (Sen. Lyons), Peter Bartlett (Throttlebottom), Don Goodspeed (Wintergreen), Susan Wood (Diana), Frank Kosik (Jenkins), Ellen Zachos (Mary), Christine Gradl (Miss Benson), Mike Danner (Justice), David A. Wood (Tour Guide), Eric Coble (Chief Flunkey), Thom Rice (Doctor), Laura Hernandez, Robbi Marchon, Madeline J. Reiss, Mary Wanamaker, Jennifer West, Jim Athens, Webster Dean, Ramond C. Harris, Kevin Weldon

FUGUE by Leonora Thuna; Director, Kenneth Frankel; Sets, Marjorie Bradley Kellogg; Costumes, Jess Goldstein; Lighting, Ann G. Wrightson CAST: Barbara Barrie (Mary), Susanne Marley (Zelda), William Atherton (Dr. Lucchesi), Myra Taylor (Dr. Oleander), Augusta Dabney (Mother), Kurt Deutsch (Noel), Mary Layne (Liz), Chelsea Altman (Tammy), Ellen Karsten (Nurse voice)

THE PHILADELPHIA STORY by Philip Barry; Director, Sheldon Epps; Sets, James Leonard Joy; Costumes, Judy Dearing; Lighting, Jeff Davis CAST: Stephanie Zimbalist (Tracy), Jessica Queller (Dinah), Ruby Holbrook (Margaret), Eric Swanson (Sandy), Daniel P. Ensel (Thomas), Gordon Connell (Uncle Willy), Amanda Carlin (Liz), Mark Hofmaier (Mike), Paul Hebron (George), Richard Bekins (Dexter), Ian Stuart (Seth), Ed Baker (Mac)

JAR THE FLOOR by Cheryl L. West; Director, Tazewell Thompson; Sets/Lighting, Joseph P. Tilford; Costumes, Kay Kurta CAST: Irma P. Hall (MaDear), Candace Hunter (Maydee), Crystal Laws Green (Lola), Susan Payne (Vennie), Josette DiCarlo (Raisa)

THE MISANTHROPE by Moliere; Translation/Adaptation, Neil Bartlett; Director, Roger T. Danforth; Sets, Bob Phillips, Jr.; Costumes, Mimi Maxmen; Lighting, Richard Winkler CAST: Morgan Lund (Alceste), Michael Early (Philinte), Adam Grupper (Oronte), Nicole Orth-Pallavicini (Celimene), Mona Wyatt (Eliante), Yolande Bavan (Arsinoe), Richard Hicks (Acaste), Eric Riley (Clitandre)

THE BUTCHER'S DAUGHTER by Wendy Kesselman; Director, Leslie Swackhamer; Sets, Tony Straiges; Costumes, Paul Tazewell; Lighting, Beverly Emmons CAST: Anney Giobbe (Celeste), Frederick Neumann (Executioner), Jane White (Nounou), Jennifer Rohn (Olympe), Jesse L. Martin (Pierrot), Beth Dixon (Executioner's Wife), Ken Kliban (de Pompignan), Jane White (Grandmother), Anthony Brown (Philippe/Actor), Billy Radin (Actor), Kitao Sakurai (Michel), Tim DeKay (Ange/Actor), Eric Coble (Actor), Julie Marie Boyd, Ellen Karsten, Canon Tate

THE HOUSE OF BLUE LEAVES by John Guare; Director, Josephine R. Abady; Sets, David Potts; Costumes, Linda Fisher; Lighting, Dennis Parichy CAST: Jack Riley (Artie), Thom Rice (Ronnie), Jane Galloway (Bunny), Barbara Eda-Young (Bananas), Kay Walbye (Corrinna), Peggy Cosgrave (Head Nun), Edwina Lewis (2nd Nun), Amanda Butterbaugh (Little Nun), Mike F. Danner (m.p.), Bryan Edward Smith (Man in White), Phillip Clark (Billy)

HEARTBEATS; Music/Lyrics/Book, Amanda McBroom; Created by Ms. McBroom and Bill Castellino; Director, Choreography, Mr. Castellino; Additional Music, Gerald Sternbach, Michele Brourman, Tom Snow, Craig Safan; Musical Supervisor/Vocal Arrangements, Mr. Sternbach; Musical Director, Ann-Carol Pence; Orchestrations, Bill Elliott; Sets, Linda Hacker; Costumes, Charlotte M. Yetman; Lighting, Richard Winkler CAST: Jan Maxwell (Annie, the Wife), Paul Harman (Steve, the Husband), Michelle Blakely, Nicholas Cokas, Teri Gibson, Ric Ryder

Richard Termine Photos

Top: Mary Layne, Barbara Barrie, William Atherton in "Fuge"
Center: Webster Dean, David A. Wood, Raymond C. Harris, Susan Wood, Jim Athens, Kevin Weldon in "Of Thee I Sing"
Bottom: Stephanie Zimbalist, Amanda Carlin, Mark Hoffmaier in "Philadelphia Story"

THE COCONUT GROVE PLAYHOUSE

Miami, Florida

Producing Artistic Director, Arnold Mittelman; Associate Producer, Lynne Peyser; Production Managers, Jay Young, Earl Hughes; Technical Director, David L. Radunsky; Production Stage Manager, Rafael V. Blanco; Marketing/Sales Director, Mark D. Sylvester; Communications Manager, Savannah Whaley

PRODUCTIONS & CASTS

GIVE 'EM HELL HARRY! by Samuel Gallu; Set, Stephen Lambert; Lighting, Todd Wren CAST: Kevin McCarthy

TANGO PASION (PREMIERE); Conceived/Supervised by Mel Howard; Choreography, Hector Zaraspe; Musical Conception/Direction, Jose Libertella, Luis Stazo; Sets/Costumes, John Falabella; Lighting, Richard Pilbrow, Dawn Chiang CAST: THE SEXTETO MAYOR: Jose Libertella, Luis Stazo, Eduardo Walczak, Mario Abramovich, Oscar Palermo, Osvaldo Aulicino, Anibal Arias, Jorge Orlando, Juan Zunini SINGERS Daniel Bouchet, Alberto Del Solar, Yeni Patino DANCERS Claudia Patricia Mendoza, Luis Castro, Daniela Arcuri, Armando Orzuza, Gustavo Marcelo Russo, Alejandra Mantina, Jorge Torres, Pilar Alvarez, Juan O. Corvalan, Viviana M. Laguzzi, Judit Aberstain, Fernando Jimenez, Veronica Gardella, Marcelo Bernandaz, Osvaldo S. Cilineto, Graciela A. Garcia, Jorge Romano, Gunilla Wingquist

LIPS TOGETHER, TEETH APART by Terrence McNally; Director, Tony Giordano; Set/Lighting, James Tilton; Costumes, Ellis Tillman CAST: Judith Delgado, Leslie Hendrix, Samuel Maupin, Michael O'Hare

DON'T DRESS FOR DINNER by Marc Camoletti; Adaptation, Robin Hawdon; Director, Pamela Hunt; Set/Lighting, James Tilton; Costumes, Ellis Tilton CAST: Alison Bevan, Jan Neuberger, Alexandra O'Karma, Max Robinson, Reno Roop, Timothy Wheeler

HIM, HER & YOU (PREMIERE); Created/Directed by Robert Shields; Tap Choreography, Lorene Yarnell; Set, James Tilton; Lighting, John McLain; Costumes, Carolyn Ford CAST: Robert Shields, Lorene Yarnell

BEAU JEST by James Sherman; Director, Robert Kalfin; Set/Lighting, James Tilton; Costumes, Ellis Tillman CAST: Marilyn Chris, Lee Wallace, Wendy Kaplan, Bob Kirsh, Joseph Adams, Michael Elich

MARRIAGE PLAY by Edward Albee; Director, Arnold Mittelman; Set, James Tilton; Lighting, Todd Wren; Costumes, Ellis Tillman CAST: Kathleen Butler, Tom Klunis

CARREÑO; Written and Performed by Pamela Ross; Original Director, Gene Frankel; Set, Stephen Lambert; Lighting, Todd Wren

SWEET JUSTICE (PREMIERE); Written/Directed by Patricia Dolan Gross; Set, Stephen Lambert; Costumes, Ellis Tillman CAST: Natashya Armer, Melanie Madison, Michael Catangay, Rafael Prieto

Jo Winstead Photos

Top Right: Tom Klunis, Kathleen Butler in "Marriage Play"
Below: Bob Kirsh, Wendy Kaplan, Lee Wallace, Marilyn Chris, Joseph Adams, Michael Elich in "Beau Jest"

Alison Bevan, Reno Roop, Jan Neuberger, Max Robinson, (top) Timothy Wheeler, Alexandra O'Karma in "Don't Dress for Dinner"

CROSSROADS THEATRE COMPANY

New Brunswick, New Jersey

Fifteenth Season

Artistic Director/Co-Founder, Ricardo Khan; Associate Producer, Kenneth Johnson; Development Director, Sydne Mahone; Managing Director, Ken McClain; Operations/Production Director, Gary Kechely; Company Manager, Cheri B. Kechely; Production Stage Manager, Doug Hosney; Press/Public Relations Director, Sandra Lanman

PRODUCTIONS & CASTS

SHEILA'S DAY by Duma Ndlovu; Co-writer, Ebony Jo-Ann CAST: Stephanie Alston, Gina Breedlove, Carla Brothers, Terry Burrell, Irene Datcher, Tina Fabrique, Thuli Dumakude, Annelen Malebo, Denise Morgan, Tu Nokwe, LaTangela Reese, Mary Twala
SLOW DANCE ON THE KILLING GROUND by William Hanley CAST: Salem Ludwig (Glas), Kevin Jackson (Randall), Bitty Schram (Rosie)
BETSEY BROWN by Ntozake Shange and Emily Mann; Music, Baikida Carroll CAST: Nicole Leach (Betsey), Keith Robert Bennett (Eugene), Vanessa A. Jones (Regina), Clarice Taylor (Vida), Gene Anthony Ray (Roscoe), Jean Cheek (Carrie), Lawrence Clayton (Mr. Jeff), Alisa Gyse-Dickens (Jane), Robert Jason Jackson (Greer), Marc Joseph (Charlie), Hillary Hawkins (Margot), Donovan Ian H. McKnight (Allard), Angela Robinson, Veronica Campbell, Wesley Alexander
THE DISAPPEARANCE (PREMIERE) by Ruby Dee; From the novel by Rosa Guy CAST: Ruby Dee (Female Narrator), Carl Lumbly (Male Narrator), Marie Thomas (Dora), Lynda Gravatt (Ann), Robinson Frank Adu (Peter), Tonia Rowe (Gail), Kharisma (Perk), Khali Kain (Imamu), Conrad Roberts (Mr. Elder), Venida Evans (Helen/Mrs. Jones/ Mrs. Dixon/Mrs. Briggs), Joseph McKenna (Sullivan/Sergeant/Titi), Isiah Whitlock, Jr. (Tenant/Brown/Mr. Miller/Police)
MOTHERS (PREMIERE) by Kathleen McGhee-Anderson CAST: Tina Lifford (Momma/ Mrs. Ellis/Mayberry), Harry Mann (Sax), Jeanne Mori (Mariko), Gretchen Oehler (Jean), Lira Angel (Penny), Meera Popkin (Tamiko), Michael Barry Greer (Doctor/Boss/Judge/Father), Takayo Fischer (Nurse/Grandmother/ Bath Woman/Fortune Teller), Elizabeth Heflin (Barbara/Donna), Monte Russell (Soldier/Customer/Terrence)
THE LATE GREAT LADIES OF BLUES & JAZZ; Conceived/Written by Sandra Reaves; Director, Ricardo Khan; Musical Director, Herschel Dwellingham; Costumes, Michael Hannah CAST: Sandra Reaves

Rich Pipeling Photos

Top: Tu Nokwe, Mary Twala, Tina Fabrique, Denise Morgan, Stephanie Alston in "Sheila's Day"
Bottom Right: Khalil Kain, Ruby Dee in "The Disappearance"

DELAWARE THEATRE COMPANY

Wilmington, Delaware

Fourteenth Season

Artistic Director, Cleveland Morris; Managing Director, David Edelman; Assistant to Artistic Director, Danny Peak; Marketing Director, Kevin Moore; Development Director, Ann Schenck; Production Stage Manager, Patricia Christian; Production Manager, Eric Schaeffer

PRODUCTIONS & CASTS

ANTIGONE by Jean Anouilh; Adaptation, Lewis Galantiere; Director, Cleveland Morris; Sets, Dan Boylen; Lighting, Curt Senie; Costumes, Marla Jurglanis CAST: KIm Sullivan (Chorus), Fanni Green (Nurse), Louise Roberts (Antigone), Jill Patterson (Ismene), Christopher Roberts (Haemon), Seth Jones (Creon), Michael Jerome Johnson, James Elliott, Kip Veasey (Guards), Erik Sherr (Messenger), Casey Saenger (Page), Liz Hutchison, Wendy Winslow Lofting (Eurydice)
MOUNTAIN by Douglas Scott; Director, John Henry Davis; Set, Philipp Jung, Peter Harrison; Costumes, David C. Woolard; Lighting, Dennis Parichy; Music/Sound, John Gromada CAST: Len Cariou (William O. Douglas), Reathel Bean (Actor), Heather Summerhayes (Actress)
THE MATCHMAKER by Thornton Wilder; Director, Cleveland Morris; Sets, Lewis Folden; Lighting, Rebecca G. Frederick; Costumes, Marla Jurglanis CAST: Dorthea Hammond (Dolly), Robert Prosky (Vandergelder), John Prosky (Cornelius), Andrew Prosky (Barnaby), Cary Barker (Irene), Nancy Daly (Minnie), Paul Morella (Ambrose), Candace Dian Leverett (Ermengarde), Georgia Southcotte (Flora), F. Gregory Tigani (Malachi), Susan Huey (Cook), Erik Sherr (Rudolf), Christopher Roberts (August), Barbara Ahern Wilhide (Gertrude), Kevin Freel (Cabman), David C. Wyeth (Scanlon/Gypsy)
THE IMMIGRANT by Mark Harelik; Conception, Mr. Harelik, Randal Myler; Director, Howard J. Millman; Sets, Lewis Folden based on Kevin Rupnik; Costumes, Maria Marrero, Marla Jurglanis; Lighting, Kevin Lapham based on Phil Monat CAST: John Sterling Arnold (Milton), Frances Tucker Kemp (Ima), Michael Oberlander (Haskell), Deborah McArthur (Leah)
THE COCKTAIL HOUR by A.R. Gurney; Director, Allan Carlsen; Set, Eric Schaeffer; Lighting, Christopher Gorzelnik; Costumes, Marla Jurglanis CAST: Gerald Richards (Bradley), Timothy Wahrer (John), Stanja Lowe (Ann), Maureen Silliman (Nina)

Richard C. Carter, Mark Garvin Photos

Top:Reathel Bean, Heather Summerhayes, Len Cariou in "Mountain"
Center: Gerald Richards, Maureen Silliman, Timothy Wahrer, Stanja Lowe in "Cocktail Hour"

Dennis T. Kleinsmith, Milfordean Luster, Sandra Love Aldridge, Geoff Safron in "Homeward Bound"

DETROIT REPERTORY THEATRE

Detroit, Michigan

Thirty-fifth Season

Artistic/Managing Director, Bruce E. Millan; Human Services Director, Dolores Andrus; Marketing Director, Dino A. Valdez; Production Manager, Richard E. Smith; Costume Director, B.J. Essen; Lighting Director, Kenneth R. Hewitt, Jr.; Scenic Artisit, John Knox

PRODUCTIONS & CASTS

HOMEWARD BOUND by Elliott Hayes; Director, William Boswell; Sets, Robert Katkowsky CAST: Sandra Love Aldridge, Howard Hogan, Bob Ketterer, Dennis T. Kleinsmith, Milfordean Luster, Geoff Safron
MY CHILDREN!MY AFRICA! by Athol Fugard; Director, Barbara Busby; Set, Marylynn Kacir CAST: Rod Johnson, Ronald Mitchell, Chris Ann Voudoukis
UNCHANGING LOVE by Romulus Linney; Director, Barbara Busby; Sets, Robert Katkowsky CAST: Sandra Love Aldridge, William Boswell, Benita Charles, Michael Hodge, Hollis Huston, F. Kwame Johnson, Marylynn Kacir, Dennis T. Kleinsmith, Milfordean Luster, Mack Palmer
THREE CARD MONTE AND THE ROYAL FLUSH by Daniel DuPlantis; Director, Bruce E. Millan; Sets, Dee Andrus CAST: William Boswell, Judy Dery, Charles W. McGraw, Mo Silverman

Bruce E. Millan Photos

138

GEORGE STREET PLAYHOUSE

New Brunswick, New Jersey

Producing Artistic Director, Gregory S. Hurst; Managing Director, Diane Claussen; Associate Artistic Director, Wendy Liscow; Press/Public Relations Director, Heidi W. Giovine; Marketing Director, Rick Engler; Business Manager, Karen Price; Development Director, Philip J. Santora; Design/Production Director, Susan Kerner; Resident Stage Manager, Thomas L. Clewell; Technical Director, Michael Reed

PRODUCTIONS & CASTS

NEAR THE END OF THE CENTURY (PREMIERE) by Tom Dulack; Director, Gregory S. Hurst; Sets, Barbara Jasien; Costumes, Barbara Forbes; Lighting, Donald Holder CAST: Michael Murphy (Richard Boyle), Greg Mullavey (Howie Stark), Catherine Curtin (Irish)
IDIOGLOSSIA by Mark Handley; Director, Tom O'Horgan; Sets, Perry Arthur Kroeger; Costumes, Barbara Forbes; Lighting, Paul Armstrong CAST: Steven Keats (Jake), Allison Janney (TC), Betsy Palmer (Claude), Deanna Deignan (Nell)
3 MEN ON A HORSE by John Cecil Holm & George Abbott; Director, Gregory S. Hurst; Sets, Atkin Pace; Costumes, Barbara Forbes; Lighting, Donald Holder CAST: Valerie Leonard (Audrey), David Malmgren (Tailor), Tom Beckett (Trowbridge), Steve Mellor (Dobbins), James Morgan (Delivery Boy), Daniel Oreskes (Harry), John Ramsey (Charlie), David S. Howard (Frankie), Scott Wentworth (Patsy), Amelia Prentice (Mabel), Adrienne Hill (Bertha), Ibi Janko (Gloria), John Bianchi (Al), Laurie Girion (Maid), Mark Hammer (Carver)
SPINE (PREMIERE); Written/Directed by Bill C. Davis; Sets, Deborah Jasien; Costumes, Sue Ellen Rohrer; Lighting, Donald Holder CAST: Heather Gottlieb (Claire), Justin Kirk (Mike Jr.), Caroline Aaron (Lois), Mark Metcalf (Mike Sr.), Sakina Jaffrey (Dr. Maru)
MORNING DEW WITH TRELLIS (PREMIERE) by Richard Browner; Director, Wendy Liscow; Sets, Atkin Pace; Costumes, Barbara Forbes; Lighting, F. Mitchell Dana CAST: Nancy Paul (Angela), Bibi Besch (Kay)
THE FIELDS OF AMBROSIA (PREMIERE) with Music by Martin Silvestri; Lyrics/Book, Joel Higgins; Based on the screenplay *The Traveling Executioner* by Garrie Bateson; Director, Gregory S. Hurst; Choreogra-phy, Lynne Taylor-Corbett; Musical Director, Sariva Goetz; Orchestrations, Harold Wheeler; Sets, Deborah Jasien; Costumes, Hillary Rosenfeld; Lighting, Howard Werner, Donald Holder CAST: Hal Davis (Pat/J.B. Tucker/Prison Super), Matthew Bennett (Stanley Mae/Samuel Pennybaker), Steve Steiner (Caleb/Rapist), Joel Higgins (Jonas Candide), Ted Stamp (Eben/Roscoe), Eddie Korbich (Jimmy Crawford), Peter Samuel (Piquant), Robert Ously (Doc), Nick Ulett (Warden Brodsky), Shaver Tillitt (Willie Herzallerliebst), Christine Andreas (Gretchen), Elisabeth S. Rodgers (Alice), Ron Lee Savin (Daddy), David Mann(Rapist), Ed Sala (Card Sharp/Bank Guard), Ron Lee Savin (Bank Manager), Peter Brown, Nicola Boyer, Debra Carozza, China Forbes, Jamie Holmes, Christopher Lynn, David Mann, Susan Peters, Shaver Tillitt
FOXFIRE by Susan Cooper and Hume Cronyn; Music, Jonathan Holtzman; Director, Matthew Penn; Sets, Deborah Jasien; Costumes, Sue Ellen Rohrer; Lighting, Donald Holder CAST: John Hickok (Dillard), Audra Lindley (Annie), James Whitmore (Hector), Terry Layman (Prince), Dorrie Joiner (Holly), John Newton (Doc)

Miguel Pagliere Photos

Joel Higgins, Eddie Korbich in "Fields of Ambrosia"

James Whitmore, Audra Lindley in "Foxfire"

Caroline Aaron, Justin Kirk in "Spine"

Jenny Bacon, Jerry Saslow, Christopher Donahue in "Baltimore Waltz"

Richard Poe, Seana Kofoed, Isaiah Washington, Pat Bowie in "Skin of Our Teeth"

Linda Stephens, Hollis Resnik in "Wings"

Shannon Cochran, Michael O'Gorman & cast in "Riverview"

GOODMAN THEATRE

Chicago, Illinois

Artistic Director, Robert Falls; Executive Director, Roche Schulfer; Associate Artistic Director, Michael Maggio; General Manager, Katherine Murphy; Associate Director, Frank Galati; Artistic Associate, Steve Scott; Affiliate Artists, Mary Zimmerman, Chuck Smith; Public Relations, Cindy Bandle, Carrie Jaeck

PRODUCTIONS & CASTS

RIVERVIEW: A Melodrama with Music (PREMIERE) by John Logan; Director, Robert Falls; Original Music/Musical Supervision/Arrangements, Larry Schanker; Orchestrations, David Siegel; Musical Director, Helen Gregory; Sets, Thomas Lynch; Costumes, Nan Cibula; Lighting, Michael S. Philippi CAST: Paul Amandes (Pa), John Beasley (Nat), Duane Boutte (Robert), Robert G. Breuler (Uncle Moe), Frederick Charles Canada (Buddy), Gary Carlson (Frankie), Shannon Cochran (Dolly), Jim Corti (Soldier), Susan Craig (Donna), Vito D'ambrosio (Genilli), Aisha De Haas (Gypsy), Leelai Demoz (Jem), Louis Dickinson (Timmy), Deidre Dolan (Lauren Bacall), Michelle Elise Duffy (Susan), Jeffery Duke (Sailor), Josh Forman (Teddy), Carole Gutierrez (Ma), Jennifer Kemp (Maria), Molly Kidder (Joanie), Jill Locnikar (Rita Hayworth), Darren Matthias (Barker), Elyse Mirto (Linda Limber), Michael O'Gorman (Jake), Kelly Prybycien (Betty Grable), Lee Raines (Rich Man), Nathaniel Sanders (Jimmt the Ape-Bot), John Scherer (Warren), Seth Swoboda (Guy), Bill Szobody (joey), Annette Thurman (RichWoman), Stanley White (King Popeye), Catherine Lee Yore (Dottie), James Zager (Sailor)

THE SKIN OF OUR TEETH by Thornton Wilder; Director, David Petrarca; Sets, Michael Yeargan; Costumes, Catherine Zuber; Lighting, Christopher Akerlind CAST: Pat Bowie (Mrs. Antrobus), Bellary Darden (E.Muse/ Conveener/Ivy), Ron Dortch (Refugee/Chair Pusher/Tremayne), Mark D. Espinoza (Refugee/Chair Pusher), Marilyn Dodds Frank (T.Muse/Conveener/Hester), Marcia Gay Harden (Sabina), Tonray Ho (M.Muse/ChairPusher), Seana Kofoed (Gladys), James McCance (Professor/Conveener/ Official), Larry Neumann, Jr. (Conveener/Fred), Daniel Oreskes (Fitzpatrick/Conveener), Dwain A. Perry (Mammoth/Conveener), Christopher Pieczynski (Homer/Conveener), Richard Poe (Antrobus), Sean A. Tate (Telegraph Boy), Lisa Tejero (Doctor/Conveener), Isiah Washington (Henry), Tom Webb (Judge/Conveener), Jacqueline Williams (Dinosaur/ Fortune Teller)

A CHRISTMAS CAROL by Charles Dickens; Adaptation, Tom Creamer; Director, Steve Scott; Music, Larry Schanker; Sets, Joseph Nieminski; Lighting, Robert Christen; Choreography, Bea Rashid CAST: Tom Mula (Scrooge), Madilynn A. Beck, E. Faye Butler, Ron Dortch, Joan Elizabeth, Christopher Erwin, Mark D. Espinoza, Ellis Foster, Terence Gallagher, Carole Gutierrez, Cheryl Hamada, Dennis Kennedy, Justina Machado, Betsy Morgan, Emeal Myles III, William J. Norris, Olumiji Olawumi, Robert Scogin, James Sie, Paul Slade Smith, Rick Snyder, James Tyrone Stewart, Steve Trussell, Christopher Vasquez, Nancy Voigts, Celeste Williams

TWO TRAINS RUNNING by August Wilson; Director, Lloyd Richards; Sets, Tony Fanning; Costumes, Chrisi Karvonides-Dushenko; Lighting, Geoff Korf CAST: Bellary Darden (Risa), Anthony Chisholm (Wolf), Paul Butler (Memphis), Roscoe Lee Browne (Holloway), Lou Ferguson (Hambone), Eriq LaSalle (Sterling), John Beasley (West)

MARVIN'S ROOM by Scott McPherson; Director, David Petrarca; Sets, Linda Buchanan; Costumes, Claudia Boddy; Lighting, Robert Christen CAST: Carol Schultz (Bessie), Tim Monsion (Dr. Wally), Jane MacIver (Ruth), Peter Rybolt (Bob), Mary Beth Fisher (Lee), JoNell Kennedy (Dr. Charlotte/Home Director), Chuck Huber (Hank), Karl Maschek (Charlie), Michael Nathanael Robinson (Marvin)

BLACK SNOW (PREMIERE) by Keith Reddin; From the novel by Mikhail Bulgakov; Director, Michael Maggio; Sets, Linda Buchanan; Costumes, Martin Pakledinaz; Lighting, James F. Ingalls; Music, Rob Milburn, Miriam Sturm, Michael Bodeen CAST: Bruce Norris (Sergei), Jordan Charney (Vasilievich), Jeffrey Hutchinson (Rvatsky-Aloysius/Bombar-dov), Seana Kofoed (Eulampia), Michael McAlister (Konkin/Fat Man/ Anton), John Mohrlein (Gavril/Shakespeare), Tom Mula (Bondarevsky/ Sophocles), Ajay K. Naidu (Young Man), William J. Norris (Likospastov/ Patrikeyev), Steve Pickering (Yegor/Strizh/Moliere), Christopher Pieczynski (Baklazhanov/Ilchin/Bakvalin/Romanus), Barbara E. Robertson (Toropetzkaya/Ludmilla), Carmen Roman (Irinia), Miriam Sturm (Muse), Marc Vann (Rudolfi/Panin/Phillippovich/Andrei)

GOODMAN STUDIO

WINGS (PREMIERE) with Music by Jeffrey Lunden; Lyrics/Book, Arthur Perlman; Based on the play by Arthur Kopit; Director, Michael Maggio; Musical Director, Brad Vieth; Sets, Linda Buchanan; Costumes, Birgit Rattenborg Wise; Lighting, Robert Christen CAST: Linda Stephens (Emily), William Brown (Doctor/Brambilla), Ora Jones (Nurse/Mrs. Timmins), Hollis Resnik (Amy), Ross Lehman (Billy)

PUDDIN 'N PETE (PREMIERE) by Cheryl L. West; Director, Gilbert Wadazaf McCauley; Set, Clay Snider; Costumes, Yslan Hicks; Lighting, Robert Shook CAST: Cheryl Lynn Bruce (Puddin), Ernest Perry, Jr. (Pete), Rebecca Tennison (Ariel), Cindy Orthal, JoNell Kennedy, Tim Rhoze, John Gegenhuber (Ensemble)

THE BALTIMORE WALTZ by Paula Vogel; Director, Mary Zimmerman; Set, Scott Bradley; Costumes, Allison Reeds; Lighting, Rita Pietraszek CAST: Jenny Bacon (Anna), Jerry Saslow (Carl), Christopher Donahue (3rd Man/Doctor)

Eric Y. Exit, Liz Lauren Photos

Marcia Gay Harden in "Skin of Our Teeth"
Top: Miriam Sturm, Bruce Norris in "Black Snow"

141

GOODSPEED OPERA HOUSE

East Haddam, Connecticut

Executive Director, Michael P. Price; Associate Producer, Sue Frost; Casting Director, Warren Pincus; Development Director, Heidi C. Freeman; Company Manager, Sean Skeehan; Public Relations Director, Michael Sandee; New York Press, Max Eisen/Madelon Rosen

PRODUCTIONS & CASTS (1992)

IT'S A BIRD, IT'S A PLANE, IT'S SUPERMAN with Music by Charles Strose; Lyrics, Lee Adams; Book, David Newman and Robert Benton; Director, Stuart Ross; Choreography, Michele Assaf; Musical Director/ Vocal Arrangements, Michael O'Flaherty; Orchestrations, Keith Levenson; Sets, Neil Peter Jampolis; Costumes, Lindsay W. Davis; Lighting, Kirk Bookman CAST: Jamie Ross (Max Mencken), Kay McClelland (Lois Lane), Gary Jackson (Clark Kent), Michael E. Gold (Perry White), Jan Neuberger (Sydney), Gabriel Barre (Dr. Sedgwick), John Schiappa (Jim Morgan), Mark Santoro, Alexander Eriksson, Randy Charleville, Mr. Gold, Bobby Miranda (Suspects), Michael McCoy (Mustafa), Cadet Bastine, Michelle Chase, Mr. Eriksson, Mr. Santoro (Fabulous Flying Fahzumis), Carla Renata Williams (Mayor), Himself (Superman), Peggy Bayer, Jennifer Lamberts, Joanne Manning

PAINT YOUR WAGON with Music by Frederick Loewe; Lyrics/Book, Alan Jay Lerner; Director, Andre Ernotte; Choreography, Tony Stevens; Misical Director/Vocal Arrangements, Michael O'Flaherty; Sets, James Noone; Lighting, Phil Monat; Costumes, John Carver Sullivan; Orchestrations, Keith Levenson, Andrew Wilder CAST: George Ball (Rumson), Marla Schaffel (Jennifer), Luke Lynch (Bullnack), Mark C. Reis (Whippany), Anthony S. Bernard (Dutchie), David Bedella (Valveras), Stephen Lee Anderson (Woodling), Liz McCartney (Elizabeth), Leigh-Anne Wencker (Sarah)

ANIMAL CRACKERS with Music/Lyrics by Bert Kalmar and Harry Ruby; Book, George S. Kaufman and Morrie Ryskind; Director, Charles Repole; Sets, John Falabella; Costumes, David Toser; Lighting, Craig Miller; Orchestrations, Russel Warner; Musical Director/Dance Arrangements, Albin Konopka; Choreography, Tony Stevens CAST: Frank Ferrante, Les Marsden, Robert Michael Baker, Craig Rubano, Celia Tackaberry, Keith Bernardo, Donald Christopher, Rieka R. Cruz, Dottie, Earle, Peter Gregus, Anna McNeely, Jeanine Meyers, Christopher Nilsson, Brenda O'Brien, Michael O'Steen, Rusty Reynolds, Hal Robinson, Jeanna Schweppe, Laurie Sheppard, Deanna Wells, Patrick Wetzel

NORMA TERRIS THEATRE

HEARTBEATS with Music/Lyrics/Book by Amanda McBroom; Creation, Ms. McBroom, Bill Castellino; Additional Music, Gerald Sternbach, Michele Brourman, Tom Snow; Director/Choreographer, Mr. Castellino; Musical Director, Ann-Carol Pence; Sets, Linda Hacker; Costumes, Charlotte Yetman; Lighting, Craig Lathrop CAST: Gilles Chiasson, Hilary James, Julie Lee Johnson, John Kozeluh, Karen Mason, Michael Rush

Diane Sobolewski Photos

Alison Bevan, John Sloman in "Rough Crossing"

Kay McClelland, Gary Jackson in "It's a Bird, It's a Plane..."

GREAT LAKES THEATRE FESTIVAL

Cleveland, Ohio

Artistic Director, Gerald Freedman; Manging Director, Mary Bill; Communications/Education Associate, Zandra Wolfgram; Set Designer, John Ezell

PRODUCTIONS & CASTS

CYRANO DE BERGERAC by Edmond Rostand; Translation, Anthony Burgess; Director, Gerald Freedman; Costumes, Jason Scott; Lighting, Thomas Skelton CAST: Robert Foxworth (Cyrano), Christopher Biebelhausen, Gloria Biegler, Judith Black, Andrew Boyer, Meredith Brickett, John Buck, Jr., Scott Caple, Johnny Lee Davenport, Marji Dodrill, Robert Haley, Francis Henry, Jim Hillgartner, Mickey Houlahan, Joel Kramer, Bryan Mason, Steve Matuszak, Kenn McLaughlin, Adam Moeller, John P. Monroe, Robert Murray, Daria Sanford, Darrell Starnik, Jeremiah Sullivan, William Verderber, Gregory Violand, Ray Virta

ROUGH CROSSING by Tom Stoppard; Music, Andre Previn; Director, Victoria Bussert; Costumes, James Scott; Lighting, Mary Jo Dondlinger; Musical Director, Nancy Gantose-Maier; Dances, John Sloman CAST: Alison Bean, Edward Conery, Steve Routman, John Sloman, John Tillotson, Charles Tuthill

A CHRISTMAS CAROL by Charles Dickens; Adaptation/Direction, Gerald Freedman; Staging, Victoria Bussert; Costumes, James Scott, Lighting, Mary Jo Dondlinger; Music, Robert Waldman; Musical Director, Stuart Raleigh CAST: Andrew Boyer, J. Michael Brennan, John Buck, Jr., David Burrington, Phillip Carroll, Amanda Chubb, Jennifer Curfman, Molly Daw, Amy DeGaetano, Danny Flave-Novak, Terri Kent, Michael Krawic, William Leach, Lisa Leigh Lewis, Kenn McLaughlin, Adam Moeller, Colin Moeller, Trista Moldovan, John P. Monroe, Maryann Nagel, Billy Radin, Candice Radin, Eric Radin, Peggy Sullivan, Charles Tuthill, William Verderber, Gregory Violand

TOM HANKS:NOW PLAYING CENTER by Tom Hanks and Randy Fechter; Staging, Gerald Freedman; Costumes, Alfred Kohout; Lighting, Mary Jo Dondlinger CAST: Tom Hanks, Christopher Biebelhausen, Meredith Brickett, Scott Caple, Ruthe Delzell, Francis Henry, Wendy James, Daria Sanford, Peggy Sullivan, Jacques Henri Taylor, Steven Waste, Rocco Scotti

SISTERS WIVES AND DAUGHTERS: Portraits of Shakespeare's Women (PREMIERE); Lighting, Cynthia Stillings CAST: Claire Bloom

OTHELLO by William Shakespeare; Conception/Direction, Harold Scott; Costumes, Daniel L. Lawson; Lighting, Jackie Manasee; Music, Lawrence "Butch" Morris CAST: Delroy Lindo (Othello), Kirk Anderson, Christopher Biebelhausen, Olivia Birkelund, Matthew Boston, John Buck, Jr., Ebani Edwards, Clement Fowler, Leland Gantt, Mickey Houlahan, Lisa Leigh Lewis, Tim McGee, John P. Monroe, Mark Niebuhr, Duane Noch, T. Ryder Smith, Gregory Suddeyh, Peggy Sullivan, Jacques Henri Taylor, Gregory Violand, Rick Williams, Kim Yancey, Jean Zarzour

Roger Mastroianni Photos

HARTFORD STAGE COMPANY

Hartford, Connecticut

Thirtieth Season

Artistic Director, Mark Lamos; Managing Director, David Hawanson; Associate Artistic Director, Rob Bundy; Literary Associate, John Dias; General Manager, Michael Ross; Public Relation Director, Howard Sherman; Production Manager, Candice Chirgotis

PRODUCTIONS & CASTS

TARTUFFE by Moliere; Translation, Richard Wilbur; Director, Mark Lamos; Sets, Christine Jones; Costumes, Tom Broecker; Lighting, Scott Zielinski CAST: Maureen Anderman (Elmire), Gerry Bamman (Orgon), Susan Gibney (Dorine), Lisa Gay Hamilton (Mariane), Harriette H. Holmes (Flipote), Patricia Kilgarriff (Madame Pernelle), David Patrick Kelly (Tartuffe), John McDonough (Loyal), Geoffrey Owens (Valere), David Rainey (Damis), Frank Raiter (Police), Keith Randolph Smith (Cleante)

PILL HILL by Samuel Kelley; Director, Marion McClinton; Sets, James D. Sandefur; Costumes, Paul Tazewell; Lighting, Allen Lee Hughes CAST: Jerome Preston Bates (Joe), Willis Burks, II (Charlie), Rafeal Clements (Tony), A. Benard Cummings (Ed), Keith Glover (Scott), Eric A. Payne (Al)

MARTIN GUERRE (PREMIERE) with Music by Roger Ames; Lyrics/Book, Laura Harrington; Director, Mark Lamos; Choreography, Liza Gennaro; Musical Director, Sue Anderson; Sets, Michael Yeargan; Costumes, Jess Goldstein; Lighting, Jennifer Tipton; Orchestrations, William Harper CAST: Patrick Cassidy (Guerre-Act II), Malcolm Gets (Guerre-Act I), Walter Charles (Guerre-the father/Boeri), Peter Samuel (Pierre Guerre), Beth Fowler (Louise), Judy Kuhn (Mireille), Cris Groendendaal (Priest), John Aller, Bill Badolato, Joan Susswein Barber, Darcy Paul Becker, Salli-Jo D. Borden, Deborah Bradshaw, Kyle Craig, David Eye, James Jaeger, Jane Kitz, Luke Lynch, Don Mayo, Veronica Mittenzwei, Peter Reardon, Lynn Shuck, Dean Stroop, Craig Waletzko, Amy M. Young

MARISOL by Jose Rivera; Director, Michael Greif; Sets, Debra Booth; Costumes, Gabriel Berry; Lighting, Kenneth Posner CAST: Doris Difarnecio (Young Woman), Cordelia Gonzalez (Marisol), Decater James (Homeless), Anne O'Sullivan (June), Phyllis Somerville (Woman with Furs), Skipp Sudduth (Golf Man/Ice Cream Man/Lenny/Scar Man), Danitra Vance (Angel)

THE COVER OF LIFE by R.T. Robinson; Director, Richard Corley; Sets, Marjorie Bradley Kellogg; Costumes, Merrily Murray-Walsh; Lighting, Kirk Bookman; Music, Randy Courts CAST: Melinda Eades (Wetsie), Kate Forbes (Tood), Libby George (Addie Mae), Leslie Hendrix (Kate), Bobo Lewis (Ola), Molly Price (Sybil), Sam Trammell (Tommy)

HERRINGBONE with Music by Skip Kennon; Lyrics, Ellen Fitzhugh; Book, Tom Cone; Adapted from Mr. Cone's play; Director, Graciela Daniele; Musical Director, Tom Fay; Set, Christopher Barreca; Costumes, Ann Hould-Ward; Lighting, Peggy Eisenauer CAST: Joel Grey (Herringbone)

T. Charles Erickson Photos

Top Right:Judy Kuhn, Patrick Cassidy in "Martin Guerre"
Bottom Left: Keith Glover, A. Bernard Cummings, Willis Burks II, Jerome Preston Bates, Eric A. Payne, Rafeal Clements in "Pill Hill"
Bottom Right: Joel Grey in "Herringbone"

HUNTINGTON THEATRE COMPANY

Boston, Massachusetts

Eleventh Season

Producing Director, Peter Altman; Managing Director, Michael Maso; Production Manager, Roger Meeker; Costume Manager, Hillary Derby; Marketing Director, Rosemary Clinton; Marketing Assistant, Deborah Gillis

PRODUCTIONS & CASTS

PAL JOEY with Music by Richard Rodgers Lyrics, Lorenz Hart; Book, John O'Hara; Adaptation, Richard Greenberg; Director, David Warren; Choreography, Thommie Walsh; Orchestrations, Bruce Coughlin; Dance Arrangements, Wally Harper; Musical Director/Vocal Arrangements, Ted Sperling; Sets, John Arnone; Costumes, Toni-Leslie James; Lighting, Peter Kaczorowski CAST: Robert Knepper (Joey), Judy Blazer (Linda), Donna Murphy (Vera), Linda Hart (Gladys), Carolee Carmello (Val), Nora Brennan (Tilda), Terrence Caza (Counterman/Armour/Workman), John Deyle (Ernest/Ted), Sara Beth Lane (Janet), Julie Ann Lynch (Patron), Rick Manning (Drummer), Richard J. McGoniagle (Pianist/Swift/Patron), Joanne McHugh (The Kid/Cigarette Girl), Kiki Moritsugu (Millie/Patron), Frederick Murdock (Waiter), Jeannette Neill (Patron), Greg Ramos (Ramon/Patron), John Shepard (Mike), Mario Soto (Bartender/Customer), David Thome (Ludlow/Patron), Amiee Turner (Cookie), Valerie Wright (Diane)

LONG DAY'S JOURNEY INTO NIGHT by Eugene O'Neill; Director, Edward Gilbert; Sets, Karl Eigsti; Costumes, Mariann Verheyen; Lighting, Nicholas Cernovitch CAST: Robert Sean Leonard (Edmund Tyrone), Jonathan Walker (James Tyrone, Jr.), Jack Aranson (James Tyrone), Patricia Conolly (Mary Cavan Tyrone), Sue-Anne Morrow (Cathleen)

A CHRISTMAS CAROL by Dickens; Director, Larry Carpenter; Sets, James Leonard Joy; Costumes, Mariann Verheyen; Lighting, Craig Miller; Music Director, Catherine Stornetta; Choreography, Daniel Pelzig CAST: Paul Benedict (Scrooge), James Javore, Darcy Pulliam, Sarah DeLima, George Ede, Maureen Silliman, Tony Aylward, John Patrick Rice, Dee Nelson, Lisa Anne Barrett, James Coelho, Paul Kirby, Michael Lesser, Nellie Palau, Kate Stevens, Jonathan Levy, Joseph Tremblay, Katie Armour, Kate Rourke, Daniel DeMarco, Douglas Gerber, Joshua Mazow

MY MOTHER SAID I NEVER SHOULD (PREMIERE); Director, Charles Towers; Sets, John Falabella; Costumes, Barbra Kravitz; Lighting, Jackie Manassee CAST: Kate Goehring (Rosie), Linda Emond (Jackie), Pauline Flanagan, Elizabeth Franz

UNDISCOVERED COUNTRY by Arthur Schnitzler; Adaptation, Tom Stoppard; Director, Jacques Cartier; Sets, LKate Edmunds; Costumes, John Falabella; Lighting, Roger Meeker CAST: Paul Roebling (Friedrich), Katie MacNichol (Erna), Kate Brubaker, Sandra Shipley, G.R. Johnson, Thomas Schall, Richard J. McGoniagle, Wendy Barie-Wilson, Jon David Weigand, Munson Hicks, Tanny McDonald, Dan Hiatt, Peter Kybart, Philip Pleasants, Karen Zippler, Chloe Leamon, Guy Chandler Roberts, Patricia Tamagini, Noel Boulanger, Todd Rosen, David P. Shannon, Andrew Goldstein, Jonathan Levy, Peter Neudell

ARMS AND THE MAN by George Bernard Shaw; Director, Larry Carpenter; Sets, James Leonard Joy; Costumes, David Murin; Lighting, Marcia Madeira; Composer, Scott Killian CAST: Katy Selverstone, Frances Cuka, Laurie Walters, Kenneth L. Marks, Robert Pemberton, Richard Russell Ramos, Humbert Allen Astredo, Jeff McCarthy

Richard Feldman Photos

Top: Jonathan Walker, Robert Sean Leonard in
"Long Day's Journey Into Night"
Bottom Left: Michele Farr, Paul Roebling, Katie MacNichol in
"Undiscovered Country"
Bottom Right: Donna Murphy, Judy Blazer in "Pal Joey"

144

ILLINOIS THEATRE CENTER

Park Forest, Illinois

Seventeenth Season

Artistic Director, Steve S. Billig; Managing Director, Etel Billig; Artistic Associate, Wayne Adams; Musical Director, Jonathan Roark; Costume Designers, Pat Decker, Leigh Ann Ruyle, Stephen and Diane Moore; Set/Lighting Directors, Mr. Adams, Mr. Roark, Archway Scenic

PRODUCTIONS & CASTS

HOMEWARD BOUND by Elliott Hayes; Directors, Steve S. Billig, Wayne Adams CAST: Claudia Hiommel, David Lewis Frisch, Steve S. Billig, Sam Nykaza-Jones, Etel Billig, Wayne Adams
AMIGO'S BLUE GUITAR by Joan MacLeod; Director, Wayne Adams CAST: Felipe Camacho, Alan Westbrook, Etel Billig, Dawn Hillman, Matt Crain
OLYMPUS ON MY MIND with Music by Grant Sturiale; Lyrics/Book, Barry Harman; Director, Steve S. Billig CAST: Stephen Stockley, Keith Heimpel, McKinley Johnson, Liz Donathan, Scott Schumacher, Ed Kross, Judy McLaughlin, Shelley Crosby, David Six
THE PIANO LESSON by August Wilson; Director, Steve S. Billig CAST: Velma Austin, A.C. Smith, Darryl Rocky Davis, Al Boswell, Reri Barrett, Kenn E. Head, Monique Cafe, Alani Hicks-Bartlett, Jamileh McKnight
OUR COUNTRY'S GOOD by Timberlake Wertenbaker; Director, Steve S, Billig CAST: Sam Nykaza-Jones, Don McGrew, Wayne Adams, David Perryam, Tom Cassidy, Morgan Fitch, Robert Cornelius, Diane Smith, Angela Friend-Smith, Carmen Severino, Paul D'Angelo, Pat Fitch
MY SON THE LAWYER IS DROWNING (PREMIERE) by Doug MacLeod; Directors, Steve S. Billig, Wayne Adams CAST: Judy McLaughlin, Fred Eberle, Etel Billig, Ed Kross, Steve S. Billig, Diane Smith
ROMANCE ROMANCE with Music by Keith Herrmann; Lyrics/Book, Barry Harman; Director, Steve S. Billig; Choreography, Blair Bybee CAST: Kenneth Paul, Shelley Crosby, Charma Ward, Blair Bybee

Glenn Davidson, Todd Panogoupolos Photos

JUPITER THEATRE

Jupiter, Florida

Executive Producer, Richard C. Akins; Artistic Director, Avery Schreiber; Producer, Brian M. Cronin; Press Director, Pamela Smith; Musical Director, Douglass G. Lutz; Set Designer, Mark Beaumont; Lighting Designer, Ginny Adams; Costume Designers, Vickie K. Bast, Billie Boston, A. Jackson Pinkney, Ellis Tillman, Patty Jensen

PRODUCTIONS & CASTS

CAROUSEL by Rodgers & Hammerstein; Director, Andrew Glant-Linden; Lighting, Stuart Reiter CAST: Nat Chandler, Michele Ragusa, Beau Allen, Michele Pigliavento, Richard Smith, Connie Day, Mary Lou Reiner, Harvey Phillips, Jilanne Marie Klaus, Wayne Steadman, Eddie Buffum, Jonathan Ridgely Lewis, Rebecca Burton, John Simpson Fairlie, Steven Garrett, Tracy Gotts, Cliff Goulet, Catrina L. Honadle, Stefan Lingenfelter, Sheila McDevitt, Elizabeth A. Nemeth, Andrea E. Rivette, Christopher Ruble, R. Matthew Ruley, Laura Sabers, Sara Winterer, James V. Marino, Marlene Elizabeth Vieira
PHANTOM by Yeston and Kopit; Director, Richard C. Akins; CAST: Richard Lissemore, Kim Lindsay, Lynn Eldredge, William McCauley, Dale Conrad Brown, Wayne Hoffman, Harvey Phillips, Wayne Steadman, Rebecca Burton, John Simpson Fairlie, Steven Flaa, Steven Garrett, Tracy Gotts, Cliff Goulet, Catrina L. Honadle, Jonathan Ridgely Lewis, Stefan Lingenfelter, Shelia McDevitt, Andrea E. Rivette, Christopher Ruble, R. Matthew Ruley, Laura Sabers, Marlene Elizabeth Vieira, Sarah Winterer, Jilanne Marie Klaus, Lauren Durning, John Tessier
I HATE HAMLET by Paul Rudnick; Director, Avery Schreiber; CAST: Robert Vaughn, Heather Lockler, Mark Arnold, Liz Torres,, Judith Granite, John Simpson Fairlie
SINGIN' IN THE RAIN by Comden, Green, Brown and Freed; Director, Richard C. Akins; Choreography, Suzanne Kaszynski CAST: Michael Cline, Pamela Cecil, B.K. Kennelly, Michelle Meade, Harvey Phillips, Wayne Steadman, Ruthann Bigley, Rebecca Burton, Brian Chenoweth, Larry Elmore, John Fairlie, Steven Flaa, Steven Garrett, Tracy Gotts, Roger Hedberg, Catrina L. Honadle, Jilanne Marie Klaus, Jonathan Ridgely Lewis, Stefan Ligenfelter, Jayme McDaniel, Sheila McDevitt, Laura Sabers, Marlene Elizabeth Vieira, Sara Winterer
RUMORS by Neil Simon; Director, Avery Schreiber; CAST: Gary Burghoff, William Christopher, Bernie Kopell, Patty McCormack, Diane Shalet, Missy McArdle, Edmond, Dante, Sheila McDevitt, John Fairlie, Catrina L. Honadle
MAN OF LA MANCHA by Mitch Leigh, Joe Darrien, Dale Wasserman; Director, Andrew Glant-Linden; CAST: David Holliday, Daniel Marcus, Angela DeCicco, David Elledge, Mark Hanley, Joshua Sussman, Hugh Hysell, Renee Dobson, Carol A. Suhr, Wayne Steadman, Missy McArdle, Brian Chenoweth, Jonathan Ridgely Lewis, Steven Garrett, Benjamin Bedenbaugh, Betsy Kelso, Ed Kuras, James F. Lawson, Kelly Mancini, Warren Moore, Lauri Pressler, Adam L. Trummel, Kit Watkins
SOUTH PACIFIC by Rodgers & Hammerstein, Josh Logan; Director, Richard C. Akins; Choreography, Kathryn Kendall; CAST: David Holliday, Patty Carver, Amy Jo Phillips, Mark Meredith, Brent Sexton, Ed Romanoff, Larry Hirschhorn, Charles Gibson, Wayne Steadman, Eileen Aranas, Keith Davis, Dale Conrad Brown, Jonathan R. Lewis, Meredith Rae, Prudencio Montesino, Christopher Ruble, Benjamin Bedenbaugh, Jenn Harris, Betsy Kelso, Ed Kuras, James F. Lawson, Kelly Mancini, Warren Moore, Lauri Pressler, Adam L. Trummel, Kit Watkins
GRAND HOTEL by Wright & Forrest, Yeston, Davis; Director/Choreographer, Andrew Glant-Linden; CAST: Brent Black, Joanne Bogart, Jill Powell, John Dewar, David Barron, Brenda O'Brien, Christopher Rath, Harvey Phillips, Wayne Steadman, Prudencio Montesino, Frances McGuckin, Carlos Landeros, Leigh Bennett, Derrick McGinty, Adam Dyer, Christopher Ruble, Benjamin Bedenbaugh, Jean Harris, Betsy Kelso, Ed Kuras, James F. Lawson, Kelly Mancini, Warren Moore, Lauri Pressler, Adam L. Trummel, Kit Watkins
CITY OF ANGELS by Coleman, Zippel and Gelbart; Director/Choreographer, Norb Joerder CAST: Marcus Neville, Dan Schiff, Jess Richards, Bertilla Baker, Renee Dobson, Janice Hamilton, Michael Licata, Tami Tappan, Timothy J. Miller, Wayne Steadman, Harvey Phillips, Joshua Sussman, Roger Keiper, Adam Dyer, Rebecca Lowry, Benjamin Bedenbaugh, Jenn Harris, Betsy Kelso, Ed Kuras, James F. Lawson, Warren Moore, Lauri Pressler, Adam L. Trummel, Kit Watkins

Greg Allikas Photos

Top Left: Robert Vaughn, Mark Arnold in "I Hate Hamlet"
Below: Keith Heimpel, Liz Donathan, Stephen Stockley, (front) McKinley Johnson in "Olympus on My Mind"

JOHN F. KENNEDY CENTER
FOR THE PERFORMING ARTS

Washington, D.C.

Chairman, James D. Wolfensohn; Managing Director, Lawrence J. Wilker

OPERA HOUSE

BUDDY: THE BUDDY HOLLY STORY; For creative credits and cast see *National Touring Companies* section

RICHARD III; with Ian McKellen; For creative credits and full cast see *National Touring Companies* section

ASPECTS OF LOVE; For creative credits and cast see *National Touring Companies* section

THE SECRET GARDEN; For creative credits and cast see *National Touring Companies* section

GUYS AND DOLLS; for creatice credits and cast see *National Touring Companies* section

EISENHOWER THEATRE

ONCE ON THIS ISLAND; For creative credits and cast see *National Touring Companies* section

1600 PENNSYLVANIA AVENUE with Music by Leonard Bernstein; Lyrics/Book, Alan Jay Lerner; Director, Erik Haagensen; Musical Directors, Robert E. Stoll, Michael Butterman; Choreography, Robert Sullivan, Sean Watters; Lighting, Allen R. White; Design, C. David Higgins; An Indiana University Opera Theatre Production CAST: William Schumacher (The President), Kathryn Foss-Pittman (The President's Wife), Alfred Bailey (Lud), Angela Brown (Seena), Joshua Huff (Little Lud), Daphne Dunston (Rachel), S. Kendrick-Smith (Henry/Uncle Sam), Timothy David Rey (Coley/Rhinestone Lilly/Simoleon), Mark Filosa (Broom/Ross/Sen. Conkling/NJ Delegate), Steven LaCosse (Auctioneer/ Secretary/Chief Justice/Cockburn/RI Delegate), Kevin Patterson, DaMar Smith, David Ackerman, Brian Kerr, David Starkey, Philip Christiansen, Jon Gruett, Michael Kelleher, Paul Vogler, Jason A. Burke, Timothy Tenhumberg, Matt Riutta, Cameron Andrews, Anntoinette Hendrix, Rebecca Cornelison, Benjamin Thompson, Sean Watters, Rosemarie Bigbee, Kiersten King, Tashnell Neal, Julius Reynolds, Demetrius Wharton, Lara Britton, Leah Creek, Patricia Domengeaux, Satoko Fujiwara, Toni Ham, Marnee Johns, Michelle Stephenson, Angela Taverner, Evelyn Winslow MUSICAL NUMBERS: Prelude, Me, On Ten Miles by the Potomac River, If I Was a Dove, Nation That Wasn't There, Welcome Home Miz Adams, Take Care of This House, President Jefferson Sunday Luncheon Party March, Seena, Sonatina, What Happened?, Lud's Wedding (I Love My Wife), Auctions, Monroviad, This Time, We Must Have a Ball, Philadelphia, Uncle Tom's Funeral/Bright and Black, Duet for One: First Lady of the Land, Hail, Money Lovin' Minstrel Show, Pity the Poor, Grand Ol' Party, The Red White and Blues, American Dreaming, Voices That Live in the Walls, To Make Us Proud

MARVIN'S ROOM by Scott McPherson; Director, David Petrarca; Sets, Linda Buchanan; Costumes, Claudia Boddy; Lighting, Richard Christen; Music, Rob Milburn CAST: Carol Schultz (Bessie), Tim Monsion (Dr. Wally), Mary Diveny (Ruth), Steve Hofvendahl (Bob), Nance Williamson (Lee), Brenda Pressley (Dr. Charlotte/Home Director)), Mark Rosenthal (Hank), Marty Zentz (Charlie), Christopher Shaw (Marvin)

ROMULUS HUNT with Music by Carly Simon; Libretto, Ms. Simon with Jacob Brackman; Music Director, Jeff Halpern; Orchestrations, Matthias Gohl; Production, Francesca Zambello; Choreography, Carmen De Lavallade; Set, Paul Steinberg; Costumes, Martin Pakledinaz; Lighting, Heather Carson CAST: Jeff Hairston, Perry Brisbon (Zoogy), Andrew Harrison Leeds, Tommy Michaels (Romulus), John Keuther (Eddie), Luretta Bybee (Joanna), Wendy Hill (Mica)

OLEANNA; For creative credits and cast see *National Touring Companies* section

THEATRE LAB

SHEAR MADNESS by Paul Portner; Director/Design, Bruce Jordan; Lighting, Daniel MacLean Wagner; Set, Kim Peter Kovac; Stage Manager, Judy Cullen CAST: Audrey Wasilewski (Barbara de Marco), Wayne Gray (Mike Thomas), Bob Lohrmann (Tony Whitcomb), Ted McAdams (Eddie Lawrence), Joseph Popp (Detective Rossetti), Diana Sowle (Mrs. Shubert)

Amelia Campbell, Harriet Harris in "Month in the Country"
Center: Karmin Murcelo, Saundra Santiago in "Once Removed"
Top Left: Lisbeth Bartlett, Leslie Lyles, Betsy Aidem, Constance Shulman,
Harriet D. Foy in "Loose Knit"
Top Right:Luis A. Laporte, Jr., Akili Prince in "Day the Bronx Died"

LONG WHARF THEATRE

New Haven, Connecticut

Twenty-eighth Season

Artistic Director, Arvin Brown; Executive Director, M. Edgar Rosenblum; Literary Consultant, John Tillinger; Artistic Administrator, Janice Muirhead; General Manager, John Conte; Associate Director, Gordon Edelstein; Development Director, Pamela Tatge; Press/Marketing Director, Robert Wildman; Press Representative, Jeffery Fickes

PRODUCTIONS & CASTS

A MONTH IN THE COUNTRY by Ivan Turgenev; Adaptation, Isaiah Berlin; Director, Arvin Brown; Sets, Loren Sherman; Costumes, Jess Goldstein; Lighting, Mark Stanley; Music, Brenton Evans CAST: David Bishins, Amelia Campbell, Donavon Dietz, Beth Dixon, Joyce Ebert, Daniel Hagen, Harriet Harris, Sean Hewitt, George Morfogen, Linda Maurel Sithole, Robert Stattel, Victor Slezak
ONCE REMOVED by Eduardo Machado; Director, John Tillinger; Sets, John Lee Beatty; Costumes, Jane Greenwood; Lighting, Pat Collins CAST: Karina Arroyave, Rafael Baez, Carlos Gomez, Karmin Murcelo, Saundra Santiago
THE DAY THE BRONX DIED (PREMIERE) by Michael Henry Brown; Director, Gordon Edelstein; Sets, Hugh Landwehr; Costumes, Candice Donnelly; Lighting, Donald Holder; Music/Sound, John Gromada CAST: Brenda Denmark, Peter Jay Fernandez, Dennis Green, Dwayne Gurley, Neal Huff, Luis A. Laporte, Jr., Aaron Martin, Curtis McClarin, Kelly Neal, Akili Prince, Herbert Rubens, Troy Winbush
THE MISANTHROPE by Moliere; Translation, Richard Wilbur; Director, Edward Gilbert; Sets/Costumes, Mark Negin; Lighting, Nicholas Cernovitch CAST: Ken Cheeseman, Marty Garcia, John Gilchrist, Scott Kealey, Caroline Lagerfelt, Diana LaMar, David Manis, Leslie Scarlett Mason, Geoffrey Owens, Doug Stender, Nicholas Woodeson
ABSURD PERSON SINGULAR by Alan Ayckbourn; Director, Arvin Brown; Sets, Michael H. Yeargan; Costumes, David Murin; Lighting, Arden Fingerhut CAST: Joyce Ebert, Patrick Horgan, Ann McDonough, John Rothman, Doug Stender, Julie White

WORKSHOPS

LOOSE KNIT by Theresa Rebeck; Director, Beth Schacter CAST: Betsy Aidem, Lisbeth Bartlett, Reed Birney, Harriet D. Foy, Leslie Lyles, Constance Shulman, Mark Tymchyshyn
THE TIMES with Music by Brad Ross; Lyrics/Book, Joe Keenan; Story, Mr. Keenan, Gordon Edelstein; Director, Mr. Edelstein; Musical Staging, Tony Stevens; Musical Director, Tom Fay; Sets, Hugh Landwehr CAST: Brooks Almy, Trent Bright, Mark Handy, Rex Hays, Jordan Leeds, Mary Gordan Murray, Gayton Scott, Cheryl Stern
COME DOWN BURNING by Kia Corthron; Director, Marya Mazor CAST: Ami Brabson, Cornell Green. Kelly Taffe, Myra Taylor, Tina Washington
THE SPRINGHILL SINGING DISASTER; Written/Performed by Karen Trott; Directed/Developed by Norman Rene

T. Charles Erickson Photos

MARRIOTT LINCOLNSHIRE THEATRE

Lincolnshire, Illinois

Producer, Kary M. Walker; Artistic Director, Dyanne Earley; Production Manager, Brigid Brown; Public Relations Director, Terry James; Marketing Director, Lauren Johnson; Musical Director, Michael Duff; Costume Designer, Nancy Missimi; Set Designer, Thomas M. Ryan; Lighting Designer, Diane Ferry Williams; Stage manager, Michael Hendricks

PRODUCTIONS & CASTS

ARTHUR: The Musical; Director/Choreographer, David H. Bell CAST INCLUDES: Gene Weygandt, Kathy Santen, William Brown
GRAND HOTEL; Director, Joe Leonardo; Choreography, Mark Hoebee CAST INCLUDES: Kurt Johns, Kathy Taylor, Kelly Prybycien, Ray Frewen, Carol Kuykendall, Malcolm Rothman, Jim Corti, Ben Yvon
THE SOUND OF MUSIC; Director, Dominic Missimi CAST INCLUDES: Kathy Santen, Ray Frewen, Ann Arvia, Guy Adkins, Kelly Prybcien
SWEENEY TODD; Director, Joe Leonardo; Musical Supervision, Kevin Stites CAST INCLUDES: Timothy Nolen, Karlah Hamilton, Robert Alan Mason, Stephen R. Buntrock, Rita Harvey, John Reeger, Blake Hammond, Mary Ernster, Mark G. Hawbecker
THE FIRST; Director, Dyanne Earley; Choreography, Mark Hoebee CAST INCLUDES: Alton Fitzgerald, Joel Hatch, Angela Lockett, Ray Frewen, Scott Schumacher, Jonathan Weir, David Conrad Schott, James A. McCammond, Stephen P. Full, Kingsley Leggs

Tom Maday Photos

Top Left: Kathy Santen, William Brown, Gene Weygandt in "Arthur"
Top Right: Alton Fitzgerald White, Joel Hatch in "The First"
Left center: Timothy Nolen, Karlah Hamilton in "Sweeney Todd"
Bottom: Kurt Johns, Jim Corti, Malcolm Rothman, Kelly Prybycien, Ray Frewen, Fred Zimmerman, Bernie Yvon, Carol Kuykendall, Kathy Taylor in "Grand Hotel"

McCARTER THEATRE

Princeton, New Jersey

Artistic Director, Emily Mann; Managing Director, Jeffrey Woodward; General Manager, Kathleen Kund Nolan; Staff Producer, Loretta Greco; Dramaturg/Literary Manager, Janice Paran; Marketing Director, David Mayhew; Publicist, Daniel Y. Bauer; Production Manager, David York; Production Stage Manager, Susie Cordon

PRODUCTIONS & CASTS

CAT ON A HOT TIN ROOF by Tennessee Williams; Director, Emily Mann; Sets, Derek McLane; Costumes, Jennifer von Mayrhauser; Lighting, Peter Kaczorowski CAST: Pat Hingle (Big Daddy), Marjorie Johnson (Sookey), Margo Martindale (Mae), Bill McIntyre (Rev. Tooker), Bill Moor (Dr. Baugh), James Morrison (Brick), Slaone Shelton (Big Mama), Skipp Sudduth (Gooper), JoBeth Williams (Margaret)
BETWEEN EAST AND WEST by Richard Nelson; Director, Jack Hofsiss; Sets, David Jenkins; Costumes, Gary Lisz; Lighting, Beverly Emmons CAST: Jeffrey Jones (Gregor), Maria Tucci (Erna)
MISS JULIE by August Strindberg; Adaptation(NEW)/Direction, Emily Mann based on literal translation by Michael Tremonte; Sets, Thomas Lynch; Costumes, Jennifer von Mayrhauser; Lighting, Pat Collins CAST: Kim Cattrall (Miss Julie), Peter Francis James (Jean), Donna Murphy (Kristin)
SWEET & HOT: The Songs of Harold Arlen (PREMIERE co-production with Asolo Theatre); Conception/Direction, Julianne Boyd; Choreography, Hope Clarke; Musical Director/Arranger, Danny Holgate; Sets, Ken Foy; Costumes, David C. Woolard; Lighting, Howell Binkley CAST: Terry Burrell, Allen Hidalgo, Jacquey Maltby, Monica Pege, Brian Quinn, Lance Roberts
MUCH ADO ABOUT NOTHING by William Shakespeare; Director, Michael Kahn; Sets, Derek McLane; Costumes, Martin Pakledinaz; Lighting, Howell Binkley CAST: Bernard K. Addison (Conrade), Yolanda Androzzo (Ursula), Firdous Bamji (Balthasar/Watch), Emery Battis (Antonio), David Birney (Benedick), Hunter Boyle (Seacoal), Alene Dawson (Hero), Edward Gero (Don John), Philip Goodwin (Verges), Eric Hoffmann (Borachio), Floyd King (Dogberry), Saundra McClain (Margaret), Robert G. Murch (Friar/Sexton), Caitlin O'Connell (Beatrice), Mark Philpot (Claudio), Jack Ryland (Don Pedro), Ted van Griethuysen (Leonato)
A CHRISTMAS CAROL by Charles Dickens; Adaptation, David Thompson; Director, Scott Ellis; Composer, Louis Rosen; Choreography, Rob Marshall; Sets, Michael Anania; Costumes, Lindsay W. Davis; Lighting, Peter Kaczorowski CAST: Robin Chadwick (Scrooge), Charles Antalosky, David Aaron Baker, Peter Birkenhead, Robert Colston, Charles Cargin, Kevin Durkin, Patricia Guinan, Steve Hofvendahl, Karen Tsen Lee, Jennifer Lopez, Charlotte Maier, Crista Moore, Audrie Neenan, Douglas Weston

T. Charles Erickson Photos

Top Right: James Morrison, JoBeth Williams in "Cat on a Hot Tin Roof"
Center: Jacquey Maltby, Allen Hidalgo, Monica Pege, Lance Roberts, Brian Quinn, Terry Burrell in "Sweet and Hot"
Bottom Left: Kim Cattrall, Peter Francis James in "Miss Julie"
Bottom Right: David Birney, Mark Philpot, Jack Ryland, Ted van Griethuysen in "Much Ado About Nothing"

OLD GLOBE THEATRE

San Diego, California

Fifty-eighth Season

Executive Producer, Craig Noel; Artistic Director, Jack O'Brien; Managing Director, Thomas Hall; Development Director, Domenick Ietto; Business Director, Derek Harrison Hurd; Public Relations Directors, Charlene Baldridge, William Eaton; Public Relations Associate, Mark Hiss

PRODUCTIONS & CASTS

THE TWO GENTLEMEN OF VERONA by William Shakespeare; Director, Laird Williamson; Sets, Richard Seger; Costumes, Andrew V. Yelusich; Lighting, Peter Maradudin CAST: Steven Flynn (Valentine), Mark Moses (Proteus), Tony Simotes (Speed), Susannah Hoffmann (Julia), Katherine McGrath (Lucetta), Richard Easton (Antonio/Duke of Milan), Phillip Charles Sneed (Panthino/Eglamour)), Jeffrey Allan Chandler (Launce), Marcia Cross (Silvia), Jonathan McMurtry (Thurio), Joanne Zipay (Ursula), Demetrio Cuzzocrea, David Huber, Steven Zubkoff, Dan Gunther, Eric Liddell, Michael Nichols, Alex Perez, Donald Sager, David Seitz, Amy Beth Cohen, Evangeline Fernandez, Andrea D. Fitzgerald, David Kirkwood, Jennifer Stratman, Courtney Jo Watson (Outlaws/Pantomimi/Guests)
INTERIOR DECORATION by William Hamilton; Director, Jack O'Brien; Sets, Ralph Funicello; Costumes, Michael Krass; Lighting, David F. Segal CAST: Tom Lacy (Gerald), Deborah Taylor (Phillipa), Deborah May (Sybil), George Deloy (William)
BREAKING UP by Michael Cristofer; Director, Stuart Ross; Sets, Richard Seger; Costumes, Michael Krass; Lighting, Ashley York Kennedy CAST: Jeffrey Hayenga (Steve), Jane Galloway (Alice)
LOST HIGHWAY: THE MUSIC AND LEGEND OF HANK WILLIAMS by Randal Myler and Mark Harelik; Director, Mr. Myler; Musical Directors, Mr. Harelik, Dan Wheetman; Sets, Richard L. Hay, Bill Curley; Costumes, Andrew V. Yelusich; Lighting, Peter Maradudin CAST: Mark Harelik, Michael Bryan French (Hank Williams), Ron Taylor (Tee-Tot), Kevin Moore (Willy), Stephanie Dunnam (Waitress), Mick Regan (Hoss), William Mesnik (Jimmy "Burrhead"), Dan Wheetman (Leon "Loudmouth"), Kathy Brady (Mama Lilly), Richard McKenzie (Pap), Sharon Schlarth (Audrey)
FROM THE MISSISSIPPI DELTA by Dr. Endesha Ida Mae Holland; Director, Seret Scott; Set, Ralph Funicello; Costumes, Robert Wojewodski; Lighting, Ashley York Kennedy CAST: Saundra Quarterman (Woman One), Pamala Tyson (Woman Two), Cheryl Lynn Bruce (Woman Three)
THE WINTER'S TALE by William Shakespeare; Director, Jack O'Brien; Sets, Ralph Funicello; Costumes, Robert Wojewodski; Lighting, David Segal; Composer, Bob James CAST: George Deloy (Leontes), Deborah May (Germione), Jed Larson (Mamillius), Hilary James (Perdita), Richard Easton (Camillo), Robert Phalen (Antigonus), Demetrio Cuzzocrea (Cleomenes), Alex Perez (Dion), Michael Nichols (Lord/Officer), David Kirkwood (Lord), Katherine McGrath (Paulina), Andrea D. Fitzgerald (Emilia), Amy Beth Cohn, Evangeline Fernandez (Ladies), Donald Sager (Gaoler), Steven Zubkoff (Mariner), Vaughn Armstrong (Polixenes), Eric Liddell (Florizel), Jonathan McMurtry (Archidamus/Shepard), Thom Sesma (Autolycus), David Huber (Clown), Joanne Zipay (Mopsa), Courtney Jo Watson (Dorcas), Dan Gunther (Servant), Carol Davis, Jennifer Stratman (Shepherdesses), Brad Upton, Marc Weston (Attendants)
LIGHT SENSITIVE by Jim Geoghan; Director, Andrew J. Traister; Set, Nick Reid; Costumes, Clare Henkel; Lighting, Barth Ballard CAST: Joel Anderson (Thomas Hanratty), Matt Landers (Lou D'Marco), Victoria Ann-Lewis (Edna Miles)
REDWOOD CURTAIN by Lanford Wilson; Director, Marshall W. Mason; Set, John Lee Beatty; Costumes, Laura Crow; Lighting, Dennis Parichy; Music, Peter Kater CAST: Jeff Daniels (Lyman), Sung Yun Cho (Geri), Debra Monk (Geneva)
GHOSTS by Henrik Ibsen; Translation, Nicholas Rudall; Director, Jack O'Brien; Sets, Ralph Funicello; Costumes, Dona Granata; Lighting, Ashley York Kennedy CAST: Christopher Collet (Osvald), Emily Bly (Regine), Jonathan McMurtry (Engstrand), Richard Easton (Pastor Manders), Patricia Conolly (Mrs. Alving)
FALSETTOS with Music/Lyrics by William Finn; Book, Mr. Finn, James Lapine; Director, Mr. lapine; Musical Director, Ben Whiteley; Set, Douglas Stein; Costumes, Ann Hould-Ward; Lighting, Frances Aronson CAST: Gregg Edelman (Marvin), Peter Reardon (Whizzer), Adam Heller (Mendel), Ramzi Khalaf (Jason), Carolee Carmello (Trina), Barbara Marineau (Charlotte), Jessica Molaskey (Cordelia)
OUT OF PURGATORY (PREMIERE) by Carol Galligan; Director, Benny Sato Ambush; Sets, Ralph Funicello; Costumes, Andrew V. Yelusich; Lighting, Ashley York Kennedy CAST: Felicity Huffman (Crista MacElroy), Bruce Nozick (Ari Ben David), Philip Sterling (Rabbi Mordechai Leventhal), Deborah Taylor (Maria Ciccone MacElroy)
MORNING'S AT SEVEN by Paul Osborn; Director, Craig Noel; Set, Richard Seger; Costumes, Andrew V. Yelusich; Lighting, Barth Ballard CAST: Mitchell Edmonds (Theodore), Roo Brown (Cora), Katherine McGrath (Aaronetta), Sada Thompson (Ida), Robert Symonds (Carl), Don Sparks (Homer), Lynne Griffin (Myrtle), Eve Roberts (Esther), Richard Kneeland (David)

Ken Howard Photos

Peter Reardon, Gregg Edelman, Carolee Carmello in "Falsettos"
Top: Patricia Conolly, Christopher Collet in "Ghosts"

151

Mark Chmiel, Michael O'Gorman, Eddie Bracken, Kelli Rabke,
Evan Bell in "Wizard of Oz"

George Hearn, Judy Kaye in "Sweeney Todd"

Caroline Lagerfelt, Simon Jones in "Don't Dress for Dinner"

PAPER MILL PLAYHOUSE

Millburn, New Jersey

Sixty-third Season

Executive Producer, Angelo Del Rossi; Artistic Director, Robert Johanson; General Manager, Geoffrey Cohen; Production Manager, Rik Kaye; Resident Stage manager, Lora K. Powell; Public Relations Director, Meara Nigro

PRODUCTIONS & CASTS

THE WIZARD OF OZ with Music by Harold Arlen; Lyrics, E.Y. Harburg; Book, John Kane, adapted from the 1939 MGM film based on L. Frank Baum's novel; Direction/Choreography, Robert Johanson, James Rocco; Musical Director, Jeff Rizzo; Sets, Michael Anania; Costumes, Gregg Barnes; Lighting, Timothy Hunter CAST: Kelli Rabke (Dorothy), Judith McCauley (Aunt Em/Glinda), Michael Hayward-Jones (Uncle Henry/ Winkie), Mark Chmiel (Hunk/Scarecrow), Michael O'Gorman (Hickory/ Tinman), Evan Bell (Zeke/Lion), Elizabeth Franz (Almira/Wicked Witch), Eddie Bracken (Marvel/Emerald City Guard/Wizard), Norma Pratt (Garden Society), Michael Anderson, Daniel Reifsnyder (Munchkin Mayor), Joyce Pratt, Gary Pratt (Barristers), Derrick McGinty (Coroner/Nikko), Michelle Caggiano, Allegra Libonati, Rebecca Lormand (Lullaby League), Faye Arthurs, Juliana Louise Biersbach, Laura Mineo (Lollipop Guild), Frances Barney, Patrick Boyd, Casey Colgan, Jodi Glaser, Gail Cook Howell, Michael Kuchar, Melody Meitrott, Fleur Phillips, Mary Ruvolo, Tim Schultheis, Christine Torre, Jamie Waggoner, John Wiltberger

SWEENEY TODD with Music/Lyrics by Stephen Sondheim; Book, Hugh Wheeler; Director, Michael Montel; Musical Director, Jeff Saver; Choreography, Sharon Halley; Sets, Eugene Lee; Costumes, Gregg Barnes; Lighting, Ken Billington CAST: George Hearn (Sweeney Todd), Jay Montgomery (Anthony), Mary Beth Peil (Beggar Woman), Judy Kaye (Mrs. Lovett), Rebecca Baxter (Johanna), Ernest C. Lewis (Seller), Nick Wyman (Turpin), Steven Harrison (Beadle), Robert Johanson (Tobias), Stephen Hanan (Pirelli), David Bryant (Fogg), David Jordan (Passerby), Lisa Albright, James Caplinger, Bill E. Dietrich, Stanley Noel Dunn, Doreen Firestone, Jim Gricar, Joy Hermalyn, Lisa Jolley, David Kelso, Melinda Klump, Michael Moore, Cara Oestreicher, Mary Sheehan, Ann Van Cleave, John Wasiniak

DON'T DRESS FOR DINNER by Marc Camoletti; Adaptation, Robin Hawdon; Director, Pamela Hunt; Sets, Michael Anania; Costumes, Gregg Barnes; Lighting, F. Mitchell Dana CAST: Simon Jones (Bernard), Alexandra O'Karma (Jacqueline), Reno Roop (Robert), Patricia Conolly (Suzette), Caroline Lagerfelt (Suzanne), Timothy Wheeler (George)

LOST IN YONKERS by Neil Simon; Director, Philip Cusack; Sets/Costumes, Santo Loquasto; Lighting, Fred Hancock CAST: Justin Walker (Jay), Eric Michael (Arty), Timothy Jerome (Eddie), Marsha Waterbury (Bella), Irene Dailey (Grandma), John Anson (Louie), Carol Harris (Gert)

MY FAIR LADY with Music by Frederick Loewe; Lyrics/Book, Alan Jay Lerner; Director, Larry Carpenter; Musical Director, Tom Helm; Choreography, Daniel Pelzig; Sets, Michael Anania; Costumes, Gregg Barnes; Lighting, Timothy Hunter CAST: Paul A. Brown, Debbi Fuhrman (Buskers), Mary C. Sheehan (Mrs. Eynsford-Hill), Judy Blazer (Eliza), Michael De Vries (Freddy), Tom Toner (Pickering), Bruce Johnson (Bystander), Simon Jones (Higgins), Robert Jensen, Michael Hayward-Jones, Ernest C. Lewis, John Wasiniak (Bystanders), John M. Wiltberger (Bartender/Footman), Russell Leib (Karparthy/Harry/Maitre d'), James Javore (Jamie/Boxington), George S. Irving (Doolittle), Pauline Flanagan (Mrs. Pearce), Mr. Hayward-Jones (Butler), Joy C. Hermalyn, Margaret Shafer, Cara Oestreicher, Ginger Thatcher (Servants), Patricia Kilgarriff (Mrs. Higgins), Anna Bergman (Lady Boxington), Stephen Casey (Constable), Jennifer Joan Joy (Flower Girl), Kevin Bogue (Lamplighter), Robert Jensen (Footman), Mary C. Sheehan (Bar Wife), Christiane Farr (Maid), Charlie Brumbly, Karen Lifshey, Kirk Ryder, Conny Lee Sasfai, Valerie Smith

PHANTOM with Music/Lyrics by Maury Yeston; Book, Arthur Kopit; Director, Robert Johanson; Musical Director, Tom Helm; Choreography, Sharon Halley; Sets, Michael Anania; Costumes, Gregg Barnes; Lighting, F. Mitchell Dana CAST: Marie-Laurence Danvers (Christine), Paul Schoeffler (Count), Patti Allison (La Carlotta), J. Courtney Pollard (Joseph Buquet), Richard White (Phantom-Erik), Jack Dabdoub (Gerard), Vince Trani (Cholet), John Wilkerson (Culture Minister), John Wiltberger (Ballet Master), Michael Hayward-Jones (Jean-Claude), Alicia Richardson (Florence), Conny Lee Sasfai (Flora), Ginger Thatcher (Fleure), Kevin Bogue (Designer/Police/Waiter), William Paul Michals (Music Director/ Baritone), Larry Grey (Inspector), Jeremy Koch (Police/Waiter), Dillon McCartney (Waiter), John Wasiniak (Oberon), Joy C. Hermalyn, Mary C. Sheehan (Divas), Christiane Farr (Dancing Belladova), Kirk Ryder (Young Carriere), Matt Fasano (Young Erik), Anna Bergman, Kristen Feeney, Cara Oestreicher, Paul Schoeffler, Margaret Shafer, Paul C. Reisman, Amanda White, Jessica Waxman

Gerry Goodstein, Jerry Dalia, Martha Swope Photos

Simon Jones, Judy Blazer in "My Fair Lady"

Richard White, Jack Dabdoub in "Phantom"

PITTSBURGH PUBLIC THEATER

Pittsburgh, Pennsylvania

Eighteenth Season

Artistic Director, Edward Gilbert; Managing Director, Dan Fallon; Stage Managers, Fred Noel, Julie Pyle; Public Relations, Elvira D. Bonta, Lisa Karmazyn

PRODUCTIONS & CASTS

THE SUM OF US by David Stevens; Director, Marshall W. Mason; Sets, John Lee Beatty; Costumes, Laura Crow; Lighting, Mal Sturchio CAST: Jordan Mott (Jeff), Russel Lunday (Harry), Anthony Meindl (Greg), Pamela Dunlap (Joyce)

MA RAINEY'S BLACK BOTTOM by August Wilson; Director, Claude Purdy; Set, Vicki Smith; Lighting, Phil Monat; Costumes, Paul Tazewell; Musical Director, Dwight Andrews CAST: William Thunhurst (Sturdyvant), Larry John Meyers (Irvin), Thomas Martell Brimm (Cutler), John Henry Redwood (Toledo), Donald Marshall (Slow Drag), Monte Russell (Levee), Sandra Reaves-Phillips (Ma Rainey), John Hall (Police), Renee Goldsberry (Dussie Mae), Ron McClelland (Sylvester)

INSPECTING CAROL by Daniel Sullivan and the Seattle Repertory Resident Co.; Director, David Saint; Sets, Loren Sherman; Lighting, Donald Holder; Costumes, Michael J. Cesario CAST: Mary Louise Wilson (M.J.), Reed Birney (Wayne), Alma Cuervo (Zorah), Andrew David Bronowski (Luther/Tiny Tim), Peggy Pope (Dorothy/Mrs. Cratchit), Ralph Williams (Sidney/Marley), Howard Samuelsohn (Phil/Cratchit), David Wolos-Fonteno (Parsons), Sam Turich (Bart), Christopher Curry (Larry/Scrooge), Kate Young (Betty), MaryBeth Munroe, Chuck Staresinic, Karen Zitnick (Stage Crew)

MAD FOREST by Caryl Churchill; Director, Mark Wing-Davey; Sets/ Costumes, Marina Draghici; Lighting, Peter Maradudin CAST: Larry John Meyers (Bogdan), Penelope Kreitzer (Irina/Grandmother/Flower Seller), Rana Haugen (Lucia/Doctor), Delia MacDougall (Florina/Student), Andrew Mutnick (Gabriel/ Student), Julia Fletcher (Rodica/ Grandmother/Flavia/ House Painter), J. Michael Flynn (Wayne/Mihai/ Dog/Bulldozer), James Carpenter (Grandfather /Old Aunt/Doctor/Priest/Vampire/Sore Throat Man/Soldier/Securitate), Sean Blackman (Radu/Soldier), Matte Osian (Ianos/Painter), Rod Gnapp (Securitate/Angel/Patient/Toma/Ghost/ Waiter/Student), Larry John Meyers (Soldier/Translator)

THE OLD LADY'S GUIDE TO SURVIVAL by Mayo Simon; Director, Alan Mandell; Costumes, Marianna Elliott; Set, Ray Recht; Lighting, Dennis Parichy CAST: Nan Martin (Netty), Shirl Bernheim (Shirl Bernheim)

COBB by Lee Blessing; Director, Lee Sankowich; Sets, Anne Mundell; Costumes, Barbara Anderson; Lighting, Phil Monat

THE SCHOOL FOR WIVES by Moliere; Director, Edward Gilbert; Sets/Costumes, Mark Negin; Lighting, Nicholas Cernovitch CAST: Kurt Knudson (Chrysalde), George Morfogen (Arnolphe), Joe Zaloom (Alain), Marceline Hugot (Georgette), Kia Christina Heath (Agnes), David Van Pelt (Horace), Charles Antalosky (Notary/Oronte), Paul Mochnick (Enrique)

Gerry Goodstein, Mark Portland , Ric Evans, Su Ellen Fitzsimmons Photos

Top Right: Reed Birney, Mary Louise Wilson, Howard Samuelsohn, Sam Turich, Peggy Pope in "Inspecting Carol"
Center: Russel Lunday, Jordon Mott in "Sum of Us"
Bottom Left: Shirl Bernheim, Nan Martin in "Old Lady's Guide to Survival"
Bottom Right: Mad Forest cast

154

PLAYMAKERS REPERTORY COMPANY

Chapel Hill, North Carolina

Producing Director, Milly S. Barranger; Associate Producing Director, David Hammond; Administrative Director, Mary Robin Wells; Production Manager, Millael Rolleri; Sets/Costumes, Sharon K. Campbell, McKay Coble, Bobbi Owen; Sound, Pamela Emerson; Stage Managers, Robert D. Russo, Tanya A. Strickland; Public Relations/Marketing Director, Sharon Broom
RESIDENT COMPANY: Gene Alper, Elizabeth Anderson, Patricia Barnett, Jef Betz, James Cartmel, Dede Corvinus, Ray Dooley, Mark Ransom Eis, Barbara Ellingson, Brett Halnu du Fretay, Paige Johnston, Cheryl Jones, Ian Jones, Michael Houston King, Nancy Lane, Brent Langdon, Charles McIver, Connan Morissey, Ronda Music, Donna Peters, Susanna Rinehart, Andrew Sellon, Alexander Yannis Stephano, Christine Suhr, Craig Turner, Ed Wagenseller, Kristine Watt
GUEST ARTISTS: (actors) Derin Altay, Christopher Armitage, Tandy Cronyn, Patrick Egan, Julie Fishell, Helen Harrelson, Herman LeVern Jones, Neil Maffin, Audrey Morgan, Christine Morris, Jeanne Ruskin, Noble Shropshire, Ken Strong, John Wojda, John Wylie; (directors) Stephen Stout, Evan Yionoulis; (design) Bill Clarke, Marcus Dilliard, Mary Louise Geiger, Ashley York Kennedy, Russell Parkman, Robert Wierzel
PRODUCTIONS: *The Little Foxes* by Lillian Hellman; Director, Stephen Stout; *Prelude to a Kiss* by Craig Lucas; Director, Ray Dooley; *The Nutcracker*: A Play by David Hammond, based on stories by E.T.A. Hoffmann; Director, Dede Corvinus; *Tartuffe* by Moliere; Director, David Hammond; *Some Americans Abroad* by Richard Nelson; Director, Evan Yionoulis; *Hamlet* by William Shakespeare; Director, David Hammond

Biar Orrell Photos

Top Left: **Elizabeth Anderson, Noble Shropshire in "Prelude to a Kiss"**
Top Right: **Tandy Cronyn, Neil Maffin in "Hamlet"**
Center: **Julie Fishell, John Wojda in "Tartuffe"**
Bottom: **Elizabeth Anderson, Ken Strong, Derin Altay, Ray Dooley in "Some Americans Abroad"**

William Peterson, Amy Morton in "Once in Doubt"

REMAINS THEATRE

Chicago, Illinois

Artistic Director, Larry Slaon; Producing Director, R.P. Sekon; Associate Artistic Director, Neel Keller; General Manager, Janis Post; Marketing Director, Christian Petersen

RESIDENT COMPANY: Gerry Becker, Lucy Childs, Holly Fulger, Kevin Hurley, Ted Levine, Mary McAuliffe, Lindsay McGee, D.W. Moffett, Amy Morton, David Alan Novak, Susan Nussbaum, Christian Petersen, William Peterson, Natalie West

PRODUCTIONS & CASTS

ONCE IN DOUBT; Written/Directed by Raymond J. Barry; Sets/Lighting, Kevin Snow; Costumes, Laura Cunningham CAST: William Peterson (Harry), Amy Morton (Flo)

OF THEE I SING by George & Ira Gershwin, George S. Kaufman, Morrie Ryskind; Director, Larry Slaon; Sets, Stephanie Gerckens; Lighting, Rita Pietraszek; Musical Director, Jeff Lewis; Costumes, Frances Maggio; Choreography, Timothy O'Slynne CAST: Darren Matthias (Wintergreen), Joan Elizabeth (Mary), Jennifer Rosin (Diana), Michelle Bernard, Bill Chamberlain, Raul Esparza, Steven Farber, Kevin Farrell, Clifford T. Fraier, David Frutkoff, Christopher Garbrecht, Kevin Hurley, Jill Loenikar, Vincent Lonergan, Mimi Manners, Rich Maxwell, Claire Morkin, Scott Putman, Joe Quinn, Dominic Rambaran, Larry Russo, Peter Siragusa, Troy West, Gary Wilmes, Sarah Worthington

SNAKEBIT (PREMIERE) by David Marshall Grant; Director, Campbell Scott; Sets, Jeff Bauer; Lighting, Kevin Snow; Costumes, Laura Cunningham CAST: D.W. Moffett (Jonathan), Talia Balsam (Jennifer), John Benjamin Hickey (Michael)

THE DAY ROOM by Don DeLillo; Director, Neel Keller; Sets/Lighting, Michael Philippi; Costumes, Frances Maggio CAST: Nathan Davis, Lawrence McCauley, Holly Wantuch, Troy West, Tracey Letts

Liz Lauren Photos

Bottom Left: Talia Balsam, John Benjamin Hickey in "Snakebit"
Bottom Right: Joan Elizabeth, Darren Matthias, Jennifer Rosin & cast in "Of Thee I Sing"

REPERTORY THEATRE OF ST. LOUIS

St. Louis, Missouri

Artistic Director, Steven Woolf; Managing Director, Mark D. Bernstein; Associate Artistic Director, Susan Gregg; Imaginary Co. Supervisor, Jeffery Scott Matthews; Development Director, Barbara Harris; Marketing Director, Gordon Alloway

PRODUCTIONS & CASTS

M.BUTTERLY by David Henry Hwang; Director, Edward Stern; Sets/Costumes, Marie Anne Chiment; Lighting, Peter E. Sargent CAST: Greg Thornton (Gallimard), Jason Ma (Song Liling), Joneal Joplin (Toulon/Judge), Anderson Matthews (Marc/Sharpless), Dina Spybey (Renee/Magazine Girl), Lucy Liu (Comrade Chin/Suzuki/Shu-Fang), Alexandra O'Karma (Helga), Fan Yi-Song, Doan Jaroenngarm, Sawako Tamishige

DRACULA by Bram Stoker; Adapted/Directed by Charles Morey; Sets, Peter B. Harrison; Costumes, John Carver Sullivan; Lighting, Max De Volder CAST: David Harum (Harker), Charles Antalosky (Van Helsing), Kathleen McCall (Mina), Katherine Leask (Lucy), Simon Brooking (Arthur), Craig Wroe (Seward), John Rensenhouse (Dracula), Zoe Vonder Haar (Mrs. Westenra), Whit Reichert (Swales/Maxwell), Lyn Liechty (Peasant/Bride), Bill Church (Reorter), Joseph Gomez (Coachman/ Reporter), Julie Eisenbeiss (Bride/Tart), Stephanie Couch (Bride)

A FUNNY THING HAPPENED ON THE WAY TO THE FORUM by Stephen Sondheim, Burt Shevelove, Larry Gelbart; Director/Choreographer, Pamela Hunt; Music Director, Larry Pressgrove; Sets, John Roslevich; Costumes, Dorothy L. Marshall; Lighting, Peter Sargent CAST: Jack Cirillo (Pseudolus), Hunter Bell, Bobby Clark, Randy Donaldson (Proteans), James Darrah (Hero), Jennifer Westfeldt (Philia), Burt Edwards (Erronius), Larry Hansen (Lycus), Paul Schoeffler (Gloriosus), Nick Corley (Hysterium), Ralston Hill (Senex), Julie J. Hafner (Domina), Janet Bushor (Gymnasia), Andree Peterson (Tintinabula), Kristen Wilson (Vibrata), Sandra Purpuro, Serena Soffer (Geminae)

SIX DEGREES OF SEPARATION by John Guare; Director, Steven Woolf; Sets, Carolyn L. Ross; Costumes, Dorothy L. Marshall; Lighting, Max De Volder CAST: Glynis Bell (Ouisa), Geoffrey Wade (Flan), Joneal Joplin (Geoffrey), John Lathan (Paul), Rob Harriell (Hustler), Darrie Lawrence (Kitty), Eric Forsythe (Larkin), Paul DeBoy (Detective), Alisha McKinney (Tess), Ian Novak (Woody), Kevin Earley (Ben), Joe Palmieri (Dr. Fine), Andrew Foster (Doug), Chad Harris (Police/Doorman), Matthew Vogel (Trent), Philip Lehl (Rick), Clea Montville (Elizabeth)

WOMAN IN MIND by Alan Ayckbourn; Director, Susan Gregg; Sets, John Ezell; Costumes, Alan Armstrong; Lighting, Dale Jordan CAST: Darrie Lawrence (Susan), Tom Cayler (Bill), Eric Forsythe (Andy), Clea Montville (Lucy), Paul DeBoy (Tony), Joe Palmieri (Gerald), Tamara Daniel (Muriel), Philip Lehl (Rick)

PYGMALION by George Bernard Shaw; Director, John Going; Sets, Joel Fontaine; Costumes, Jeffrey Struckman; Lighting, Allen Lee Hughes CAST: Stacey Miller (Clara), Zoe Vonder Haar (Mrs. Eynsford-Hill), Wm Daniel File (Bystander), Matt Bradford Sullivan (Freddy), Katherine Leask (Eliza), Burt Edwards (Pickering), Martin LaPlatney (Higgins), Robert F. D'Haene (Sarcastic Man), Jenny Turner (Mrs. Pearce), Donald Ewer (Doolittle), Ruby Holbrook (Mrs. Higgins), Gillian McNally (Maid), Kitty Armour, Carol Brynac, Eric Conners, Jeffrey Cox, Teresa Doggett, Jennifer Jonassen, Patti Lewis, Ian Novak, Brenda Robertson-Suhre, Tom Schiller, Barbara Size, David S. Stewart

SHOW AND TELL by Anthony Clarvoe; Director, Susan Gregg; Sets/Lighting, Max De Volder; Costumes, J. Bruce Summers; Music/Sound, Stephen Burns Kessler CAST: Susan Ericksen (Corey), Jim Abele (Seth), Mickey Hartnett (Iris/Lucy), Kim Sebastian (Ann/Gail), Brenda Denmark (Sharon/ Erinn), R. Ward Duffy (Farsted)

THE MYSTERY OF IRMA VEP by Charles Ludlam; Director, Tony Martin; Sets, William F. Schmiel; Costumes, J. Bruce Summers; Lighting, Glenn Dunn CAST: Jim Abele, John Resenhouse

SIGHT UNSEEN by Donald Margulies; Director, Steven Woolf; Sets/ Costumes, Michael Ganio; Lighting, John Wylie CAST: Joneal Joplin (Nick), David Harum (Jonathan), Kathleen Mahony-Bennett (Patricia), Clea Montville (Grete)

Judy Andrews Photos

Top Left: Philip Lehl, Clea Montville, John Lathan in
"Six Degrees of Separation"
Center: Jim Abele, Susan Ericksen in "Show and Tell"
Bottom: Jason Ma, Greg Thornton in "M. Butterfly"

SEATTLE REPERTORY THEATRE

Seattle, Wahington

Thirtieth Season

Artistic Director, Daniel Sullivan; Managing Director, Benjamin Moore; Associate Artistic Director, Douglas Hughes; Artistic Associate/Literary Manager, Kurt Beattie; Public Relations Manager, M. Mark Bocek

PRODUCTIONS & CASTS

THE TRAGEDY OF JULIUS CAESAR by William Shakespeare; Directors, Douglas Hughes and Liz Diamond; Sets, Andrei Both; Costumes, Caryn Neman; Lighting, Peter Maradudin CAST: Jonathan Adams, Lisa Arrindell, John Aylward, Lisa Carswell, James M. Davenport, Stefan Enriquez, George A. Franz, Tamu Gray, Torrey Hanson, Tamara Harris, Ron Heneghan, Hunt Holman, John Holyoke, Suzy Hunt, Robert M. James, Carol Johnson, Darren Lay, Anthony Lee, John Patrick Lowrie, James Ludwig, Vivian Majowski, Jessica Marlowe, Bob Morrisey, Masaye Okano Nakagawa, Mark Nelson, Timothy McCuen Piggee, Marcus Rolland, Robert J. Sehorn, Jr., Mark Kenneth Smaltz, Rick Tutor, R. Hamilton Wright, Adam Weiner

INSPECTING CAROL by Daniel Sullivan and the Resident Acting Company; Director, Mr. Sullivan; Sets, Andrew Wood Boughton; Costumes, Robert Wojewodski; Lighting, Rick Paulsen; Composer, Norman Durkee CAST: John Aylward, Jeannie Carson, Barbara Dirickson, William Biff McGuire, Jessica Marlowe, Bob Morrisey, Marianne Owen, Mark Kenneth Smaltz, Daniel Spiegelman, John Sullivan, Rick Tutor, R. Hamilton Wright

LIPS TOGETHER, TEETH APART by Terrence McNally; Director, David Saint; Sets, James Noone; Costumes, David Murin; Lighting, Kenneth N. Posner CAST: John Aylward, Barbara Dirickson, Laurie Kennedy, R. Hamilton Wright

THE FLYING KARAMAZOV BROTHERS in **THE BROTHERS KARAMAZOV** by Paul Magid; Director, Daniel Sullivan; Music/Musical Direction, Doug Wieselman and Gina Leishman; Lyrics, Howard Patterson; Sets, Andrew Wood Boughton; Costumes, Caryn Neman; Lighting, Allen Lee Hughes; Co-Produced with Arena Stage CAST: Bob Amaral, Larry Block, Joanna Glushak, David LaDuca, Paul Magid, Howard Patterson, Michael Preston, Cathy Sutherland, Sam Williams

HEARTBREAK HOUSE by George Bernard Shaw; Director, Adrian Hall; Sets, Eugene Lee; Costumes, Cathy Zuber; Lighting, Natasha Katz CAST: John Aylward, Jeannie Carson, Barbara Dirickson, William Biff McGuire, Bob Morrisey, John Morrison, Marianne Owen, Rick Tutor, Nance Williamson, R. Hamilton Wright

THE PIANO LESSON by August Wilson; Director, Lloyd Richards; Sets, E. David Cosier, Jr.; Costumes, Costanza Romero; Lighting, York Kennedy CAST: Ed Bernard, Denise Burse-Mickelbury, Danny Robinson Clark, Rosalyn Coleman, Michael Jayce, Christina Mitchell, W. Allen Taylor, Isiah Whitlock, Jr.

THE SUBSTANCE OF FIRE by Jon Robin Baitz; Director, Michael Bloom; Set, Bill Clarke; Costumes, Rose Pederson; Lighting, Brian Gale CAST: Rob Gomes, Allan Miller, Michael Ornstein, Marianne Owen, Dulcy Rogers

SPUNK by Zora Neale Hurston; Adaptation, George C. Wolfe; Music, Chic Street Man; Director, Jacqueline Moscou; Sets/Costumes, Michael Olich; Lighting, Meg Fox CAST: LeLand Gantt, Michael Jayce, Anthony Lee, Chic Street Man, Shona Tucker, Sybil Walker

EYE OF GOD (PREMIERE) by Tim Blake Nelson; Director, Douglas Hughes; Set, Andrew Wood Boughton; Costumes, Rose Pederson; Lighting, Greg Sullivan; Music/Sound, Michael Roth CAST: Garret Dillahunt, Jamie Harrold, William Biff McGuire, Todd Jefferson Moore, Bob Morrisey, Marianne Owen, Angie Phillips, Susan Riddiford, Rick Tutor

Chris Bennion Photos

Top: Angie Phillips, Garret Dillahunt in "Eye of God"
Center: Mario Arrambide, Rick Tutor, (bottom) John Aylward, (top)
Mark Kenneth Smaltz in "Julius Caesar"
Bottom: Isiah Whitlock, Jr., Danny Robinson Clark, Michael Jzyce,
Ed Bernard in "The Piano Lesson"

SOUTH COAST REPERTORY

Costa Mesa, California

PRODUCTIONS: *The Man Who Came to Dinner* by Kaufman and Hart; Director, William Ludel; *Our Country's Good* by Timberlake Wertenbaker; Director, Martin Benson; *A Christmas Carol* by Dickens; Adaptation, Jerry Patch; Director, John-David Keller; *The Miser* by Moliere; Translation/Direction, David Chambers; *Great Day in the Morning* (PREMIERE) by Thomas Babe; Director, David Emmes; *Hay Fever* by Noel Coward; Director, William Ludel; *Shadowlands* by William Nicholson; Director, William Nicholson; Director, Martin Benson; *Let's Play Two* (PREMIERE) by Anthony Clarvoe; Director, Michael Bloom; *Odd Jobs* by Frank Moher; Director, David Emmes; *Intimate Exchanges* by Alan Ayckbourn; Director, Mark Rucker; *Waiting for Godot* by Samuel Beckett; Director, Martin Benson; *So Many Words* (PREMIERE) by Roger Rueff; Director, Mark Rucker

Charlaine Brown, Ron Stone Photos

Top Left: Jeff Allin, I.M. Hobson, Laurie Walters in "The Man Who Came to Dinner"
Bottom Left: Timothy Landfield, Kandis Chappell in "Hay Fever"
Bottom Right: Susan Cash, Arye Gross in "Let's Play Two"

159

STUDIO ARENA THEATRE

Buffalo, New York

Thirty-eighth Season

Producing Director, Raymond Bonnard; Artistic Director, Gavin Cameron-Webb; Development Director, Anne E. Hays; Marketing Director, Courtney J. Walsh; Stage managers, Julia P. Jones, Sally Ann Wood

PRODUCTIONS & CASTS

LEND ME A TENOR by Ken Ludwig; Director, Kent Thompson; Set, Jim Maronek; Costumes, Gail Brassard; Lighting, Rachel Budin CAST: Brad Bellamy, Keith Curran, Brenda Foley, Suzanne Grodner, Bob Kirsh, Leilani Mickey, Philip Pleasants, Joan Ulmer

LOST ELECTRA by Bruce E. Rodgers; Director, Gavin Cameron-Webb; Sets/Costumes, G.W. Mercier; Lighting, Richard Devin CAST: Monica Bell, Sean P. Fagan, Julian Gamble, Daren Kelly, Monique Morgan

A CHRISTMAS CAROL by Charles Dickens; Adaptation, Amlin Gray; Original Direction, David Frank; Staging, Gavin Cameron-Webb; Sets/Lighting, Paul Wonsek; Costumes, Mary Ann Powell; Choreography, Linda H. Swiniuch CAST: Robert Spencer (Scrooge), Kevin Donovan, Martin Kildare, Saul Elkin, Ron O.J. Parson, Arn Weiner, Meghan Rose Krank, Jeffrey Nicoloff, Brenda Foley, Lorna C, Hill, Terrance Brown, D. Cameron Hartney, Bobby De La Plante, Adam Van Volkenburg, Mia Kai Simone Moody, Renee Pastel, Allison Dinsmore, Marlena Franke, Antwan Barlow, Brian Michael Fitzgerald, Emily Dinsmore, Angel Steele, Jeremy Hoeltke, Adam Saffron, Carolyn De Lorenzo, Sarah Iacono, A. Luana Kenyatta, Christopher M. Verel

THE DINING ROOM by A. R. Gurney; Director, Nagle Jackson; Set, Bill Clarke; Costumes, Donna Massimo; Lighting, Q. Brian Sickels CAST: Laurinda Barrett, Corinna May, Jim Mohr, Corliss Preston, Virgil Roberson, John Scherer

THE BUSINESS OF MURDER by Richard Harris; Director, Frederick King Keller; Set/Lighting, Paul Wonsek; Costumes, Charlotte M. Yetman; Music, Robert Volkman CAST: Roger Forbes, Marcia Kash, Faran Tahir

MISS EVERS' BOYS by David Feldshuh; Director, Edward G. Smith; Set, Harry A. Feiner; Costumes, Lauren K. Lambie; Lighting, William H. Grant, III CAST: Oliver Barrero, Christine Campbell, Laverne Clay, Stephen McKinley Henderson, Martin Kildare, Ron O.J. Parson, Eric A. Payne

THE VOYAGE OF MARY C. by Laurence Carr; Director, Gavin Cameron-Webb; Set, Robert M. Cothran; Costumes, Lauren K. Lambie; Lighting, Harry A. Feiner CAST: Sean Cullen, Ellen Fiske

A...MY NAME IS STILL ALICE; Conception/Original Direction, Joan Micklin Silver and Julianne Boyd; Director/Choreography, Darwin Knight; Set, Peter B. Harrison; Costumes, Lauren K. Lambie; Lightingm Victor En Yu Tan; Musical Director, Randall Kramer CAST: Jo Ann Cunningham, Frances Ford, Tonye Patano, Karyn Quackenbush, Cheryl Stern

K.C. Kratt Photos

Roger Forbes, Marcia Kash, Faran Tahir in "Business of Murder"
Top: Bob Kirsh, Philip Pleasants in "Lend Me a Tenor"

THE STUDIO THEATRE

Washington, D.C.

Fifteenth Season

Artistic/Managing Director, Joy Zinoman; Associate Managing Director, Keith Alan Baker; Dramaturg, Maynard Marshall; Public Relations Director, Marilyn Newton; Production Manager, Tracey L. Prinz; Stage Manager, Serge Seiden

PRODUCTION & CASTS

THE BRIGHT AND THE BOLD by Peter Whelan CAST: Carla Harting (Violet), Kryztov Lindquist (Devlin), Sarah Marshall (Jesse), Elizabeth Michele Schasffer (Ada), Emily K. Townley (Joyce), Marty McDonough (Hector), John Leonard Thompson (Jim), Isabel Keating (Mabel), Helen Headman (Grace), Scott Harrison (Raymond)

THE LISBON TRAVIATA by Terrence McNally CAST: Philip Goodwin (Stephen), Floyd King (Mendy), Michael Chaban (Mike), Firdous Bamji (Paul)

ROSENCRANTZ AND GUILDENSTERN ARE DEAD by Tom Stoppard CAST: Jim Shanklin (Rosencrantz), Ezra Knight (Guilderstern), Lawrence Redmond (Player), Rick Hammerly, Matthew Howe, Kevin Roach, Sheira Venetianer (Tragedians), Jordan Young (Alfred), Tom Kearney (Hamlet), Mary Melyssa Hall (Ophelia), David Johnson (Claudius), Rosemary Regan (Gertrude), David Harsheid (Polonius), Ramin Ackert (Horatio), Larry Fish (Ambassador)

IMAGINE DROWNING by Terry Johnson CAST: Nancy Robinette (Brenda), Alan Wade (Buddy), Mary Tucker (Jane), Paul Morella (David), John Leonard Thompson (Tom), Isaac Butler (Sam)

Stan Barouh Photos

Left: John Leonard Thompson, Sarah Marshall in "Bright and Bold Design"

SYRACUSE STAGE

Syracuse, New York

Twentieth Season

Producing Director, James A. Clark; Artistic Director, Tazewell Thompson; Development Director, Shirley Lockwood; Business Manager, Diana Coles; Marketing Director, Barbara Beckos; Press Director, Barbara Haas; Company Manager, Peter Sandwall; Stage Managers, Martha Donaldson, Megan Schneid

PRODUCTIONS & CASTS

LEND ME A TENOR by Ken Ludwig; Director, Arthur Storch; Set, James Noone; Costumes, Pamela Scofield; Lighting, Phil Monat CAST: Deanna Dunmyer (Maggie), Bill Randolph (Max), Christopher Wynkoop (Saunders), Giulia Pagano (Maria), Curt Karibalis (Tito), Russell Goldberg (Bellhop), Luba Gregus (Diana), Rica Martens (Julia)
A CHRISTMAS CAROL by Charles Dickens; Adaptation, Gerardine Clark; Director, William S. Morris; Sets, Bob Barnett; Costumes, Maria Marrero; Lighting, Victor En Yu Tan CAST: Kermit Brown (Scrooge), Mel Duane Gionson, Patrick Mulcahy, Russ Jolly, Malcolm Ingram, John Leighton, Cheryl Gaysunas, Amy Hohn, David Ponting, Gerardine Clark, Kia Christina Heath, Leslie Noble, Elizabeth Ingram
HYSTERICS by Le Clanche du Rand; Director, Will Osborne; Set, Kerry Sanders; Costumes, Randall E. Klein; Lighting, Sandra Schilling CAST: Le Clanche du Rande (Storyteller)
"MASTER HAROLD"...AND THE BOYS by Athol Fugard; Director, Jamie Brown; Sets, James Noone; Costumes, Barbara Jenks; Lighting, Phil Monat CAST: Daryl Edwards (Sam), Allen Gilmore (Willie), Benjamin White (Hally)
AWAKE AND SING! by Clifford Odets; Director, Arthur Storch; Sets, R. Michael Miller; Costumes, Pamela Scofield; Lighting, Marc B. Weiss CAST: David S. Howard (Myron), Lynn Cohen (Bessie), Joel Friedman (Jacob), Shanna Riss (Hennie), Tony Gillan (Ralph), Ed Cannan (Schlosser), Arnie Mazer (Moe), Robert Ari (Morty), Steve Routman (Sam)
JAR THE FLOOR by Cheryl L. West; Director, Tazewell Thompson; Sets/Lighting, Joseph P. Tilford; Costumes, Kay Kurta CAST: Irma P. Hall (MaDear), Brenda Pressley (MayDee), Crystal Laws Green (Lola), Susan Payne (Vennie), Stephanie Silverman (Raisa)

Doug Wonders Photos

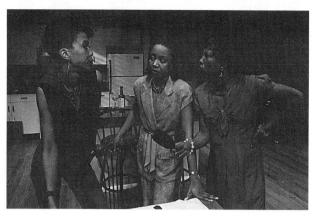

Susan Payne, Brenda Pressley, Crystal Laws Green in "Jar the Floor"

Anne Scurria, Janice Duclos, Timothy Crowe, Olympia Dukakis in "Hope Zone"

TRINITY REPERTORY COMPANY

Providence, Rhode Island

Artistic Director, Richard Jenkins; Resident Designer, Eugene Lee; Resident Costume Designer, William Lane; Sets, Robert D. Soule; Lighting, Michael Giannitti, Jeff Clark; Production Manager, Mr. Clark; General Manager, Dennis Conway; Development Director, Kibbe Reilly; Public Relations Director, Margaret Melozzi; Guest Directors, Clinton Turner Davis; David Petrarca, Ralph Waite

PRODUCTIONS & CASTS

THE SEAGULL by Anton Chekhov; Adaptation, Tori Haring-Smith; Director, Richard Jenkins CAST: Barbara Blossom, Christopher Nyrnes, Robert J. Colonna, Timothy Crowe, William Damkoehler, Jennifer Dundas, Jonathan Fried, Julia Sheridan Langham, Brian McEleney, Allen Oliver, Margo Skinner, Jennifer Wiltsie, Clare Vadeboncoeur
LIPS TOGETHER, TEETH APART by Terrence McNally; Director, Leonard Foglia CAST: Anne Scurria, Ed Shea, Cynthia Strickland, Fred Sullivan, Jr.
A CHRISTMAS CAROL; Adaptation, Adrian Hall and Richard Cumming CAST: Stephen Berenson, Barbara Blossom, Robert J. Colonna, Timothy Crowe, William Damkoehler, Wyatt Paul Davis, Janice Duclos, Julie Galdieri, Phyllis Kay, Ricardo Pitts-Wiley, John Thompson, Clare Vadeboncoeur, Dan Welch, Jeanine White
NORTHEAST LOCAL (PREMIERE) by Tom Donaghy CAST: Rengin Altay, Jane MacIver, Allen Oliver, Ed Shea
THE HOPE ZONE (PREMIERE) by Kevin Heelan; Director, Richard Jenkins CAST: Robert J. Colonna, Timothy Crowe, Janice Duclos, Olympia Dukakis, Anne Scurria
COME BACK, LITTLE SHEBA by William Inge CAST: Donald Berry, Barbara Blossom, Tom Buckland, Christopher Byrnes, Richard Donnelly, Jennifer Dundas, James O'Brien, Barbara Orson, Alton Starr, Dan Welch
TWELFTH NIGHT or WHAT YOU WILL by William Shakespeare CAST: Judy Bard, Stephen Berenson, Marc Carver, Robert J. Colonna, Timothy Crowe, William Damkoehler, Tony Fross, Phyllis Kay, Henrik Kromann, Rachel Maloney, Leecia Manning, Brian McEleney, Kevin Moriarty, Anne Scurria, Ed Shea, Dan Sulger, Christopher Turner, Jeanine White
THE GOOD TIMES ARE KILLING ME by Lynda Barry CAST: Brienin Bryant, Janice Duclos, Jennifer Dundas, Wendy Hodgson, Lisa Lane, Howard London, Carol Anne Parker, Ricardo Pitts-Wiley, Cynthia Strickland, Fred Sullivan, Jr., John Thompson, Rose Weaver

Mark Morelli Photos

VIRGINIA STAGE COMPANY

Norfolk, Virginia

Thirteenth Season

Artistic Director, Tom Gardner; Managing Director, Doug Perry; Production Manager, Amanda Graham; Stage Manager, Bo Wilson; Development Director, Barbara Peck; Marketing/Public Relations Director, Julie Stafford

PRODUCTIONS & CASTS

THE LION IN WINTER by James Goldman; Director, Tom Gardner; Sets, Donald Eastman; Costumes, Lisa Vollrath; Lighting, James F. Ingalls CAST: Grant Albrecht (Richard), John Dawson Beard (John), Wesley Bishop (Henry II), Bill Camp (Geoffrey), Kandis Chappell (Eleanor), Alec Phoenix (Philip), Katy Selverstone (Alais)
FROM THE MISSISSIPPI DELTA by Dr. Endesha Ida Mae Holland; Director, Seret Scott; Set, Debra Booth; Costumes, Lisa Vollrath; Lighting, Pat Dignan CAST: Kim Brockington (Woman Two), Kena Tangi Dorsey (Woman One), Shelia Ramsey (Woman Three)
THE IMMIGRANT by Mark Harelik; Director, Tom Gardner; Set, Donald Eastman; Costumes, Dona Granata; Lighting, Brian MacDevitt CAST: Twyla Hafermann (Leah), Gordon G. Jones (Milton), Margery Shaw (Ima), Richard Topol (Haskell)
PUMP BOYS AND DINETTES by John Foley, Mark Hardwick, Debra Monk, Cass Morgan, John Schimmel, Jim Wann; Director, Jason Edwards; Set, Mark Cheney; Costumes, Guinevere W. Lee; Lighting, Kenton Yeager CAST: Jason Edwards (Jim), Tina Johnson (Prudie), Lonnie Rowell (Eddie), Guy Strobel (L.M.), Barry Tarallo (Jackson), Elizabeth Ward (Rhetta)
LOVE LETTERS by A. R. Gurney; Director, Ted Weiant CAST: Charlton Heston (Andrew), Lydia Clarke Heston (Melissa)

Echard Wheeler Photos

Guy Strobel, Elizabeth Ward, Lonnie Rowell, Barry Tarallo, Tina Johnson in "Pump Boys and Dinettes"

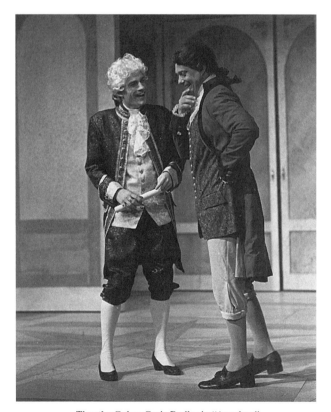

Timothy Gulen, Craig Dudley in "Amadeus"

WAYSIDE THEATRE

Middletown, Virginia

Thirty-first Season

Artistic Director, Christopher Owens; General Manager, Donna Johnson; Stage Manager, Liz Reddick; Administrative Assistant, Sharon Gochenour; Costumes, Harriet Engler; Lighting, John Demaree

PRODUCTIONS & CASTS

STAGE STRUCK by Simon Gray; Director, James B. Nicola; Sets, John Ervin; CAST: Nick Stannard (Robert), Jeffrey D. Eiche (Herman), Kathy Lichter (Anne), Michael Burg (Widdecombe)
OTHER PEOPLE'S MONEY by Jerry Sterner; Director, Christopher Owens; Sets, John Ervin; CAST: Nick Stannard (William), Dana Bate (Andrew), Kathy Lichter (Bea), Michael Burg (Garfinkle), Wendy Welch (Kate)
AMADEUS by Peter Shaffer; Director/Sound, Christopher Owens; Sets, Keith Belli CAST: Craig Dudley (Salieri), Timothy Gulan (Mozart), Joanne Lessner (Constanze), Nick Stannard (Joseph II), Alan Gilbert (Van Strack), Alan Furlan (Orsini-Rosenberg), Nick Nerangis (Baron Swieten), Kevin Connell, Jenny Maguire, Tod S. Williams (Venticelli), Jocelyn Beam (Katherina), Vanessa Jennings Lock (Teresa), Fraser Scorgie (Guiseppe), Jeremiah Fletcher, Robert Schnettler (Servants), Richard Bennett (Valet), Ellen Nichols (Cook)
TAKING STEPS by Alan Ayckbourn; Director, Richard Harden; Set, John Ervin CAST: Wendy Welch (Elizabeth), Nick Stannard (Mark), Kevin Connell (Tristram), Dana Bate (Roland), Alan Gilbert (Leslie), Jenny Maguire (Kitty)

YALE REPERTORY THEATRE

New Haven, Connecticut

Artistic Director, Stan Wojewodski, Jr.; Managing Director, Benjamin Mordecai; Associate Artistic Director, Mark Bly; Resident Dramaturg, Gitta Honegger; General Manager, Caroline F. Turner; Development Director, Marcia Winter; Marketing Director, Joan Channick; Press/ Publications Director, Joyce Friedmann; Stage Managers, Karen Carpenter, Wendy Beaton

PRODUCTIONS & CASTS

HAMLET by William Shakespeare; Director, Stan Wojewodski, Jr.; Sets, Todd Andrew Rosenthal; Costumes, Katherine Roth; Lighting, Robert Wierzel CAST: Dallas Adams, Roxanna Augesen, Earl Baker, Karen Angela Bishop, Buzz Bovshow, Enrico Colantoni, Brendan Corbalis, Reginald Lee Flowers, Melody J. Garrett, Sean Haberle, James Hallett, Mary Magdalena Hernandez, James Kall, Declan Lane, Julie Lawrence, Craig Mathers, Tom McCarthy, Gregory McClure, Drew Richardson, Reg Rogers, Michael Strickland

THE COLORED MUSEUM by George C. Wolfe; Director, Donald Douglass; Composer/Musical Director, Kysia Bostic; Sets, Monica Raya; Costumes, Elizabeth Michal Fried; Lighting, Trui Malten CAST: Demitri Corbin, Chanelle Diane Dumas, Charlette Renee Hammett, Pamela Harley, Pamela Isaacs, JoNell Kennedy, Kelly Neal

CHILDREN OF PARADISE: SHOOTING A DREAM by Steven Epp; Felicity Jones, Dominique Serrand and Paul Walsh; based on the work of Marcel Carne; Director, Dominique Serrand; Sets, Vincent Gracieux; Music, Chandler Poling; Lighting, Frederic Desbois; Costumes, Trina Mrnak CAST: Dallas Adams, Michael Belfiore, Michael Collins, Sarah Corzatt, Barbara Berlovitz Desbois, John Clark Donahue, Steven Epp, Laura Esping, Vincent Gracieux, Nancy Hogetvedt, Aimee Jacobson, Eric Jensen, Felicity Jones, Ben Kernan, Angie Lewis, Robert Rosen, Joel Sass, Robert Schneider, Charles Schuminski, Dominique Serrand, Brian Sostek

SAINT JOAN OF THE STOCKYARDS by Bertolt Brecht; Translation, Paul Schmidt; Director, Liz Diamond; Music/Sound, Dan Moses Schreier; Sets, Adam Scher; Costumes, Lisa Tomczeszyn; Lighting, Jennifer Tipton CAST: Dallas Adams, Christopher Bauer, Tom Bloom, Amy Brenneman, David Chandler, Brendan Corbalis, Jane Eden, Melody J. Garrett, Paul Giamatti, Ben Halley, Jr., Rodney Scott Hudson, Sarah Knowlton, Camryn Manheim, Alessandro Nivola, Nicky Paraiso, Michael Potts, Daniel J. Roth, Tim Salamandyk, Paul Schmidt, Peter Schmitz, Scott Sherman, Christina Sibul

ESCAPE FROM HAPPINESS by George F. Walker; Director, Irene Lewis; Co-Produced with Center Stage; Sets, Michael Yeargan; Costumes, Jess Goldstein; Lighting, Stephen Strawbridge CAST: Alexandra Gersten, Annette Helde, Marin Hinkle, Dan Moran, James Noah, Pippa Pearthree, Liev Schreiber, Lois Smith, Jack Wallace, William Youmans

THE BALTIMORE WALTZ by Paula Vogel; Director, Stan W Wojewodski, Jr.; Sets, David Maxine; Costumes, Denise Hudson; Lighting, Lynne Chase CAST: Tim Blake Nelson, Mary Shultz, Jonathan Walker

T. Charles Erickson, Michael Daniel, Richard Anderson Photos

Top Right: Felicity Jones, Robert Rosen in "Children of Paradise"
Below: Tim Blake Nelson, Mary Scultz,
Jonathan Walker in "Baltimore Waltz"
Bottom Left: (front) Sean Haberle, Melody J. Garrett in "Hamlet"
Bottom Right: Brendan Corbalis, David Chandler, Ben Haley, Jr. in "Saint Joan of the Stockyards"

Alexandra Gersten in "Escape from Happiness"

ANNIE GET YOUR GUN

Music/Lyrics, Irving Berlin; Book, Herbert and Dorothy Fields; Director, Susan H. Schulman; Choreography, Michael Lichtefeld; Musical Director, Brian W. Tidwell; Orchestrations, Robert Russell Bennet, Michael Gibson, Mr. Tidwell; Sets, Heidi Landesman, Joel Reynolds; Costumes, Catherine Zuber; Lighting, Ken Billington; Stage Manager, Bryan Young; Executive Producer, George MacPherson; Presented by Tom McCoy, Tom Mallow, ATP/Dodger, Pace Theatrical Group and Kennedy Center; Press, Laura Matalon

CAST

Charlie Davenport	Paul V. Ames
Doll Tate	K.T. Sullivan
Mac	Marty McDonough
Foster Wilson/Conductor/Pawnee	Mike O'Carroll
Frank Butler	Brent Barrett
Annie Oakley	Cathy Rigby
Little Jake	Ryan Mason
Nellie	Theresa McCoy
Jessie	Kaitlin McCoy
Buffalo Bill	Erick Devine
Porter	John Walden
Cowboy/Footman	John Anthony
Chief Sitting Bull	Mauricio Bustamante
Stillwater	Joe Bowerman
Indian Girl	Catherine Gardner
Pawnee's Messenger	Robert Preston Smith
Mrs. Sylvia Potter-Porter	Robin Lusby
Mrs. Schuyler Adams	Lynn Shuck
Mr. Schuyler Adams	Bill Bateman
Mrs. Ernest Henderson	Wendy Piper
Ensemble	Ana Maria Andricain, John Anthony

Bill Bateman, Stephen Bourneuf, Joe Bowerman, Catherine Gardner, Lisa Hanna Robin Lusby, Ryan Mason, Kaitlin McCoy, Theresa McCoyMarty McDonough Sharon Moore, Wendy Piper,Hugh B. RichardsLynn Shuck Roger Preston Smith, John Walden, Leigh-Anne Wencker

UNDERSTUDIES: Bill Bateman, Marty McDonough (Charlie), Lynn Shuck, Robin Lusby (Dolly), Craig Waletzko, Jow Bowerman (Mac), Mr. Bateman, Roger Preston Smith (Foster/Pawnee/Sitting Bull), John Anthony (Frank Butler/Messenger), Ana Maria Andricain (Annie Oakley/Mrs. Adams/ Mrs. Henderson), Catherine Gardner (Jake/Nellie/Jessie), Mike O'Carroll (Buffalo Bill), Craig Waletzko (Porter/Conductor/Footman/Mr. Adams), Stephen Bourneuf (Cowboy), Mr. Waletzko, Hugh B. Richards (Stillwater), Ms. Shuck, Leigh Anne Wencker (Potter-Porter), Theresa McCoy (Indian Girl)

MUSICAL NUMBERS: Col. Buffalo Bill, I'm a Bad Bad Man, Doin' What Comes Natur'lly, Girl That I Marry, You Can't Get a Man with a Gun, There's No Business Like Show Business, Moonshine Lullaby, They Say It's Wonderful, Wild West Pitch Dance, My Defenses are Down, Indian Ceremonial, I Got Lost in His Arms, I Got the Sun in the Morning, Anything You Can Do, Finale

The 1946 musical in two acts.

Joan Marcus Photos

Top Right: Theresa McCoy, Ryan Mason, Cathy Rigby, Kaitlin McCoy
Center: Cathy Rigby, Brent Barrett
Bottom: "There's No Business Like Show Business"

ANNIE WARBUCKS

Music, Charles Strouse; Lyrics/Director, Martin Charnin; Book, Thomas Meehan; Choreography, Peter Gennaro; Musical Director, Keith Levenson; Orchestrations, Harold Wheeler; Sets, Ming Cho Lee; Lighting, Ken Billington; Sound, Tony Meola; Costumes, Garland W. Riddle; General Manager, John C. Breckenridge; Stage Manager, Randy William Charnin; Presented by San Bernardino Civic Light Opera and The National Alliance of Musical Theatre Producers

CAST

Annie Warbucks ....Lauren Gaffney
Sandy ....Chelsea
Oliver Warbucks ....Harve Presnell
Franklin Delano Roosevelt..Raymond Thorne
Grace Farrell ....Margueritte MacIntyre
Drake...*..Harvey Evans
Mrs. Pugh..Carol Woodbury
Orphans
Molly ....Lindsay Ridgeway
Duffy ....Kathryn Zaremba
Tessie ....Jeanette Brox
July ....Alexis Dale Fabricant
Pepper ....Missy Goldberg
Simon Whitehead ....Joel Hatch
Warbucks' Accountants ....Edward Conery, Erick Devine
Commiss.Harriet Stark ....Alene Robertson
Miss Jones ....Trisha Gorman
Miss Sherman/Wagstaff/Gladys ....Nancy Sinclair
Peaches ....Christine Flores
Mrs. Sheila Kelly ....Cass Morgan
Dr. Whittleby ....Lizanne Schader
Alice's Voice ....Trisha Gorman
Tim's Voice/NBC Announcer/McCall ....Paul Ainsley
Usherette ....Carol Woodbury
Fletcher ....Charles Douglas
Alberta ....Anita Jackson
Harry/Gabriel Heatter/Ray Billy /Lillianthal/Bert Healy...........Erick Devine
Trainman/Stanley/Howe/Hat Man/Guard ....Edward Conery
C.G. Paterson ....LaShayla Logan
Alvin T. Peterson ....M.W. Reid
Ella Paterson ....Ellia English
Piano Player ....Charles Douglas
UNDERSTUDIES: Alexis Dale Fabricant (Annie), Erick Devine (Warbucks), Paul Ainsley (FDR), Trisha Gorman (Grace), Edward Conery (Drake), Missy Goldberg (Peaches), Jeffrey Wilkins (Whitehead), Carol Woodbury (Stark), Nancy Sinclair (Sheila), Christine Flores (C.G.), Charles Douglas(Paterson), Anita Jackson (Ella)

MUSICAL NUMBERS: A New Deal for Christmas, The Best Thing of All, My Valentine, Above the Law, Changes, The Other Woman, That's the Kind of Woman, A Younger Man, When You Smile, But You Go On, I Got Me, Love, Somebody's Gotta Do Somethin', All Dolled Up, When We Get Ours, Tenement Lullaby, It Would Have Been Wonderful, I Guess Things Happen for the Best, The Day They Say I Do, Finale

   A musical in two acts with sixteen scenes. The action takes place in New York, Tennessee and Washington, D.C., 1933-34. See *Theatre World* Vol. 48 for previous version of this production.

Tom Maday Photos

**Top Right: Harve Presnell, Lauren Gaffney
Center: Lauren Gaffney, Raymond Thorne
Bottom: Lauren Gaffney**

ASPECTS OF LOVE

Music/Book Adapatation, Andrew Lloyd Webber; Lyrics, Don Black, Charles Hart; Based on the novel by David Garnett; Director, Robin Phillips; Music Supervisor, Michael Reed; Orchestrations, David Cullen, Mr. Lloyd Webber, Larry Wilcox; Sets, Phillip Silver; Costumes, Ann Curtis; Lighting, Louise Guinand; Sound, Martin Levan; Stage manager, Clayton Phillips; Presented by Broadway in Concert, LIVENT and Really Useful Theatre Co. (Canada)

CAST

Rose Vibert	Linda Balgord, Sarah Brightman (L.A.)
	Alice M. Vienneau (alternate)
Alex Dillingham	Ron Bohmer
George Dillingham	Barrie Ingham
Giulietta Trapani	Kelli James Chase
Marcel Richard	David Masenheimer
Jenny Dillingham	
younger	Maryke Hendrikse
older	Lori Alter
Elizabeth	Suzanne Briar
Hugo Le Meunier	Stephen Foster
Jerome	David Chaney

Ensemble ....Elizabeth Beeler, Suzanne Briar, David Chaney, Stephen Foster, Maryke Hendrikse, Rob Lorey, Brian Lynch, David Masenheimer, Bonnie Schon, Merri Sugarman

UNDERSTUDIES: Rob Lorey (Alex alternate), Stephen Foster (Alex), David Chaney (George), Bonnie Schon (Giuletta), Brian Lynch (Marcel), Whitney Webster (Young Jenny), Elizabeth Beeler, Dana Lynn Caruso (Older Jenny), Merri Sugarman (Elizabeth), Brad Drummer (Hugo)

MUSICAL NUMBERS: Love Changes Everything, Parlez-vous francais, Seeing is Believing, Memory of a Happy Moment, Chanson d'enfance, Everybody Loves a Hero, She'd Be Far Better Off with You, Stop Wait Please, Leading Lady, Other Pleasures, There is More to Love, Mermaid Song, First Man You Remember, Journey of a Lifetime, Falling, Hand Me the Wine and the Dice, Anything But Lonely

A musical in two acts. The action takes place in France, 1947-64.

Robert C. Ragsdale Photos

Linda Balgord, Barrie Ingham

BREAKING LEGS

By Tom Dulack; Director, John Tillinger; Set, James Noone; Costumes, David C. Woolard; Lighting, Ken Billington; General Manager, Ralph Roseman; Stage Manager, Elliott Woodruff; Presented by Elliot Martin, Bud Yorkin and James & Maureen O'Sullivan; Tour opened in the Wilber Theatre, Boston on September 29, 1992

CAST

Lou Graziano	Vincent Gardenia succeeded by Harry Guardino
Angie	Karen Valentine
Terence O'Keefe	Gary Sandy
Mike Fransisco	Joseph Mascolo
Tino De Felice	Vince Viverito
Frankie Salvucc	Larry Storch

A comedy in two acts. The action takes place in a University town restaurant.

Janet Van Ham Photos

Left: Gary Sandy, Vince Viverito, Vincent Gardenia, Joseph Mascolo, Larry Storch

BUDDY: THE BUDDY HOLLY STORY

Music/Lyrics, Buddy Holly, Various; Book, Alan James, Director, Rob Bettinson; Musical Director, Paul Jury; Design, Andy Walmsley, Michael Hotopp; Costumes, Bill Butler; Lighting, Ken Billington; Sound, Rick Price, John Kilgore; Asst. Director, Steven Bloom, Stage Manager, Allen McMullen; Executive Producer, George MacPherson; Presented by Tom Mallow, ATP/Dodger, Pace Theatrical Group in association with Paul Elliott, Laurie Mansfield, Greg Smith & David Mirvish

Chip Epstein

CAST

Buddy	Chip Esten
Shirley	Cheryl Allison
Decca Musicians	Alex Bourne, Todd Eastland, Brian Tiernan
Vi Petty	Jo Lynn Burks
Murray Deutch	Thom Culcasi
Hipockets Duncan	Tony Gilbert
Peggy Sue/Mary Lou Sokoloff	Anastasia Glasheen
Jerry Allison	Colin Gray
Norm Petty	Robin Haynes
Apollo Singers	Vanessa A. Jones, Ramona Keller, Fredi Walker
Ritchie Valens/DJ	Alex Paez
Joe B. Mauldin	Bobby Prochaska
Big Bopper/Producer	Brian Ruf
Maria's Aunt	Gayton Scott
Apollo Performer	Horace Scott
Clearlake MC	Kim Story
Maria Elena	Lauree Taradah
English DJ/Jack Daw	Billy Ward

UNDERSTUDIES: Alex Bourne (Buddy alternate), Brian Tiernan (Maudlin), Todd Eastland (Jerry), Billy Ward (Hipockets/Petty/Valens), Thom Culcasi (Bopper/MC), Cheryl Allison (Vi/Mary Lou), Anastasia Glasheen (Maria/Aunt), John Simonson (4th Cricket/SWING)

MUSICAL NUMBERS: Texas Rose, Flower of My Heart, Ready Teddy, That's All Right, That'll Be the Day, Looking for Someone to Love, Mailman Bring Me No More Blues, Maybe Baby, Everyday, Sweet Love, Not Fade Away, Peggy Sue, Words of LOve, Oh Boy, Listen to Me, Well All Right, It's So Easy to Fall in Love, Think It Over, True Love Ways, Why Do Fools Fall in Love, Chantilly Lace, Maybe Baby, Peggy Sue Got Married, Heartbeat, La Bamba, Raining in My Heart, It Doesn't Matter Anymore, Rave On, Johnny B. Goode

    A musical in two acts. For original 1990 Broadway version see Theatre World Vol.47.

Michael Lamont Photo

Robert Goulet

CAMELOT

Music, Frederick Loewe; Lyrics/Book, Alan Jay Lerner; Based on The Once and Future King by T.H. White; Director/Choreographer, Norbert Joerder; Musical Director, John Visser; Sets/Lighting, Neil Peter Jampolis; Costumes, Franne Lee; Sound, Tom Morse; Presented by Music Fair; Press, Jeffrey Richards; Tour opened in the Fisher Theatre, Detroit on September 9, 1992

CAST

Sir Dinadan	Richard Smith
Sir Lionel	Virl Andrick
Merlyn/Pellinore	James Valentine
Arthur	Robert Goulet
Sir Sagramore	Cedric D. Cannon
Lady Anne	Jean Mahlmann
Guenevere	Patricia Kies
Nimue	Vanessa Shaw
Sir Lancelot	Steve Blanchard
Dap	Newton R. Gilchrist
Mordred	Kenneth Boys
Tom of Warwick	Justin March
Ensemble	Steve Asciolla, Greg Brown, Ben Starr

Coates, William Thomas Evans, Lisa Guignard, Theresa Hudson, Brian Jefferey Hurst, Donald Ives, Ted Keegan, Stephanie Park, Raymond Sage, Barbara Scanlon, Verda Lee Tudor, Kimberley Wells

    The 1960 musical in two acts. Robert Goulet played Lancelot in the original production with Richard Burton (Arthur) and Julie Andrews (Guenevere).

Scott Windus Photo

CRAZY FOR YOU

For creative credits see B*roadway Calendar-Past Seasons* ; General Managers, Gatchell & Neufeld; Press, Bill Evans; Opened in the Music Hall, Dallas on May 13, 1993

CAST

Tess	Cathy Susan Pyles
Bobby Child	James Brennan
Bela Zangler	Stuart Zagnit
Irene Roth	Kay McClelland
Mother	Lenka Peterson
Polly Baker	Karen Ziemba
Everett Baker	Carleton Carpenter
Lank Hawkins	Christopher Council

Ensemble..........Sally Boyett, Sharon Ferrol, Heather Douglas, Nora Brennan, Angie L. Schworer, Lori Hart, Laura Catalano, John Boswell, Bobby Clark, Alan Gilbert, Gary Kirsch, Frederick J. Boothe, Keith Savage, Bill Brassea, Stephen Reed, Ron DeVito, Geoffrey Wade, Jeanette Landis

A musical comedy inspired by *Girl Crazy* (1930), in two acts with 17 scenes. The action takes place in New York City and Deadrock, Nevada in the 1930s.

Karen Ziemba, James Brennan

DAVID'S MOTHER

By Bob Randall; Director, Josephine R. Abady; Sets, David Potts; Lighting, Marc B. Weiss; Costumes, Susan Denison Geller; Sound, Jeffrey Montgomere; Music, Steve Orich; Stage Manager, Theresa Bentz; Opened in the Pasadena Playhouse on September 11, 1992.

CAST

Sally	Ellen Greene
David	Karl Maschek
Gladys	Peggy Blow
Bea	Carol Locatell
Susan	Leah Remini
Phillip	Vasili Bogazianos
John	Norman Snow
Justine	Jennifer Blanc

A drama in two acts. The action takes place on New York's west side

Left: Norman Snow, Ellen Greene, Vasili Bogazianos
Craig Schwartz Photo

FALSETTOS-COMPANY #1

For creative credits see Broadway Calendar-Past Seasons ; Musical Director, Ben Whiteley; Production Supervisor, Craig Jacobs; Stage Manager, Robert Currie; Presented by Pace Theatrical Group; Performed in Ft. Lauderdale; Palm Beach; Pittsburgh and Stamford, Ct.

CAST

Marvin...Adrian Zmed
Whizzer...Ray Walker
Mendel..Stuart Zagnit
Jason...Jeffrey Landman
Trina...Carolee Carmello
Charlotte...Barbara Marineau
Cordelia..Yvette Lawrence

A musical in two acts. The action takes place in 1979 and 1981.

FALSETTOS-COMPANY #2

For creative credits and musical numbers see *Broadway Calendar-Past Seasons* ; Company Manager, Ken Silverman; Stage Manager, Maureen F. Gibson; Presented by Fran and Barry Weissler; Press, Pete Sanders/Ian Rand

CAST

Marvin...Gregg Edelman
Whizzer...Stephen Bogardus
Mendel..Adam Heller
Jason...Sivan Cotel
Brett Tabisel (matinees)
Trina...Carolee Carmello
Charlotte...Heather Mac Rae
Cordelia..Julie Prosser
STANDBYS: Gary Moss (Marvin/Mendel), Jay Montgomery (Whizzer), Dana Moore (Charlotte/Cordelia)

Gregg Edelman, Ramzi Khalaf, Carolee Carmello
Ken Howard Photo

FOREVER PLAID-COMPANY I

For creative credits see *Productions that played through this season* section; Musical Director, Steven Freeman; Sound, Tony Tait; Stage Managers, Peter Van Dyke, Evan Ensign; Presented by Gene Wolsk, Steven Suskin; Theatre Corp. of America and The Old Globe Theatre

CAST

Jinx ....Stan Chandler
Smudge...David Engel
Sparky ....Larry Raben
Francis...Guy Stroman

The original New York cast.

FOREVER PLAID-COMPANY II

Musical Director, Seth Rudetsky; Sound, Marc Salzberg; Presented by Gene Wolsk, Laura Stein and Steven Suskin

A musical for the "good guys". The action takes place in 1964 and now.

CAST

Paul Binotto
Gregory Jbara
Neil Nash
Michael Winther

A musical for the "good guys". The action takes place in 1964 and now.

Craig Schwartz Photo

Guy Stroman, David Engel, Stan Chandler, Larry Raben

GUYS AND DOLLS

For creative credits and musical numbers see *Broadway Calendar-Past Seasons* ; Production Supervisor, Steven Beckler; Musical Director, Randy Booth; Production Manager, Peter Fulbright; Executive Producer, George MacPherson; Presented by ATP/Dodger, Roger Berlind, Kardana Productions, Tom Mallow and Kennedy Center for the Performing Arts; Tour opened in the Bushnell Theatre, Hartford, CT on September 15, 1992

CAST

Nicely-Nicely Johnson ....Kevin Ligon
Benny Southstreet ....Al DeCristo
Rusty Charlie ....Jay Brian Winnick
Sarah Brown..Patricia Ben Peterson
Arvide Abernathy..MacIntyre Dixon
Agatha..Patricia Grace Kennedy
Calvin...Steven Bogard
Martha..Heather Lee
Harry the Horse .... James Dybas
Lt. Brannigan...Andy Umberger
Nathan Detroit ....Lewis J. Stadlen succeeded
by David Garrison
Angie the Ox..Charles Cermele
Miss Adelaide ....Lorna Luft
Sky Masterson ....Richard Muenz
Joey Biltmore ....David Hart
Mimi ....Michele O'Steen
Gen. Matilda B. Cartwright ....Joy Franz
Big Jule...Lyle Kanouse
Drunk...David Vosburgh
Guys.............Andy Blankenbuehler, Steven Bogard, Charles Cermele, John Crutchman
Christopher Gattelli, David Earl Hart, Jack Hayes, Darren Lee
Kenneth McMullen, Sergio Trujillo, Jerome Vivona
David Vosburgh, Jay Brian Winnick
Dolls ....Roxanne Barlow, Lisa Dawn Cave, Kriss Dias
Patricia Grace Kennedy, Heather Lee, Michelle O'Steen
UNDERSTUDIES: Steven Bogard (Sky), Lisa Dawn Cave (Mimi), Charles Cermele (Benny/Harry), Paul DePasquale (Sky/Nicely/Nathan), David Hart, Ken McMullen (Jule/Brannigan), Patricia Grace Kennedy (Cartwright), Heather Lee (Adelaide/Sarah), Beth McVey (Adelaide/ Cartwright/Agatha/Martha), Andy Umberger (Nathan), David Vosburgh (Arvide/Harry), Jay Brian Winnick (Benny/Nicely) SWINGS: Mary MacLeod, Bill Burns, Beth McVey, Paul DePasquale

A new production of the 1950 musical in two acts. The action takes place in "Runyonland" around Broadway, and in Havana, Cuba.

Martha Swope Photos

Lorna Luft
Top: Richard Muenz and cast

JESUS CHRIST SUPERSTAR

Music, Andrew Lloyd Webber; Lyrics, Tim Rice; Director/Choreographer, Tony Christopher; Asst. Director, James O'Neil; Musical Director, Michael Rapp; Sets, Bill Stabile; Costumes, David Paulin; Lighting, Rick Belzer; Sound, Jonathan Deans; Special Effects, Gregg Stephens; Stage Manager, Alan Hall; Executive Producer, Forbes Candlish; Presented by Landmark Entertainment Group, Magic Promotions and TAP Prods.; Opened in the Morris A. Mechanic Theatre, Baltimore on December 15, 1992

CAST

Jesus of Nazareth ....Ted Neeley
Judas Iscariot...Carl Anderson
Mary Magdalene..Irene Cara
Caiphas ....David Bedella
Annas ....Danny Zolli
Pontius Pilate ....Dennis DeYoung
Peter ....Kevin R. Wright
King Herod ....Laurent Giroux
Ensemble.....James O'Neil, Nathanial Sanders, Stephen X. Ward, Kate L. Snyder, Amy Splitt, Kirsten Young, David Marques, J. Steven Campbell, Dawn Feusi, Laurie Carter, Leesa Richards Humphrey, Steve Campanella, Curtis Clark, Michelle DeJean, Steve Geary, Eileen Kaden, Joseph P. McDonnell, Tracy-Lynn Neff SWINGS: Larry Vickers, Michelle Wylie

A new production of the 1971 musical featuring Neeley and Anderson recreating their roles from the 1973 film version.

Right: Ted Neeley

JOSEPH AND THE AMAZING TECHNICOLOR DREAMCOAT

Music, Andrew Lloyd Webber; Lyrics, Tim Rice; Director, Steven Pimlott; Musical Supervisor, Michael Reed; Musical Director, Paul Bogaev; Design, Mark Thompson; Choreography, Anthony Van Laast; Lighting, Andrew Bridge; Sound, Martin Levan; Orchestration, John Cameron; General Management, Gatchell & Neufeld; Stage Manager, Jeff Lee; Production Manager, Peter Fulbright; Opened in the Pantages Theatre, Hollywood on February 25, 1993

CAST

Joseph ....Michael Damian
Narrator ....Kelli Rabke
Jacob/Potiphar/Guru ....Clifford David
Pharaoh/Levi...Robert Torti
Butler/Gad...Glenn Sneed
Baker/Issachar ....Bill Nolte
Mrs. Potiphar, Napthali's Wife..Julie Bond
Apache Dancers ....Tina Ou, Tim Schultheis
Reuben ....Marc Kuddish
Simeon ....Neal Ben-Ari
Napthali ....Danny Bolero Zaldivar
Asher...Willy Falk succeeded by Timothy Smith
Dan ....Joseph Savant
Zebulun ....Tim Schultheis
Benjamin ....Ty Taylor
Judah..Gerry McIntyre succeeded by Gordy Owens
Reuben's Wife ....Michelle Murlin
Simeon's Wife ....Mindy Franzese
Levi's Wife ....Jocelyn Vodovoz Cook
Issachar's Wife ....Jacquie Porter
Asher's Wife ....Lisa Akey
Zebulun's Wife ....Diana Brownstone
Gad's Wife ....Betsy Chang
Benjamin's Wife ....Tina Ou
Judah's Wife..Susan Carr George
UNDERSTUDIES: Willy Falk, Ty Taylor, Matthew Zarley (Joseph), Lisa Akey, Susan Carr George, Kelli Severson (Narrator), Bill Nolte, Glenn Sneed (Jacob/Potiphar/Guru), Marc Kudisch, Joseph Savant (Pharoah) SWINGS: Ron Kellum, Andrew Makay, Janet Rothermel, Kelli Severson, Gina Trano, Matthew Zarley

MUSICAL NUMBERS: Overture, Prologue, Any Dream Will Do, Jacob and Sons/Joseph's Coat, Joesoph's Dreams, Poor Poor Joseph, One More Angel in Heaven, Potiphar, Close Every Door, Go Go Go Joseph, Entr'acte, Pharaoh Story, Poor Poor Pharaoh/Song of the King, Pharaoh's Dream Explained, Stone the Crows, Those Canaan Days, Brothers Came to Egypt /Grovel Grovel, Who's the Thief, Benjamin Calypso, Joseph All the Time, Jacob in Egypt, Any Dream Will Do, Joseph Megamix

Michael Damian
Jay Thompson/Craig Schwartz Photo

MY FAIR LADY

Music, Fredrick Loewe; Lyrics/Book, Alan Jay Lerner; Director, Howard Davies; Music/Vocal Direction, Jack Lee; Choreography, Donald Saddler; Sets, Ralph Koltai; Costumes, Patricia Zipprodt; Lighting, Natasha Katz; Sound, Peter Fitzgerald; Musical Coordinator, John Monaco; Production Supervisor, Craig Jacobs; Presented by Barry and Fran Weissler, Jujamcyn Theatres, Pace Theatrical Group, Tokyo Broadcasting System and Martin Rabbett; Press, Richard Kornberg/Anita Dloniak; Opened in the Barbara B. Mann Performing Arts Hall, Fort Meyers, Fl. on April 3, 1993

CAST

Eliza Doolittle ....Melissa Errico
        Meg Tolin(during Errico illlness)
Freddie Eynsford Hill...Robert Stella
Mrs. Eynsford-Hill...Lisa Merrill McCord
Colonel Pickering...Paxton Whitehead
Professor Henry Higgins...Richard Chamberlain
"Loverly" Quartet ...Jeffrey Wilkins, Bruce Moore, Michael Gerhart, Jamie MacKensie
George, the bartender...David Bryant
Jamie..Michael J. Farina
Harry/Zoltan Karpathy ....James Young
Mrs. Pearce ....Glynnis Bell
Butler/Lord Boxington..Jeffrey Wilkins
Alfred P. Doolittle ....Julian Holloway
Servants ....Michael Gerhart, Marilyn Kay Huelsman
    Edwardyne Cowan, Corinne Melancon, Leslie Bell
Charles, the Chauffeur ....Michael Gerhart
Mrs. Higgins..Dolores Sutton
Lady Boxington...Marnee Hollis
Policeman ....Ron Schwinn
Flower Girl ....Corinne Melancon
Footman..Ben George
Queen of Transylvania..Patti Karr
Mrs. Higgins Maid..Sue Delano
Ensemble ....Leslie Bell, David Bryant, Edwardyne Cowan, Laurie Crochet
    Sjoerd de Jong, Sue Delano, Rebecca Downing, Michael J. Farina
    Ben George, Michael Gerhart, Marnee Hollis, Marilyn Kay Huelsman
    Patti Karr, Tom Kosis, John Vincent Leggio, Jamie MacKenzie
    Lisa Merrill McCord, Corine Melancon, Bruce Moore
    Ron Schwinn, James Young, Jeffrey Wilkins

UNDERSTUDIES: Paxton Whitehead (Higgins), Edwardyne Cowan (Eliza), James Young (Doolittle), Jeffrey Wilkins (Pickering), Patti Karr (Mrs. Higgins), Michael Gerhart (Freddie), Lisa Merrill McCord (Mrs. Pearce) SWINGS: Newton Cole, Wendy Oliver, John Scott

MUSICAL NUMBERS: Why Can't the English, Wouldn't It Be Loverly, With a Little Bit of Luck, I'm an Ordinary Man, Just You Wait, Servant's Chorus, Rain in Spain, I Could Have Danced All Night, Ascot Gavotte, On the Street Where You Live, Embassy Waltz, You Did It, Show Me, Get Me to the Church, Hymn to Him, Without You, I've Grown Accustomed to Her Face

A new production of the 1956 musical in two acts. The action takes place in London, 1912.

Carol Rosegg/Martha Swope Photos

Richard Chamberlain, Melissa Errico, Paxton Whitehead in "My Fair Lady"

NUNSENSE II: THE SECOND COMING

Music/Lyrics/Book/Direction by Dan Goggin; Choreography, Felton Smith; Musical Director, Michael Rice; Orchestrations, Mr. Rice, David Nyberg; Set, Barry Axtell; Lighting, Paul Miller; Sound, Snow Sound; Stage Manager, Paul J. Botchis; Opened in the Hamilton Pavilion, Waterbury, CT. on November 20, 1992

CAST

Sister Robert Anne ....Christine Anderson
Sister Mary Amnesia ....Semina De Laurentis
Sister Mary Hubert..Mary Gillis
Sister Mary Regina..Kathy Robinson
Sister Mary Leo..Lyn Vaux

MUSICAL NUMBERS: Jubilate Deo, Nunsense the Magic Word, Winning is Just the Beginning, Prima Ballerina, Biggest Ain't the Best, I've Got Pizzazz, The Country Nun, Look Ma I Made It, Padre Polka, The Classic Queens, A Hat and Cane Song, Angeline, We're the Nuns to Come To, What Would Elvis Do?, Yes We Can, I am Here to Stay, Oh Dear What a Catastrophe, No One Ever Cared the Way You Do, There's Only One Way to End Your Prayers, Finale

Premiere of a musical comedy sequel in two acts.

OLEANNA

For creative credits see *Off Broadway Calendar* ; Press, Bill Evans; Tour opened in the Stamford Center for the Arts on April 6, 1993

CAST

John ....William H. Macy
Carol...Debra Eisenstadt

Three scenes performed in two acts.

Gerry Goodstein Photo

ONCE ON THIS ISLAND

Music, Stepehn Flaherty; Lyrics/Book, Lynn Ahrens; Based on novel *My Love My Love* by Rosa Guy; Director/Choreographer, Graciela Daniele; Orchestrations, Michael Starobin; Musical Director, Mark Lipman; Musical Supervisor, Steve Marzullo; Sets, Loy Arcenas; Costumes, Judy Dearing; Lighting, Allen Lee Hughes; Sound, Scott Lehrer; Asst. Choreographer, Willie Rosario; Stage Manager, Bryan Young; Executive Producer, George MacPherson; Presented by Tom Mallow, ATP/Dodger, Pace Theatrical Group, John F. Kennedy Center, in association with The Shubert Organization, Capital Cities/ABC, Suntory Int'l, James Walsh and Playwrights Horizons

CAST

Erzulie, Goddess of Love ....Natalie Venetia Belcon
Andrea ....Monique Cintron
Daniel..Darius de Haas
Asaka, Mother of the Earth ....Alvaleta Guess
Little Ti Moune ....Nilyne Fields
Mama Euralie..Sheila Gibbs
Ti Moune...Vanita Harbour
Papa Ge, Demon of Death...Gerry McIntyre
Agwe, God of Water..James Stoval
Armand...Keith Tyrone
Tonton Julian ....Miles Watson
STANDBYS: Euschia Walker (Mama/Asaka), Tonya L. Dixon (Ti Moune/ Andrea/Erzulie), LaShonda Hunt (Little Ti), Keith Tyrone (Daniel), James Stovall (Tonton), Steven Cates (Papa/Agwe/Armand)

MUSICAL NUMBERS:We Dance, One Small Girl, Waiting for Life, And the Gods Heard Her Prayer, Rain, Pray, Forever Yours, Sad Tale of the Beauxhommes, Ti Moune, Mama Will Provide, Some Say, Human Heart, Some Girls, The Ball, A Part of Us, Why We Tell the Story

A musical performed without intermission. The action takes place in the French Antilles during a night storm. For original 1990 Broadway production see *Theatre World* Vol. 47.

Martha Swope Photos

Vanita Harbour, Gerry McIntyre, James Stovall
Top: The Company

THE PHANTOM OF THE OPERA

Music, Andrew Lloyd Webber; Lyrics, Charles Hart, Richard Stilgoe; Book, Mr. Stilgoe, Lloyd Webber; Based on the novel by Gaston Leroux; Director, Harold Prince; Musical Staging/Choreography, Gillian Lynne; Production Design, Maria Bjornson; Lighting, Andrew Bridge; Sound, Martin Levan; Musical Director, Roger Cantrell; Orchestrations, David Cullen, Lloyd Webber; Musical Supervision/Direction, David Caddick; Production Supervisor, Mitchell Lemsky; General Management, Alan Wasser; Presented by Cameron Mackintosh and The Really Useful Theatre Co.; Press, Merle Frimark, Marc Thibodeau; Opened at the Ahmanson Theatre, Los Angeles on May 31, 1989 and still playing on May 31, 1993.

CAST

The Phantom of the Opera	Davis Gaines
Christine Daae	Dale Kristien
Raoul, Vicomte de Chagny	Michael Piontek
Carlotta Giudicelli	Leigh Munro
Monsieur Andre	Norman Large
Monsieur Firmin	Calvin Remsberg
Madame Giry	Barbara Lang
Ubaldo Piangi	Gualtiero Negrini
Meg Giry	Elisabeth Stringer
Monsieur Reyer	D.C. Anderson
Auctioneer	Richard Gould
Porter/Marksman	Sean Smith
Monsieur Lefevre/Don Attilio/Passarino	Gary Marshal
Joseph Buquet	Gene Brundage
Firechief	Kris Pruet
Slave Master (Hannibal)	David Loring
Flunky/Stagehand	Stephen Moore
Policeman	Peter Atherton
Confidante (Il Muto)	Rhonda Dillon
Porter/Fireman	William Scott Brown
Page (Don Juan Triumphant)	Candace Rogers-Adler
Wardrobe Mistress	Gail Land Hart
Princess (Hannibal)	Jani Neuman
Madame Firmin	Rio Hibler-Kerr
Innkeeper's Wife (Don Juan Triumphant)	Catherine Caccavallo
Ballet Chorus of the Opera Populaire	Leslie-Noriko Beadles, Madelyn Berdes Mary Alyce Laubacher, Natasha MacAller Sylvia Rico, Connie, Versteeg
Ballet Swing	Irene Cho
Swings	Karen Benjamin, Joseph Dellger, Brad Scott

UNDERSTUDIES: Norman Large (Phantom), Joseph Dellger (Phantom, Andre/Raoul), Jani Neuman (Christine), Stephen Moore (Raoul), Sean Smith (Raoul/Andre), Richard Gould, Gary Marshal (Firmin), Brad Scott (Andre), Catherine Caccavallo, Rio Hibler-Kerr (Carlotta), Rhonda Dillon (Carlotta/ Madame Giry), Karen Benjamin (Madame Giry), William Scott Brown, Kris Pruet (Piangi), Irene Cho, Mary Alyce Laubacher, Natasha MacAller (Meg), Tamra Shaker (Christine Standby), Elkin Antoniou (Ballet Swing)

A musical in two acts and a prologue. For musical numbers see BROADWAY CALENDAR. On Aug.6, 1992, Davis Gaines became L.A.'s longest running Phantom with 515 performances to date.

Joan Marcus, Michael Lamont, Robert Millard Photos

Top: Davis Gaines, Dale Kristien
Bottom: Davis Gaines

RICHARD III

By William Shakespeare; Director, Richard Eyre; Design, Bob Crowley; Lighting, Jean Kalman; Music, Dominic Muldowney; Stage/Company Manager, John Caulfield; Presented by the Royal National Theatre of Great Britain; Press, Chris Boneau/Adrian Bryan-Brown; Tour opened at Brooklyn Academy of Music on June 9, 1992.

CAST

Richard III	Ian McKellen
Robert Brackenbury/Scrivner	Keith Bartlett
Marquess of Dorset	Paul Bazely
William Catesby	David Beames
Lord Mayor/Henry VI Ghost	Sam Beazley
Prince Edward/Page	Simon Blake, Oliver Grig, Tom Penta, Richard Puddifoot
Lord Stanley	Richard Bremmer
Richard, Duke of York	Sebastian Brennan, James Graves, Richard Lawrence, Marco Williamson
Queen Elizabeth	Charlotte Cornwell
Henry/Lord Grey	Peter Darling
Bishop/James Blunt	David Foxxe
Lady Anne	Anastasia Hille
Murderer/Lord Lovel	Dominic Hingorani
Duchess of York	Rosalind Knight
Second Murderer	Phil McKee
Sir James Tyrrel	Tim McMullan
Queen Margaret	Antonia Pemberton
Lord Rivers	Alain Perrin
King Edward/Earl of Oxford	Bruce Purchase
Duke of Buckingham	Terence Rigby
Lord Hastings/Walter Herbert	Richard Simpson
Duke of Clarence	Malcolm Sinclair
Keeper/Citizen	Chris Walker
Maid/Nurse/Mistress	Olivia Williams
Richard Ratcliffe	Tristram Wynmark

John Haynes Photo

176

THE SECRET GARDEN

Music, Lucy Simon; Lyrics/Book, Marsha Norman; Based on the novel by Frances Hodgson Burnett; Director, Susan H. Schulman; Musical Director, Constantine Kitsopoulos; Choreography, Michael Lichtefeld; Orchestrations, William D. Brohn; Musical Supervision, Michael Kosarin; Sets, Heidi Landesman; Costumes, Theoni V. Aldredge; Lighting, Tharon Musser; Sound, Otts Munderloh; Company Manager, John Pasinato; Stage Manager, Dan W. Langhofer; Executive Producer, George MacPherson; Presented by Heidi Landesman, Rick Steiner, Jujamcyn Theatres/TV Asahi, Tom Mallow, ATP/Dodger, Pace Theatrical Group; Press, Laura Matalon; Tour opened in the Palace Theatre, Cleveland, Ohio on April 28, 1992

CAST

Lily	Anne Runolfsson
Mary Lenox	Melody Kay, Kimberly Mahon (alternate)
Fakir	Andy Gale
Ayah	Audra Ann McDonald
Rose (Mary's mother)	Jacquelyn Piro
Capt. Albert Lennox	Kevin Dearinger
Lt. Peter Wright	Ken Land
Lt. Ian Shaw	Mark Agnes
Major Holmes	Marc Mouchet
Claire/Mrs. Winthrop	Roxann Parker
Alice (Rose's friend)	Mary Illes
Archibald Craven(Mary's uncle)	Kevin McGuire
Dr. Neville Craven (his brother)	Douglas Sills
Mrs. Medlock (housekeeper)	Mary Fogarty
Martha (a chambermaid)	Tracey Ann Moore
Dickon (her brother)	Roger Bart
Ben (the gardner)	Jay Garner
Colin	Sean Considine, Luke Hogan
William	James Barbour
Betsy	Jill Patton
Timothy	Ty Hreben

UNDERSTUDIES: Jacquelyn Piro(Lily), Mary Illes (Lily/Rose), Douglas Sills (Archibald), Marc Mouchet (Archibald/Ben), James Barbour (Neville/Lennox/Wright/Shaw/Holmes), Ken Land (Neville), Roxann Parker (Medlock), Susie McMonagle, Jill Patton (Rose/Ayah/Claire/Winthrop/ Alice/Betsy), Ty Hreben (Dickon), Oliver Woodall (Dickon/Fakir/Wright/ Shaw/William/Betsy), Mark Agnes (Lennox/Fakir), Todd Murray (Wright/ Shaw/Holmes/William/Betsy) SWINGS: Susie McMonagle, Oliver Woodall, Todd Murray

MUSICAL NUMBERS: Openeing Dream, There's a Girl, House Upon the Hill, I Heard Someone Crying, A Fine White Horse, A Girl in the Valley, It's a Maze, Winter's on the Wing, Show Me the Key, A Bit of Earth, Storm, Lily's Eyes, Round-Shouldered Man, Final Storm, The Girl I Mean to Be, Quartet, Race to the Top of the Morning, Wick, Come to My Garden, Come Spirit Come Charm, Disappear, Hold On, Letter Song, Where in the World, How Could I Ever Know, Fianle

A musical in two acts with 18 scenes and prologue. The action takes place in Colonial India and at Misselthwaite Manor, North Yorkshire, England in 1906.

Carol Rosegg/Martha Swope Photos

Top Left: Roger Bart, Melody Kay
Bottom: Anne Runolfsson, Kevin McGuire

SIX DEGREES OF SEPARATION

By John Guare; Director, Jerry Zaks; Sets, Tony Walton; Costumes, William Ivey Long; Lighting, Paul Gallo; Sound/Stage Manager, Christopher Bond; Presented by Richard Martini, Albert Nocciolino, Allen Spivak and Larry Magid; Press, Smyth Katzen/Molly Smyth; Tour opened in the James A. Doolittle Theatre, Los Angeles on October 11, 1992

CAST

Ouisa ....Marlo Thomas
Flan ....Ned Schmidtke,John Cunningham(LA)
Paul ....Ntare Mwine
Kitty ....Holly Barron
Police/Doorman ....Ian Blackman
Doug..David Burke
Geoffrey...Richard Clarke, Sam Stoneburner
Hustler...James DuMont
Rick ....Patrick Fabian
Detective ....Allen Fitzpatrick, Brian Evers
Larkin..Philip LeStrange
Dr. Fine ....David Little, Victor Raider-Wexler
Elizabeth ....Deirdre Lovejoy
Woody ....Colin Mitchell
Ben..Adam Philipson
Tess..Isabel Rose
Trent ....Richard Wofford

A play performed without intermission. The action takes place in New York City.For original 1990 Broadway production see *Theatre World* Vol.47.

Schwartz/Thompson Photos

Top Right: Ntare Mwine, Marlo Thomas
Bottom Left: Richard Wofford, Ntare Mwine
Bottom Right: Patrick Fabian, Ntare Mwine, Deirdre Lovejoy

STATE FAIR

Music, Richard Rodgers; Lyrics, Oscar Hammerstein II; Book, Tom Briggs and Louis Mattioli; Based on screenplay by Hammerstein and novel by Phil Strong; Director/Choreographer, Randy Skinner; Musical Director, John McDaniel; Orchestrations, Bruce Pomahac; Dance Arrangements, Scot Wooley; Sets, James L. Joy; Costumes, Michael Bottari, Ronald Case; Lighting, Natasha Katz; Sound, Jonathan Deans; Stage Manager, John M. Gallo; Production Manager, Gene O' Donovan; Opened in the Stevens Center, North Carolina on July 17, 1992

CAST

Abel Frake	Michael McCarty succeeded by Lenny Wolpe
Gus	Eric Gunhus
Melissa Frake	Jan Pessano
Wayne Frake	Michael Hayden succeeded by Lewis Cleale
Dave Miller/Judge	Charles Goff
Eleanor	Karen Lifshey
Margy Frake	Susan Egan
Harry	Philip Lehl
Pat Gilbert	Michael Halpin
Charlie	Robert Loftin
Hoop-La Barker	Tina Johnson
Emily Arden	Lisa Akey
Astounding Stralenko/Lem	Tom Hafner
Cooch Dancers	Kelli Barclay, Ms. Johnson
Clay	Edward Badrak

Han Masters, Stefanie Morse, Cori Lanting McCormick, Jacquiline Rohrbacker, Michael Lee Scott

UNDERSTUDIES: Tom Hafner (Abel/Dave), Tina Johnson (Melissa/Mrs. Metcalf), Eric Gunhus (Wayne/Hank), Stephanie Morse (Margy), Robert Loftin (Harry/Judge), Michael Lee Scott (Pat/Chief/MC), K.C. Masters (Charlie), David Burnham (Stralenko/Barker/Lem/Clay), Karen Lifshey (Emily)

MUSICAL NUMBERS: Our State Fair, It Might as Well Be Spring, That's for Me, Isn't It Kinda Fun?, More Than Just a Friend, You Never Had It So Good, When I Go Walking with My Baby, This Isn't Heaven, It's a Grand Night for Singing, Marriage Type Love, Tha Man I Used to Be, All I Owe Ioway, That's the Way It Happens, I Haven't Got a Worry in the World, There's a Music in You, Boys and Girls Like You and Me, The Next Time It Happens, Finale

A two-act stage adaptation of the 1945 and 1962 film musicals with additional songs.

Robert Loftin, Eric Gunhus, Lisa Akey, Michael Lee Scott, David Burnham

Carol Channing

TWO LADIES OF BROADWAY

Conductors, Robert Wendel, Terry Cavari; Presented by Columbia Artisits Festivals and Bushnell; Opened in the Mortensen Hall, Hartford, CT on October 1, 1992

CAST

Carol Channing
Rita Moreno
Steven Mancuso
Robert Tatad

A revue in two acts.

THE WILL ROGERS FOLLIES

For creative credits and musical numbers see *Broadway Calendar-Past Seasons* ; Musical Director, Kay Cameron; Stage manager, Mark S. Krause

CAST

Will Rogers ....Keith Carradine succeeded by Mac Davis
Betty Blake ....Dee Hoty
Clem Rogers..George Riddle
Ziegfeld's Favorite ....Leigh Zimmerman
Voice of Ziegfeld...Gregory Peck
COMPANY ....Paulette Braxton, Blaine Mastalir, Stacie James
Christine Tarallo, Ron Kidd, Abe Reybold, Jeff Williams, Michael Lee Wright
Laurel Lynn Collins, Sutton Foster, Dana Leigh Jackson, Gina Keys
Julie Lamar, Lisa Mandel, Bob Moore, Jeanne Moore, Philip Deyer
Moriah Snyder, Christy Romano, Spencer Liff, Michael Lee Wright
Tomas Garcilazo, Holly Cruikshank, Wendy Leahy, Wendy Palmer
Francie, Provine, Jane Sonderman, Tracy Terstriep, Victoria L. Waggoner

A musical in two acts. For original 1991 Broadway production see Theatre World Vol 47.

Right: Keith Carradine (center)

Karen Ziemba, John Ruess

THE WORLD GOES 'ROUND

Music, John Kander; Lyrics, Fred Ebb; Director, Scott Ellis; Choreography, Susan Stroman; Orchestrations, David Krane; Musical Direction, David Loud; Set, Bill Hoffman; Costumes, Lindsay W. Davis; Lighting, Phil Monat; Sound, Gary Stocker; Production Supervisor, Michael A. Clarke; Presented by Gary McAvay, Aldo Scrofani, R. Tyler Gatchell, Jr., Peter Neufeld, Pace Theatrical Group, James M. Nederlander and Rosekram Productions; Press, Ainta Dloniak

CAST

Joel Blum Shelley Dickinson Marin Mazzie John Ruess Karen Ziemba
UNDERSTUDIES: Karen Babcock, Jeanne Croft, Bobby Smith

MUSICAL NUMBERS: The World Goes Round, Yes, Coffee in a Cardboard Cup, The Happy Time, Colored Lights, Sara Lee, Arthur in the Afternoon, My Coloring Book, I Don't Remember You, Sometimes a Day Goes By, All That Jazz, Class, Mr. Cellophane, Me and My Baby, There Goes the Ball Game, How Lucky Can You Get, The Rink, Ring Them Bells, Kiss of the Spider Woman, Only Love, Marry Me, Quiet Thing, When It All Comes True dance, Pain, Grass is Always Greener, We Can Make It, Maybe This Time, Isn't This Better, Money Money, Cabaret, New York New York

A musical revue of Kander and Ebb theatre and movie songs in two acts. Original 1991 New York Production *(Theatre World Vol. 47)* titled *And the World Goes 'Round: The Songs of Kander & Ebb.*

Joan Marcus Photos

1993 THEATRE WORLD RECIPIENTS
(Outstanding New York Debut)

Brent Carver
of "Kiss of the Spider Woman"

Marcia Gay Harden
of "Angels in America"

Stephanie Lawrence
in "Blood Brothers"

Michael Cerveris
of "The Who's Tommy"

Andrea Martin
of "My Favorite Year"

Liam Neeson
of "Anna Christie"

Stephen Rea
of "Someone Who'll Watch Over Me"

Natasha Richardson
of "Anna Christie"

Diana Spybey
of "Five Women Wearing The Same Dress"

Martin Short
of "The Goodby Girl"

Stephen Spinella
of "Angels in America"

Jennifer Tilly
of "One Shoe Off"

THEATRE WORLD AWARDS presented Monday , May 31, 1993
Top: Presenters (all former recipients): Brian Mitchell, Marcus Chong, Jane Alexander, Christopher Walken, Eileen Heckart, Cliff
Robertson(center), Dorothy Loudon, Ron Leibman, Bernadette Peters, Ben Vereen, Lucie Arnaz, Gianarlo Esposito Below: Dina Spyby, Giancarlo
Esposito, Jane Alexander, Christopher Walken, Eileen Eckart, Cliff Robertson, Michael Cerveris Bottom Row: Dorothy Loudon with Brent Carver,
Brian Mitchell, Martin Short(accepting for Andrea Martin), Natacha Richardson, Liam Neeson, Bernadette Peters Above: Lucie Arnaz, Ron
Liebman, Marcia Gay Harden, Stephanie Lawrence, Christopher Walken,
Photos by Michael Riordan, Michael Viadë, Peter Warrack, Van Williams

Top: John Leguizamo, Giancarlo Esposito, Stephen Spinella, Rosetta LeNoire, Ben Vereen, Marcus Chong, Below: Martin Short (accepting his own award), Eileen Heckart, Cliff Robertson, Dorothy Loudon, Brent Carver Bottom: Morristown (TN) High School Chorus performing medley from "Guys and Dolls," Derector Gerald Maloy (also above)
Photos by Drew Eliot, Michael Riordon, Michael Viadë, Peter L. Warrack, Van Williams

Julie Andrews

Alec Baldwin

Bonnie Franklin

PREVIOUS THEATRE WORLD AWARD RECIPIENTS

1944-45: Betty Comden, Richard Davis, Richard Hart, Judy Holliday, Charles Lang, Bambi Linn, John Lund, Donald Murphy, Nancy Noland, Margaret Phillips, John Raitt
1945-46: Barbara Bel Geddes, Marlon Brando, Bill Callahan, Wendell Corey, Paul Douglas, Mary James, Burt Lancaster, Patricia Marshall, Beatrice Pearson
1946-47: Keith Andes, Marion Bell, Peter Cookson, Ann Crowley, Ellen Hanley, John Jordan, George Keane, Dorothea MacFarland, James Mitchell, Patricia Neal, David Wayne
1947-48: Valerie Bettis, Edward Bryce, Whitfield Connor, Mark Dawson, June Lockhart, Estelle Loring, Peggy Maley, Ralph Meeker, Meg Mundy, Douglass Watson, James Whitmore, Patrice Wymore
1948-49: Tod Andrews, Doe Avedon, Jean Carson, Carol Channing, Richard Derr, Julie Harris, Mary McCarty, Allyn Ann McLerie, Cameron Mitchell, Gene Nelson, Byron Palmer, Bob Scheerer
1949-50: Nancy Andrews, Phil Arthur, Barbara Brady, Lydia Clarke, Priscilla Gillette, Don Hanmer, Marcia Henderson, Charlton Heston, Rick Jason, Grace Kelly, Charles Nolte, Roger Price
1950-51: Barbara Ashley, Isabel Bigley, Martin Brooks, Richard Burton, Pat Crowley, James Daley, Cloris Leachman, Russell Nype, Jack Palance, William Smithers, Maureen Stapleton, Marcia Van Dyke, Eli Wallach
1951-52: Tony Bavaar, Patricia Benoit, Peter Conlow, Virginia de Luce, Ronny Graham, Audrey Hepburn, Diana Herbert, Conrad Janis, Dick Kallman, Charles Proctor, Eric Sinclair, Kim Stanley, Marian Winters, Helen Wood
1952-53: Edie Adams, Rosemary Harris, Eileen Heckart, Peter Kelley, John Kerr, Richard Kiley, Gloria Marlowe, Penelope Munday, Paul Newman, Sheree North, Geraldine Page, John Stewart, Ray Stricklyn, Gwen Verdon
1953-54: Orson Bean, Harry Belafonte, James Dean, Joan Diener, Ben Gazzara, Carol Haney, Jonathan Lucas, Kay Medford, Scott Merrill, Elizabeth Montgomery, Leo Penn, Eva Marie Saint
1954-55: Julie Andrews, Jacqueline Brookes, Shirl Conway, Barbara Cook, David Daniels, Mary Fickett, Page Johnson, Loretta Leversee, Jack Lord, Dennis Patrick, Anthony Perkins, Christopher Plummer
1955-56: Diane Cilento, Dick Davalos, Anthony Franciosa, Andy Griffith, Laurence

Harvey, David Hedison, Earle Hyman, Susan Johnson, John Michael King, Jayne Mansfield, Sara Marshall, Gaby Rodgers, Susan Strasberg, Fritz Weaver
1956-57: Peggy Cass, Sydney Chaplin, Sylvia Daneel, Bradford Dillman, Peter Donat, George Grizzard, Carol Lynley, Peter Palmer, Jason Robards, Cliff Robertson, Pippa Scott, Inga Swenson
1957-58: Anne Bancroft, Warren Berlinger, Colleen Dewhurst, Richard Easton, Tim Everett, Eddie Hodges, Joan Hovis, Carol Lawrence, Jacqueline McKeever, Wynne Miller, Robert Morse, George C. Scott
1958-59: Lou Antonio, Ina Balin, Richard Cross, Tammy Grimes, Larry Hagman, Dolores Hart, Roger Mollien, France Nuyen, Susan Oliver, Ben Piazza, Paul Roebling, William Shatner, Pat Suzuki, Rip Torn
1959-60: Warren Beatty, Eileen Brennan, Carol Burnett, Patty Duke, Jane Fonda, Anita Gillette, Elisa Loti, Donald Madden, George Maharis, John McMartin, Lauri Peters, Dick Van Dyke
1960-61: Joyce Bulifant, Dennis Cooney, Sandy Dennis, Nancy Dussault, Robert Goulet, Joan Hackett, June Harding, Ron Husmann, James MacArthur, Bruce Yarnell
1961-62: Elizabeth Ashley, Keith Baxter, Peter Fonda, Don Galloway, Sean Garrison, Barbara Harris, James Earl Jones, Janet Margolin, Karen Morrow, Robert Redford, John Stride, Brenda Vaccaro
1962-63: Alan Arkin, Stuart Damon, Melinda Dillon, Robert Drivas, Bob Gentry, Dorothy Loudon, Brandon Maggart, Julienne Marie, Liza Minnelli, Estelle Parsons, Diana Sands, Swen Swenson
1963-64: Alan Alda, Gloria Bleezarde, Imelda De Martin, Claude Giraud, Ketty Lester, Barbara Loden, Lawrence Pressman, Gilbert Price, Philip Proctor, John Tracy, Jennifer West
1964-65: Carolyn Coates, Joyce Jillson, Linda Lavin, Luba Lisa, Michael O'Sullivan, Joanna Pettet, Beah Richards, Jaime Sanchez, Victor Spinetti, Nicolas Surovy, Robert Walker, Clarence Williams III
1965-66: Zoe Caldwell, David Carradine, John Cullum, John Davidson, Faye Dunaway, Gloria Foster, Robert Hooks, Jerry Lanning, Richard Mulligan, April Shawhan, Sandra Smith, Leslie Ann Warren
1966-67: Bonnie Bedelia, Richard Benjamin, Dustin Hoffman, Terry Kiser, Reva Rose,

Elizabeth McGovern

Brian Kerwin

Vivian Reed

Marcus Chong

Donna Kane

Laurence Fishburne

Robert Salvio, Sheila Smith, Connie Stevens, Pamela Tiffin, Leslie Uggams, Jon Voight, Christopher Walken
1967-68: David Birney, Pamela Burrell, Jordan Christopher, Jack Crowder (Thalmus Rasulala), Sandy Duncan, Julie Gregg, Stephen Joyce, Bernadette Peters, Alice Playten, Michael Rupert, Brenda Smiley, Russ Thacker
1968-69: Jane Alexander, David Cryer, Blythe Danner, Ed Evanko, Ken Howard, Lauren Jones, Ron Leibman, Marian Mercer, Jill O'Hara, Ron O'Neal, Al Pacino, Marlene Warfield
1969-70: Susan Browning, Donny Burks, Catherine Burns, Len Cariou, Bonnie Franklin, David Holliday, Katharine Houghton, Melba Moore, David Rounds, Lewis J. Stadlen, Kristoffer Tabori, Fredricka Weber
1970-71: Clifton Davis, Michael Douglas, Julie Garfield, Martha Henry, James Naughton, Tricia O'Neil, Kipp Osborne, Roger Rathburn, Ayn Ruymen, Jennifer Salt, Joan Van Ark, Walter Willison
1971-72: Jonelle Allen, Maureen Anderman, William Atherton, Richard Backus, Adrienne Barbeau, Cara Duff-MacCormick, Robert Foxworth, Elaine Joyce, Jess Richards, Ben Vereen, Beatrice Winde, James Woods
1972-73: D'Jamin Bartlett, Patricia Elliott, James Farentino, Brian Farrell, Victor Garber, Kelly Garrett, Mari Gorman, Laurence Guittard, Trish Hawkins, Monte Markham, John Rubinstein, Jennifer Warren, Alexander H. Cohen (Special Award)
1973-74: Mark Baker, Maureen Brennan, Ralph Carter, Thom Christopher, John Driver, Conchata Ferrell, Ernestine Jackson, Michael Moriarty, Joe Morton, Ann Reinking, Janie Sell, Mary Woronov, Sammy Cahn (Special Award)
1974-75: Peter Burnell, Zan Charisse, Lola Falana, Peter Firth, Dorian Harewood, Joel Higgins, Marcia McClain, Linda Miller, Marti Rolph, John Sheridan, Scott Stevensen, Donna Theodore, Equity Library Theatre (Special Award)
1975-76: Danny Aiello, Christine Andreas, Dixie Carter, Tovah Feldshuh, Chip Garnett, Richard Kelton, Vivian Reed, Charles Repole, Virginia Seidel, Daniel Seltzer, John V. Shea, Meryl Streep, A Chorus Line (Special Award)
1976-77: Trazana Beverley, Michael Cristofer, Joe Fields, Joanna Gleason, Cecilia Hart, John Heard, Gloria Hodes, Juliette Koka, Andrea McArdle, Ken Page, Jonathan Pryce, Chick Vennera, Eva LeGallienne (Special Award)
1977-78: Vasili Bogazianos, Nell Carter, Carlin Glynn, Christopher Goutman, William Hurt, Judy Kaye, Florence Lacy, Armelia McQueen, Gordana Rashovich, Bo Rucker, Richard Seer, Colin Stinton, Joseph Papp (Special Award)
1978-79: Philip Anglim, Lucie Arnaz, Gregory Hines, Ken Jennings, Michael Jeter, Laurie Kennedy, Susan Kingsley, Christine Lahti, Edward James Olmos, Kathleen Quinlan, Sarah Rice, Max Wright, Marshall W. Mason (Special Award)

1979-80: Maxwell Caulfield, Leslie Denniston, Boyd Gaines, Richard Gere, Harry Groener, Stephen James, Susan Kellermann, Dinah Manoff, Lonny Price, Marianne Tatum, Anne Twomey, Dianne Wiest, Mickey Rooney (Special Award)
1980-81: Brian Backer, Lisa Banes, Meg Bussert, Michael Allen Davis, Giancarlo Esposito, Daniel Gerroll, Phyllis Hyman, Cynthia Nixon, Amanda Plummer, Adam Redfield, Wanda Richert, Rex Smith, Elizabeth Taylor (Special Award)
1981-82: Karen Akers, Laurie Beechman, Danny Glover, David Alan Grier, Jennifer Holliday, Anthony Heald, Lizbeth Mackay, Peter MacNicol, Elizabeth McGovern, Ann Morrison, Michael O'Keefe, James Widdoes, Manhattan Theatre Club (Special Award)
1982-83: Karen Allen, Suzanne Bertish, Matthew Broderick, Kate Burton, Joanne Camp, Harvey Fierstein, Peter Gallagher, John Malkovich, Anne Pitoniak, James Russo, Brian Tarantina, Linda Thorson, Natalia Makarova (Special Award)
1983-84: Martine Allard, Joan Allen, Kathy Whitton Baker, Mark Capri, Laura Dean, Stephen Geoffreys, Todd Graff, Glenne Headly, J.J. Johnston, Bonnie Koloc, Calvin Levels, Robert Westenberg, Ron Moody (Special Award)
1984-85: Kevin Anderson, Richard Chaves, Patti Cohenour, Charles S. Dutton, Nancy Giles, Whoopi Goldberg, Leilani Jones, John Mahoney, Laurie Metcalf, Barry Miller, John Turturro, Amelia White, Lucille Lortel (Special Award)
1985-86: Suzy Amis, Alec Baldwin, Aled Davies, Faye Grant, Julie Hagerty, Ed Harris, Mark Jacoby, Donna Kane, Cleo Laine, Howard McGillin, Marisa Tomei, Joe Urla, Ensemble Studio Theatre (Special Award)
1986-87: Annette Bening, Timothy Daly, Lindsay Duncan, Frank Ferrante, Robert Lindsay, Amy Madigan, Michael Maguire, Demi Moore, Molly Ringwald, Frances Ruffelle, Courtney B. Vance, Colm Wilkinson, Robert DeNiro (Special Award)
1987-88: Yvonne Bryceland, Philip Casnoff, Danielle Ferland, Melissa Gilbert, Linda Hart, Linzi Hately, Brian Kerwin, Brian Mitchell, Mary Murfitt, Aidan Quinn, Eric Roberts, B.D. Wong
1988-89: Dylan Baker, Joan Cusack, Loren Dean, Peter Frechette, Sally Mayes, Sharon McNight, Jennie Moreau, Paul Provenza, Kyra Sedgwick, Howard Spiegel, Eric Stoltz, Joanne Whalley-Kilmer, Special Awards: Pauline Collins, Mikhail Baryshnikov
1989-90: Denise Burse, Erma Campbell, Rocky Carroll, Megan Gallagher, Tommy Hollis, Robert Lambert, Kathleen Rowe McAllen, Michael McKean, Crista Moore, Mary-Louise Parker, Daniel von Bargen, Jason Workman, Special Awards: Stewart Granger, Kathleen Turner
1990-91: Jane Adams, Gillian Anderson, Adam Arkin, Brenda Blethyne, Marcus Chong, Paul Hipp, LaChanze, Kenny Neal, Kevin Ramsey, Francis Ruivivar, Lea Salonga, Chandra Wilson, Special Awards: Tracey Ullman, Ellen Stewart

Michel Rupert

Dianne Wiest

B.D. Wong

PULITZER PRIZE PRODUCTIONS

1918-Why Marry?, **1919**-No award, **1920**-Beyond the Horizon, **1921**-Miss Lulu Bett, **1922**-Anna Christie, **1923**-Icebound, **1924**-Hell-Bent fer Heaven, **1925**-They Knew What They Wanted, **1926**-Craig's Wife, **1927**-In Abraham's Bosom, **1928**-Strange Interlude, **1929**-Street Scene, **1930**-The Green Pastures, **1931**-Alison's House, **1932**-Of Thee I Sing, **1933**-Both Your Houses, **1934**-Men in White, **1935**-The Old Maid, **1936**-Idiot's Delight, **1937**-You Can't Take It with You, **1938**-Our Town, **1939**-Abe Lincoln in Illinois, **1940**-The Time of Your Life, **1941**-There Shall Be No Night, **1942**-No award, **1943**-The Skin of Our Teeth, **1944**-No award, **1945**-Harvey, **1946**-State of the Union, **1947**-No award, **1948**-A Streetcar Named Desire, **1949**-Death of a Salesman, **1950**-South Pacific, **1951**-No award, **1952**-The Shrike, **1953**-Picnic, **1954**-The Teahouse of the August Moon, **1955**-Cat on a Hot Tin Roof, **1956**-The Diary of Anne Frank, **1957**-Long Day's Journey into Night, **1958**-Look Homeward, Angel, **1959**-J.B., **1960**-Fiorello!, **1961**-All the Way Home, **1962**-How to Succeed in Business without Really Trying, **1963**-No award, **1964**-No award, **1965**-The Subject Was Roses, **1966**-No award, **1967**-A Delicate Balance, **1968**-No award, **1969**-The Great White Hope, **1970**-No Place to Be Somebody, **1971**-The Effect of Gamma Rays on Man-in-the-Moon Marigolds, **1972**-No award, **1973**-That Championship Season, **1974**-No award, **1975**-Seascape, **1976**-A Chorus Line, **1977**-The Shadow Box, **1978**-The Gin Game, **1979**-Buried Child, **1980**-Talley's Folly, **1981**-Crimes of the Heart, **1982**-A Soldier's Play, **1983**-'night, Mother, **1984**-Glengarry Glen Ross, **1985**-Sunday in the Park with George, **1986**-No award, **1987**-Fences, **1988**-Driving Miss Daisy, **1989**-The Heidi Chronicles, **1990**-The Piano Lesson, **1991**-Lost in Yonkers, **1992**-The Kentucky Cycle, **1993**-Angels in America: Millenium Approaches

NEW YORK DRAMA CRITICS CIRCLE AWARDS

1936-Winterset, **1937**-High Tor, **1938**-Of Mice and Men, Shadow and Substance, **1939**-The White Steed, **1940**-The Time of Your Life, **1941**-Watch on the Rhine, The Corn Is Green, **1942**-Blithe Spirit, **1943**-The Patriots, **1944**-Jacobowsky and the Colonel, **1945**-The Glass Menagerie, **1946**-Carousel, **1947**-All My Sons, No Exit, Brigadoon, **1948**-A Streetcar Named Desire, The Winslow Boy, **1949**-Death of a Salesman, The Madwoman of Chaillot, South Pacific, **1950**-The Member of the Wedding, The Cocktail Party, The Consul, **1951**-Darkness at Noon, The Lady's Not for Burning, Guys and Dolls, **1952**-I Am a Camera, Venus Observed, Pal Joey, **1953**-Picnic, The Love of Four Colonels, Wonderful Town, **1954**-Teahouse of the August Moon, Ondine, The Golden Apple, **1955**-Cat on a Hot Tin Roof, Witness for the Prosecution, The Saint of Bleecker Street, **1956**-The Diary of Anne Frank, Tiger at the Gates, My Fair Lady, **1957**-Long Day's Journey into Night, The Waltz of the Toreadors, The Most Happy Fella, **1958**-Look Homeward Angel, Look Back in Anger, The Music Man, **1959**-A Raisin in the Sun, The Visit, La Plume de Ma Tante, **1960**-Toys in the Attic, Five Finger Exercise, Fiorello!, **1961**-All the Way Home, A Taste of Honey, Carnival, **1962**-Night of the Iguana, A Man for All Seasons, How to Succeed in Business without Really Trying, **1963**-Who's Afraid of Virginia Woolf?, **1964**-Luther, Hello Dolly!, **1965**-The Subject Was Roses, Fiddler on the Roof, **1966**-The Persecution and Assassination of Marat as Performed by the Inmates of the Asylum of Charenton under the Direction of the Marquis de Sade, Man of La Mancha, **1967**-The Homecoming, Cabaret, **1968**-Rosencrantz and Guildenstern Are Dead, Your Own Thing, **1969**-The Great White Hope, 1776, **1970**-The Effect of Gamma Rays on Man-in-the-Moon Marigolds, Borstal Boy, Company, **1971**-Home, Follies, The House of Blue Leaves, **1972**-That Championship Season, Two Gentlemen of Verona, **1973**-The Hot l Baltimore, The Changing Room, A Little Night Music, **1974**-The Contractor, Short Eyes, Candide, **1975**-Equus, The Taking of Miss Janie, A Chorus Line, **1976**-Travesties, Streamers, Pacific Overtures, **1977**-Otherwise Engaged, American Buffalo, Annie, **1978**-Da, Ain't Misbehavin', **1979**-The Elephant Man, Sweeney Todd, **1980**-Talley's Folley, Evita, Betrayal, **1981**-Crimes of the Heart, A Lesson from Aloes, Special Citation to Lena Horne, The Pirates of Penzance, **1982**-The Life and Adventures of Nicholas Nickleby, A Soldier's Play, no musical honored, **1983**-Brighton Beach Memoirs, Plenty, Little Shop of Horrors, **1984**-The Real Thing, Glengarry Glen Ross, Sunday in the Park with George, **1985**-Ma Rainey's Black Bottom (no musical), **1986**-A Lie of the Mind, Benefactors, no musical, Special Citation to Lily Tomlin and Jane Wagner, **1987**-Fences, Les Liaisons Dangereuses, Les Misérables, **1988**-Joe Turner's Come and Gone, The Road to Mecca, Into the Woods, **1989**-The Heidi Chronicles, Aristocrats, Largely New York (Special), (no musical), **1990**-The Piano Lesson, City of Angels, Privates on Parade, **1991**-Six Degrees of Separation, The Will Rogers Follies, Our Country's Good, Special Citation to Eileen Atkins, **1992**-Two Trains Running, Dancing at Lughnasa, **1993**-Angels in America: Millenium Approaches, Someone Who'll Watch Over Me, Kiss of the Spider Woman

AMERICAN THEATRE WING ANTOINETTE PERRY (TONY) AWARD PRODUCTIONS

1948-Mister Roberts, **1949**-Death of a Salesman, Kiss Me, Kate, **1950**-The Cocktail Party, South Pacific, **1951**-The Rose Tattoo, Guys and Dolls, **1952**-The Fourposter, The King and I, **1953**-The Crucible, Wonderful Town, **1954**-The Teahouse of the August Moon, Kismet, **1955**-The Desperate Hours, The Pajama Game, **1956**-The Diary of Anne Frank, Damn Yankees, **1957**-Long Day's Journey into Night, My Fair Lady, **1958**-Sunrise at Campobello, The Music Man, **1959**-J.B., Redhead, **1960**-The Miracle Worker, Fiorello! tied with The Sound of Music, **1961**-Becket, Bye Bye Birdie, **1962**-A Man for All Seasons, How to Succeed in Business without Really Trying, **1963**-Who's Afraid of Virginia Woolf?, A Funny Thing Happened on the Way to the Forum, **1964**-Luther, Hello Dolly!, **1965**-The Subject Was Roses, Fiddler on the Roof, **1966**-The Persecution and Assassination of Marat as Performed by the Inmates of the Asylum of Charenton under the Direction of the Marquis de Sade, Man of La Mancha, **1967**-The Homecoming, Cabaret, **1968**-Rosencrantz and Guildenstern Are Dead, Hallelujah Baby!, **1969**-The Great White Hope, 1776, **1970**-Borstal Boy, Applause, **1971**-Sleuth, Company, **1972**-Sticks and Bones, Two Gentlemen of Verona, **1973**-That Championship Season, A Little Night Music, **1974**-The River Niger, Raisin, **1975**-Equus, The Wiz, **1976**-Travesties, A Chorus Line, **1977**-The Shadow Box, Annie, **1978**-Da, Ain't Misbehavin', Dracula, **1979**-The Elephant Man, Sweeney Todd, **1980**-Children of a Lesser God, Evita, Morning's at Seven, **1981**-Amadeus, 42nd Street, The Pirates of Penzance, **1982**-The Life and Adventures of Nicholas Nickleby, Nine, Othello, **1983**-Torch Song Trilogy, Cats, On Your Toes, **1984**-The Real Thing, La Cage aux Folles, **1985**-Biloxi Blues, Big River, Joe Egg, **1986**-I'm Not Rappaport, The Mystery of Edwin Drood, Sweet Charity, **1987**-Fences, Les Misérables, All My Sons, **1988**-M. Butterfly, The Phantom of the Opera, **1989**-The Heidi Chronicles, Jerome Robbins' Broadway, Our Town, Anything Goes, **1990**-The Grapes of Wrath, City of Angels, Gypsy, **1991**-Lost in Yonkers, The Will Rogers' Follies, Fiddler on the Roof, **1992**-Dancing at Lughnasa, Crazy For You, Guys & Dolls, **1993**-Angels in America: Millenium Approaches, Kiss of the Spider Woman

| Polly Adams | Terry Alexander | Brooks Almy | David Aaron Baker | Jodi Baker | Brian Batt |

BIOGRAPHICAL DATA ON THIS SEASON'S CASTS
(JUNE 1, 1992-MAY 31, 1993)

ACKERMAN, LONI. Born April 10, 1949 in NYC. Attended New School. Bdwy debut 1968 in George M!, followed by No, No Nanette, So Long 174th Street, The Magic Show, Evita, Cats, OB in *Dames at Sea, Starting Here Starting Now, Roberta in Concert, Brownstone, Diamonds.*

ADAMS, JANE. Born April 1, 1965 in Washington, DC. Juilliard graduate. Debut 1986 OB in The Nice and the Nasty, followed by Young Playwrights Festival, Bdwy in I Hate Hamlet for which she received a Theatre World Award, The Crucible.

ADAMS, J. B. Born September 29, 1954 in Oklahoma City, OK. Graduate Okla.City U. Debut 1980 OB in *ELT's Plain and Fancy,* followed by *Balancing Act.*

ADAMS, POLLY. Born in Nashville, TN. Graduate Stanford U., Columbia U. Bdwy debut 1976 in *Zalmen, or the Madness of God,* OB in *Ordway Ames-gay, The Free Zone.*

ADAMSON, ELLEN. Born July 13, 1956 in Atlanta, GA. Graduate Neighborhood Playhouse, Stanford U. Debut 1983 OB in *The Triptych* followed by *The Park, A Midsummer Night's Dream, Real Family, Me. MacAdam Travelling Theatre.*

ADLER, BRUCE. Born November 27, 1944 in NYC. Attended NYU. Debut 1957 OB in *It's a Funny World,* followed by *Hard to Be a Jew, Big Winner, The Golden Land, The Stranger's Return, The Rise of David Levinsky, On Second Avenue,* Bdwy in *A Teaspoon Every Four Hours* (1971), *Oklahoma!* (1979), *Oh, Brother!, Sunday in the Park with George, Broadway, Those Were the Days, Crazy for You.*

A'HEARN, PATRICK. Born September 4, 1957 in Chappaqua, NY. Graduate Syracuse U. Debut 1985 OB in Pirates of Penzance, followed by Forbidden Broadway, followed by Bdwy in Les Misºrables (1987).

AIDEM, BETSY. Born October 28, 1957 in East Meadow, NY. Graduate NYU. Debut 1981 OB in The Trading Post, followed by *A Different Moon, Balm in Gilead, Crossing the Bar, Our Lady of the Tortilla, Steel Magnolias, Road, 5 Women Wearing the Same Dress.*

ALDERSON, WILLIAM. Born August 18, 1935 in Bratt, Fl. Graduate Sacramento Col. OB in Andromaque, Glass Menagerie, Yellow Jack, Simon, Huui, Huui, Between Two Thieves, The Shadow, Breakfast, Seize the Day, Rivalry of Dolls, The Roads to Home.

ALDREDGE, TOM. Born February 28, 1928 in Dayton, OH. Attended Daton U. Goodman Theatre. Bdwy debut 1959 in *The Nervous Set,* followed by *UTBU, Slapstick Tragedy, Everything in the Garden, Indians, Engagement Baby, How the Other Half Loves, Sticks and Bones, Where's Charley?, Leaf People, Rex, Vieux Carre, St. Joan, Stages, On Golden Pond, The Little Foxes, Into the Woods, Two Shakespearean Actors, Lost, Troilus and Cressida,Tthe Butter and Egg Man, Ergo, Boys in the Band, Twelfth Night, Colette, Hamlet, The Orphan, King Lear, The Iceman Cometh, Black Angel, Getting Along Famously, Fool for Love, Neon Psalms, Richard II, The Last Yankee.*

ALEXANDER, JANE. Born October 28, 1939 in Boston, MA. Attended Sarah Lawrence Col, U. Edinburgh. Bdwy debut 1968 in *The Great White Hope,* for which she received a Theatre World Award, followed by *6 Rms Riv Vu, Find Your Way Home, Hamlet* (LC), *The Heiress, First Monday in October, Goodbye Fidel, Monday after the Miracle, Shadowlands, The Visit.* OB in *Losing Time, Approaching Zanzibar.*

ALEXANDER, TERRY. Born March 23, 1959 in Detroit, MI. Graduate Wayne State U. Bdwy debut 1971 in *No Place to Be Somebody,* OB in *Rashomon, The Glass Menagerie, Breakout, Naomi Court, Streamers, Julius Caesar, Nongogo, Sus, Playboy of the West Indies.*

ALEXIS, ALVIN. Born July 5 in NYC. Debut 1976 OB in *In the Wine of Time,* followed by *Rear Column, Class Enemy, Zooman and the Sign, Painting a Wall, The Flatbush Faithful, The Amen Corner, Teens Today, Time Wasted, Monk 'n' Bud.*

ALFORD, DAVID. Born December 20, 1964 in Nashville, TN. Graduate Austin State U. Juilliard. Debut 1993 OB in *Traps.*

ALLINSON, MICHAEL. Born in London, England. Attended RADA. Bdwy debut 1960 in *My Fair Lady,* followed by *Hostile Witness, Come Live With Me, Coco, Angel Street, My Fair Lady* (1981), *Oliver!, Shadowplay,* OB in *The Importance of Being Earnest, Staircase, Loud Bang on June 1st, Good and Faithful Servant, The Best of Friends.*

ALMY, BROOKS. Born July 15 in Fort Belvoir, VA. Attended U. Hawaii. Bdwy debut 1981 in *Little Prince and the Aviator,* followed by *Play Me a Country Song, NYC Opera's Music Man, Candide, Sweeney Todd, and Pajama Game, A Change in the Heir, Grand Hotel,* OB in Shylock, *Nunsense, Bright Hearts and Broken Lights, Annie Warbucks.*

ANDERSON, CHRISTINE. Born August 6 in Utica, NY. Graduate U. Wis. Bdwy debut in *I Love My Wife* (1980), OB in *I Can't Keep Running in Place, On the Swing Shift, Red, Hot and Blue, A Night at Texas Guinan's, Nunsense.*

ANDERSON, LAWRENCE. Born May 18, 1964 in Poughkeepsie, NY. Graduate U Col. Bdwy debut 1992 in *Phantom of the Opera followed by Les Miserables.*

ANDRES, BARBARA. Born February 11, 1939 in NYC. Graduate Catholic U. Bdwy debut 1969 in *Jimmy,* followed by *The Boy Friend, Rodgers and Hart, Rex, On Golden Pond, Threepenny Opera, Landscape of the Body, Harold Arlen's Cabaret, Suzanna Andler, One-Act Festival, Company, Marathon '87, Arms and the Man, A Woman without a Name, First is Supper, Fore!.*

ANDREWS, GEORGE LEE. Born October 13, 1942 in Milwaukee, WI. Debut OB in *Jacques Brel Is Alive and Well ...,* followed by *Starting Here Starting Now, Vamps and Rideouts, The Fantasticks,* Bdwy in *A Little Night Music* (1973), *On the 20th Century, Merlin, The Phantom of the Opera, A Little Night Music* (NYCO).

ANDREWS, JULIE. Born Oct.1, 1935 in Walton-on-Thames, England. Bdwy debut 1954 in *The Boy Friend* followed by *My Fair Lady, Camelot* OB 1993 in *Putting It Together*

ANTON, SUSAN. Born October 12, 1950 in Yucaipa, CA. Attended Bernardino Col. Bdwy debut 1985 in *Hurlyburly,* followed by *The Will Rogers Follies, OB's Xmas a Go-Go.*

ARCARO, ROBERT. (a.k.a. Bob), Born August 9, 1952 in Brooklyn, NY. Graduate Wesleyan U. Debut 1977 OB in *New York City Street Show, followed by Working Theatre Festival, Man with a Raincoat, Working One-Acts, Henry Lumpur, Special Interests, Measure for Measure, Our Lady of Perpetual Danger, Brotherly Love, I Am a Man.*

ARI, ROBERT/BOB. Born July 1, 1949 in NYC. Graduate Carnegie-Mellon U. Debut 1976 OB in *The Boys from Syracuse* followed by *Gay Divorce, Devour the Snow, Carbondale Dreams, Show Me Where the Good Times Are, CBS Live.*

ARKIN, ADAM. Born August 19, 1956 in Brooklyn, NY. Bdwy debut 1991 in *I Hate Hamlet* for which he received a Theatre World Award followed *Guys and Dolls,* OB in *Sight Unseen, A Christmas Memory.*

ARNAZ, LUCIE. Born July 17, 1951 in Los Angeles, CA. Bdwy debut 1979 in *They're Playing Our Song* for which she received a Theatre World Award, followed by *Lost in Yonkers* (1992).

ARNOTT, MARK. Born June 15, 1950 in Chicago, IL. Graduate Dartmouth Col. Debut 1981 in *The Hunchback of Notre Dame* followed by *Buddies, Love's Labour's Lost, Two Gentlemen of Verona, The Dining Room, The Knack, Marmalade Skies, The Homecoming,* Bdwy debut 1992 in *A Small Family Business.*

AROESTE, JOEL. Born April 10, 1949 in NYC. Graduate SUNY. Bdwy debut 1986 in *Raggedy Ann,* OB in *Beauty and the Beast, Slow Dance on the Killing Ground.*

ARRINDELL, LISA. Born March 24, 1969 in Bronx, NY. Juilliard graduate, Debut OB 1990 in *Richard III,* followed by *Earth and Sky, Mixed Babies, Heliotrope Bouquet.*

ARTHUR, DAVID. Born October 3, 1955 in Chicago, IL. Graduate Goodman School, DePaul U. Debut 1993 OB in *Carnival,* followed by *Jack the Ripper Revue.*

ASH, RANDL. Born September 15, 1959 in Elmhurst, IL. Attended Central CT State Col. Debut 1977 OB in *The Comic Strip,* followed by *Elegies for Angels Punks and Raging Queens, Pageant.*

ASHFORD, ROBERT. Born November 19, 1959 in Orlando, FL. Attended Washington & Lee U. Bdwy debut 1987 in *Anything Goes,* followed by *Radio City Music Hall Christmas Spectacular, The Most Happy Fella* (1992), *My Favorite Year.*

ATLEE, HOWARD. Born May 14, 1926 in Bucyrus, OH. Graduate Emerson Col. Debut 1990 OB in *Historical Prods,* followed by *The 15th Ward, The Hells of Dante, What a Royal Pain in the Farce.*

BACON, KEVIN. Born July 8, 1958 in Philadelphia, PA Debut 1978 OB in *Getting Out*, followed by *Glad Tidings, Album, Flux, Poor Little Lambs, Slab Boys, Men without Dates, Loot, The Author's Voice, Road, Spike Heels, The Normal Heart* (Benefit reading).

BACKER, BRIAN. Born December 5, 1956 in NYC. Attended Neighborhood Playhouse. Bdwy debut 1981 in *The Floating Light Bulb* for which he received a Theatre World Award. OB in *December 7th, Circumstantial Evidence*.

BAGNERIS, VERNEL. Born July 31, 1949 in New Orleans, LA. Graduate Xavier U. Debut 1979 OB in *One Mo' Time*, followed by *Staggerlee, Further Mo', Jelly Roll Morton: A Me-Morial* all of which he wrote.

BAILEY, ADRIAN. Born September 23, in Detroit, MI. Graduate U. Detroit. Bdwy debut 1976 in *Your Arms Too Short to Box with God*, followed by *Prince of Central Park, Jelly's Last Jam,* OB in *A Thrill a Moment*

BAKER, DAVID ARON. Born August 14, 1963 in Durham, NC. Graduate U.Texas, Juilliard. Bdwy debut 1993 in *White Liars/Black Comedy,* OB in *Richard III, 110 in the Shade* (NYCO).

BAKER, JODI. Born August 26, 1967 in Salt Lake City, UT. Graduate Cal. State U. Fresno, N'tl Theatre Consv. Debut 1992 OB in *God of Vengeance.*

BAKER, ROBERT MICHAEL. Born February 28, 1954 in Boston, MA. Attended Boston U.AADA. Debut 1984 OB in *Jessie's Land* followed by *Enter Laughing , Happily Ever After, Company, The Education of Hyman Kaplan, Yiddle with a Fiddle, Carnival,* Bdwy in *Guys and Dolls* (1992).

BALDWIN, ALEC. Born April 3, 1958 in Massepequa, NY. Attended George Washington U. NYU. Bdwy debut 1986 in *Loot* for which he received a Theatre World Award, followed by *Serious Money, A Streetcar Named Desire,* OB in *Prelude to a Kiss.*

BALLINGER, JUNE. Born November 15, 1949 in Camden, NJ. Attended Briarcliff Col. Debut 1980 OB in *Mr. Wilson's Peace of Mind*, followed by *Dona Rosita, A Man in the House, Human Nature, Sound Bytes.*

BARANSKI, CHRISTINE. Born May 2, 1952 in Buffalo, NY. Graduate Juilliard. Debut OB 1978 in *One Crack Out*, followed by *Says I Says He, The Trouble with Europe, Coming Attractions, Operation Midnight Climax, Sally and Marsha, A Midsummer Night's Dream, It's Only a Play, Marathon '86, Elliot Loves, Lips Together Teeth Apart, A Christmas Memory,* Bdwy in *Hide and Seek* (1980), *The Real Thing, Hurlyburly, House of Blue Leaves, Rumors, Nick & Nora.*

BARAY, JOHN. Born November 29, 1944 in San Antonio, TX. Graduate Trinity U. Debut 1981 OB in *The Red Mill* followed by *Babes in Toyland, The Mikado, The Pirates of Penzance, Pacific Overtures, Gashiram, Cambodia Agonistes.*

BARON, EVALYN. Born Apr. 21, 1948 in Atlanta, GA. Graduate Northwestern U., U. Min. Debut 1979 OB in *Scrambled Feet*, followed by *Hijinks, I Can't Keep Running in Place, Jerry's Girls, Harvest of Strangers, Quilters,* Bdwy in *Fearless Frank* (1980), *Big River, Rages, Social Security, Les Miserables.*

BARRE, GABRIEL. Born August 26, 1957 in Brattleboro, VT. Graduate AADA. Debut 1977 OB in *Jabberwock* followed by *T.N.T., Bodo, The Baker's Wife, The Time of Your Life, Children of the Sun, Wicked Philanthropy, Starmites, Mistress of the Inn, Gifts of the Magi, The Tempest, Return to the Forbidden Planet, The Circle, Where's Dick?, Forever Plaid, Jacques Brel,* Bdwy in *Rags* (1986), *Starmites, Anna Karenina, Ain't Broadway Grand.*

BARTENIEFF, GEORGE. Born January 24, 1933 in Berlin, Germany. Bdwy debut 1947 in *The Whole World Over*, followed by *Venus Is, All's Well That Ends Well, Quotations from Chairman Mao Tse-Tung, The Death of Bessie Smith, Cop-Out, Room Service, Unlikely Heroes,* OB in *Walking in Waldheim, Memorandum, The Increased Difficulty of Concentration, Trelawny of the Wells, Charley Chestnut Rides the IRT, Radio (Wisdom): Sophia Part I, Images of the Dead, Dead End Kids, The Blonde Leading the Blonde, The Dispossessed, Growing Up Gothic, Rosetti's Apologies, On the Lam, Samuel Beckett Trilogy, Quartet, Help Wanted, A Matter of Life and Death, The Heart That Eats Itself, Coney Island Kid, Cymbeline, Better People.*

BARTON, STEVE. Born in Arkansas. Graduate U. Texas. Bdwy debut 1988 in *Phantom of the Opera*, followed by OB's *Six Wives, The Hunchback of Notre Dame.*

BATT, BRYAN. Born March 1, 1963 in New Orleans, LA. Graduate Tulane U. Debut 1987 OB in *Too Many Girls*, followed by *The Golden Apple, Jeffrey,* Bdwy in *Starlight Express* 1987

BAUER, STEVEN. (aka Steven Echevarria, Rocky Bauer) Born December 2, 1956 in Havana, Cuba. Attended U. Miami. Debut 1980 OB in *Waiting for Lefty* followed by *Balm in Gilead, 3rd Annual Heart o' Texas Eczema Telethon.*

BEACH, DAVID. Born February 20, 1964 in Dayton, OH. Attended Dartmouth Col., LAMDA. Debut 1990 OB in *Big Fat and Ugly with a Moustache* followed by *Modigliani, Octoberfest, Pets.*

BEAL, JOHN. Born August 13, 1909 in Joplin, MO. Graduate U. PA. His many credits include *Wild Waves, Another Language, She Loves Me Not, Russet Mantle, Soliloquy, Miss Swan Expects, Liberty Jones, Voice of the Turtle, Lend an Ear, Teahouse of the August Moon, Calculated Risk, Billy, Our Town* (1970), *The Crucible, The Master Builder, A Little Hotel on the Side, The Sea Gull, Three Men on a Horse,* OB in *Wilder's Triple Bill, To Be Youn Gifted and Black, Candyapple, Long Day's Journey into Night, Rivers Return.*

BECKER, GERRY. Born April 11, 1951 in St. Louis, MO. Graduate U. MO. St. Louis U. Bdwy debut 1993 in *Song of Jacob Zulu.*

BEDDOW, MARGERY. Born December 13, 1937 in Grosse Pointe, MI. Attended HB Studio. Bdwy debut 1959 in *Redhead* followed by *Fiorello!, Show Boat, The Conquering Hero, We Take the Town, Take Me Along, Little Me, Here's Love, Ulysses in Nighttown,* OB in *Sing Melancholy Baby, Anyone Can Whistle.*

BEECHMAN, LAURIE. Born April 4, 1954 in Philadelphia, PA. Attended NYU. Bdwy debut 1977 in *Annie*, followed by *Pirates of Penzance, Joseph and the Amazing Technicolor Dreamcoat* for which she received a Theatre World Award, *Cats, Les*

Miserables, OB in Some Enchanted Evening, Pal Joey in Concert.

BELIS, TINA. Born January 8, 1963 in Pennsylvania. Bdwy debut 1984 in *The Three Musketeers*, followed by *Camelot* (1993).

BENJAMIN, P. J. Born September 2, 1951 in Chicago, IL. Attended Loyola U., Columbia U. Bdwy debut 1973 in *Pajama Game*, followed by *Pippin, Sarava, Charlie and Algernon, Sophisticated Ladies, Torch Song Trilogy, Wind in the Willows, Ain't Broadway Grand,* OB in *Memories of Riding with Joe Cool.*

BELMONTE, VICKI. Born January 20, 1947 in U.S.A. Bdwy debut 1960 in *Bye Bye Birdie*, followed by *Subways Are for Sleeping, All American, Annie Get Your Gun* (LC), OB in *Nunsense.*

BENSON, CINDY. Born October 2, 1951 in Attleboro, MA. Graduate St. Leo Col, U. IL. Debut 1981 OB in *Some Like It Cole*, followed by *Eating Raoul, Balancing Act, Bdwy Les Miserables* (1987).

BENSON, JODI. Born October 10, 1961 in Rockford, IL. Attended Millkin U. Bdwy debut 1983 in *Marilyn, An American Fable* followed by *Smile, Welcome to the Club, Crazy for You,* OB in *Hurry! Hurry! Hollywood!*

BENTLEY, MARY DENISE. Born December 28 in Indianapolis, IN. Graduate Ind. U. Bdwy debut 1983 in *Dreamgirls,* OB in *Little Shop of Horrors* (1987) followed by *Forbidden Broadway.*

BERGER, STEPHEN. Born May 16, 1954 in Philadelphia, PA. Attended U. Cinn. debut 1982 in *Little Me,* OB in *Nite Club Confidential, Mowgli, Isn't It Romantic, Hello Muddah Hello Fadduh.*

BERNHARD, SANDRA. Born June 6 1955 in Flint, MI. Debut 1988 OB in *Without You I'm Nothing* followed by *Giving Till It Hurts.*

BERNHEIM, SHIRL. Born September 21, 1921 in NYC. Debut 1967 OB in *A Different World* followed by *Stage Movie, Middle of the Night, Come Back, Little Sheba, One-Act Festival, EST Marathon 93.*

BERQUE, BARBARA. Born August 31, 1953 OB in St. Louis, MO. Debut 1983 OB in *El Salvador* followed by *The Wonder Years, What does a Blind Leopard See?, The Enclave, Measure for Measure, The Hot 1 Baltimore, You Never Can Tell, The Best of Sex and Violence, Are You Now or Have You Ever Been?*

BERRESSE, MICHAEL. Born August 15, 1964 in Holyoke, MA. Bdwy debut 1990 in *Fiddler on the Roof* followed by *Guys and Dolls.*

BERTISH, SUZANNE. Born August 7, 1951 in London, Endland. Attended London Drama School. Bdwy debut 1981 in *Nicholas Nickleby*, followed by *Salome,* OB in *Skirmishes* for which she received a Theatre World Award, followed by *Rosemersholm, Art of Success.*

BEVERLEY, TRAZANA. Born Aug. 9, 1945 in Baltimore, MD. Graduate NYU. Debut 1969 OB in *Rules for Running*, followed by *Les Femmes Noires, Geronimo, Antigone, The Brothers, God's Trombones, Marathon '91,* Bdwy in *My Sister My Sister, For Colored Girls Who Have Considered Suicide* for which she received a Theatre World Award, *Death and the King's Horseman* (LC), *The Crucible.*

BIANCHI, JAMES R. Born June 21, 1949 in Cleveland, OH. Attended Bowling Green State U. Debut 1991 OB in *Twelft Night*, followed by *St. Joan, The Tempest.*

BILLECI, JOHN. Born April 19, 1957 in Brooklyn, NY Graduate Loyola Marymount U. Debut 1993 OB in 3 by *Wilder,* Bdwy 1993 in *Wilder Wilder Wilder.*

BISCOE, DONNA. Born September 30, 1955 in Fort Benning, GA. Graduate Clark Col. Debut 1993 OB in *Heliotrope Bouquet.*

BISHOP, KELLY (formerly Carole). Born Feb. 28, 1944 in Colorado Springs, CO. Bdwy debut 1967 in *Golden Rainbow*, followed by *Promises Promises, On the Town, Rachel Lily Rosenbloom, A Chorus Line, Six Degrees of Separation,* OB in *Piano Bar, Changes, The Blessing, Going to New England, Six Degrees of Separation, Pterodactyl.*

BLACK, BONNIE. Born September 21 in Brooklyn, NY. Attended SUNY/Brockport. Debut 1981 OB in *A Song for All Saints*, followed by *Comedy of Errors, Them Within Us.*

BLAISDELL, NESBITT. Born December 6, 1928 in NYC. Graduate Amherst, Columbia U. Debut 1978 OB in *Old Man Joseph and His Family*, followed by *Moliere in Spite of Himself, Guests of the Nation, Chekov Sketch Book, Elba, Ballad of Soapy Smith, Custom of the Country, A Cup of Coffee, The Immigrant, Yokohama Duty, Quincy Blues,* Bdwy in *Cat on a Hot Tin Roof* (1990).

BLAKELY, MICHELLE. Born July 27, 1969 in Harrisonburg, VA. Graduate NYU. Debut 1992 OB in *Day Dreams.*

BLANCHARD, STEVE. Born December 4, 1958 in York, PA. Attended UMd. Bdwy debut 1984 in T*he Three Musketeers* followed by *Camelot* OB in *Moby Dick.*

BLATT, BETH. Born November 27, 1957 in Wilmette, IL. Graduate Dartmouth Col. Debut 1983 OB in *She Loves Me* followed by *One Touch of Venus, The Last Musical Comedy, Lightin Out.*

BLOCK, LARRY. Born October 30, 1942, in NYC. Graduate URI. Bdwy debut 1966 in *Hail Scrawdyke*, followed by *La Turista,* OB in *Eh?, Fingernails Blue as Flowers, Comedy of Errors, Coming Attractions, HenryIV Part 2, Feuhrer Bunker, Manhattan Love Songs, Souvenirs, The Golem, Responsible Parties, Hit Parade, Largo Desolato, The Square Root of 3, Young Playwrights Festival, Hunting Cockroaches, Two Gentlemen of Verona, Yell Dog Contract, Temptation, Festival of 1 Acts, The Faithful Brethern of Pitt Street, Loman Family Picnic, One of the All-Time Greats, Pericles, Comedy of Errors.*

BLOOM, TOM. Born November 1, 1944 in Washington, D.C. Graduate Western MD Col., Emerson Col. Debut 1989 OB in T*he Widow's Blind Date*, followed by *A Cup of Coffee, Major Barbara, A Perfect Diamond,* Bdwy in *Lips Together Teeth Apart.*

BLUE, ARLANA. Born November 15, 1948 in Passaic, NJ. Attended NY School of Ballet. Debut 1971 OB in *Fear of Love* followed by *Paranoia Pretty, Sgt. Pepper's Lonely Hearts Club Band, Life During Wartime.*

BLUM, MARK. Born May 14, 1950 in Newark, NJ. Graduate U. PA, U. MN. Debut 1976 OB in The Cherry Orchard, followed by Green Julia, Say Goodnight Gracie, Table Settings, Key Exchange, Loving Reno, Messiah, It's Only a Play, Little Footsteps, Cave of Life, Gus & Al, Laureen's Whereabouts, Bdwy in Lost in Yonkers (1991).

BOBBIE, WALTER. Born November 18, 1945 in Scranton, PA. Graduate U. Scranton, Catholic U. Bdwy debut 1971 in Frank Merriwell, followed by The Grass Harp, Grease, Tricks, Going Up, History of the American Film, Anything Goes, Getting Married, Guys and Dolls, OB in Drat!, She Loves Me, Up from Paradise, Goodbye Freddy, Cafe Crown, Young Playwrights '90.

BODLE, JANE. Born November 12 in Lawrence, KS. Attended U. Utah. Bdwy debut 1983 in Cats, followed by Les Miserables, Miss Saigon.

BOGARDUS, STEPHEN. Born March 11, 1954 in Norfolk, VA. Princeton graduate. Bdwy debut 1980 in West Side Story, followed by Les Miserables, Falsettos, OB in March of the Falsettos, Feathertop, No Way to Treat a Lady, Look on the Bright Side, Falsettoland.

BOGOSIAN, ERIC. Born April 24, 1953 in Woburn, MA. Graduate Oberlin Col. Debut 1982 OB in Men Inside/Voices of America, followed by Funhouse, Drinking in America, Talk Radio, Sex Drugs Rock & Roll, Notes from Underground, The Normal Heart (Benefit reading).

BOSCO, PHILIP. Born September 26, 1930 in Jersey City, NJ. Graduate Catholic U. Credits: Auntie Mame, Rape of the Belt, Ticket of Leave Man, Donnybrook, A Man for All Seasons, Mrs. Warren's Profession, with LCRep in A Great Career, In the Matter of J. Robert Oppenheimer, The Miser, The Time of Your Life, Camino Real, Operation Sidewinder, Amphitryon, Enemy of the People, Playboy of the Western World, Good Woman of Setzuan, Antigone, Mary Stuart, Narrow Road to the Deep North, The Crucible, Twelfth Night, Enemies, Plough and the Stars, Merchant of Venice, A Streetcar Named Desire, Henry V, Threepenny Opera, Streamers, Stages, St. Joan, The Biko Inquest, Man and Superman, Whose Life Is It Anyway?, Major Barbara, A Month in the Country, Bacchae, Hedda Gabler, Don Juan in Hell, Inadmissible Evidence, Eminent Domain, Misalliance, Learned Ladies, Some Men Need Help, Ah Wilderness!, The Caine Mutiny Court Martial, Heartbreak House, Come Back Little Sheba, Loves of Anatol, Be Happy for Me, Master Class, You Never Can Tell, Devil's Disciple, Lend Me a Tenor, Breaking Legs.

BOVE, ELIZABETH. Born September 30 in Melbourne, Aust. Graduate U. Texas. Debut 1986 OB in Witness for the Prosecution followed by House of Bernarda Alba, The Country Girl, The Maids, Roundheads and Peakheads, The Dream Cure, The House of the Dog.

BOYD, JULIE. Born January 2 in Kansas City, MO. Graduate U. Utah, Yale. Bdwy debut 1985 in Noises Off, followed by OB in Only You, Working 1 Acts, Hyde in Hollywood, Nowhere, A Distance from Calcutta.

BOYNTON, PETER. Born November 4, 1955 in Damariscotta, ME. Attended U. Mass. Debut 1980 OB in The Golden Apple, followed by The Wonder Years, Bdwy in She Loves Me (1993)

BRANNUM, TOM. Born June 17, 1941 in Shawnee, PA. Bdwy debut 1961 in Once There Was a Roman, followed by Take Here She's Mine, We Bombed in New Haven, Room Service, OB in Mystery Play, Shaft of Love, Make Up Your Mind.

BRENNAN, MAUREEN. Born October 11, 1952 in Washington, DC. Attended U. Conn. Bdwy debut 1974 in Candide for which she received a Theatre World Award, followed by Going Up, Knickerbocker Holiday, Little Johnny Jones, Stardust, OB in Shakespeare's Cabaret, The Cat and the Fiddle, Nuts and Bolts: Tightened.

BRENNAN, NORA. Born December 1, 1953 in East Chicago, IN. Graduate Purdue U. Bdwy debut 1980 in Camelot, followed by Cats.

BRILL, FRAN. Born September 30 in PA. Attended Boston U. Bdwy debut 1969 in Red White and Maddox, OB in What Every Woman Knows, Scribes, Naked, Look Back in Anger, Knuckle, Skirmishes, Baby with the Bathwater, Holding Patterns, Festival of One Acts, Taking Steps, Young Playwrights Festival, Claptrap, Hyde in Hollywood, Good Grief.

BRODERICK, MATTHEW. Born March 21, 1963 in New York City. Debut 1981 OB in Torch Song Trilogy, followed by The Widow Claire, A Christmas Memory Bdwy 1983 in Brighton Beach Memoirs for which he received a Theatre World Award, followed by Biloxi Blues.

BRODY, JONATHAN. Born June 16, 1963 in Englewood, NJ. Debut 1982 OB in Shulamith, followed by The Desk Set, Eating Raoul, Theda Bara and the Frontier Rabbi, Bdwy in Me and My Girl (1986).

BROGGER, IVAR. Born January 10 in St. Paul, MN. Graduate U. Minn. Debut 1979 OB in In The Jungle of Cities, followed by Collected Works of Billy the Kid, Mean Time, Cloud 9, Richard III, Clarence, Madwoman of Chaillot, Seascapes with Sharks and Dancer, Second Man, Twelfth Night, Almost Perfect, Up 'N' Under, Progress, Juno, Bdwy in Macbeth (1981), Pygmalion (1987), Saint Joan (1983), Blood Brothers.

BROOKES, JACQUELINE. Born July 24, 1930 in Montclair, NJ. Graduate U. Iowa, RADA. Bdwy debut 1955 in Tiger at the Gates, followed by Watercolor, Abelard and Heloise, A Meeting by the River, OB in The Cretan Woman (1954) for which she received a Theatre World Award, The Clandestine Marriage, Measure for Measure, The Duchess of Malfi, Ivanov, 8 Characters in Search of an Author, An Evening's Frost, Come Slowly Eden, The Increased Difficulty of Concentration, The Persians, Sunday Dinner, House of Blue Leaves, Owners, Hallelujah, Dream of a Black-listed Actor, Knuckle, Mama Sang the Blues, Buried Child, On Mt. Chimorazo, Winter Dancers, Hamlet, Old Flames, The Diviners, Richard II, Vieux Carre, Full Hookup, Home Sweet Home/Crack, Approaching Zanzibar, Ten Blocks on the Camino Real.

BROOKING, SIMON. Born December 23, 1960 in Edinburgh, Scot. Graduate SUNY/Fredonia, U. Wash. Debut 1989 OB in American Bagpipes, followed by The Mortality Project, Prelude & Liebestod, Rough Crossing, Rumor of Glory, King Lear, Bdwy 1993 in Candida.

BROOKS, JEFF. Born April 7, 1950 in Vancouver, Can. Attended Portland State U. Debut 1976 OB in Titanic, followed by Fat Chances, Nature and Purpose of the Universe, Actor's Nightmare, Sister Mary Ignatius Explains It All, Marathon 84, The Foreigner, Talk Radio, Washington Heights, Bdwy in A History of the American Film (1978), Lend Me A Tenor, Gypsy, Nick & Nora, Guys & Dolls.

BROWN, DARCY. Born April 7, 1968 in Poughkeepsie, NY. Graduate Brown U. Debut 1992 OB in Cowboy in His Underwear, followed by Loose Ends, Arms and the Man, The Rain Always Falls.

BROWN, GRAHAM. Born October 24 in NYC. Graduate Howard U. OB in Widowers Houses (1959), The Emperor's Clothes, Time of Storm, Major Barbara, Land Beyond the River, The Blacks, Firebugs, God Is a (guess Who?), Evening of 1-Acts, Man Better Man, Behold Cometh the Vanderkellans, Ride a Black Horse, The Great MacDaddy, Eden, Nevis Mountain Dew, Season Unravel, The Devil's Tear, Sons and Father of Sons, Abercrombie Apacolypse, Ceremonies in Dark Old Men, Eyes of the American, Richard II, Taming of the Shrew, A Winter's Tale, Black Eagles, Henry V, Bdwy in Weekend (1968) Man in the Glass Booth, River Niger, Pericles, Black Picture Show, Kings, Lifetimes, Burners' Frolic, Jonquil, Talented Tenth.

BROWN, ROBIN LESLIE. Born January 18, in Canandaigua, NY. Graduate LIU. Debut 1980 OB in The Mother of Us All, followed by Yours Truly, Two Gentlemen of Verona, Taming of the Shrew, The Mollusc, The Contrast, Pericles, Andromache, Macbeth, Electra, She Stoops to Conquer, Berneice, Hedda Gabler, A Midsummer Night's Dream, Three Sisters, Major Barbara, The Fine Art of Finesse, 2 Schnitzler One-Acts, As You Like It, Ghosts, Chekhov Very Funny, God of Vengeance, Good Natured Man.

BROWN, ROO. Born July 22, 1932 in Pittsburgh, PA. Graduate Smith Col. Debut 1984 OB in A.. My Name is Alice, followed by A..My Name is Still Alice.

BROWN, WILLIAM SCOTT. Born March 27, 1959 in Seattle, WA. Attended U. WA. Debut 1986 OB in Juba, Bdwy in Phantom of the Opera (1988).

BROWNING, SUSAN. Born February 25, 1941 in Baldwin, NY. Graduate Penn. State. Bdwy debut 1963 in Love and Kisses, followed by Company for which she received a Theatre World Award, Goodtime Charley, Big River, OB in Jo, Dime a Dozen, Seventeen, The Boys from Syracuse, Collision Course, Whiskey, As You Like It, Removalists, Africanus Instructus, The March on Russia.

BRUSH, KEITH. Born October 20, 1961 in Columbus, OH. Graduate Thomas More Col., U. Cinn., RADA. Debut 1992 OB in Lake Street Extension.

BRYANT, DAVID. Born May 26, 1936 in Nashville, TN. Attended TN State U. Bdwy debut 1974 in Don't Play Us Cheap, followed by Bubbling Brown Sugar, Amadeus, Les Miserables, OB in Up in Central Park, Elizabeth and Essex, Appear and Show Cause.

BRYDON, W. B. Born September 20, 1933 in Newcastle, Eng. Debut 1962 OB in The Long and the Short and the Tall, followed by Live Like Pigs, Sgt. Musgrave's Dance, The Kitchen, Come Slowly Eden, The Unknown Soldier and His Wife, Moon for the Misbegotten, The Orphan, Possession, Total Abandon, Madwoman of Chaillot, The Circle, Romeo and Juliet, Philadelphia Here I Come, Making History, Spinoza, Mme. MacAdam Traveling Theatre, Bdwy in The Lincoln Mask, Ulysses in Nighttown, The Father.

BRYGGMAN, LARRY. Born December 21, 1938 in Concord, GA. Attended CCSF, Am. Th. Wing. Debut 1962 OB in A Pair of Pairs, followed by Live Like Pigs, Stop You're Killing Me, Mod Donna, Waiting for Godot, Ballymurphy, Marco Polo Sings a Solo, Brownsville Raid, Two Small Bodies, Museum, Winter Dancers, Resurrection of Lady Lester, Royal Bob, Modern Ladies of Guanabacoa, Rum and Coke, Bodies Rest and Motion, Blood Sports, Class 1 Acts, Spoils of War, Coriolanus, Prelude to a Kiss, Macbeth, Henry IV Parts 1 and 2, The White Rose, Nothing Sacred, As You Like It, Bdwy in Ulysses in Nighttown (1974), Checking Out, Basic Training of Pavlo Hummel, Richard III, Prelude to a Kiss.

BUELL, BILL. Born September 21, 1952 in Paipai, Taiwan. Attended Portland State U. Debut 1972 OB in Crazy Now, followed by Declassee, Lorenzaccio, Promenade, The Common Pursuit, Coyote Ugly, Alias Jimmy Valentine, Kiss Me Quick, Bad Habits, Groundhog, On the Bum, Bdwy in Once a Catholic (1979), The First, Welcome to the Club, The Miser, Taking Steps.

BULLOCK, ANGELA. Born July 5 in NYC. Graduate Hunter Co. Debut 1993 OB in Washington Square Moves, followed by John Brown.

BULOS, YUSEF. Born September 14, 1940 in Jerusalem. Attended American U., AADA. Debut 1965 OB with American Savoyards in rep, followed by Saints, The Trouble with Europe, The Penultimate Problem of Sherlock Holmes, In the Jungle of Cities, Hermani, Bertrano, Duck Variations, Insignificance, Panache, Arms and the Man,Tthe Promise, Crowbar, Hannah 1939, Strange Feet, Bdwy in Indians (1970), Capt. Brassbound's Conversion.

BURKE, MAGGIE. Born May 2, 1936 in Vay Shore, NY. Graduate Sarah Lawrence Col. OB in Today is Independence Day, Lovers and Other Strangers, Jules Feiffer's Cartoons, Fog, Home is the Hero, King John, Rusty & Rico and Lena, Friends, Butterfaces, Old Times, Man with a Raincoat, Hall of North American Forests, Carla's Folks, A Betrothal, Driving Miss Daisy, The Innocents Crusade, Approaching Zanzibar, Born Guilty, Bdwy in Brighton Beach Memoirs (1985), Cafe Crown.

BURK, TERENCE. Born August 11, 1947 in Lebanon, IL. Graduate S. IL. U. Bdwy debut 1976 in Equus, OB in Religion, The Future, Sacred and Profane Love, Crime and Punishment.

BURKHARDT, GERRY. Born June 14, 1946 in Houston, TX. Attended Lon Morris col. Bdwy debut 1968 in Her First Roman, followed by The Best Little Whorehouse in Texas, Crazy for You, OB in Girl Crazy, Leave it to Me.

BURNETT, ROBERT. Born February 28, 1960 in Goshen, NY. Attended HB Studio. Bdwy debut 1985 in Cats.

BURNHAM, MARGARET. Born May 29 in Gainsville, OH. Graduate Wooster Col. Debut 1988 OB in *Midsummer Night's Dream* followed by *Reckonings, The Former Mrs. Meis, Pericles, Love's Labour's Lost.*

BURRELL, FRED. Born September 18, 1936. Graduate UNC, RADA. Bdwy debut 1964 in Never Too Late, followed by Illya Darling, OB in The Memorandum, Throckmorton, Texas, Voices in the Head, Chili Queen, The Queen's Knight, In Pursuit of the Song of Hydrogen, Unchanging Love, More Fun Than Bowling, A Woman without a Name, The Sorrows of Fredrick, The Voice of the Prairie, Spain, Democracy and Esther.

BURRELL, PAMELA. Born August 4, 1945 in Tacoma, WA. Bdwy debut 1966 in *Funny Girl,* followed by *Where's Charley?, Strider, Sunday in the Park with George,* OB in *Arms and the Man* for which she received a Theatre World Award, *Berkeley Square, The Boss, Biography: A Game, Strider: Story of a Horse, A Little Madness, Spinoza, After the Dancing in Jericho.*

BURROWS, VINIE. Born November 15, 1928 in NYC. Graduate NJY. Bdwy in *The Wisteria Trees, Green Pastures, Mrs. Patterson, The Skin of Our Teeth,* OB in *Walk Together Children, Her Talking Drum, Sister Sister.*

BURSE-MICKLEBURY, DENISE. Born January 13 in Atlanta, GA. Graduate Spellman Col., Atlanta U. Debut 1990 OB in *Ground People* for which she received a Theatre World Award, followed by *A Worm in the Heart, Robert Johnson: Trick the Devil.*

BURSTEIN, DANNY. Born June 16, 1964 in NYC. Graduate UCal/San Diego. Moscow Art Theatre. Debut 1991 OB in The Rothschilds, A Weird Romance, Bdwy in A Little Hotel on the Side (1992). The Sea Gull, Saint Joan, Three Men on a Horse.

BURSTYN, MIKE. (Formerly Burstein) Born July 1, 1945 in the Bronx, NY. Bdwy debut 1968 in The Megilla of Itzak Manger followed by Inquest, Barnum, Ain't Broadway Grand, OB in Wedding in Shtetl, Prisoner of Second Avenue, The Rothschilds.

BURTON, ARNIE. Born September 22, 1958 in Emmett, ID. Graduate U. Ariz. Bdwy debut 1983 in *Amadeus,* OB in *Measure for Measure, Major Barbara, Schnitzler One Acts, Tartuffe, As You Like It, Ghosts, Othello, Moon for the Misbegotten.*

BURTON, KATE. Born September 10, 1957 in Geneva, Switz. Graduate Brown U., Yale. Bdwy debut 1982 in *Present Laughter,* followed by *Alice in Wonderland, Doonesbury, Wild Honey, Some Americans Abroad, Jake's Women,* OB in *Winners* for which she received a 1983 Theatre World Award, *Romeo and Juliet, The Accrington Pals, Playboy of the Western World, Measure for Measure.*

BUSCH, CHARLES. Born August 23, 1954 in New York City. Graduate Northwestern U. Debut OB 1985 in *Vampire Lesbians of Sodom,* followed by *Times Square Angel, Psycho Beach Party, The Lady in Question, Red Scare on Sunset,* all of which he wrote. The Charles Busch Revue.

BUSHMANN, KATE. Born October 6, 1961 in Ft. Smith, AR. Graduate Stephens Col. Debut 1992 OB in *Move It and It's Your's,* followed by *Roleplay.*

BUTT, JENNIFER. Born May 17, 1958 in Valparaiso, IN. Stephens Col. Graduate. Debut 1983 OB in The Robber Bridegroom, followed by Into the Closet, Bdwy in Les Miserables (1987).

BUTTERFIELD, CATHERINE. Born February 5 in NYC. Graduate SMU. Debut 1983 OB in *Marmalade Skies,* followed by *Bobo's Birthday, Joined at the Head.*

CAHN, LARRY. Born December 19, 1958 in Valparaiso, IN. Stephens Col. Graduate. Debut 1983 OB in The Robber Bridegroom, followed by Into the Closet, Bdwy in Les Miserables (1987).

CAIN, WILLIAM. Born May 27, 1931 in Tuscaloosa, AL. Graduate U. Wash., Catholic U. Debut 1962 OB in Red Roses for Me, followed by Jericho Jim Crow, Henry V, Antigone, Relatively Speaking, I Married an Angel in Concert, Buddha, Copperhead, Forbidden City, Fortinbras, Bdwy in Wilson in the Promise Land (1970), You Can't Take It with You, Wild Honey, The Boys in Autumn, Mastergate, A Streetcar Named Desire.

CALABRESE, MARIA. Born December 7, 1967 in Secone, PA. Bdwy debut 1991 in *The Will Rogers Follies, My Favorite Year.*

CALDWELL, ZOE. Born September 14, 1933 in Melbourne, Aust. Attended Methodist Ladies col. Bdwy debut 1965 in *The Devils,* followed by *Slapstick Tragedy* for which she received a Theatre World Award, *The Prime of Miss Jean Brodie, The Creation of the World and Other Business, Medea* (1982), OB in *Colette, Dance of Death, Long Day's Journey into Night, A Perfect Ganesh.*

CALLAWAY, LIZ. Born April 13, 1961 in Chicago, IL. Debut 1980 OB in Godspell, followed by The Matinee Kids, Brownstone, No Way to Treat a Lady, Marry Me a Little, 1-2-3-4-5, Bdwy in Merrily We Roll Along (1981), Baby, The Three Musketeers, Miss Saigon, Cats.

CALUD, ANNETTE Y. Born November 1963 in Milwaukee, WI. Graduate IL. Col. of Optometry. Bdwy debut 1991 in *Miss Saigon.*

CAMP, JOANNE. Born Apr. 4, 1951 in Atlanta, GA. Graduate Fl. Atlantic U., Geo. Wash. U. Debut 1981 OB in *The Dry Martini,* followed by *Geniuses* for which she received a Theatre World Award, *June Moon, Painting Churches, Merchant of Venice, Lady from the Sea, The Contrast, Coastal Disturbances, Andromache, Electra, Uncle Vanya, She Stoops to Conquer, Hedda Gabler, The Heidi Chronicles, Importance of Being Earnest, Medea, Three Sisters, A Midsummer Night's Dream, School for Wives, Measure for Measure, Dance of Death, Two Schnitzler One-Acts, Tartuffe, Lips Together Teeth Apart, As You Like It, Moon for the Misbegotten, Phaedra,* Bdwy in *The Heidi Chronicles* (1989).

CAMPBELL, AMELIA. Born August 4, 1965 in Montreal, Can. Graduate Syracuse U. Debut 1988 OB in *Fun,* followed by *Member of the Wedding, Tunnel of Love, Five Women Wearing the Same Dress,* Bdwy in *Our Country's Good* (1991), *A Small Family Business.*

CANAAN, ROBERT. Born January 30, 1963 in NYC. Graduate NYU. Debut 1988 OB in *Turpentine Twist,* followed by *Hunting Cockroaches, Nagasaki Muru, Stand-Ins,*

Cake & Sippin Whiskey, Bdwy in *Conversations with My Father* (1993).

CARABUENA, PHILIP LEE. Born October 18, 1986 in NYC. Bdwy debut 1991 in *Miss Saigon.*

CARHART, TIMOTHY. Born December 24, 1953 in Washington, DC. Graduate U. IL. Debut 1984 OB in The Harvesting, followed by The Ballad of Soapy Smith, Hitchhikers, Highest Standard of Living, Festival of 1-Acts, Bdwy in A Streetcar Named Desire (1992).

CARNAHAN, KIRSTI. Born June 29 in Evanston, IL. Attended U. Cinn. Bdwy debut 1983 in *Baby,* followed by *The Three Musketeers, Kiss of the Spider Woman,* OB in *Hang on to the Good Times, Mortally Fine.*

CARRADINE, KEITH. Born August 8, 1949 in San Mateo, CA. Attended Col. State U. Bdwy debut 1969 in *Hair,* followed by *Foxfire, The Will Rogers Follies,* OB in *Wake Up It's Time to Go to Bed.*

CARROLL, NANCY E. Born in Haverhill, MA. Graduate Cin. Convervatory. Debut 1990 OB in *Nunsense,* followed by *Balancing Act.*

CARROLL, PAT. Born May 5, 1927 in Shreveport, LA. Attended Catholic U. Debut 1950 OB in *Come What May* followed by *On the Town, Gertrude Stein Gertrude Stein,* Bdwy in *Catch a Star* (1955), *Dancing in the End Zone, The Show-Off.*

CARTER, CAITLIN. Born February 1 in San Francisco, CA. Graduate Rice U., NC School of Arts. Bdwy debut 1993 in *Ain't Broadway Grand.*

CARVER, BRENT. Born November 17, 1951 in Cranbrook, BC, Canada. Attended UBC. Bdwy debut 1993 in *Kiss of the Spider Woman* for which he received a Theatre World Award.

CASSIDY, DAVID. Born April 12, 1950 in NYC. Bdwy debut 1969 in *Fig Leaves Are Falling,* followed by *Joseph and the Amazing Technicolor Dreamcoat, Blood Brothers.*

CASSIDY, SHAUN. Born September 27, 1958 in Los Angeles, CA. Bdwy debut 1993 in *Blood Brothers.*

CASTANOS, LUZ. Born July 15, 1935 in NYC. Graduate CUNY. Debut 1959 OB in *Last Visit,* followed by *Eternal Sabbath, Finis for Oscar Wilde, Young and Fair, La Dama Duende, A Media Luz Los Tres, Yerma, Words Divine.*

CASTAY, LESLIE. Born December 11, 1963 in New Orleans, LA. Graduate Tulane U. Debut 1985 OB in *The Second Hurricane.* followed by *Too Many Girls, The Hunchback of Notre Dame,* Bdwy in *Threepenny Opera* (1989).

CAVISE, JOE ANTONY. Born January 7, 1958 in Syracuse, NY. Graduate Clark U. Debut 1981 OB in *Street Scene,* followed by Bdwy 1984 in *Cats.*

CEA, KIM. Born April 15, 1964 in Pittsburgh, PA. Graduate Point Park Col. Debut 1988 OB in *On the Prowl,* followed by *CBS Live.*

CERULLO, JONATHAN. Born December 21, 1960 in NYC. Graduate Emerson Col. Bdwy debut 1988 in *Legs Diamond,* followed by *Anna Karenina,* OB in *Gigi.*

CHAIKEN, STACIE. Born December 6 in Hagerstown, MD. Graduate U. Minn., U. Cal/Berkeley. Debut 1987 OB in *A Midsummer Night's Dream* followed by *Down in the Hole, Flaming Idiots, The Wise Men of Chelm.*

CHALFANT, KATHLEEN. Born January 14, 1945 in San Francisco, CA. Graduate Stanford U. Bdwy debut 1975 in *Dance with Me,* followed by *M. Butterfly, Angels in America,* OB in *Jules Feiffer's Hold Me, Killings on the Last Line, The Boor, Blood Relations, Signs of Life, Sister Mary Ignatius Explains it All, Actor's Nightmare, Faith Healer, All the Nice People, Hard Times, Investigation of the Murder in El Salvador, 3 Poets, The Crucible, The Party.*

CHAMBERLIN, KEVIN. Born November 25, 1963 in Baltimore, MD. Graduate Rutgers U., Debut 1990 OB in *Neddy,* followed by *Smoke on the Mountain,* Bdwy in *My Favorite Year* (1992).

CHAMPION, KELLY. Born February 14, 1952 in Syracuse, NY. Graduate Northwestern U. Debut 1982 OB in *Wives,* followed by *A Worm in the Heart.*

CHANNING, STOCKARD. Born February 13, 1944 in NYC. Attended Radcliffe Col. Debut 1970 in *Adaptation/Next,* followed by *The Lady and the Clarinet, The Golden Age, Woman in Mind, Six Degrees of Separation, The Normal Heart* (benefit reading) Bdwy in *Two Gentlemen of Verona, They're Playing Our Song, The Rink, Joe Egg, House of Blue Leaves, Six Degrees of Separation, Four Baboons Adoring the Sun.*

CHAPMAN, KAREN. Born February 29, 1960 in Virginia Beach, VA. Attended U. Del. Math/Eng. Debut 1989 OB in *Enrico IV,* Bdwy in *A Little Hotel on the Side* (1992).

CHARLES, WALTER. Born April 4, 1945 in East Stroudsburg, PA. Graduate Boston U. Bdwy debut 1973 in *Grease,* followed by *1600 Pennsylvania Avenue, Knickerbocker Holiday, Sweeney Todd, Cats, La Cage aux Folles, Aspects of Love, Me and My Girl, 110 in the Shade* (NYCO).

CHENG, KAM. Born March 28, 1969 in Hong Kong. Attended Muhlenberg Col. Bdwy debut 1991 in *Miss Saigon.*

CHO, SUNG YUN. Born April 24, 1971 in Seoul, Korea. Graduate SUNY/Puchase. Bdwy debut 1993 in *Redwood Curtain.*

CHONG, MARCUS. Born July 8, 1967 in Seattle, WA. Attended Santa Monica City Col. Bdwy debut 1990 in *Stand-Up Tragedy* for which he received a *Theatre World Award.*

CHRIS, MARILYN. Born May 19, 1939 in NYC. Bdwy debut 1966 in The Office, followed by Birthday Party, 7 Descents of Myrtle, Lenny, OB in Nobody Hears a Broken Drum, Fame, Juda Applause, Junebug Graduates Tonight, Man is Man, In the Jungle of Cities, Good Soldier Schweik, The Tempest, Ride a Black Horse, Screens, Kaddish, Lady from the Sea, Bread, Leaving Home, Curtains, Elephants, The Upper Depths, Man Enough, Loose Connections, Yard Sale, God of Vengeance.

CHRISTAKOS, JERRY. Born September 9, 1960 in Chicago, IL. Attended U. Ariz. Bdwy debut 1993 in *Kiss of the Spider Woman.*

CHRISTIAN, WILLIAM Born September 30, 1955 in Washington, DC. Graduate Catholic U. & American U. OB in *She Stoops to Conquer, A Sleep of Prisoners, American Voices, Member of the Wedding, Them That's Got.*

CHRISTOPHER, THOM. Born October 5, 1940 in Jackson Heights, NY. Attended Ithaca Col., Neighborhood Playhouse. Debut 1972 OB in *One Flew Over the Cuckoo's Nest*, followed by *Tamara, Investigation of the Murder in El Salvador, Sublime Lives*, Bdwy in *Emperor Henry IV* (1973), *Noel Coward in Two Keys* for which he received a Theatre World Award, *Caesar and Cleopatra*.

CHRYST, GARY. Born in 1959 in LaJolla, CA. Joined Joffrey Ballet in 1968. Bdwy debut 1979 in *Dancin*, followed by *A Chorus Line, Guys & Dolls*, OB in *One More Song One More Dance, Music Loves Me.*

CIULLA, CELESTE. Born September 10, 1967 in NYC. Graduate Northwestern U., Harvard. Debut 1992 OB in *Othello*, followed by *The Good Natured Man, Phaedra.*

CLANCY, JOE. Born November 3, 1962 in Springfield, MO. Graduate Catholic U. Debut 1992 in *Dog Logic.*

CLARK, PETULA. Born November 15, 1932 in Epson, Eng. Bdwy debut 1993 in *Blood Brothers.*

CLAVEAU, SHARON. Born November 8, 1949 in Duluth, MN. Attended U. Minn. Fordham. U. Debut 1992 OB in *Wuthering Heights.*

CLAYTON, LAWRENCE. Born September 10, 1956 in Mocksville, NC. Attended NC Central U. Debut 1980 in *Tambourines to Glory*, followed by *Skyline, Across the Universe, Two by Two, Romance in Hard Times, Juba, Tapestry*, Bdwy in *Dreamgirls* (1984), *High Rollers.*

CLOW, JAMES. Born April 15, 1965 in White Plains, NY. Graduate Syracuse U. LAMDA. Debut 1992 OB in *Juno*, Bdwy in *Blood Brothers* (1993).

COCKRUM, ROY. Born June 29, 1956 in Knoxville, TN. Graduate Northwestern U. Debut 1991 OB in *The Broken Pitcher*, followed by *Vampire Lesbians of Sodom, Red Scare on Sunset.*

COHEN, IAN. Born in Brooklyn, NY. Debut 1991 OB in *The Beauty Part*, followed by *Free Zone.*

COHEN, MARGERY. Born June 24, 1947 in Chicago, IL. Attended U. Wis, U. Chicago. Bdwy debut 1968 in *Fiddler on the Roof*, followed by *Jacques Brel is Alive*, OB in *Berlin to Broadway, By Bernstein, Starting Here Starting Now, Unsung Cole, Paris Lights, Pere Goriot, The Consuming Passions of Lydia Pinkham, Jacques Brel is Alive.*

COHEN, SAMUEL D. Born March 10, 1963 in Memphis, TN. Graduate Penn State. Debut 1989 OB in *The Witch*, followed by *Lover's Labour's Lost.*

COHENOUR, PATTI. Born September 17, 1952 in Albuquerque, NM. Attended U. NM. Bdwy debut 1982 in *A Doll's Life*, followed by *Pirates of Penzance, Big River, The Mystery of Edwin Drood, Phantom of the Opera*, OB in *La Boheme* for which she received a Theatre World Award.

COKAS, NICK. Born April 11, 1965 in San Francisco, CA. Graduate UCLA. Bdwy debut 1993 in *Blood Brothers.*

COLE, NORA. Born September 10, 1953 in Louisville, KY. Attended Beloit Col., Goodman School. Debut 1977 OB in *Movie Buff*, followed by *Cartoons for a Lunch Hour, Boogie-Woogie Rumble, Ground Hog*, Bdwy in *Your Arms Too Short to Box with God* (1982), *Inacent Black, Runaways, Jelly's Last Jam.*

COLLINS, COURTENAY. Born September 20 in Rome, GA. Graduate Converse Col., Juilliard. Debut 1992 OB in *Say Something Funny*, followed by *West Memphis Mojo, Life on the Third Rail, Campaigning Dames, A Rag on a Stick and a Star, Eating Raoul, The Cover of Life, Love's Labour's Lost.*

COLLINS, STEPHEN. Born October 1, 1947 in Des Moines, IA. Graduate Amherst Col. Bdwy debut 1972 in *Moonchildren*, followed by *No Sex Please We're British, The Ritz, Censored Scenes from King Kong, Loves of Anatol*, OB in *Twelfth Night, More Than You Deserve, Macbeth, The Last Days of British Honduras, BAM Co's New York Idea, Three Sisters, and The Play's the Thing, Beyond Therapy, One of the Guys, The Old Boy, Putting it Together.*

COLON, MIRIAM. Born in 1945 in Ponce, PR. Attended UPR, Actors Studio. Bdwy debut 1953 in *In the Summer House*, OB in *Me Candido, The OX Cart, The Passion of Antigona Perez, Julius Caesar, Fanlights, Simpson Street, The Boiler Room.*

CONNELL, JANE. Born October 27, 1925 in Berkeley, CA. Bdwy debut in New Faces of 1956, followed by Drat! The Cat!, Mame(1966/1983), Dear World, Lysistrata, Me and My Girl, Lend a Tenor, Crazy for You, OB in Shoestring Revue, Threepenny Opera, Pieces of Eight, Demi-Dozen, She Stoops to Conquer,, The Real Inspector Hound, The Rivals, The Rise and Rise of Daniel Rocket, Laughing Stock, The Singular Dorothy Parker, No No Nanette in Concert*

CONNELL, TIM. Born May 3, 1961 in Philadelphia, PA. Bdwy debut 1991 in *Nick and Nora*, OB in *Anyone Can Whistle, Pets, Sharon.*

CONOLLY, PATRICIA. Born August 29, 1933 in Tabora, E. Africa. Attended U. Sydney. With APA in *You Can't Take it with You,. Peace, School for Scandal, The Wild Duck, Right You Are, We Comrades Three, Pantagleize, Exit the King, The Cherry Orchard, The Misanthrope, The Cocktail Party, and Cock-a-doodle Dandy*, followed by *A Streetcar Named Desire, The Importance of Being Earnest, The Circle, A Small Family Business, The Real Inspector Hound, 15 Minute Hamlet*, OB in *Blithe Spirit, Woman in Mind.*

CONROY, FRANCES. Born in 1953 in Monroe, GA. Attended Dickinson Col., Juilliard, Neighborhood Playhouse. Debut 1978 OB with the Acting Co. in *Mother Courage, King Lear, and The Other Half*, followed by *All's Well That Ends Well, Othello, Sorrows of Stephen, Girls Girls Girls, Zastrozzi, Painting Churches, Uncle Vanya, Romance Language, To Gillian on Her 37th Birthday, Man and Superman, Zero Positive, Secret Rapture, Some Americans Abroad, Bright Room Called Day, Lips Together Apart, The Last Yankee, The Lady from Dubuque* (1980), *Our Town* (1989), *The Secret Rapture, Some Americans Abroad, Two Shakespearean Actors.*

CONWAY, KEVIN. Born May 29, 1941 in NYC. Debut 1968 in *Muzeeka*, followed by *Saved, The Plough and the Stars, One Flew Over the Cuckoo's Nest, When You Comin Back, Red Ryder, Long DayÆs Journey into Night, Other Places, King John*,

Other People's Money, The Man Who Fell in Love with His Wife, Ten Below, Bdwy in *Indians* (1969), *Moonchildren, Of Mice and Men, The Elephant Man.*

COOPER, CHUCK. Born November 8, 1954 in Cleveland, OH Graduate Ohio U. Debut 1982 OB in *Colored People's Time*, followed by *Riff Raff Revue, Primary English Class, Break/Agnes/Eulogy/Lucky* Bdwy in *Amen Corner* (1983), *Someone Who'll Watch Over Me.*

COPELAND, JOAN. Born June 1, 1922 in NYC. Attended Brooklyn Col., AADA. Debut 1945 OB in *Romeo and Juliet*, followed by *Othello, Conversation Piece, Delightful Season, End of Summer, American Clock, The Double Game, Isn't it Romantic? Hunting Cockroaches, Young Playwrights Festival, The American Plan, Rose Quartet, Another Time*, Bdwy in *Sundown Beach, Detective Story, Not for Children, Hatful of Fire, Something More, The Price, Two by Two, Pal Joey, Checking Out, The American Clock.*

COPOLA, SAM. Born July 31, 1935 in New Jersey. Attended Actors Studio. Debut 1968 OB in *A Present from Your Old Man*, followed by *Things That Almost Happen, Detective Story, Jungle of Cities, Pals, Fore!*, Bdwy in *The Caine Mutiny Court Martial* (1983).

CORBO, GEORGINA. Born September 21, 1965 in Havana, Cuba. Attended SUNY/Purchase. Debut 1988 OB in *Ariano*, followed by *Born to Rumba, Mambo Louie and the Dancing Machine.*

CORMIER, TONY. Born November 2, 1951 in Camp Roberts, CA. Attended Pierce Col., Wash. State U. Debut 1984 in *Kennedy at Colonus*, followed by *Something Cloudy Something Clear, Three Sisters*, OB *Love's Labour's Lost, Angel in the House.*

CORSAIR, BILL. Born September 5, 1940 in Providence, RI. Debut 1984 OB in *Ernie and Arnie*, followed by *In the Boom Boom Room, The Constituent, New Jersey/New York.*

COUNCIL, RICHARD E. Born October 1, 1947 in Tampa, FL. Graduate U. Fl. Debut 1973 OB in *Merchant of Venice*, followed by *Ghost Dance, Look We've Come Through. Arms and the Man, Isadora Duncan Sleeps with the Russian Navy, Arthur, The Winter Dancer, The Prevalence of Mrs. Seal, Jane Avril, Young Playwrights Festival, Sleeping Dogs, The Good Coach, Subfertile*, Bdwy in *Royal Family* (1975), *Philadelphia Story, I'm Not Rappaport, Conversations with My Father.*

COUNTRYMAN, MICHAEL. Born September 15, 1955 in St. Paul, MN. Graduate Trinity Col., AADA. Debut 1983 OB in *Changing Palettes*, followed by *June Moon, Terra Nova, Out!, Claptrap, The Common Pursuit, Woman in Mind, Making Movies, The Tempest, Tales of the Lost Formicans, Marathon '91, The Stick Wife, Lips Together Teeth Apart*, Bdwy in *A Few Good Men* (1990), *Face Value.*

COWLING, GARY. Born November 4, 1961 in Newport News, Va. Graduate William & Mary Col., West Va. U. Debut 1987 OB in *Spoon River*, followed by *Billy Budd, Love's Labour's Lost, Comedy of Errors, School for Scandal, Othello, Off the Beat and Path 2.*

CRAMPTON, GLORY. Born March 30, 1964 in Rockville Center, NY. Graduate NYU. Debut 1988 OB in *The Fantasticks*, followed by *Carnival.*

CREAGHAN, DENNIS. Born May 1, 1942 in London, England. Attended Hofstra U., HB Studio. Debut 1973 OB in *Hamlet*, followed by *The Tempest, Edward II, The Servant, Pterodactyls*, Bdwy in *The Elephant Man* (1979).

CRIVELLO, ANTHONY. Born Aug 2, 1955 in Milwaukee, WI. Bdwy debut 1982 in *Evita*, followed by *The News, Les Miserables*, OB in *The Juniper Tree, The Spider Woman.*

CROMWELL, J.T. Born March 4, 1935 in Ann Arbor, MI. Graduate U. Cinn. Bdwy debut 1965 in *Half a Sixpence*, followed by *Jacques Brel is Alive..., 1600 Pennsylvania Avenue*, OB in *Pageant.*

CROUSE, LINDSAY. Born May 12, 1948 in New York City. Graduate Radcliffe Col. Bdwy debut 1972 in *Much Ado About Nothing*, followed by *A Christmas Carol*, OB in *The Foursome, Fishing, Long Day's Journey into Night, Total Recall, Father's Day, Hamlet, Reunion, Twelfth Night, Childe Byron, Richard II, Serenading Louie, Prairie/Shawl, The Stick Wife*, Bdwy 1991 in *The Homecoming* for which she received a Theatre World Award.

CROXTON, DARRYL. Born April 5, 1948 in Baltimore, MD. Attended AADA. Bdwy debut 1969 in *Indians* followed by *Sly Fox, Hamlet*, OB in *Volpone, Murder in the Cathedral, The Taking of Miss Janie, The Glorious Monstef, MacBeth, Julius Caesar, Cabal of Hypocrites, De Obeah Mon, Jack Gelber's New Play, Threepenny Opera, Benito Cereno, Rehearsal.*

CRUTCHFIELD, BUDDY. Born June 4, 1957 in Dallas, TX. Graduate SMU. Debut 1979 *Radio City Christmas Spectacular*, followed by OB *HMS Pinafore, Pirates of Penzance, Tent Show, A Church is Born, Senior Discretion, The Widow Clair, Six Wives*, Bdwy in *The Most Happy Fella* (1992).

CRUZ, FRANCIS J. Born September 4, 1954 in Long Beach, CA. Attended F.I.D.M. Bdwy debut 1991 in *Miss Saigon.*

CULLITON, JOSEPH. Born January 25, 1948 in Boston, MA. Attended Cal State U. Debut 1982 OB in *Francis*, followed by *Flirtations, South Pacific (LC), Julius Caesar, King John, Company, On a Clear Day*, Bdwy 1987 in *Broadway.*

CULLIVER, KAREN. Born December 30, 1959 in Florida. Attended Stetson U. Bdwy debut 1983 in *Show Boat* followed by *The Mystery of Edwin Drood, Meet Me in St. Louis, Phantom of the Opera*, OB in *The Fantasticks.*

CUNNINGHAM, JOHN. Born June 22, 1932 in Auburn, NY. Graduate Yale, Dartmouth U. OB in *Love Me a Little, Pimpernel, The Fantasticks, Love and Let Love, The Bone Room, Dancing in the Dark, Father's Day, Snapshot, Head Over Heels, Quartermaine's Terms, Wednesday, On Approval, Miami, Perfect Party, Birds of Paradise, Six Degrees of Separation*, Bdwy in *Hot Spot* (1963), *Zorba, Company, 1776, Rose, The Devil's Disciple, Six Degrees of Separation, Anna Karenina, The Sisters Rosensweig.*

CUNNINGHAM, T. SCOTT. Born December 15 in Los Angeles, CA. Graduate NC School of Arts. Debut 1992 OB in *Pterodactyls*, followed by *Takes on Women.*

CURLESS, JOHN. Born September 16 in Wigan, Eng. Attended Central Schl. of Speech. NY debut 1982 OB in *The Entertainer,* followed by *Sus, Up 'n' Under, Progress, Prin, Nightingale, Absent Friends, Owners/Traps,* Bdwy in *A Small Family Business* (1992).

CURRY, TIM. Born April 19, in 1947 in Cheshire, England. Attended U. Birmingham. Bdwy debut 1975 in *The Rocky Horror Show,* followed by *Travesties, Amadeus, Me and My Girl, My Favorite Year,* OB in *The Art of Success.*

CURTIS, KEENE. Born February 15, 1925 in Salt Lake City UT. Graduate U. Utah. Bdwy debut 1949 in *Shop at Sly Corner,* with *APA in School for Scandal, The Tavern, Anatole, Scapin, Right You Are, Importance of Being Earnest, Twelfth Night, King Lear, Seagull, Lower Depths, Man and Superman, Judith, War and Peace, You Can't Take It with You, Pantaglieze, Cherry Orchard, Misanthrope, Cocktail Party, Cock-a-Doodle Dandy, Hamlet, A Patriot for Me, The Rothschilds, Night Watch, Via Galactica, Annie, Division Street, La Cage aux Folles,* OB in *Colette, Ride Across Lake Constance, The Cocktail Hour.*

CWIKOWSKI, BILL. Born August 4, 1945 in Newark, NJ. Graduate Smith and Monmouth Col. Debut 1972 OB in *Charlie the Chicken,* followed by *Summer Brave, The Desperate Hours, Mandrogola, Two by Noonan, Soft Touch, Innocent Pleasures, 3 from the Marathon, Two Part Harmony, Bathroom Plays, Little Victories, Dolphin Position, Cabal of Hypocrites, Split Second, Rose Cottages, The Good Coach, Marathon '88, Tunnel of Love.*

DAHLIA, RICHARD. Born May 22 in Peekskill, NY. Attended West Chester CC. Debut 1984 OB in *Sacraments* followed by *Trumpets and Drums, Night Watch, The Jew of Malta, The Knights of the Round Table.*

DAILY, DANIEL. Born July 25, 1955 in Chicago, IL. Graduate Notre Dame, U. Wash. Debut 1988 OB in *Boy's Breath,* followed by *A Ronde, Iron Bars, Chekhov Very Funny, Macbeth, As You Like It, Free Zone.*

DALEY, R.F. Born April 16, 1955 in Denver, Co. Attended N. Co. U. Bdwy debut 1988 in *Chess,* followed by *Sweeney Todd, Guys and Dolls.*

DALY, JOSEPH. Born April 7, 1944 in Oakland, CA. Debut 1959 OB in *Dance of Death,* followed by *Roots, Sgt. Musgrave's Dance, Viet Rock, Dark of the Moon, Shadow of a Gunman, Hamlet, The Ride Across Lake Constance, A Doll's House, Native Bird, Yeats Trio, Mecca, Marching to Georgia, Comedians, A Country of Old Men, Falsies, Taming of the Shrew, Working One Acts, The Window Man,* Bdwy in *Mastergate* (1989).

DALY, TYNE. Born February 21, 1947 in Madison, WI. Attended Brandeis U., AMDA, Debut 1966 OB in *The Butter and Egg Man followed by A Christmas Memory,* Bdwy in *That Summer That Fall* (1967), *Gypsy* (1989/1991), *The Sea Gull* (1992).

DANNER, BRADEN. Born in 1976 in Indianapolis, IN. Bdwy debut 1984 in *Nine,* followed by *Oliver!, Starlight Express, Les Miserables,* OB in *Genesis.*

DANSON, RANDY. Born April 30, 1950 in Plainfield NJ. Graduate Carnegie-Mellon U. Debut 1978 OB in *Gimme Shelter,* followed by *Big and Little, The Winter Dancers, Time Steps, Casualties, Red and Blue, The Resurrection of Lady Lester, Jazz Poets at the Grotto, Plenty, Macbeth, Blue Window, Cave Life, Romeo and Juliet, One-Act Festival, Mad Forest.*

DANZA, TONY. Born April 21, 1951 in Brooklyn, NY. Attended U. Dubuque. Debut 1993 OB in *Wrong Turn at Lungfish.*

D'ARCY, MARY. Born in 1956 in Yardville, NJ. Graduate Glassboro State Col. Bdwy debut 1980 in *The Music Man* followed by *Sunday in the Park with George, The Phantom of the Opera,* OB in *Florodora, Upstairs at O'Neal's, Backers Audition.*

DAUGHERTY, BILL. Born April 5, 1961 in St. Louis, MO. Graduate Webster U. Debut 1990 OB in *Daugherty & Field Off Broadway,* followed by *Over the Rainbow.*

DAVID, KEITH. Born May 8, 1954 in NYC, Julliard Graduate. Debut 1979 OB in *Othello,* followed by *The Haggadah, Pirates of Penzance, Macbeth, Coriolanus, Titus Andronicus,* Bdwy in *Jelly's Last Jam* (1992).

DAVIS, BRUCE ANTHONY. Born March 4, 1959 in Dayton, OH. Attended Juilliard. Bdwy debut 1979 in *Dancin',* followed by *Big Deal, A Chorus Line, High Rollers,* OB in *Carnival.*

DAVIS, HOPE. Born March 23, 1964 in Englewood, NJ. Graduate Vassar Col. Debut 1991 OB in *Can-Can. Goodnight Desdemona, Pterodactyls,* followed by Bdwy in *Two Shakespearean Actors* (1991).

DAVIS, MAC. Born January 21, 1942 in Lubbock, TX. Attended Emory U. Bdwy debut 1992 in *The Will Rogers Follies.*

DAVIS, MARY BOND. Born June 3, 1958 in Los Angeles, CA. Attended Cal. State U./Northridge, LACC. Debut 1985 in *Trousers,* Bdwy in *Mail* (1988), *Jelly's Last Jam.*

DAVIS, MELISSA ANNE. Born November 14 in Nashville, TN. Attended Belmont U. Bdwy debut 1990 in *Les Miserables.*

DAVYS, EDMUND C. Born January 21, 1947 in Nashua, NH. Graduate Oberlin Col. Debut 1977 OB in *Othello,* Bdwy in *Crucifer of Blood* (1979), *Shadowlands, A Small Family Business, The Show-off, St. Joan, Three Men on a Horse.*

DAWSON, DAVID. Born February 22, 1922 in Brooklyn, NY. Debut 1965 OB in *Hogan's Goat* followed by *Some Rain, About Face July Festival, Homesick, Tom and Viv,* Bdwy in The Freaking Out of Stephanie Blake(1967).

DAWSON, SUZANNE. Born January 19, 1951 in Montreal, Canada. Debut 1980 OB in *Chase a Rainbow,* followed by *New Faces of 1952, The Last Musical Comedy, The Great American Backstage Musical, CBS Live,* Bdwy in *Rumors* (1988).

DEAN, LAURA. Born May 27, 1963 in Smithtown, NY. Debut 1973 OB in *The Secret Life of Walter Mitty,* followed by *A Village Romeo and Juliet, Carousel, Hey Rube, Landscape of the Body, American Passion, Feathertop, Personals, Godspell, Festival of One-Acts, Catch Me If I Fall, A..., My Name is Still Alice,* Bdwy in *Doonesbury* (1983), for which she received a Theatre World Award.

DEAN, LOREN. Born July 31, 1969 in Las Vegas, NV. Debut 1989 OB in *Amulets against the Dragon Forces,* for which he received a Theatre World Award, followed by *Beggars in the House of Plenty.*

DeGONGE, MARCY. Born May 4, 1957 in Newark, NJ. Graduate Hart Col. Bdwy debut 1989 in *Cats.*

DELAINE, SHERI. Born September 15, 1953 in Iron wood, MI. Graduate U. Wisc. Debut 1988 OB in *Tartuffe* followed by *French Gray, Pericles, The Rover, Zastrozzi, Shaviana, Off the Beat and Path 2.*

DELLA PIAZZA, DIANE. Born September 3, 1962 in Pittsburgh, PA. Graduate Cincinnati Consv. Bdwy debut 1987 in *Les Miserables.*

DeMUNN, JEFFREY. Born April 15, 1947 in Buffalo, NY. Graduate Union Col. Debut 1975 OB in *Augusta* followed by *A Prayer for My Daughter, Modigliani, Chekhov Sketchbook, A Midsummer Night's Dream, Total Abandon, The Country Girl, Hands Of Its Enemy, One Shoe Off,* Bdwy in *Comedians* (1976), *Bent, K2, Sleight of Hand, Spoils of War.*

DePAUL, JULIE. Born June 7 in North Canton, OH. Graduate Ohio State U., Southern Methodist U. Debut 1993 OB in *Widowers Houses.*

DeRAEY, DANIEL. Born April 2, 1946 in NYC. Graduate Fordham U. Debut 1979 OB in *Class Enemy* followed by *The Return of Pinocchio, Nothing Sacred.*

DeSHIELDS, ANDRE. Born January 12, 1946 in Baltimore, MD. Graduate U. Wis. Bdwy debut 1973 in *Warp,* followed by *Rachel Lily Rosenbloom, The Wiz, Ain't Misbehavin'* (1978/1988), *Haarlem Nocturne, Just So, Stardust, OB in 2008-1/2, Jazzbo Brown, The Soldier's Tale, The Little Prince, Haarlem Nocturne, Sovereign State of Boogedy Boogedy, Kiss Me When It's Over, Saint Tous, Ascension Day, Casino Paradise, The Wiz.*

DeVRIES, JON. Born March 26, 1947 in NYC. Graduate Bennington Col., Pasadena Playhouse. Debut 1977 OB in *The Cherry Orchard,* followed by *Agamemnon, The Ballad of Soapy Smith, Titus Andronicus, The Dreamer Examines his Pillow, Sight Unseen Patient A,* Bdwy in *The Inspector General, Devour the Snow, Major Barbara, Execution of Justice.*

DeWOLF, CECILIA. Born May 9, 1952 in Glen Cove, NY. Graduate Denver U. PennState U., Columbia OB in *Beautiful Dreamer* (1986), followed by *Family Life, Julie Johnson, EST Marathon 93, Jackie.*

DIENER, JOAN. Born February 24, 1934 in Cleveland, OH. Attended Sarah Lawrence Col., Bdwy debut 1948 in *Small Wonder,* followed by *Season in the Sun, Kismet,* for which she received a Theatre World Award, *Cry for Us All, Man of LaMancha* (1965/1992), *Home Sweet Home.*

DILLON, MIA. Born July 9, 1955 in Colorado Springs, CO. Graduate Penn State U. Bdwy debut 1977 in *Equus,* followed by *Da, Once a Catholic, Crimes of the Heart, The Corn is Green, Hay Fever, The Miser,* OB in *The Crucible, Summer, Waiting for the Parade, Crimes of the Heart, Fables for Friends, Scenes from La Vie de Boheme, Three Sisters, Wednesday, Roberta in Concert, Come Back Little Sheba, Vienna Notes, George White's Scandals, Lady Moonsong, Mr. Monsoon, Almost Perfect, The Aunts, Approximating Mother, Remembrance, Lauren's Whereabouts.*

DiPASQUALE, FRANK. Born July 15, 1955 in Whitestone, NY. Graduate USC. Bdwy debut in *La Cage aux Folles* (1983), followed by *Radio City Christmas Spectacular 1990, The Secret Garden,* OB in *Theda Bara and the Frontier Rabbi.*

DIVENY, MARY. Born in Elmira, NY. Attended Elmira Col., AADA. Bdwy debut 1946 in *The Playboy of the Western World,* followed by *Crime and Punishment, Life with Mother,* OB in *The Matchmaker, Marvin's Room.*

DIXON, ED. Born September 2, 1948 in Oklahoma. Attended U. Okla. Bdwy in *The Student Prince,* followed by *No No Nanette, Rosalie in Concert, The Three Musketeers, Les Miserables,* OB in *By Bernstein, King of the Schnorrers, Rabboni, Moby Dick, Shylock, Johnny Pye and the Foolkiller.*

DOERR, MARK. Born July 6, 1965 in Ann Arbor, MI. Graduate U. Mich. Juilliard. Debut 1991 OB in *Unchanging Love,* followed by *Rodgers & Hart: A Celebration, The Perpetrator, Sharon,* Bdwy in *The Visit* (1992).

DOHI, SYLVIA. Born Feb. 2, 1965 in Hollywood, Ca. Attended UCLA, Portland CC. Bdwy debut 1991 in *Miss Saigon.*

DOTRICE, ROY. Born May 26, 1925 in Guernsey, Channel Islands. Bdwy debut 1967 in *Brief Lives,* followed by *A Return Engagement in 1974, Mr. Lincoln, A Life, Hay Fever, The Homecoming,* OB in *An Enemy of the People, The Best of Friends.*

DOUGLAS, DIANA. Born January 22, 1923 in Devonshire, Bermuda. Attended American Academy. Bdwy debut 1953 in *Sabrina Fair,* followed by *The Highest Tree, Critics Choice, Cactus Flower, Everything in the Garden,* OB in *Best of Friends.*

DOWNING, REBECCA. Born November 30, 1962 in Birmingham, AL. Graduate Oklahoma City U. Debut 1989 OB in *Wonderful Town,* Bdwy in *The Will Rogers Follies* (1991).

DOYLE, JACK. Born June 7, 1954 in Brooklyn, NY. Graduate Adelphi U. Debut OB in *New Faces* followed by *Tomfoolery,* Bdwy in The Will Rogers Follies (1991).

DRAKE, DAVID. Born June 27, 1963 in Baltimore, Md. Attended Essex Col., Peabody Consv. Debut 1984 in *Street Theatre,* followed by *Pretty Boy, Vampire Lesbians of Sodom, The Life, The Night Larry Kramer Kissed Me, Pageant, The Normal Heart* (benefit reading).

DUDLEY, CRAIG. Born January 22, 1945 in Sheepshead Bay, NY. Graduate AADA, AmThWing. Debut 1970 OB in *Macbeth,* followed by Zou, *I Have Always Believed in Ghosts, Othello, War and Peace, Dial "M" for Murder, Misalliance, Crown of Kings, Trelawny of 'the Wells, Ursula's Permanent.*

DUELL, WILLIAM. Born August 30, 1923 in Corinth, NY. Attended Il. Wesleyan, Yale. OB 1962 in *Portrait of the Artist as a Young Man/Barroom Monks,* followed by *A Midsummer Night's Dream, Henry IV, Taming of the Shrew, The Memorandum, Threepenny Opera, Loves of Cass Maguire, Romance Language, Hamlet, Henry IV (I & II), On the Bum,* Bdwy in *A Cook for Mr. General, Ballad of the Sad Cafe, Ilya Darling, 1776, Kings, Stages, The Inspector General, The Marriage of Figaro, Our Town.*

DUKAKIS, OLYMPIA. Born June 20, 1931 in Lowell, MA. Debut 1960 OB in *The Breaking Wall,* followed by *Nourish the Beast, Curse of the Starving Class, Snow Orchid, The Marriage of Bette and Boo, A Christmas Memory,* Bdwy in *The Aspern Papers* (1962), *Abraham Cochran, Who's Who in Hell, Social Security.*

DUKES, DAVID. Born June 6, 1945 in San Francisco, CA. Attended Mann Col. Bdwy debut 1971 in *School for Wives*, followed by *Don Juan, The Play's the Thing, The Visit, Chemin de Fer, Holiday, Rules of the Game, Love for Love, Travesties, Dracula, Bent, Amadeus, M. Butterfly, Love Letters, Someone Who'll Watch over Me*, OB in *Rebel Women*.

DUNNE, GRIFFIN. Born June 8, 1955 in NYC. Attended Neighborhood Playhouse. Debut 1974 OB in *White Album*, followed by *Coming Attractions, Hooters*, Bdwy in *Search and Destroy* for which he received a Theatre World Award.

DURANG, CHRISTOPHER. Born January 2, 1949 in Montclair, NJ. Graduate Harvard, Yale. Debut 1976 OB in *Das Lusitania Songspiel*, followed by *The Hotel Play, Sister Mary Ignatius Explains It All, The Birthday Present, The Marriage of Bette and Boo, Laughing Wild, Ubu, Putting It Together, A Christmas Memory*.

DuSOLD, ROBERT. Born June 7, 1959 in Waukesha, WI. Attended U. Cinn. Consv. Bdwy debut in *Les Miserables* (1991).

EAGAN, DAISY. Born November 4, 1979 in Brooklyn, NY. Attended Neighborhood Playhouse. Debut 1988 OB in *Tiny Tim's Christmas Carol*, followed by *The Little Prince*, Bdwy in *Les Miserables* (1989), *The Secret Garden*.

EARLE, DÔTTIE. Born October 6, 1962 in Norwalk, CT. Graduate U. Mass. Debut 1989 OB in *Up Against It, Radio City Christmas Spectacle*, Bdwy in *The Will Rogers Follies* (1993)

EASTLY, KEELY. Born February 18, 1957 in New Albany, IN. Attended U. Nev. Debut 1981 OB in *The Lesson*, followed by *I Am a Camera, Flesh Flash and Frank Harris, Journal of Albion Moonlight, Split, Walking the Blonde, Tales from Hollywood*.

EDELMAN, GREGG. Born September 12, 1958 in Chicago, IL. Graduate Northwestern U. Bdwy debut 1982 in *Evita*, followed by *Oliver!, Cats, Cabaret, City of Angels, Falsettos, Anna Karenina*, OB in *Weekend, Shop on Main Street, Forbidden Broadway, She Loves Me, Babes in Arms*.

EDWARDS, NAZ (formerly Nazig). Born February 2, 1952 in Philadelphia, PA. Debut 1981 OB in *Oh Johnny!*, followed by *Olympus on My Mind*, Bdwy in *Zorba, Anna Karenina*.

EIGENBERG, DAVID M. Born May 17, 1964 in Manhasset, NY. Graduate AADA. Debut 1989 OB in *Young Playwright's Festival/Finnagan's Funeral Parlor & Ice Cream Shop*, followed by *Six Degrees of Separation, The My House Play, EST Marathon '92, Tunnel of Love*, Bdwy in *Six Degrees of Separation* (1990).

EIKENBERRY, JILL. Born January 21, 1947 in New Haven, Ct. Attended Yale U. Bdwy debut 1972 in *Moonchildren*, followed by *Uncommon Women and Others, Watch on the Rhine, Onward Victoria, Holiday*, OB in *Saints* (1976), *Porch*.

EISNER, JOHN. Born December 13, 1959 in NYC. Graduate Amherst, Nt'l Theatre Consv. Debut 1987 OB in *The Dybbuk*, followed by *Mississippi Crossing, Romeo and Juliet, Come as You Are, The Male Animal, King of Hearts, Bedroom Farce*.

ELDARD, RON. Born in 1964 in New York City. Attended HS Performing Arts. Bdwy debut 1986 in *Biloxi Blues*, OB in *Tony 'n' Tina's Wedding*, followed by *Servy-n-Bernice 4 Ever, The Years, Aven'U Boys*.

ELDER, DAVID. Born July 7, 1966 in Houston, TX. Attended U. Houston. Bdwy debut 1992 in *Guys and Dolls*.

ELLIS, BRAD. Born September 5, 1960 in Lexington, MA. Attended Berklee Col. Debut 1990 OB in *Forbidden Broadway, Forbidden Broadway 10th Anniversary Forbidden Broadway 1993*.

ENGEL, DAVID. Born September 19, 1959 in Orange, CA. Attended U. Cal/Irvine. Bdwy debut 1983 in *La Cage aux Folles*, OB in *Forever Plaid*.

ERBE, KATHRYN. Born in 1965 in NYC. Graduate NYU. Bdwy debut 1990 in *Grapes of Wrath*, followed by *The Speed of Darkness*, OB in T*he My House Play, Down the Shore*.

ERRICO, MELISSA. Born March 23, 1970 in NYC. Graduate Yale U. BADA. Bdwy debut 1992 in *Anna Karenina*, OB in *After Crystal Night, Spring Awakening*.

ESHELMAN, DREW. Born October 12, 1946 in Long Beach, CA. Graduate Shimer Col., AmCons Th. Broadway debut 1987 in *Les Miserables*.

ESPINOSA, BRANDON. Born August 9, 1982 in Queens, NYC. Bdwy debut 1993 in *The Will Rogers Follies*.

ESPOSITO, GIANCARLO. Born April 26, 1958 in Copenhagen, Den. Bdwy debut 1968 in *Maggie Flynn*, followed by *The Me Nobody Knows, Lost in the Stars, Seesaw, Merrily We Roll Along, Don't Get God Started, 3 Penny Opera*, OB in *Zooman and the Sign* for which he received a 1981 Theatre World Award, *Keyboard, Who Loves the Dancer, House of Ramon Iglesias, Do Lord Remember Me, Balm in Gilead, Anchorman, Distant Fires, The Root*.

ESTABROOK, CHRISTINE. Born September 13 in Erie, PA. OB credits include *Pastorale, Win/Lose/Draw, Ladyhouse Blues, Baby with the Bathwater, Blue Windows, North Shore Fish, The Boys Next Door, For Dear Life, The Widow's Blind Date, What a Man Weighs*, Bdwy in *I'm Not Rappaport* (1978), *The Sisters Rosensweig*.

ESTERMAN, LAURA. Born April 12 in NYC. Attended Radcliffe Col., LAMDA. Debut 1969 OB in *The Time of Your Life*, followed by *Pig Pen, Carpenters, Ghosts, Macbeth, The Sea Gull, Rubbers, Yankees 3 Detroit 0, Golden Boy, Out of Our Father's House, The Master and Margarita, Chinchilla, Dusa, Fish, Stas and Vi, A Midsummer Night's Dream, The Recruiting Officer, Oedipus the King, Two Fish in the Sky, Mary Barnes, Tamar, Marvin's Room*, Bdwy in *Waltz of the Toreadors, The Show-off*.

ESTEY, SUELLEN. Born November 21 in Mason City, IA. Graduate Stephens Col., Northwestern U. Debut 1970 OB in *Some Other Time*, followed by *June Moon, Buy Bonds Buster, Smile Smile Smile, Carousel, Lullaby of Broadway, I Can't Keep Running, The Guys in the Truck, Stop the World..., Bittersuite—One More Time, Passionate Extremes, Sweeney Todd, Love in Two Countries*, Bdwy in *The Selling of the President* (1972), *Barnum, Sweethearts in Concert, Sweeney Todd* (1989).

EVANS, HARVEY. Born January 7, 1941 in Cincinnati, OH. Bdwy debut 1957 in *New Girl in Town*, followed by *West Side Story, Redhead, Gypsy, Anyone Can Whistle,*

Hello Dolly!, George M!, Our Town, The Boy Friend, Follies, Barnum, La Cage aux Folles, OB in *Sextet, Annie Warbucks*.

EWING, GEOFFREY C. Born August 10, 1951 in Minneapolis, MN. Graduate U. Minn. Bdwy debut 1983 in *Guys in the Truck*, followed by *Cork*, OB in *The Leader/The Bald Soprano, Ali*.

FABER, RON. Born February 16, 1933 in Milwaukee, WI. Graduate Marquette U., OB Debut 1959 in *An Enemy of the People*, followed by *The Exception* and the *Rule, America Hurrah, They Put Handcuffs on Flowers, Dr. Selavy's Magic Theatre, Troilus and Cressida, The Beauty Part, Woyzeck, St. Joan of the Stockyards, Jungle of Cities, Scenes from Everyday Life, Mary Stuart, 3 by Pirandello, Times and Appetites of Toulouse-Lautrec, Hamlet, Johnstown Vendicator, Don Juan of Seville, Between the Acts, Baba Goya, Moving Targets, Arturo Ui, Words Divine*, Bdwy in *Medea* (1973), *First Monday in October*.

FAIR, TONY. Born May 18, 1962 in NYC. Attended Fordham U. Debut 1992 OB in *Lightin' Out*.

FALK, WILLY. Born July 21 in New York City. Harvard, LAMDA graduate. Debut 1982 OB in *The Robber Bridegroom*, followed by *Pacific Overtures, The House in the Woods, Elizabeth and Essex*, Bdwy in *Marilyn: An American Fable, Starlight Express, Les Miserables, Miss Saigon*.

FARDON, JOSHUA. Born October 23, 1965 in Kansas City, MO. Graduate Yale U., Northwestern U. Debut 1991 OB in *Othello*, followed by *Scapin*.

FARINA, MARILYN J. Born April 9, 1947 in New York City. Graduate Sacred Heart Col. Debut 1985 OB in *Nunsense*.

FARINA, MICHAEL. Born August 22, 1958 in The Bronx, NY. Attended NY Inst. of Techn., Mercy Col., Bdwy debut 1990 in *Fiddler on the Roof*, OB in *Gifts of the Magi*.

FAUGNO, RICHARD (Rick). Born November 8, 1978 in New York City. Bdwy debut 1991 in *The Will Rogers Follies*, followed by *Conversations with my Father*.

FAYE, JOEY. Born July 12, 1910 in NYC. Bdwy debut 1938 in *Sing Out the News*, followed by *Room Service, Meet the People, The Man Who Came to Dinner, The Milky Way, Boy Meets Girl, Streets of Paris, Allah Be Praised, The Duchess Misbehaves, Tidbits of 1948, High Button Shoes, Top Banana, Tender Trap, Man of La Mancha, 70 Girls 70, Grind, 3 Men on a Horse*, OB in *Lyle, Naomi Court, Awake and Sing, Coolest Cat in Town, The Ritz, Enter Laughing, 1-2-3-4-5*.

FAYE, PASCALE. Born January 6, 1964 in Paris, France. Bdwy debut 1991 in *Grand Hotel*, followed by *Guys and Dolls*.

FEAGAN, LESLIE. Born January 9, 1951 in Hinckley, OH. Graduate Ohio U., Debut 1978 OB in *Can-Can*, followed by *Merton of the Movies, Promises Promises, Mowgli*, Bdwy in *Anything Goes* (1978), *Guys and Dolls*.

FELDON, BARBARA. Born March 12, 1941 in Pittsburgh, PA. Attended Carnegie Tech. Bdwy debut 1960 in *Caligula*, followed by *Past Tense*, OB in *Faces of Love/Portrait of America, Cut the Ribbons*.

FELDSHUH, TOVAH. Born December 28, 1953 in New York City. Graduate Sarah Lawrence Col., U. Minn. Bdwy debut 1973 in *Cyrano*, followed by *Dreyfus in Rehearsal, Rodgers and Hart, Yentl* for which she received a Theatre World Award, *Sarava, Lend Me a Tenor*, OB in *Yentl the Yeshiva Boy, Straws in the Wind, Three Sisters, She Stoops to Conquer, Springtime for Henry, The Time of Your Life, Children of the Sun, The Last of the Red Hot Lovers, Mistress of the Inn, A Fierce Attachment, Custody, Six Wives, Hello Muddah Hello Faddah*.

FERGUSON, LOU. Born August 8, 1944 in Trinidad, W.I. Debut 1970 OB in *A Season in the Congo*, followed by *Night World, La Gente, Shoe Shine Parlor, The Defense, Rum an' Coca Cola, Remembrance, Raisin in the Sun, Member of the Wedding, Playboy of the West Indies*.

FERLAND, DANIELLE. Born January 31, 1971 in Derby, CT. OB Debut 1983 in *Sunday in the Park with George*, followed by *Paradise, Young Playwrights Festival, Camp Paradox*, Bdwy in *Sunday in the Park with George* (1984), *Into the Woods* for which she received a Theatre World Award, *A Little Night Music* (NYCO/LC), *Crucible, A Little Hotel on the Side*.

FERRONE, RICHARD. Born May 7, 1946 in Newton, MA. Graduate Holy Cross Col., Boston Law Col. Debut 1980 OB in *The Caine Mutiny Court-Martial*, followed by *Romeo and Juliet*, Bdwy in *The Crucible* (1991), *A Little Hotel on the Side*.

FIEDLER, JOHN. Born February 3, 1925 in Plateville, WI. Attended Neighborhood Playhouse. OB in *The Sea Gull, Sing Me No Lullaby, The Terrible Swift Sword, The Rasberry Picker, The Frog Prince, Raisin in the Sun, Marathon '88, Human Nature*, Bdwy in *One Eye Closed (1954), Howie, Raisin in the Sun, Harold, The Odd Couple, Our Town, The Crucible, A Little Hotel on the Side*.

FIELD, CRYSTAL. Born December 10, 1942 in NYC. Attended Juilliard, Hunter Col., Debut 1960 OB in *A Country Scandal*, followed by *A Matter of Life and Death, The Heart That Eats Itself, Ruzzante Returns from the Wars, An Evening of British Music Hall, Ride That Never Was, House Arrest, Us, Beverly's Yard Sale, Bruno's Donuts, Coney Island Kid, Till The Eagle Hollars, The Rivalry of Dolls, Pineapple Face*.

FIELD, ROBIN. Born April 13, 1947 in Los Angeles, CA. Attended San Fernando Valley Col., Orange Coast Col. Debut 1967 OB in *Your Own Thing*, followed by *Look Me UP, Speed Gets the Poppys, Babes in Arms, Broadway A Hundred Years Ago, Daugherty & Field, Over the Rainbow*.

FIERSTEIN, HARVEY. Born June 6, 1954 in Brooklyn, NY. Graduate Pratt Inst. Debut 1971 OB in *Pork*, followed by *International Stud, Figures in a Nursery, Haunted Host, Pouf Positive, Safe Sex*, Bdwy in *Torch Song Trilogy f*or which he recieved a Theatre World Award, *Safe Sex*.

FINE, ROSEMARY. Born December 9, 1961 in Limerick, Ireland. Graduate Trinity Col./Dublin. Bdwy debut 1988 in *Juno and the Paycock*. OB in *Grandchild of Kings* (1992), *Mme. MacAdam*.

| Cindy Benson | Danny Burstein | SandraBernhard | Stephen Collins | Donna Biscoe | Keene Curtis |

| Bonnie Black | Tim Connell | Roo Brown | Anthony Crivello | Kate Bushmann | Tim Curry |

| Annette Calud | Jeffrey De Munn | Nancy E. Carroll | André De Shields | Pat Carroll | Christopher Durang |

| Leslie Castay | John Eisner | Celeste Ciulla | David Engel | Courtney Collins | Brandon Espinoza |

| Melissa Ann Davis | Harvey Evans | Suzanne Dawson | Willy Falk | Julie DePaul | Rick Faugno |

FINKEL, JOSHUA. Born October 29, 1963 in Los Angeles, CA. Graduate U. Cal. Bdwy debut 1993 in *Kiss of the Spider Woman.*

FINN, JOHN. Born September 30, 1952 in NYC. Debut 1985 OB in *The Last of the Knucklemen,* followed by Bdwy in *Biloxi Blues* (1987).

FIORDELLISI, ANGELINA. Born March 15, 1955 in Detroit, MI. graduate U. Detroit. Bdwy debut 1983 in *Zorba,* OB in *An Ounce of Prevention, Have I Got a Girl for You, The View From Here.*

FIRE, NORMA. Born June 9, 1937 in Brooklyn, NY. Graduate Brooklyn Col. Debut 1982 OB in *3 Acts of Recognition,* followed by *Merry Wives of Windsor, Henry V, It's All Talk, Macbeth, The Mysteries?*

FISHBURNE, LAURENCE "LARRY". Born July 30, 1961 in Augusta, GA. Attended NYC High School of Performing Arts. Debut 1976 OB in *Eden,* followed by *In My Many Names and Days.* Bdwy 1992 in *Two Trains Running* for which he received a Theatre World Award.

FITZPATRICK, JIM. Born November 26, 1950 in Omaha, NE. Attended U. NE. Debut 1977 OB in *Arsenic and Old Lace,* followed by *Merton of the Movies, Oh Boy!, Time and the Conways, Street Scene, The Duchess of Malfi, Comedy of Errors, Much Ado about Nothing, Cinderella, Anyone Can Whistle.*

FLAGG, TOM. Born March 30 in Canton, OH. Attended Kent State U., AADA. Debut 1975 OB in *The Fantasticks,* followed by *Give Me Liberty, The Subject Was Roses, Lola, Red Hot and Blue, Episode 26, Dazy, Dr. Dietrick's Process,* Bdwy in *Legend* (1976), *Shenandoah, Players, The Will Rogers Follies.*

FLETCHER, SUSANN. Born September 7, 1955 in Wilmington, DE. Graduate Longwood Col., Bdwy debut 1980 in *The Best Little Whorehouse in Texas,* followed by *Raggedy Ann, Jerome Robbins' Broadway, The Goodbye Girl.*

FLORENTINO, LEILA. Born August 12 in the Philippines. Attended U. Philippines. Bdwy debut 1992 in *Miss Saigon.*

FOLLANSBEE, JULIET. Born in September 1919 in Chicago, IL. Graduate Bryn Mawr Col. Debut 1949 OB in *The Fifth Horseman,* followed by *Luminosity without Radiance, Johnny Doesn't Live Here Anymore, Epitaph for George Dillon, Maromichaelis, Brothers Karamozov, Excelsior, In the Summer House, Road to the Graveyard, Day of the Dolphin, Bell Book and Candle, Crime and Pinishment, Pas de Deux, Brightness Falling, Heathen Valley, Somewhere I Have Never Traveled.*

FORMAN, LORRAINE. Born May 25, 1929 in Vancouver, BC, Canada. Bdwy debut 1989 in *Oklahoma,* followed by *Kiss of the Spider Woman.*

FORMAN, KEN. Born September 22, 1961 in Boston, MA. Attended NYU. Debut 1985 OB in *Measure for Measure,* followed by *Rosencrantz and Guildenstern Are Dead, Macbeth, I Stand Before You Naked, Romeo and Juliet, 3 by Wilder,* Bdwy in *Wilder Wilder Wilder* (1983).

FOSTER, HERBERT. Born May 14, 1936 in Winnipeg, Can. Bdwy in *Ways and Means, A Touch of the Poet, The Imaginary Invalid, Henry V, Noises Off, Me and My Girl, Lettice and Lovage,* OB in *Afternoon Tea, Papers, Mary Stuart, Gifts of the Magi, Heliotrope Bouquet.*

FOWLER, SCOTT. Born March 22, 1967 in Medford, MA. Debut 1989 on Bdwy in *Jerome Robbins' Broadway,* followed by *Brigadoon* (NYCO/LC), *Ain't Broadway Grand.*

FOXWORTH, ROBERT. Born November 1, 1941 in Houston, TX. Graduate Carnegie Tech. Bdwy debut 1969 in *Henry V,* followed by *The Crucible,* for which he received a Theatre World Award, *Candida,* OB in *Terra Nova.*

FRANCIS-JAMES, PETER. Born September 16, 1956 in Chicago, IL. Graduate RADA. Debut 1979 OB in *Julius Caesar,* followed by *Long Day's Journey into Night, Antigone, Richard II, Romeo and Juliet, Enrico IV, Cymbeline, Hamlet, Learned Ladies, 10th Young Playwrights Festival.*

FRANKLIN, BONNIE. Born January 6, 1944 in Santa Monica, CA. Attended Smith Col. UCLA. Debut 1968 OB in *Your Own Thing,* followed by *Dames at Sea, Drat!, Carousel, Frankie and Johnny in the Claire de Lune, Love and Shrimp,* Bdwy in *Applause* (1970) for which she received a Theatre World Award.

FRANKLYN-ROBBINS, JOHN. Born December 14, 1951 in Wiltshire, Eng. Graduate U. Birmingham, RADA. Bdwy debut 1968 in *Measure for Measure,* followed by *All's Well That Ends Well, The Sea Gull, Saint Joan, 3 Men on a Horse.*

FRANZ, ELIZABETH. Born June 18, 1941 in Akron, OH. Attended AADA. Debut 1965 in *In White America,* followed by *One Night Stands of a Noisey Passenger, The Real Inspector Hound, Augusta, Yesterday Is Over, Actor's Nightmare, Sister Mary Ignatius Explains It All, The Time of Your Life, Children of the Sun,* Bdwy in *Rosencrantz and Guildenstern Are Dead, The Cherry Orchard, Brighton Beach Memoirs, The Octette Bridge Club, Broadway Bound, The Cemetery Club, Getting Married.*

FRASER, ALISON. Born July 8, 1955 in Natick, MA. Attended Carnegie-Mellon, Boston Consv. Debut 1979 OB in *In Trousers,* followed by *March of the Falsettos, Beehive, Four One-Act Musicals, Tales of Tinseltown, Next Please!, Up Against It,* Bdwy in *The Mystery of Edwin Drood* (1986), *Romance Romance, The Secret Garden.*

FRENCH, ARTHUR. Born in New York City and attended Brooklyn Col. Debut 1962 OB in *Raisin' Hell in the Sun,* followed by *Ballad of Bimshire, Day of Absence, Happy Ending, Brotherhood, Perry's Mission, Rosalee Pritchett, Moonlight Arms, Dark Tower, Brownsville Raid, Nevis Mountain Dew, Julius Caesar, Friends, Court of Miracles, The Beautiful LaSalles, Blues for a Gospel Queen, Black Girl, Driving Miss Daisy, The Spring Thing, George Washington Slept Here, Ascension Day, Boxing Day Parade, A Tempest, The Hills of Massabielle,* Bdwy in *Ain't Supposed to Die a Natural Death, The Iceman Cometh, All God's Chillun Got Wings, The Resurrection of Lady Lester, You Can't Take It with You, Design for Living, Ma Rainey's Black Bottom, Mule Bone.*

FRIDAY, BETSY. Born April 30, 1958 in Chapel Hill, NC. Graduate NC School of Arts. Bdwy debut 1980 in *The Best Little Whorehouse in Texas,* followed by *Bring Back Birdie, The Secret Garden,* OB in *I Ought to Be in Pictures, Smile, Ace of Diamonds.*

GAINES, BOYD. Born May 11, 1953 in Atlanta, GA. Graduate Juilliard. Debut 1978 OB in *Spring Awakening,* followed by *A Month in the Country* for which he received a Theatre World Award, BAM Theatre Co.'s *Winter's Tale, The Barbarians, Johnny on a Spot, Vikings, Double Bass, The Maderati, The Heidi Chronicles, The Extra Man, The Comedy of Errors,* Bdwy in *The Heidi Chronicles* (1989).

GALANTICH, TOM. Born in Brooklyn, NY. Debut 1985 OB in *On the 20th Century,* followed by *Mademoiselle Colombe,* Bdwy in *Into the Woods* (1989), *City of Angels.*

GALINDO, RAMON. Born June 3 in San Francisco, CA. Graduate U. of Calif. Berkeley. Bdwy debut 1979 in *Carmelina,* followed by *Merlin, Cats, Song and Dance, Jerome Robbins' Broadway,* OB in *Funny Feet* (1987).

GANUN, JOHN. Born August 23, 1966 in Blissfeld, MI. Graduate U. Mich. Bdwy debut 1991 in *The Will Rogers Follies.*

GARBER, VICTOR. Born March 15, 1949 in London, Can. Debut 1973 OB in *Ghosts* for which he received a Theatre World Award, followed by *Joe's Opera, Cracks, Wenceslas Square, Love Letters, Assassins,* Bdwy in *Tartuffe, Deathtrap, Sweeney Todd, They're Playing Our Song, Little Me, Noises Off, You Never Can Tell, Devil's Disciple, Lend Me a Tenor, Two Shakespearean Actors.*

GARDENIA, VINCENT. Born January 7, 1923 in Naples, It. Debut 1955 OB in In April Once, followed by *Man with the Golden Arm, Volpone, Brothers Karamazov, Power of Darkness, Machinal, Gallows Humor, Theatre of the Absurd, Lunatic View, Little Murders, Passing Through from Exotic Places, Carpenters, Buried Inside Extra, Breaking Legs,* Bdwy in *The Visit* (1958), *Rashomon, The Cold Wind and the Warm, Only in America, The Wall, Daughter of Silence, Seidman & Son, Dr. Fish, The Prisoner of Second Avenue, God's Favorite, California Suite, Ballroom, Glengarry Glen Ross.*

GARRETT, RUSSELL (formerly Giesenschlag). Born July 8, 1959 in San Diego, CA. Attended San Diego State U. Bdwy debut 1982 in *Seven Brides for Seven Brothers,* followed by *42nd Street,* OB in *Girl Crazy, Pageant.*

GELFER, STEVEN. Born February 21, 1949 in Brooklyn, NY. Graduate NYU, Ind. U. Debut 1968 OB and Bdwy in *The Best Little Whorehouse in Texas,* followed by *Cats.*

GEORGE, BEN. Born June 7, 1947 in Oxford, Eng. Attended Leeds Music Col. Debut 1984 OB in *Last of the Knucklemen,* Bdwy in *The Best Little Whorehouse in Texas* (1985), *Grand Hotel.*

GEORGIANA, TONI. Born December 14, 1963 in Uniontown, PA. Attended Juilliard. Bdwy debut 1991 in *The Will Rogers Follies.*

GERACI, FRANK. Born September 8, 1939 in Brooklyn, NY. Attended Yale. Debut 1961 OB in *Color of Darkness,* followed by *Mr. Grossman, Balm in Gilead, The Fantasticks, Tom Paine, End of All Things Natural, Union Street, Uncle Vanya, Success Story, Hughie, Merchant of Venice, Three Zeks, Taming of the Shrew, The Lady from the Sea, Rivals, Deep Swimmer, The Imaginary Invalid, Candida, Hedda Gabler, Serious Co., Berenice, The Philanderer, All's Well That Ends Well, Three Sisters, A Midsummer Night's Dream, Medea, The Importance of Being Earnest, Major Barbara, Measure for Measure, The Fine Art of Finesse, Two Schnitzler One Acts, Peace in a Traveling Heart, Tartuffe,* Bdwy in *Love Suicide at Schofield Barracks* (1972).

GERARD, DANNY. Born May 29, 1977 in New York City. Bdwy debut 1986 in *Into the Light,* followed by *Les Miserables, Lost in Yonkers,* OB in *Today I Am a Fountain Pen, Second Hurricane, Falsettoland.*

GIBBS, SHEILA. Born Feb. 16, 1947 in New York City. Graduate NYU. Debut 1971 in *Two Gentlemen of Verona, followed by Runaways, Once on This Island,* OB in *Last Days of British Honduras, Poets from the Inside, Once on This Island.*

GIBSON, JULIA. Born June 8, 1962 in Norman, OK. Graduate U. Iowa, NYU. Debut 1987 OB in *A Midsummer Night's Dream, followed by Love's Labor Lost, Crucible, The Man Who Fell in Love with His Wife, Learned Ladies, Candide.*

GIONSON, MEL DUANE. Born February 23, 1954 in Honolulu, HI. Graduate U. HI. Debut 1979 OB in *Richard II,* followed by *Sunrise, Monkey Music, Behind Enemy Lines, Station J, Teahouse, A Midsummer Night's Dream, Empress of China, Chip Shot, Manoa Valley, Ghashiram, Shogun, Macbeth, Life of the Land, Noiresque, Three Sisters, Lucky Come Hawaii, Henry IV Parts 1 & 2, Working 1-Acts '91.*

GIOSA, SUE. Born November 23, 1958 in Connecticut. Graduate Queens Col. RADA, LAMDA. Debut OB 1988 in *Tamara,* followed by *Breaking Legs.*

GLEASON, JOANNA. Born June 2, 1950 in Toronto, Can. Graduate UCLA. Bdwy debut 1977 in *I Love My Wife* for which she received a Theatre World Award, followed by *The Real Thing, Social Security, Into the Woods, Nick & Nora,* OB in *A Hell of a Town, Joe Egg, It's Only a Play, Eleemosynary.*

GLUSHAK, JOANNA. Born May 27, 1958 in New York City. Attended NYU. Debut 1983 OB in *Lenny and the Heartbreakers,* followed by *Lies and Legends, Miami, Unfinished Song, A Little Night Music* (NYCO), Bdwy in *Sunday in the Park with George* (1984), *Rags, Les Miserables.*

GOETHALS, ANGELA. Born May 20, 1977 in NYC. Bdwy debut 1987 in *Coastal Disturbance,* followed by *Four Baboons Adoring the Sun,* OB in *Positive Me, Approaching Zanzibar, The Good Times are Killing Me.*

GOLDSTEIN, STEVEN. Born September 22, 1963 in New York City. Graduate NYU. Debut 1987 OB in *Boy's Life,* followed by *Oh Hell, Three Sisters, Marathon '91, Angel of Death, Five Very Live, Casino Paradise,* Bdwy in *Our Town* (1988).

GOLER-KOSARIN, LAUREN. Born November 10, 1961 in Washington, DC. Bdwy debut 1980 in *Happy New Year,* followed by *Onward Victoria!, Smile, Late Night Comic, Ain't Broadway Grand,* OB in *Joseph, Eating Raoul.*

GOODWIN, AARON. Born November 8, 1966 in Macon, GA. Graduate Furman U. Debut 1991 OB in *Macbeth* followed by Fridays, *Tales from Hollywood, God's Country, Greetings.*

GOODNESS, JOEL. Born January 22, 1962 in Wisconsin Rapids, WI. Graduate U. Wisc. Debut 1991 OB in *Custody* followed by *Georgy,* Bdwy in *Crazy for You* (1992).

GORDY, WAYNE. Born December 26 in Philadelphia, PA. Graduate Hofstra U., Richmond Col/London. Debut 1988 OB in *Fiorello*, followed by *A Christmas Carol*.

GORNEY, KAREN LYNN. Born January 28, 1945 in Los Angeles, CA. Graduate Carnegie Tech, Bradeis U. Debut 1972 OB in *Dylan* followed by *Life on the Third Rail, Academy Street, Unconditional Communication*.

GOTTSCHALL, RUTH. Born April 14, 1957 in Wilmington, DE. Bdwy debut 1981 in *The Best Little Whorehouse in Texas* followed by *Cabaret, Legs Diamond, Prince of Central Park, The Goodbye Girl*.

GOULD, ELLEN. Born December 30, 1950 in Worcester, MA. Graduate Brandeis U., NYU. Debut 1979 OB in *Confessions of a Reformed Romantic*, followed by *Gewandter Songs, Three Irish No Plays, Yeats Trio, Heat of Reentry, Bubbe Meises*, Bdwy in *Macbeth* (81).

GRAAE, JASON. Born May 15, 1958 in Chicago, IL. Graduate Cincinnati Consv. Debut 1981 OB in *Godspell*, followed by *Snoopy, Heaven on Earth, Promenade, Feathertop, Tales of Tinseltown, Living Color, Just So, Olympus on My Mind, Sitting Pretty in Concert, Babes in Arms, The Cat and the Fiddle, Forever Plaid, A Funny Thing Happened on the Way to the Forum, 50 Million Frenchmen, Rodgers and Hart Revue, A Grand Night for Singing, Hello Muddah Hello Faddah*, Bdwy in *Falsettos* (1993), *A Grand Night for Singing*.

GRACE, EILEEN. Born July 25 in Pittsburgh, PA. Graduate Point Park Col. Bdwy debut in *42nd Street*, followed by *My One and Only, The Will Rogers Follies*.

GRAFF, RANDY. Born May 23, 1955 in Brooklyn, NY. Graduate Wagner Col. Debut 1978 OB in *Pins and Needles*, followed by *Station Joy, A...My Name Is Alice, Once on a Summer's Day*, Bdwy in *Sarava, Grease, Les Miserables, City of Angels, Falsettos*.

GRANT, DAVID MARSHALL. Born June 21, 1955 in New Haven, Ct. Attended Conn. Col., Yale U. Debut 1978 OB in *Sganarelle*, followed by *Table Settings, The Tempest, Making Movies, Naked Rights*, Bdwy in *Bent* (1979), *The Survivor, Angels in America*.

GRANT, JEANNE. Born December 18, 1925 in Chicago, IL. Graduate U. Chicago. Bdwy debut in *Brigadoon* (1947) followed by *The King and I, Damn Yankees, A Tree Grows in Brooklyn, The Consul, The Saint of Bleecker Street, 3 Wishes for Jamie, Goldilocks, The Gay Life, Fiddler on the Roof* (1976) , *The High Life* (in concert/1993).

GRANT, SEAN. Born July 13, 1966 in Brooklyn, NY. Attended NC School of Arts. Bdwy debut 1987 in *Starlight Express* followed by *Prince of Central Park, The Goodbye Girl*.

GRAVITTE, DEBBIE SHAPIRO. Born September 29, 1954 in Los Angeles, CA. Graduate LACC. Bdwy debut 1979 in *They're Playing Our Song*, followed by *Perfectly Frank, Blues in the Night, Zorba, Jerome Robbins' Broadway, Ain't Broadway Grand* OB in *They Say It's Wonderful, New Moon* (in concert).

GRAY, DOLORES. Born June 7, 1924 in Hollywood, CA. Bdwy debut 1944 in *Seven Lively Arts* followed by *Are You With It?, Annie Get Your Gun, Carnival in Flanders, Destry Rides Again, Sherry!, 42nd Street*, OB in *Money Talks, Make Someone Happy*.

GRAY, KEVIN. Born February 25, 1958 in Westport, CT. Graduate Duke U. Debut 1982 OB in *Lola*, followed by *Pacific Overtures, Family Snapshots, The Baker's Wife, The Knife, Magdalena* in Concert, Bdwy in *The Phantom of the Opera* (1989).

GRAY, SAM. Born July 18, 1923 in Chicago, IL. Graduate Columbia U. Bdwy debut 1955 in *Deadfall* followed by *Six Fingers in a Five Finger Glove, Saturday Sunday Monday, Golda, A View from the Bridge*, OB in *The Ascent of F-6* followed by *Family Portrait, One Tiger on a Hill, Shadow of Heroes, The Recruiting Officer, The Wild Duck, Jungle of Cities, 3 Acts of Recognition, Returnings, A Little Madness, The Danube, Dr. Cook's Garden, Child's Play, Kafka Fathers and Son, Dennis, Panache, Marathon 89, Bitter Friends, Arturo Ui, Blackout, King of Carpets*.

GREEN, AMANDA. Born December 29, 1963 in NYC. Debut 1984 OB in *The New Yorkers* followed by *Sheik of Avenue B*.

GREEN, ANDREA. Born September 31 in New York City. Graduate Queens Col./CUNY. Bdwy debut 1980 in *They're Playing Our Song*, followed by *Little Me*, OB in *And the World Goes Round, Yiddle with a Fiddle, Song of Singapore, Jacques Brel*.

GREEN, DAVID. Born June 16, 1942 in Cleveland, OH. Attended Kan. State U. Bdwy debut 1980 in *Annie*, followed by *Evita, Teddy and Alice, The Pajama Game* (LC), OB in *Once on a Summer's Day, Miami, On the 20th Century, What About Luv?, Tom and Viv*.

GREENE, ELLEN. Born February 22, 1950 in NYC. Attended Ryder Col. Debut 1973 on Bdwy in *Rachel Lily Rosenbloom*, followed by *The Little Prince and the Aviator, 3 Men on a Horse*, OB in *In the Boom Boom Room, Threepenny Opera, Disrobing the Bride, Little Shop of Horrors, Starting Monday, Weird Romance*.

GREGG, CLARK. Born April 2, 1962 in Boston, MA. Graduate NYU. Debut 1987 OB in *Fun* followed by *The Detective, Boy's Life,Three Sisters, The Old Boy, Nothing Sacred*, Bdwy in *A Few Good Men (1990)*.

GREGORIO, ROSE. Born in Chicago, IL. Graduate Northwestern, Yale U. Debut 1962 OB in *The Days and Nights of Beebee Fenstermaker* followed by *Kiss Mama, The Balcony, Bivouac at Lucca, Journey to the Day, Diary of Anne Frank, Weekends Like Other People, Curse of the Starving Class, Dreams of a Blacklisted Actor, The Last Yankee, King Richard*, Bdwy in *The Investigation, Daphne in Cottage D, The Owl and the Pussycat, The Cuban Thing, Jimmy Shine, The Shadow Box, A View from the Bridge* (1983), *M. Butterfly*.

GRIESEMER, JOHN. Born December 5, 1947 in Elizabeth, NJ. Graduate Dickinson Col, URI. Debut 1981 OB in *Turnbuckle*, followed by *Death of a Miner, Little Victories, Macbeth, A Lie of the Mind, Kate's Diary, Little Egypt, EST Marathon 93, Woyzeck, Born Guilty*, Bdwy in *Our Town(1989)*.

GRIFFITH, KRISTIN. Born September 7, 1953 in Odessa, TX. Graduate Juilliard. Bdwy debut 1976 in *Texas Trilogy*, OB in *Rib Cage, Character Lines, 3 Friends, 2 Rooms, A Month in the Country, Fables for Friends, The Trading Post, Marching in Georgia, American Garage, A Midsummer Night's Dream, Marathon '87, Bunker Reveries, On the Bench, EST Marathon '92 and 93, The Holy Terror*.

GROENER, HARRY. Born September 10, 1951 in Augsburg, Germany, Graduate U. Washington. Bdwy debut 1979 in *Oklahoma!* for which he received a Theatre World Award, followed by *Oh, Brother!, Is There Life after High School, Cats, Harrigan 'n' Hart, Sunday in the Park with George, Sleight of Hand, Crazy for You*, OB in *Beside the Seaside*.

GROVE, GREGORY. Born December 15, 1949 in Ada, OK. Graduate SMU, HB Studio. Debut 1977 OB in *K: Impressions of Kafka's Trial* followed by *Early one Evening at the Rainbow Bar and Grill, Human Nature, Bargains*, Bdwy in *Lone Star/Privat W* (1979).

GUNDERSON, STEVE. Born June 9, 1957 in San Diego, CA. Attended SD State U. Debut 1982 OB in *Street Scene* followed by *The Three Sisters, Topsy and Bunker, Butley, Forever Plaid, Back to Bacharach*, Bdwy in *Suds* (1989).

GUTTMAN, RONALD. Born August 12, 1952 in Brussels, Belg. Graduate Brussels U. Debut 1986 OB in *Coastal Disturbances*, followed by *Modigliano, Free Zone*, Bdwy in *Coastal Disturbances* 1987.

HACK, STEVEN. Born April 20, 1958 in St. Louis, MO. Attended Cal. Arts, AADA. Debut 1978 OB in *The Coolest Cat in Town*, followed by Bdwy in *Cats* (1982).

HADARY, JONATHAN. Born September 11, 1948 in Chicago, IL. Attended Tufts U. Debut 1974 OB in *White Nights*, followed by *El Grande de Coca Cola, Songs from Pins and Needles, God Bless You Mr. Rosewater, Pushing 30, Scrambled Feet, Coming Attractions, Tom Foolery, Charley Bacon and Family, Road Show, 1-2-3-4-5, Wenceslas Square, Assassins, Lips Together Teeth Apart, Weird Romance, The Destiny of Me*, Bdwy in *Gemini* (1977 also OB), *Torch Song Trilogy, As Is, Gypsy*.

HAMILTON, LAUREN. Born November 10, 1959 in Boston, MA. Graduate Bard Col., Neighborhood Playhouse. Debut 1988 OB in *Famine Plays*, followed by *Tiny Dimes, Rodents and Radios, Hunger, Homo Sapien Shuffle, Famine Plays, A Murder of Crows, A Vast Wreck*.

HANDLER, EVAN. Born January 10, 1961 in New York City. Attended Juilliard. Debut 1979 OB in *Biography A Game*, followed by *Striker, Final Orders, Marathon '84, Found a Peanut, What's Wrong with This Picture?, Bloodletters, Young Playwrights Festival, Human Nature, Six Degrees of Separation, Marathon '91, Big Al, Time on Fire*, Bdwy in *Solomon's Child* (1982), *Biloxi Blues, Brighton Beach Memoirs, Broadway Bound, Six Degrees of Separation, I Hate Hamlet*.

HARAN, MARY-CLEERE. Born May 13, 1952 in San Francisco, CA. Attended San Francisco State U. Bdwy debut 1979 in *The 1940's Radio Hour*, followed by OB in *Hollywood Opera, What a Swell Party!, Swinging on a Star*.

HARDING, JAN LESLIE. Born in 1956 in Cambridge, MA. Graduate Boston U. Debut 1980 OB in *Album*, followed by *Sunday Picnic, Buddies, The Lunch Girls, Marathon '86, Traps, Father Was a Peculiar Man, A Murder of Crows, David's Red-haired Death, Strange Feet, Impassioned Embraces*.

HARDY, MARK. Born September 25, 1961 in Reidsville, NC. Graduate UNC/Greensboro. Debut 1990 OB in *The Rothschilds*, followed by *Juba*, Bdwy in *Les Miserables* (1990).

HARRIS, BAXTER. Born November 18, 1940 in Columbus, KS. Attended U. Kan. Debut 1967 OB in *America Hurrah*, followed by *The Serpent, Battle of Angels, Down by the River..., Ferocious Kisses, The Three Sisters, The Dolphin Position, Broken Eggs, Paradise Lost, Ghosts, The Time of Your Life, The Madwoman of Chaillot, The Reckoning, Wicked Women Revue, More Than You Deserve, Him, Pericles, Selma, Gradual Clearing, Children of the Sun, Marathon '90, Go to Ground, EST Marathon '92&93,Long Ago and Far Away* Bdwy in *A Texas Trilogy* (1976), *Dracula, The Lady from Dubuque*

HARRIS, JULIE. Born December 2, 1925 in Grosse Pointe, MI. Yale graduate. Bdwy debut 1945 in *It's a Gift*, followed by *Henry V. Oedipus, Playboy of the Western World, Alice in Wonderland, Macbeth, Sundown Beach* for which she received a Theatre World Award, *The Young and the Fair, Magnolia Alley, Montserrat, A Member of the Wedding, I Am a Camera, Mlle. Colombe, The Lark, Country Wife, Warm Peninsula, Little Moon of Alban, A Shot in the Dark, Marathon '33, Ready When You Are C. B., Hamlet (CP), Skyscraper, 40 Carats, And Miss Reardon Drinks a Little, Voices, The Last of Mrs. Lincoln, Au Pair Man, In Praise of Love, Belle of Amherst, Mixed Couples, Break a Leg, Lucifer's Child, A Christmas Carol*.

HARRIS, MEL. Born July 12, 1958 in Bethlehem, PA. NY debut 1992 OB in *Empty Hearts* for which she received a Theatre World Award.

HAYDEN, SOPHIE. Born February 23 in Miami, FL. Graduate Northwestern U. Bdwy debut 1979 in *Whoopee!*, followed by *Barnum, Comedy of Errors, The Most Happy Fella* (1992), *The Show-Off, Jessie's Land, Passover, Lies My Father Told Me, Torpedo Bra, Fun*.

HAYS, REX. Born June 17, 1946 in Hollywood, CA. Graduate San Jose State U., Brandeis U. Bdwy debut 1975 in *Dance with Me*, followed by *Angel, King of Hearts, Evita, Onward Victoria!, Woman of the Year, La Cage aux Folles, Grand Hotel*, OB in *Charley's Tale, Six Wives*.

HEALD, ANTHONY. Born August 25 1944 in New Rochelle, NY. Graduate Mich. State U. Debut 1980 OB in *Glass Menagerie*, followed by *Misalliance* for which he recieved a Theatre World Award, *The Caretaker, The Fox, Quartermaine's Terms, The Philanthropist, Henry V, Digby, Principia Scriptoriae, Lisbon Traviata, Elliot Loves, Pygmalion, Lips Together Teeth Apart, Later Life*, Bdwy in *Wake of Jamey Foster* (1982), *Marriage of Figaro, Anything Goes, A Small Family Business*.

HEINSOHN, ELISA. Born September 11, 1962 in Butler, PA. Debut 1984 OB in *Oy Mama Am I in Love*, followed by *Scandal*, Bdwy in *42nd Street* (1985), *Smile, Phantom of the Opera*.

HELLER, ADAM. Born June 8, 1960 in Englewood, NJ. Graduate NYU. Debut 1984 OB in *Kuni-Leml*, followed by *The Special, Half a World Away, Encore!*, Bdwy in *Les Miserables* (1989).

HENRITZE, BETTE. Born May 23 in Betsy Layne, KY. Graduate U. TN. OB in *Lion in Love, Abe Lincoln in Illinois, Othello, Baal, A Long Christmas Dinner, Queens of France, Rimers of Eldritch, Displaced Person, Acquisition, Crime of Passion, Happiness Cage, Henry VI, Richard III, Older People, Lotta, Catsplay. A Month in the Country. The Golem, Daughters, Steel Magnolias,* Bdwy in *Jenny Kissed Me* (1948), *Pictures in the Hallway, Giants Sons of Giants, Ballad of the Sad Cafe, The White House, Dr. Cook's Garden, Here's Where I Belong, Much Ado about Nothing, Over Here, Angel Street, Man and Superman, Macbeth* (1981) *,Present Laughter, The Octette Bridge Club, Orpheus Descending, Lettuce and Lovage, On Borrowed Time.*

HIBBERT, EDWARD. Born September 9, 1955 in NYC. Attended Hurstpierpont Col, RADA. Bdwy debut 1982 in *Alice in Wonderland,* followed by *Me and My Girl,* OB in *Candide in Concert, Dandy Dick, Privates on Parade, Lady Bracknell's Confinement, Candide, Jeffrey.*

HADGE, MICHAEL. Born June 6, 1932 in Greensboro, NC. Bdwy bow 1958 in *The Cold Wind and the Warm* followed by *Lady of the Camelias, Impossible Years,* OB in *Local Stigmatic, The Hunter, The Roads to Home.*

HAGEN, DANIEL. Born September 29 in Storm Lake, IA. Graduate U. Iowa. Bdwy debut 1987 in *The Nerd,* OB in *Pillow Talk* (1988) followed by *Variations on the Death of Trotsky, Stay Carl Stay, A Distance from Calcutta.*

HAGERTY, JULIE. Born June 15, 1955 in Cincinnati, OH. Attended Juilliard. Debut 1979 OB in *Mutual Benefit Life,* followed by *Wild Life, House of Blue Leaves* (1979), *The Years,* Bdwy in *House of Blue Leaves* (1986) for which she received a Theatre World Award, *Front Page, 3 men on a Horse.*

HAMLET, MARK. Born February 5, 1954 in Rockville Centre, NY. Graduate Adelphi U. Debut 1989 OB in *Urban Planning,* follwed by *A New Game, Lucia di Lammermoor, The Merry Widow.*

HAMLIN, HARRY. Born October 30, 1951 in Pasadena, CA. Yale graduate. Bdwy debut 1984 in *Awake and Sing,* OB in *The Normal Heart* (benefit reading).

HANAN, STEPHEN. Born January 7, 1947 in Washington, DC. Graduate Harvard, LAMDA. Debut 1978 OB in *All's Well That Ends Well,* followed by *Taming of the Shrew, Rabboni, Comedy of Errors,* Bdwy in *Pirates of Penzance(1978), Cats, Peter Pan.*

HANELINE, THOM. Born February 24, 1952 in Berea, OH. Graduate Kent State U. Debut 1992 OB in *Love's Labour's Lost,* followed by *Measure for Measure.*

HANSEN, LARRY. Born March 11, 1952 in Anacortes, WVA. Graduate Western Wash. U. Debut 1978 OB in *Can-Can,* Bdwy in *Show Boat* (1983), *Anna Karenina.*

HARDEN, MARCIA GAY. Born August 14, 1959 in La Jolla, CA. Graduate U. MD., U. TX, NYU. Debut 1989 OB in *The Man Who Shot Lincoln* followed by *One of the Guys, The Years,* Bdwy in *Angels in America* for which she received a 1993 Theatre World Award.`

HARLAN, HEATHER. Born October 20, 1970 in Richmond, VA. Bdwy debut 1992 in *A Little Hotel on the Side,* followed by *The Master Builder, 3 Men on a Horse.*

HARMAN, PAUL. Born July 29, 1952 in Mineola, NY. Graduate Tufts U. Bdwy debut 1980 in *It's So Nice to be Civilized,* followed by *Les Miserables, Chess,* OB in *City Suite, Sheik of Avenue B.*

HARRINGTON, DELPHI. Born August 26 in Chicago, IL. Graduate Northwestern U. Debut 1960 OB in *A Country Scandal* followed by *Moon for the Misbegotten, A Baker's Dozen, The Zykovs, Character Lines, Richie, American Garage, After the Fall, Rosencrantz and Guildenstern Are Dead, Good Grief,* Bdwy in *Thieves* (1974), *Everything in the Garden, Romeo and Juliet, Chapter Two, The Sea Gull.*

HARRIS, STEVE. (formerly Steven Michael) Born August 31, 1957 in Fall River, MA. Attended Pasadena City Col., Clown Col. Bdwy debut 1980 in *Barnum* followed OB in *Heliotrope Bouquet.*

HARSHAW, CEE-CEE. Born May 1, 1970 in Hickory, NC. Graduate Boston Consv. Bdwy debut 1992 in *Jelly's Last Jam* OB in *Fire's Daughters.*

HARTLEY, MARIETTE. Born June 21, 1940 in NYC. Debut 1988 OB in *King John* followed by *Love and Shrimp.*

HATCHER, ROBYN. Born September 8, 1956 in Philadelphia, PA. Graduate Adelphi U. Debut OB 1983 in *Macbeth* followed by *Edward II, Deep Sleep, Flatbush Faithful, Pardon Permission, Welcome Signs, Them That's Got.*

HAWKE, ETHAN. Born November 6, 1970 in Austin, TX. Debut 1991 OB in *Casanova* followed by *A Joke, Sophistry* Bdwy in *The Sea Gull* (1992).

HAWLEY, LYNN. Born November 12, 1965 in Sharon, CT. Graduate Middlebury Col. Debut 1992 OB in *Woyzeck* followed by *Owners.*

HAYENGA, JEFFREY. Born August 13 in Sibledy, IO. Graduate U. Min. Bdwy in *The Elephant Man* followed by *Ah Wilderness, Long Day's Journey into Night,* OB in *King Lear, Mother Courage, The Actor's Nightmare, Burkie, Brand, Hamlet, Breaking Up, Two Rooms, Patient A, Jeffrey.*

HAYNES, ROBIN. Born July 20, 1953 in Lincoln, NE. Graduate U. Wash. Debut 1976 OB in *Touch of the Poet* followed by *She Loves Me, Romeo and Juliet, Twelfth Night, Billy Bishop Goes to War, Max and Macie,* Bdwy in *The Best Little Whorehouse in Texas* (1978), *Blood Brothers.*

HEALY, DAVID. Born December 17, 1960 in NYC. Graduate George Washington U. Debut 1985 OB in *Love as We Know It,* Bdwy in *The Real Inspector Hound, 15 Minute Hamlet* (1992).

HEARD, ERIKA L. Born October 21 in Evanston, IL. Attended IL State U. Bdwy debut 1993 in *The Song of Jacob Zulu.*

HEARD, JOHN. Born March 7, 1946 in Washington, DC. Graduate Clark U. Debut 1974 OB in *The Wager* followed by *Macbeth, Hamlet, Fishing, G.R. Point* for which he received a Theatre World Award, *The Creditors, The Promise, Othello, Split, Chekov Sketchbook, Love Letters, The Last Yankee, Marathon 91,* Bdwy in *Warp* (1973), *Total Abandon.*

HECHT, BJARNE. Born June 4, 1958 in Copenhagen, Denmark. Graduate Royal Danish Ballet, Neighborhood Playhouse. Debut 1993 OB in *3 by Wilder,* Bdwy in *Wilder Wilder Wilder*(1993).

HENRY, SPRUCE. Born April 14, 1962 in Covington, LA. Graduate Clinch Valley Col., AADA. Debut 1989 OB in *Pericles* followed by *Off the Beat and Path 2.*

HENSLEY, DALE. Born April 9, 1954 in Nevada, MO. Graduate Southwest MO. State U. Debut 1980 OB in *Annie Get Your Gun,* Bdwy in *Anything Goes* (1987), *Guys and Dolls* (1992).

HERNANDEZ, PHILIP. Born December12, 1959 in Queens, NY. Graduate SUNY. Debut 1987 OB in *The Gingerbread Lady* followed by *Ad Hock,* Bdwy in *Kiss of the Spider Woman* (1993).

HIGGINS, JOHN MICHAEL. Born February 12, 1963 in Boston, MA. Graduate Amherst Col. Debut 1986 in *National Lampoon's Class of '86,* followed by *Neddy, Self-torture and Strenuous Exercise, Trumps, Comic Safari, Maids of Honor, Beau Jest, Comedy of Errors, Jeffrey,* Bdwy in *Mastergate* (1990), *La Bete.*

HILER, KATHERINE. Born November 5, 1952 in Evanston, IL. Graduate Deniston U. Debut 1977 OB in *Essential Shepard,* followed by Bdwy in *They're Playing Our Song, Little Me, Woman of the Year, Crazy for You.*

HINES, GREGORY. Born February 14, 1946 in NYC. Bdwy debut 1954 in *The Girl in Pink Tights,* followed by *Eubie!* for which he received a Theatre World Award, *Comin' Uptown, Black Broadway, Sophisticated Ladies, Jelly's Last Jam,* OB in *Twelfth Night, A Christmas Memory.*

HIPKINS, BILLY. Born May 18, 1961 in Verona, NJ. Attended AADA. Debut 1988 OB in *Alias Billy Valentine,* Bdwy in *Anna Karenina* (1992).

HIRSCH, JUDD. Born March 15, 1935 in NYC. Attended AADA. Bdwy debut 1966 in *Barefoot in the Park,* followed by *Chapter Two, Talley's Folly, Conversations with My Father,* OB in *On the Necessity of Being Polygamous, Scuba Duba, Mystery Play, The Hot I Baltimore, Prodigal, Knock Knock, Life and/or Death, Talley's Folly, The Sea Gull, I'm Not Rappaport, Conversations with My Father.*

HIRSCHHORN, LARRY. Born August 31, 1958 in Oceanside, NY. Graduate Ithaca Col. Debut 1983 OB in *Promises Promises* followed by *Gingerbread Lady, The Wise Men of Chelm.*

HOCK, ROBERT. Born May 20, 1931 in Phoenixville, PA. Yale graduate. Debut 1982 OB in *The Caucasian Chalk Circle* followed by *The Adding Machine, Romeo and Juliet, Edward II, Macbeth, Kitty Hawk, Heathen Valley, Comedy of Errors, Phaedra, The Good Natur'd Boy.*

HODGES, BEN. Born September 17, 1969 in Morristown, TN. Graduate Otterbein Col. Debut OB 1992 in *Loose Ends.*

HOFF, CHRISTIAN. Born April 21, 1968 in Berkeley, CA. Attended Stella Adler Consv. Bdwy debut 1993 in *The Who's Tommy.*

HOFFMAN, JANE. Born July 24 in Seattle, WA. Graduate U. Cal. Bdwy debut 1940 in *Tis of Thee,* followed by *Crazy with the Heat, Something for the Boys, One Touch of Venus, Calico Wedding, Mermaids Singing, Temporary Island, Story for Strangers, Two Blind Mice, The Rose Tattoo, The Crucible, Witness for the Prosecution, Third Best Sport, Rhinoceros, Mother Courage and Her Children, Fair Game for Lovers, A Murderer Amoung Us. Murder Among Friends, Some Americans Abroad, Lost in Yonkers,* OB in *American Dream, Sandbox, Picnic on the Battlefield, Theatre of the Absurb, Child Buyer, A Corner of the Bed, Slow Memories, Last Analysis, Dear Oscar, Hocus Pocus, Lessons, The Art of Dining, Second Avenue Rag, One Tiger to a Hill, Isn't It Romantic, Alto Part, Frog Prince, Alterations, The Grandma Plays, The Mysteries.*

HOFFMAN, PHILIP. Born May 12, 1954 in Chicago, IL. Graduate U.Ill. Bdwy debut 1981 in *The Moony Shapiro Songbook,* followed by *Is There Life after High School?, Baby, Into the Woods, Falsettos,* OB in *The Fabulous 50's, Isn't It Romantic, 1-2-3-4-5, Rags.*

HOLBROOK, ANNA. Born April 18, in Fairbanks, Alaska. Attended Trinity U., U. AZ. Debut 1988 OB in *St. Hugo of Central Park* followed by *The Great Nebulain Orion, The Dolphin Project.*

HOLLIDAY, DAVID. Born August 4, 1937 in Illinois. Attended Carthage Col. Bdwy debut 1968 in *Man of La Mancha,* followed by *Coco* for which he received a Theatre World Award, *Music Is, Perfectly Frank, Man of La Mancha* (1991), OB in *Nevertheless They Laugh.*

HOLLIS, TOMMY. Born March 27, 1954 in Jacksonville, TX. Attended Lon Morris Col., U. Houston. Debut 1985 OB in *Diamonds,* followed by *Secrets of the Lava Lamp, Paradise, Africanus Instructus, The Colored Museum,* Bdwy 1990 in *The Piano Lesson* for which he received a Theatre World Award.

HOLMES, RICHARD. Born March 16, 1963 in Philadelphia, PA. Graduate Gettysburg Col., NY Debut 1990 OB in *Richard III* followed by *Othello, Shadow of a Gunman, Mr. Parnell,* Bdwy in *Saint Joan* (1993).

HONDA, ERIKA. Born March 28, 1946 in NYC. Graduate Sarah Lawrence Col. Debut OB in *1992 Young Playwrights Festival.*

HOPE, SHARON. Born in NYC. Graduate Baruch Col. Debut 1987 OB in *A Star Ain't Nothing but a Hole in Heaven* followed by *Black Medea, Capital Cakewalk, The Trial, Them That's Got.*

HORVATH, JAMES. Born August 14, 1954 in Chicago, IL. Graduate Triton Col., Butler U. Debut 1978 OB in *Can-Can* followed by Bdwy in *Can-Can* (1981), *Ain't Broadway Grand.*

HOTY, DEE. Born August 16, 1952 in Lakewood, OH. Graduate Otterbein Col. Debit 1979 in *The Golden Apple,* followed by *Ta-Dah!, Personals,* Bdwy in *The 5 O'Clock Girl* (1981), *Shakespeare Cabaret, City of Angels, The Will Rogers Follies.*

HOTY, TONY. Born September 29, 1949 in Lakewood, OH. Attended Ithaca Col., U. WVA., Debut 1974 OB in *Godspell* (also Bdwy 1976) followed by *Joseph and the Amazing Technicolor Dreamcoat, Robin Hood, Success and Succession, The Root,* Bdwy in *Gypsy* (1989).

HOWARD, CELIA. Born August 23, 1937 in Oakland, CA. Graduate Stanford U. Debut OB in *Cat and the Canary* (1965), followed by *Whitsuntide, Last Summer at Blue Fish Cove, After the Rain, Midsummer, Heathen Valley, Fortinbras.*

HOWER, NANCY. Born May 11 in Wyckoff, NJ. Graduate Rollins Col., Juilliard. Debut 1991 OB in *Othello* followed by *As You Like It, The Years.*

HOWLAND, BETH. Born May 28, 1941 in Boston, MA. Debut 1960 OB in *Once upon a Mattress* followed by *Impassioned Embraces,* Bdwy in *Bye Bye Birdie, High Spirits, Drat! The Cat!, Darling of the Day, Company.*

HOXIE, RICHMOND. Born July 21, 1946 in NYC. Graduate Dartmouth Col., LAMDA. Debut 1975 OB in *Shaw for an Evening* followed by *The Family, Landscape with Waitress, 3 from the Marathon, The Slab Boys, Vivien, Operation Midnight Climax, The Dining Room, Daddies, To Gillian on Her 37th Birthday, Dennis, Traps, Sleeping Dogs, Equal Wrights, EST Marathon '93, The Dolphin Project.*

HOYT, LON. Born April 6, 1958 in Roslyn, NY. Graduate Cornell U. Bdwy debut 1982 in *Rock 'n' Rool* followed by *Baby, Leader of the Pack, Starlight Express, OB in Tapestry.*

HUFFMAN, CADY. Born February 2, 1965 in Santa Barbara, CA. Debut 1983 OB in *They're Playing Our Song,* followed by *Festival of 1 Acts, Oh Hell!,* Bdwy 1985 in *La Cage aux Folles,* followed by *Big Deal, The Will Rogers Follies.*

HUGOT, MARCELINE. Born February 10, 1960 in Hartford, CT. Graduate Brown U. Cal/San Diego. Debut 1986 OB in *The Maids* followed by *Measure for Measure, Them within Us.*

HUNT, ANNETTE. Born January 31, 1938 in Hampton, Va. Graduate Va. Intermont Col. Debut 1957 OB in *Nine by Six,* followed by *Taming of the Shrew, Medea, Anatomist, The Misanthrope, The Cherry Orchard, Electra, Last Resort, The Seducers, A Sound of Silence, Charades, Dona Rosita, Rhinestones, Where's Charley?, The White Rose of Memphis, M. Amilcar, The Sea Gull, Rutherford & Son,* Bdwy in *All the Girls Came Out to Play* (1972), *Lemonade.*

HURST, MELISSA. Born June 8, 1955 in Cleveland, OH. Graduate NYU. Debut 1980 OB in *Dark Ride* followed by *A Walk on Lake Erie, The Houseguests, Reunion, American Camera, Enter the Greek, Basic Black and Pearls, Grover Bob Loves You, One Neck.*

HURT, MARY BETH. Born September 26, 1948 in Marshalltown, IA. Attended U. Iowa, NYU. Debut 1972 OB in *More Than You Deserve,* followed by *As You Like It, Trelawny of the Wells, The Cherry Orchard, Love for Love, A Member of the Wedding, Boy Meets Girl, Secret Service, Father's Day, Nest of the Wood Grouse, The Day Room, Secret Rapture, Othello, One Shoe Off,* Bdwy in *Crimes of the Heart* (1981), *The Misanthrope, Benefactors.*

HYMAN, EARLE. Born September 11, 1926 in Rocky Mount, NC. Attended New School, American Theatre Wing. Bdwy debut 1943 in *Run Little Chillun,* followed by *Anna Lucasta, Climate of Eden, Merchant of Venice, Othello, Julius Caesar, The Tempest, No Time for Sargeants, Mr. Johnson* for which he received a Theatre World Award, *St. Joan, Hamlet, Waiting for Godot, The Duchess of Malfi, Les Blancs, The Lady from Dubuque, Execution of Justice, Death of the King's Horseman, The Master Builder,* OB in *The White Rose and the Red, Worlds of Shakespeare, Jonah, Life and Times of J. Walter Smintheus, Orrin, The Cherry Orchard, House Party, Carnival Dreams, Agamemnon, Othello, Julius Caesar, Coriolanus, Pygmalion.*

ILLES, MARY. Born January 20, 1962 in Dayton, OH. Graduate OH State U. Debut.../. 1992 OB in *Chess,* Bdwy in *She Loves Me* (1992).

INGRAM, TAD. Born September 11, 1948 in Pittsburgh, PA. Graduate Temple U., LAMDA. Debut 1979 OB in *Biography: A Game* followed by *The Possessed, Gospel According to Al, The Death of Von Richthofen,* Bdwy in *The Most Happy Fella* (1992).

IRWIN, BILL. Born April 11, 1950 in California. Attended UCLA, Clown Col. Debut 1982 OB in *The Regard of Flight* followed by *The Courtroom, Waiting for Godot,* Bdwy in *5-6-7-8 Dance* (1983), *Accidental Death of an Anarchist, Regard of Flight, Largely New York, Fool Moon.*

ISHEE, SUZANNE. Born October 15 in High Point, NC. Graduate NCU., Manhattan School of Music. Bdwy debut 1983 in *Show Boat* followed by *Mame, La Cage Aux Folles, Phantom of the Opera.*

IVES, DONALD. Born October 25, 1962 in Salem, MO. Attended Southwest MO. State, Webster Col., Southern IL. U. Bdwy debut 1993 in *Camelot.*

IVEY, DANA. Born August 12 in Atlanta, GA. Graduate Rollins Col., LAMDA. Bdwy debut 1981 in *Macbeth* (LC), followed by *Present Laughter, Heartbreak House, Sunday in the Park with George, Pack of Lies, Marriage of Figaro,* OB in *A Call from the East, Vivien, Candida in Concert, Major Barbara in Concert, Quartermaine's Terms, Baby with the Bathwater, Driving Miss Daisy, Wenceslas Square, Love Letters, Hamlet, The Subject Was Roses, Beggars in the House of Plenty.*

JACOBY, MARK. Born May 21, 1947 in Johnson City, TN. Graduate GA State U., FL State U., St. John's U. Debut 1984 OB in *Bells Are Ringing,* Bdwy in *Sweet Charity* for which he received a Theatre World Award, *Grand Hotel, The Phantom of the Opera.*

JAMES, KELLI. Born March 18, 1959 in Council Bluffs, IA. Bdwy debut 1987 in *Les Miserables.*

JAMES, PETER FRANCIS. (See FRANCIS-JAMES, PETER.)

JANKO, IBI. Born February 18, 1966 in Carmel, CA. Graduate Yale U. debut 1993 OB in *Somewhere I Have Never Travelled* followed by *Vinegar Tom, Waiting, Your Mom's a Man.*

JARRETT, BELLA. Born February 9, 1931 in Adairsville, GA. Graduate Wesleyan Col. Debut 1958 OB in *Waltz of the Toreadors* followed by *Hedda Gabler, The Browning Version, Cicero, Pequod, Welcome to Andromeda, The Trojan Women, Phaedra, The Good Natur'd Man,* Bdwy in *Once in a Lifetime* (1978), *Lolita.*

JASON, JOHN. Born August 25, 1962 in Middletown, CT. Attended East Conn. Col., Mesa Col. Debut 1991 OB in *Body and Soul* followed by *Wyoming Blizzard, Boys in the Back Room, Murder in Disguise,* Bdwy in *The Visit* (1992).

JENNEY, LUCINDA. Born April 23, 1954 in Long Island City, NY. Graduate Sarah Lawrence Col. Debut 1981 OB in *Death Takes a Holiday* followed by *Ground Zero Club, True to Life, Aven'U Boys,* Bdwy in *Gemini* (1981).

JENNINGS, KEN. Born September 10, 1947 in Jersey City, NJ. Graduate St. Peter's Col. Bdwy debut 1975 in *All God's Chillun Got Wings,* followed by *Sweeney Todd* for which he received a Theatre World Award, *Present Laughter, Grand Hotel, OB in Once on a Summer's Day, Mayor, Rabboni, Gifts of the Magi, Carmilla, Sharon*

JOHANSON, DON. Born October 19, 1952 in Rock Hill, SC. Graduate USC. Bdwy debut 1976 in *Rex* followed by *Cats, Jelly's Last Jam,* OB in *The American Dance Machine.*

JOHN, TAYLOR. Born November 25, 1981 in NYC. Bdwy debut 1991 in *Les Miserables.*

JOHNSON, DANNY. Born in Lafayette, IN. Graduate Goodman/DePaul U. Bdwy debut 1993 in *The Song of Jacob Zulu.*

JOHNSON, PAGE. Born August 25, 1930 in Welch, WV. Graduate Ithaca Col. Bdwy bow 1951 in *Romeo and Juliet,* followed by *Electra, Oedipus, Camino Real, In April Once for which he received a Theatre World Award, Red Roses for Me, The Lovers, Equus, You Can't Take It with You* OB in *The Enchanted Guitar, 4 in 1, Journey of the Fifth Horse, APA's School for Scandal, The Tavern, and The Seagull, Odd Couple, Boys in the Band, Medea, Deathtrap, Best Little Whorehouse in Texas, Fool for Love, East Texas,Brush Arbor Revival.*

JOHNSON, TINA. Born October 27, 1951 in Wharton, TX. Graduate N. TX State U. Debut 1979 OB in Festival followed by *Blue Plate Special, Just So,* Bdwy in *The Best Little Whorehouse in Texas, South Pacific, She Loves Me.*

JOHNSTON, NANCY. Born January 15, 1949 in Statesville, NC. Graduate Carson Newman Col., UNC/Greensboro. Debut 1987 OB in *Olympus on My Mind,* followed by *Nunsense, Living Color, White Lies,* Bdwy in *The Secret Garden.*

JONES, CHERRY. Born November 21, 1956 in Paris, TN. Graduate Carnegie-Mellon. Debut 1983 OB in *The Philanthropist,* followed by *He and She, The Ballad of Soapy Smith, The Importance of Being Earnest, I Am a Camera, Claptrap, Big Time, Light Shining in Buckinghamshire, The Baltimore Waltz, Goodnight Desdemona, And Baby Makes 7,* Bdwy in *Stepping Out* (1986), *Our Country's Good.*

JONES, JAY AUBREY. Born March 30, 1954 in Atlantic City, NJ. Graduate Syracuse U. Debut 1981 OB in *Sea Dream,* followed by *Divine Hysteria, Inacent Black and the Brothers, La Belle Helene,* Bdwy in *Cats* (1986).

JONES, JEN. Born March 23, 1927 in Salt Lake City, UT. Debut 1960 OB in *Dreams Under the Window* followed by *The Long Voyage Home, Diff'rent, The Creditors, Look at Any Man, I Knock at the Door, Pictures in the Hallway, Grab Bag, Bo Bo, Oh Dad Poor Dad, Henhouse, Uncle Vanya, Grandma's Play, A Distance from Calcutta,* Bdwy in *Dr. Cook's Garden* (1967), *But Seriously, Eccentricities of a Nightingale, The Music Man* (1980), *The Octette Bridge Club.*

JONES, SIMON. Born July 27, 1950 in Wiltshire, Eng. Attended Trinity Hall. NY debut 1984 OB in *Terra Nova* followed by *Magdalena in Concert, Woman in Mind, Privates on Parade,* Bdwy in *The Real Thing* (1984), *Benefactors, Getting Married, Private Lives, The Real Inspector Hound/15 Minute Hamlet.*

JONES, WALKER. Born August 27, 1956 in Pensacola, Fl. Graduate Boston U., Yale U. Debut 1989 OB in *Wonderful Town* followed by *Scapin.*

JOSLYN, BETSY. Born April 19, 1954 in Staten Island, NY. Graduate Wagner Col. Debut 1976 OB in *The Fantasticks* followed by *Light Up the Sky, Collette Collage,* Bdwy in *Sweeney Todd* (1979), *A Doll's Life, The Goodbye Girl.*

JOY, ROBERT. Born August 17, 1951 in Montreal, Can. Graduate Oxford U. Debut 1978 OB in *The Diary of Anne Frank,* followed by *Fables for Friends, Lydie Breeze, Sister Mary Ignatius Explains It All, Actor's Nightmare, What I Did Last Summer, The Death of von Ricthofen, Lenny and the Heartbreakers, Found a Peanut, Field Day, Life and Limb, Hyde in Hollywood, The Taming of the Shrew, Man in His Underwear, Goodnight Desdemona,* Bdwy in *Hay Fever* (1985), *The Nerd, Shimada.*

JOYCE, JOE. Born November 22, 1957 in Pittsburgh, PA. Graduate Boston U. Debut 1981 OB in *Close Enough for Jazz,* followed by *Oh Johnny!, They Came from Planet Mirth, Encore!, You Die at Recess, Forever Plaid, Pageant.*

KADEN, EILEEN. Born February 25, 1968 in Rahway, NJ. Graduate Carnegie-Mellon U. Debut 1991 OB in *Company* followed by *Anyone Can Whistle.*

KAHN, MADELINE. Born September 29, 1942 in Boston, MA. Graduate Hofstra U. Bdwy debut in *New Faces of 1968* followed by *Two by Two, She Loves Me, On the 20th Century, Born Yesterday* (1988), *The Sisters Rosensweig,* OB in *Promenade, The Boom Boom Room, Marco Polo Sings a Solo, What's Wrong with This Picture?, A Christmas Memory.*

KANE, BRAD. Born September 29, 1973 in New Rochelle, NY. Debut 1982 OB in *Scraps* followed by *A Winter's Tale, Sunday in the Park with George, Titus Andronicus,* Bdwy in *Evita* (1983), *She Loves Me* (1993).

KANE, DONNA. Born August 12, 1962 in Beacon, NY. Graduate Mt. Holyoke Col. Debut 1985 OB in *Dames at Sea* for which she received a Theatre World Award, followed by *The Vinegar Tree, Johnny Pye and the Foolkiller, Babes in Arms, Young Rube, Go to Ground,* Bdwy in *Meet Me in St. Louis, Les Miserables.*

KANTOR, KENNETH. Born April 6, 1949 in the Bronx, NY. Graduate SUNY, Boston U. Debut 1974 OB in *Zorba,* followed by *Kiss Me Kate, A Little Night Music, Buried Treasure, Sounds of Rodgers and Hammerstein, Shop on Main Street, Kismet, The Fantasticks, Colette Collage, Philemon,* Bdwy in *The Grand Tour* (1979), *Brigadoon* (1980), *Mame* (1983), *The New Moon* (NYCO), *Me and My Girl, Guys and Dolls* (1992).

KAPLAN, JOHNATHAN. Born July 5, 1980 in Detroit, MI. Debut 1991 OB in *Rags,* Bdwy in *Falsettos* (1992) for which he received a Theatre World Award.

KATIMS, ROBERT. Born April 22, 1927 in Brooklyn, NY. Attended Brooklyn Col. Debut 1953 OB in *The Penguin* followed by *The Invasion of Aratooga, Shmulnik's Waltz, On the Wing, No Conductor.*

| Diana Douglas | John Fiedler | Naz Edwards | Robin Field | Angelina Fiordellisi | Tom Galantich |

| Leila Florentino | John Ganun | Elizabeth Franz | Wayne Gordy | Alison Fraser | Sean Grant |

| Toni Georgiana | Evan Handler | Karen Lynn Gorney | Ethan Hawke | Amanda Green | Bjarne Hecht |

| Mary Cleere Haran | John Michael Higgins | Heather Harlan | Billy Hipkins | Delphi Harrington | Ben Hodges |

| Erika L. Heard | Christian Hoff | Erika Honda | Donald Ives | Melissa Hurst | Thomas Keith |

201

KATZMAN, BRUCE. Born December 19, 1951 in NYC. Graduate Ithaca Col., Yale U. Debut 1990 OB in *Richard III* followed by *Othello,* Bdwy in *The Crucible* (1991), *A Little Hotel on the Side.*

KAYE, JUDY. Born September 11, 1948 in Phoenix, AZ. Attended UCLA, Ariz. State U. Bdwy debut 1977 in *Grease,* followed by *On the 20th Century* for which she received a Theatre World Award, *Moony Shapiro Songbook, Oh Brother!, Phantom of the Opera, The Pajama Game* (LC) OB in *Eileen in Concert, Can't Help Singing, Four to Make Two, Sweethearts in Concert, Love, No No Nanette in Concert, Magdalena in Concert, Babes in Arms, Desire Under the Elms, The Cat and the Fiddle, What about LUV?*

KAZAN, LAINIE. Born May 15, 1943 in Brooklyn, NY. Attended Hofstra U. Bdwy debut 1992 in *My Favorite Year.*

KEACH, STACY. Born June 2, 1941 in Savannah, GA. Graduate U. Cal., Yale U., LAMDA. Debut 1967 OB in *MacBird* followed by *Niggerlovers, Henry IV, Country Wife, Hamlet,* Bdwy in *Indians* (1969)., *Deathtrap, Solitary Confinement.*

KEHR. DONNIE. Born September 18, 1963 in Washington, DC. attended AM. Ballet School. Debut 1982 OB in *American Passion* followed by *The Human Comedy, The Mystery of Edwin Drood,* Bdwy in *Legend* (1975), *The Human Comedy, Edwin Drood, Tommy*

KEITH, LAWRENCE/LARRY. Born March 4, 1931 in Brooklyn, NY. Graduate Brooklyn Col., Ind. U. Bdwy debut 1960 in *My Fair Lady* followed by *High Spirits, I Had a Ball, Best Laid Plans, Mother Lover,* OB in *The Homecoming, Conflict of Interest, The Brownsville Raid, M. Amilcar, The Rise of David Levinsky, Miami, Song for a Saturday, Rose Quartet, I Am a Man.*

KEITH, THOMAS. Born January 1, 1961 in Cleveland, OH. Graduate Ohio U. Debut 1985 OB in *Goatman* followed by *Art, The Scooter Cycle, Futz!, the Histories of Gladys, The Depression Show.*

KELLER, JEFF. Born September 8, 1947 in Brooklyn, NY. Graduate Monmouth Col. Bdwy 1974 in *Candide* followed by *Fiddler on the Roof, On the 20th Century, The 1940's Radio Show, Dance a Little Longer, Phantom of the Opera,* OB in *Bird of Paradise, Charlotte Sweet, Roberta in Concert, Personals.*

KELLY, JOHN-CHARLES. Born April 28, 1946 in Salem, OR. Graduate U. Or., U. AZ., Debut 1984 OB in *Bells Are Ringing* followed by *The High Life* (in concert).

KENYON, LAURA. Born November 23, 1948 in Chicago, IL. Attended U. SCal. Debut 1970 OB in *Peace* followed by *Carnival, Dementos, The Trojan Women, Have I Got a Girl for You, Desire, The Hunchback of Notre Dame,* Bdwy in *Man of LaMancha* (1971), *On the Town, Nine.*

KEPROS, NICHOLAS. Born November 8, 1932 in Salt Lake City, Ut. Graduate U UT., RADA. Debut 1958 OB in *The Golden Six* followed by *Wars of Roses, Julius Caesar, Hamlet, Henry IV, She Stoops to Conquer, Peer Gynt, Octaroon, Endicott and the Red Cross, The Judas Applause, Irish Hebrew Lesson, Judgement in Havana, The Millionairess, Androcles and the Lion, The Redempter, Othello, The Times and Appetites of Toulouse-Lautrec, Two Fridays, Rameau's Nephew, Good Grief,* Bdwy in *Saint Joan* (1968/1993), *Amadeus, Execution of Justice.*

KERR, PATRICK. Born January 23, 1956 in Wilmington, Del. Graduate Temple U. Debut 1980 OB in *Jerry* followed by *Romeo and Juliet, The Warrior Ant, A Midsummer Night's Dream, Jeffrey.*

KERSHAW, WHITNEY. Born April 10, 1962 in Orlando, FL. Attended Harkness/Joffrey Ballet Schools. Debut 1981 OB in *Francis,* Bdwy in *Cats.*

KERWIN, BRIAN. Born October 25, 1949 in Chicago, IL. Graduate U. S. Cal. Debut 1988 OB in *Emily* for which he received a Theatre World Award, followed by *Lips Together Teeth Apart, One Shoe Off.*

KHALAF, RAMZI. Born January 17, 1982 in Lebanon. Debut 1993 OB in *The Little Prince.*

KIARA, DOROTHY. Born June 27, 1954 in Providence, RI. Graduate Boston Consv, Bdwy debut 1980 in *They're Playing Our Song* followed by *Nine,* OB in *Forbidden Broadway* ('88/89/93).

KIES, PATRICIA. Born September 1, 1952 in Camp Atterbury, IN. Attended U. Utah. Bdwy debut 1993 in *Camelot.*

KILEY, JÚLIA. Born July 20, 1959 in New Britain, CT. Graduate CCNY. Debut 1990 OB in *Assassins* followed by *A Charles Dickens Christmas, Marry Me a Little.*

KIM, DANIEL DAE. Born August 4, 1968 in Korea. Graduate Haverford Col. Debut 1991 OB in *Romeo and Juliet* followed by *Love Letters from a Student Revolutionary, A Doll House.*

KIMBROUGH, CHARLES. Born May 23, 1936 in St. Paul, MN. Graduate Ind. U., Yale U. Bdwy debut 1969 in *Cop-Out* followed by *Company, Love for Love, Rules of the Game, Candide, Mr. Happiness, Same Time Next Year, Sunday in the Park with George, Hay Fever,* OB in *All for Love, Struts and Frets, Troilus and Cressida, Secret Service, Boy Meets Girl, Drinks before Dinner, The Dining Room, Later Life.*

KIND, ROSLYN. Born in Brooklyn, NY. Bdwy debut 1992 in *3 From Brooklyn* followed by OB in *Show 'em Where the Good Times Are* (1993).

KING, CLEO. Born August 21, 1967 in St. Louis, MO. Attended U. MO. Debut 1992 OB in *A...My Name is Still Alice.*

KINGSLEY, GRETCHEN. Born October 6, 1961 in Washington, DC. Attended Tulane U. Debut 1985 OB in *Mowgli* followed by *This Could Be the Start, A Backer's Audition,* Bdwy in *Les Miserables* (1987), *Sweeney Todd.*

KINSEY, RICHARD. Born March 22, 1954. Attended Cal. State U./Fullerton, Bdwy debut 1991 in *Les Miserables.*

KLEIN, ROBERT. Born February 8, 1942 in NYC. Graduate Alfred U.,. Yale U. OB in *Six Characters in Search of an Author, Second City Returns, Upstairs at the Downstairs,* Bdwy in *The Apple Tree, New Faces of 1968, Morning Noon and Night, They're Playing Our Song, The Robert Klein Show, Robert Klein* on Broadway, *The Sisters Rosensweig.*

KLIBAN, KEN. Born July 26, 1943 in Norwalk, CT. Graduate U. Miami, NYU. Bdwy debut 1967 in *War and Peace* followed by *As Is,* OB in *War and Peace, Puppy Dog Tails, Istanbul, Persians, Home, Elizabeth the Queen, Judith, Man and Superman, Boom Boom Room, Ulysses in Traction, Lulu, The Beaver Coat, Troilus and Cressida, Richard II, The Great Grandson of Jedediah Kohler, It's Only a Play, Time Framed, Love's Labour's Lost, Wild Blue, Lips Together Teeth Apart.*

KLUGMAN, JACK. Born April 17, 1925 in Philadelphia, PA. Attended Carnegie Tech., AmThWing. Bdwy debut 1952 in *Golden Boy* followed by *A Very Special Baby, Gypsy, Tchin-Tchin, The Odd Couple, The Sudden and Accidental Re-Education of Horse Johnson, I'm Not Rappaport, 3 Men on a Horse,* OB in *Coriolanus, Stevedore, St. Joan, Bury the Dead.*

KNIGHT, LILY. Born November 30, 1949 in Jersey City, NJ. Graduate NYU. Debut 1980 OB in *After the Revolution,* followed by *The Wonder Years, The Early Girl, Musical Comedy Murders* of 1940, *The Holy Terror, The View from Here,* Bdwy in *Agnes of God* (1983).

KOLINSKI, JOSEPH. Born June 26 1953 in Detroit, MI. Attended U. Detroit. Bdwy debut 1980 in *Brigadoon* followed by *Dance a Little Closer, The Three Musketeers, Les Miserables,* OB in *Hijinks!, The Human Comedy* (also Bdwy), *Picking Up the Pieces.*

KONG, PHILIP. Born September 23, 1986 in Lattingtown, NY. Bdwy debut 1991 in *Miss Saigon.*

KORBICH, EDDIE. Born November 6, 1960 in Washington, DC. Graduate Boston Consv. Debut 1985 OB in *A Little Night Music,* followed by *Flora the Red Menace, No Frills Revue, The Last Musical Comedy, Godspell, Sweeney Todd* (also Bdwy 1989), *Assassins, Eating Raoul, Casino Paradise, Gifts of the Magi,* Bdwy in *Singin' in the Rain* (1985), .

KOREY, ALIX (formerly Alexandra). Born May 14 in Brooklyn, NY. Graduate Columbia U. Debut 1976 OB in *Fiorello!,* followed by *Annie Get Your Gun, Jerry's Girls, Rosalie in Concert, America Kicks Up Its Heels, Gallery, Feathertop, Bittersuite, Romance in Hard Times, Songs You Might Have Missed, Forbidden Broadway 10th Anniversary, Casino Paradise, Gifts of the Magi,* Bdwy in *Hello Dolly!* (1978), *Show Boat* (1983), *Ain't Broadway Grand.*

KORF, MIA. Born November 1, 1965 in Ithaca, NY. Attended Cornell U. Ithaca Col Debut 1987 *OB in Two Gentlemen of Verona* followed by *The Seagull, Godspell, Young Playwrights 90,* Bdwy in *Face Value* (1993).

KRAKOWSKI, JANE. Born September 11, 1968 in New Jersey. Debut 1984 OB in *American Passion,* followed by *Miami, A Little Night Music,* Bdwy in *Starlight Express* (1987), *Grand Hotel, Face Value.*

KREPPEL, PAUL. Born June 20 in Kingston, NY. Attended Emerson Col. Debut 1974 OB in *The Proposition* followed by *Godspell, Joseph and the Amazing Technicolor Dreamcoat, Tuscaloosa's Calling Me, The Comedy of Errors, Alice in concert, Agamemnon, Hello Muddah Hello Faddah.*

KRISTIEN, DALE. Born May 18 in Washington, DC. Graduate Ithaca Col. Bdwy debut 1981 in *Camelot,* followed by *Show Boat, Radio City Music Specials, Phantom of the Opera.*

KUBALA, MICHAEL. Born February 4, 1958 in Reading, PA. Attended NYU. Bdwy debut 1978 in *A Broadway Musical followed by Dancin', Woman of the Year, Marilyn, Jerome Robbins' Broadway, Crazy for You,* OB in *Double Feature* (1981).

KUHN, BRUCE W. Born December 7, 1955 in Davenport, IA. Graduate U. W. Va., U. Wash. Bdwy debut 1987 in *Les Miserables.*

KUHN, JUDY. Born May 20, 1958 in NYC. Graduate Oberlin Col. Debut 1985 OB in *The Mystery of Edwin Drood, Rodgers and Hart Revue,* Bdwy in *Edwin Drood* (1985), *Rags, Les Miserables, Chess, Two Shakespearean Actors, She Loves Me.*

KURTZ, SWOOSIE. Born September 6, 1944 in Omaha, NE. Attended U.S. Cal., LAMDA. Debut 1968 OB in *The Firebugs,* followed by *The Effect of Gamma Rays..., Enter a Free Man, Children, Museum, Uncommon Women and Others, Wine Untouched, Summer, The Beach House, Six Degrees of Separation, Lips Together Teeth Apart,* Bdwy in *Ah Wilderness!* (1975), *Tartuffe, A History of the American Film, 5th of July, House of Blue Leaves.*

KUX, BILL. Born June 26, 1953 in Detroit, MI. Graduate Cal Inst. Arts, Yale U. Debut 1984 OB in the *Philanthropist,* followed by *Loose Ends, Absent Friends, The Mysteries?,* Bdwy in *Ain't Broadway Grand* (1993).

LaCHANZE. Born December 16, 1961 in St. Augustine, FL. Attended Morgan State U., Philadelphia Col. Bdwy debut 1986 in *Uptown It's Hot,* followed by *Dreamgirls* (1987), *Once on This Island* for which she received a 1991 Theatre World Award, OB in *Once on This Island.*

LACHOW, STAN. Born December 20, 1931 in Brooklyn, NY. Graduate Roger Williams Col. Debut 1977 OB in *Come Back, Little Sheba* followed by *The Diary of Anne Frank, Time of the Cuckoo, Angelus, The Middleman, Charley Bacon and Family, Crossing the Bar, Today I Am a Fountain Pen, The Substance of Fire,* Bdwy in *On Golden Pond* (1979), *The Sisters Rosensweig.*

LAGE, JORDAN. Born February 17, 1963 in Palo Alto, CA. Graduate NYU. Debut 1988 OB in *Boy's Life,* followed by *Three Sisters, The Virgin Molly, Distant Fires,* Bdwy in *Our Town* (1989).

LAGERFELT, CAROLINE. Born September 23 in Paris. Graduate AADA. Bdwy debut 1971 in *The Philanthropist* followed by *4 on a Garden, Jockey Club Stakes, The Constant Wife, Otherwise Engaged, Betrayal, The Real Thing, A Small Family Business,* OB in *Look Back in Anger, Close of Play, Sea, Anchor, Quartermaine's Terms, Other Places, Phaedra Britanica, Swim Visit, Creditors.*

LaGIOIA, JOHN. Born November 24, 1937 in Philadelphia, PA Graduate Temple U. OB in *Keyhole, Lovers in the Metro, The Cherry Orchard, Titus Andronicus, Henry VI, Richard III, A Little Madness, Rubbers, Right You Are, Pavlo Hummel,* Bdwy in *Henry V* (1969), *Gemini, Doubles, On Borrowed Time* (1991).

MARTENS, LORA JEANNE. Born in Glen Ellyn, IL. Graduate IllWesleyanU. Bdwy debut 1980 in *Onward Victoria* followed by *The 5 O'Clock Girl*, OB in *Skyline, Choices.*

MARTIN, ANDREA. Born January 15, 1947 in Portland, ME. Graduate StephensCol., EmersonCol., Sorbonne/Paris. Debut 1980 OB in *Sorrows of Stephen* followed by *Hardsell, She Loves Me*, Bdwy in My *Favorite Year* (1992) for which she received a Theatre World Award.

MARTIN, GEORGE N. Born August 15, 1929 in NYC. Bdwy debut 1970 in *Wilson in the Promise Land*, followed by *The Hothouse, Plenty, Total Abandon, Pack of Lies, The Mystery of Edwin Drood, The Crucible, A Little Hotel on the Side*, OB in *Painting Churches, Henry V, Springtime for Henry.*

MARTIN, LEILA. Born August 22, 1932 in New York City. Bdwy debut 1944 in *Peepshow*, followed by *Two on the Aisle, Wish You Were Here, Guys and Dolls, Best House in Naples, Henry Sweet Henry, The Wall, Visit to a Small Planet, The Rothschilds, 42nd Street, The Phantom of the Opera*, OB in *Ernest in Love, Beggar's Opera, King of the U.S., Philemon, Jerry's Girls.*

MARTIN, LUCY. Born February 8, 1942 in NYC. Graduate Sweet Briar College. Debut 1962 OB in *Electra*, followed by *Happy as Larry, The Trojan Women, Iphigenia in Aulis, Wives, The Cost of Living, The Substance of Fire*, Bdwy in *Shelter* (1973) *Children of a Lesser God, Pygmalion, The Sisters Rosensweig.*

MARTINEZ, TONY. Born January 27, 1920 in Santurce, PR. Attended UPR. Bdwy debut 1967 in *Man of La Mancha* and in 1972, 1977, 1992 *Revivals.*

MASON, CRAIG. Born July 1, 1950 in Rochester, MN. Graduate YaleU. Debut 1978 in *Allegro* followed by *On a Clear Day You Can See Forever, The Tempest.*

MASTERS, PATRICIA. Born December 8, 1952 in Washington, DC. Graduate UMd. Debut 1984 OB in *Forbidden Broadway* followed by *Tomfoolery, CBS Live, The High Life* (in concert).

MAUGANS, WAYNE. Born September 26, 1964 in Harrisburg, PA. Graduate NYU. Debut 1990 OB in *Lusting after Pipino's Wife*, followed by *Ancient Boys, Take It to Bed.*

MAYES, SALLY. Born August 3 in Livingston, TX. Attended UHouston. Bdwy debut 1989 in *Welcome to the Club* for which she received a Theatre World Award, followed by *She Loves Me*, OB in *Closer Than Ever.*

MAZZIE, MARIN. Born October 9, 1960 in Rockford, IL. Graduate W. MI. U. Debut 1983 OB in *Where's Charley?, And the World Goes Round*, Bdwy in *Big River* (1986).

MAZZILLI, LEE. Born March 25, 1955 in NYC. Debut 1992 OB in *Tony and Tina's Wedding.*

McALLEN, KATHLEEN ROWE. Born November 30 in the Bay area, CA. Attended UCB, UCLA. Debut 1981 OB in *Joseph and the Amazing Technicolor Dreamcoat*, followed by *Chess*, Bdwy in *Joseph and...* (1982), followed by *Aspects of Love* for which she received a Theatre World Award.

McCANN, CHRISTOPHER. Born September 29, 1952 in New York City. Graduate NYU. Debut 1975 OB in *The Measures Taken*, followed by *Ghosts, Woyzeck, St. Joan of the Stockyards, Buried Child, Dwelling in Milk, Tongues, 3 Acts of Recognition, Don Juan, Michi's Blood, Five of Us, Richard III, The Golem, Kafka Father and Son, Flatbush Faithful, Black Market, King Lear, The Virgin Molly, Mad Forest, Ladies of Fisher Cove*

McCLARNON, KEVIN. Born August 25, 1952 in Greenfield,IN. Graduate ButlerU,LAMDA. Debut 1977 OB in *The Homecoming* followed by *Heaven's Gate, A Winter's Tale, Johnny on a Spot, The Wedding, Between Daylight and Boonville, Macbeth, The Clownmaker, Cinders, The Ballad of Soapy Smiith, Better Days, The Showoff.*

McCLENDON, DAWN. Born February 17, 1965 in Norwalk, CT. Graduate DukeU. Debut OB 1993 in *Washington Square Moves*, followed by *Life during Wartime, Julius Caesar.*

McCLINTOCK, JODIE LYNNE. Born April 7, 1955 in Pittsburgh, PA. Graduate WestminsterCol. Debut 1983 OB in *As You Like It* followed by *1984* , *The Art of Success, Free Zone*, Bdwy in *Long Day's Journey into Night.*

McCONNELL, DAVID. Born February 12, 1962 in Los Alamos, NM. Graduate AADA. OB in *You Never Can Tell, The Hot 1 Baltimore, Cloud 9, Working, The Normal Heart, The Winter's Tale, This One Thing I Do, The Rivers and Ravines, Anima Mundi, Aunt Mary.*

McCORMICK, CAROLYN. Born September 19, 1959 in Texas. Graduate Williams Col. Debut 1988 OB in *In Perpetuity Throughout the Universe*, followed by *Lips Together Teeth Apart, Laureen's Whereabouts.*

McCORMICK, MICHAEL. Born July 24, 1951 in Gary, IN. Graduate NorthwesternU. Bdwy debut 1964 in *Oliver!* followed by *Kiss of the Spider Woman*, OB *Coming Attractions, Tomfoolery, The Regard of Flight, Charlotte's Secret, World Away, In a Pig's Valise, I'Arturo Ui, Scapin. .*

McCOWEN, ALEC. Born May 26, 1925 in Tunbridge Wells, England Attended RADA. Bdwy debut 1951 in *Antony and Cleopatra* followed by *Caesar and Cleopatra, King Lear, Comedy of Errors, After the Rain, Hadrian VII, The Philanthropist, The Misanthrope, Equus, Kipling, Someone Who'll Watch over Me*, OB in *Mark's Gospel.*

McCRADY, TUCKER. Born September 24, 1965 in Sewanee, TN. Graduate HarvardU, Juilliard. Bdwy debut 1993 in *Camelot.*

McCRANE, PAUL. Born January 19, 1961 in Philadelphia, PA. Debut 1977 OB in *Landscape of the Body*, followed by *Dispatches, Split, Hunting Scenes, Crossing Niagara, Hooters, Fables for Friends, Moonchildren, Right Behind the Flag, Human Nature, Six Degrees of Separation, The Country Girl, Group, The Years*, Bdwy in *Runaways* (1978), *Curse of an Aching Heart, The Iceman Cometh* (1985).

McCUNE, ROD. Born October 12, 1962 in Jasper, IN. Graduate PurdueU, ButlerU. Bdwy debut 1993 in *Ain't Broadway Grand.*

McDANIEL, KEITH. Born March 29, 1956 in Chicago, IL. Attended ColumbiaCol. Bdwy debut 1985 in *Leader of the Pack* followed by *Kiss of the Spider Woman.*

McDANIEL, JAMES. Born March 25, 1958 in Washington, DC. Attended U. PA. Debut 1982 OB in *A Soldier's Play* followed by *E.S.T. Marathon, The Harvesting, Caligula, The Mound Builders, Incredibly Famous Willy Rivers, Diamonds, Balm in gilead, Before It Hits Home*, Bdwy in *Joe Turner's Come and Gone, Six Degrees of Separation (Also OB), Someone Who'll Watch Over Me.*

McDERMOTT, SEAN. Born October 23, 1961 in Denver, CO. Attended Loretto Heights. Debut 1986 on Bdwy in *Starlight Express* followed by, *Miss Saigon, Falsettos.*

McDONALD, BETH. Born May 25, 1954 in Chicago, IL. Graduate Juilliard. Debut 1981 OB in *A Midsummer Night's Dream* followed by *The Recruiting Officer, Jungle of Cities, Kennedy at Colonus, Our Own Family, Ancient History*, Bdwy 1993 in *Angels in America.*

McDONALD, TANNY. Born February 13 in Princeton, NJ. Graduate Vassar Col. Debut 1961 OB in *American Savoyards* followed by *All in Love, To Broadway with Love, Carricknabauna, The Beggar's Opera, Brand, Goodbye, Dan Bailey, Total Eclipse, Gorky, Don Juan Comes Back fron the War, Vera with Kate, Francis, On Approval, A Definite Maybe, Temptation, Titus Andronicus, Hamlet, June*, Bdwy in*Fiddler on the Roof, Come Summer, The Lincoln Mask, Clothes for a Summer Hotel, Macbeth, Man of La mancha.*

McDORMAND, FRANCES. Born in 1958 in the South. Debut 1983 OB in *Painting Churches* followed by *On the Verge*, Bdwy in *Awake and Sing* (1984), *A Streetcar Named Desire* (1988), *The Sisters Rosensweig.*

McDOWELL, MALCOLM. Born June 15, 1943 in Leeds, England Debut 1980 OB in *Look Back in Anger* followed by *In Celebration, Another Time.*

McFARQUHAR, ERICA. Born August 9, 1959 in Jamaica, West Indies. Graduate Princeton. Debut 1993 OB in *The Knights of the Round Table* followed by *The Evening Shift, Ice Cold, A Midsummer Night's Dream.*

McGANN, JOHN MICHAEL. Born February 2, 1952 in Cleveland, Ohio, Debut 1975 OB in *Three Musketeers*, followed by *Panama Hattie, A Winter's Tale, Johnny-on-a-Spot, Barbarians, A Midsummer Night's Dream, The Wild Duck, Jungle of Cities, The Tempest, Hamlet, The Hunchback of Notre Dame.*

McGILLIN, HOWARD. Born November 5, 1953 in Los Angeles, CA. Graduate U. Cal./Santa Barbara. Debut 1984 OB in *La Boheme*, followed by Bdwy in *The Mystery of Edwin Drood* for which he received a Theatre World Award, *Sunday in the Park with George, Anything Goes, 50 Million Frenchmen in Concert, The Secret Garden, She Loves Me, Kiss of the Spider Woman.*

McGOVERN, ELIZABETH. Born July 18, 1961 in Evanston, IL. Attended Juilliard. Debut 1981 OB in *To Be Young Gifted and Black*, followed by *Hotel Play, My Sister in This House* for which she received a Theatre World Award, *Painting Churches, Hitch-Hikers, Map of the World, Two Gentlemen of Verona, Maids of Honor, As You Like It* (CP) Bdwy in *Love Letters* (1989), *Hamlet* (1992).

McGRATH, MATT. Born June 11, 1969 in NYC. Attended FordhamU. Bdwy debut 1978 in *Working* followed by *A Streetcar Named Desire*, OB in *Dalton's Back* (1989), *Amulets against the Dragon Forces, Life during Wartime, The Old Boy, Nothing Sacred, The Dadshuttle.*

McKECHNIE, DONNA. Born in November 1944 in Detroit, MI. Bdwy debut 1961 in *How to Succeed in Business* followed by *Promises Promises, Company, On the Town, Music!Music!, A Chorus Line*, OB in *Wine Untouched, Cut the Ribbons.*

McKELLEN, IAN. Born May 25, 1939 in Burnley, England. Bdwy debut 1967 in *The Promise* followed by *Amadeus, Wild Honey, Richard III* (BAM).

McKERRACHER, MARK. Born February 21, 1956 in Pasadena, CA. Graduate Santa Barbara U. Bdwy debut 1991 in *Les Miserables.*

McLACHLAN, RODERICK. Born September 9, 1960 in Detroit, MI. Graduate NorthwesternU Debut 1987 in *Death and the King's Horseman* (LC) followed by Bdwy in *Our Town, The Real Inspector Hound, Saint Joan*, OB in *Madame Bovary, Julius Caesar, Oh Hell!, Hauptmann, Make Up Your Mind.*

McNABB, BARRY. Born August 26, 1960 in Toronto, Can. Graduate U. Ore. Bdwy debut 1986 in *Me and My Girl*, followed by *The Phantom of the Opera.*

McNIGHT, SHARON. Born December 18 in Modesto, CA. Graduate San Fran. State Col. Debut 1977 OB in *Murder at the Rutherford House* followed by *A Looney Experience*, Bdwy 1989 in *Starmites* for which she received a Theatre World Award.

McROBBIE, PETER. Born January 31, 1943 in Hawick, Scotland. Graduate Yale U. Debut 1976 OB in *The Wobblies*, followed by *The Devil's Disciple, Cinders, The Ballad of Soapy Smith, Rosmersholm, American Bagpipes, Richard III*, Bdwy in *Whose Life Is It Anyway?* (1979), *Macbeth* (1981), *The Mystery of Edwin Drood, The Master Builder* (1992), *Saint Joan.*

McVETY, DREW. Born April 16, 1965 in Port Huron, MI. Graduate NYU. Debut OB 1988 in *The Heidi Chronicles* followed by *The Substance of Fire*, Bdwy 1989 in *The Heidi Chronicles.*

McVEY, J. MARK. Born January 6, 1958 in Huntington, W. Va. Graduate Marshall U. Bdwy debut 1991 in *Les Miserables*, OB in *Cafe A Go-Go, Chess, Hey Love.*

MEISLE, KATHRYN. Born June 7 in Appleton, WI. Graduate Smith Col., UNC/Chapel Hill. Debut 1988 OB in *Dandy Dick* followed by *Cahoots, Othello, As You Like It* (CP).

MELLOR, STEPHEN. Born September 17, 1954 in New Haven, CT. Graduate Boston U. Debut 1980 OB in *Paris Lights*, followed by *Coming Attractions, Plenty, Tooth of Crime, Shepard Sets, A Country Doctor, Harm's Way, Brightness Falling, Terminal Hip, Dead Mother, A Murder of Crows, Seven Blowjobs, Pericles, Terminal Hip, Strange Feet*, Bdwy in *Big River.*

MENENDEZ, HENRY. Born August 14, 1965 in Atlantic City, NJ. Graduate Boston Consv. Bdwy debut 1991 in *Miss Saigon.*

Cherry Jones

Don Kehr

Madeline Kahn

Patrick Kerr

Laura Kenyon

Ramzi Khalaf

Dorothy Kiara

Charles Kimbrough

Patricia Kies

Joseph Kolinski

Julia Kiley

Andrew Harrison
Leeds

Judy Kuhn

Hal Linden

Sara Laub

Delroy Lindo

Mary Layne

John R. Little

Katherine Leask

Joe Locarro

Lenore Loveman

Victor Love

Roxie Lucas

Stephen Mailer

Nora Mae Lyng

Matt McGrath

Crysta Maria
Macalush

Albert Macklin

Heather MacRae

Timothy Nolen

206

MEREDIZ, OLGA. Born February 15, 1956 in Guantanamo, Cuba. Graduate Tulane U. Bdwy debut 1984 in *The Human Comedy*, OB in *El Bravo!, Women without Men, El Grande de Coca-Cola, The Blessing, The Lady from Havana, 10th Young Playwrights Festival.*

MERKERSON, S. EPATHA. Born November 28, 1952 in Saginaw, MI. Graduate Wayne State U. Debut 1979 OB in *Spell #7*, followed by *Home, Puppetplay, Tintypes, Every Goodbye Ain't Gone, Hospice, The Harvesting, Moms, Lady Day at Emerson's Bar and Grill, 10th Young Playwrights Festival,* Bdwy in *Tintypes* (1982), *The Piano Lesson.*

MERLIN, JOANNA. Born July 15 in Chicago, Il. Attended UCLA. Debut 1958 OB in *The Breaking Wall,* followed by *Six Characters in Search of an Author, Rules of the Game, A Thistle in My Bed, Canadian Gothic/American Modern, Family Portrait, Brooklyn Trojan Women,* Bdwy in *Becket* (1961) *A Far Country, Fiddler on the Roof, Shelter, Uncle Vanya, The Survivor, Solomon's Child.*

MILLER, REBECCA. Born in Roxbury, CT in 1962. Attended YaleU. Debut 1988 OB in *The Cherry Orchard* followed by *The American Plan, The Years.*

MILLS, ELIZABETH. Born August 3, 1967 in San Jose, CA. Attended San Jose StateU. Bdwy debut 1993 in *Ain't Broadway Grand.*

MILLS, STEPHANIE. Born in 1959 in Brooklyn, NY. Bdwy debut 1975 in *The Wiz* followed by 1984 revival, and OB revival in 1993.

MINOFF, TAMMY. Born October 4, 1979 in New York City. Debut 1988 OB in *The Traveling Man,* followed by *1-2-3-4-5,* Bdwy in *The Will Rogers Follies* (1991), *The Goodbye Girl.*

MINOT, ANNA. Born in Boston, MA. Attended Vassar Col. Bdwy debut 1942 in *The Strings My Lord Are False,* followed by *The Russian People, The Visitor, The Iceman Cometh, An Enemy of the People, Love of Four Colonels, The Trip to Bountiful, Tunnel of Love, Ivanov,* OB in *Sands of the Niger, Gettin Out, Vieux Carre, State of the Union, Her Great Match, Rivals, Hedda Gabler, All's Well That Ends Well, Tarfuffe, The Good Natured Man.*

MITCHELL, BRIAN. Born October 31, 1957 in Seattle, WA. Bdwy debut 1988 in *Mail* for which he received a Theatre World Award, followed by *Oh Kay!, Jelly's Last Jam, Kiss of the Spider Woman.*

MITCHELL, GREGORY. Born December 9, 1951 in Brooklyn, NY. Graduate Juilliard, Principle with Eliot Feld Ballet before Bdwy debut 1983 in *Merlin,* followed by *Song and Dance, Phantom of the Opera, Dangerous Games, Aspects of Love, Man of La Mancha (1992), Kiss of the Spider Woman,* OB in *One More Song One More Dance, Tango Apasionado.*

MITCHELL, JOHN CAMERON. Born April 21, 1963 in El Paso, TX. Attended Northwestern U. Bdwy debut 1985 in *Big River,* followed by *Six Degrees of Separation, The Secret Garden,* OB in *Six Degrees of Separation, Destiny of Me.*

MIXON, ALAN. Born March 15, 1933 in Miami, FL. Attended UMiami. Bdwy debut 1962 in *Something about a Soldier* followed by *Sign in Sidney Brustein's Window, The Devils, The Unknown Soldier and His Wife, Love Suicide at Schofield Barracks, Equus, Saint Joan,* OB in *Suddenly Last Summer, Desire under the Elms, The Trojan Women, The Alchemist, Child Buyer, Mr. & Mrs. Lyman, Whitman Portrait, Iphigenia in Aulis, Small Craft Warnings, Mourning Becomes Electra, The Runner Stumbles, Old Glory, The Gathering, Ballad of the Sad Cafe, One Tiger to a Hill, The Butler Did It.*

MOFFAT, DONALD. Born December 26, 1930 in Plymouth, England. Attended RADA. Bdwy debut 1957 in *Under Milk Wood* followed by *Much Ado about Nothing, The Tumbler, Duel of Angels, Passage to India, The Affair, Father's Day, Play Memory, The Wild Duck, Right You Are, You Can't Take It with You, War and Peace, The Cherry Orchard, CockaDoodle Dandy, Hamlet, The Iceman Cometh,* OB in *The Bald Soprano, Jack, The Caretaker, Misalliance, Painting Churches, Henry IV Part I, Titus Andronicus, As You Like It.*

MOGENTALE, DAVID. Born December 28, 1959 in Pittsburgh, PA. Graduate AuburnU. Debut 1987 OB in *The Signal Season of Dummy Hoy* followed by *The Holy Note, Killers, Battery, Necktie Breakfast, Under Control, 1 Act Festival.*

MOKAE, ZAKES. Born August 5, 1935 in Johannesburg, S.Af. Attended St. Peter's Col., RADA. Debut 1970 OB in *Boesman and Lena* followed by *Fingernails Blue as Flowers, The Cherry Orchard, Trial of Vessey, Last Days of British Honduras, A Lesson from Aloes,* Bdwy in *Master Harold and the Boys.., Blood Knot, The Song of Jacob Zulu.*

MONK, DEBRA. Born February 27, 1949 in Middletown, OH. Graduate Frostburg State Col., SouthernMethodistU. Bdwy debut 1982 in *Pump Boys and Dinettes* followed by *Prelude to a Kiss, Redwood Curtain,* OB in *Young Playwrights Festival, A Narrow Bed, Oil City Symphony, Prelude to a Kiss, Assassins, Man in His Underwear, Innocents Crusade, Three Hotels.*

MONTANO, ROBERT. Born April 22 in Queens, NYC. Attended Adelphi U. Bdwy debut 1985 in *Cats* followed by *Chita Rivera + Two, Legs Diamond, Kiss of the Spider Woman,* OB in *The Chosen* (1987), *The Torturer's Visit, How Are Things in Costa del Fuego?, Picture Perfect.*

MOOR, BILL. Born July 13, 1931 in Toledo, OH. Attended Northwestern, Denison U. Bdwy debut 1964 in *Blues for Mr. Charlie,* followed by *Great God Brown, Don Juan, The Visit, Chemin de Fer, Holiday, P.S. Your Cat Is Dead, Night of the Tribades, Water Engine, Plenty, Heartbreak House, The Iceman Cometh, Two Shakespearean Actors,* OB in *Dandy Dick, Love Nest, Days and Nights of Beebee Fenstermaker, The Collection, The Owl Answers, Long Christmas Dinner, Fortune and Men's Eyes, King Lear, Cry of Players, Boys in the Band, Alive and Well in Argentina, Rosmersholm, The Biko Inquest, A Winter's Tale, Johnny on a Spot, Barbarians, The Purging, Potsdam Quartet, Zones of the Spirit, The Marriage of Bette and Boo, Temptation, Devil's Disciple, Happy Days, Lemonade.*

MOORE, CRISTA. Born September 17 in Washington, DC. Attended Am. Ballet Th. Schl. Debut 1987 OB in *Birds of Paradise, Rags,* followed by Bdwy in *Gypsy* (1989) for which she received a Theatre World Award, *EST Marathon '93, Long Ago and Far Away, 110 in the Shade* (LC/NYCO).

MOORE, DANA. Born in Sewickley, PA. Bdwy debut 1982 in *Sugar Babies,* followed by *Dancin', Copperfield, On Your Toes, Singin' in the Rain, Sweet Charity, Dangerous Games, A Chorus Line, The Will Rogers Follies.*

MOORE, MAUREEN. Born August 12, 1951 in Wallingford, CT. Bdwy debut 1974 in *Gypsy,* followed by *The Moonie Shapiro Songbook, Do Black Patent Leather Shoes Really Reflect Up?, Amadeus, Big River, I Love My Wife, Song and Dance, Les Miserables, Amadeus, Jerome Robbins' Broadway, A Little Night Music* (NYCO), *Falsettos,* OB in *Godspell, Unsung Cole, By Strouse.*

MORAN, MARTIN. Born December 29, 1959 in Denver, CO. Attended Stanford U., AmCons Theatre. Debut 1983 OB in *Spring Awakening,* followed by *Once on a Summer's Day, 1•2•3•4•5, Jacques Brel Is Alive* (1992), Bdwy in *Oliver!* (1984), *Big River.*

MOREAU, JENNIE. Born November 19, 1960 in Lewisburg, PA. Graduate NC School of Arts. Debut 1988 OB in *Tony N' Tina's Wedding* followed by *Rimers of Eldritch, Eleemosynary* for which she received a Theatre World Award, *The Good Times Are Killing Me, Young Playwrights Festival 92, Born Guilty.*

MORFOGEN, GEORGE. Born March 30, 1933 in New York City. Graduate Brown U., Yale. Debut 1957 OB in *The Trial of D. Karamazov,* followed by *Christmas Oratorio, Othello, Good Soldier Schweik, Cave Dwellers, Once in a Lifetime, Total Eclipse, Ice Age, Prince of Homburg, Biography: A Game, Mrs. Warren's Profession, Principia Scriptoriae, Tamara, Maggie and Misha, The Country Girl, Othello,As You Like It* (CP), Bdwy in *The Fun Couple* (1962), *Kingdoms, Arms and the Man.*

MORSE, ROBIN. Born July 8, 1963 in New York City. Bdwy debut 1981 in *Bring Back Birdie,* followed by *Brighton Beach Memoirs, Six Degrees of Separation,* OB in *Greenfields,* December 7th, Class I Acts, Eleemosynary, One Act Festival, Six Degrees of Separation, Patient A.

MOSTEL, JOSHUA. Born December 21, 1946 in NYC. Graduate Brandeis U. Debut 1971 OB in *The Proposition* followed by *More Than You Deserve, The Misanthrope, Rocky Road, The Boys Next Door, A Perfect Diamond,* Bdwy in *Unlikely Heroes, American Millionaire, Texas Trilogy, 3 Penny Opera, My Favorite Year.*

MUENZ, RICHARD. Born in 1948 in Hartford, CT. Attended Eastern Baptist Col. Bdwy debut 1976 in *1600 Pennsylvania Avenue,* followed by *The Most Happy Fella, Camelot, Rosalie in Concert, Chess, The Pajama Game* (LC), *Nick and Nora, 110 in the Shade* (LC).

MULLINS, MELINDA. Born April 20, 1958 in Clanton, AL. Graduate Mt. Holyoke Col. Juilliard. Bdwy debut 1987 in *Sherlock's Last Case,* followed by *Serious Money, Mastergate,* OB in *Macbeth, The Hideaway Hilton, Traps/Owners.*

MURAOKA, ALAN. Born August 10, 1962 in Los Angeles, CA. Graduate UCLA. Bdwy debut 1988 in *Mail* followed by *Shogun: The Musical, My Favorite Year.*

MURPHY, CHRISTOPHER. Born June 1944 in Troy, NY. Graduate FordhamU, NYU. Debut 1961 OB in *The Hostage* followed by *Heloise, The Tavern, The Oedipus Chronicles.*

MURPHY, DONNA. Born March 7, 1959 in Corona, NY. Attended NYU. Bdwy debut 1979 in *They're Playing Our Song, followed by The Human Comedy, The Mystery of Edwin Drood, Passion,* OB in *Francis, Portable Pioneer and Prairie Show, Little Shop of Horrors, A ... My Name Is Alice, Showing Off, Privates on Parade, Song of Singapore.*

MURRAY, BRIAN. Born October 9, 1939 in Johannesburg, SA. Debut 1964 OB in *The Knack* followed by *King Lear, Ashes, The Jail Diary of Albie Sachs, A Winter's Tale, Barbarians, The Purging, A Midsummer Night's Dream, The Recruiting Officer, The Arcata Promise, Candide in Concert, Much Ado about Nothing, Hamlet,* Bdwy in *All in Good Time* (1965), *Rosencrantz and Guildenstern Are Dean, Sleuth, Da, Noises Off, A Small Family Business.*

MURTAUGH, JAMES. Born October 28, 1942 in Chicago, Il. Debut OB in *The Firebugs* followed by *Highest Standard of Living, Marathon '87, Other People's Money, Marathon '88, I Am a Man,* Bdwy in *Two Shakespearean Actors* (1991).

NADLER, MARK. Born October 14, 1961 in Waterloo, IA.Attended Interlochen Arts Academy. Debut 1990 OB in *7 O'Clock at the Top of the Gate* followed by *The Sheik of Avenue B.*

NAKAHARA, RON. Born July 20, 1947 in Honolulu, HI. Attended UHi, UTenn. Debut 1981 OB in *Danton's Death* followed by *Flowers and Household Gods, Rohwer, A Midsummer Night's Dream, Teahouse, Song for Nisei Fishermen, Eat a Bowl of Tea, Once Is Never Enough, Noiresque, Play Ball, Three Sisters, And the Soul Shall Dance, Earth and Sky, Cambodia Agonistes, A Doll House,* Bdwy in *A Few Good Men* (1989).

NALBACH, DANIEL. Born May 20, 1937 in Buffalo, NY. Graduate Canisius Col.,U. Pittsburgh. Debut 1986 OB in *Murder on Broadway* followed by *The Thirteenth Chair, The Cellar.*

NASH, NEIL. Born May 23, 1963 in Long Beach, CA. Graduate Pepperdine U. Debut 1987 OB in *The Fantasticks* followed by *Forever Plaid.*

NASTASI, FRANK. Born January 7, 1923 in Detroit, MI. Graduate WayneU, NYU. Bdwy debut 1963 in *Lorenzo* followed by *Avanti,* OB in *Bonds of Interest, One Day More, Nathan the Wise, The Chief Things, Cindy, Escurial, The Shrinking Bride, Macbird, Cakes with the Wine, Metropolitan Madness, Rockaway Boulevard, Scenes from La Vie de Boheme, Agamemnon, Happy Sunset Inc, 3 Last Plays of O'Neill, Taking Steam, Lulu, Body! Body!, Legend of Sharon Shashanova, Enrico IV, Stealing Fire.*

NEESON, LIAM. Born June 7, 1952 in Ballymena, N. Ireland. Attended Queens Col. Bdwy debut 1992 in *Anna Christie* for which he received a Theatre World Award.

NEIDEN, DANIEL. Born July 9, 1958 in Lincoln, NE. Graduate DrakeU. Debut 1980 OB in *City of Life* followed by *Ratman and Wilbur, Nuclear Follies, Pearls, Sophie, The Witch, A Rag on a Stick and a Star.*

NELSON, MARK. Born Sept. 26, 1955 in Hackensack, NJ. Graduate PrincetonU. Debut 1977 OB in *The Dybbuk* followed by *Green Fields, The Keymaker, The Common Pursuit, Flaubert's Latest,Cabaret Verbotten* Bdwy in *Amadeus* (1981), *Brighton Beach Memoirs, Biloxi Blues, Broadway Bound, Rumours, A Few Good Men*
NEUSTADT, TED. Born May 28, 1954 in Baltimore, MD. Graduate NYU, FordhamU. Debut 1990 OB in *Money Talks* followed by *Jackie, Fore!, EST Marathon 93.*
NEVARD, ANGELA. Born March 19, 1963 in Montreal, Can. Graduate Skidmore Col. Debut 1988 OB in *Faith Hope and Charity* followed by *3 by Wilder, Macbeth, The Balcony, Harm's Way, Judgement Day, Tartuffe, Morning Song, Who Will Carry the Word, The Sea Plays, Twelfth Night, Camino Real,* Bdwy in *Wilder Wilder Wilder* (1993).
NEVILLE, JOHN. Born May 2, 1925 in London, England. Attended RADA. Bdwy debut 1956 in *Romeo and Juliet* followed by *Richard II, Hamlet, Twelfth Night, Sherlock Holmes, Ghosts, Saint Joan.*
NEVINS, KRISTINE. Born October 9, 1951 in Champaign, IL. Graduate KanStateU. Debut 1986 OB in *Charley's Tale,* followed by *Starmites, Kiss Me Quick before the Lava Reaches the Village, Midsummer Nights, A Mind Is a Terrible Thing to Lose.*
NICHOLAW, CASEY. Born October 6, 1992. Attended UCLA. Debut 1986 in *The Pajama Game,* Bdwy in *Crazy for You* (1992).
NIXON, CYNTHIA. Born April 9, 1966 in New York City. Debut 1980 in *The Philadelphia Story* (LC) for which she received a Theatre World Award, OB in *Lydie Breeze, Hurlyburly, Sally's Gone She Left Her Name, Lemon Sky, Cleveland and Half-Way Back, Alterations, Young Playwrights, Moonchildren, Romeo and Juliet, The Cherry Orchard, The Balcony Scene, Servy-n-Bernice 4Ever, On the Bum,* Bdwy in *The Real Thing* (1983), *Hurlyburly, The Heidi Chronicles, Angels in America.*
NIXON, MARNI. Born February 22 in Altadena, CA. Attended LACC, U.S. Cal., Pasadena Playhouse. Bdwy debut 1952 in *The Girl in Pink Tights* followed by *My Fair Lady* (1964), OB in *Thank Heaven for Lerner and Loewe, Taking My Turn, Opal, Romeo and Juliet.*
NOLEN, TIMOTHY. Born July 9, 1941 in Rotan, TX. Graduate Trenton State, Col., Manhattan School of Music. Debut in *Sweeney Todd* (1984) with NYC Opera. Bdwy in *Grind* (1985) followed by *Phantom of the Opera.*
NOONAN, TOM. Born April 12, 1951 in Greenwich, CT. Graduate Yale U. Debut 1978 OB in *Buried Child* followed by *The Invitational, Farmyard, The Breakers, Five of Us, Spookhouse, Marathon 88, What Happened Was.*
NORCIA, PATRIZIA. Born April 6, 1954 in Rome, Italy. Graduate HofstraU., YaleU Debut 1978 OB in *Sganarelle* followed by *The Master and Margarita, The Loves of Cass Maguire, Fanshen, The Price of Genius, Taming of the Shrew, Epic Proportions, Oklahoma Samivar, Rough Crossing, The World of Ruth Draper.*
NORMAN, JOHN. Born May 13, 1961 in Detroit, MI. Graduate Cinn. Consv. Bdwy debut 1987 in *Les Miserables.*
NORTH, ALAN. Born December 23, 1927 in NYC. Attended Columbia U. Bdwy debut 1955 in *Plain and Fancy* followed by *South Pacific, Summer of the 17th Doll, Requiem for a Nun, Never Live over a Pretzel Factory, Dylan, Spofford, The American Clock, Marilyn, Conversations with My Father,* OB in *Finian's Rainbow, The Music Man, Annie Get Your Gun, The American Clock, Comedians.*
NOVIN, MICHAEL J. Born April 21 in Baltimore, MD. Graduate NYU. Debut 1987 0B in *Give My Regards to Broadway* followed by *Hannah Senesh,* Bdwy in *Camelot* (1993).
O'BRIEN, ERIN J. Born October 15 in Shakopee, MN. Graduate UMn, NYU. Debut 1992 OB in *Juno.*
O'BRIEN, FRANK. Born April 28 in NYC. Graduate Georgetown U. Bdwy debut 1971 in *Two Gentlemen of Verona,* OB in *Juno.*
ODO, CHRIS. Born February 7, 1954 in Kansas City, MO. Attended Southwest MoStateU. Debut 1984 OB in *A Midsummer Night's Dream* followed by *Oedipus, Sleepless City, Summer Face Woman, White Cotton Sheets,* Bdwy in *M. Butterfly* (1988).
O'HARA, JENNY. Born February 24 in Sonora, CA. Attended CarnegieTech. Bdwy debut 1964 in *Dylan* followed by *The Odd Couple* (1985) OB in *Hang Down Your Head and Die, Play with a Tiger, Arms and the Man, Sambo, My House Is Your House, The Kid, The Fox. EST Marathon 93, Bed and Breakfast.*
O'KELLY, AIDEEN. Born in Dalkey, Ireland. Member Dublin's Abbey Theatre. Bdwy debut 1980 in *A Life* followed by *Othello,* OB in *The Killing of Sister George, Man Enough, Resistance, Remembrance, Somewhere I Have Never Traveled*
O'LEAR, THOMAS JAMES. Born June 21, 1956 in Windsor Locks, CT. Graduate U. Conn. Bdwy debut 1991 in *Miss Saigon.*
OLIVER, ROCHELLE. Born April 15, 1937 in NYC. Attended Brooklyn Col. Bdwy debut 1960 in *Toys in the Attic* followed by *Harold, Who's Afraid of Virginia Woolf?, Happily Never After,* OB in *Brothers Karamazov, Jack Knife, Vincent, Stop You're Killing Me, Enclave, Bits and Pieces, Roads to Home, A Flower Palace, Fayebird.*
OLSON, MARCUS. Born September 21, 1955 in Missoula, MT. Graduate Amherst Col. Debut 1986 OB in *Personals* followed by *Where the Cookie Crumbles, Assassins, Them within Us.*
O'MARA, MOLLIE. Born September 5, 1960 in Pittsburgh, PA. Attended Catholic U. Debut 1989 OB in *Rodents and Radios,* followed by *Crowbar, Famine Plays, Homo Sapien Shuffle.*
O'NEILL, CON. Born in 1964 in Ireland. Bdwy debut 1993 in *Blood Brothers.*
O'REILLY, CIARAN. Born March 13, 1959 in Ireland. Attended Carmelite Col., Juilliard. Debut 1978 OB in *Playboy of the Western World* followed by *Summer, Freedom of the City, Fannie, The Interrogation of Ambrose Fogarty, King Lear, Shadow of a Gunman, The Marry Month of May, I Do Not Like Thee Dr. Fell, The Plough and the Stars, Yeats: A Celebration!, Philadelphia Here I Come, Making*

History, The Mme. MacAdam Traveling Theater.
ORESKES, DANIEL. Born in NYC. Graduate UPa., LAMDA. Debut 1990 OB in *Henry IV* followed by *Othello, Tis Pity She's a Whore,* Bdwy in *Crazy He Calls Me* (1992).
ORMAN, ROSCOE. Born June 11, 1944 in NYC. Debut 1962 OB in *If We Grew Up* followed by *Electronic Nigger, The Great McDaddy, The Sirens, Every Night When the Sun Goes Down, The Last Street Play, Julius Caesar, Coriolanus, The 16th Round, 20 Years Friends, Talented Tenth, The Confessions of Stepin Fetchit,* Bdwy in *Fences* (1988).
O'ROURKE, KEVIN. Born January 25, 1956 in Portland, OR. Graduate Williams Col. Debut 1981 OB in *Declassee* followed by *Sister Mary Ignatius.., Submariners, A Midsummer Night's Dream, Visions of Kerouac, Self Defense, Spoils of War, The Spring Thing, Joined at the Head, Laureen's Whereabouts,* Bdwy in *Alone Together* (1984), *Cat on a Hot Tin Roof, Spoils of War* (1988).
OSCAR, BRAD. Born September 22, 1964 in Washington, DC. Graduate Boston U. Bdwy debut 1990 in *Aspects of Love,* OB in *Forbidden Broadway 1993.*
O'SHEA, MILO. Born June 2, 1926 in Dublin, Ire. Bdwy debut 1968 in *Staircase* followed by *Dear World, Mrs. Warren's Profession, Comedians, A Touch of the Poet, Mass Appeal, Corpse, Meet Me in St. Louis,* OB in *Waiting for Godot, Mass Appeal, The Return of Herbert Bracewell, Educating Rita, Alive Alive Oh!, Remembrance.*
O'SULLIVAN, ANNE. Born February 6, 1952 in Limerick City, Ire. Debut 1977 OB in *Kid Champion,* followed by *Hello Out There, Fly Away Home, The Drunkard, Dennis, Three Sisters, Another Paradise, Living Quarters, Welcome to the Noon, The Dreamer Examines His Pillow, Mama Drama, Free Fall, The Magic Act, The Plough and the Stars, Marathon '88, Bobo's Guns, Marathon '90, Festival of I Acts, Marathon '91, A Murder of Crows.*
O'SULLIVAN-MOORE, EMMETT. Born October 3, 1919 in New Orleans, LA. Graduate LaStateU. Debut 1982 OB in *Bottom of the Ninth* followed by *Who'll Save the Plowboy?, EST Marathon 90, The Roads to Home.*
OLIENSIS, ADAM. Born March 22, 1960 in Passaic, NJ. Graduate U. Wis. Debut 1985 OB in *Inside-Out* followed by *Little Blood Brother, Macbeth, 3 by Wilder,* Bdwy in *Wilder Wilder Wilder* (1993).
OVERBEY, KELLIE. Born November 21, 1964 in Cincinnati, OH. Graduate Northwestern U. Debut 1988 OB in *The Debutante Ball,* followed by *The Second Coming, Face Divided, The Melville Boys.*
OWENS, GORDON. Born February 23, 1959 in Washington, DC. Attended UNC. Schl of Arts. Bdwy debut 1984 in *Dreamgirls,* followed by *A Chorus Line, Starlight Express, Miss Saigon.*
PAEPER, ERIC. Born September 20, 1965 in NYC. Gradllate SUNY/Purchase. Debut 1992 OB in *Pageant* followed by *The Night Larry Kramer Kissed Me.*
PANARO, HUGH. Born February 19, 1964 in Philadelphia, PA. Graduate Temple U. Debut 1985 OB in *What's a Nice Country Like You Doing in a State Like This,* followed by *I Have Found Home, Juba, Splendora,* Bdwy in *Phantom of the Opera* (1990).
PAPPAS, EVAN. Born August 21, 1958 in San Francisco, CA. Attended Cal.Jr.Col. Bdwy debut 1982 in *A Chorus Line* followed by *My Favorite Year,* OB in *I Can Get It for You Wholesale* (1991)
PARKER, COREY. Born July 8, 1965 in NYC. Attended NYU. Debut 1984 OB in *Meeting the Winter Bikerider* followed by *Red Storm Flower, Been Taken, Losing Battles, The Bloodletters, Orphans, Blind Date, Rose Cottages, Ring of Men.*
PARKER, ELLEN. Born September 30, 1949 in Paris, Fr. Graduate Bard Col. Debut 1971 OB in *James Joyce Liquid Theatre* followed by *Uncommon Women and Others, Dusa Fish Stas and Vi, A Day in the Life of the Czar, Fen, Isn't It Romantic?, The Winter's Tale, Aunt Dan and Lemon, Cold Sweat, The Heidi Chronicles, Absent Friends, Joined at the Head,* Bdwy in *Equus, Strangers, Plenty.*
PARKER, MARY-LOUISE. Born August 2, 1964 in Ft. Jackson, SC. Graduate NC Schl. of Arts. Debut 1989 OB in *The Art of Success,* followed by *Prelude to a Kiss, Babylon Gardens, EST Marathon '92,* Bdwy in *Prelude to a Kiss* for which she received a 1990 *Theatre World Award.*
PARKER, SARAH JESSICA. Born March 25, 1965 in Nelsonville, OH Bdwy debut 1978 in *Annie,* OB in *The Innocents, One-Act Festival, To Gillian on Her 37th Birthday, Broadway Scandals of 1928, The Heidi Chronicles, Substance of Fire.*
PARSONS, ESTELLE. Born November 20, 1927 in Lynn, MA. Attended Boston U., Actors Studio. Bdwy debut 1956 in *Happy Hunting* followed by *Whoop Up, Beg Borrow or Steal, Mother Courage, Ready When You Are C.B., Malcolm, Seven Descents of Myrtle, And Miss Reardon Drinks a Little, The Norman Conquests, Ladies at the Alamo, Miss Marguerida's Way, Pirates of Penzance,* OB in *DemiDozen, Pieces of Eight, The Threepenny Opera, Automobile Graveyard, Mrs. Dally Has a Lover* (1963) for which she received a Theatre World Award, *Next Time I'll Sing to You, Come to the Palace of Sin, In the Summer House, Monopoly, The East Wind, Galileo, Peer Gynt, Mahagonny, People Are Living There, Barbary Shore, Oh Glorious Tintinnabulation, Mert and Paul, Elizabeth and Essex, Dialogue for Lovers, New Moon* (in concert), *Orgasmo Adulto Escapes from the Zoo, The Unguided Missile Baba Goya, Extended Forecast.*
PASSELTINER, BERNIE. Born November 2l, 1931 in NYC. Graduate Catholic U. OB in *Square in the Eye, Sourball, As Virtuously Given, Now Is the Time for All Good Men, Rain, Kaddish, Against the Sun, End of Summer, Yentl the Yeshiva Boy, Heartbreak House, Every Place Is Newark, Isn't It Romantic?, Buck, Pigeons on the Walk, Waving Goodbye, The Sunshine Boys, Free Zone, God of Vengeance,* Bdwy in *The Office, The Jar, Yentl.*
PATTERSON, KELLY. Born February 22, 1964 in Midland, TX. Attended Southern Methodist U. Debut 1984 OB in *Up in Central Park* followed by *Manhattan Serenade, The Golden Apple, Weekends in the Country,* Bdwy in *Sweet Charity* (1986), *Jerome Robbins' Broadway.*

PATTISON, LIANN. Born April 12 in Chico, CA. Attended CalStateU/Chico,UWash. Debut 1985 OB in *I'm Not Rappaport, A Burning Beach, Tamara, Camp Paradox*, Bdwy in *Serious Money* (1988).

PATTON, LUCILLE. Born in New York City. Attended Neighborhood Playhouse. Bdwy debut 1946 in *Winter's Tale*, followed by *Topaze, Arms and the Man, Joy to the World, All You Need is One Good Break, Fifth Season, Heavenly Twins, Rhinoceros, Marathon 33, The Last Analysis, Dinner at 8, La Strada, Unlikely Heroes, Love Suicide at Schofield Barracks, The Crucible, A Little Hotel on the Side*, OB in *Ulysses in Nighttown, Failures, Three Sisters, Yes Yes No No, Tango, Mme. de Sade, Apple Pie, Follies, Yesterday Is Over, My Prince My King, I Am Who I Am, Double Game, Love in a Village, 1984, A Little Night Music, Cheri, Till the Eagle Hollers, Money Talks, EST Marathon '92.*

PEACOCK, CHIARA. Born September 19, 1962 in Ann Arbor, MI. Graduate Sarah LawrenceCol. Debut 1985 OB in *Yours Anne* followed by *Maggie Magalita, Fantasma, Romance in Hard Times, A Shayna Maidel*, Bdwy in *The Sisters Rosensweig.*

PEARLMAN, STEPHEN. Born February 26, 1935 in New York City. Graduate Dartmouth Col. Bdwy debut 1964 in *Barefoot in the Park*, followed by *La Strada, Six Degrees of Separation*, OB in *Threepenny Opera, Time of the Key, Pimpernel, In White America, Viet Rock, Chocolates, Bloomers, Richie, Isn't It Romantic, Bloodletters, Light Up the Sky, Perfect Party, Come Blow Your Horn, A Shayna Madel, Value of Names, Hyde in Hollywood, Six Degrees of Separation.*

PENNINGTON, GAIL. Born October 2, 1957 in Kansas City, MO. Graduate SMU. Bdwy debut 1980 in *The Music Man* followed by *Can-Can, America, Little Me* (1982), *42nd Street, The Most Happy Fella*, OB in *The Baker's Wife.*

PEPE, NEIL. Born June 23, 1963 in Bloomington, IN. Graduate Kenyon Col. Debut 1988 OB in *Boys' Life* followed by *Three Sisters, Virgin Molly, Return to Sender, Five Very Live, Down the Shore.*

PEREZ, LUIS. Born July 28, 1959 in Atlanta, GA. With Joffrey Ballet before 1986 Bdwy debut in *Brigadoon* (LC), followed by *Phantom of the Opera, Jerome Robbins' Broadway, Dangerous Games, Grand Hotel, Man of La Mancha* (1992), *Ain't Broadway Grand*, OB in *Wonderful Ice Cream Suit, Tango Apasionada.*

PERKINS, CAROL. Born December 29, 1957 in Sarasota, FL. Bdwy debut 1991 in *Penn & Teller Refrigerator Tour*, OB in *Penn & Teller Rot in Hell.*

PERKINS, PATTI. Born July 9 in New Haven,CT. Attended AMDA. Debut 1972 OB in *The Contrast* followed by *Fashion, Tuscaloosa's Calling Me, Patch, Shakespeare's Cabaret, Maybe I'm Doing It Wrong, Fabulous LaFontaine, Hannah 1939, Free Zone*, Bdwy in *All Over Town, Shakespeare's Cabaret.*

PERRY, ELIZABETH. Born October 18, 1937 in Pawtucket, RI. Attended RIStateU.,AmThWing. Bdwy debut 1956 in *Inherit the Wind* followed by *The Women*, with AP in *The Misanthrope, Hamlet, The King Dies, Macbeth, and Chronicles of Hell, Present Laughter, 84 Charing Cross Road, Coastal Disturbances, Musical Comedy Murders*, OB in *Royal Gambit, Here Be Dragons, Lady from the Sea, Heartbreak House, him, All the Way Home, The Frequency, Fefu and Her Friends, Out of the Broom Closet, Ruby Ruby Sam Sam, Did You See the Elephant?, Last Stop Blue Jay Lane, A Difficult Borning, Presque Isle, Isn't It Romantic?, The Chairs, Joined at the Head.*

PESCE, VINCE. Born December 3, 1966 in Brooklyn NY. Bdwy debut 1993 in *Guys and Dolls*, OB in *The Hunchback of Notre Dame.*

PETERSON, CHRIS. Born November 29 in Princeton, NJ. Attended Westminster Choir Col. Bdwy debut 1984 in *Cats*, followed by *The Phantom of the Opera.*

PETTIT, DODIE. Born December 29, in Princeton, NJ. Attended Westminster Choir col. Bdwy debut 1984 in *Cats*, followed by *The Phantom of the Opera.*

PEVSNER, DAVID. Born December 31, 1958 in Skokie, IL. Graduate Carnegie-Mellon U. Debut 1985 OB in *A Flash of Lightning*, followed by *Rags, A Rag on a Stick and a Star*, Bdwy in *Fiddler on the Roof* (1990).

PHILLIPS, ETHAN. Born February 8, 1950 in Rockville Center, NY. Graduate Boston U. Cornell U. Debut 1979 OB in *Modigliani*, followed by *Eccentricities of a Nightingale, Nature and Purpose of the Universe, The Beasts, Dumb Waiter, The Indian Wants the Bronx, Last of the Red Hot Lovers, Only Kidding, Almost Perfect, Theme and Variations, Marathon '91, Lips Together Teeth Apart, Young Playwrights Festival*, Bdwy in *My Favorite Year* (1992).

PHILLIPS, GARRISON. Born October 8, 1929 in Tallahasee, Fl. Graduate U. W.Va. Debut 1956 OB in *Eastward in Eden* followed by *Romeo and Juliet, Time of the Cuckoo, Triptych, After the Fall, Two Gentlemen of Verona, Ambrosio, The Sorrows of Frederick, La Ronde,Playing with Fire(After Frankstein)*, Bdwy in *Clothes for a Summer Hotel* (1980).

PIDGEON, REBECCA. Born October 25, 1965 in Edinburgh, Scotland. Attended RADA. Debt 1992 OB in *Oleanna.*

PIEHL, MICHAEL. Born June 25, 1967 in Seattle, Wa. Bdwy debut 1991 in *Grand Hotel.*

PIERCE, VERNA. Born in New Jersey. Attended UKan., AADA. Bdwy debut 1974 in *A Little Night Music* followed by *Pippin, OB in Fiorello!, The Elephant Man, Juno.*

PIERSON, GEOFF. Born June 16, 1949 in Chicago, IL. Graduate FordhamU., YaleU. Debut 1978 OB in *Wings* followed by *Playing with Fire, Crossing Delancey, The Yes Word, Miss Julie, Etta Jenks, The Yes Word*, Bdwy in *Tricks of the Trade* (1980).

PIETROPINTO, ANGELA. Born February 4 in NYC. Graduate NYU. OB in *Henry IV, Alice in Wonderland, Endgame, The Sea Gull, Jinx Bridge, The Mandrake, Marie and Bruce, Green Card Blues, 3 by Pirandello, The Broken Pitcher, Cymbeline, Romeo and Juliet, A Midsummer Night's Dream, Twelve Dreams, The Rivals, Cap and Bells, Thrombo, Lies My Father Told Me, Sorrows of Stephen, Between the Wars, The Hotel Play, Rain Some Fish No Elephants, Young Playwrights 90, Tunnel of Love, Thanksgiving Day*, Bdwy in *The Suicide*, (1980), *Eastern Standard.*

PHOENIX, ALEC. Born September 9, 1964 in Bristol, England Graduate Swarthmore Col., Juilliard. Debut 1992 OB in *Henry V* followed by *Love's Labour's*

Lost, Bdwy in *Timon of Athens* (1993)., *A Government Inspector.*

PIGEON, BELINDA. Born August 12, 1967 in Santa Barbara, CA. Graduate Eastman School of Music, Manhattan School of Music. Debut 1993 OB in *Orpheus in Love.*

PINE, LARRY. Born March 3, 1945 in Tucson, Az. Graduate NYU. Debut 1967 OB in *Cyrano* followed by *Alice in Wonderland, Mandrake, Aunt Dan and Lemon, The Taming of the Shrew, Better Days, Dolphin Project*, Bdwy in *End of the World* (1984).

PINHASIK, HOWARD. Born June 5, 1953 in Chicago, IL. Graduate OhioU. Debut 1978 OB in *Allegro* followed by *Marya, The Meechans, Street Scene, Collette Collage, Hopscotch.*

PINKINS, TONYA. Born May 30, 1962 in Chicago Il. Attended Carnegie-Mellon U. Bdwy debut 1981 in *Merrily We Roll Along*, followed by *Jelly's Last Jam*, OB in *Five Points, A Winter's Tale, An Ounce of Prevention, Just Say No, Mexican Hayride, Young Playwrights '90, Approximating Mother.*

PIRO, JACQUELYN. Born January 8, 1965 in Boston, MA. Graduate Boston U. Debut 1987 OB in *Company*, followed by Bdwy in *Les Miserables* (1990).

PITONIAK, ANNE. Born March 30, 1922 in Westfield, MA. Attended UNC Women's Col. Debut 1982 OB in *Talking With*, followed by *Young Playwrights Festival, Phaedra, Steel Magnolias, Pygmalion, The Rose Quartet*, Bdwy in *'night, Mother* (1983) for which she received a Theatre World Award, *The Octette Bridge Club.*

PITTU, DAVID. Born April 4, 1967 in Fairfield, CT. Graduate NYU. Debut 1987 OB in *Film is Evil:Radio Is Good* followed by *Five Very Live, White Cotton Sheets, Nothing Sacred.*

PLAYTEN, ALICE. Born August 28, 1947 in New York City. Bdwy debut 1960 in *Gypsy*, followed by *Oliver!, Hello Dolly!, Henry Sweet Henry* for which she received a Theatre World Award, *George M.!, Spoils of War, Rumors*, OB in *Promenade, The Last Sweet Days of Isaac, National Lampoon's Lemmings, Valentine's Day, Pirates of Penzance, Up from Paradise, A Visit, Sister Mary Ignatius Explains It All, An Actor's Nightmare, That's It Folks, 1-2-3-4-5, Spoils of War, Marathon '90 and '93, The Mysteries?.*

PLOTNICK, JACK. Born October 30, 1968 in Somerset, NJ. Graduate CarnegieMellonU Debut 1991 OB in *Pageant* followed by *Class Clown, The News in Revue*, Bdwy in *Sheik of Avenue B* (1992).

PLUNKETT, MARYANN. Born in 1953 in Lowell, MA. Attended U. NH. Bdwy debut 1983 in *Agnes of God* followed by *Sunday in the Park with George, Me and My Girl, The Crucible, The Master Builder, A Little Hotel on the Side, Saint Joan, The Sea Gull*, OB in *Aristocrats.*

POCHOS, DEDE. Born April 27, 1960 in Lake Forest, IL. Graduate U.Penn. Bdwy debut 1993 in *Wilder Wilder Wilder*. OB in *A Midsummer Night's Dream, Macbeth, Tomorrow Was War, Judgment Day, Tartuffe, Who Will Carry the Word?*

POE, RICHARD. Born January 25, 1946 in Portola, CA. Graduate U. San Francisco, U. Cal./Davis Debut 1971 OB in *Hamlet*, followed by *Seasons Greetings, Twelfth Night, Naked Rights, Approximating Mother, Jeffrey*, Bdwy in *Broadway* (1987), *M. Butterfly, Our Country's Good.*

POLETICK, ROBERT. Born February 28 in Brooklyn, NY. Debut 1988 OB in *Brotherhood* followed by *Beyond the Horizon, Hamlet, Holding Out, Them, Those People.*

POPE, STEPHANIE. Born April 8, 1964 in NYC. Debut 1983 OB in *The Buck Stops Here* followed by *Shades of Harlem*, Bdwy in *Big Deal* (1986), *Jelly's Last Jam.*

PORTER, ADINA. Born February 18, 1963 in NYC. Attended SUNY/Purchase. Debut 1988 OB in *The Debutante Ball* followed by *Inside Out, Tiny Mommie, Footsteps in the Rain, Jersey City, The Mysteries?*

POWELL, MICHAEL WARREN. Born January 22, 1937 in Martinsville, VA. Attended Goodman Theatre Schol. Debut 1954 OB in *Home Free?*, followed by *This is the Rill Speaking, Balm in Gilead, The Gingham Dog, Thank You Miss Victoria, Futz, Tom Paine, Amulets Against the Dragon Forces, Dirty Talk, On the Wing, The Weather Outside, Prelude to a Kiss, Tales from Hollywood.*

PRATT, SEAN. Born December 26, 1965 in Oklahoma City, OK. Graduate Santa Fe Col. BADA. Debut OB 1993 in *The Good Natured Man* followed by *Phaedra, Widowers Houses.*

PRENTICE, AMELIA. Born September 14 in Toronto, Can. Graduate AADA, LAMDA, Bdwy debut 1987 in *Starlight Express*, followed by *Anna Karenina*, OB in *Hooray for Hollywood, Lenny Bruce Revue, Broadway Jukebox, Little Me.*

PRESCOTT, JENNIFER. Born February 19, 1963 in Portland, OR. Graduate NYU, AMDA. Bdwy debut 1987 in *Starlight Express* followed by *Fiddler on the Roof*, OB in *On a Clear Day You Can See Forever, 3 Americanisms.*

PRICE, BRIAN DAVID. Born March 6, 1966 in Washington, DC. Graduate YaleU. Debut OB 1989 in *Philoctetes* followed by *Women and Wallace.*

PRINCE, FAITH. Born August 5, 1957 in Augusta, GA. Graduate U. Cinn. Debut OB 1981 in *Scrambled Feet*, followed by *Olympus on My Mind, Groucho, Living Color, Bad Habits, Falsettoland*, Bdwy in *Jerome Robbins Broadway (1989), Nick & Nora, Guys and Dolls* (1992).

PUGH, RICHARD WARREN. Born October 20, 1950 in New York City. Graduate Tarkio Col. Bdwy debut 1979 in *Sweeney Todd*, followed by *The Music Man, The Five O'Clock Girl, Copperfield, Zorba* (1983), *Phantom of the Opera*, OB in *Chase a Rainbow.*

PULLIAM, DARCY. Born November 15, 1943 in Schenectady, NY. Graduate TuftsU.,Wayne StateU. Bdwy debut 1986 in *La Cage aux Folles* followed by *Anna Karenina*, OB in *American Bagpipes, The Royal Game, Werewulf.*

PURSLEY, DAVID. Born July 13, 1938 in Lewisburg, PA. Graduate Harvard U., Baylor U. Debut 1969 OB in *Peace* followed by *The Faggot, Wings, The Three Musketeers*, Bdwy in *Happy End* (1977), *Snow White, Anything Goes, 3 Penny Opera, Anna Karenina.*

QUIGLEY, BERNADETTE. Born November 10, 1960 in Coldspring, NY Debut 1983 OB in *Ah Wilderness* followed by *Relative Values, God of Vengeance.*

QUILLIN, MIMI CICHANOWICZ. Born March 26 on Staten Island, NY. Graduate Boston Consv. Bdwy debut 1986 in *Sweet Charity* followed by *Ain't Broadway Grand,* OB in *Promises Promises* (1983), *The Balcony, Carnal Knowledge, Any Place but Here.*

QUINN, COLLEEN. Born April 24 in Lindenhurst, NY. Debut 1988 OB in *Borderlines* followed by *Keeping an Eye on Louie, Octoberfest, Dutchman, Beauty Marks, Midsummer, Program for Murder.*

QUINN, PATRICK. Born February 12, 1950 in Philadelphia, PA. Graduate Temple U. Bdwy Debut 1976 in *Fiddler on the Roof* followed by *A Day in Hollywood/A Night in the Ukraine, Oh, Coward!, Lend Me a Tenor,* OB in *It's Better with a Bank, By Strouse, Forbidden Broadway, The Best of Forbidden Broadway, Raft of Medusa, Forbidden Broadway's 10th Anniversary.*

QUINTERO, JOE. Born August 27, 1969 in Paterson, NJ. Graduate Rutgers U. Debut 1993 OB in *The Boiler Room* followed by *Washington Square Moves.*

RAEBECK, LOIS. Born in West Chicago, IL. Graduate Purdue U. Debut 1986 OB in *Rule of Three* followed by *Cork, Between Time and Timbuktu, The Women in the Family, All's Well That Ends Well, Necktie Breakfast, The Hour of the Dog.*

RAIKEN, LAWRENCE/LARRY. Born February 5, 1949 on Long Island, NY. Graduate William & Mary Col.,UNC. Debut 1979 OB in *Wake Up It's Time to Go to Bed* followed by *The Rise of David Levinsky, Bells Are Ringing, Pageant,* Bdwy in *Woman of the Year* (1981), *Sheik of Avenue B.*

RAITER, FRANK. Born January 17, 1932 in Cloquet, MN. Yale graduate. Bdwy debut 1958 in *Cranks,* followed by *Dark at the Top of the Stairs, J.B., Camelot, Salome,* OB in *Soft Core Pornographer, The Winter's Tale, Twelfth Night, Tower of Evil, Endangered Species, A Bright Room Called Day, Learned Ladies, 'Tis Pity She's A Whore, Othello, Comedy of Errors.*

RALPH, SHERYL LEE. Born December 30, 1957 in NYC. Graduate Rutgers U. Debut 1977 OB in *Eden* followed by *One Night Only,* Bdwy in *Reggae* (1980), *The Goodbye Girl.*

RAMSAY, REMAK. Born February 2, 1937 in Baltimore, MD. Graduate Princeton U. Debut 1964 OB in *Hang Down Your Head and Die,* followed by *The Real Inspector Hound, Landscape of the Body, All's Well That Ends Well* (CP), *Rear Column, The Winslow Boy, The Dining Room, Save Grand Central, Quartermaine's Terms,* Bdwy in *Half a Sixpence, Sheep on the Runway, Lovely Ladies Kind Gentlemen, On the Town, Jumpers, Private Lives, Dirty Linen, Every Good Boy Deserves Favor, Devil's Disciple, Woman in Mind, Nick and Nora, Saint Joan.*

RAMSEY, KEVIN. Born September 24, 1959 in New Orleans, LA. Graduate NYU. Bdwy debut in *Black and Blue* (1989), followed by *Oh Kay!* for which he received a Theatre World Award, *5 Guys Named Moe,* OB in *Liberation Suite, Sweet Dreams, Prison Made Tuxedos, Staggerlee, Juba.*

RANDALL, TONY. Born February 26, 1920 in Tulsa, OK. Attended Northwestern, Columbia, Neighborhood Playhouse. Bdwy debut 1947 in *Antony and Cleopatra* followed by *To Tell You the Truth, Caesar and Cleopatra, Oh Men! Oh Women!, Inherit the Wind, Oh! Captain!, UTBU, M. Butterfly, A Little Hotel on the Side, 3 Men on a Horse.*

RASHAD, PHYLICIA. Born June 19, 1948 in Houston, TX. Graduate HowardU. Debut 1968 OB in *Miss Weaver* followed by *Zora, The Sirens, The Duplex,* Bdwy in *Ain't Supposed to Die a Natural Death* (1972), *The Wiz, Dreamgirls, Into the Woods, Jelly's Last Jam.*

RASHOVICH, GORDANA. Born September 18 in Chicago, Il. Graduate Roosevelt U., RADA. Debut 1977 OB in *Fefu and Her Friends* for which she received a Theatre World Award, followed by *Selma, Couple of the Year, Mick Sonata, Class One-Acts, Morocco, A Shayna Maidel, The Misanthrope, EST Marathon '93,* Bdwy in *Conversations with My Father* (1992).

RAWLS, HARDY. Born November 18, 1952 in Jacksonville, FL. Graduate FlAtlanticU., UCLA. Debut 1982 OB in *Who'll Save the Plowboy?* followed by *A Thurber Carnival, CBS Live.*

REA, STEPHEN. Born October 31, 1948 in Belfast, Ire. Graduate Queen's U., Abbey Theatre School. Bdwy debut 1992 in *Someone Who'll Watch over Me* for which he received a Theatre World Award.

REBHORN, JAMES. Born September 1, 1948 in Philadelphia, PA. Graduate WittenbergU. ColumbiaU. Debut 1972 OB in *Blue Boys* followed by *Are You Now.., The Trouble with Europe, Othello, The Hunchback of Notre Dame, Period of Adjustment, The Freak, Half a Lifetime, Touch Black, To Gillian on Her 37th Birthday, Rain, The Hasty Heart, Husbandry, Isn't It Romantic?, Blind Date, Cold Sweat, Spoils of War, Marathon 88, Ice Cream with Her Fudge, Life during Wartime, Innocents Crusade, On the Bum,* Bdwy in *I'm Not Rappaport, Our Town* (1989) .

REDGRAVE, LYNN. Born March 8, 1943 in London, England. Attended Central School. Bdwy debut 1967 in *Black Comedy* followed by *My Fat Friend, Mrs. Warren's Profession, Knock Knock, St. Joan, Aren't We All?, Love Letters, The Master Builder, A Little Hotel on the Side, Shakespeare for My Father*

REED, BOBBY. Born September 26, 1956 in NYC. Attended AMDA. Debut 1975 OB in *Boy Meets Boy* followed by *The Hunchback of Notre Dame, Der Ring Gott Farblonjet, Big Hotel, A Christmas Carol, At Home with the TV, White Cotton Sheets.*

REED, MAGGI-MEG. Born in Columbus, OH. Graduate Harvard U. Debut 1984 OB in *She Stoops to Conquer* followed by *Playboy of the Western World, Triangles, Beyond the Window.*

REED, VIVIAN. Born June 6, 1947 in Pittsburgh, PA. Attended Juilliard. Bdwy debut 1971 in *That's Entertainment* followed by *Don't Bother Me I Can't Cope, Bubbling Brown Sugar* for which she received a Theatre World Award, *It's So Nice to Be Civilized, High Rollers.*

REEHLING, JOYCE. Born March 5, 1949 in Baltimore, MD. Graduate NC School of Arts. Debut 1976 OB in *The Hot 1 Baltimore* followed by *Who Killed Richard Cory?, Lulu, 5th of July, The Runner Stumbles, Life and/or Death, Back in the Race, Time Framed, Extremities, Hands of the Enemy, Reckless, Prelude to a Kiss, On the Bum,* Bdwy in *A Matter of Gravity* (1976), *5th of July, Prelude to a Kiss.*

REEVES, MARC. Born November 6, 1956 in Wichita, KS. Graduate WichitaStateU, OhioU. Debut 1992 OB in *The Depression Show*

RESNIK, HOLLIS. Born June 1, 1957 in Euclid, OH. Graduate Denison U. Debut 1993 OB in *Wings.*

REYNOLDS, RUSTY. Born September 13, 1968 in Summit, NJ. Attended UIowa, Manhattan School of Music. Debut 1993 OB in *Carnival* followed by *The Littlest Clown.*

RHOADS, KURT. Born October 17, 1957 in Columbus, GA. Graduate EastIllU, UChicago, Goodman School. Debut 1992 OB in *Othello* followed by *The Good Natur'd Man, Them That's Got.*

RICHARD, TANIA. Born September 1, 1969 in Chicago, IL. Graduate IllStateU. Bdwy debut 1993 in *The Song of Jacob Zulu.*

RICHARDS, CAROL. Born December 26 in Aurora, IL. Graduate Northwestern U., Columbia U. Bdwy debut 1965 in *Half a Sixpence,* followed by *Mame, Last of the Red Hot Lovers, Company, Cats.*

RICHARDS, GARY. Born December 16, 1953 in NYC. Graduate Union Col. Debut 1981 OB in *Catch22* followed by *Ladies in Retirement, My Three Angels, Play It Again Sam, Lies My Father Told Me, The Root.*

RICHARDSON, NATASHA. Born May 11, 1963 in London, Eng. Graduate Central School of Speech and Drama. Bdwy debut 1992 in *Anna Christie* for which she received a Theatre World Award.

RICKMAN, ALLEN L. Born February 4, 1960 in Far Rockaway, NY. Attended Brooklyn Col. Debut 1988 OB in *Faithful Brethern of Pitt Street* followed by *Dr. Dietrich's Process, The Big Winner, Tony 'n' Tina's Wedding, Theda Bara and the Frontier Rabbi.*

RIEBLING, TIA. Born July 21, 1954 in Pittsburgh, PA. Attended NYU, CarnegieMellon. Debut 1983 OB in *American Passion* followed by *Preppies, Hamelin, Wish You Were Here,* Bdwy in *Smile* (1986), *Fiddler on the Roof, Les Miserables.*

RIFKIN, RON. Born October 31, 1939 in New York City. Graduate NYU. Bdwy debut 1960 in *Come Blow Your Horn,* followed by *The Goodbye People, The Tenth Man,* OB in *Rosebloom, The Art of Dining, Temple, Substance of Fire.*

RIGOL, JOEY. Born January 6, 1979 in Miami, FL. Debut 1988 OB in *The Chosen,* followed by *The Voyage of the Beagle, The Music Man, Stop the World, Sympathy, Radio City Christmas Spectacular,* Bdwy in *Les Miserables* (1989).

RILEY, ROB. Born April 6, 1945 in Concordia, KS.. Graduate UMi. Debut 1986 OB in *Paul Sills & Company* followed by *Wild Men!*(1993).

RINEHART, ELAINE. Born August 16, 1958 in San Antonio, TX. Graduate NC Schl. Arts. Debut 1975 OB in *Tenderloin,* followed by *Native Son, Joan of Lorraine, Dumping Ground, Fairweather Friends, The Color of the Evening Sky, The Best Little Whorehouse in Texas, The Wedding of the Siamese Twins, Festival of 1 Acts, Up 'n' Under, Crystal Clear, Black Market, 1 Act Comedies, Raft of the Medusa, I Can't Stop Screaming, King of Carpets.*

RINGHAM, NANCY. Born November 16, 1954 in Minneapolis, MN. Graduate St. Olaf Col, Oxford U. Bdwy debut in *My Fair Lady* (1981), *3 Penny Opera, The Will Rogers Follies,* OB in *That Jones Boy, Bugles at Dawn, Not-so-new Faces of 1982, Trouble in Tahiti, Lenny and the Heartbreakers, 4 one-act Musicals, Esther: A Vaudeville Megillah.*

RIPLEY, ALICE. Born December 14, 1963 in San Leandro, CA. Graduate Kent State U. Bdwy debut 1993 in *The Who's Tommy.*

RIVERA, CHITA. Born January 23, 1933 in Washington, DC. Bdwy debut 1950 in *Guys and Dolls* followed by *Call Me Madam, Can-Can, Seventh Heaven, Mr. Wonderful, West Side Story, Bye Bye Birdie, Bajour, Chicago, Bring Back Birdie, Merlin, The Rink, Jerry's Girls, Kiss of the Spider Woman,* OB in *Shoestring Revue.*

RIVERA, MANUEL. Born January 27, 1959 in NYC. Debut 1984 OB in *Cuban Swimmer/Dog Lady* followed by *She First Met Her Parents on the Subway, Beyond the Outer Circle.*

ROBB, R.D. Born March 31, 1972 in Philadelphia, PA Bdwy debut 1980 in *Charlie and Algernon,* followed by *Oliver!, Les Miserables.*

ROBBINS, REX. Born in Pierre, SD. Bdwy debut 1964 in *One Flew over the Cuckoo's Nest* followed by *Scratch, The Changing Room, Gypsy, Comedians, An Almost Perfect Person, Richard III, You Can't Take It with You, Play Memory, Six Degrees of Separation, The Sisters Rosensweig,* OB in *Servant of Two Masters, The Alchemist, Arms and the Man, Boys in the Band, A Memory of Two Mondays, They Knew What They Wanted, Secret Service, Boy Meets Girl, Three Sisters, The Play's The Thing, Julius Caesar, Henry IV Part I, The Dining Room, Urban Blight.*

ROBERTS, BEN. Born November 9, 1961 in Alice, TX. Graduate Tyler Jr. Col. UMs. Debut 1993 OB in *Widowers' Houses.*

ROBERTS, TONY. Born October 22, 1939 in New York City. Graduate Northwestern U. Bdwy debut 1962 in *Something about a Soldier,* followed by *Take Her She's Mine, Last Analysis, Never Too Late, Barefoot in the Park, Don't Drink the Water, How Now Dow Jones, Play It Again Sam, Promises Promises, Sugar, Absurd Person Singular, Murder at the Howard Johnson's, They're Playing Our Song, Doubles, Brigadoon* (LC), *South Pacific* (LC), *Love Letters, Jerome Robbins' Broadway, The Sisters Rosensweig, The Sea Gull,* OB in *The Cradle Will Rock, Losing Time, The Good Parts, Time Framed, The Normal Heart* (benefit reading) *Brigadoon* (NYCO/LC).

ROBERTSON, ALENE. Born December 9 in Hartford, CT. Debut 1993 OB in *Annie Warbucks.*

ROBINSON, LANCE. Born June 21, 1979 in Salisbury, MD. Bdwy debut 1989 in *Gypsy,* followed by *Shadowlands, The Will Rogers Follies.*

ROCHE, TUDI. Born July 19, 1955 in Lubbock, TX. Attended TxChristianU. Bdwy debut 1980 in *A Day in Hollywood/A Night in the Ukraine* followed by *Harrigan 'n' Hart*, OB in *Preppies* (1983), *Man Enough, The View from Here.*

ROGERS, GIL. Born February 4, 1934 in Lexington, KY. Attended Harvard U. OB in *The Ivory Branch, Vanity of Nothing, Warrior's Husband, HellBent fer Heaven, Gods of Lightning, Pictures in a Hallway, Rose, Memory Bank, A Recent Killing, Birth, Come Back Little Sheba, Life of Galileo, Remembrance, Mortally Fine, Frankie, The History of President JFK Part 1*, Bdwy in *The Great White Hope, The Best Little Whorehouse in Texas, The Corn Is Green* (1983).

ROONEY, MICKEY. Born September 23, 1920 in Brooklyn, NY. Bdwy debut 1979 in *Sugar Babies* for which he received a Special Theatre World Award, followed by *The Will Rogers Follies.*

ROSS, BERTRAM. Born November 14, 1920 in Brooklyn, NY. Attended Oberlin Col. With Martha Graham Co. before 1983 debut OB in *The Tempest* followed by *An Evening with Bertram Ross, One Night in Manhattan.*

ROSS, JAN. Born February 5, 1948 in Long Beach, CA. Graduate Brandeis U. Debut 1972. OB in *Two If by Sea* followed by *The Cellar.*

ROSS, NATALIE. Born January 24, 1932 in Minneapolis, MN. Graduate U.Wash., RADA. Bdwy debut 1961 in *Come Blow Your Horn*, OB in *Butterfly Dream* (1966), *Dietrich Process, Tales from Hollywood.*

ROTH, TISHA. Born February 28, 1961 in Norristown, PA. Graduate NC School of Arts. Debut 1986 OB in *Movie Queen* followed by *The Age of Pie, The Early Girl, The Mysteries?*

ROWAN, RICHARD. Born June 7, 1965 in NYC. Graduate Northwestern U. Debut 1992. OB in *The News in Revue.*

ROZNOWSKI, ROBERT. Born July 16, 1963 in Baltimore, MD. Graduate Point Park Col., Ohio State U. Debut 1992 OB in *Lightin' Out* followed by *Young Abe Lincoln.*

RUBANO, CRAIG. Born in St. Louis, MO. Graduate YaleU., ColumbiaU. Debut 1989 OB in *The Pirates of Penzance*, followed by *Charlotte's Web, Ernest in Love*, Bdwy in *Les Miserables* (1993).

RUCK, PATRICIA. Born September 11, 1963 in Washington, DC. Attended Goucher Col. Bdwy debut 1986 in *Cats.*

RUCKER, BO. Born August 17, 1948 in Tampa, Fl. Debut 1978 OB in *Native Son* for which he received a Theatre World Award, followed by *Blues for Mr. Charlie, Streamers, Forty Deuce, Dustoff, Rosetta Street*, Bdwy in *Joe Turner's Come and Gone* (1988).

RUEHL, MERCEDES. Born in 1950 in Jackson Heights, NY. Attended New Rochelle Col. Debut 1985 OB in *Coming of Age in SoHo* followed by *The Marriage of Bette and Boo, Other People's Money*, Bdwy in *I'm Not Rappaport* (1985), *Lost in Yonkers.*

RUIVIVAR, FRANCIS. Born December 21, 1960 in Hong Kong, China. Graduate Loretto Heights Col. Bdwy debut 1988 in *Chess*, followed by *Starlight Express, Shogun: The Musical* for which he received a Theatre World Award, *Miss Saigon*, OB in *Promised Land.*

RULE, CHARLES. Born August 4, 1928 in Springfield, MO. Bdwy debut 1951 in *Courtin' Time*, followed by *Happy Hunting, Oh Captain!, The Conquering Hero, Donnybrook, Bye Bye Birdie, Fiddler on the Roof, Henry Sweet Henry, Maggie Flynn, 1776, Cry for Us All, Gypsy, Goodtime Charley, On the 20th Century, Phantom of the Opera*, OB in *Family Portrait.*

RUPERT, MICHAEL. Born October 23, 1951 in Denver, CO. Attended Pasadena Playhouse. Bdwy debut 1968 in *The Happy Time* for which he received a *Theatre World Award*, followed by *Pippin, Sweet Charity* (1986), *Mail, City of Angels, Falsettos*, OB in *Festival, Shakespeare's Cabaret, March of the Falsettos, Falsettoland.*

RYAN, AMY. Born May 3, 1968 in NYC. Debut OB 1988 in *A Shayna Maidel* followed by *Rimers of Eldritch, Eleemosynary*, Bdwy (1993) in *The Sisters Rosensweig.*

RYAN, STEVEN. Born June 19, 1947 in New York City. Graduate Boston U., U. Minn. Debut 1978 OB in *Winning Isn't Everything*, followed by *The Beethoven, September in the Rain, Romance Language, Love's Labour's Last, Love and Anger, Approximating Mother*. Bdwy in *I'm Not Rappaport* (1986), *Guys and Dolls* (1992).

RYNN, MARGIE. Born in Princeton, NJ. Graduate U. Cal/Berkeley, ULA. Debut 1988 OB in *Autobahn* followed by *The Bed Experiment, Suite Sixteen, Les Miserables.*

SALONG, LEA. Born February 22, 1971 in Manila, PI. Attended Manila U. Bdwy debut 1991 in *Miss Saigon* for which she received a Theatre World Award.

SALVATORE, JOHN. Born November 3, 1961 in Rockville Center, NY. Attended Adelphi U. Bdwy debut 1986 in *A Chorus Line*, OB in *Pageant.*

SAMUELSON, HOWARD. Born October 21, 1958 in Philadelphia, PA. Graduate NYU. Debut 1985 OB in *Measure for Measure* followed by *The Job Search, The Emperor's New Clothes, The Racket, Vampire Lesbians of Sodom, A Midsummer Night's Dream, Comedy of Errors, I Am a Man*, Bdwy in *Blood Brothers* (1993).

SANCHEZ, JAIME. Born December 19, 1938 in Rincon, PR. Attended Actors Studio. Bdwy debut 1957 in *West Side Story* followed by *Oh Dad Poor Dad.., A Midsummer Night's Dream, Richard III*, OB in *The Toilet/Conerico Was Here to Stay* for which he received a Theatre World Award, *The Ox Cart, The Tempest, Merry Wives of Windsor, Julius Caesar, Coriolanus, He Who Gets Slapped, State without Grace, The Sun Always Shines for the Cool, Othello, Elektra, Domino, The Promise, Rising Sun Falling Star, Academy Street.*

SANDERS, JAY O. Born April 16, 1953 in Austin, TX. Graduate SUNY/Purchase. Debut 1976 OB in *Henry V*, followed by *Measure for Measure, Scooping, Buried Child, Fables for Friends, In Trousers, Girls Girls Girls, Twelfth Night,Geniuses, The Incredibly Famous Willy Rivers, Rommel's Garden, Macbeth, Heaven on Earth*, Bdwy in *Loose Ends* (1979), *The Caine Mutiny Court Martial, Saint Joan.*

SANTORO, MICHAEL. Born November 23, 1957 in Brooklyn, NY. Attended Lee Strasberg Inst. Debut 1985 OB in *The Normal Heart* followed by *Homesick, There Is an Angel in Las Vegas, Pokey, Who Collects the Pain?, Things That Should Be Said*

SATTA, STEVEN. Born December 25, 1964 in The Bronx, NYC. Graduate NYU. Debut 1991 OB in *Macbeth* followed by *Chekhov Very Funny*, Bdwy in *A Little Hotel on the Side* (1992).

SCANLAN, JOHN. Born April 3, 1924 in Milwaukee, Wi. Graduate ColumbiaU., AADA. OB in *The Plough and the Stars, The Mousetrap, To Bury a Cousin, A Christmas Carol, Beyond Desire, Geese, As You Like It.*

SCHARFMAN, WENDY. Born December 13, 1950 in Albany, NY. Graduate Wheeler Col. UNC/Chapel Hill, Asolo Consv. Debut 1991 OB in *The Dropper* followed by *Betrayal, A Kind of Alaska, A Midsummer Night's Dream, Last Chance Texaco, Tides, Dando Bohica.*

SCHEINE, RAYNOR. Born November 10 in Emporia, VA. Graduate VaCommonwealthU. Debut 1978 OB in *Curse of the Starving Class*, followed by *Blues for Mr. Charlie, Salt Lake City Skyline, Mother Courage, The Lady or the Tiger, Bathroom Play , Wild Life, RePo, Almost a Man, Heaven on Earth, Bargains*, Bdwy in *Joe Turner's Come and Gone* (1988).

SCHNEIDER, HELEN. Born December 23 in NYC. Bdwy debut 1989 in *Ghetto*,OB in *What a Swell Party!, Friday.*

SCHOEFFLER, PAUL. Born November 21, 1958 in Montreal, Can. Graduate UCa/Berkley, CarnegieMellon, UBrussels. Debut 1988 OB in *Much Ado about Nothing* followed by *The Cherry Orchard, Carnival.*

SCHREIBER, LIEV. Born October 4, 1967 in San Francisco, CA. Graduate Hampshire Col., YaleU., RADA. Debut 1992 OB in *Goodnight Desdemona Good Morning Juliet.*

SCHULMAN, CRAIG. Born March 1, 1956 in Weisbaden, W. Ger. Graduate SUNY/Oswego. Debut 1980 OB in *Pirates of Penzance, Light Opera of Manhattan, Gilbert & Sullivan Players*, Bdwy in *Les Miserables* (1990).

SCHWARTZ, GARY. Born November 20, 1964 in Englewood, NJ. Attended Hofstra U., Debut 1987 OB in *The Chosen* followed by *What's a Nice Country Like You Doing in a State Like This?*, Bdwy in *Fiddler on the Roof* (1990), *Kiss of the Spider Woman.*

SCOTT, CAMPBELL. Born July 19, 1962 in NYC. Attended Lawrence U. Bdwy debut 1985 in *Hay Fever* followed by *The Real Thing, Long Day's Journey into Night, Ah Wilderness!*, OB in *Measure for Measure, Copperhead, A Man for all Seasons, The Last Outpost, Pericles, On the Bum.*

SCOTT, GEORGE C. Born October 18, 1927 in Wise, VA. Attended U. Mo. Debut 1957 OB in *Richard III* for which he received a Theatre World Award, followed by *As You Like It, Merchant of Venice, Children of Darkness, Desire Under the Elms, Wrong Turn at Lungfish,Bdwy in Comes a Day, The Andersonville Trial, The Wall, General Seegar, The Little Foxes, Plaza Suite, All God's Children Got Wings, Uncle Vanya, Death of a Salesman, Sly Fox, Tricks of the Trade, Present Laughter, Boys in Autumn, On Borrowed Time.*

SELDES, MARIAN. Born August 23, 1928 in NYC. Attended Neighborhood Playhouse. Bdwy debut 1947 in *Medea* followed by *Crime and Punishment, That Lady, Town Beyond Tragedy, Ondine, On High Ground, Come of Age, The Chalk Garden, The Milk Train Doesn't Stop Here Anymore, The Wall, A Gift of Time, A Delicate Balance, Before You Go, Father's Day, Equus, The Merchant, Deathtrap*, OB in *Different, Ginger Man, Mercy Street, Isadora Duncan Sleeps with the Russian Navy, Painting Churches, Gertrude Stein and Companion, Richard II, The Milk Train Doesn't Stop.., A Bright Room Called Day, Another Time, Three Tall Women.*

SENNETT, DAVID. Born July 7, 1954 in Champaign, IL. Attended Brandeis U., ANTA. Debut 1983 OB in *Buck* followed by *Frankenstein, Wakefield Plays, Room Service, Three Sisters, A Winter's Tale, Dorian, Them within Us.*

SERRA, RAYMOND. Born August 13, 1937 in NYC. Attended Rutgers U., Wagner Col. Debut 1975 OB in *The Shark* followed by *Mama's Little Angels, Manny, Front Page*, Bdwy in *The Wheelbarrow Closers* (1976), *Marlowe, The Accidental Death of an Anarchist, Legs Diamond, 3 from Brooklyn.*

SESMA, THOM. Born June 1, 1955 in Sasebo, Japan, Graduate U. Cal. Bdwy debut 1983 in *La Cage aux Folles* followed by *Chu Chem, Search and Destroy, Nick and Nora*, OB in *In a Pig's Valise, Baba Goya, Chu Chem, Hey Love.*

SETRAKIAN, ED. Born October 1, 1928 in Jenkinstown, W.Va. Graduate Concord Col., NYU. Debut 1966 OB in *Dreams in the Night* followed by *Othello, Coriolanus, Macbeth, Hamlet, Baal, Old Glory, Futz, Hey Rube, Seduced, Shout across the River, American Days, Sheepskin, Inserts, Crossing the Bar, The Boys Next Door, The Mensch, Adoring the Madonna*, Bdwy in *Days in the Trees* (1976) *St. Joan, The Best Little Whorehouse in Texas.*

SEVERS, WILLIAM. Born January 8, 1932 in Britton, OK. Attended Pasadena Playhouse, Columbia Col. Bdwy debut 1960 in *Cut of the Axe* followed by *On Borrowed Time* (1991), OB in *The Moon Is Blue, Lulu, Big Maggie, Mixed Doubles, The Rivals, The Beaver Coat, Twister, Midnight Mass, Gas Station, Firebugs, Fellow Travelers, The Iowa Boys.*

SHABALALA, JOSEPH. Born August 28, 1940 in Ladysmith, S.Africa. Bdwy debut in *The Song of Jacob Zulu* (1993).

SHALHOUB, TONY. Born October 9, 1953 in Green Bay, WI. Graduate Yale U. Bdwy debut 1985 in *The Odd Couple*, followed by *The Heidi Chronicles, Conversations with My Father*, OB in *Richard II, One Act Festival, Zero Positive, Rameau's Nephew, For Dear Life.*

SHANNON, MARK. Born December 13, 1948 in Indianapolis, IN. Attended U. Cin. Debut 1969 OB in *Fortune and Men's Eyes*, followed by *Brotherhood, Nothing to Report, When You Comin' Back Red Ryder?, Serenading Louie, Three Sisters, K2, Spare Parts, Lips Together Teeth Apart, Tales from Hollywood.*

SHAPIRO-GRAVITTE, DEBBIE. Born September 29, 1954 in Los Angeles, CA. Graduate LACC. Bdwy debut 1979 in *They're Playing Our Song* followed by *Perfectly Frank, Blues in the Night, Zorba, Jerome Robbins' Broadway, Ain't Broadway Grand*, OB in *They Say It's Wonderful, New Moon in Concert.*

SHAVER, HELEN. Born February 24, 1952 in St. Thomas, Ont., Can. Bdwy debut 1992 in *Jake's Women,* for which she received a Theatre World Award.

SHAWHAN, APRIL. Born April 10, 1940 in Chicago, IL. Debut 1964 OB in *Jo* followed by *Hamlet, Oklahoma!, Mod Donna, Journey to Gdansk, Almost in Vegas, Bosoms and Neglect, Stella, The Vinegar Tree, Ghosts,* Bdwy in *Race of Hairy Men, 3 Bags Full* for which she received a Theatre World Award, *Dinner at 8, Cop-Out, Much Ado about Nothing, Over Here, Rex, A History of the American Film.*

SHAY, MAUREEN. Born May 6, 1978 in Rochester, MN. Debut 1992 OB in *On the Bum.*

SHELL, CLAUDIA. Born September 11, 1959 in Passaic, NJ. Debut 1980 OB in *Jam.* Bdwy in *Merlin,* followed by *Cats.*

SHELLEY, CAROLE. Born August 16, 1939 in London, England. Bdwy debut 1965 in *The Odd Couple* followed by *The Astrakhan Coat, Loot, Noel Coward's Sweet Potato, Hay Fever, Absurd Person Singular, The Norman Conquests, The Elephant Man, The Misanthrope, Noises Off, Stepping Out, The Miser,* OB in *Little Murder , The Devil's Disciple, The Play's the Thing, Double Feature, Twelve Dreams, Pygmalion in Concert, A Christmas Carol, Jubilee in concert, Waltz of the Toreadors, What the Butler Saw, Maggie and Misha, Later Life, The Destiny of Me.*

SHERMAN, JONATHAN MARC. Born October 10, 1968 in Morristown, NJ. Attended CarnegieMellon U., AADA. Debut 1986 OB in *The Chopin Playoffs* followed by *A Joke, Sophistry* (also author).

SHERWELL, YVONNE. Born May 27, 1934 in Waterbury, CT. Attended Columbia U. Debut 1970 OB in *Contributions* followed by *One Night in Manhattan.*

SHEW, TIMOTHY. Born February 7, 1959 in Grand Forks, ND. Graduate Millikin U., U. Mich. Debut 1987 OB in *The Knife,* Bdwy in *Les Miserables.*

SHIMIZU, KEENAN. Born October 22, 1956 in New York City. Bdwy debut 1965 in *South Pacific,* followed by *The King and I,* OB in *Rashomon, The Year of the Dragon, The Catch, Peking Man, Flowers and Household Gods, Behind Enemy Lines, Station J, Rosie's Cafe, Boutique Living, Gonza and Lancer, Letters to a Student Revolutionary, Fairy Bones.*

SHINER, DAVID. Born September 13, 1953 in Boston, MA. Debut 1990 OB in *Cirque du Soleil* followed by *Serious Fun!,* Bdwy in *Fool Moon* (1993).

SHORT, MARTIN. Born March 26, 1950 in Hamilton, Ont. Canada. Graduate McMaster U. Bdwy debut 1993 in *The Goodbye Girl* for which he received a Theatre World Award.

SHULL, RICHARD. Born February 24, 1929 in Evanston, Il. Graduate State U. Iowa. Debut 1953 OB in *Coriolanus,* followed by *Purple Dust, Journey to the Day, American Hamburger League, Frimbo, Fade the Game, Desire under the Elms, The Marriage of Betty and Boo, The Front Page* (LC), *One of the All-Time Greats,* Bdwy in *Black-eyed Susan* (1954), *Wake Up Darling, Red Roses for Me, I Knock at the Door, Pictures in the Hallway, Have I Got a Girl for You, Minnie's Boys, Goodtime Charley, Fools, Oh, Brother!, Ain't Broadway Grand.*

SHULMAN, MICHAEL. Born December 31, 1981 in New York City. Debut 1989 OB in *Gardenia,* followed by *Assassins, The House That Goes on Forever,* Bdwy in *Four Baboons Adoring the Sun* (1992).

SILLIMAN, MAUREEN. Born December 3 in New York City. Attended Hofstra U. Bdwy debut 1975 in *Shenandoah,* followed by *I Remember Mama, Is There Life After High School?,* OB in *Umbrellas of Cherbourg, Two Rooms, Macbeth, Blue Window, Three Postcards, Pictures in the Hall, The Voice of the Prairie, Picking Up the Pieces, Democracy and Esther.*

SIMES, DOUGLAS. Born April 21, 1949 in New Salem, NY. Graduate Lehigh U, YaleU. Debut 1974 OB in *The Lady's Not for Burning* followed by *The Dumbwaiter, The Revenger's Tragedy, The Lady from the Sea, Between Time and Timbuktu, A Chast Maid and Cheapside, Measure for Measure, Exit Music.*

SIMMONS, J.K. (formerly Jonathan) Born January 9, 1955 in Detroit, MI. Graduate U. Mont. Debut 1987 OB in *Birds of Paradise,* followed by *Dirty Dick,* Bdwy in *A Change in the Heir* (1990), *A Few Good Men, Peter Pan* (1990/1991), *Guys and Dolls.*

SMITH, LOUISE. Born February 8, 1955 in NYC. Graduate Antioch Col. Debut 1981 OB in *The Haggadah* followed by *Salt Speaks, The Tempest, Betty and the Blenders, Life Simulated, Coyote Ugly, The White Whore and the Bit Player.*

SMITH, ROBERT VINCENT. Born April 13, 1950 in Lafayette, IN. Graduate Ind. U. Debut on Bdwy in *Show Boat* (1983), OB in *The Fantasticks* (1987) followed by *The Pajama Game, Marry Me a Little.*

SISTO, ROCCO. Born February 8, 1953 in Bari, Italy. Graduate U. Ill, NYU. Debut 1982 OB in *Hamlet,* followed by *The Country Doctor, Times and Appetites of Toulouse-Lautrec, The Merchant of Venice, What Did He See, A Winter's Tale, The Tempest, Dream of a Common Language, 'Tis Pity She's a Whore.*

SLAFF, JONATHAN. Born October 29, 1950 in Wilkes-Barre, PA. Graduate Yale U., Columbia. Debut 1988 OB in *One Director Against His Cast,* followed by *Futz!*

SLEZAK, VICTOR. Born July 7, 1957 in Youngstown, OH. Debut 1979 OB in *Electra Myth,* followed by *Hasty Heart, Ghosts, Alice and Fred, Widow Claire, Miracle Worker, Talk Radio, Marathon '88, One Act Festival, Marathon '90, Young Playwrights, Marathon '91, Appointment with a High Wire Lady, Sam I Am, The White Rose, Born Guilty.*

SMITH, ANNA DEAVERE. Born September 18, 1950 in Baltimore, MD. Graduate Beaver Col., AmConsvTheatre. Debut 1980 OB in *Mother Courage* followed by *Mercenaries, Fires in the Mirror.*

SMITH, LOIS. Born November 3, 1930 in Topeka, Ks. Attended U.W.Va. Bdwy debut 1952 in *Time Out for Ginger,* followed by *The Young and the Beautiful, The Wisteria Trees, The Glass Menagerie, Orpheus Descending, Stages, The Grapes of Wrath,* OB in *A Midsummer Night's Dream, Non Pasquale, Promenade, La Boheme, Bodies Rest and Motion, Marathon '87, Gus and Al, Marathon '88 Measure for Measure, Spring Thing, Beside Herself, Sam I Am, Dog Logic.*

SMITH, SHEILA. Born April 3, 1933 in Coneaut, OH. Attended Kent State U.,

Cleveland Play House, Bdwy debut 1963 in *Hot Spot* followed by *Mame* for which she received a Theatre World Award, *Follies, Company, Sugar, Five O'Clock Girl, 42nd Street,* OB in *Taboo Revue, Anything Goes, Best Foot Forward, Sweet Miami, Fiorello!, Taking My Turn, Jack and Jill, M. Amilcar, The Sunset Gang, Backers Audition.*

SMITH-CAMERON, J. Born September 7 in Louisville, KY. Attended Fla. State U. Bdwy debut 1982 in *Crimes of the Heart,* followed by *Wild Honey, Lend Me A Tenor, Our Country's Good, Real Inspector Hound/15 Minute Hamlet,* OB in *Asian Shade, The Knack, Second Prize: 2 Weeks in Leningrad, Great Divide, Voice of the Turtle, Women of Manhattan, Alice and Fred, Mi Vida Loca, Little Egypt, On the Bum, Traps/Owners.*

SOCKWELL, SALLY. Born June 14 in Little Rock, AR. Debut 1976 OB in *Vanities* followed by *Bargains.*

SOLO, WILLIAM. Born March 16, 1948 in Worcester, Ma. Graduate U. Mass. Bdwy debut 1987 in *Les Miserables.*

SOMMER, JOSEF. Born June 26, 1934 in Griefswald, Germany Graduate CarnegieTech. U. Bdwy debut 1970 in *Othello* followed by *Children Children, Trial of the Catonsville 9, Full Circle, Who's Who in Hell, Whose Life Is It Anyway?,* OB in *Enemies, Merchant of Venice, The Dog Ran Away, Drinks before Dinner, Lydie Breeze, Black Angel, The Lady and the Clarinet, Love Letters on Blue Paper, Largo Desolato, Hamlet, Later Life.*

SOPHIEA, CYNTHIA. Born October 26, 1954 in Flint, MI. Bdwy debut 1981 in *My Fair Lady* followed by *She Loves Me,* OB in *Lysistrata, Sufragette, The Golden Apple.*

SPACEY, KEVIN. Born July 26, 1959 in South Orange, NJ. Attended LACC, Juilliard. Debut 1981 OB in *Henry IV Part I* followed by *Barbarians, Uncle Vanya, The Robbers, Life and Limb, As It Is in Heaven, Playland,* Bdwy in *Ghosts* (1982), *Hurlyburly, Long Day's Journey into Night.*

SPAISMAN, ZYPORA. Born January 2, 1920 in Lublin, Poland. Debut 1955 OB in *Lonesome Ship* followed by *My Father's Court, A Thousand and One Nights, Eleventh Inheritor, Enchanting Melody, Fifth Commandment, Bronx Express, The Melody Lingers On, Yoshke Musikant, Stempenya, Generations of Green Fields, Shop, A Play for the Devil, Broome Street America, The Flowering Peach, Riverside Drive, Big Winner, The Land of Dreams, Father's Inheritance, At the Crossroads.*

SPELLMAN, KERRIANNE. Born January 7, 1966 in NJ. Graduate AMDA, AADA. Bdwy debut 1993 in *Les Miserables.*

SPIELBERG, DAVID. Born March 6, 1940 in Mercedes, TX. Graduate U.TX. Debut 1963 OB in *A Man's a Man* followed by *Two Executioners, Funnyhouse of a Negro, MacBird, Persians, Trial of the Catonsville 9, Sleep, Friends, The Destiny of Me,* Bdwy in *Thieves* (1974).

SPIELBERG, ROBIN. Born November 20, 1962 in New Jersey. Attended Mich. State U., NYU. Debut 1988 OB in *Boys' Life,* followed by *Marathon '90, Three Sisters, 5 Very Live, Cocktails and Camp, Nothing Sacred.*

SPIEWAK, TAMARA ROBIN. Born February 20, 1980 in Bridgeport, CT. Bdwy debut 1990 in *Les Miserables.*

SPINELLA, STEPHEN. Born October 11, 1956 in Naples, Italy. Graduate NYU. Debut 1982 OB in *The Age of Assassins* followed by *Dance for Me Rosetta, Bremen Coffee, The Taming of the Shrew, L'Illusion, Burrhead,* Bdwy 1993 in *Angels in America* for which he received a Theatre World Award.

SPIVAK, ALICE. Born August 11, 1935 in Brooklyn, NY. Debut 1954 OB in **Early Primrose** followed by *Of Mice and Men, Secret Concubine, Port Royal, Time for Bed, House of Blue Leaves, Deep Six the Briefcase, Selma, Ferry Tales, Temple, A Backer's Audition.*

SPIVEY, TOM. Born January 28, 1951 in Richmond, VA. Graduate Wm & Mary, Penn State. Debut 1989 OB in *The Thirteenth Chair,* followed by *The Rover, Off the Beat and Path 2.*

SPOLAN, JEFFREY. Born July 14, 1947 in New York City. Graduate Adelphi U. Debut 1982 OB in *Yellow Fever,* followed by *Savage in Limbo, Three Sisters, East of Evil.*

SPORE, RICHARD. Born March 23, 1948 in Chicago, IL. Debut 1982 OB in *The Frances Farmer Story,* followed by *Counselor-at-Law, Troilus and Cressida, Motions of History, Henry IV, Comedy of Errors.*

SPRINGLE, RICHARD DAVIS. Born November 18, 1947 in Norfolk, VA. Attended Old Dominion U. Debut 1993 OB in *Einstein.*

SPYBEY, DINA. Born August 29, 1965 in Columbus, OH. Graduate OhStateU,Rutgers. Debut 1993 OB in *Five Women Wearing the Same Dress* for which she received a Theatre World Award.

STAHL, MARY LEIGH. Born August 29, 1946 in Madison, WI. Graduate Jacksonville State U. Debut 1974 OB in *Circus,* followed by *Dragons, Sullivan and Gilbert, The World of Sholem Aleichem,* Bdwy in *The Phantom of the Opera* (1988).

STANTON, ROBERT. Born March 8, 1963 in San Antonio, Tx. Graduate George Mason U., NYU. Debut 1985 OB in *Measure for Measure,* followed by *Rum and Coke, Cheapside, Highest Standard of Living, One Act Festival, Best Half-Foot Forward, Sure Thing, Emily, Ubu, Casanova, Owners/Traps,* Bdwy in *A Small Family Business* (1992).

STANLEY, DOROTHY. Born November 18 in Hartford, CT. Graduate Ithaca Col., CarnegieMellon U. Debut 1978 OB in *Gay Divorce* followed by *Dames at Sea,* Bdwy in *Sugar Babies* (1980), *Annie, 42nd Street, Broadway, Jerome Robbins' Broadway, Kiss of the Spider Woman.*

STANLEY, GORDON. Born December 20, 1951 in Boston, MA. Graduate Brown U., TempleU. Debut 1977 OB in *Lyrical and Satirical* followed by *Allegro, Elizabeth and Essex, Red Hot and Blue, Two on the Isles, Moby Dick, Johnny Pye and the Foolkiller, The Golden Apple, Gifts of the Magi, Big Fat and Ugly with a Moustache, Lightin' Out,* Bdwy in *Onward Victoria* (1980), *Joseph and the Amazing Technicolor Dreamcoat, Into the Light, Teddy and Alice.*

   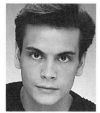  

| Jean Marie | Gordon Owens | Kellie Overbey | Eric Paeper | Tia Riebling | Rusty Reynolds |

| Angela Nevard | Michael Piehl | Carole Shelley | Steven Satta | Myra Taylor | Jonathon Marc Sherman |

| Lillias D. White | Stan Taffel | Jennifer Dorr White | James Waterston | Sarah McCord Williams | Patrick White |

| Ruth Williamson | EdmundWilkinson | Lou Williford | Glen Williamson | Shán Willis | Kelly Woodruff |

     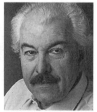

| Lynne Wintersteller | Michael York | Christina Youngman | Craig Zakarian | Karen Ziemba | Louis Zorich |

213

STAPLETON, JEAN. Born January 19, 1923 in NYC. Attended Hunter Col., AmThWing. Bdwy debut 1953 in *In the Summer House* followed by *Damn Yankees, Bells Are Ringing, Juno, Rhinoceros, Funny Girl, Arsenic and Old Lace*, OB in *Mountain Language/The Birthday Party, Learned Ladies, The Roads to Home.*

STEENBURGEN, MARY. Born Feb.8, 1953 in Newport, AR. Attended Neighborhood Playhouse. Bdwy debut 1993 in *Candida.*

STEHLIN, JACK. Born June 21, 1936 in Allentown, PA. Graduate Juilliard. Debut 1984 OB in *Henry V* followed by *Gravity Shoes, Julius Caesar, Romeo and Juliet, Phaedra Britannica, Don Juan of Seville, Uncle Vanya, Henry IV Part I, Life off Earth, Danton's Death, Casanova, Washington Square Moves.*

STEINBORN, CARLY JANE. Born August 14, 1984 in San Diego, CA. Bdwy debut 1993 in *The Who's Tommy.*

STERN, CHERYL. Born July 1, 1956 in Buffalo, NY. Graduate Northwestern U. Debut 1984 OB in *Daydreams* followed by *White Lies, Pets.*

STERN, JEFFREY. Born May 21, 1983 in Manhasset, NY. Bdwy debut 1992 in *The Will Rogers Follies.*

STERNHAGEN, FRANCES. Born January 13, 1932 in Washington, DC. Graduate Vassar Col. OB in *The Admirable Bashful, Thieves Carnival, Country Wife, Ulysses in Nighttown, Saintliness of Margery Kemp, The Room, A Slight Ache, Displaced Person, Playboy of the Western World, The Prevalence of Mrs. Seal, Summer, Laughing Stock, The Return of Herbert Bracewell, Little Murders, Driving Miss Daisy, Remembrance, A Perfect Ganesh*, Bdwy in *Great Day in the Morning, The Right Honourable Gentleman*, with APA in *The Cocktail Party*, and *CockaDoodle Dandy, The Sign in Sidney Brustein's Window, Enemies, The Good Doctor, Equus, Angel, On Golden Pond, The Father, Grownups,Home Front, You Can't Take It withYou.*

STILLMAN, ROBERT. Born December 2, 1954 in NYC. Graduate Princeton U. Debut 1981 OB in *The Haggadah*, followed by *Street Scene, Lola, No Frills Revue, Six Wives*, Bdwy in *Grand Hotel* (1989).

STILLER, JERRY. Born June 8, 1931 in NYC. Graduate USyracuse. Debut 1953 OB in *Coriolanus* followed by T*he Power and the Glory, The Golden Apple, Measure for Measure, The Taming of the Shrew, The Carefree Tree, Diary of a Scoundrel, Romeo and Juliet, As You Like It, Two Gentlemen of Verona, Passione, Hurlyburly, Prairie/Shawl, Much Ado about Nothing*, Bdwy in *The Ritz* (1975), *Unexpected Guests, Passione, Hurlyburly, 3 Men on a Horse.*

STEVENS, FISHER. Born November 27, 1963 in Chicago, IL. Attended NYU. Bdwy debut 1982 in *Torch Song Trilogy* followed by *Brighton Beach Memoirs*, OB in *A Darker Purpose, A Perfect Ganesh.*

STOCKTON, ROSE. Born in Urbane, OH. Graduate Antioch Col. Debut 1983 OB in *Primal Time* followed by *The Three Zeks, Arms and the Man, Antigone, Two Gentlemen of Verona, The Rivals, The Imaginary Invalid, Candida, The Diaries of Adam and Eve, Othello.*

STOLARSKY, PAUL. Born February 18, 1933 in Detroit, MI. Graduate WayneStateU, U.Mich. Debut 1972 OB in *Bluebird* followed by *Let Yourself Go, Rocket to the Moon, D, My Mother My Father and Me, Me and Molly, Shlemiel the First, The Rachel Plays,*

STOLTZ, ERIC. Born in 1961 in California. Attended U.S. Cal, Debut 1987 OB in *The Widow Claire* followed by *The American Plan*, Bdwy in *Our Town* for which he received a 1989 Theatre World Award, *Two Shakespearean Actors.*

STONEBURNER, SAM. Born February 24, 1934 in Fairfax, VA. Graduate Georgetown U., AADA. Debut 1960 OB in *Ernest in Love*, followed by *Foreplay, Anyone Can Whistle, Twilight Cantata, Six Degrees of Separation, Flaubert's Latest*, Bdwy in *Different Times* (1972), *Bent, Macbeth* (1981), *The First, Six Degrees of Separation.*

STOUT, MARY. Born April 8, 1952 in Huntington, WVa. Graduate MarshallU. Debut 1980 OB in *Plain and Fancy* followed by *The Sound of Music, Crisp, A Christmas Carol, Song for a Saturday, Prizes, The Golden Apple*, Bdwy in *Copperfield* (1981), *A Change in the Heir, My Favorite Year.*

STOUT, STEPHEN. Born May 19, 1952 in Huntington, WVa. Graduate SMU. Bdwy debut 1981 in *Kingdoms* followed by *The Heidi Chronicles, The Sisters Rosensweig*, OB in *Cloud 9, A Midsummer Night's Dream, Loose Ends.*

STRAM, HENRY. Born September 10, 1954 in Layfayette, IN. Attended Juilliard. Debut 1978 OB in *King Lear*, followed by *Shout and Twist, The Cradle Will Rock, Prison-made Tuxedos, Cinderella/Cendrillon, The Making of Americans, Black Sea Follies, Eddie Goes to Poetry City, A Bright Room Called Day, The Mind King, On the Open Road.*

STRASSER, ROBIN. Born May 7, 1945 in NYC. Bdwy debut 1963 in *The Irregular Verb to Love* followed by *The Country Girl, Chapter Two*, OB in *A Meeting by the River, Loving Reno, The News in Revue.*

SULLIVAN, BRAD. Born November 18, 1931 in Chicago, IL. Graduate U.Me., AmThWing. Debut 1961 OB in *Red Roses for Me* followed by *South Pacific, Hot House, Leavin' Cheyenne, The Ballad of Soapy Smith, Cold Sweat, As You Like It, Somewhere I Have Never Travelled*, Bdwy in *The Basic Training of Pavlo Hummel* (1977), *Working, The Wake of Jamie Foster, The Caine Mutiny Court Martial, Orpheus Descending.*

SULLIVAN, K.T. Born October 31, 1953 in Coalgate, OK. Graduate OklaU. OB 1992 in *A..My Name Is Still Alice*, Bdwy in *3 Penny Opera* (1989).

SUMMERHAYS, JANE. Born October 11, In Salt Lake City, UT. Graduate UUtah, Catholi U. Debut 1980 OB in *Paris Lights* followed by *On Approval, One Act Festival, Taking Steps, Noel and Gertie*, Bdwy in *Sugar Babies* (1980), *A Chorus Line, Me and MyGirl, Rent Me A Tenor*, Born March 8, 1958 in NYC. Graduate BrownU, YaleU. Debut 1981 OB in Steel on Steel, Bdwy in Angels in America (1993).

SUSSMAN, MATTHEW. Born March 8, 1958, in NYC. Graduate Brown U. Yale U. Debut 1981 in *Steel on Steel, Angels in America(1993).*

SUTORIUS, JAMES. Born Dember 14, 1944 in Euclid, OK. Graduate IllWesleyan, AMDA. Bdwy debut 1970 in *The Cherry Orchard* followed by *The Changing Room,*

The November People, Hamlet, Conversations with My Father, OB in *Servant of Two Masters, Hamlet, Sexual Perversity in Chicago, Other People's Money.*

SWANSEN, LARRY. Born November 10, 1930 in Roosevelt, OK. Graduate U. OK. Bdwy debut 1966 in T*hose That Play the Clowns*, followed by *The Great White Hope, The King and I*, OB in *Dr. Faustus Lights the Lights, Thistle in My Bed, A Darker Flower, Vincent, MacBird, The Unknown Soldier and His Wife, The Sound of Music, The Conditioning of Charlie One, Ice Age, Prince of Homburg, Who's There?, Heart of a Dog, Grandma Pray for Me, Frankenstein, Knights of the Round Table.*

TAFFEL, STAN. Born December 6, 1962 in NYC. Graduate Boston U. Debut 1987 OB in *Lenny Bruce Revue* followed by *Speakeasy, Noo Yawk Tawk, The News in Revue.*

TALYN, OLGA. Born December 5 in West Ger. Attended Syracuse U., U. Buffalo. Debut 1973 OB in *The Proposition*, followed by *Corral, Tales of Tinseltown, Shop on Main Street*, Bdwy in A *Doll's House, The Phantom of the Opera.*

TATE, ROBERT. Born April 30, 1964 in Albuquerque, N. Mx. Graduate Yale U. Debut OB 1988 in *Ten Percent Revue*, followed by *Harold and the Purple Dragon, Nefertiti, Rags, Lightin' Out.*

TATUM, MARIANNE. Born February 18, 1951 in Houston, TX. Attended Manhattan Schl. of Music. Debut 1971 OB in *Ruddigore*, followed by *The Gilded Cage, Charley's Tale, Passionate Extremes*. Bdwy in *Barnum* (1980) for which she received a Theatre World Award, *The Three Musketeers, The Sound of Music* (NYCO/LC)

TAYLOR, ANDY. Born October 3 in Eugene, OR. Graduate Oberlin Col.UMon. Debut 1990 OB in *Romeo and Juliet* followed by *Rodgers and Hart, On the Open Road, Juno.*

TAYLOR, DREW. Born March 9, 1955 in Milwaukee, WI. Attended AADA. Debut 1985 OB in *She Loves Me*, followed by *Kiss Me Kate, You Can Be a New Yorker Too,* Bdwy in *The Secret Garden* (1991).

TAYLOR, GEORGE. Born September 18, 1930 in London, England. Attended AADA. Debut 1972 OB in *Hamlet*, followed by *Enemies, The Contractor, Scribes, Says I Says He, Teeth 'n' Smiles, Viaduct, Translations, Last of the Knucklemen, The Accrington Pals, Ragged Trousered Philanthropists, Brightness Falling*. Bdwy in *Emperor Henry IV* (1973), *The National Health, Loot, City of Angels.*

TAYLOR, MYRA. Born July 9, 1960 in Ft. Motte, SC. Graduate Yale U. Debut 1985 OB in *Dennis* followed by *The Tempest, Black Girl, Marathon 86, Phantasie, Walking the Dead, I Am a Man*, Bdwy in *A Streetcar Named Desire* (1988), *Mule Bone.*

TAYLOR, SCOTT. Born June 29, 1962 in Milan, TN. Attended Miss. State U. Bdwy in *Wind in the Willows* (1985), followed by *Cats.*

TELLER. Born in 1948 in Philadelphia, PA. Graduate Amherst Col. Debut 1985 OB in *Penn & Teller*, Bdwy in same (1987), followed by *Refrigerator Tour*, OB in *Penn & Teller Rot in Hell.*

TELLES, RICK. Born November 10, 1962 in Oakland, CA. Graduate UCLA, LAMDA. Debut 1992 OB in *Lake Street Extension.*

TEMPERLEY, STEPHEN. Born July 29, 1949 in London, England. Attended AADA. Debut 1968 OB in *Invitation to a Beheading*, followed by *Henry IV Parts I & II, Up Against It*, Bdwy in *Crazy for You* (1992).

TERRY SUSAN. Born May 30, 1953 in New Haven, CT. Graduate U. NH. Bdwy debut 1979 in *Evita*, followed by *Zorba*, OB in *Insert Foot, Follies in Concert, Forbidden Broadway, A Little Night Music (NYCO/LC).*

TESTA, MARY. Born June 4, 1955 in Philadelphia, PA. Attended URI. Debut 1979 OB in In *Trousers* followed by *Company, Life Is Not a Doris Day Movie, Not-So-New Faces of 1982, American Princess, Mandrake, 4 One-Act Musicals, Next, Please!, Daughters, One-Act Festival, The Knife, Young Playwrights Festival, Tiny Mommy, Finnegan's Funeral and Ice Cream Shop, Peter Breaks Through, Lucky Stiff, 1-2-3-4-5, Scapin, Hello Muddah Hello Faddah*, Bdwy in *Barnum* (1980), *Marilyn, The Rink.*

THACKER, RUSS. Born June 23, 1946 in Washington, DC. Attended Montgomery Col. Bdwy debut 1967 in *Life with Father* followed by *Music! Music!, The Grass Harp, Heathen, Home Sweet Homer, Me Jack You Jill, Do Black Patent Leather Shoes Really Reflect Up?*, OB in *Your Own Thing* for which he received a Theatre World Award, *Dear Oscar, Once I Saw a Boy Laughing, Tip-Toes, Oh, Coward!, New Moon in concert, The Firefly in Concert, Rosalie in Concert, Some Enchanted Evening, Roberta in Concert, Ilio, Genesis, Little Me.*

THOMAS, JOHN NORMAN. Born May 13, 1961 in Detroit, MI. Graduate Cinn. Consv. Bdwy debut 1987 in *Les Miserables*, followed by *The Merchant of Venice, Kiss of the Spider Woman.*

THOMAS, RAYMOND ANTHONY Born December 19, 1956 in Kentwood, LA. Graduate U. Tex/El Paso. Debut 1981 OB in *Escape to Freedom*, followed by *The Sun Gets Blue, Blues for Mr. Charlie, The Hunchback of Notre Dame, Ground People, The Weather Outside, One Act Festival, Caucasian Chalk Circle, The Virgin Molly, Black Eagles, Distant Fires.*

THOME, DAVID. Born July 24, 1951 in Salt Lake City, UT. Bdwy debut 1971 in *No No Nanette*, followed by *Different Times, Good News, Rodgers and Hart, A Chorus Line, Dancin', Dreamgirls* (1981/1987), *Peter Pan* (1990/1992).

THOMPSON, EVAN. Born September 3, 1931 in NYC. Graduate UCal. Bdwy debut 1969 in *Jimmy* followed by *1776, City of Angels*, OB in *Mahogonny, Treasure Island, Knitters in the Sun, HalfLife, Fasnacht Dau, The Importance of Being Earnest, Under the Gaslight, Henry V, The Fantasticks, Walk the Dog Willie, Macbeth, 1984, Leave It to Me, Earth and Sky, No Conductor.*

THOMPSON, WEYMAN. Born December 11, 1950 in Detroit, MI. Graduate WayneStateU, UDetroit. Bdwy debut 1980 in *Clothes for a Summer Hotel* followed by *Dreamgirls, Shakespeare's Cabaret, 5 Guys Named Moe*, OB in *Daddy Goodness, Jelly Belly.*

THORSON, LINDA. Born June 18, 1947 in Toronto, Can. Graduate RADA. Bdwy debut 1982 in *Steaming* for which she received a Theatre World Award, followed by *Noises Off, Zoya's Apartment, Getting Married, City of Angels.*

TICOTIN, NANCY. Born September 4, 1957 in NYC. Bdwy debut 1980 in *West Side Story* followed by *Jerome Robbins' Broadway*, OB in *The King and I* (CC), *A..My Name is Still Alice*.

TILLY, JENNIFER. Born 1958 in Harbour City CA. Graduate Stephens Col. Debut 1993 OB in *One Shoe Off* for which she received a Theatre World Award.

TIMPANARO, NANCY. Born December 30, 1952 in Patterson, NJ. Attended SUNY/Albany. Debut 1991 OB in *Tony 'n' Tina's Wedding*, followed by *Totie*.

TITONE, THOMAS. Born March 24, 1959 in Secaucus, NJ. Attended NCar School of Arts. With AMBallet Theatre before Bdwy debut in *The Most Happy Fella* (1992), followed by *My Favorite Year*, OB in *The Hunchback of Notre Dame*.

TOMEI, MARISA. Born December 4, 1964 in Brooklyn, NY. Attended Boston U., NYU. Debut 1986 OB in *Daughters* for which she received a Theatre World Award, followed by *Class I Act, Evening Star, What the Butler Saw, Marathon '88, Sharon and Billy, Chelsea Walls, The Summer Winds, Comedy of Errors*.

TOMPOS, DOUG. Born January 27, 1962 in Columbus, OH. Graduate Syracuse U., LAMDA. Debut 1985 OB in *Very Warm for May*, followed by *A Midsummer Night's Dream, Mighty Fine Music, Muzeeka, Wish You Were Here, Vampire Lesbians of Sodom*, Bdwy in *City of Angels*.

TONER, THOMAS. Born May 25, 1928 in Homestead, PA. Graduate UCLA. Bdwy debut 1973 in *Tricks*, followed by *The Good Doctor, All Over Town, The Elephant Man, California Suite, A Texas Trilogy, The Inspector General, Me and My Girl, The Secret Garden*, OB in *Pericles, The Merry Wives of Windsor, A Midsummer Night's Dream, Richard III, My Early Years, Life and Limb, Measure for Measure, Little Footsteps*.

TORN, RIP. Born February 6, 1931 in Temple, TX. Graduate UTx. Bdwy debut 1956 in *Cat on a Hot Tin Roof* followed by *Sweet Bird of Youth* for which he received a Theatre World Award, *Daughter of Silence, Strange Interlude, Blues for Mr. Charlie, The Country Girl, The Glass Menagerie, Anna Christie* (1992). OB in *Chapparal, The Cuban Thing, The Kitchen, Deer Park, Dream of a Blacklisted Actor, Dance of Death, Macbeth, Barbary Shore, The Creditors, Seduced, The Man and the Fly, Terrible Jim Fitch, Village Wooing*.

TOY, CHRISTINE. Born December 26, 1959 in Scarsdale, NY. Graduate Sarah Lawrence Col. Debut 1982 OB in *Oh Johnny!*, followed by *Pacific Overtures, Genesis, Festival of One Acts , Balancing Act*.

TRUCCO, ED. Born June 3, 1963 in NYC. Attended HB Studio. Debut 1988 OB in *Ariano* followed by *The Boiler Room*.

TRUE, BETSY. Born April 19, 1960 in Cincinnati, OH. Graduate Boston Conv. Bdwy debut 1989 in *Les Miserables*.

TSOUTSOUVAS, SAM. Born August 20, 1948 in Santa Barbara, CA. Attended U. Cal., Juilliard. Debut 1969 OB in *Peer Gynt*, followed by *Twelfth Night, Timon of Athens, Cymbeline, School for Scandal, The Hostage, Women Beware Women, Lower Depths, Emigre, Hello Dali, The Merchant of Venice, The Leader, The Bald Soprano, The Taming of the Shrew, Gus & Al, Tamara, The Man Who Shot Lincoln, Puppetmaster of Lodz, Richard III*, Bdwy in *Three Sisters, Measure for Measure, Beggar's Opera, Scapin, Dracula, Our Country's Good, The Misanthrope*.

TUCCI, LOUIS. Born May 16, 1962 in Toronto, Canada. Graduate Hunter Col. Bdwy debut 1990 in *The Buddy Holly Story*, OB in *Return of the Forbidden Planet, Woyzeck*.

TUCCI, MARIA. Born June 19, 1941 in Florence, It. Attended Actors Studio. Bdwy debut 1963 in *The Milk Train Doesn't Stop Here Anymore*, followed by *The Rose Tattoo, The Little Foxes, The Cuban Thing, The Great White Hope, School for Wives, Lesson from Aloes, Kingdoms, Requiem for a Heavyweight, The Night of the Iguana*, OB in *Corruption in the Palace of Justice, Five Evenings, Trojan Women, White Devil, Horseman Pass By, Yerma, Shepherd of Avenue B., The Gathering, A Man for All Seasons, Love Letters, Substance of Fire*.

TULL, PATRICK. Born July 28, 1941 in Sussex, England. Attended LAMDA. Bdwy debut 1967 in *The Astrakhan Coat* followed by *The Crucible, The Master Builder, Getting Married, Ten Little Indians, The Tamer Tamed, Brand, Frankenstein, What the Butler Saw, She Stoops to Conquer, The Art of Success*.

TUNE, TOMMY. Born February 28, 1939 in Wichita Falls, TX. Graduate UTx. Bdwy debut 1965 in *Baker Street* followed by *A Joyful Noise, How Now Dow Jones, Seesaw, My One and Only, Tommy Tune Tonite!*, OB in *Ichabod*.

TURNER, GLENN. Born September 21, 1957 in Atlanta, GA. Bdwy debut 1984 in *My One and Only*, followed by *A Chorus Line, Grand Hotel, 5 Guys Named Moe*.

TURPIN, BAHNI. Born June 4 in Pontiac, MI. Attended Howard U., NYU. Debut 1990 OB in *Ground People* followed by *Who Collects the Pain?, Young Playwrights Festival 1991*.

TURTURRO, JOHN. Born February 28, 1957 in Brooklyn, NY. Graduate SUNY/New Paltz, LaU. Debut 1984 OB in *Danny and the Deep Blue Sea* for which he received a Theatre World Award, followed by *Men without Dates, Chaos and Hard Times, Steel on Steel, Tooth of the Crime, Of Mice and Men, Jamie's Gang, Marathon 86, The Bald Soprano/The Leader, La Puta Vita Trilogy, Italian American Reconciliation, Arturo Ui, The Normal Heart* (benefit reading), Bdwy in *Death of a Salesman* (1984).

ULISSEY, CATHERINE. Born August 4, 1961 in NYC. Attended Ntl. Academy of Arts. Bdwy debut 1986 in *Rags* followed by *The Mystery of Edwin Drood, Phantom of the Opera*.

UNGER, JUDY. Born August 22, 1970 in NYC. Bdwy debut 1977 in *Golda*, OB in *Cornerpieces*.

VAN BENSCHOTEN, STEPHEN. Born August 27, 1943 in Washington, DC. Graduate LaSalle Col., Yale U. Debut 1967 OB in *King John* followed by *The Tempest, Program for Murder, Murder*, Bdwy in *Unlikely Heroes* (1971), *Grease*.

VANCE, DANA. Born June 23, 1952 in Steubenville, OH. Graduate UWVa. Debut 1981 OB in *An Evening with Sheffman and Vance* followed by *A Backer's Audition, CBS Live*, Bdwy in *Teaneck Tanzi*.

VAN DYCK, JENNIFER. Born December 23, 1962 in St. Andrews, Scotland.

Graduate Brown U. Debut OB 1977 in *Gus and Al*, followed by *Marathon '88, Secret Rapture, Earth and Sky, A Man in His Underwear*, Bdwy in *Secret Rapture, Two Shakespearean Actors, Dancing at Lughnasa*.

VAUGHAN, MELANIE. Born September 18 in Yazoo City, MS. Graduate LaStateU. Bdwy debut 1976 in *Rex* followed by *Sunday in the Park with George, On the 20th Century, Music Is, Starlight Express, The Most Happy Fella* (1992), OB in *Canterbury Tales*.

VENNEMA, JOHN C. Born August 24, 1948 in Houston, TX. Graduate Princeton U., LAMDA, Bdwy debut 1976 in *The Royal Family*, followed by *The Elephant Man, Otherwise Engaged*, OB in *Loot, Statements after an Arrest, The Biko Inquest, No End of Blame, In Celebration, Custom of the Country, The Basement, A Slight Ache, Young Playwrights Festival, Dandy Dick, Nasty Little Secrets, Mountain, Light Up the Sky, Joined at the Head*.

VEREEN, BEN. Born October 10, 1946 in Miami, FL. Debut 1965 OB in *Prodigal Son*, Bdwy in *Sweet Charity, Golden Boy, Hair, Jesus Christ Superstar* for which he received a Theatre World Award, *Pippin, Grind, Jelly's Last Jam*.

VICKERY, JOHN. Born in 1951 in Alameda, CA. Graduate UCal/Berkely, UCal/Davis. Debut 1981 OB in *Macbeth* followed by *Ned and Jack, Eminent Domain, The Real Thing, The Sisters Rosensweig*, OB in *American Days, A Call from the East, Henry IV Part 1, Looking Glass, The Death of Von Richtofen, Vampires*.

VINCENT, A. J. Born May 26 in Darby, PA. Attended NYU, Marquette U., TempleU. Debut 1987 OB in *Psycho Beach Party* followed by *Did You Ever Go to PS 43?, Girls We Have Known, Vampire Lesbians of Sodom*, Bdwy in *The Will Rogers Follies* (1993).

VIVIANO, SAL. Born July 12, 1960 in Detroit, MI. Graduate E.Ill.U. Debut 1985 OB in *Hot Times and Suicide* followed by *The Fantasticks, Miami, Romance/Romance, Hamlet: The Opera, Broadway Jukebox, Catch Me If I Fall, Weird Romance, Beau Jest*, Bdwy in *The Three Musketeers* (1984), *Romance/Romance, City of Angels, Falsettos*.

VOGEL, DAVID. Born October 19, 1922 in Canton, OH. Attended U. PA. Bdwy debut 1984 in *Ballet Ballads* followed by *Gentlemen Prefer Blondes, Make A Wish, Desert Song*, OB in *How to Get Rid of It, The Fantasticks, Miss Stanwyck Is Still in Hiding, Marya, She Loves Me, The Male Animal, The Mind Is a Terrible Thing to Lose*.

VOIGHT, JON. Born December 29, 1938 in Yonkers, NY. Graduate Catholic U. Debut 1960 OB in *O Oysters!* followed by *A View from the Bridge*, Bdwy in *Sound of Music* (1959), *That Summer That Fall* for which he received a Theatre World Award, *The Sea Gull* (1992).

VON BARGEN, DANIEL. Born June 5, 1950 in Cincinnati, OH. Graduate Purdue U. Debut 1981 OB in *Missing Persons*, followed by *Macbeth, Beggars in the House of Plenty, Angel of Death*, Bdwy debut in *Mastergate* (1989) for which he received a Theatre World Award.

VIDNOVIC, MARTIN. Born January 4, 1948 in Falls Church, Va. Graduate CinConsv of Music. Debut 1972 OB in *The Fantasticks* followed by *Lies and Legends, Some Enchanted Evening*, Bdwy in *Home Sweet Homer* (1976), *The King and I, Oklahoma* (1979), *Brigadoon* (1980), *Baby*.

WADE, STEPHEN. Born February 13, 1953 in Chicago, IL. Bdwy debut 1980 in *Banjo Dancing*, OB in *On the Way Home* (1993).

WAGNER, CHUCK. Born June 20, 1958 in Nashville, TN. Graduate USCal. Bdwy debut 1985 in *The Three Musketeers* followed by *Into the Woods, Les Miserables*.

WAGNER, HANK. Born March 12, 1969 in New York City. Graduate London Central Schl. Debut 1990 OB in *Measure for Measure*, followed by *Cork, The Fine Art of Finesse, Two Schnitzler One-Acts, As You Like It, Tartuffe*.

WALDROP, MARK. Born July 30, 1954 in Washington, DC. Graduate CinConsv. Debut 1977 OB in *Movie Buff* followed by *Hey Love*, Bdwy in *Hello Dolly!* (1978), *The Grand Tour, Evita, La Cage aux Folles*.

WALKER, MICHAEL. Born March 11, 1950 in Kenya. Bdwy debut 1974 in *Sherlock Holmes*, OB in *Open Admission*.

WALKER, RAY. Born August 13, 1963 in St. Johnsbury, VT. Graduate NYU. Debut 1985 OB in *Christmas Spectacular*, followed by *Merrily We Roll Along, Chess*, Bdwy 1977 in *Les Miserables*.

WALLACE, JACK. Born August 11, 1933 in Pekin, IL. Debut OB in *Bleacher Bums* (1978) followed by *Edmond, Front Page, Baba Goya, The Road, House of Blue Leaves, Lie of the Mind, Chelsea Walls, Reunion, One Big Shot*, Bdwy in *Glengary Glen Ross* (1984).

WALLACE, LEE. Born July 15, 1930 in NYC. Attended NYU. Debut 1966 OB in *Journey of the 5th Horse*, followed by *Saturday Night, An Evening with Garcia Lorca, Macbeth, Booth Is Back in Town, Awake and Sing, Shepherd of Avenue B, Basic Training of Pavlo Hummel, Curtains, Elephants, Goodnight Grandpa, Jesse's Land, The Sunshine Boys, Taking Stock, God of Vengeance*, Bdwy in *Secret Affairs of Mildred Wild, Molly, Zalmen or the Madness of God, Some of My Best Friends, Grind, The Cemetery Club*.

WALLER, KENNETH. Born April 12, 1945 in Atlanta, GA. Graduate Piedmont Col. Debut 1976 in *Boys from Syracuse*, Bdwy in *Sarava* (1979), *Onward Victoria, Me and My Girl, Phantom of the Opera*.

WALLOWITCH, JOHN. Born February 11 in Philadelphia, PA. Graduate TempleU., Juilliard. Debut OB in *Big Charlotte* followed by *Cracked Cups, The World of Wallowitch, One Night in Manhattan*.

WALSH, BARBARA. Born June 3, 1955 in Washington, DC. Attended Mongomery Col. Bdwy debut 1982 in *Rock 'n' Roll: The First 5000 Years*, followed by *Nine, Falsettos, Blood Brothers*, OB in *Forbidden Broadway*.

WALSH, M. EMMET. Born March 22, 1935 in Ogdensburg, NY. Graduate Clarkson Col. AADA. OB in, *Old Glory, Shepards on the Shelf, Death of the Well Loved Boy, 3 from Column A*, Bdwy in *Beauty Part, Does a Tiger Wear a Necktie?, That Championship Season, Fore!*

WARD, DOUGLAS TURNER. Born May 5, 1930 in Burnside, LA. Attended UMich. Bdwy debut 1959 in *Raisin in the Sun* followed by *One Flew over the Cuckoo's Nest, Last Breeze of Summer*, OB in *The Iceman Cometh, The Blacks, Pullman Car Hiawatha, Bloodknot, Happy Ending, Day of Absence, Kongi's Harvest, Ceremonies in Dark Old Men, The Harangues, The Reckoning, Frederick Douglas, River Niger, The Offering, Old Phantoms, The Michigan. About Heaven and Earth, Louie and Ophelia, Lifetimes, The Little Tommy Parker Celebrated Minstrel Shows, Last Night at Ace High.*

WARING, WENDY. Born December 7, 1960 in Melrose, MA. Attended Emerson Col., Debut 1987 OB in *Wish You Were Here*, Bdwy in *Legs Diamond* (1988), T*he Will Rogers Follies.*

WARNER, MARILEE. Born April 24, 1960 in Erie, PA. Graduate UMiami. Debut 1992 OB in *The Mystery of Anna O* followed by *Who Will Carry the Word?*, Bdwy in *Anna Karenina* (1992)

WASHINGTON, SHARON. Born September 12, 1959 in New York City. Graduate Dartmouth Col., Yale U. Debut 1988 OB in *Coriolanus* followed by *Cymbeline, Richard III, The Balcony, Caucasian Chalk Circle, Before It Hit Home.*

WATERSON, JAMES. Debut 1993 OB in *Another Time* followed by *Good Evening* (dir)

WEAVER, FRITZ. Born January 19, 1926 in Pittsburgh, PA. Graduate U. Chicago. Bdwy debut 1955 in *The Chalk Garden* for which he received a Theatre World Award, followed by *Protective Custody, Miss Lonelyhearts, All American, Lorenzo, The White House, Baker Street, Child's Play, Absurd Person Singular, Angels Fall, The Crucible* (1991), *A Christmas Carol*, OB in *The Way of the World, White Devil, The Doctor's Dilemma, Family Reunion, The Power and the Glory, The Great God Brown, Peer Gynt, Henry IV, My Fair Lady* (CC), *Lincoln, The Biko Inquest, The Price, Dialogue for Lovers, A Tale Told, Time Framed, Wrong Turn at Lungfish.*

WEBER, ANDREA. Born in Midland, MI. Graduate IndU, Hunter Col. Debut 1981 OB in *Inadmissible Evidence* followed by *Childhood, Festival of One Acts, Comedy of Errors*, Bdwy in *Macbeth* (1983).

WEBER, JAKE. Born March 12, 1963 in London, Eng. Graduate Middlebury Col. Juilliard Debut 1988 OB in *Road*, followed by *Twelfth Night, Maids of Honor, Richard III, The Big Funk, Othello, Mad Forest, As You Like it* (CP) *Othello*, Bdwy in *A Small Family Business* (1992).

WEISS, GORDON JOSEPH. Born June 16, 1949 in Bismarck, ND. Attended Moorhead State Col. Bdwy debut 1974 in *Jumpers* followed by *Goodtime Charley, King of Hearts, Raggedy Ann, Ghetto, Jelly's Last Jam*, OB in *A Walk on the Wild Side.*

WEISS, JEFF. Born in 1940 in Allentown, PA. Debut 1986 OB in *Hamlet* followed by *The Front Page, Casanova*, Bdwy in *Macbeth* (1988), *Our Town, Mastergate, Face Value, The Real Inspector Hound/15 Minute Hamlet.*

WELLS, CRAIG. Born July 2, 1955 in Newark, NJ. Graduate Albion Col. Debut 1985 OB in *Forbidden Broadway*, followed by *The Best of Forbidden Broadway, Closer Than Ever, Collette Collage, Balancing Act*, Bdwy in *Chess* (1988), *Les Miserables.*

WELLS, DEANNA. Born August 7, 1962 in Milwaukee, WI. Graduate NorthwesternU. Debut OB in *On the 20th Century* followed by *After These Messages, The Fantasticks, Sharon*, Bdwy in *Smile, South Pacific* (LC)

WESTON, CELIA. Born in South Carolina. Attended Salem Col., NC School of Arts. Bdwy debut 1979 in *Loose Ends*, OB in *Bargains.*

WESTON, DOUGLAS. Born January 13, 1960 in London, England Graduate Princeton U., RADA. Debut. 1991 OB in *Whitestones* followed by Bdwy in *Blood Brothers* (1993)

WESTENBERG, ROBERT. Born October 26, 1953 in Miami Beach, FL. Graduate U. Cal/Fresno. Debut 1981 OB in *Henry IV Part I*, followed by *Hamlet, The Death of von Richthofen*, Bdwy in *Zorba* (1983) for which he received a Theatre World Award, *Sunday in the Park with George, Into the Woods, Les Miserables, The Secret Garden.*

WEXLER, KAREN. Born July 26, 1965 in Buffalo, NY. Graduate Vassar Col. Debut 1990 OB in *Once in a Lifetime* followed by *The Tempest, A Midsummer Night's Dream, What the Butler Saw, Dark of the Moon, Craig's Wife, Senior Prom.*

WHALEY, FRANK. Born July 20, 1963 in Syracuse, NY. Graduate, SUNY/Albany. Debut 1986 OB in *Tigers Wild* followed by *The Years.*

WHITE, AL. Born May 17, 1942 in Houston, TX. Graduate San Fran CC. Bdwy debut 1992 in *Two Trains Running* for which he received a Theatre World Award.

WHITE, AMELIA. Born September 14, 1954 in Nottingham, England. Attended London Central School. Debut 1984 OB in *The Accrington Pals* for which she received a Theatre World Award, followed by *American Bagpipes*, Bdwy in *Crazy for You* (1992).

WHITE, DAISY. Born January 7, 1966 in Paris, France. Graduate Bennington Col., RADA. Debut 1991 OB in *The Christmas Rules*, followed by *A Shayna Maidel*, Bdwy in *A Little Hotel on the Side* (1992), *The Sea Gull.*

WHITE, JENNIFER DORR. Born August 16, 1959 in Atlanta, Ga. Graduate WilliamsCo Ntl Theatre Consv. Debut 1990 OB in *Women of Manhattan* followed by *Bedroom Farce, Dando Bohica, State of the Art, Romeo and Juliet.*

WHITE, LILLIAS D. Born July 21, 1951 in Brooklyn, NYC. Graduate NYCC. Debut 1975 OB in *Solidad Tetrad* followed by *The Life, Romance in Hard Times, Back to Bacharach*, Bdwy in *Barnum* (1981), *Dreamgirls, Rock n' Roll: The First 5000 Years, Once on This Island, Carrie.*

WHITE, PATRICK. Born September 9, 1963 in Albany, NY. Graduate AADA. Debut 1988 OB in *Male Animal*, followed by *After the Rain, Take the Waking Slow, Anima Mundi, Bedroom Farce.*

WHITEHEAD, PAXTON. Born in Kent, England. Attended Webber-Douglas Acad. Bdwy debut 1962 in *The Affair* followed by *Beyond the Fringe, Candida, Habeas Corpus, Crucifer of Blood, Camelot, Noises Off, Run for Your Wife, Artist Descending A Staircase, Lettice and Lovage, A Little Hotel on the Side*, OB in *Gallows Humor, One Way Pendulum, A Doll's House, Rondelay.*

WILDER, ALAN. Born September 24, 1953 in Chicago, IL. Graduate Il. StateU. Bdwy debut 1986 in *The Caretaker*, followed by *The Song of Jacob Zulu* (1993).

WILKINSON, EDMUND. Born November 14, 1962 in The Bronx, NY. Graduate RutgersU. Debut 1992 OB in *Othello* followed by *The Good Natur'd Man, Widowers' Houses*

WILKOF, LEE. Born June 25, 1951 in Canton, OH. Graduate U. Cinn. Debut 1977 OB in *Present Tense*, followed by *Little Shop of Horrors, Holding Patterns, Angry Housewives, Assassins, Born Guilty*, Bdwy in *Sweet Charity* (1986), *The Front Page, She Loves Me.*

WILLIAMS, ALLISON. Born September 26, 1958 in NYC. Debut 1977 OB in *Present Tense*, followed by *Young Gifted* and *Broke, Thrill a Moment*, Bdwy in *The Wiz* (1977), *Dreamgirls, Sweet Charity, Jelly's Last Jam.*

WILLIAMS, DARNELL. Born in London in 1955. Debut 1993 on Bdwy in *Angels in America.*

WILLIAMS, ELLIS. Born June 28, 1951 in Brunswick, GA. Graduate Boston U. Debut 1977 OB in *Intimation*, followed by *Spell #7, Mother Courage, Ties That Bind, Kid Purple, The Boys Next Door, Avenue X*, Bdwy in *The Basic Training of Pavlo Hummel, Pirates of Penzance, Solomon's Child, Trio, Requiem for a Heavyweight, Once on This Island.*

WILLIAMS, MEL. Born November 15, 1947 in Philadelphia, PA. Graduate Cheyney State Antioch U. Debut 1992 OB in *Spindrift.*

WILLIAMS, SARAH McCORD. Born February 18, 1963 in Greenwich, CT. Attended RISD. Debut 1989 OB in *Don Juan* followed by *Revenge of the Mother, Wet Dreams, Overruled, Scapin.*

WILLIAMS, TREAT. Born December 1, 1951 in Rowayton, CT. Bdwy debut 1974 in *Grease* followed by *Over Here, Once in a Lifetime, Pirates of Penzance, Love Letters*, OB in *Maybe I'm Doing It Wrong, Love Letters, Some Men Need Help, Oh Hell!, Oleanna.*

WILLIAMSON, GLEN. Born September 10, 1959 in Greeley, CO. Graduate UCal/Santa Cruz., Juilliard. Debut 1992 OB in *The Boy Who Saw True.*

WILLIFORD, LOU. Born August 14, 1957 in Dallas, TX. Graduate Trinity U. Debut 1990 OB in *The Brass Jackal*, followed by *Lips Together Teeth Apart, Gifts of the Magi*, Bdwy in *Fiddler on the Roof* (1990).

WILLIS, SHAN. Born in the USA. Graduate NYU. Bdwy debut 1992 in *The Real Inspector Hound/15 Minute Hamlet*, OB in *As You Like It, The Taming of the Shrew, Dark of the Moon, A Midsummer Night's Dream, Voices.*

WILLISON, WALTER. Born June 24, 1947 in Monterey Park, CA. Bdwy debut 1970 in *Norman Is That You?*, followed by *Two by Two* for which he received a Theatre World Award, *Wild and Wonderful, A Celebration of Richard Rodgers, Pippin, A Tribute to Joshua Logan, A Tribute to George Abbott, Grand Hotel*, OB in *South Pacific in Concert, They Say It's Wonderful, Broadway Scandals of 1928 and Options*, both of which he wrote, *Aldersgate 88.*

WILLIAMSON, RUTH. Born January 25, 1954 in Baltimore, MD. Graduate U. Md. Bdwy debut 1981 in *Annie*, followed by *Smile, Guys and Dolls*, OB in *Preppies, Bodo.*

WILLIS, RICHARD. Born in Dallas, TX. Graduate Cornell U., Northwestern U. Debut 1986 OB in *Three Sisters* followed by *Nothing to Report, The Rivalry of Dolls.*

WILLS, RAY. Born September 14, 1960 in Santa Monica, CA. Graduate Wichita St. U. Brandeis U. Debut 1988 OB in *Side by Side by Sondheim*, followed by *Kiss Me Quick, The Grand Tour, The Cardigans, The Rothschilds, Little Me, A Backers Audition*, Bdwy in *Anna Karenina* (1993).

WILSON, CHANDRA. Born August 27, 1969 in Houston, TX. Graduate NYU. Debut 1991 OB in *The Good Times Are Killing Me* for which she received a Theatre World Award.

WINANT, BRUCE. Born April 9, 1957 in Santa Monica, CA. Graduate U.S. Intl. U. Bdwy debut 1991 in *Miss Saigon.*

WING, VIRGINIA. Born November 9 in Marks, Ms. Graduate MissCol. Debut 1989 OB in *Two by Two* followed by *Food and Shelter, Cambodia Agonistes.*

WINSON, SUZI. Born February 28, 1962 in New York City. Bdwy debut 1980 in *Brigadoon*, followed by OB in *Moondance, Nunsense.*

WINSTON, LEE. Born March 14, 1941 in Great Bend. KS. Graduate U. Kan, Debut 1966 OB in *The Drunkard*, followed by *Little Mahagony, The Good Soldier Schweik, Adopted Moon, Miss Waters to You, Christmas Bride, The Elephant Piece, Cornerpieces, Knights of the Round Table*, Bdwy in *Showboat* (1966), *1600 Pennsylvania Avenue.*

WINTERSTELLER, LYNNE. Born September 18, 1955 in Sandusky, OH. Graduate UMd. Bdwy debut 1982 in *Annie* followed by OB's *Gifts of the Magi* (1984), T*he Rise of David Levinsky, Nunsense, 'Closer Than Ever.*

WONG, B. D. Born October 24, 1962 in San Francisco, CA. Debut 1981 OB in *Androcles and the Lion* followed by *Applause, The Tempest*, Bdwy in *M. Butterfly* for which he received a Theatre World Award, *Face Value.*

WOODARD, CHARLAYNE. Born December 29 in Albany, NY. Graduate GoodmanTh.Sch., SUNY. Debut 1975 OB in *Don't Bother Me I Can't Cope* followed by *Dementos, Under Fire, A ... My Name Is Alice, Twelfth Night, Hang on to the Good Times, Paradise, Caucasian Chalk Circle, Pretty Fire*, Bdwy in *Hair* (1977), *Ain't Misbehavin'* (1978/1988).

WOODRUFF, KELLY. Born August 12, 1957 in Johnson City, TN. Attended FlaStateU. Debut 1984 OB in *Bells Are Ringing* followed by *Buskers, George White's Scandals*, Bdwy in *The Will Rogers Follies* (1991).

WOODS, CAROL. Born November 13, 1943 in Jamaica, NY. Graduate Ithica Col. Debut 1980 OB *One Mo' Time* followed by *Blues in the Night*, Bdwy in *Grind* (1985), *Big River, Stepping Out, The Crucible, A Little Hotel on the Side, The Goodbye Girl.*

WOODS, RICHARD. Born May 9, 1923 in Buffalo, NY. Graduate Ithica Col. Bdwy in *Beg Borrow or Steal, Capt. Brassbound's Conversion, Sail Away, Coco, Last of Mrs. Lincoln, Gigi, Sherlock Holmes, Murder Among Friends, Royal Family, Deathtrap, Man and Superman, Man Who Came to Dinner, The Father, Present Laughter, Alice in Wonderland, You Can't Take It with You, Design for Living, Smile, The Show-Off,* OB in *The Crucible, Summer and Smoke, American Gothic, Four-in-One, My Heart's in the Highlands, Eastward in Eden, Long Gallery, Year Boston Won the Pennant, In the Matter of J. Robert Oppenheimer,* with APA in *You Can't Take It with You, War and Peace, School for Scandal, Right You Are, Wild Duck, Pantagleize, Exit the King, Cherry Orchard, Cock-a-doodle Dandy,* and *Hamlet, Crimes and Dreams, Marathon '84, Much Ado about Nothing, Sitting Pretty in Concert, The Cat and the Fiddle, The Old Boy.*

WOODSON, JOHN. Born May 12, 1950 in Des Moines, IA. Attended NC Schl. of Arts. Debut 1990 OB in *King Lear,* followed by *The Sorrows of Frederick, Democracy and Esther.*

WOPAT, TOM. Born in 1950 in Lodi, WI. Attended U. Wis. Debut 1978 OB in *A Bistro Car on the CNR,* followed by *Oklahoma!, The Robber Bridegroom, Olympus on My Mind,* Bdwy in *I Love My Wife* (1979), *City of Angels, Guys and Dolls.*

WORKMAN, JASON. Born October 9, 1962 in Omaha, Neb. Attended U. Ky., Goodman School. Bdwy debut 1989 in *Meet Me in St. Louis* for which he received a Theatre World Award. OB in *Haunted Host, Safe Sex.*

WORKMAN, SHANELLE. Born August 3, 1978 in Fairfax, VA. Bdwy debut 1988 in *Les Miserables.*

WRIGHT, AMY. Born April 15, 1950 in Chicago, IL. Graduate Beloit Col. Debut 1977 OB in *The Stronger* followed by *Nightshift, Hamlet, Miss Julie, Slacks and Tops, Terrible Jim Fitch, Village Wooing, The Stronger, Time Framed, Trifles, Words from the Moon, Prin, Born Guilty,* Bdwy in *5th of July,* (1980), *Noises Off.*

WYCHE, MIMI. Born December 2, 1955 in Greenville, SC. Graduate Stanford U. Debut 1986 OB in *Once on a Summer's Day,* followed by *Senor Discretion, Juan Darien, The Golden Apple,* Bdwy in *Cats* (1988).

WYMAN, NICHOLAS. Born May 18, 1950 in Portland, ME. Graduate Harvard U. Bdwy debut 1975 in *Very Good Eddie,* followed by *Grease, The Magic Show, On the 20th Century, Whoopee!, My Fair Lady* (1981), *Doubles, Musical Comedy Murders of 1940, Phantom of the Opera,* OB in *Paris Lights, When We Dead Awaken, Charlotte Sweet, Kennedy at Colonus, Once on a Summer's Day, Angry Housewives, The Hunchback of Notre Dame.*

WYNKOOP, CHRISTOPHER. Born December 7, 1943 in Long Branch, NJ. Graduate AADA. Debut 1970 OB in *Under the Gaslight,* followed by *And So to Bed, Cartoons for a Lunch Hour, Telecast, Fiorello!, The Aunts,* Bdwy in *Whoopee!* (1979), *City of Angels, Anna Christie.*

YANCEY, KIM. Born September 25, 1959 in NYC. Graduate CCNY. Debut 1978 OB in *Why Lillie Won't Spin* followed by *Escape to Freedom, Dacha, Blues for Mr.Charlie, American Dreams, Ties That Bind, Walking Through, Raisin in the Sun, Don Juan of Seville, Heliotrope Bouquet.*

YEOMAN, JO ANN. Born March 19, 1948 in Phoenix, AZ. Graduate Ariz. St. U., Purdue U. Debut 1974 OB in *The Boy Friend,* followed by *Texas Starlight, Ba Ta Clan, A Christmas Carol.*

YORK, MICHAEL. Born March 27, 1942 in Fulmer, England. Attended Oxford U. Bdwy debut 1973 in *Outcry* followed by *Bent* (1980), *The Little Prince and the Aviator, The Crucible, Someone Who'll Watch Over Me.*

YOUNG, DAVID. Born July 14, 1947 in Kansas City, MO. Graduate UKs. Debut 1973 OB in *The Raree Show* followed by *Inexhaustible Banquet, Times Like These, The Night Boat, Rabboni, Madison Avenue, Exit Music,* Bdwy in, *Into the Light* (1986).

YOUNG, KAREN. Born September 29., 1958 in Pequonnock, NJ. Attended Douglas Col., Rutgers U. Debut 1982 OB in *Three Acts of Recognition* followed by *A Lie of the Mind, Dog Logic.*

YOUNGMAN, CHRISTINA. Born September 14, 1963 in Philadelphia, PA. Attended Point Park Col. Debut 1983 OB in *Emperor of My Baby's Heart,* followed by *Carouselle des Folles,* Bdwy in *Starlight Express* (1987), *Largely New York, The Will Rogers Follies, My Favorite Year.*

ZAKARIAN, CRAIG. Born September 17, 1960 in Kent Island, MD. Graduate Shepherd Col. Debut 1993 OB in *3 by Wilder,* Bdwy in *Wilder Wilder Wilder* (1993).

ZALOOM, PAUL. Born December 14, 1951 in Brooklyn, NY. Graduate Goddard Col. Debut 1979 OB in *Fruit of Zaloom,* followed by *Crazy as Zaloom, Return of the Creature from the Blue Zaloom, Theatre of Trash, House of Horrors, My Civilization, Sick but True.*

ZARISH, JANET. Born April 21, 1954 in Chicago, Il. Graduate Juilliard. Debut 1981 OB in *The Villager,* followed by *Playing with Fire, Royal Bob, An Enemy of the People, A Midsummer Night's Dream, Festival of 1-Acts, Other People's Money, Human Nature, Selling Off, EST Marathon '93.*

ZEMON, TOM. Born January 13, 1964 in Hartford, CT. Graduate U. Hartford, Bdwy debut 1988 in *Les Miserables.*

ZIEMBA, KAREN. Born November 12 in St. Joseph, MO. Graduate U. Akron, Debut 1981 OB in *Seesaw,* followed by *I Married an Angel, Sing for Your Supper, 50 Million Frenchmen, And the World Goes Round, 110 In The Shade* (NYCO/LC), *A Grand Night for Singing.*

ZIEN, CHIP. Born March 20, 1947 in Milwaukee, WI. Attended U. Penn. OB in *You're a Good Man Charlie Brown,* followed by *Kadish, How to Succeed ..., Dear Mr. G., Tuscaloosa's Calling, Hot L Baltimore, El Grande de Coca Cola, Split, Real Life Funnies, March of the Falsettos, Isn't It Romantic, Diamonds, Falsettoland,* Bdwy in *All Over Town* (1974), *The Suicide, Into the Woods, Grand Hotel, Falsettos.*

ZINDEL, LIZABETH. Born October 30, 1976 in New York City. Debut 1989 OB in *Essence of Margrovia,* followed by *Last Night, Come Again, Common Clay, David's Mother, Night Sky, EST Marathon '92.*

ZISKIE, DANIEL. Born in Detroit MI. Debut 1970 OB in *Second City* followed by *The Sea Gull, Ballymurphy The Rivals, Listen to the Lions, Halloween, Bandit, Mamet Plays, At Home, The Castaways, EST Marathon 93, Bed and Breakfast,* Bdwy in *Mornings at 7, Breakfast with Les and Bess, I'm Not Rappaport.*

ZISKIE, KURT. Born April 16, 1956 in Oakland, CA. Graduate Stanford U., Neighborhood Playhouse. Debut 1985 OB in *A Flash of Lightning* followed by *Ulysses in Nighttown, Three Sisters, EST Marathon '92,* Bdwy in *Broadway* (1987).

ZORICH, LOUIS. Born February 12, 1924 in Chicago, IL. Attended Roosevelt U. OB in *Six Characters in Search of an Author, Crimes and Crimes, Henry V, Thracian Horses, All Women Are One, The Good Soldier Schweik, Shadow of Heroes, To Clothe the Naked, A Memory of Two Mondays, They Knew What They Wanted, The Gathering, True West, The Tempest, Come Day Come Night, Henry IV Parts 1 & 2* Bdwy in *Becket, Moby Dick, The Odd Couple, Hadrian VII, Moonchildren, Fun City, Goodtime Charley, Herzl, Death of a Salesman, Arms and the Man,The Marriage of Figaro, She Loves Me.*

| Stella Adler | Peter Allen | John Anderson | Shirley Booth |

OBITUARIES

(JUNE 1, 1992-MAY 31, 1993)

JOSEPH ABALDO Jr, 47, Philadelphia-born actor and founder of Abaldo/Richin Casting, died on December 4, 1992 in New York of AIDS. He was a founding member of the New Repertory Company and appeared in many productions there. He starred in *The Magic Show* on Broadway for over two years. As a casting director, his credits include *Rothchilds, Pageant, Nunsense* and he was working on the upcoming *The Life* when he died. Survived by his companion, parents, and three brothers.

STELLA ADLER, 91, influential Manhattan-born actress and teacher, died on December 21, 1992 in Los Angeles. After studying with Stanislavsky, she revised his theories to stress the actor create by imagination rather than personal emotion and memory. She came to prominence in the 1930s as a Group Theatre member in plays such as *Success Story, Awake and Sing* and *Paradise Lost.* Later plays include *He Who Gets Slapped* (1946) and *Oh Dad Poor Dad* (London). Directing credits include *Golden Boy* (tour) and *Johnny Johnson* (1956). She wrote *Stella Adler on Acting* and her students included Marlon Brando, Ellen Burstyn, Robert DeNiro, Candice Bergen and Elaine Stritch. Survived by her daughter, sister, two grandchildren, and stepdaughter.

THOMAS J. AGUILAR, 41, actor, died of AIDS on May 7, 1993. He played Paul in *A Chorus Line* in London and on Broadway.

PETER ALLEN, 48, Australian-born entertainer and Grammy and Academy Award-winning songwriter, died on June 18, 1992 in San Diego of AIDS. Discovered by Judy Garland in 1964, he began as opening act for her concerts and flourished as a cabaret and concert headliner. Bdwy debut in 1970's *Soon* , followed by *Up in One*. He wrote the score for and starred in the 1988 musical *Legs Diamond* . He also had several popular engagements at Radio City Music Hall. Married in 1967 to Liza Minnelli (separated 1971), he is survived by his mother and a sister.

MALCOLM ALLEN, 58, leading general manager, company manager and actor, died February 22, 1993 in Manhattan of lung cancer. Bdwy debut in 1947's *A Young Man's Fancy* before switching to management on shows including *A Funny Thing Happened...*(1972),*My Fair Lady* (1976), *Best Little Whorehouse in Texas* . No reported survivors.

JOHN ANDERSON, 69, Illinois-born stage, film and tv actor, died August 7, 1992 in Sherman Oaks, CA. Made Bdwy debut in *Cat on a Hot Tin Roof* followed by many Off-Bdwy and touring shows. At the time of death, he was preparing New York production of *In the Sweet By and By* which he performed in L.A. Survived by two sisters, two children, five grand-children and a great grandson.

BERT ANDREWS, 63, Chicago-born photographer, died January 25, 1993 in New York of stomach cancer. He chronicled the history of black theatre from the 1950s to the 1990s. His work was collected in the 1990 book *In the Shadow of the Great White Way: Images from the Black Theatre.* No survivors.

JOSEPH ANTHONY, 80, Milwaukee-born actor and director, died January 20, 1993 in Hyannis, MA. Directing credits include *Best Man, Under the Yum-Yum Tree, Rhinoceros, Mary Mary, The Lark, Most Happy Fella, Marriage Go-Round, 110 in the Shade* and *Rainmaker* . Acting credits include *Professor Mamlock, On the Rocks,*

Liberty Jones, Lady in the Dark, Truckline Cafe, Skipper Next to God, Montserrat, Peer Gynt (1951), *Country Girl* (also 1966 revival), *Flight Into Egypt, Camino Real* . Survived by wife, actress Perry Wilson, a son, daughter, and two grandchildren.

MALCOLM ATTERBURY, 85, stage, film and tv actor, died August 23, 1992 in Beverly Hills. He owned and operated the Tamarack Playhouse and the Playhouse in Albany, NY. He appeared on Bdwy in 1963's *One Flew Over the Cuckoo's Nest* . Survived by his wife, three children, and five grandchildren.

PATRICIA BARCLAY (PATRICIA B. EWELL), 93, actress, died October 25, 1992 in Dennis, MA. She appeared in Broadways plays of the 1920s, 30s, and 40s along with regional theatre. Survived by husband, Richard Ewell, a retired actor.

EDWIN LOUIS BATTLE, 33, actor, died February 23, 1993 in Toronto of a stroke. He was appearing in the Toronto production of *Joseph and the ...Dreamcoat.* Bdwy credits include *Show Boat and Big River.* Other credits include *Juba, Sugar Hill, Machinal, Elegies for Angels, Angels in America* and *The Life.* Survived by his parents, 2 sisters and 2 brothers.

SHIRLEY BOOTH (THELMA BOOTH FORD), 94, NYC-born stage, tv and film actress, died October 16, 1992 in No. Chatham , MA. of natural causes. A three time Tony Award winner, for *Come Back Little Sheba, Goodbye My Fancy* and *Time of the Cuckoo,* she was also the original Dolly Levi in *The Matchmaker.* A versatile talent, she also starred in the musicals *A Tree Grows in Brooklyn, Juno, By the Beautiful Sea,* and *Look to the Lillies.* Bdwy debut 1925 in *Hells Bells* followed by *Bye Bye Baby, Laff That Off, War Song, Too Many Heroes, Three Men on a Horse, Excursion, Philadelphia Story, My Sister Eileen, Tomorrow the World, Hollywood Pinafore, Land's End, Love Me Long, Miss Isobel, Second String* , and *Hay Fever.* She also recreated *"..Little Sheba"* on film, winning an Oscar, and was a popular tv star from 1961 to 1966 with *Hazel.* Survived by her sister.

RICHARD BRANDA, 57, stage, film and tv actor, died January 7, 1993 in L.A. of colon cancer. New York credits include *Great White Hope* and *Dr. Faustus.* He worked with the Stratford Shakespeare Festival in the early 1960s. Survived by his wife, three daughters, and two brothers.

PATRICIA BROOKS, 59, singer/actress, died January 22, 1993 in Mt. Kisco, NY of multiple sclerosis. Jose Quintero cast her in *The Grass Harp* and in *Iceman Cometh.* After singing in the nun chorus in *Sound of Music* she decided to switch to opera where she achieved much success. Survived by her husband, Theodore D. Mann, her mother, two sons, a stepbrother, and a sister.

GEORGIA BROWN, 58, English-born singer/actress, died June 6, 1992 in London after a brief illness. Best known for creating the part of Nancy in *Oliver* , introducing "As Long As He Needs Me" in London and New York. After appearing in *Threepeny Opera* in London (1956), she succeeded Lotte Lenya in the New York company. Other New York credits include *Greek, Side By Side By Sondheim,* and the title musical roles of *Carmelina* and *Roza* (1987). She returned to London in *42nd St.* and *Greek.* Survived by a son.

STEPHEN BURKS, 36, Illinois-born actor, died November 26, 1992 in L.A. Bdwy debut 1980 in *Division Street.* He worked Off-Bdwy in *Steel on Steel* and *Lady's Not for Burning* and also appeared at the Mark Taper Forum in L.A. Survived by his parents, brothers and sisters, stepparents, and a grandmother.

ERIC BURROUGHS, 81, stage and radio actor, died November 12, 1992 in New York of natural causes. Orson Welles cast him in 1935's *Macbeth* for the Federal

Georgia Brown   Steven Burks

Sammy Cahn   Charlles Honi Coles

Negro Theatre project. Stage roles included *Long Way From Home, Set My People Free, Petrified Forest, Mrs. Patterson* and *Cleopatra.* Survived by third wife, daughter and son.

JOSEPH R. BURSTIN, 85, producer, died on December 27, 1992. He produced *To Be Young Gifted and Black* and *Raisin in the Sun* among others. He was a major force in the Yiddish theatre of the 1940s. Survived by his wife, daughter, son, and four grandchildren.

SAMMY CAHN (COHEN), 79, NYC-born lyricist, died January 15, 1993 of heart failure in L.A. Best known for his movie songs, Cahn's theatre lyrics include 1947's *High Button Shoes* followed by *Skyscraper ,Walking Happy* and *Look To The Lilies* . In 1974 he made his Bdwy debut as a performer in a revue of his songs, *Words and Music*, which won him a *Theatre World* Award. Survived by his wife, son, daughter, and two grandchildren.

JOYCE CAREY, 94, British born stage and film actress, died February 28, 1993 in London. She made her stage debut in 1916 in an all-female production of *Henry V.* She made her Bdwy debut in 1927's *Road To Rome* and worked on New York stages for the next 7 years. On her return to London, she began an association with Noel Coward performing in many of his plays and films. She worked through the 1980's. She also wrote *Sweet Aloes* (1934) under the pseudonym Jay Mallory. She was awarded the OBE in 1982 and never married. No survivors.

MORRIS CARNOVSKY, 94, St. Louis-born actor died September 1, 1992 in Easton, CT. Starting in the 1920s he appeared with the Theatre Guild in such plays as *Brothers Karamazov, Marco Millions, Volpone, Uncle Vanya* and the premieres of *Saint Joan* and *Apple Cart.* He joined the Group Theatre in 1931 where he was in *Golden Boy* and *Awake and Sing.* He worked in films but came under attack by the right-wing House Committee on Un-American Activities. He returned to theatre in 1953's *World of Sholem Aleichem,* followed by *Tiger at the Gates, The Lovers, Taming of the Shrew, Measure for Measure, Nude with Violin, Cold Wind and the Warm, Family Affair* and many Shakespearean productions with the American Shakespeare Festival in Stratford, CT. He was elected to the Theatre Hall of Fame in 1979. Survived by his wife, son, two sisters, and niece.

CONSTANCE CARPENTER, 87, English-born actress, died December 26, 1992 in New York of a stroke. Bdwy debut in 1924's *Charlot's Revue* followed by *A Connecticut Yankee* and she succeeded Gertrude Lawrence upon her 1952 death in *King and I* . Carpenter played the role of Anna for 621 performances. Married 4 times, she left no survivors.

JUNE CLAYWORTH, 80, stage and film actress, died January 7, 1993 in Woodland Hills, CA. On Bdwy, she appeared in *Are You Decent?, Torch Song* and *Once in a Lifetime.* Survived by her son.

CHARLES (HONI) COLES, 81, Philadelphia-born dancer/singer/actor, died November 12, 1992 in New York of cancer. Debut 1933 Off-Bdwy in *Humming Sam* . Bdwy in *Gentlemen Prefer Blondes, Hello Dolly* , *Bubbling Brown Sugar* and *Black Broadway.* Biggest Bdwy triumph, and 1983 supporting actor Tony Award in *My One and Only* which gave him new recognition for his elegant tap-dancing. Survived by his wife, daughter and son.

FREDERICK COMBS, 57, Virginia-born actor/director/playwright, died September 19, 1992 in Los Angeles of AIDS. Best known for creating the role of Donald in 1968's *Boys in the Band* and re-creating the role in the 1970 film, he also played the role in London. Bdwy debut 1961 in *Taste of Honey* followed by *Midsummer Night's Dream ,The Knack* (both with NY Shakespeare Festival) and Zeffirelli's *Lady of the Camellias* . In 1973 his play *The Children's Mass* opened Off-Bdwy and in 1979 he founded the L.A. Actor's Lab where he teught. Survived by a sister.

KEN CORY, 51, actor, died January 15 in New York of AIDS. Credits include *Mame* and *Company* . No survivors.

WILLIAM DARRID, 69, producer/writer/actor, died July 11, 1992 in Santa Monica, CA. of respiratory failure. As an actor he appeared in Bdwy's *Inherit the Wind, Men of Distinction* and *Reclining Figure* before producing *The Disenchanted, Andersonville Trial* and *Cook for Mr. General* . He married actress Diana Douglas in 1956 and helped raise Michael and Joel Douglas. Also survived by his brother and step-grandson.

DOUG DELAUDER, 38, actor, died June 30, 1992 of AIDS. He appeared in the long running *Perfect Crime* .

FLORENCE DESMOND (DAWSON), 87, entertainer/impersonator, died January 16, 1993 in Guildford England. She performed in New York with Noel Coward in *This Year of Grace* and was popular in nightclubs. She was a major legit star in London and also worked in films. Survived by second husband.

GERALD LINCOLN DOLIN, 79, composer/music director, died December 31, 1992. Writing credits include *Smile at Me* and *Dancing Coed.* He was musical director for Frank Loesser's *Where's Charley?* and is credited with composing the introduction to "Once in Love with Amy". Survived by a son, two daughters, and four grandchildren.

Alfred Drake   Denholm Elliot

Billl Elverman   Constance Ford

WILLIAM DOUGLAS-HOME, 80, English playwright, died September 28, 1992 in Winchester, England. A prolific comedy writer in London, several of his plays reached Bdwy including *The Chiltern Hundreds, Yes M'Lord, Reluctant Debutante* and *The Kingfisher.* He was court-martialed in 1944 for failing to obey a command to continue firing upon soldiers whose commander would not surrender unconditionally. He spent a year in prison. Survived by his wife, a son, and three daughters.

ALFRED DRAKE (CAPURRO), 78, NYC-born actor/singer, died July 25, 1992 in New York of heart failure. The versatile performer and major star created the lead roles in the classic musicals *Oklahoma* (1943), *Kiss Me Kate* (1948), and *Kismet* (1953, Tony Award-1954,1965 revival). Drake made his Bdwy debut in 1935's *Mikado,* followed by *White Horse Inn, Babes in Arms, Two Bouquets, One for the Money, Two for the Show, Straw Hat Revue, Out of the Frying Pan, As You Like It, Yesterday's Magic, Sing Out Sweet Land, Beggar's Holiday, Cradle Will Rock, Joy to the World, The Liar, The Gambler, King and I, Kean, Lorenzo, Hamlet* (with Richard Burton), *Those That Play the Clowns, Song of the Grasshopper, Gigi, Skin of Our Teeth* . He received a special Tony Award in 1990 and was president of the Players' Club for many years. Survived by second wife Esther, a fellow cast member in *Oklahoma* , two daughters, and two grandchildren.

JOHN PAUL DUFFY, 42, New Jersey-born director/actor/writer, died March 28, 1993, an apparent suicide. He directed or acted in more than 50 New York plays and managed the Copacabana nightclub. Survived by his parents and a brother.

HARRY ELLERBE, South Carolina-born actor/director, died December 3, 1992 in Atlanta. Bdwy debut 1913 in title role of *Philip Goes Forth,* followed by *Thoroughbred, Strange Orchestra, Ghosts, Hedda Gabbler, Outward Bound, Whiteoaks, Cocktail Party, Oh Mr Meadowbrook, Desk Set, Man on Stilts, Junior Miss* and *The Show-Off* Off-Bdwy. After directing *For Love or Money* he directed regionally and on tv. Survived by a sister.

DENHOLM ELLIOTT, 70, London-born stage and screen actor, died October 6, 1992 of AIDS. Best known for the Merchant-Ivory films *A Room with a View, Maurice,* and Spielberg's *Indiana Jones* series, he debuted on Bdwy with 1951's *Ring 'Round the Moon* followed by *Green Bay Tree, Monique, Write Me a Murder, Seagull, Imaginary Invalid, Touch of the Poet, Tonight at 8:30,* BAM's *New York Idea* and *Three Sisters.* His many London credits include acting opposite Laurence Olivier in *Venus Observ'd* and *A Life in the Theatre* . Survived by second wife, a son and daughter.

BILL ELVERMAN, 40, playwright/actor, died August 13, 1992 in New York. His play *Rock County* won the 1985 Joseph Kesselring Award for best unproduced play. Produced plays include *Particular Friendships/ True Lies, Sever Reservations, The Team, Watercress, After the Party* and *The Mask* (1992, Nat Horne Theatre). Survived by his parents, a sister and two brothers.

HENRY EPHRON, 81, Bronx-born playwright/screenwriter/producer, died September 6, 1992 in L.A. Theatre includes *Three's a Family* (1943) and *Take Her She's Mine,* both written with wife Phoebe, who died in 1971. Survived by daughter Nora Ephron, a writer/director, three other daughters, and seven grandchildren.

BERNARD FRAWLEY, 63, Irish-born actor, died December 17, 1992 in New York of throat cancer. Bdwy credits include *Mass Appeal,* Off-Bdwy includes *Philadelphia Here I Come* and *Ballymurphy* as well as much regional theatre. Survived by his wife and daughter.

LILLIAN VALLISH FOOTE, 69, producer, died August 5, 1992 in Princeton, NJ after a short illness. She worked closely with husband-playwright Horton Foote on his projects. She also produced *Roads To Home* Off-Bdwy. Survived by her husband, and four children.

CONSTANCE FORD, 69, stage and tv actress, died February 26, 1993 in New York of cancer. Bdwy debut as the prostitute in the original 1949 *Death of a Salesman,* followed by *See The Jaguar, Say Darling, Golden Fleecing* and *Nobody Loves an Albatross.* She appeared for 25 years on the tv soap opera *Another World.* No survivors.

JUNE JOYCE LEWIS FRASER, 75, actress/director/former stripper, died November 28, 1992 in Englewood, NJ. After working with Sally Rand and Gypsy Rose Lee, she appeared in *Earl Caroll's Vanities.* She later started an Off-Bdwy acting troupe called the Troupers and directed/produced *The Trouble in July* .

SYLVIA FRIEDLANDER (ROBINS), 74, producer, died November 7, 1992 in Manhattan. Although she mainly worked in tv, she produced *Bathsheba* the Bdwy play introducing James Mason in 1947, Survived by her husband, two daughters and a brother.

DAVID GALLEGLY, 42, Texas-born actor/singer, died February 15, 1993 of AIDS. Stage includes originating Guy Rose in *Boy Meets Boy* (1975).

Vincent Gardenia

Ray Gill

Lillian Gish

VINCENT GARDENIA (SCOGNAMIGLIO), 71, Italian-born stage, film and tv actor, died December 9, 1992 of a heart attack in Philadelphia, where he was appearing in *Breaking Legs.* Off-Bdwy debut in 1955's *In April Once* followed by *Man with the Golden Arm, Volpone, Brothers Karamazov, Power of Darkness, Machinal* (Obie Award, 1960),*Gallows Humor, Theatre of the Absurd, Lunatic View, Little Murders, Passing Through from Exotic Places* (Obie Award,1970), *Carpenters, Buried inside Extra, Breaking Legs* . Bdwy shows include *The Visit* (1958), *Roshoman, Cold Wind and the Warm, Only in America, The Wall, Daughter of Silence, Seidman & Son, Dr. Fish, Prisoner of Second Ave.* (Tony Award, 1972), *God's Favorite, California Suite, Ballroom, Glengarry Glen Ross* . He worked extensively in film and tv. Survived by a brother.

JOY GARRETT, 47, Texas-born stage and tv actress, died February 11, 1993 in Los Angeles of liver failure. Off-Bdwy debut in 1969's *Gertrude Stein's First Reader* followed by *Drunkard, Candyapple, One for the Money* and *Silver Queen Saloon.* Bdwy debut 1971 in *Inner City.* For seven years she played on the soap opera *Young and Restless.* Survived by her parents.

MINNIE GENTRY, 77, Virginia-born stage and tv actress, died May 6, 1993 in Manhattan. Bdwy debut 1946 in *Lysistrata* . She and husband Lloyd Gentry formed Cleveland's Karamu Playhouse. In the 1960s she returned to New York appearing in *The Blacks, Amen Corner, Ain't Supposed to Die a Natural Death, Black Girl, Georgia Georgia, Gentleman Caller/Black Quartet, Sunshine Boys, All God's Chillun Got Wings, Raisin in the Sun* (1979) and the title role in *Media* . Also known for playing the grandmother on tv's *Cosby Show.* Survived by a daughter, three grandchildren, nine great grandchildren, and three great-great grandchildren.

LILLIAN GISH, 99, Ohio-born film, stage, and tv actress, one of the towering figures of early film, died February 27, 1993 in Manhattan of heart failure. Acting from the age of 5 onward, she was billed as Baby Lillian in 1902's *In Convict Stripes* with Walter Huston. She debuted on Bdwy in David Belasco's production *The Good Little Devil* with Mary Pickford. After her film stardom she returned to the stage for *Uncle Vanya* (1930 Helena, again in 1973 as the nurse), *Camille,* Ophelia to John Gielgud's *Hamlet* (1936), *Life with Father* (Chicago), *The Trip to Bountiful, All the Way Home, Passage to India, Romeo and Juliet, I Never Sang for My Father,* and *A Musical Jubilee* (1975). She made over 100 films between 1912 and 1987. Her actress sister Dorothy died in 1968. She never married and leaves no survivors.

RAY GILL, 42, New Jersey-born actor, died September 27, 1992 in Saylorsburg, PA. of AIDS. Bdwy debut 1978 in *On the 2oth Century* followed by *Pirates of Penzance, The First, They're Playing Our Song, Sunday in the Park with George, Cat on a Hot Tin Roof.* Off Bdwy he created the role of Boolie in *Driving Miss Daisy* . Other Off-Bdwy includes *Bundle of Nerves* and *Romance in Hard Times.* He played the Baker in the first *Into the Woods* tour.Survived by his parents and two sisters.

MICHAEL GORDON, 83, Baltimore-born stage and film director, died April 29, 1993 in L.A. From 1935-40 he worked with the Group Theatre. In the mid-40s he started directing stage productions including *Home of the Brave, Laura, Gods Sit Back* then went to Hollywood. After being blacklisted by the House Commitee on Un-American activities, he returned to New York and directed Bdwy productions including *Male Animal, His and Hers* and *Tender Trap.* He directed the film version of *Cyrano de Bergerac* with Jose Ferrer. Survived by a son, two daughters, and three grandsons.

SIDNEY GORDON, 72, actor/agent, died June 23, 1992 in Palm Springs, CA. He began his career in *Boys from Syracuse* (1938) and *Too Many Girls* before becoming an agent. Survived by two brothers and three sisters.

JOHN GRANGER, 69, Oklahoma-born stage, film and tv actor, died May 31, 1993 in Doylestown, PA. of a cerebral hemorrage. Bdwy debut 1953 in *Little Hut* followed by *Cherie, Auntie Mame.* Off-Bdwy included *The Screens* . Survived by his partner.

EDWARD G. GREER, 73, Massachusetts-born director, died May 7, 1993 in Manhattan of heart failure. He directed the American premiere of Beckett's *After the Fall,* and many Equity Library and New School productions including *Murder in the Cathedral, Dr. Faustus, Tempest, Electra, Music at Night* (NY premiere). Survived by a sister.

MARTIN GREGG, 51, Maine-born actor/producer, died October 11, 1992 in San Diego, CA. of AIDS. He toured with Yul Brynner in *King and I* for 2 years as the young prince. He co-founded the Robert F. Kennedy Theatre for Children in NY and owned the Ritz theatre before founding the California Performing Arts Center for Children in San Diego. In 1990, he established the North Park Theatre Foundation. Survived by his companion, mother, two sisters and a brother.

PAUL HAAKON, 80, Danish-born dancer, died August 16, 1992 in Manhattan of cancer. Bdwy debut in 1933's *Champagne Sec* followed by *At Home Abroad, The Show is On, Hooray for What!* and choreographed *Mexican Hayride* (1944). Considered by many to be among the great male ballet dancers of the century, he also danced ballet in Europe and America and danced and choreographed film. Survived by his wife, son, two daughters, a brother, a sister, and nine grandchildren.

OLIVER HAILEY, 60, Texas-born playwright/tv writer, died January 23, 1993 in L.A. of cancer. He wrote three Bdwy plays, *First One Asleep Whistle, Father's Day,* and *I Won't Dance* . Off-Bdwy includes *Who's Happy Now* and *Hey You Light Man!.* Survived by his wife and two daughters.

Helen Hayes

Audrey Hepburn

HELEN HAYES (BROWN), 92, Washington D.C.-born actress, the first lady of the American theatre, died March 17, 1993 in Nyack, NY. Hayes made her professional debut at age 5 playing Prince Charles in *The Royal Family* at the National Theatre. Bdwy debut 1909 as Little Mimi in *Old Dutch* followed by *Summer Widowers, Penrod, Dear Brutus , Pollyanna* (tours),*Clarence* (1919), *Bab, To the Ladies, We Moderns, Dancing Mothers, Caesar and Cleopatra, What Every Woman Knows* (1926, favorite role), *Coquette, Mary of Scotland* and *Victoria Regina* (where she aged from girlhood to widowhood), *Twelfth Night, Candle in the Wind, Harriet, Happy Birthday* (Tony Award, 1947), *Glass Menagerie* (London, 1948, later City Center), *The Wisteria Trees, Mrs. McThing, Skin of Our Teeth, Time Remembered* (Tony Award, 1958), *A Touch of the Poet, Program for Two Players, The White House, School for Scandal, Right You Are, We Comrades Three, The Show-Off* (1967), *The Front Page* (1969), and *Harvey* (1970). In 1955 the Fulton Theatre was re-named for her, and upon that buildings demolition, the Little Theatre became the Helen Hayes. She won Oscars in 1931 and 1970 for her film work and an Emmy for her TV work. Married to playwright Charles MacArthur from 1928 till his death in 1956. Survived by actor son James MacArthur. Her daughter died in 1949 from polio. In tribute to Miss Hayes, the lights on Broadway theatres were dimmed at 8 p.m. on the night she died.

AUDREY HEPBURN, 63, Belgium-born stage and film actress, a legendary movie star, died January 20, 1993 of colon cancer in Tolochenaz, Switzerland. After London stage debut in *High Button Shoes* (1948), she debuted on Bdwy with 1951's *Gigi* which won her a *Theatre World* Award. In 1954 *Ondine* won her a Tony Award, the same year she won an Oscar for 1953's *Roman Holiday.* She starred in film versions of the plays *My Fair Lady, Wait Until Dark, Sabrina Fair* and *The Children's Hour* . A special Tony Award was presented to Miss Hepburn in 1968, and in the 1980s she became a special ambassador for the United Nations Childrens Fund. In 1990 she gave a staged reading of Anne Frank's diary at the U.N. in New York. Divorced from *Ondine* co-star Mel Ferrer, she is survived by her companion, and two sons.

HAL HESTER, 63, Kentucky-born composer/playwright, died September 13, 1992 in Puerto Rico of diverticulitis. Mr. Hester created the 1968 Off-Bdwy hit *Your Own Thing* with Danny Apolinar and Donald Driver. In recent years he wrote for regional theatre and ran nightclubs and guesthouses. He is survived by his companion, father, and two sisters.

PHYLLIS HILL (FERRER OVERTON), 72, NYC-born actress/ballerina, died in L.A. of lung cancer. Bdwy includes *Rosalinda, Sons and Soldiers, What's Up, Helen Goes to Troy, Volpone, Angel Street, Alchemist, Insect Comedy, The Shrike, Fifth Season,* and co-starring with then-husband Jose Ferrer in *Cyrano de Bergerac* . She was the daughter of actress Peggy Johnson Hill and niece of actor Nolan Leary.

LOUISE HOFF, 69, actress, died June 1, 1992 in Bethlehem, PA. after an illness. On Bdwy, she appeared in *Phoenix '55,* and *Fallen Angel.* Other credits include *The Bandwagon* (revival), *From A to Z, Tunnel of Love, Cloud 7, Invitation to a March* and *Bon Voyage.* Known also for comedy act with sister Jean Dillon, She is survived by her sister, husband, and daughter.

JOHN HOLLAND, 85, Nebraska-born stage, tv and film actor, died May 21, 1993 in Woodland Hills, CA. On Bdwy he appeared in Mary Martin's *Peter Pan* and toured with *Caine Mutiny Court Martial.* No survivors.

HANYA HOLM, 99, German-born choreographer, a major contributer to Bdwy dance, died November 3, 1992 in New York of pneumonia. In addition to her modern dance work, she choreographed *Kiss Me Kate, Out of This World, My Fair Lady ,Camelot, My Darling Aida, Golden Apple, Insect Comedy, Blood Wedding, The Liar* and others. Bdwy debut 1948 with *Ballet Ballads.* In 1952 she became the first choreographer to copyright her dances, for *Kiss Me Kate* and *Out of This World* . Survived by her son, and three granddaughters.

CHARLES HORNE, 48, playwright, died on September 2, 1992 in Syracuse, NY of AIDS. His plays include *The Smoking Room* . Survived by his companion, parents, and three brothers.

CY HOWARD(SEYMOUR HOROWITZ), 77, Milwaukee-born comedy writer/ director, died April 29, 1993 in L.A. of heart failure. Although best known as a radio and film writer, he started as an actor in 1944's *Storm Operation.* Survived by third wife, a daughter, and a sister.

KATHERINE HYNES (d'GROOT), 88, English-born actress, died March 27, 1993 in Englewood, NJ from a stroke. Bdwy includes *Lovers and Friends, Point of No Return, Red Roses for Me, Apple Cart* (1956) and Off-Bdwy in *Cretan Woman* . She outlived her husband and daughter, leaving no survivors.

PAUL JBARA, 44, Brooklyn-born actor and Academy Award-winning songwriter, died September 29, 1992 in L.A. of AIDS. He made his debut in the original cast of Bdwy's *Hair* (1968) and appeared in the London casts of *Jesus Christ Superstar* and *Rocky Horror Show* . He wrote the music, lyrics and book for *Rachel Lily Rosenblum* which closed in previews in 1973. Survived by two sisters.

GERALD E. JACOBSON (JAKE EVERETT), 46, Oregon-born actor/arts administrator, died December 26, 1992 in San Diego of AIDS. Everett made a 1974 Bdwy debut in *Tubstrip* followed by *Roomers* . Survived by his companion, parents, and a sister.

Charlotte Jones

Ruby Keeler

Jack Kelly

ALLAN JONES, 84 , Pennsylvania-born singer/actor, died June 27, 1992 in New York of lung cancer. Though best known for the 1936 film of *Show Boat* and other film musicals, he played Sky in the original *Guys and Dolls* road company and toured *Man of La Mancha* in the 1970s. Survived by his son, singer Jack Jones, his fourth wife, a second son, a stepdaughter, and two great-grandchildren.

DAVID C. JONES, 76, actor, died September 14, 1992 of cancer. He played nearly 90 roles at the Trinity Repertory of Providence, RI. including Candy in *Of Mice and Men,* Harry Hope in *Iceman Cometh* and the servant in *Cherry Orchard* . Bdwy includes *No Time for Sergeants* . No survivors.

CHARLOTTE JONES (NATHANSON), 76, Chicago-born actress, died November 6, 1992 in Toms River, NJ of heart disease. Bdwy debut 1952 in *Buttrio Square* followed by *Camino Real, Mame, How Now Dow Jones, A Matter of Gravity, Skin of Our Teeth, Johnny Johnson;* Off Bdwy includes *False Confessions, Sign of Jonah, Girl on the Via Flamina, Red Roses for Me, Night in Black Bottles, Camino Real, Plays for Bleeker St., Pigeons, Great Scott!, Sjt. Musgrave's Dance, Papers, Beggar's Opera, 200 Years of American Furniture, Belle Femme, Heat of Re-entry, Appointment with Death* . Survived by her husband, a son, a daughter, five grandchildren, and three great-grandchildren.

KEVIN JOHNSON, 74, actor/dancer/tv director, died July 12, 1992 in Arlington, VA. of cancer. Bdwy includes *This Is the Army* and *High Button Shoes* . Survived by four children.

PHILIPP C. JUNG, 43, Cleveland-born set designer, died December 12, 1992 in San Luis Obispo, CA. of AIDS. His work includes *Eastern Standard, Mastergate, Closer Than Ever, Madwoman of Central Park West, Major Barbara, Dark at the Top of the Stairs, Banana Box, Panama Hattie, Lisbon Traviata, Molly Mademoiselle Colombe* and *It's a Man's World* . Survived by his companion, his mother, and sister.

ABEN KANDEL, 96, playwright/screenwriter, died January 28, 1993 in L.A. of heart failure. His play's include 1931's *Hot Money* along with many screenplays including the film of *Dinner at Eight* . Survived by a son and daughter.

MICHAEL KANIN, 83, Rochester-born playwright, director/screenwriter /producer, died March 12, 1993 in L.A. of heart failure. With his wife, Fay Mitchell Kanin, he co-wrote *Rashoman, His and Hers, The Gay Life* and many films, including *Woman of the Year* which won him and Ring Lardner Jr. Oscars. Survived by his wife, his son, his brother, writer Garson Kanin, and two grandaughters.

RUBY KEELER, 83, Canadian-born dancer actress, a film star of the 1930s, died February 28, 1993 in Rancho Mirage, CA. of cancer. Bdwy debut 1923 in *Rise of Rosie O'Reilly* followed by *Show Girl, Bye Bye Bonnie, Lucky, Sidewalks of New York,* and 1940's *Hold on to Your Hats* with then-husband Al Jolson(she left the trial run when he adlibbed references to their marital problems). She returned to Bdwy with great success in 1971's revival of *No No Nanette* . Films include the influential *42nd St.* Survived by five children and 14 grandchildren.

JACK KELLY, 65, stage, tv and film actor, died November 7, 1992 in Huntington Beach, CA. after a stroke. Best known for the tv series *Marvrick*, he started as a child actor in *Swing Your Lady* and *Schoolhouse on the Lot* . Survived by his wife and a daughter.

LOIS KIBBEE, 71, stage/tv actress and writer, died October 18, 1992 of a brain tumor. On Bdwy she appeared in *Man for All Seasons* and *Venus Is* . She wrote biographies of Joan Bennett and Christine Jorgensen. Known for her appearances on soap operas, she is survived by her mother, sister, and three brothers.

MICHAEL KING (RICHARD C. WEGENER), 69, actor/puppeteer, died June 1, 1992 in Tarzana, CA. Bdwy includes *Young Man's Fancy, Hellzapoppin, Tobacco Road* and *Catherine Was Great* . Survived by his wife, daughter, and three sisters.

LOU KRUGMAN, 78, New Jersey-born stage, radio, film and tv actor, died August 8, 1992 in Burbank, CA. of cancer. Bdwy debut in 1933's *Yoshe Kalb* followed by *Twelfth Night, Midsummer Night's Dream, Cafe Crown, Peer Gynt* and *Diary of Anne Frank* . Survived by his wife, two daughters, and grandson.

DONALD KVARES, 57, playwright, died May 4, 1993 in NYC of diabetes. A pioneer of the Off Off Bdwy movement, he had over 100 plays produced at Cafe Cino, LaMama and other theatres. Plays include *Wuziz, Couchmates, Springtime for Mahler, Freudian Memoirs of Viola Pickins, Smoking Pistols* and *Doctor's Office Disco.* Survived by a sister.

JIM LAMB, 29, actor, died February 18, 1993 in New York of AIDS. Associated with the Ridiculous Theatre Co. where he was in *Big Hotel, Der Ring Gott Farblonjet, Camille* and *Brother Truckers,* he also appeared in *Soul Survivor* and *Don Juan in New York* . Survived by his parents and two brothers.

ROBERT LARKIN, 61, New Jersey-born press agent/writer, died January 21, 1993 in New York of AIDS. As a press agent and senior member of the Shirley Herz firm, he publicized numerous Bdwy and Off-Bdwy shows as well as New York City Ballet and other dance troupes. His last show was the recent *Gypsy* revival. Survived by three brothers.

Willian LeMassena

Eugene Leontovich

BRIAN ALAN LASSER, 40, Chicago-born songwriter/musical director, died November 20, 1992 in New York of AIDS. His songs were heard in *Matinee Kids, Bundle of Nerves, Black Tulip,* and *No-Frill Revue* . As an actor he appeared *As Is* Off-Bdwy and was perhaps best known for his 16 year partnership with Karen Mason as her arranger/musical director. Survived by his parents and two sisters.

IRVING ALLEN LEE, 43, NYC-born stage and tv actor, died September 5, 1992 in Manhattan of AIDS. He was "Big Daddy" in the revival of *Sweet Charity* and replaced Ben Vereen in *Pippin* . 1969 debut Off Bdwy in *Kiss Now* followed by *Ride the Winds, Visit with Death* and *Changes.* Other Bdwy:*Rock-a-Bye Hamlet, A Broadway Musical* and *Ain't Misbehavin'* (us). He directed Off-Bdwy and regionally, taught theatre arts and acted on tv soaps. Survived by his parents and two brothers.

WILLIAM LeMASSENA, 76, New Jersey born actor, died January 19, 1993 in New Suffolk, NY of lung cancer. Bdwy debut 1940 with Alfred Lunt and Lynn Fontanne in *Taming of the Shrew* followed by *There Shall Be No Night, The Pirate, Hamlet, Call Me Mister, Annie Get Your Gun, Inside U.S.A., I Know My Love, Dream Girl, Nina, Ondine, Fallen Angels, Redhead, Conquering Hero, Beauty Part, Come Summer, Grin and Bare It, All Over Town, Texas Trilogy, Deathtrap, Blithe Spirit* and *Night of the Iguana.* Off Bdwy includes *The Coop, Brigadoon, Life with Father, F. Jasmine Addams, Dodge Boys, Ivanov* . Survived by his companion.

EUGENIE LEONTOVICH, 93, Moscow-born actress/teacher/playwright, died April 3, 1993 in Manhattan. Bdwy debut in 1928's *And So to Bed* followed by *Grand Hotel, Twentieth Century, Dark Eyes* (co-writer), *Obsession, Anastasia* and *Cave Dwellers.* Off-Bdwy includes *Anna K* which she also directed.

CLEAVON LITTLE, 53, Oklahoma-born stage, film and tv actor, died October 22, 1992 In Sherman Oaks, CA of colon cancer. A Tony Award winner for *Purlie* his other Bdwy credits include *Jimmy Shine, All Over Town, Poison Tree* and *I'm Not Rappaport.* Off-Bdwy includes debuting in 1967's *Macbird,* followed by *Hamlet, Someone's Coming Hungry, Ofay Watcher, Scuba Duba, Narrow Road to the Deep North, Great MacDaddy, Joseph and the...Dreamcoat, Resurrection of Lady Lester, Keyboard* and recently *All God's Dangers* . He was well known for his role in the film *Blazing Saddles* and also for tv work. Survived by his daughter, father, stepmother, two sisters and two brothers.

CARY SCOTT LOWENSTEIN, 30, dancer/singer/actor, died November 20, 1992 in Boca Raton, FL of AIDS. Bdwy debut 1980 in *A Chorus Line* followed by *Tap Dance Kid* and *Song and Dance.* He toured in *Sophisticated Ladies* and *Chorus Line* and danced in videos. His wife, actress/dancer Lynn Gendron died of a brain tumor October 9, 1991. Survived by his parents and three sisters.

ROGER MacDOUGALL, 82, Glasgow-born playwright/screenwriter, died May 27, 1993. He and Stanley Mann wrote 1957's *Hide and Seek* . Other plays include *Escapade* . Survived by a son, daughter, and two grandchildren.

SIR KENNETH McMILLAN, 62, English choreographer, died October 29, 1992 backstage at the Royal Opera House in Covent Garden of AIDS. Besides being the Royal Ballet's resident choreographer, he was working on the National Theatre production of *Carousel* at the time of his death. Knighted in 1983, he is survived by his wife and daughter.

MERCER McCLOUD, 86, English-born actor, died January 20, 1993 in New York of heart failure. Bdwy includes *Green Bay Tree, Apple Cart* and *Half a Sixpence* . He toured with *Man for All Seasons* . Survived by his second wife, foster son, and two grandsons.

MICHAEL AUSTIN McDONALD, 39, actor, died July 4, 1992 in L.A. of AIDS. Bdwy includes *No No Nanette, Good News* and Bobby in *Chorus Line* . Survived by his parents and sister.

GARY MASCARO, 43, choreographer, died December 2, 1992 of AIDS. Credits include New York and L.A. productions of *Tamara* .

SCOTT McPHERSON, 33, Ohio-born playwright/actor, died November 7, 1992 in Chicago of AIDS. He wrote the award winning play *Marvin's Room* which had success in New York and Chicago. His other plays include *Till the Fat Lady Sings, Scrape,* and *Legal Briefs.* Chicago acting credits include *Normal Heart* . Survived by his mother, brother, two stepbrothers, and three stepsisters.

MICHAEL MERRITT, 47, set designer, died August 3, 1992 in Chicago of colon and liver cancer. He designed David Mamet's plays including *American Buffalo* and *Speed-the-Plow* . He also designed for Steppenwolf and other Chicago theatres.Survived by his parents, a brother and sister.

HOPE MILLER (LESSMAN), 63, former actress/real estate executive, died July 25, 1992 in Manhattan. She appeared on Bdwy including *Now I Lay Me Down to Sleep* (1950). She retired from acting in 1953. Survived by her son and father.
ROGER MILLER, 56, songwriter/singer, died October 25, 1992 in L.A. of cancer. After a string of hit records in the 1960s, he wrote 1985's musical *Big River* which won him a Tony and revitalized his career. Survived by his wife, seven children and seven grandchildren.

Cleavon Little

Roudolf Nureyev

TIMOTHY MILLET, 37, dancer, died November 17, 1992. Bdwy includes *Dreamgirls* and *Chorus Line* . He also worked on tv. Survived by his wife, a son, three sisters, two brothers and his mother.

JAMES MILLHOLLIN, 77, stage, screen and tv actor, died May 23, 1993 in Biloxi, MS of cancer. On Bdwy he appeared in *Saratoga, Girls in 509,* and *No Time for Sergeants.* Survived by a sister.

GEORGE MINAMI Jr., 53, died December 28, 1992 in Hayward, CA of heart failure. He was a principal dancer in 1958's *Flower Drum Song* . He toured with the show then directed several Las Vegas shows. Survived by his father and sister.

ELIZABETH MONTGOMERY, 91, English-born costume/set designer, died May 15, 1993 in London. She and Margaret Harris were the American branch of "Motley", a design group. American credits include *Romeo and Juliet* (Laurence Olivier, Vivien Leigh), *Doctor's Dilemma, Three Sisters, Anne of the Thousand Days, Peter Pan, South Pacific, Most Happy Fella, Paint Your Wagon, Can-Can* and *First Gentleman* (Tony Award). Survived by a son and four stepdaughters.

MICHAEL DAVID MORRISON, 33, stage and tv actor, died February 18, 1993 in New York of an accidental drug overdose. Stage includes *Breaking the Code* (us), *Beirut* (1987), *Tigers Wild,* and *Twelfth Night* . He was one of the leads on tv's *As the World Turns* . Survived by his wife, actress Amy McDonald, and their son.

PAUL MORSE, 45, actor/composer/author, died August 7, 1992 in L.A. of AIDS. He toured with *Zorba* and won the 1967 Samuel French Playwriting contest with *Coming of Age.* He had many plays done in Southern California including *Children of the Universe, Letters to Harriet Tubman, Two Friends/Dos Amigos,* and *Roughing It* . Survived by his father and sister.

PETER B. MUMFORD, 48, production stage manager, died March 28, 1993 in Manhattan of AIDS. His last show was *Lost in Yonkers* preceded by *Buddy, Heidi Chronicles, Legs Diamond, Dreamgirls, Dancin', Baby, Little Shop of Horrors, Gin Game, Same Time Next Year* and others. Survived by his mother and sister.

DAVID MUSSELMAN, 38, production manager/producer/actor, died September 23, 1992 in Washington, D.C. of AIDS. He was in the original cast of *Let My People Come* before managing *Pacific Overtures, Stepping Out, Les Liasons Dangereuses ,Les Miserables* and the *Lettice & Lovage* tour. He co-produced *Oil City Symphony* . Survived by his companion.

RUTH NELSON, 87, Michigan-born stage, film and tv actress, died September 12, 1992 in New York of cancer. A Group theatre member, she debuted in 1931's *House of Connelly* followed by *Waiting for Lefty, Solitaire, Skin of Our Teeth* (1966), *To Grandmother's House We Go* and Off-Bdwy productions including *Collette, Scenes from the Everyday Life, 3 Acts of Recognition, Imagination Dead Imagine* and *The Crucible.* Divoreced from actor William Challee, she was then married to film director John Cromwell till his death. Survived by two sisters, a stepson, and four grandchildren.

ROBERT NIGRO, 45, stage/tv director, died August 5, 1992 in New York of AIDS. He directed Bdwy's *Is There Life After High School* and Off-Bdwy productions of *P.S. Your Cat Is Dead, Apple Tree,* ELT's *Fiorello, Company* and *Elephant Man* . His last production, which he co-authored, was *Twenty Fingers Twenty Toes* at the WPA Theatre. Survived by his companion, brother and three sisters.

RUDOLF NUREYEV, 54, Russian-born legendary dancer, died January 6, 1993 in Paris of AIDS. After his extraordinary ballet career, he toured in the lead role of *The King and I.* He also acted occasionally in films.

MORTIMER J. (SNOOKS) O'BRIEN, 82, Rochester-born dancer/stage manager, died June 18, 1992 after an auto accident. With his twin brother, Chet O'Brien, he danced in vaudeville and on Bdwy in *Face the Music, Of Thee I Sing, Great Waltz* and *As Thousands Cheer.* Switching to stage management, he worked on *The Gay Divorce, Connecticut Yankee* and *One Touch of Venus* . Survived by brother, Wife, daughter, son, sister and two grandchildren.

DAVID OLIVER, 30, stage/tv actor, died November 12, 1992 in L.A. of AIDS. Stage work includes many parts with San Diego Civic Light Opera and at the Edinburgh Festival. He was in L.A. productions of *Elegies* , an AIDS drama. Best known for the tv shows *Year in the Life* and *Another World* , he is survived by his companion, mother, stepfather, father and seven brothers and sisters.

FREDERICK O'NEAL, 86, Mississippi-born actor and president Emeritus of Actors' Equity, died August 25, 1992 in New York after a long illness. New York debut 1936 with Civic Repertory Theatre. He was one of the founders of the American Negro Theatre in 1940, and later the British Negro Theatre. He won the Clarence Derwent Award for his Bdwy role in 1944's *Anne Lucasta* followed by *Take a Giant Step, House of Flowers, Lost in the Stars* and *Ballad for Bimshire* among others. Survived by his wife.

Anthony Perkins

Vivienne Segal

EREN OZKER, 44, Turkish-born actress and puppeteer with the Muppets, died February 25, 1993 in New York of cancer. In the 1970s she worked at the Roundabout, Public Theatre and New Dramatists Guild. In 1976 she joined tv's *Muppet Show* and worked with puppet theatre and film after that. Survived by her husband and four sisters.

MITCHELL PARISH, 92, Lithuania-born lyricist, died March 31, 1993 in New York of a stroke. Known for "Stardust" and many other standards, his lyrics were celebrated the 1987 Bdwy revue *Stardust* which has also had an Off-Bdwy production and several tours. Survived by a daughter and son.

MARIE PAXTON, London-born actress, died in New York City after a brief illness. As a child actress she appeared in U.S. productions of *Pickwick* (1927), and *Napoleon* (1928). She moved to NYC in the 1940s and appeared on Bdwy in *Three Sisters, Chalk Garden, O Mistress Mine* and *Hadrian VII* among others. She was Mrs. Higgins in the first *Fair Lady* tour and her last Bdwy role was in the 1970 *Boy Friend* . Survived by a niece.

PATRICIA PEARDON, 69, actress/sculptor, died April 22, 1993 in New York of pneumonia. Discovered by Moss Hart, she made her Bdwy debut in 1941's *Junior Miss*. She returned in 1955's *Desperate Hours* and toured extensively with the American Shakespeare Festival players and later worked with the Institute for Advanced Studies in the Theatre Arts. Survived by two daughters and a grandson.

ED PECK, 75, actor, died September 12, 1992 in L.A. of a heart attack. Bdwy credits include *No Time for Sergeants* . No survivors.

ANTHONY PERKINS, 60, NYC-born stage, film and tv actor/director, died September 12, 1992 in Hollywood of AIDS. He won a *Theatre World* Award for his 1954 Bdwy debut in *Tea and Sympathy* followed by *Look Homeward Angel, Greenwillow, Harold, Star Spangled Girl, Equus* and *Romantic Comedy* . Off-Bdwy includes *Steambath* . Best known for his film role in 1960's horror film *Psycho*, he was a versatile talent who sang on stage and recordings, played comedy and drama, wrote film scripts and also directed. The son of actor Osgood Perkins, he is survived by his wife and two sons.

ALAN PETERSON, 54, dancer/choreographer, died December 30, 1992 of AIDS. He danced in *Funny Girl* and in films.

DONALD PHELPS, 61, actor, died February 16, 1993 in West Hollywood of AIDS. New York stage includes *Streets of New York, Fantasticks* and *Tom Jones* . Survived by his sister.

JOSEPH PORELLO, 56, Long Island-born entertainer/teacher, died June 22, 1992 in Manhattan of AIDS. He appeared in the *Zorba* tour among others and performed in opera and cabaret. Survived by four sisters and three brothers.

NANCY QUINN, 46, California-born artistic director of Young Playwrights, died April 24, 1993 in Brooklyn of a heart attack. She began assisting on *No Place to Be Somebody* at the Public Theatre, then supported young playwrights with the National Playwrights Conference, Arena Stage, and the annual Young Playwrights Festival. Survived by her husband, mother, a sister and brother.

LOU RAMOS, 51, actor, died June 23, 1992 in New York after a brief illness. He appeared on Bdwy in *Gloria and Esperanza* and at LaMama and other Off-Bdwy theatres. Survived by his companion, sister and three brothers.

DONALD RANDOLPH, 87. South African-born stage and film actor, died March 16, 1993 in L.A. of pneumonia. Bdwy debut 1932 in *Fatal Alibi* followed by more than 35 shows including *Richard III, Hamlet, Henry IV, Lady in the Dark* and *Life with Father* .

CHARLES A. READE, actor/dancer, died August 29, 1992 in Saugus, MA. following a two year hospitalization from a stroke. He debuted in the *Ziegfeld Follies of 1927* followed by *This Is the Army* along with vaudeville and tv. Survived by his wife.

TAYLOR REED, 60, actor, died March 24, 1993 in New York of a heart attack. Stage includes the 1970's *Man of La Mancha, A Mother's Kisses, Pickwick* and touring with *Guys and Dolls* (w/Milton Berle).Survived by his mother and four sisters.

KATE REID, 62, London-born stage, tv and film actress, died March 27, 1993 in Ontario of cancer. Bdwy debut 1962 in the matinee cast of *Who's Afraid of Virginia Woolf?* followed by *Dylan, Slapstick Tragedy, The Price, Freedom of the City, Cat on a Hot Tin Roof* (1974), *Bosoms and Neglect, Morning's at 7* and *Death of a Salesman* (1984). She worked extensively at the Stratford Festival in Canada. Twice divorced, she is survived by a son and daughter.

ALBERT BOSCO REYES, 51, playwright/director/Founder of Nat Horne Musical Theatre, died October 26, 1992 in Manhattan of AIDS. He directed at the Nat Horne and many regional theatres and won eight Peabody awards for his TV work. Survived by his parents, three brothers and a sister.

KENNY SACHA, 39, Bronx-born actor/impressionist, died August 1, 1992 in Hollywood of AIDS. A frequent club performer, he performed in Radio City Music Hall's 1983 revue *Five Six Seven Eight Dance* and the touring *French Dressing*. Survived by his parents and a sister.

GUS SCHIRMER, 73, producer/director, died June 10, 1992 in Culver City, CA. of kidney failure. Debut directing *New Faces of 1934* (Imogene Coca, Henry Fonda) followed by *Dear Charles* and City Center versions of *Pal Joey* (Bob Fosse) and *Wonderful Town* (Elaine Stritch). Other stage includes *Party with Comden and Green* (1958), *Gay Divorce* (1960) and *The Boy Friend* (1970). He was a casting director for film and tv in later years. Survived by two aunts and a cousin.

BUDDY SCHWAB, 62, dancer/choreographer/director, died December 1, 1992 in Detroit of lung cancer. Starting as a dancer in Bdwy's *As the Girls Go* followed by *Guys and Dolls* and others, he switched to choreography working on *No Strings* and *Mack and Mabel* (as associate) and Bdwy revivals of *Boy Friend* and *Camelot*. He directed *Barnum* in London and worked on film and tv dance. Survived by his mother and sister.

SAMMY SCHWARTZ, 86, actor, died August 13, 1992 in Pittsburgh of a heart attack. He replaced Sam Levene in *Guys and Dolls* and also played Nathan Detroit on the road. Bdwy includes *Foxy*. Survived by two nieces.

VIVIENNE SEGAL, 95, Philadelphia-born musical star, died December 29, 1992 in Beverly Hills of heart failure. Bdwy debut 1915 in *The Blue Paradise* followed by *Little Whopper, Ziegfeld Follies* (1924), *Oh Lady Lady, Yankee Princess, Adrienne, Castles in the Air, Desert Song, Chocolate Soldier, Three Musketeers, I Married an Angel, No No Nanette, Connecticut Yankee, Music in My Heart,* and *Glad to Be Alive*. Her most notable role was the hard-boiled Vera in *Pal Joey*. After creating the part in 1940, she repeated it in the 1952 revival winning a NY Drama Critics Award. Married twice, she is survived by a sister.

ROBERT SHAYNE (ROBERT SHAEN DAWE), 92, Yonkers, NY-born actor, died November 29, 1992 in Woodland Hills, CA. of lung cancer. Bdwy includes *The Rap, Yellow Jack, Cat and the Canary, Whiteoaks* in the 1930s and *Without Love* with Kathrine Hepburn in 1942. He acted in almost 100 films and on tv. Survived by his wife, three daughters, eleven grandchildren and nine great-grandchildren.

KEN SIMMONS (SIMINSKI), 41, stage manager/actor/director, died March 22, 1993 in Manhattan of AIDS. Off-Bdwy he managed *Approaching Zanzibar* and *Coastal Disturbances*. Survived by his companion, two brothers, sister and mother.

ROBERT F. SIMON, 83, stage, film and tv actor, died November 29, 1992 in Tarzana, CA. of a heart attack. Beginning at the Cleveland Playhouse in the 1930s, he then debuted on Bdwy with *Clash By Night* followed by *Russian People, All My Sons,* and *Death of a Salesman* (succeeding Lee J. Cobb). Other stage includes *No For an Answer* and *Of Thee I Sing*. Survived by two daughters, two sons and three grandchildren.

RICHARD SMART, 79, Hawaii-born actor/singer, died November 12, 1992 in Hawaii of cancer. Bdwy includes *Two for the Show, All for Love, Merry Widow* and starring with Mary Fabray in *Bloomer Girl*. Moving back to Hawaii he owned a large cattle ranch but built a community theatre there and occasionally worked, most recently in a one-man musical *Richard Smart Remembers*. Survived by two sons and three grandchildren.

GEORGE SPOTA, 75, producer/manager, died April 30, 1993 in L.A. of cancer. He conceived, created and produced Bdwy's *Will Rogers U.S.A.,* and *Bully* among others. Survived by his wife, a daughter, three brothers and three grandchildren.

SAM STICKLER, 37, stage manager/production supervisor, died August 31, 1992 in Albany of AIDS. His shows include *Oliver* (1984), *Song and Dance, Les Miserables, The Real Thing* and *Hurlyburly*. Survived by his parents and a sister.

DANNY STRAYHORN, actor/dancer, died November 1, 1992 of AIDS. Bdwy includes the recent *Grand Hotel* and *Starlight Express*. Other Bdwy includes *Dr. Jazz, Honky Tonk Nights, Sophisticated Ladies* and *The Wiz*.

KAY SWIFT, 95, NYC-born composer, died January 28, 1993 in Southlington, CT. of Alzheimer's disease. A rehearsal pianist for *Connecticut Yankee* she cracked Bdwy with her songs for 1929's *Little Show* including the hit "Can't We Be Friends?". In 1930 *Fine and Dandy*, lyrics by husband Paul James, Was the first Bdwy score composed completely by a woman and yielded "Fine and Dandy" and "Can This Be Love". Other work includes *Garrick Gaieties* and *Paris '90*. Survived by two daughters and six grandchildren.

ALBERT TAVARES, 39, casting director, died July 28, 1992 in Taunton, MA. of AIDS. He cast the musicals *Smile* and *Little Shop of Horrors* as well as Disney films and directed Off-Bdwy. Survived by his parents, two sisters and two brothers.

ROUBEN TER-ARUTUNIAN, 72, Russian-born designer, died October 17, 1992 in New York of lymphoma of the brain. He moved to New York in 1951, worked for the American Shakespeare Festival, then made his Bdwy debut with 1957's *New Girl in Town*. Other Bdwy includes *Who Was That Lady I Saw You With?, Redhead* (1959

Tony Award), *Advise and Consent, Deputy, Lady From the Sea* as well as City Ballet's annual *Nutcracker* and many other ballets and operas. No survivors.

RUTH TESTER (CAROTHERS), 89, singer/dancer, died March 21, 1993 in Weston, MA. She appeared in many Bdwy musicals of the 1920s and 30s including *Second Little Show, Garrick Gaieties of 1930, Lollipop, Lucky Break, The Ramblers, Bunk of 1926* and *The Gang's All Here*. Survived by a son and two granddaughters.

TED THOMAS (THEODORE HERTZL THOMASHEFSKY), 88, stage and film producer, died October 28, 1992. He began his career as assistant stage manager on Max Reinhardt's *The Miracle*, stage managed *Four Saints in Three Acts* (1934) and moved into producing with 1937's *Cradle Will Rock*. Survived by his son, conductor Michael Tilson Thomas, his wife and a brother.

ANN TODD, 82, English-born actress, died May 6, 1993 in London of a stroke. Bdwy debut in 1957's *Four Winds* after success on British stages. Also known for her films including *The Seventh Veil*. Survived by a son and daughter.

CHRISTOPHER TODD, 30, actor/dancer, died August 9, 1992 of AIDS. Stage includes Bdwy and touring *Starlight Express*.

VICTOR VALENTINE(WILMES), 40, director/choreographer, died in Santa Monica of AIDS. Beginning as an actor/dancer in regional productions of *Dames at Sea, Little Night Music* and *Cabaret* he moved into directing regional/tour versions of *Little Shop of Horrors* and *Jesus Christ Superstar*. In 1988 he directed/produced *The Broadway Benefit* at BAM for Gay Men's Health Crisis. Survived by his longtime companion, mother, stepfather and grandmother.

NETTIE VELIE, 96, actress/singer, died December 17, 1992 in Mount Vernon, NY. in 1915 she rose from chorus girl to leading lady in *The Only Girl* followed by *Going Up, La La Lucille* and the title role in George M. Cohan's *Mary* (1920).

RICHARD WARING, 82, English-born actor, died January 18, 1993 on City Island, NY. Best known for creating Morgan Evans in *The Corn is Green*, he debuted in 1931's *Romeo and Juliet* followed by *Camille, Cradle Song, Boy Meets Girl, Henry VIII, What Every Woman Knows, Alice in Wonderland, Gramercy Ghost, Measure for Measure, Edwin Booth, Portrait of a Queen* and *Androcles and the Lion*. He did work Off-Bdwy(*Cherry Orchard* , *The Actors*) and many roles at the American Shakespeare Festival. Survived by a brother.

FREDERIC WARRINER, 76, Pasadena-born actor, died November 10, 1992 in Middletown, CT. of a brain hemorrhage. Bdwy debut 1950 in *King Lear* followed by *Getting Married* (Clarence Derwent Award), *Speak of the Devil, Mr. Pickwick, Taming of the Shrew, Getting Married, St. Joan* (1951), *Pin to See the Peepshow, Wayward Saint, Caligula, Major Barbara, Time Remembered, Oliver, Man For All Seasons, Portrait of a Queen, Two Gentlemen of Verona* (1971 musical) and Off-Bdwy including *Invitation to a Beheading* and *Trelawny of the Wells*. He performed with many regional theatres including Barter Theatre (VA) and American Shakespeare Festival. Divorced from actress/playwright Elinor Wright in the 1950s, he leaves no survivors.

ANITA WEBB, 89, actress, died on January 2, 1993 in New York. Bdwy includes *Harvey* and *Damn Yankees* . In later years becoming blind, she represented the disabled as a council member of Actors Equity.

RONNIE WELSH, 52, actor/cabaret performer, died January 5, 1993 in New York of brain cancer. Stage work includes *Sleeping Prince, Take Her She's Mine, Father of the Bride* and succeeding Robert Morse in *How to Succeed in Business...*

ANNE G. WILDER, 63, producer, died September 27, 1992 in New York of a heart attack. An advocate for Playwrights Horizons, she was its chairwoman for the past 11 years. Other Off-Bdwy productions included *A...My Name Is Alice* and *Win/Lose/Draw*. Survived by her husband, a daughter, two sons, a sister and granddaughter.

KATE WILKINSON, 76, San Francisco-born actress, died February 9, 1993 in New York of bone cancer. Bdwy includes *Little Murders* (1967), *Johnny No Trump, Watercolor, Postcards, Ring Round the Bathtub, Last of Mrs. Lincoln, Man and Superman, Frankenstein* and *Man Who Came to Dinner.* Off-Bdwy includes 1959's *La Madre, Ernest in Love, Story of Mary Surratt, Bring Me a Warm Body, Child Buyer, Rimers of Eldritch, Doll's House, Hedda Gabler, Real Inspector Hound, Contractor, When the Old Man Died, Overcoat, Villager, Good Help Is Hard to Find, Lumiere, Rude Times* and most recently *Steel Magnolias*. She worked regionally and on tv and is survived by two sons.

LESTER WILSON, 51, choreographer/dancer, died February 14, 1993 in L.A. Bob Fosse cast him in the 1963 *Pal Joey* and he danced in the London *Golden Boy*. He choreographed 1975's *Me and Bessie* followed by shows like *Grind* and *Three Musketeers* as well as films like *Saturday Night Fever* and *Sister Act* . Survived by his mother and sister.

MAXINE WOOD (FINSTERWALD), 87, playwright, died April 7, 1993 in Oakland, CA. of heart failure. Best known for her 1946 Bdwy play *On Whitman Avenue* which dealt with racial discrimination. Other plays include *Severed Cord, Seven Against One* and *Sandals and Golden Heels* . Survived by a sister.

EARL WRIGHTSON, 77, Baltimore-born singer/tv host, died March 7, 1993 in East Norwich, CT. of heart failure. For three years in the 1950s he hosted an afternoon tv show *The American Musical Theatre* and with his companion, Lois Hunt, performed theatre music in concerts and recordings. Bdwy includes *Firebrand of Florence* (1945), *Kiss Me Kate, Paint Your Wagon, I Do I Do!, Man of La Mancha, South Pacific, Can-Can, Silk Stockings, Fiddler on the Roof, Gigi* and *A Little Night Music.* Recently Wrightson and Hunt performed *Sound of Music* in a 97 city tour. In addition to Miss Hunt, he is survived by an estranged wife, daughter and granddaughter.

HOWARD YOUNG, 81, producer, died April 19, 1993 in Santa Barbara, CA. With his partner Russell Lewis, he produced 8 Bdwy and 27 touring shows before founding the Sacramento Music Circus in the 1950s. Bdwy includes *Tonight at 8:30, Lady Windemere's Fan, Desert Song, Trial of Mary Suratt* and *Curious Savage.* Survived by his wife, three daughters and five grandchildren.

INDEX

248

Wilkes, Dorothy, 125
Wilkinson, Edmund, 117, 216
Wilkof, Lee, 105, 216
Will Rogers Follies, The, 35, 60, 180
Williams, Allison M., 56
Williams, Allison, 35, 216
Williams, Bruce, 126
Williams, Carla Renata, 142
Williams, Celeste, 141
Williams, Curt, 102
Williams, Darnell, 49, 216
Williams, Darryl, 102
Williams, Diane Ferry, 149
Williams, Elizabeth, 52
Williams, Gareth, 88
Williams, Heathcote, 74
Williams, Jacqueline, 141
Williams, JoBeth, 150
Williams, Karren, 71
Williams, Kelli, 92
Williams, Khea, 90
Williams, Kyle, 89
Williams, Lynnard Edwin, 92
Williams, Marshall, 91
Williams, Matt, 93
Williams, Mel, 83, 216
Williams, Olivia, 106, 134, 176, 188
Williams, Ralph, 37, 154
Williams, Rick, 142
Williams, Sam, 128, 158
Williams, Sandra Lea, 113
Williams, Sarah McCord, 107, 213, 216
Williams, Shelley, 125
Williams, Tennessee, 74, 128, 150
Williams, Tod S., 162
Williams, Treat, 80, 216
Williamson, David, 132
Williamson, Glen, 83, 213, 216
Williamson, Laird, 151
Williamson, Marco, 106, 176, 188
Williamson, Nance, 147, 158
Williamson, Peter, 104
Williamson, Ruth, 55, 213, 216
Williamson, Tish, 90
Williford, Lou, 87, 213, 216
Willinger, David, 104
Willis Burks, II, 143
Willis, Hilda, 91
Willis, Jack, 127
Willis, John, 5, 99
Willis, Scott, 62
Willis, Shan, 6, 216
Willoughby, Joe, 54
Wills, Ray, 7, 105, 216
Wilmes, Gary, 156
Wilson, August, 141, 145, 154, 158
Wilson, Bo, 162
Wilson, Darlene, 35, 50
Wilson, Erin Cressida, 85, 90
Wilson, Felicia, 118
Wilson, Jonathan, 134
Wilson, Kathryn Gay, 134
Wilson, Kristen, 157
Wilson, Lanford, 34, 72, 151
Wilson, Mary Louise, 118, 154
Wilson, Michael, 125
Wilson, Morrow, 78
Wilson, Rainn, 132
Wilson, Randolph F., 74
Wilson, Robert, 72, 125
Wilson, Sandy, 130
Wilson, Sirocco D., 74
Wilson, Tristan, 82, 93
Wiltberger, John M., 152
Wiltberger, John, 152
Wiltsie, Jennifer, 161
Wimmer, Nephi Jay, 58
Winant, Bruce, 16, 58, 216
Winbush, Troy, 148
Window Man, The, 78

Wineman, J. Christopher, 122
Wines, Halo, 128
Wing, Virginia, 83, 216
Wing-Davey, Mark, 112, 116, 154
Wingquist, Gunilla, 45, 136
Wings, 115, 140-141
Wink, Chris, 67
Winkler, Chuck, 125
Winkler, Richard, 120, 135
Winnick, Jay Brian, 73, 170
Winniford, Dustye, 73, 104
Winston, Joel, 134
Winston, Lee, 71, 98, 216
Winter Lies, 95
Winter's Tale, The, 151
Winter, Marcia, 163
Winterer, Sara, 145
Winterer, Sarah, 145
Winters, Catherine, 89
Wintersteller, Lynne, 95, 213, 216
Winther, Michael, 64, 169
Wirth, David Joe, 99
Wise Men Of Chelm, The, 88
Wise, Birgit Rattenborg, 115, 141
Wise, Peter Ashton, 99
Wise, Savannah, 57
Wise, Scott, 26, 55
Wiseman, Kieran, 115
Witte, Paige, 125
Witten, Matthew, 74, 102
Wittstein, Ed, 62
Wiz, The, 98
Wizard Of Oz, The, 152
Wizoreck, Barry, 88
Wodtke, Nicholas Cross, 31
Wojcik, Randy, 35, 50
Wojda, John, 155
Wojewodski, Robert, 51, 151, 158
Wojtas, Tom, 123
Wolf, Catherine, 61
Wolf, Don, 54
Wolf, Kelley, 133
Wolf, Kerry, 70
Wolfe, Cathleen, 121
Wolfe, David, 19
Wolfe, George C., 49, 56, 118, 158, 163
Wolfe, Jesse, 89
Wolfe, Tom, 101
Wolfe, Wayne, 95, 103-104
Wolfensohn, Adam, 90
Wolff, Patricia, 80
Wolfgram, Zandra, 142
Wolfson, David, 72
Woliner, Jason, 51
Wolk, James, 77, 90, 105
Wolos-Fonteno, David, 74, 154
Woman In Mind, 157
Womble, Terence, 31, 66, 82, 95, 100
Wong, Anthony, 74, 100
Wong, B.D., 27, 187, 216
Wong, Don Sterling, 134
Wong, Lily-Lee, 50
Wonsek, Paul, 105, 160
Woo, Jenny, 126
Wood, Bill, 72, 103
Wood, David A., 135
Wood, Karen S., 133
Wood, Kimberly, 90
Wood, Sally Ann, 160
Wood, Susan, 27, 135
Woodall, Sandra, 126
Woodard, Charlayne, 113, 216
Woodard, Greer, 98
Woodbury, Richard, 115
Woodeson, Nicholas, 148
Woodman, Jeff, 117
Woodruff, Kelly, 35, 213, 216
Woodruff, Robert, 126
Woodruff, Virginia Ann, 98
Woods, Carol, 26-27, 35, 216

Woods, Richard, 9, 217
Woods, Steve, 89
Woodson, John, 78, 134, 217
Woodward, Jeffrey, 150
Woolard, David C., 41, 79, 96, 120, 125, 138, 150, 166
Wooley, Michael Leon, 54
Wooley, Scot, 39, 179
Woolf, Stephen, 157
Wopat, Tom, 55, 130, 217
Words Divine, 85
World Of Kurt Weill, The, 72
World Of Ruth Draper, The, 82
Worm In The Heart, A, 91
Worrall, Brian, 122-123
Worthington, Sarah, 156
Woyzeck, 115
Wren, Todd, 136
Wright & Forrest, 128, 145
Wright, Amy, 105, 217
Wright, Crystal Simone, 128
Wright, David C., 84
Wright, Jeffrey, 49
Wright, Michael, 102
Wright, Miller, 64-65, 89, 95, 97, 110
Wright, R. Hamilton, 158
Wright, Rae C., 100
Wright, Randel, 98
Wright, Valerie, 144
Wright, Wendell, 128
Wrightson, Ann G., 135
Wroe, Craig, 157
Wrong Turn At Lungfish, 92
Wrubel, Bill, 82
Wrubel, Mr., 82
Wyatt, Mona, 134-135
Wyeth, David C., 138
Wyler, Stephen, 72
Wylie, John, 155, 157
Wyman, Nick, 101, 152
Wymark, Tristram, 106
Wynkoop, Christopher, 21, 161, 217
Wynn, Larry, 54
Wyrtch, Kenneth J., 70
Wyss, Patti, 75
Xoregos, Shela, 70, 78, 85
Yancey, Kim, 119, 142, 217
Yancy, Kim, 118
Yaney, Denise, 34
Yarnell, Lorene, 136
Yassur, Moshe, 98
Yates, Tiffany, 92
Yawitz, Lizzie, 95
Yeager, Kenton, 162
Yearby, Marlies, 71
Yeargan, Michael, 141, 143, 148, 163
Yeargun, Lisa, 101
Years, The, 112
Yelusich, Andrew V., 151
Yen, Sandy, 87
Yes Word, The, 77
Yeston, Maury, 130, 145, 152
Yetman, Charlotte M., 135, 160
Yetman, Charlotte, 142
Yetter, Douglas, 87
Yi-Song, Fan, 157
Yionoulis, Evan, 155
Yoda, Ingrid, 106
Yore, Catherine Lee, 141
York Theatre Company, 121
York, David, 150
York, Emily, 125
York, Mark, 73
York, Michael, 12, 213, 217
York, Rachel, 57, 113
You Could Be Home Now, 114
Youmans, James, 96, 120
Youmans, William, 76, 131, 163
Young, Amy M., 143
Young, Billy Joe, 71

Young, Cedric, 30-31
Young, Damian, 81-82
Young, David, 130, 171, 217
Young, Jane, 77
Young, Jay, 136
Young, Joellyn Cox, 130
Young, Jordan, 160
Young, Karen, 76, 82, 217
Young, Kate, 154
Young, Nancy, 89
Young, Richard H., 125
Young, Robert L., 98
Young, William, 127
Youngman, Christina, 16, 35, 60, 213, 217
Youngs, Hazel, 91
Yourgrau, Tug, 31
Yung, Hai Wah, 83
Yvon, Ben, 149
Zabel, David, 82
Zacek, Dennis, 61
Zachos, Ellen, 135
Zager, James, 141
Zahn, Steve, 119
Zahorsky, Kate, 104
Zaionz, Craig, 70
Zak, Scott, 79
Zakarian, Craig, 40, 88, 213, 217
Zakem, Daniel, 122
Zakowska, Donna, 126
Zaks, Jerry, 27, 38, 55, 132, 178
Zaleski, Robert, 72
Zaloom, Joe, 154
Zamarripa, Todd, 58
Zambello, Francesca, 127, 147
Zangara, Michelle, 87
Zapp, Peter, 122-123
Zaraspe, Hector, 45, 136
Zaremby, Justin, 78
Zarish, Janet, 102, 217
Zarzour, Jean, 142
Zaslow, Michael, 121
Zeidman, Jeff, 100
Zeisler, Ellen, 70, 72, 88, 99
Zeisler, Mark, 127
Zerkle, Greg, 124
Zieger, Scott, 41
Zielinski, Scott, 85, 127, 129, 143
Ziemba, Karen, 71, 73, 95, 168, 180, 213, 217
Zien, Chip, 53, 217
Zigler, Scott, 122-123
Ziman, Richard, 76
Zimbalist, Stephanie, 135
Zimberg, Stuart, 78
Zimmerman, James, 60
Zimmerman, Mark, 27
Zimmerman, Mary, 141
Zingalis, Rosi, 77
Zinn, David, 104
Zinoman, Joy, 160
Zinsser, Sarah, 82
Zipay, Joanne, 151
Zippel, David, 26
Zippler, Karen, 144
Zipprodt, Patricia, 16, 172
Ziskie, Daniel, 102, 217
Zitnick, Karen, 154
Zito, Chuck, 77
Zito, Ron, 75
Zito, Torrie, 26
Zollo, Frederick, 49, 80, 94
Zuber, Catherine, 127, 141, 164
Zuber, Cathy, 158
Zubkoff, Steven, 151
Zuckerman, Mort, 60
Zuckerman, Stephen, 120
Zuniga, Jose, 79
Zunini, Juan, 136
Zweigbaum, Steven, 52